AQA A-level

Economics

2

Ray Powell

James Powell

Approval message from AQA

This textbook has been approved by AQA for use with our qualification. This means that we have checked that it broadly covers the specification and we are satisfied with the overall quality. Full details of our approval process can be found on our website.

We approve textbooks because we know how important it is for teachers and students to have the right resources to support their teaching and learning. However, the publisher is ultimately responsible for the editorial control and quality of this book.

Please note that when teaching the **AQA A-level Economics** course, you must refer to AQA's specification as your definitive source of information. While this book has been written to match the specification, it cannot provide complete coverage of every aspect of the course.

A wide range of other useful resources can be found on the relevant subject pages of our website: www.aqa.org.uk.

DYNAMIC
LEARNING

HODDER
EDUCATION
AN HACHETTE UK COMPANY

Hodder Education, an Hachette UK company, Carmelite House, 50 Victoria Embankment, London EC4Y 0DZ

Orders

Bookpoint Ltd, 130 Park Drive, Milton Park, Abingdon, Oxfordshire OX14 4SE
tel: 01235 827827
fax: 01235 400401
e-mail: education@bookpoint.co.uk
Lines are open 9.00 a.m.–5.00 p.m., Monday to Saturday, with a 24-hour message answering service.
You can also order through the Hodder Education website: www.hoddereducation.co.uk

ISBN 978-1-4718-2984-0

Impression number	5	4	3		
Year	2020	2019	2018	2017	2016

The publishers would like to thank the following for permission to reproduce photographs:

p.1 Ilya Genkin/Fotolia; **p.6** lecic/Fotolia; **p.19** Roberto Herrett/Alamy; **p.45** © John Lewis; **p.46** © Apple; **p.83** Richard Villalon/Fotolia; **p.129** Image Works; **p.148** Rosemary Roberts/Alamy Stock Photo; **p.167** Julie Fryer Images/Alamy Stock Photo; **p.187** vichie81/Fotolia; **p.190** World History Archive/Alamy Stock Photo; **p.213** Matthew Chattle/Alamy Stock Photo; **p.227** Norma Joseph/Alamy Stock Photo; **p.253** epa european pressphoto agency b.v./Alamy Stock Photo; **p.269** Fotolia; **p.299** © The Coca-Cola Co.; **p.321** Fotolia; **p.338** Fotolia

All website addresses included in this book are correct at the time of going to press but may subsequently change.

The front cover image is reproduced by permission of Fotolia.

Typeset in 11/13 pt ITC Berkeley Oldstyle Std Book by Integra Software Services Pvt. Ltd., Pondicherry, India
Printed in Italy

Hachette UK's policy is to use papers that are natural, renewable and recyclable products and made from wood grown in sustainable forests. The logging and manufacturing processes are expected to conform to the environmental regulations of the country of origin.

Get the most from this book

This textbook has been tailored explicitly to cover the content of the AQA specification for the second year of the A-level course. The book is divided into two parts, each covering the sections that make up the AQA programme of study.

The text provides the foundation for studying AQA economics, but you will no doubt wish to keep up to date by referring to additional topical sources of information about economic events. This can be done by reading the serious newspapers, visiting key sites on the internet and reading such magazines as *Economic Review*.

Special features

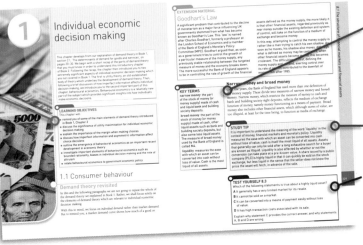

Learning outcomes
A statement of the intended learning objectives for each chapter.

Key terms
Clear, concise definitions of essential key terms where they first appear and a list at the end of each section.

Study tips
Short pieces of advice to help you present your ideas effectively and avoid potential pitfalls.

Test yourself
Exercises to provide active engagement with economic analysis.

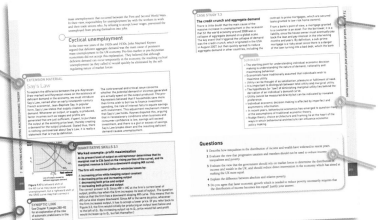

Extension material
Extension points to stretch your understanding.

Quantitative skills
Worked examples of quantitative skills that you will need to develop.

Synoptic links
Connections between different areas of economics are highlighted to help improve your overall understanding of the subject.

Case studies
Case studies to show economic concepts applied to real-world situations.

Summaries
Bulleted summaries of each topic that can be used as a revision tool.

Practice questions
Practice questions are provided at the end of each section to help you check your knowledge and understanding of the topics you have covered within each chapter.

Contents

Introduction vi

Breakdown of the examinations ix

Part 1 Microeconomics

1 Individual economic decision making

1.1 Consumer behaviour 2
1.2 Imperfect information 11
1.3 Aspects of behavioural economic theory 12
1.4 Behavioural economics and economic policy 18

2 Production, costs and revenue

2.1 Developing short-run production theory: the law of diminishing returns 25
2.2 Developing long-run production theory: returns to scale 30
2.3 Marginal cost and marginal revenue 35
2.4 Profit 42
2.5 Technological change 45

3 Perfect competition, imperfectly competitive markets and monopoly

3.1 Market structures 55
3.2 The objectives of firms 59
3.3 Perfect competition 63
3.4 Monopoly and monopoly power 66
3.5 Monopolistic competition 72
3.6 Oligopoly 76
3.7 Price discrimination 83
3.8 The dynamics of competition and competitive market processes 87
3.9 Contestable and non-contestable markets 88
3.10 Consumer and producer surplus 90

4 The labour market

4.1 The demand for labour — marginal productivity theory 93
4.2 The supply of labour 98
4.3 Perfectly competitive labour markets 102
4.4 Imperfectly competitive labour markets 104
4.5 The influence of trade unions in determining wages and levels of employment 107
4.6 The national minimum wage 109
4.7 Discrimination in the labour market 112

5 The distribution of income and wealth: poverty and inequality

5.1 The distribution of income and wealth 118
5.2 The problem of poverty 129
5.3 Government policies to alleviate poverty and to influence the distribution of income and wealth 132

6 Revisiting market failure and government intervention in markets

6.1 Marginal analysis and market failure 141
6.2 Environmental market failures 155
6.3 Property rights 156
6.4 Competition policy 157
6.5 Public ownership 163
6.6 Privatisation 164
6.7 Regulation and deregulation of markets 169
Microeconomics key terms 174
Microeconomics practice questions 182

Part 2 Macroeconomics

7 Revisiting and developing macroeconomic theory

7.1 Introducing the national and international economy 189
7.2 Circular flow and *AD/AS* revisited 193
7.3 Economic growth revisited 203
7.4 A further look at employment and unemployment issues 206
7.5 Inflation, the Phillips curve and the quantity theory of money revisited 213

8 Financial markets and monetary policy

8.1 The structure of financial markets and financial assets 226
8.2 Commercial banks and investment banks 238
8.3 Central banks and monetary policy 246
8.4 The regulation of the financial system 258

9 Revisiting fiscal policy and supply-side policies

9.1 Fiscal policy 265
9.2 Supply-side policies 291

10 The international economy

10.1 Globalisation 298
10.2 Trade 304
10.3 The balance of payments 322
10.4 Exchange rate systems 340
10.5 Economic growth and development 355
Macroeconomics key terms 369
Macroeconomics practice questions 376

Index 384

v

Introduction

Welcome back to economics and to your second year of A-level study. Our principal aim is to help you develop further your understanding of the subject to turn you into a good economist.

To assist you to get the most out of your studies, we have included extension material in all the chapters of the book. Much of the extension material goes beyond the basic demands of the A-level specification, introducing you to new theories and to recent developments of existing theories.

There are also many case studies in the book. These enable you to link theory to up-to-date events taking place in the UK economy and in the wider international economy.

The organisation of the book is similar to that of the A-level specification, in that it is split into two main sections: microeconomics and macroeconomics. However, as the specification states, 'students should appreciate that microeconomics and macroeconomics are not entirely distinct areas of study. For example, microeconomic principles often provide fundamental insights into understanding aspects of the macroeconomy. Similarly, economic issues and problems often contain both a microeconomic and a macroeconomic dimension.'

This is reflected in the three A-level examination papers, and particularly in Paper 3: Economic principles and issues. The details of Paper 3, and also Paper 1: Markets and market failure and Paper 2: National and international economy, are explained in the section 'Breakdown of the examination'.

Book 2 and Book 1

Book 2 has been written to follow on from Book 1, the book which we assume you used during the first year of your A-level course. In Book 2, where we have considered it necessary, we have revisited and summarised essential elements of Book 1, before developing them further by adding the rather more difficult topics which appear in the A-level specification.

Here are four examples, the first two selected from Book 2's microeconomic chapters and the latter two from the macroeconomic chapters.

1   We begin Book 2, Chapter 1 by revisiting the demand theory you learnt when reading Book 1, Chapter 2. However, we then go on to explain a more advanced element of demand theory called utility theory. The

chapter then introduces you to a relatively new part of modern economics known as behavioural economics.

2 Market failure was an important topic explained in Book 1, Chapter 5. We revisit this topic in Book 2, Chapter 6, before investigating various market failures using an important technique known as marginal analysis, which is introduced in Book 2, Chapters 2 and 3.

3 In Chapter 7, which is titled 'Revisiting and developing macroeconomic theory', we develop further your understanding of the aggregate demand/aggregate supply (*AD/AS*) macroeconomic model, and your understanding of employment and unemployment issues, which we first explained in Book 1, Chapters 7 and 8.

4 Book 1, Chapter 9 introduced you to macroeconomic policy. In Chapter 8 of Book 2, we investigate the role of financial markets in the economy and develop your understanding of monetary policy and how it is implemented in the UK. Likewise, in Chapter 9, we provide a more in-depth explanation of certain key aspects of fiscal policy and supply-side policy, which we first covered in Book 1.

Although Book 1 was largely devoted to the national economy, some mention was made of the importance of trade for an economy such as the UK. Book 1 also introduced you to the current account of the balance of payments. In this book, we will revisit the balance of payments, before investigating parts of the balance of payments other than the current account, and exploring the links between the balance of payments and exchange rates. We will introduce you to important elements of trade theory, to the effects of globalisation on the national economy, and to some of the key topics in development economics. We will also discuss how the UK's membership of the EU and external events in the international economy affect the performance of the UK economy.

How much maths do I need to know?

As we stated in the introduction to Book 1, at the beginning of an economics course, students often seek advice about the amount of mathematics they need to know or must learn to help them with their studies. For A-level economics, it is not important to learn any more maths skills over and above those that you learnt at GCSE, but you do need to develop analytical and quantitative skills in economics when 'selecting, interpreting and using appropriate data from a range of sources'.

Quantitative skill requirements

In order to develop your skills, knowledge and understanding in economics, you need to have acquired competence in the quantitative skills that are relevant to the subject content and which are applied when answering an economics question at A-level. These skills include:

- calculating, using and understanding ratios and fractions
- calculating, using and understanding percentages and percentage changes
- understanding and using the terms 'mean' and 'median' and relevant quantiles
- constructing and interpreting tables and a range of standard graphical forms (line graphs, bar graphs and pie charts)
- calculating and interpreting index numbers
- making calculations of elasticity and interpreting the result

- calculating cost, revenue and profit (marginal, average and total) from given data
- making calculations to convert data from money to real terms
- interpreting, applying and analysing information in written, graphical and numerical forms

The assessment of quantitative skills represents a minimum of 20% of the overall A-level marks.

As was the case in Book 1, as you proceed through this book, you will be introduced to economics graphs and to the different ways of presenting and calculating statistics, and you will be reminded that economics contains a large number of abstract ideas and concepts, similar to those employed in mathematics. A logical mind, capable of handling abstractions, will be of great help if you are to become a good economist.

Finally, for answers to case studies, test yourself questions etc. featured in this book, please visit **https://www.hoddereducation.co.uk/Product?Product=9781471829789** and click 'Download answers'.

Breakdown of the examinations

Scheme of assessment

The AS and A-level specifications are designed to be studied over 1 year and 2 years respectively with all assessments taken at the end of the course. Both qualifications are linear. To achieve the award, students must complete all exams in May/June in a single year. All assessments must be taken in the same series.

The assessment objectives and aims

The **assessment objectives (AOs)** are set by the GCE regulator, Ofqual, and are the same for all AS and A-level economics specifications and all exam boards. The exams measure how well students achieve the following AOs:

- **AO1:** Demonstrate knowledge of terms/concepts and theories/models to show an understanding of the behaviour of economic agents and how they are affected by and respond to economic issues
- **AO2:** Apply knowledge and understanding to various economic contexts to show how economic agents are affected by and respond to economic issues
- **AO3:** Analyse issues within economics, showing an understanding of their impact on economic agents
- **AO4:** Evaluate economic arguments and use qualitative and quantitative evidence to support informed judgements relating to economic issues

The **assessment aims** are set by the GCE examining board, AQA. For both the AS and A-level courses, the assessment aims are to encourage students to:

- develop an interest in and enthusiasm for economics
- appreciate the contribution of economics to the understanding of the wider economic and social environment
- develop an understanding of a range of concepts and an ability to use those concepts in a variety of different contexts
- use an enquiring, critical and thoughtful approach to the study of economics and develop an ability to think as an economist
- understand that economic behaviour can be studied from a range of perspectives
- develop analytical and quantitative skills, together with qualities and attitudes which will equip economics students for the challenges, opportunities and responsibilities of adult and working life

During your course you should develop a critical approach to economic models and methods of enquiry. You should build up a good knowledge and understanding of developments in the UK economy and government policies over the 15 years before you sit the exams. You should also be aware of earlier events where this helps to give recent developments a longer-term perspective.

The examination structure

As an A-level student, you are assessed through *three* examination papers, each of which is 2 hours long.

- **Paper 1: Markets and market failure** will examine mainly microeconomic topics.
- **Paper 2: National and international economy** will examine mainly macroeconomic topics.
- **Paper 3: Economic principles and issues** will examine both microeconomic and macroeconomic topics.

In Paper 1 and Paper 2, the question structure is the same. Section A contains two data-response questions, which are identified as Context 1 and Context 2. You should answer *either* Context 1 *or* Context 2, but not both. Section B contains three essay questions, of which you should answer one. Each essay is in two parts, respectively carrying 15 and 25 marks. The first part of each essay tests AO1 to AO3, whereas the second part tests all four AOs.

Paper 3 is different in coverage and structure from Papers 1 and 2. It includes topics from both the microeconomic and macroeconomic sections of the specification and, particularly when answering questions linked to the case study in the question, you are expected to recognise when it is appropriate to use microeconomic and/or macroeconomic models.

Section A of Paper 3 contains 30 compulsory objective test questions, which assess both microeconomic and macroeconomic topics. Section B contains a single compulsory case study question which over-arches the whole A-level specification. The details of the case study are provided in a separate source booklet, which you read at the start of the exam. The source booklet is *not* pre-released before the exam. The source booklet contains extracts on the theme of the case study. The extracts include both numerical and textual data. The exam paper contains three questions which you answer as if you are an economist giving advice to a client. The client you are advising could be a company, a government minister or a labour organisation, although there are other possibilities.

Mark allocation

The mark allocation for the A-level examination is as follows.

Papers 1 and 2:

- Section A: 2, 4, 9 and 25 are the maximum marks for each of the four parts of the data-response question, for which the maximum mark is 40
- Section B: 15 and 25 are the maximum marks for each of the two parts of the essay question, for which the maximum mark is 40

The maximum mark for Papers 1 and 2 is 80.

Paper 3:

- Section A: 1 mark per objective test question, with a maximum mark of 30 for the section
- Section B: 10, 15 and 25 are the maximum marks for each of the three parts of the investigation in the case study, for which the maximum mark is 50

The maximum mark for Paper 3 is 80.

1

Microeconomics

1 Individual economic decision making

This chapter develops from our explanation of demand theory in Book 1, section 2.1, 'The determinants of demand for goods and services', on pages 20–30. We begin with a short recap of the parts of demand theory that you must know in order to understand this introductory chapter of Book 2. Following the recap, the chapter then introduces you to two extremely significant aspects of individual economic decision making which are not covered in Book 1. The first is utility theory, an old-established body of theory which underlies the development of demand theory. Then, following a brief discussion of how imperfect information affects individual decision making, we introduce you to the second important part of this chapter, behavioural economics. Behavioural economics is a relatively new part of the subject which provides significant insights into how individuals make economic decisions.

LEARNING OBJECTIVES
This chapter will:

● remind you of some of the main elements of demand theory introduced in Book 1, Chapter 2
● discuss the significance of utility maximisation for individual economic decision making
● explain the importance of the margin when making choices
● discuss how imperfect information and asymmetric information affect choice decisions
● outline the emergence of behavioural economics as an important recent development in economic theory
● investigate important elements of behavioural economics such as bounded rationality, biases in individual decision making and the role of altruism
● relate behavioural economics to government economic policy

1.1 Consumer behaviour

Demand theory revisited

In this and the following paragraphs we are not going to repeat the whole of the demand theory we explained in Book 1. Rather, we shall focus solely on the elements of demand theory which are relevant to individual economic decision making.

With this in mind, we focus on *individual demand* rather than market demand. But to remind you, a market demand curve shows how much of a good or

KEY TERMS

individual demand curve shows how much of a good or service the consumer plans to demand at different possible prices.

law of demand as a good's price falls, more is demanded.

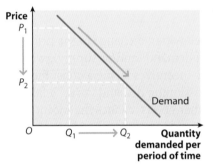

Figure 1.1 An individual's demand curve

STUDY TIP

Make sure you understand the relationship between market demand and individual demand.

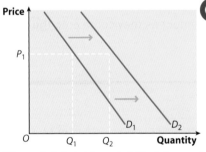

Figure 1.2 A rightward shift of demand

service *all* the consumers in the market plan to demand at all the different possible prices of the good or service, whereas an **individual's demand curve** shows how much a single consumer in the market plans to demand at all the different possible prices of the good or service. (Remember that the market demand curve is simply the sum of all the individual demand curves in the market.)

We introduced you in Book 1 to the **law of demand**, which states that as a good's price falls, more is demanded. An individual's demand curve thus shows an inverse relationship between price and quantity demanded. This relationship is shown in Figure 1.1, which is a repeat of Book 1, Figure 2.1, except that in this case the demand curve shows how a single consumer behaves in the market rather than all consumers taken together.

Having explained the 'law' of demand in Book 1, we then went on to distinguish between a **shift of a demand curve** to a new position (an **increase in demand** or a **decrease in demand**) and a movement or adjustment along a demand curve, in response to a change in the good's price. The latter we called an **extension of demand** or a **contraction of demand**. A demand curve will shift if any of the factors influencing demand, *other than the good's own price*, changes. These factors, which are sometimes called the **conditions of demand**, include income, tastes and preferences, and the prices of substitute goods and complementary goods. An increase in income shifts demand curves rightward — but only for normal goods. A normal good is defined as a good for which demand increases when income increases. By contrast, an inferior good is a good (such as poor-quality food) for which demand falls as income increases. If the good is inferior, an increase in income shifts the demand curve leftward. Figure 1.2 below shows a rightward shift of demand from D_1 to D_2, caused perhaps by a fall in the price of a good in joint demand (a complementary good) or by a successful advertising campaign for the product.

KEY TERMS

shift of a demand curve the movement of a demand curve to a new position.

increase in demand a rightward shift of the demand curve.

decrease in demand a leftward shift of the demand curve.

extension of demand an adjustment or movement down a demand curve following a fall in the good's price.

contraction of demand an adjustment or movement up a demand curve following an increase in the good's price.

condition of demand a determinant of demand, other than the good's own price, that fixes the position of the demand curve. A change in one or more of the conditions of demand leads to a shift of demand.

STUDY TIP

Make sure you understand the difference between a shift of a demand (or supply) curve and an adjustment in response to a price change along a demand (or supply) curve.

Rational economic decision making and economic incentives

At the heart of traditional or orthodox demand theory is the assumption that the members of households or consumers always act rationally. **Rational behaviour** means people try to make decisions in their self-interest or to maximise their private benefit. When a choice has to be made, people always choose what they think at the time is the best alternative, which means that the second best or next best alternative is rejected. For households and the individuals within them, rational behaviour is attempting to maximise the welfare, satisfaction or utility gained from the goods and services consumed.

Given the assumption of rational economic behaviour, a change in the price of any good and a change in the conditions of demand (and/or supply), which leads to a change in price, alters the economic incentives facing a consumer. As we have seen, with a traditional downward-sloping demand curve, a fall in the price of a good, relative to the prices of other goods, creates the incentive to demand more of the good. Likewise, an increase in the good's relative price creates an incentive to demand less of the good.

KEY TERM

rational behaviour acting in pursuit of self-interest, which for a consumer means attempting to maximise the welfare, satisfaction or utility gained from the goods and services consumed.

SYNOPTIC LINK

At this point, go back to Book 1, pages 24–30, and remind yourself, first, of how on occasion an individual's demand curve may slope upward, and second, of how price elasticity of demand and cross elasticity of demand affect the incentives consumers face when prices change.

TEST YOURSELF 1.1

Which of the following provides the best reason why consumers become early adopters of a new innovation such as a smart watch, even though they know that they will be paying a high price for the good?

Early adopters are people who:

A like technological gadgets

B get up early to buy in a sale

C base their consumption decisions on the reviews submitted online by existing users

D want to be the first to get new types of product as they come onto the market

Explain your answer.

Utility theory: total and marginal utility, and diminishing marginal utility

What is utility?

We mentioned in the previous section on rational economic decision making that consumers attempt to maximise the welfare or utility they gain from the goods and services they decide to consume. We shall explore this further in the next section, on utility maximisation. In economics, **utility** is usually defined as the economic welfare or satisfaction obtained from consumption.

KEY TERMS

utility the satisfaction or economic welfare an individual gains from consuming a good or service.

marginal utility the additional welfare, satisfaction or pleasure gained from consuming one extra unit of a good.

The relationship between total utility and marginal utility

Let us imagine a thirsty child who drinks six glasses of lemonade on a hot sunny afternoon, deriving successively 8, 6, 4, 2, 0 and –2 'units of utility' from each glass consumed. This information is shown in the total and marginal utility schedules in Table 1.1, from which the total and marginal utility curves drawn in Figure 1.3 are plotted. Note that marginal utility is plotted at 'halfway' points.

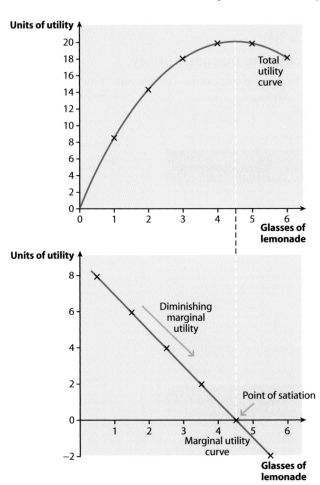

Figure 1.3 An example of total utility and marginal utility curves

Table 1.1 Total and marginal utility schedules for lemonade

Glasses of lemonade	Total utility (units of utility)	Marginal utility (units of utility)
0	0	
		8
1	8	
		6
2	14	
		4
3	18	
		2
4	20	
		0
5	20	
		–2
6	18	

It is important to realise that the total and marginal utility schedules and, likewise, the total and marginal utility curves show exactly the same information, but they show it in different ways. The total utility schedule and the total utility curve show the data cumulatively — for example, when drinking two glasses of lemonade, the thirsty child gains 14 'units of utility' in total. After three glasses, total utility rises to 18 'units of utility', and so on.

In contrast, the marginal utility schedule and the marginal utility curve plot the same data as separate observations, rather than cumulatively. The last unit consumed is always the marginal unit and the utility derived from it is the marginal utility. So, after two drinks, the second glass of lemonade is the marginal unit consumed, yielding a marginal utility of 6 'units of utility'. But when three glasses of lemonade are consumed, the third glass becomes the marginal unit, from which the still partially thirsty child gains a marginal utility of just 4 'units of utility'.

Economists refer to the utility of a good: in this case, how much satisfaction can be received from consuming glasses of lemonade

In Figure 1.3, diminishing marginal utility is shown both by the diminishing rate of increase of the slope of the total utility curve drawn in the upper panel of the diagram and by the negative or downward slope of the marginal utility curve in the lower panel. Notice that we have drawn a 'point of satiation' on the diagram, which is reached as the fifth glass of lemonade is drunk. The fifth glass of lemonade yields zero marginal utility. At this point, when marginal utility is zero, total utility is maximised. In the context of food and drink, satiation means being 'full up'. Even if lemonade is free to the consumer, it would be irrational for our 'no-longer-thirsty' child to drink a sixth glass of lemonade. He or she would experience negative marginal utility (or marginal disutility), which is shown by the downward slope of the total utility curve and by the negative position of the lower section of the marginal utility curve.

STUDY TIP

The relationships between marginal values and total values of an economic variable must be understood when studying production theory, cost theory and revenue theory, as well as when studying utility theory. With production theory, cost theory and revenue theory, you must also understand the relationships between marginal and average returns, marginal and average cost and marginal and average revenue.

QUANTITATIVE SKILLS 1.1

Worked example: calculating marginal utility

An 8-year-old boy decides to enter a competition to see how many jam doughnuts can be eaten in 15 minutes. Table 1.2 shows how many he ate and his total utility schedule.

Table 1.2 Total utility for doughnuts

Jam doughnuts	Total utility (units of utility)	Marginal utility (units of utility)
0	0	
1	6	
2	10	
3	12	
4	12	
5	8	
6	3	

Complete the boy's marginal utility schedule.

The boy's marginal utility schedule is shown in Table 1.3.

Table 1.3 Total and marginal utility for doughnuts

Jam doughnuts	Total utility (units of utility)	Marginal utility (units of utility)
0	0	
1	6	6
2	10	4
3	12	2
4	12	0
5	8	−4
6	3	−5

The hypothesis (or 'law') of diminishing marginal utility

The numerical examples in Tables 1.1–1.3, and the graph in Figure 1.3, illustrate a very famous economic hypothesis, which some would call an economic law: the **hypothesis of diminishing marginal utility**. This simply states that as a person increases consumption of a good — while keeping consumption of other products constant — there is a decline in the marginal utility derived from consuming each additional unit of the good.

> **KEY TERM**
>
> **hypothesis of diminishing marginal utility** for a single consumer the marginal utility derived from a good or service diminishes for each additional unit consumed.

> **SYNOPTIC LINK**
>
> In the context of economic methodology, Book 1, Chapter 1 explained the difference between a hypothesis and a theory. To remind you, whereas a hypothesis is a proposed explanation for something, a theory is when a hypothesis is tested and survives the test.

CASE STUDY 1.1

Adam Smith's diamonds and water paradox

In 1776 the great classical economist Adam Smith wrote about the diamonds and water paradox (or the paradox of value) in his famous book *The Wealth of Nations*. Smith wrote:

> Nothing is more useful than water: but; scarce any thing can be had in exchange for it. A diamond, on the contrary, has scarce any value in use; but a very great quantity of other goods may frequently be had in exchange for it.

In most countries, water has a low price but a piece of diamond jewellery has a high price. Why does an economy put a much lower value on something vital to sustaining life compared to something that simply looks good? Smith pointed out that practical things that we use every day have a *value in use*, but often have little or no *value in exchange*. On the other hand, some of the things that often have the greatest value in the market or in exchange, such as a drawing by Picasso, have little or no practical use other than, in this case, as ornamentation.

Understanding the diamonds and water paradox comes through first understanding the economic terms 'marginal utility' and 'scarcity'. Scarcity relates to how little of a good there is compared to what people are demanding. Marginal utility is the additional welfare a person gains from using or purchasing an additional unit of the good. People are willing to pay a higher price for goods with greater marginal utility.

Relating this to water and diamonds, water is not scarce in most of the world, which means people can consume water up to the point at which the marginal utility they gain from the last drop consumed is very low. They aren't willing to pay a lot of money for one more drink of water. Diamonds, by contrast, are scarce. Because of their limited supply, the marginal utility typically gained from adding one more diamond to a person's collection is much higher than for one extra drink of water. However, if one is dying of thirst, then this paradox breaks down. In this situation, the marginal utility gained from another drink of water would be much higher than the additional satisfaction of owning an extra diamond — at least until the thirst was quenched.

Follow-up questions

1 Define the terms 'scarcity' and 'marginal utility'.
2 Can you think of two other goods which generally illustrate the paradox of value?

7

EXTENSION MATERIAL

Marginal utility and an individual's demand curve

If lemonade were available completely free (at zero price), it would be rational for our thirsty boy to drink exactly five glasses of lemonade in the course of a hot, sunny afternoon. He would consume up to the point of satiation, beyond which no further utility can be gained. But because lemonade is an economic good which is scarce in supply and which has an opportunity cost, it is reasonable to assume that the child (or his parents) must pay for his drinks. Suppose that the price of lemonade is equal to the marginal utility gained from the fourth glass. At this price, P_4 represents the opportunity cost of the fourth glass of lemonade: that is, the utility that could be gained if the price were spent on some other good, say a bar of chocolate. To maximise utility at this price, the thirsty child should drink four glasses of lemonade, but no more. It would be irrational to consume a fifth glass at this price, since the extra utility gained would be less than the opportunity cost represented by the price P_4.

Figure 1.4 below shows the effect of the price rising from P_4, successively to P_3, P_2 and P_1. These prices equal the marginal utility derived by the child from the third, second and first glasses of lemonade. When the price rises to P_3, our thirsty child reduces demand to three glasses, so as to maximise utility in the new situation. At price P_2 demand is again reduced to two drinks, and so on. The higher the price, the lower the quantity demanded, which is exactly what a demand curve shows.

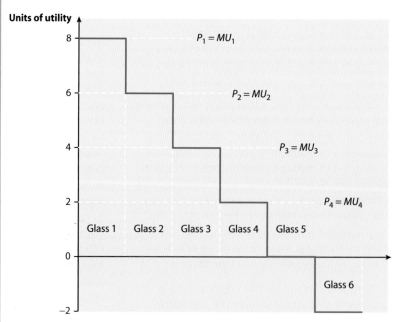

Figure 1.4 Relating marginal utility to changes in price and to the shape of a demand curve

Utility maximisation

As we noted in Book 1, the assumption of maximising behaviour by economic agents (consumers, workers, firms and even the government) is central to orthodox or traditional economic theory. Economic agents decide their market plans so as to maximise a target objective or goal which is believed to be consistent with the pursuit of self-interest. In demand theory, the objective which households are assumed to wish to maximise is the utility, or welfare, obtained from the set of goods and services consumed.

EXTENSION MATERIAL

Maximising versus minimising behaviour

It is worth noting that any maximising objective can always be recast as a minimising objective. Thus a household's assumed objective of *'maximising the utility gained from the set of goods and services consumed'* can be restated as *'minimising the outlay, expenditure or cost of obtaining the same combination or bundle of goods and services'*. Whether we set up an assumed objective in maximising or minimising terms depends on our convenience. It is more usual to investigate maximising objectives, but for some purposes a consideration of the minimising principle can shed interesting light on economic behaviour.

Maximisation subject to constraints

If all goods were free, or if households had unlimited income and capacity to consume all goods, a consumer would maximise utility by obtaining all the goods which yield utility, up to the point of satiation. As we have already indicated, satiation occurs when no more utility can be gained from consuming extra units of a good. Any further consumption would yield only disutility at the margin (negative utility, dissatisfaction or displeasure).

However, because of the problem of scarcity, consumers face a number of constraints which restrict the choices they make in the market place. The constraints are:

● **Limited income.** Consumers, even the very rich, do not possess an unlimited income, or stock of wealth that can be converted into income, with which to purchase all the goods and services that could possibly yield utility. Income spent on one good cannot be spent on some other good or service.
● **A given set of prices.** Very often, consumers can't by their own actions influence the market prices they have to pay to obtain the goods and services they buy. Given this assumption, consumers are 'price-takers' rather than 'price-makers'.
● **The budget constraint.** Taken together, limited income and the set of prices faced impose a budget constraint on consumers' freedom of action in the market place. If we assume that all income is spent and not saved, that there is no borrowing, and that stocks of wealth are not run down, a consumer can only purchase more of one good by giving up consumption of some other good or service, which represents the opportunity cost of consumption.
● **Limited time available.** Even when goods are free, consumer choices must still be made because it is often impossible to consume more than one good at a time or to store more than a limited number of goods for future consumption.

Importance of the margin when making choices

Along with assumptions such as rational economic behaviour and opportunity cost, the 'margin' is one of the key concepts in traditional or orthodox economic theory. Given consistent tastes and preferences, rational consumers choose between available goods and services in such a way as to try to maximise total utility, welfare or satisfaction derived from consumption of the goods. Along with the relative prices that must be paid for each of the goods, the marginal utilities gained from the consumption of the last unit of each good determine the combination of goods the consumer must choose in order to maximise total utility.

As we shall see in later chapters in Part 1 of this book, in orthodox economic theory, the margin is equally important in other areas of economic choice. For example, we shall see how when firms choose how much of a good to produce and sell, they take account of the marginal sales revenue received from selling the last unit of the good, and the marginal cost of producing the last unit. Generalising across all choice situations, we shall explain how in order to maximise a desired objective, an economic agent must undertake the activity involved up to the point at which the marginal private benefit received equals the marginal private cost incurred. For example, a utility-maximising consumer must choose to consume or demand a good up to the point at which $MU = P$. Marginal utility or MU is, of course, the marginal private benefit derived from consuming the last unit of the good, while the good's price, P, is its opportunity cost in consumption, at the margin.

STUDY TIP

The margin is one of the key concepts in A-level microeconomics. Make sure you understand and can apply the concept.

EXTENSION MATERIAL

Can utility be measured?

On several occasions we have referred to 'units of utility' as a unit of measurement for the happiness, pleasure, satisfaction or fulfilment of need which an individual derives from consuming a good or service. However, in real life there is no way in which an individual can mathematically work out the utility to be gained from every unit of a good consumed. Economists have found it impossible to measure directly units of satisfaction, pleasure or fulfilment through which comparisons can be made across individuals.

To get around this problem, the famous economist Paul Samuelson introduced the concept of 'revealed preference'. What revealed preference theory does is work backward from observing how consumers actually behave to observing their preferences. Consumers reveal their preferences by choosing, at given prices and for given levels of income, the bundles or combinations of goods they end up buying.

1.2 Imperfect information

The importance of information for decision making

So far in this chapter, we have assumed that consumers possess perfect information — for example, about the goods that are available to buy, their prices and quality, and about the utility which will be derived from their consumption.

However, when attempting to maximise total utility, more often than not consumers possess imperfect information. As a result, they make 'wrong' decisions. We saw in Book 1, Chapter 5, section 5.5 how consumers may choose to under-consume a merit good such as education and over-consume a demerit good such as tobacco because they possess imperfect information about the long-term consequences of their choices. We shall investigate this further in Chapter 6, section 6.1 of this book, and we shall also touch on this issue in our coverage of behavioural economics in the next section of this chapter.

On a more mundane level, a student may spend £100 on a ticket for a rock concert, believing in advance that she would thoroughly enjoy the entertainment. However, she may come out of the stadium in which the event was held believing that she has wasted her hard-earned money and would be far better off if she had spent the £100 on other goods, such as a meal in a high-class restaurant. This is an example of a 'wrong' choice, but it was also a rational choice because she believed *in advance* that the concert would be good.

The significance of asymmetric information

Sometimes, one party to a market transaction, either the buyer or the seller, suffers from imperfect information about the nature of the transaction. **Asymmetric information** arises when either the buyer or the seller involved in a potential transaction knows something that is not observable to the other party. One of the ways in which asymmetric information can manifest itself is through the process known as *adverse selection*, which is a feature of many market transactions. For example, in the sale and purchase of a second-hand computer, the seller of the good knows more about the computer's defects than a potential purchaser. However, to avoid paying too high a price for an inferior product which contains lots of defects, potential purchasers often offer low prices on *all* second-hand computers, regardless of the fact that some of the computers are good.

The problem of asymmetric information possessed by buyers and sellers is described in a classic article by George Akerlof on the market for 'lemons' — a 'lemon' being American slang for a poor-quality second-hand car.

11

CASE STUDY 1.2

The market for lemons

In 2001 George Akerlof was awarded the Nobel Prize in Economics, largely in response to a 13-page academic paper he published in 1970 titled 'The market for lemons'. Back in 1970, Akerlof found it difficult to get his paper published. Two leading academic journals rejected the paper on the ground that asymmetric information in the market for second-hand cars was too trivial an economic issue. However, by 2001 things had changed.

On receiving his Nobel Prize, Akerlof said:

'Lemons' deals with a problem as old as markets themselves. It concerns how horse traders respond to the natural question: 'if he wants to sell that horse, do I really want to buy it?' Such questioning is fundamental to the market for horses and used cars, but it is also at least minimally present in many market transactions.

Here is an extract from what Akerlof wrote in his 1970 paper:

From time to time one hears either mention of or surprise at the large price difference between new cars and those which have just left the showroom.

The usual lunch table justification for this phenomenon is the pure joy of owning a 'new' car.

We offer a different explanation. Suppose that there are just four kinds of cars. There are new cars and used cars. There are good cars and bad cars (which in America are known as 'lemons'). A new car may be a good car or a lemon, and of course the same is true of used cars.

The individuals in this market buy a new automobile without knowing whether the car they buy will be good or a lemon. After owning a specific car, however, for a length of time, the car owner can form a good idea of the quality of this machine.

An asymmetry of information has developed: for the sellers have more knowledge about the quality of a car than the buyers. But good and bad used cars must still sell at the same price, since it is impossible for a buyer to tell the difference between a good and a bad car.

It is apparent that a used car cannot have the same valuation as a new car — if it did, it would clearly be advantageous to trade a lemon at the price of a new car, at a high probability of the new car being a good car. Most used cars traded will be 'lemons', and good used cars may not be traded at all. The 'bad cars tend to drive out the good (in much the same way that bad money drives out the good).'

Follow-up questions

1 Akerlof asked the question 'if he wants to sell that horse, do I really want to buy it?'. Explain how this question relates to the market for second-hand cars.
2 Suggest two other markets, other than the markets for second-hand cars, used computers and horses, in which market outcomes are affected by asymmetric information.

1.3 Aspects of behavioural economic theory

Emergence of behavioural economics

> **KEY TERM**
>
> **behavioural economics** a method of economic analysis that applies psychological insights into human behaviour to explain how individuals make choices and decisions.

Behavioural economics is a field of study that has attracted a great deal of attention since the beginning of the 21st century. Most of the research in the field has come from universities in the USA, but in recent years UK university economics departments have been offering courses in the subject.

Behavioural economics is built on the insights of psychologists seeking to understand human behaviour and decision making. This research field can be traced back to 1931 when L. L. Thurstone conducted experiments to determine consumer preferences by asking participants to choose repeatedly between alternative bundles of goods. Two of the most influential psychologists are the Israeli academics Amos Tversky and Daniel

Kahneman, who spent decades studying how people think and provided a major contribution to decision research and psychological theory. In 2002 Kahneman was awarded the Nobel Memorial Prize in economics and in 2011 he published *Thinking, Fast and Slow* in which he credits Tversky (who died in 1996) for helping with much of his work.

In 2008 the Chicago economist Richard Thaler and the legal scholar Cass Sunstein published *Nudge: Improving Decisions about Health, Wealth and Happiness*, which is a highly accessible overview of behavioural economics. Having read *Nudge*, immediately on becoming prime minister in 2010, David Cameron set up the UK government's Behavioural Insights Team (BIT), which was initially based in the Cabinet Office in Downing Street. The creation of the BIT, and of a similar body advising the US president, marked the growing influence that behavioural economics was having on government policy-makers.

On its website, the BIT writes:

> We coined the term 'behavioural insights' in 2010 to help bring together ideas from a range of inter-related academic disciplines (behavioural economics, psychology, and social anthropology). These fields seek to understand how individuals take decisions in practice and how they are likely to respond to options. Their insights enable us to design policies or interventions that can encourage, support and enable people to make better choices for themselves and society.

The BIT's website is worth reading to find out about projects that the team runs in government. The web address is: **www.behaviouralinsights.co.uk**. You might also access a BIT publication, *Better Choices: Better Deals*, otherwise known as the Government's consumer empowerment strategy, which recommends how government policy can attempt to influence consumer behaviour. It can be found at **www.behaviouralinsights.co.uk/publications/better-choices-better-deals-behavioural-insights-team-paper**.

STUDY TIP

Try and read Thaler and Sunstein's *Nudge: Improving Decisions about Health, Wealth and Happiness*, and also some of the Behavioural Insight Team's publications, which can be accessed on the internet.

EXTENSION MATERIAL

Squaring the circle between traditional and behavioural economic theory

In his excellent book *Predictably Irrational*, Dan Ariely stated that traditional economics is about creating a theory and using it to explain actual behaviour, whereas behavioural economics is about observing actual behaviour and then coming up with a theory.

Traditional theories are often attacked by behavioural economists on the ground that the simplifying assumptions on which the theories are built are unrealistic. In particular, in the context of what orthodox economists call the 'theory of the firm', behavioural economists query the 'profit-maximising assumption'. This is the assumption that entrepreneurs make business decisions solely on the basis of whether the decisions will lead to larger profits.

However, in a very famous essay, *The Methodology of Positive Economics*, published in 1953, the great pro-

free market economist Milton Friedman defended the traditional approach. Friedman wrote: 'Truly important and significant hypotheses will be found to have "assumptions" that are wildly inaccurate descriptive representations of reality, and, in general, the more significant the theory, the more unrealistic the assumptions.'

Friedman rejected testing a theory solely on the realism of its assumptions. He agreed that assumptions such as utility maximisation and profit maximisation are unrealistic. Friedman argued that a theory should be tested and then accepted or rejected on the basis of the validity and fruitfulness of its predictions. If unrealistic assumptions led to wrong conclusions, he would have argued that the theory should be rejected or modified. But if assumptions are unrealistic because of the need

13

to abstract from a complex reality, but still lead to sound predictions which survive scientific testing, they can be justified. In summary, if members of households act 'as if' they are utility maximisers and likewise the entrepreneurs who run firms act 'as if' they are profit maximisers, the predictive power of traditional theories can still be good.

In the traditional theory of the firm, entrepreneurs are assumed to produce and sell output up to the point at which marginal revenue equals marginal cost, yet real-world business people seldom make such decisions when running their businesses. Friedman argued that this does not matter. If Friedman had lived to the present day (he died at the age of 94 in 2006), he might be using similar reasoning to defend traditional economic theory from the attacks of behavioural economists.

SYNOPTIC LINK
Oligopolistic pricing behaviour is explained in Chapter 3, pages 82–87.

SYNOPTIC LINK
The traditional theory of the firm and profit maximisation are explained in depth in Chapter 2.

KEY TERM
rule-of-thumb a rough and practical method or procedure that can be easily applied when making decisions.

STUDY TIP
Make sure you understand the key differences between traditional economic theory and behavioural economics.

Rational economic behaviour revisited

Bounded rationality

So far in this chapter, and also in Book 1, we have assumed that when exercising choice, individuals are perfectly rational, in the sense that they make decisions in a context of being fully informed, with perfect logic and aiming to achieve the maximum possible economic gain. However, in real life, individuals are seldom if ever perfectly rational. In the world in which we live, decisions are made in conditions of **bounded rationality**, which means that individuals, however high or low their intelligence, make decisions subject to three unavoidable constraints: imperfect information about possible alternatives and their consequences; limited mental processing ability; and a time constraint which limits the time available for making decisions. In complex choice situations, bounded rationality often results in *satisficing* rather than *maximising* choices.

KEY TERMS
bounded rationality when making decisions, an individual's rationality is limited by the information they have, the limitations of their minds, and the finite amount of time available in which to make decisions.

bounded self-control limited self-control in which individuals lack the self-control to act in what they see as their self-interest.

SYNOPTIC LINK
The difference between satisficing and maximising is explained in Chapter 3, pages 62–63.

Bounded self-control

Bounded rationality is closely linked to the related concept of **bounded self-control**. Traditional or orthodox economic theory implicitly assumes that when making choices, individuals have complete self-control. Behavioural economists, by contrast, believe that individuals have bounded (or limited) self-control. Making New Year resolutions in the period immediately after Christmas provides many good examples. Having put on weight during the Christmas festivities, people may decide to go for a daily jog early in the morning before going to work each day after 1 January. For many, this may work well for a few days, but the first bout of bad weather often leads to the resolution being broken.

Thinking fast and thinking slow

The Nobel prize-winning psychologist Daniel Kahneman has been one of the most influential figures in the development of behavioural economics. Kahneman introduced economists to the idea that human beings think in two different ways. The first, which Kahneman called System 1 or 'thinking fast', is intuitive and instinctive. Decisions are made quickly and little effort is used to analyse the situation. This is automatic thinking.

The second, which Kahneman called System 2, is 'thinking slow'. In this method of thinking, which is also known as reflective thinking, concentration and mental effort are required to work through a problem before a decision can be made.

For example, when learning to play a new game such as golf, an individual will 'think slow' when deciding on the appropriate golf club to select for a particular stroke, and on how to grip the club and to take a swing at the ball. Because the decision making is relatively slow, involving careful, logical thought about every decision, the process can be tiring. However, the more often the game is played and the more practice is put in, the less will golfers have to think about minor decisions. Automatic thinking takes over. Professional golf players often play quickly with decisions made on the basis of habit. Through years of repetitive training, their automatic systems have learnt to respond to situations promptly and effectively. In big-game situations they can, of course, suffer if they stop to think. When this happens, they switch to System 2 or the reflective system, over-thinking the situation, which can mean that bad decisions lead to disastrous consequences.

Many of our everyday economic decisions will be taken by our automatic system. Buying a coffee at a train station, buying groceries in a supermarket and ordering drinks in a bar will often be quick, intuitive decisions. Bigger and more important decisions tend to be taken by our reflective system. Deciding whether to buy a car or a house, and choosing an insurance policy, will normally result from reflective decisions.

KEY TERM

cognitive bias a mistake in reasoning or in some other mental thought process occurring as a result of, for example, using rules-of-thumb or holding onto one's preferences and beliefs, regardless of contrary information.

ACTIVITY

Make a list of all the things you bought the last time you went on a serious shopping expedition. How many of your decisions to buy were undertaken by your reflective system and how many by your automatic system?

Biases in decision making

Behavioural economics argues that the decisions people make when exercising choice are often heavily biased. This is because decisions are made on the basis of one's own likes, dislikes and past experiences. Psychologists use the term **cognitive bias** to describe this situation.

A cognitive bias is a mental error that is consistent and predictable. There are many kinds of cognitive bias, one of which is *confirmation bias*. This is the tendency to seek only information that matches what one already believes. It stems from the often unconscious act of listening only to opinions which back up our pre-existing views, while at the same time ignoring or dismissing opinions — no matter how valid — that threaten our views.

EXTENSION MATERIAL

The AQA specification advises that you understand some of the reasons why an individual's economic decisions may be biased. Here are ten examples of cognitive bias additional to confirmation bias, which we have already described:

Ten cognitive biases

Status-quo bias: This is where people generally prefer that things remain the same, or change as little as possible. It is the belief that changing the status quo is likely to be inferior or make things worse.

Memory bias: People are likely to possess accurate memories associated with significant emotions or events (such as the memory of what one was doing when a grandchild was born or when a catastrophe such as the assassination of a world leader occurred). Memory bias influences what and how easily one remembers.

Observational selection bias: The effect of suddenly noticing things not noticed much before and wrongly assuming that the frequency of the observation has increased.

In-group bias: We forge tighter bonds with friends similar to ourselves (our in-group), while being suspicious of others. We value our immediate group at the expense of people we don't really know.

Positive expectation bias: The sense that luck will eventually change for the better — which often fuels gambling addictions. A run of bad luck has to change eventually and better times lie ahead.

Post-purchase rationalisation: Believing after the purchase of an unnecessary, faulty or overly expensive good that buying the product was a good idea, thus justifying a bad decision.

Neglecting probability: The inability to grasp a proper sense of peril and risk, which can lead to overstating the risks of relatively harmless activities and understating the risks of more dangerous ones — for example, air travel versus car travel or cycling risks.

Negativity bias: People tend to pay more attention to bad news than to good news. We perceive negative news as being more important or profound.

Bandwagon effect bias: People succumb to 'group-think' or herd behaviour.

Current moment bias: Preferring pleasure or gratification at the current moment to pleasure in the future. The pain can be left for later.

ACTIVITY

Make a list of all the significant decisions you have made in the last week. To what extent, if any, do these decisions embody one or more of the ten cognitive biases listed above?

KEY TERM

availability bias occurs when individuals make judgements about the likelihood of future events according to how easy it is to recall examples of similar events.

The availability bias

The **availability bias** occurs when individuals place too much weight on the probability of an event happening because they can recall vivid examples of similar events. For example, after reading several news reports about car thefts, an individual may judge that vehicle theft is much more common than it really is in the local area.

Consider also the economic decision to buy a lottery ticket. The probability of selecting the winning numbers in the most popular draw is outrageously long at over 45 million/1. It is irrational to believe that buying a ticket is a sound economic decision because the chance of winning the jackpot is so improbable. However, in October 2014 UK National Lottery tickets sales totalled £649.4 million, an increase of £134.0 million on the same period in 2013. No doubt, when buying a ticket most players do not think about the odds but instead focus on the news stories of people winning the jackpot. The lucky winners of large jackpots are publicised in the national media and their tales are promoted by Camelot, the business that runs the National Lottery. Since its launch in 1994 the National Lottery claims to have created 3,700 millionaires in the UK.

The availability bias often leads to decisions that are not based on logical reasoning. The media will report stories that stick in our mind and affect our reasoning process. Humans will often believe that the probability of an extreme weather event, such as a hurricane or severe flooding, is more likely than empirical statistical analysis bears out. In October 2014 Ipsos MORI's published research highlighting how the general public in 14 countries held preconceptions on the make-up of their societies that were significantly detached from the reality. In the UK, for example, the average citizen believed that 24% of the population were immigrants when the real figure is 13%; and likewise that 24% of the working age population was unemployed when in fact it was less than 7%.

Quickly recalling examples that come to mind is an automatic system response. It will often lead to an overly cautious decision that over-estimates the probability of an outcome occurring.

Anchoring

Anchoring is an example of a predictable bias in individual decision making. Most people have a tendency to compare and contrast only a limited set of items. This is called the anchoring effect. A good example is provided by restaurant menus, which sometimes feature very expensive main courses, while also including more (apparently) reasonably priced alternatives. We are lured into choosing the cheaper items, even though their prices are still quite high. When given a choice, we often tend to pick the middle option, believing it's not too expensive, but also not too cheap.

Biases based on social norms

Human beings are social animals and as a result the behaviour of other people influences our own behaviour. By unconsciously learning from the behaviour of other people, **social norms** are established.

Negative social norms include attitudes towards drinking alcohol. Many young adults often drink heavily because they think it is what people of their age are expected to do. By presenting statistical data showing that the majority of young adults do not engage in regular heavy drinking, behavioural economists would seek to *nudge* young drinkers into different patterns of behaviour.

Positive social norms can be seen in the way in which social attitudes have altered toward smoking in the last 30 years. In the 1980s it was socially acceptable to smoke in all public places including libraries, trains and the London Underground. Concerted health campaigns which provided the general public with better information about the risks of smoking have altered social attitudes toward smoking. As a result people became much more willing to accept laws which restricted their right to smoke. The laws banning smoking in public places are **economic sanctions** (used by government policy-makers) and not **nudges**. Critics of behavioural economics point out that sanctions,

KEY TERMS

anchoring a cognitive bias describing the human tendency when making decisions to rely too heavily on the first piece of information offered (the so-called 'anchor'). Individuals use an initial piece of information when making subsequent judgements.

social norms forms or patterns of behaviour considered acceptable by a society or group within that society.

economic sanctions restrictions imposed by regulations and/or laws that restrict an individual's freedom to behave in certain ways. Breaking a sanction can lead to punishment.

nudges factors which encourage people to think and act in particular ways. Nudges try to shift group and individual behaviour in ways which comply with desirable social norms.

17

such as the smoking ban, are more effective at changing behaviour and improving public health than nudges, which only alter the behaviour of some people. Nevertheless, government reports in Ireland claim that since smoking in public places was banned people are also less likely to smoke in other people's houses because it is now considered to be socially unacceptable.

ACTIVITY

Give examples of some of the social norms that affect your behaviour when at home and when attending school or college.

TEST YOURSELF 1.3

Which of the following provides the best definition of a norm?

Norms are:

A laws that attempt to discourage excessive consumption

B informal rules that govern human behaviour

C formal rules that govern human behaviour

D formal rules about how to buy goods and services

Explain your answer.

Altruism and fairness

Altruism is when we act to promote someone else's wellbeing, even though we may suffer as a consequence, either in terms of a financial or time loss, or by incurring personal risk. Before the development of behavioural economics, economists generally assumed that individuals were not altruistic and acted only in their self-interest. Nevertheless, altruism could still be accommodated within maximising theory — for example, by assuming that individuals derive pleasure as a result of giving to others. More recently, behavioural economists have drawn attention to the fact that for many if not most people, their first impulse is to cooperate with each other rather than to compete. Very young children are frequently observed helping other children around them, out of a genuine concern for their welfare. Animals have also been observed displaying altruism.

Altruistic behaviour often results from people's perceptions of **fairness**. This being a normative term incorporating value judgements, different people have a range of different views on the meaning of fairness. A popular view is that fairness involves treating people equally or in a way that is right or reasonable.

KEY TERMS

altruism concern for the welfare of others.

fairness the quality of being impartial, just, or free of favouritism. It can mean treating everyone the same. Fairness involves treating people equally, sharing with others, giving others respect and time, and not taking advantage of them.

SYNOPTIC LINK
Go back to Book 1, Chapter 1 to remind yourself of the meaning of normative statements.

1.4 Behavioural economics and economic policy

As we mentioned in our introduction to aspects of behavioural economics, UK and US governments have recently been introducing the insights of behavioural economics into practical policy making. In the context of the impact of behavioural economics on government economic policy making, you need to consider how behavioural economics might influence the design of a variety of government policies which aim to reduce or eliminate particular economic problems.

At times in this chapter, we have tended to portray traditional or orthodox economics and behavioural economics as if they are completely opposed to each other, implying that if one is correct, the other is inevitably wrong. However, this is a somewhat misguided way of viewing the two very important branches of economic theory. It is better to think of behavioural economics as complementing and improving traditional economic theory by allowing governments and decision makers to design policy interventions, such as healthcare interventions, to enable them to achieve policy goals more effectively.

Behavioural economics argues that individuals are not fully rational in the way traditional economic theory assumes. As a result, individuals regularly suffer from behavioural biases that make it difficult for them to achieve the results they actually prefer. In this situation, government intervention should aim at helping individuals to achieve an outcome that is in their own best interest.

Choice architecture and framing

Choice architecture

Choice architecture is the term used by behavioural economists to describe how government policy-makers can lead people into making particular choices. Government can use behavioural insights to design choice architectures so that citizens are *nudged* to opt for choices that are deemed to be in their best interest, so as to achieve a socially desirable outcome. For example, countries that require people to opt out of organ donations generally have a much higher proportion of the population willing to donate than countries that ask people to opt in.

This introduces us to a key behavioural concept known as **default choice**. When framing policy on issues such as organ donation, individuals who, in the event of their death, might donate body organs such as hearts or livers, can be asked whether to opt in or opt out of organ donation using a tick box. In this context, if opt out is the default choice, the tick box should allow the user to opt in, i.e. to reject the default choice by ticking the box. Unless the user ticks the box, healthcare organisations such as the NHS cannot make use of the user's organs. For a behavioural economist, the benefits of opt-out over opt-in are clear: the supply of donated organs rises to be closer to the demand for them and the nation's public health improves.

Policy-makers can improve social welfare by designing government programmes that select as a default an option that can be considered in an individual's best long-term interest. A number of examples of this approach have been trialled and introduced by the UK government's Behavioural Insights Team. One of these is automatic pension enrolment (see case study 1.3).

> **KEY TERMS**
>
> **choice architecture** a framework setting out different ways in which choices can be presented to consumers, and the impact of that presentation on consumer decision making.
>
> **default choice** an option that is selected automatically unless an alternative is specified.

NHS
Blood and Transplant

Have you joined the Organ Donor Register?

In most of the UK, signing up to the NHS Organ Donor Register is an opt-in choice, but people resident in Wales have to tick a box to opt out of organ donation

Automatic pension enrolment

There is a broad consensus among economists in the UK that too many workers are saving too little for their retirement in old age. In an effort to solve this problem the BIT and the Department for Work and Pensions (DWP) introduced a policy of automatic enrolment in October 2012. Previously the default position for workers was that they would not pay into a pension fund unless they made the choice to opt into a scheme. Under automatic enrolment the default position is that workers pay into a pension system unless they choose to opt out. Opting-in is the default choice.

Initially the scheme started with the UK's biggest employers (firms that have over 250 workers) but it is being rolled out to include all employers by 2018. After the first 6 months the BIT reported that overall participation in pension schemes increased from 61% to 83%. This saw 400,000 extra workers saving income for retirement. By December 2014 the DWP reported that 5 million workers were included in automatic enrolment and that 9 out of 10 workers had not exercised their right to opt out of the system.

Follow-up questions

1 Why is it desirable for social and economic policy for governments to base pension policy on an opting-in default choice?
2 Research the BIT website to find other examples of policy being changed to incorporate this default choice.

Framing

> **KEY TERM**
> **framing** how something is presented (the 'frame') influences the choices people make.

People are influenced by how information is presented. **Framing** is the tendency for people to be influenced by the context in which the choice is presented when making a decision. Advertisers have for many years presented consumers with choices in a manner that frames their products in a favourable light. Consider the label on food products that read: '90% fat-free'. Would they sell as well if the label read: '10% fat'?

Politicians will often frame (or spin) economic statements in a manner that is favourable to the argument they are trying to make. For example, in December 2014 the chancellor of the exchequer George Osborne said that the Government had more than halved the UK's budget deficit since taking office in May 2010. This message was printed on Conservative Party campaign posters in January 2015. Osborne was trying to frame his government in the voters' mind as one of economic competence. This statement is true if you measure the size of the budget deficit as a ratio of GDP. However, if you measure the budget deficit in money terms, it has only been reduced by around 40%.

Table 1.4 UK budget deficit, 2009/10 and 2014/15

Year	UK budget deficit (£bn)	UK budget deficit as a % of GDP
2009/10	153.0	10.2
2014/15	91.3	5.0

Source: OBR, *A Brief Guide to the UK Public Finances*, 3 December 2014

Mandated choices

> **KEY TERM**
> **mandated choice** people are required by law to make a decision.

A variation of default choice is **mandated choice**; this is where people are required by law to make a decision. A mandated or required choice is when a choice architect designs a system that forces individuals to make an explicit decision and not merely go ahead with a default position. This system is favoured by libertarians who philosophically oppose the notion that well-meaning government officials should guide citizens into making the 'correct' choice favoured by the government, especially if this is the default option.

An everyday example of a mandated choice outside of government policy is the Microsoft software installation boxes that appear on our computer screens. The Microsoft choice architects force computer users to make choices and select various options before they can move onto the next step and complete the installation process. Most people will choose the recommended settings but they have to make an active decision to do so. Mandated choices work well with simple yes/no decisions but less well with complex decisions.

Restricted choice

Restricted choice means offering people a limited number of options, on the basis that offering too many choices is unhelpful and leads to poor decisions. Most people can't, or can't be bothered to, evaluate a large number of choices. The policy of requiring the energy companies to simplify their pricing structures and restrict the number of options offered to consumers is an example of 'restricted choice' in action.

Government policy-makers should consider behavioural insights when designing systems. A well-designed system should make it easier for citizens to pay for government services by setting up direct debits, using accessible language and sending text messages or e-mails to remind people to complete requests. Evidence from the BIT shows that personalised letters increase response rates, whilst asking respondents to sign forms at the top of the page and not the bottom results in more honest answers.

Choice architecture: some further implications for government policy

When making a choice, individuals need to understand the decision that they are making. Simple decisions such as ordering a meal in a restaurant are easy to understand. More complex decisions, such as taking out a mortgage or insurance policy, can be difficult to understand due to complex clauses, intricate pricing tariffs, and baffling legal terminology. Government regulation of business behaviour should try to ensure that companies make their products as straightforward and transparent as possible for consumers to exercise choice. Individuals need to have as great an understanding as possible of the consequences of any decisions and choices they make.

Well-designed choice architecture helps people to make good intuitive decisions. For example, pedestrians are told by the writing painted on the roads to *look right* or *look left* when crossing a road. This choice architecture helps reduce accidents, especially in tourist areas where a large number of pedestrians are not initially familiar with the 'rules of the road'.

However, as choices become more complex, people have greater difficulty in understanding the information presented to them. By providing an individual with information about the choices made by similar people in similar situations, it is possible for an individual to benefit from 'collaborative filtering'. Accessing the preferences of like-minded people reduces the chance that individual decisions are made on the basis of imperfect knowledge, though to some extent this advantage may be offset by people's tendency to 'join the herd' without considering the disadvantages of doing so.

The best way to help an individual's decision-making process is to provide feedback that enables them to learn from their past performance. In a school environment, good teachers do this all the time. Constructive feedback helps people to make better decisions and choices. However, negative feedback is

> **KEY TERM**
> **restricted choice** offering people a limited number of options so that they are not overwhelmed by the complexity of the situation. If there are too many choices, people may make a poorly thought-out decision or not make any decision.

typically misperceived or rejected. Constructive feedback enhances people's feelings of competence and self-control. Feedback is most useful when individuals actively participate in the feedback session. By contrast, destructive feedback tends to cause conflict and reduce personal motivation.

Choice architects need to build incentives — sometimes based on monetary rewards — into the choice architecture they design. People often respond to such incentives. According to traditional economic theory, individuals value money and other tangible rewards and try hard to gain them. People go to work to earn money, so we expect them to work harder when there is more money at stake. Reward incentives — particularly monetary incentives — can motivate individuals to behave in ways they would otherwise avoid.

However, behavioural economics has made two important advances with regard to reward incentives and how they affect economic behaviour. First, it has suggested that not all incentives are equally important. As we saw earlier, individuals feel losses more severely than equivalent gains. Second, behavioural economics has shown that in certain situations, individuals respond in perverse ways to reward incentives. Monetary incentives, for example, may cause individuals to respond in the workplace with less effort rather than more. Behavioural economics recognises that people are not only motivated by financial gain; social norms and perceptions of fairness, for example, exert a powerful influence on people's behaviour.

Revisiting nudge theory

As explained earlier, a nudge tries to alter people's behaviour in a predictable way without forbidding any options or significantly changing economic incentives. A nudge is not a legal requirement.

When used as a part of government policy, nudges must be open and transparent to the general public. Governments should be honest with the public and ensure that they explain why they have introduced a nudge, but still allow individuals to make a choice.

Nudges versus shoves

'Nudge' policies seek to lead people by providing them with helpful information and language that then allows them to make an informed choice. By contrast, 'shove' policies instruct people to behave in certain ways, often by their responding to financial incentives and disincentives that reward or punish different decisions.

Government policies based on traditional economic theories have generally sought to shove people into altering their behaviour rather than to nudge them into the desired direction.

Table 1.5 Nudges versus shoves

Nudge	Shove
• Provides information for people to respond to. • Opt-out schemes rather than opt-in schemes and default choices. • Active choosing by individuals.	• Uses taxation and subsidies to alter incentives and on occasion, in the case of taxes to punish people. • Uses fines, laws banning activities and regulations.

ACTIVITY

School rules, which may not have changed significantly for many years, are often based on the 'shove' principle. These include punishments for lateness and bad behaviour. Get together with a group of fellow students and discuss how, and the extent to which, the school might move away from 'shove' to 'nudge'. Then see what happens, both immediately and in the future, when you submit your proposals to the school authorities — for example, at a School Council meeting.

SUMMARY

- The starting point for understanding individual economic decision making is understanding the nature of demand, rationality and maximising behaviour.
- Economists have traditionally assumed that individuals wish to maximise utility.
- Utility can be thought of as satisfaction, pleasure or fulfilment of need.
- It is important to distinguish between total utility and marginal utility.
- The hypothesis (or 'law') of diminishing marginal utility lies behind the derivation of an individual's demand curve.
- Utility cannot be measured directly but can be indicated by revealed preference.
- Individual economic decision making is affected by imperfect and asymmetric information.
- In recent years, behavioural economics has emerged to question many of the assumptions of traditional economic theory.
- Nudge theory, choice architecture and framing lie at the heart of the ways in which behavioural architecture can influence economic policy making.

Questions

1 Describe the main features of an individual's demand curve for a good.

2 What is meant by maximisation subject to constraints?

3 Explain the difference between maximising and satisficing behaviour.

4 Discuss the similarities of, and the differences separating, the orthodox and the behavioural theories of individual economic decision making.

5 What is a 'nudge'? Explain how a food business might use nudges to promote healthy eating.

6 Outline two ways in which the insights of behavioural economics can be incorporated into government economic policy.

2 Production, costs and revenue

To understand production, costs and revenue in greater depth than was the case in Book 1, it is necessary to understand how the 'building blocks' of the theory of the firm, which are shown in Figure 2.1, link together. This and the next chapter explain these linkages.

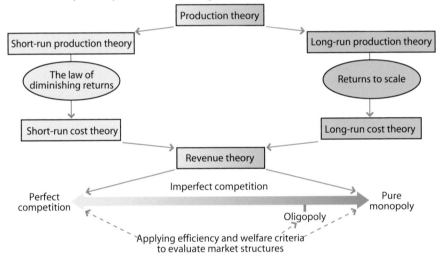

Figure 2.1 The 'building blocks' of the theory of the firm

A theme running through Chapters 2 and 3 is that it is difficult and sometimes impossible to understand properly market structures such as perfect competition and monopoly (shown in the final part of Figure 2.1) without first understanding the nature of production, costs and revenue. More narrowly, cost theory cannot be fully understood without understanding the first 'building block' in the flow chart, production theory.

In this chapter, we explain in more detail the concept, first used in Chapter 1, of 'the margin', which we use to explain production, cost and revenue curves in a more rigorous way than was the case in Book 1. The margin is one of the most important economic concepts in the A-level economics specification, especially in microeconomics.

Figure 2.1 reminds us of the distinction explained in Book 1 between short-run and long-run production and cost theory. However, in this chapter we explain how the law of diminishing returns determines the shape of the marginal returns curve (in short-run production theory) and the marginal cost curve (in short-run cost theory). Likewise, we explain how the long-run concept of returns to scale is a major determinant of the shape of long-run cost curves.

In contrast to production and cost curves, a firm's revenue curves are determined by the competitiveness and structure of the market in which the firm sells its output. The main forms of market structure, shown in the lower part of Figure 2.1, are explained and analysed in Chapter 3.

This chapter will:

- remind you of the difference between the short run and the long run
- explain the law diminishing marginal returns in the context of short-run production theory
- describe how a firm's short-run marginal cost curve is derived from short-run production theory
- describe how a firm's long-run cost curves are affected by the production theory concept of returns to scale
- explain how a firm's revenue curves are dependent on the type of market structure in which the firm sells its output
- discuss the role of profit in the economy
- examine how technological change can affect production and costs, and also competitiveness and market structure

2.1 Developing short-run production theory: the law of diminishing returns

What is a firm?

Before we delve further into the nature of production theory, first in the short run and then in the long run, we shall first remind you of the nature of a **firm**. A firm is a business enterprise that either produces or deals in and exchanges goods or services. Unlike non-business productive organisations, such as many charities, firms are commercial, earning revenue to cover the production costs they incur.

KEY TERM

firm a productive organisation which sells its output of goods or services commercially.

CASE STUDY 2.1

Ronald Coase and the nature of the firm

Way back in 1937, Professor Ronald Coase, who much later in 1991 received the Nobel Prize in Economics for his insights, set out to explain why firms exist. Coase's starting point was that 'production could be carried on without any organisation at all', and could be determined solely by the price mechanism. Coase then asked 'why do firms exist?' His answer was that firms exist because they reduce transaction costs, such as search and information costs, bargaining costs, costs of keeping trade secrets, and policing and enforcement costs.

Coase then asked 'why then don't firms become bigger and bigger? Why isn't all world production

carried on by a single big firm?' Coase gave two main reasons. 'First, as a firm gets larger, there may be decreasing returns to the entrepreneurial function, that is, the costs of organising additional transactions within the firm may rise...Secondly... as the transactions which are organised increase, the entrepreneur...fails to make the best use of the factors of production.' At a certain point, the gains from economies of scale are defeated by the costs of bureaucracy.

For further information on Coase and the nature of the firm, and on the different views of later economists, access on the internet the article by Steve Denning, 'Did Ronald Coase get economics wrong?', published in *Forbes Magazine* on 25 September 2013.

Follow-up question

1 Explain the meaning of the following terms mentioned in the passage: the entrepreneurial function; transaction costs; bargaining costs; and enforcement costs.

The short run and the long run

As we explained in Book 1, Chapter 3, the short run is defined as the time period in which, in the course of production, at least one of the factors of production is fixed and cannot be varied. (By contrast, in the long run, the scale of all the factors of production can be changed.) As a simplification, we shall assume that only two inputs or factors of production are needed for production to take place — capital and labour. We shall also assume that in the short run, capital is fixed. It follows that the only way the firm can increase output in the short run is by adding more of the variable factor of production, labour, to the fixed capital.

Table 2.1 Short-run production with fixed capital

Fixed capital	Variable labour										
	0	1	2	3	4	5	6	7	8	9	10
Total returns	0	1	8	18	32	50	64	70	72	68	60
Average returns	–	1	4	6	8	10	10.7**	10	9	7.6	6
Marginal returns		1	7	10	14	18*	14	6	2	–4	–8

* The point of diminishing marginal returns
** The point of diminishing average returns
Note: Total, average and marginal returns are often called total, average and marginal product.
For example, in Table 2.1 the 'marginal returns of labour' can be called the 'marginal product of labour'.

Table 2.1 shows what might happen in a small musical instrument workshop assembling guitars when the number of workers employed increases from 0 to 10. The first worker employed assembles 1 guitar a day, and the second and third workers respectively add 7 and 10 guitars to the workshop's total daily output. These figures measure the marginal returns (or marginal product) of each of the first three workers employed. The **marginal returns of labour** are the addition to total output brought about by adding one more worker to the labour force.

In Table 2.1, the first five workers benefit from increasing marginal returns (or increasing marginal productivity). An additional worker increases total output by more than the amount added by the previous worker. Increasing marginal returns are very likely when the labour force is small. In this situation, employing an extra worker allows the workforce to be organised more efficiently. By dividing the various tasks of production among a greater number of workers, the firm benefits from specialisation and the division of labour. Workers become better and more efficient in performing the particular tasks in which they specialise, and time is saved that otherwise would be lost as a result of workers switching between tasks.

But as the firm adds labour to fixed capital, eventually the **law of diminishing marginal returns** (or law of diminishing marginal productivity) sets in. In this example, the law sets in when the sixth worker is employed. The marginal return of the fifth worker is 18 guitars, but the sixth worker adds only 14 guitars to total output. Diminishing marginal returns set in because labour is being added to fixed capital. When more and more labour is added to fixed plant and machinery, eventually workers begin to get in each other's way and the marginal returns of labour fall, though not often at a labour force as small as six workers.

KEY TERMS

marginal returns of labour the change in the quantity of total output resulting from the employment of one more worker, holding all the other factors of production fixed.

law of diminishing returns a *short-term* law which states that as a variable factor of production is added to a fixed factor of production, eventually both the marginal and average returns to the variable factor will begin to fall. It is also known as the law of diminishing marginal (and average) productivity.

Note that the impact of diminishing marginal returns does not mean that an extra worker joining the labour force is any less hardworking or motivated than his or her predecessors. (In microeconomic theory we often assume that workers and other factors of production are completely interchangeable and homogeneous.) Any further specialisation and division of labour eventually become exhausted as more labour is added to a fixed amount of capital or machinery.

Whereas marginal returns are the addition to total output attributable to taking on the last worker added to the labour force, the **average returns** at any level of employment are measured by dividing the total output of the labour force by the number of workers employed. The average returns of the labour force employed in the guitar workshop are shown by the middle row of data in Table 2.1. Note that in the table, the point of diminishing *average* returns occurs after the sixth worker is taken on, whereas diminishing marginal returns set in after the fifth worker is employed. The relationship between the marginal returns and the average returns of labour is illustrated in the lower panel of Figure 2.2 below.

The law of diminishing returns shown on a diagram

Figure 2.2 illustrates the law of diminishing marginal returns. In the upper panel of the diagram, the law begins to operate at point A. Up to this point, the slope of the total returns curve increases, moving from point to point up the curve. This shows the labour force benefiting from increasing marginal returns. When diminishing marginal returns set in, the **total returns** curve continues to rise as more workers are combined with capital, but the curve becomes less steep from point to point up the curve. Point Y shows where total returns begin to fall. Beyond this point, additional workers begin to get in the way of other workers, to such an extent that the marginal returns to labour become negative.

It is important to understand that all three curves (and all three rows in Table 2.1) contain the same information, but the information is used differently in each curve (and row). The total returns curve plots the information *cumulatively*, adding the marginal returns of the last worker employed to the total returns before the worker joined the labour force. By contrast, the marginal returns curve plots the same information *non-cumulatively*, or as separate observations. Finally, at each level of employment, the average returns curve shows the total returns of the labour force divided by the number of workers employed.

In the lower panel of Figure 2.2, the law of diminishing marginal returns sets in at point B, at the highest point on the marginal returns curve. Before this point, increasing marginal returns are shown by the rising (or positively sloped) marginal returns curve, while beyond this point, diminishing marginal returns are depicted by the falling (or negatively sloped) marginal returns curve. Likewise, the point of diminishing average returns is located at the highest point of the average returns curve at point C. Finally, marginal returns become negative beyond point W.

> **KEY TERMS**
>
> **average returns of labour** total output divided by the total number of workers employed.
>
> **total returns of labour** total output produced by all the workers employed by a firm.

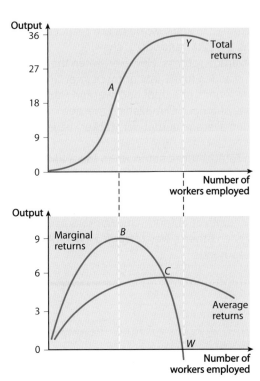

Figure 2.2 Total, marginal and average returns curves

QUANTITATIVE SKILLS 2.1

Worked example: diminishing returns to labour

A firm has a fixed amount of capital and land, and increases output by employing additional labour according to the schedule in Table 2.2.

Table 2.2 Diminishing returns to labour

Labour	Output
1	20
2	42
3	68
4	93
5	100
6	90

1 When do diminishing marginal returns set in?
2 When do diminishing average returns set in?
3 When do diminishing total returns set in?

1 Diminishing marginal returns set in when the marginal returns or marginal productivity falls for an extra worker added to the labour force. The marginal returns of the second worker, which are calculated by subtracting total output when only one worker is employed from total output when two workers are employed, are 22 units of output. Via a similar calculation, the marginal returns of the third worker are 26 units of output. However, diminishing marginal returns set in when a fourth worker is added to the labour force. The marginal returns of the fourth worker are 25 units of output.

2 For each size of labour force, average returns are calculated by dividing total output by the number of workers employed. Average returns when the labour force is 1, 2, 3 and 4 workers are respectively outputs of 20, 21, 22.67 and 23.25, showing increasing average returns. However, when the fifth worker is added to the labour force, marginal returns fall to 7 units of output and average returns fall to 20 units of output. Diminishing average returns (falling average output per worker) have now set in.

3 Diminishing total returns set in when the addition of an extra worker causes total output to fall. This happens when the sixth worker is added to the labour force. Note that marginal returns are now negative (−10 units of output). The workers are getting into each other's way to such an extent that total output falls.

EXTENSION MATERIAL

The relationship between marginal returns and average returns

The relationship between the marginal returns of labour and the average returns of labour is an example of a more general relationship that you need to know. (Shortly, we shall provide a second example, namely the relationship between marginal costs and average costs of production.)

Marginal and average curves plotted from the same set of data always display the following relationship:

- When the marginal is greater than the average, the average rises.
- When the marginal is less than the average, the average falls.
- When the marginal equals the average, the average is constant, neither rising nor falling.

It is vital to understand this relationship. It does *not* state that an average will rise when a marginal is rising; nor does it state that an average will fall when a marginal falls. As we saw in Figure 2.2, marginal returns begin to fall as soon as the law of diminishing marginal returns sets in. Nevertheless, as long as marginal returns are greater than the average returns of labour, the latter continue to rise. When marginal returns exceed average returns, the average returns curve is 'pulled up', even when the marginal returns curve is falling. But when the marginal returns curve cuts through the average returns curve (at point *C* in Figure 2.2), beyond that point the average returns of labour begin to fall. The marginal returns curve cuts through the average returns curve at the latter's highest point. Beyond this point, the marginal returns curve continues to fall, and because marginal returns are less than average returns, they 'pull down' the average returns curve.

EXTENSION MATERIAL

The importance of productivity

Book 1, Chapter 3 introduced you to the very important economic concept of **productivity**, focusing in the main on **labour productivity**, or output per worker. The chapter then looked at a big problem which has adversely affected UK economic performance in recent years: the failure of labour productivity to recover from a relatively low level, compared to other countries such as Germany and the USA, in the years following the 2008/2009 recession. This has been the called the 'productivity puzzle'. Why has the UK economy performed less well than competitor countries in increasing labour productivity?

Among the explanations of the productivity puzzle that have been put forward are: inadequate investment in new capital goods, relatively low wages in the UK economy and employers 'hoarding' rather than laying off workers in the recession, which, with depressed output, inevitably means that labour productivity falls. With regard to the latter argument, the fall in labour productivity has helped employment in the UK in the short run, but the long-run consequences of low productivity growth may be much less favourable. For further information on productivity, labour productivity and related concepts such as the UK's productivity gap, re-read Book 1, pages 55–58.

2.2 Developing long-run production theory: returns to scale

Returns to scale

Figure 2.3, which is an extended version of Figure 3.3 in Book 1, page 61, illustrates the important distinction between returns to a variable factor of production, which occur in the short run, and **returns to scale**, which operate only in the economic long run. Suppose that a firm's fixed capital is represented by **plant** size 1 in the diagram. Initially, the firm can increase production in the short run, by moving along the horizontal arrow *A*, employing more variable factors of production such as labour. To escape the impact of short-run diminishing marginal returns which eventually set in, the firm may make the long-run decision to invest in a larger production plant, such as plant size 2. The movement from plant size 1 to plant size 2 is shown by the movement along the vertical arrow *X* in the diagram. Once plant size 2 is in operation, the firm is in a new short-run situation, able to increase output by moving along arrow *B*. But again, the impact of short-run diminishing returns may eventually cause the firm to expand the scale of its operations to plant size 3 in the long run.

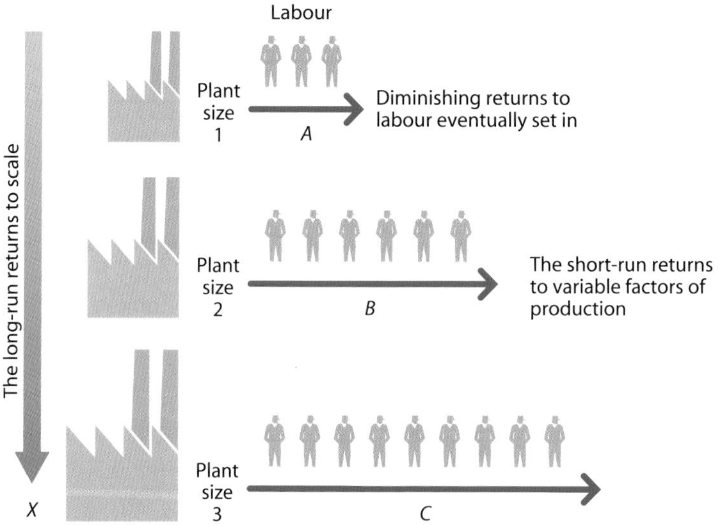

Figure 2.3 Contrasting short-run and long-run production

It is important to avoid confusing returns to scale, which occur in the long run when the scale of *all* the factors of production can be altered, with the short-run returns that occur when at least one factor is fixed. With returns to scale there are three possibilities:

- **Increasing returns to scale.** If an increase in the scale of all the factors of production causes a more than proportionate increase in output, there are increasing returns to scale.
- **Constant returns to scale.** If an increase in the scale of all the factors of production causes the same proportionate increase in output, there are constant returns to scale.
- **Decreasing returns to scale.** If an increase in the scale of all the factors of production causes a less than proportionate increase in output, there are decreasing (or diminishing) returns to scale.

KEY TERMS

returns to scale the rate by which output changes if the scale of all the factors of production is changed.

plant an establishment, such as a factory, a workshop or a retail outlet, owned and operated by a firm.

KEY TERMS

increasing returns to scale when the scale of all the factors of production employed increases, output increases at a faster rate.

constant returns to scale when the scale of all the factors of production employed increases, output increases at the same rate.

decreasing returns to scale when the scale of all the factors of production employed increases, output increases at a slower rate.

Economies and diseconomies of scale

Just as it is important to avoid confusing short-run returns to the variable factors of production with long-run returns to scale, so returns to scale must be distinguished from a closely related concept: economies and diseconomies of scale. Returns to scale refer to the *technical* relationship in production between *inputs* and *outputs* measured in physical units. For example, increasing returns to scale occur if a doubling of a car firm's factory size and its labour force and other factors of production enables the firm to more than double its output of cars. There is no mention of money costs of production in this example of increasing returns to scale. Returns to scale are part of long-run production theory, but economies and diseconomies of scale are part of long-run cost theory. **Economies of scale** occur when **long-run average cost** (*LRAC*) falls as output increases. **Diseconomies of scale** occur when *LRAC* rises as output increases.

STUDY TIP

Increasing returns to scale and economies of scale are often treated as interchangeable terms, though strictly speaking, returns to scale are part of long-run production theory whereas economies of scale are part of long-term cost theory. You must understand the relationship between returns to scale and economies or diseconomies of scale. The AQA A-level specification advises: 'Students should appreciate that both the law of diminishing returns and returns to scale explain relationships between inputs and output. They should also understand that these relationships have implications for costs of production.'

The link between returns to scale and economies and diseconomies of scale is that increasing returns to scale lead to falling long-run average costs or economies of scale, and likewise decreasing returns to scale bring about rising long-run average costs or diseconomies of scale. The effect of increasing returns to scale on long-run average costs can be explained in the following way: output increases faster than inputs, so if wage rates and other factor prices are the same at all levels of output, the money cost of producing a unit of input must fall. Likewise, with decreasing returns to scale, output increases at a slower rate than inputs, and the money cost of producing a unit of output rises.

There are other reasons for falling long-run average costs besides the impact on costs of increasing returns to scale. These include the effect of 'bulk buying' reducing the cost of raw materials and components.

Bringing together long-run average cost and short-run average cost

In Book 1 we described and explained various possible shapes of *LRAC* curve. In this chapter, we go a stage further by explaining the relationship between a firm's *LRAC* curve and the associated *SRATC* curves.

Figure 2.4 shows a number of short-run average total cost (*SRATC*) curves, each representing a particular firm size. In the long run, a firm can move from one short-run cost curve to another, for example from $SRATC_1$ to $SRATC_2$, with each curve associated with a different scale of capacity that is fixed in the short run. The line drawn as a tangent to the family or set of *SRATC* curves is the *LRAC* curve.

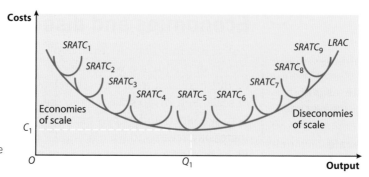

Figure 2.4 A U-shaped *LRAC* curve and its related *SRATC* curves

Optimum firm size

The size of firm at the lowest point on the firm's *LRAC* curve is known as the **optimum firm size**. In Figure 2.4, we can identify a single optimum firm size, occurring after economies of scale have been gained, but before diseconomies of scale set in. In the graph, optimum firm size is shown by the short-run cost curve $SRATC_5$, with optimum output at Q_1.

Other shapes of *LRAC* curve

The *LRAC* curve need not be symmetrically U-shaped, with a single identifiable optimum size of firm, as illustrated in Figure 2.4. Four other possibilities are depicted in Figures 2.5, 2.6, 2.7 and 2.8. Figure 2.5 is a variant of Figure 2.4, but with a horizontal section to the *LRAC* curve inserted between the sections of the curve showing economies and diseconomies of scale.

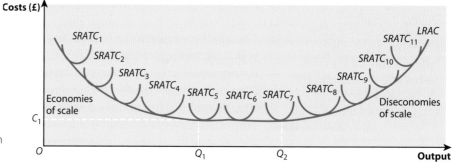

Figure 2.5 A 'three-section' long-run average cost curve

In this diagram, the *LRAC* curve comprises three sections: a downward-sloping section showing economies of scale; a horizontal mid-section; and finally, an upward-sloping section which begins when diseconomies of scale set in. With this shape of the *LRAC* curve, it is not possible to identify a single optimum firm size. Long-run average costs of production would be the same for any size of firm producing at the lowest points on $SRATC_5$, $SRATC_6$ and $SRATC_7$, between and including the levels of output Q_1 and Q_2.

Figure 2.6 illustrates an important concept in production and cost theory: **minimum efficient scale** (*MES*). *MES* is the lowest output at which long-run average costs have been reduced to the minimum level that can be achieved, which means that the firm has benefited to the full from economies of scale. In Figure 2.6, all firm sizes to the left of the $SRATC_3$ curve are below minimum efficient scale, incurring higher average costs than can be achieved at the lowest point on $SRATC_3$. By contrast, there would be no further reductions in long-run production costs for any firms producing levels of output above Q_1. In the diagram, the MES level of output is Q_1, with average costs minimised at C_1.

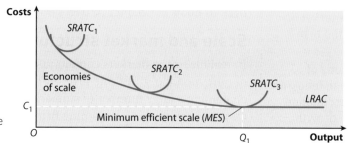

Figure 2.6 An 'L'-shaped $LRAC$ curve and minimum efficient scale (MES)

Another possibility is illustrated by Figure 2.7: an $LRAC$ curve which is horizontal throughout its length. This curve depicts a market or industry in which firms neither benefit from economies of scale nor suffer the consequences of diseconomies of scale.

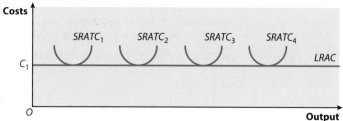

Figure 2.7 Constant long-run average costs

Figure 2.8 helps to explain why small firms are common in industries supplying services, such as those provided by hairdressers and personal trainers. The markets in which these services are provided typically possess economies of small-scale production. Diseconomies of scale may set in early in such industries, resulting in an $LRAC$ curve in which the optimum-sized firm, depicted by the short-run average cost curve $SRATC_2$, is relatively small. The MES, Q_1, is at a low level of output.

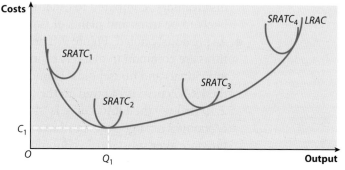

Figure 2.8 The $LRAC$ curve in an industry with economies of small-scale production

External economies and diseconomies of scale

The scale economies and diseconomies referred to so far in this chapter have been **internal economies and diseconomies of scale**. These occur when a firm, or a plant within the firm itself, increases its scale and size. By contrast, **external economies of scale** occur when average or unit costs of production fall, not because of the growth of the firm or plant itself, but because of the growth of the industry or market of which the firm is a part. Likewise,

KEY TERM

internal economies and diseconomies of scale
changes in long-run average costs of production resulting from changes in the size or scale of a firm or plant.

external diseconomies of scale occur when average costs of production increase because of the growth of the whole industry or market. To find out more about external economies and diseconomies of scale, and also about the various types of internal economy and diseconomy of scale, you should refer back to Book 1, Chapter 3, pages 65–67.

Scale and market structure

In real life, some markets contain just a few firms — in the extreme case of pure monopoly, just one firm. At the other extreme there are markets containing a large number of similarly sized small firms. Between these extremes are markets containing firms of a variety of sizes — some large firms but also some small firms.

The existence or non-existence of increasing returns to scale and economies of scale provide one explanation for variability in the size of firm in different market or industry structures. This section brings together some conclusions that can be drawn from Figures 2.6, 2.7 and 2.8.

- Figure 2.9, which is the same as Figure 2.6 but with a vertical line added to show the maximum size of the market, can be used to explain natural monopoly. Natural monopoly occurs when there is room in a market for only one firm benefiting to the full from economies of scale. In Figure 2.9 this is shown by the firm producing on the short-run average cost curve, $SRATC_3$.

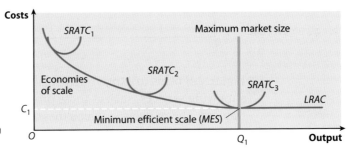

Figure 2.9 Circumstances in which natural monopoly arises

- The horizontal *LRAC* curve in Figure 2.7 illustrates a market in which large, medium-sized and small firms or plants can coexist and compete against each other. No firm or plant gains a cost advantage, or suffers a cost disadvantage, compared to other firms or plants in the market. There are likely to be firms and plants of varying size in such a market.
- As previously noted, Figure 2.8 helps to explain why small plants or firms are common in markets or industries supplying personal services to individuals and households. Economies of small-scale production mean that the *LRAC* curve is 'skewed' to the left of the diagram. By contrast, in Figure 2.10 (below) the *LRAC* curve is 'skewed' to the right of the diagram, showing economies of large-scale production. Diseconomies of scale eventually set in, but only after substantial economies of scale have been achieved.

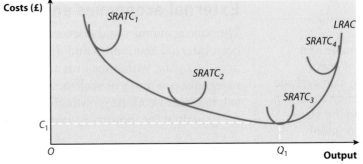

Figure 2.10 The *LRAC* curve in an industry with economies of large-scale production

There are, of course, other factors, apart from the existence or non-existence of scale economies and diseconomies, which contribute to markets containing different sizes of firm. A factor that has been becoming increasingly important in recent decades is firms 'contracting out' the provision of services, previously provided 'in house' by managers and workers employed by the firms themselves, to 'outside' suppliers of the same services. The outside suppliers range from small independent firms such as a local sandwich shop to large-scale specialist firms providing services such as catering, accountancy and ICT maintenance.

2.3 Marginal cost and marginal returns

How a firm's short-run marginal cost curve is derived from short-run production theory

Early in this chapter, we explained the shape of a firm's marginal returns curve in relation to the impact of the short-run law of diminishing returns. In this section, we use the law of diminishing returns to explain, in the short run, the shape of a firm's **marginal cost** (*MC*) curve, before linking the *MC* curve to its short-run **average variable cost** (*AVC*) and **average fixed cost** (*AFC*) curves, which are explained in Book 1, Chapter 3, pages 62–63, and finally its short-run **average total cost** (*ATC*) curve.

Marginal cost is the extra cost a firm incurs when it produces one extra unit of output. Short-run marginal costs are determined solely by changes in variable costs of production since, by definition, in the short run, fixed costs don't change when the level of output changes. For the sake of simplicity, assuming labour is the only variable factor of production, variable costs are simply wage costs. If all workers receive the same hourly wage, total wage costs rise in exact proportion to the number of workers employed. However, if to start with the firm is benefiting from increasing marginal returns to labour, the total variable cost of production rises at a slower rate than output. This causes the marginal cost of producing an extra unit of output to fall. In Figure 2.11, the *increasing marginal returns of labour* (shown by the *positive* slope of the marginal returns curve in the upper graph) cause *marginal costs* to fall (shown by the *negative* slope of the *MC* curve in the lower of the two graphs).

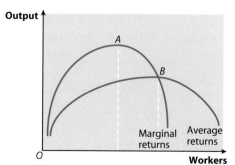
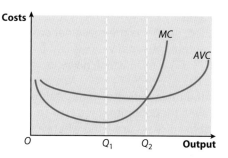

Figure 2.11 Deriving the *MC* and *AVC* curves from short-run production theory

However, once the law of diminishing marginal returns has set in, short-run marginal costs rise as output increases. The wage cost of employing an extra worker is still the same, but each extra worker is now less productive than the previous worker. Total variable costs rise faster than output, so short-run marginal costs also rise. Again in Figure 2.11, the diminishing marginal returns of labour (shown by the *negative* slope of the marginal revenue curve in the right-hand side of the upper graph) cause marginal costs to rise (shown by the *positive* slope of the *MC* curve in the right-hand side of the lower graph).

35

Relating marginal cost to average variable cost and average total cost

Just as a firm's short-run *MC* curve is derived from the marginal returns of the variable factors of production, so the firm's average variable cost (*AVC*) curve (illustrated in the lower panel of Figure 2.11 and also in panel (a) of Figure 2.12) is explained by the average returns curve (shown in the upper panel of Figure 2.11). When increasing average returns are experienced, with the labour force *on average* becoming more efficient and productive, the *AVC* per unit of output must fall as output rises. But once diminishing *average* returns set in at point *B* in Figure 2.11, the *AVC* curve begins to rise with output.

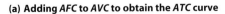

(a) Adding *AFC* to *AVC* to obtain the *ATC* curve

(b) The U-shaped *ATC* curve

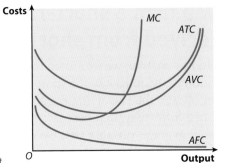

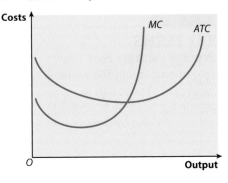

Figure 2.12 The relationships between marginal cost, average variable cost and average total cost

To see a fuller explanation of the *AVC* curve (and also the average fixed cost and short-run average total cost curves), you should re-read Book 1, pages 62–63. However, at this point we should add that the marginal cost curve cuts through from below *both* the *AVC* and *SRATC* curves at the lowest points of these curves. This is a further example of the mathematical relationship between the marginal and average values of a variable which we explained in the extension material on page 29.

QUANTITATIVE SKILLS 2.2

Worked example: calculating marginal and average variable costs

Table 2.3 shows the total cost of producing different levels of output in the short run.

Table 2.3 Total cost of different output levels

Output	Total cost (£)
0	100
1	115
2	140
3	175
4	220

Calculate:

a **the marginal cost of the first unit of output**
b **average variable cost when output is 4 units**

a Total cost increases by £15 when the first unit of output is produced, so this is the marginal cost of the first unit of output. Alternatively we can use the equation $TC_1 - TC_0 = MC_1$, which gives us the same answer, £15.

b The first row in the table indicates that total fixed costs are £100 even though output is zero. This means that total fixed costs are £100 whatever the level of output. To calculate average variable cost when 4 units are produced, we divide total variable cost (£220 – £100, which is £120) by total output, which is 4: £120/4 = £30. Thus *AVC* = £30.

Long-run marginal cost and long-run average cost

The mathematical relationship just described also holds in the long run, in this case between **long-run marginal cost** and **long-run average cost**. If the *LRAC* curve is U-shaped, as in Figure 2.13, the long-run marginal cost curve cuts through the lowest point of the *LRAC* curve. (Note that, for the sake of simplicity, *SRATC* curves have not been included in Figure 2.13.)

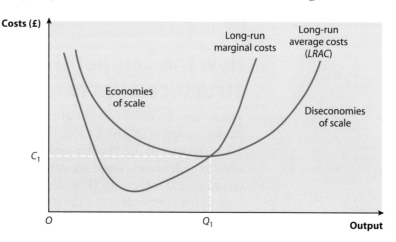

Figure 2.13 A long-run marginal cost curve cutting through a U-shaped *LRAC* curve

TEST YOURSELF 2.2
Apply the mathematical rule of the relationship between the marginal and average values of a variable (see page 29) to Figures 2.5, 2.6 and 2.7. Copy the diagrams (but leave out the *SRATC* curves in each diagram) and then draw on each diagram the long-run marginal cost curve that fits the diagram.

Explaining the revenue curves facing firms

Book 1, page 70 introduced you to the total revenue a firm earns when selling its output, and also to a firm's average revenue. This chapter takes you deeper into revenue theory, by introducing the key concept of marginal revenue, and then by relating revenue curves to the two extreme market structures of perfect competition and monopoly. First, however, we shall summarise what you should already know about revenue from reading Book 1.

The meaning of revenue

Revenue is the money that a firm earns when selling its output. **Total revenue** (*TR*) is *all* the money a firm earns from selling the total output of a product. By contrast, at any level of output, **average revenue** (*AR*) is calculated by dividing total revenue by the size of output. Stated as an equation:

$$\text{average revenue} = \frac{\text{total revenue}}{\text{output}} \text{ or } AR = \frac{TR}{Q}$$

Marginal revenue (*MR*) is the addition to total revenue resulting from the sale of one more unit of output. Stated as an equation:

$$\text{marginal revenue} = \frac{\Delta \text{ total revenue}}{\Delta \text{ output}} \text{ or } MR = \frac{\Delta TR}{\Delta Q}$$

where Δ is the symbol used to indicate the changes in total revenue and the change in total output.

How the competitiveness of a market structure affects a firm's revenue curves

The nature of a firm's revenue curves depends on the competitiveness of the market structure in which the firm sells its output. The final row of Figure 2.1 at the start of this chapter sets out the four market structures that you need to understand. These are perfect competition, monopolistic competition, oligopoly and monopoly. However, we shall leave until Chapter 3 the imperfectly competitive market structures of monopolistic competition and oligopoly. This means that this chapter considers only the two extreme market structures of perfect competition and monopoly.

In the latter part of Chapter 3, we shall also investigate the dynamics of competition and the competitive market processes existent in real-world markets. In this chapter, however, and in the early parts of Chapter 3, we consider solely the type of competition known as *price competition*. This focuses on the price or prices that firms charge, in pursuit of a single assumed business objective: profit maximisation. (Other types of competition include quality competition and after-sales service competition.) In this chapter we look at revenue curves, first in perfect competition and then in monopoly.

Average revenue and marginal revenue in perfect competition

A perfectly competitive market is defined by a number of conditions or characteristics that the market must possess. These conditions, which we shall revisit in Chapter 3, are:

- a very large number of buyers and sellers
- all buyers and sellers possess perfect information about what is going on in the market
- consumers can buy as much as they wish to purchase and firms can sell as much as they wish to supply at the ruling market price set in the market as a whole
- an individual consumer or supplier cannot affect the ruling market price through its own actions
- an identical, uniform or homogeneous product
- no barriers to entry into, or exit from, the market in the long run

Taken together, the six listed conditions tell us that a perfectly competitive firm, which is depicted in panel (a) of Figure 2.14, faces a perfectly elastic demand curve for its product. (Figure 2.14 is the same as Figure 4.2 in Book 1, page 77.) The demand curve facing the firm is located at the ruling market price, P_1, which itself is determined through the interaction of market demand and market supply in panel (b) of the diagram. Note that the horizontal axis in the panel (b) diagram shows millions of units of output being produced. This is because panel (b) depicts the whole market, comprising very large numbers of both consumers and firms. In equilibrium, where market demand equals market supply, the ruling market price is P_1, and the equilibrium quantity is Q_1 millions of units. In panel (a), the horizontal axis is labelled 'hundreds', to reflect the fact that in perfect competition a single firm is only a tiny part of the total market.

The assumption that a perfectly competitive firm can sell whatever quantity it wishes at the ruling market price P_1, but that it cannot influence the ruling market price by its own action, means that all firms in perfectly competitive markets are passive **price-takers**.

KEY TERM

price-taker a firm which is so small that it has to accept the ruling market price. If the firm raises its price, it loses all its sales; if it cuts its price, it gains no advantage.

The labels 'No sales' and 'No sense' placed on Figure 2.14(a), respectively above and below the price line P_1, help to explain why a perfectly competitive firm is a price-taker. 'No sales' indicates that if the firm raises its selling price above the ruling market price, customers desert the firm to buy the identical products (perfect substitutes) available from other firms at the ruling market price. 'No sense' refers to the fact that, although a perfectly competitive firm *could* sell its output below the price P_1, doing so is inconsistent with the profit-maximising objective. No extra sales can result, so selling below the ruling market price inevitably reduces both total sales revenue and therefore profit, given the fact that the firm can sell any quantity it wants at the ruling market price.

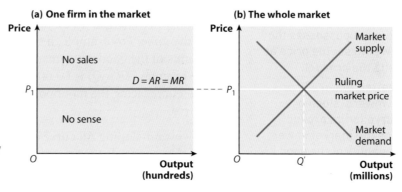

Figure 2.14 Deriving a perfectly competitive firm's average and marginal revenue curves

It follows from this that the ruling market price facing each firm in the market is both the firm's average revenue curve and its marginal revenue curve. Each unit of the good is sold at a price of £1 (average revenue), and selling an extra unit of the good always increases total revenue by £1 (marginal revenue). The horizontal price line is also the perfectly elastic demand curve for the firm's output. It is perfectly elastic because the good produced by *all* the firms in the market, being uniform or homogeneous, are perfect substitutes for each other. In summary, for a firm, $D = AR = MR$, as depicted in Figure 2.14(a).

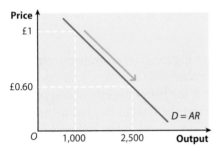

STUDY TIP

Note that Figure 2.14 contains two demand curves. On the one hand, the market demand curve, drawn in panel (b) of the diagram, slopes downward, reflecting the fact that in the market as a whole a fall in price will lead to an increase in the quantity sold; with a straight-line market demand curve, the price elasticity of demand falls from point to point moving down the demand curve. Goods produced in other markets are partial, though not perfect, substitutes for goods produced in this market. By contrast, the demand curve for the output of any one firm *within* the market is perfectly elastic, and hence horizontal, because other firms *within* the market produce identical goods which are perfect substitutes for the goods produced by any one firm in this market.

Average revenue and marginal revenue in monopoly

It is worth repeating that the demand curve facing a perfectly competitive firm, besides being located at the ruling market price, is also the firm's *AR* curve and its *MR* curve. By contrast, the demand curve for a monopolist's output is the monopolist's *AR* curve, but it is *not* the monopolist's *MR* curve.

To understand why the market demand curve is the monopolist's average revenue (*AR*) curve, consider Figure 2.15, which shows two prices, £1 and £0.60, which can be charged by a monopolist for the good it produces.

At a price of £1, 1,000 units are demanded. At this price, the monopolist's total revenue is £1000. Average revenue, or total revenue divided by output (*TR* ÷ *Q*), is £1, which is of course the same as price. This is the case at all prices: the price charged for all units of the good and average revenue are always the same. For example, if the monopolist sets the price at £0.60, 2,500 units of the good are demanded; total sales revenue is £1,500 and average revenue (*TR* ÷ *Q*) is £0.60. The downward-sloping market demand curve facing the monopolist is therefore the firm's average revenue (*AR*) curve.

The downward-sloping *AR* curve can affect the monopoly in two different ways. If the monopolist is a **price-maker**, choosing to set the price at which the product is sold, the demand curve dictates the maximum output that can be sold at this price. For example, if the price is set at P_1 in Figure 2.16, the maximum quantity that can be sold at this price is Q_1. But if the monopolist cuts the price it charges to P_2, sales increase to Q_2. Alternatively, if the monopolist is a **quantity-setter** rather than a price-maker, the demand curve dictates the maximum price at which a chosen quantity of the good can be sold. If the monopolist wants to sell Q_2, the market demand curve shows that the maximum price at which this quantity can be sold is P_2. To summarise, if the monopolist sets the price, the market demand curve dictates the maximum quantity the firm can sell. Conversely, if the monopolist sets the quantity, the market demand curve determines the maximum price the firm can charge. However, for any one good it produces, a firm cannot be a price-maker and a quantity-setter at the same time.

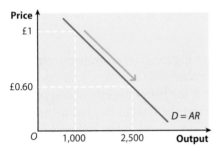

Figure 2.15 Price equalling average revenue (*AR*) in monopoly

KEY TERMS

price-maker when a firm faces a downward-sloping demand curve for its product, it possesses the market power to set the price at which it sells the product.

quantity-setter when a firm faces a downward-sloping demand curve for its product, it possesses the market power to set the quantity of the good it wishes to sell.

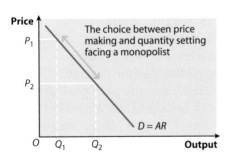

Figure 2.16 The choice between price making and quantity setting facing a monopolist

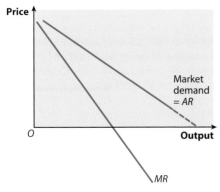

Figure 2.17 Monopoly average revenue (*AR*) and marginal revenue (*MR*) curves

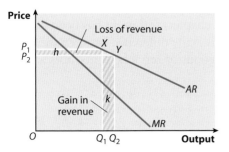

Figure 2.18 Explaining a monopolist's marginal revenue (*MR*) curve

However, to understand why marginal revenue and average revenue are *not* the same in monopoly, you must remember that when the *marginal* value of a variable is less than the *average* value of the variable, the *average* value falls.

Because the market demand curve or average revenue curve falls as output increases, the monopolist's marginal revenue curve *must* be below its average revenue curve. Figure 2.17 shows the relationship between the *AR* and the *MR* curves. You should see, however, that the *MR* curve is not only below the *AR* curve — it has also been drawn twice as steep. This is always the case whenever the *AR* curve is a downward-sloping straight line.

The relationship between *AR* and *MR* curves is illustrated again in Figure 2.18. The monopolist initially charges a price of P_1 and sells the level of output Q_1. However, to increase sales by an extra unit to Q_2, the downward-sloping *AR* curve forces the monopolist to reduce the selling price to P_2. This reduces the price at which *all* units of output are sold. Total sales revenue increases by the area k in Figure 2.18, but decreases by the area h. Areas k and h respectively show the revenue gain (namely, the extra unit sold multiplied by price P_2) and the revenue loss resulting from the fact that, in order to sell more, the price has to be reduced for *all* units of output, not just the extra unit sold. Marginal revenue, which is the revenue gain minus the revenue loss (or $k - h$), must be less than price or average revenue (area k) at the new level of output.

EXTENSION MATERIAL

Elasticity and revenue curves

We mentioned earlier in the chapter that the horizontal price line facing a perfectly competitive firm is also the perfectly elastic demand curve for the firm's output. The explanation for this lies in the word 'substitutability'. When studying elasticity, you learnt that the availability of substitutes is the main determinant of price elasticity of demand. In perfect competition, because of the assumptions of a uniform product and perfect information, the output of every other firm in the market is a perfect substitute for the firm's own product. If the firm tries to raise its price above the ruling market price, it loses all its customers.

In monopoly, by contrast, providing the demand curve is a straight line as well as downward sloping, price elasticity of demand falls moving down the demand curve. Demand for the monopolist's output is elastic in the top half of the curve, falling to be unit elastic exactly half way down the curve, and inelastic in the bottom half of the curve. This is shown in

Figure 2.19. Demand is elastic between *A* and *B*, unit elastic at *B*, and inelastic between *B* and *C*.

We shall revisit the significance of elasticity in the next chapter, when comparing profit maximisation with revenue maximisation.

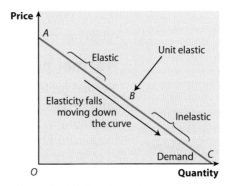

Figure 2.19 Price elasticity of demand and a monopolist's demand or average revenue (*AR*) curve

2.4 Profit

Defining profit

We mentioned in Book 1, Chapter 3 that students often confuse profit and revenue, mistakenly believing that the two terms have the same meaning. In fact, profit and revenue are different. Revenue has already been explained in some depth in the previous sections of this chapter, and profit has been briefly mentioned on a number of occasions. **Profit** is the difference between the sales revenue the firm receives when selling the goods or services it produces and the costs of producing the goods.

total profit = total revenue – total costs

> **KEY TERM**
> **profit** the difference between total sales revenue and total cost of production.

The difference between normal and abnormal (supernormal) profit

We have mentioned on several occasions in this chapter, and also in Book 1, page 30, that economists often assume that firms have a single business objective: **profit maximisation**. This means producing the level of output at which profit (revenue minus costs) is greatest. (Firms may also have other objectives, such as survival, growth and increasing their market share.)

> **KEY TERM**
> **profit maximisation** occurs at the level of output at which total profit is greatest.

In the next chapter, we shall explain how profit maximisation is achieved in the different market structures of perfect competition, monopoly, monopolistic competition and oligopoly. When explaining profit maximisation, we shall apply two profit concepts, used frequently by economists undertaking microeconomic analysis, but rarely used outside the field of microeconomic theory. These are *normal profit* and *abnormal profit*. (Abnormal profit is also called *supernormal profit* and *above-normal profit*.)

Normal profit

Normal profit is the minimum level of profit necessary to keep incumbent firms in the market, rewarding the time, decision making and entrepreneurial risk taking 'invested' into production. However, the normal profit made by incumbent firms, or firms already established in the market, is insufficient to attract new firms into the market. Economists treat normal profit as an opportunity cost, which they include in firms' average cost curves. In the long run, firms unable to make normal profit leave the market. Normal profit varies from one industry to another, depending on the risks facing firms.

> **KEY TERMS**
> **normal profit** the minimum profit a firm must make to stay in business, which is, however, insufficient to attract new firms into the market.
>
> **abnormal profit** profit over and above normal profit. Also known as supernormal profit and above-normal profit.

Abnormal profit

Abnormal profit, or supernormal profit, is extra profit over and above normal profit. In the long run, and in the absence of entry barriers, abnormal profit performs the important economic function of attracting new firms into the market.

QUANTITATIVE SKILLS 2.3

Worked example: calculating revenue and profit

Table 2.4 provides information about the short-run output, costs and revenue of a firm.

Table 2.4 Short-run output, costs and revenue

Output per week	Total revenue (£000s)	Total cost (£000s)
0	0	10
1	20	14
2	38	19
3	54	28
4	68	44
5	80	80
6	90	93

From the information in the table, calculate:

a **marginal revenue when output per week increases from 4 to 5 units**
b **the level of output at which the firm would make normal profit but not abnormal profit**
c **the profit-maximising level of output per week**

a The marginal revenue, which is the change in the total revenue, is £80,000 – £68,000, which is £12,000.

b Assuming that normal profit is being treated as a cost of production, the firm makes normal profit, but not abnormal profit, when total revenue equals total cost. This is at a level of output of 5 units per week.

c Profits are maximised at the level of output at which (*TR* – *TC*) is greatest. This is at a level of output of 3 units per week, when total profit equals £54,000 – £28,000, which is £26,000.

TEST YOURSELF 2.3

Using the information in Table 2.4, draw on a piece of graph paper the firm's average revenue and marginal revenue curves.

The role of profit in a market economy

Profit performs a number of roles in a market economy. These include the creation of business, worker and shareholder incentives. Profit also influences the allocation of resources, it is an efficiency indicator, and it is a reward for innovation and for risk taking. Finally, profits also provide an important source of business finance.

The creation of business incentives

As we have noted on several occasions both in this book and in Book 1, traditional or orthodox microeconomic theory assumes that profit maximisation is the most important business objective. Not only do rising profits, and the hope of higher profits in the future, provide the incentive for managers within a firm to work harder to make the business even more profitable, but also they create incentives for other firms to enter the market. Abnormal profit acts as a 'magnet' attracting new entrants into a market or industry. If market entry is easy and/or relatively costless, new firms joining the market should lead to an increase in market supply. We shall explain in the next chapter how the entry of new firms triggers a process which actually reduces both abnormal profit and prices, with the latter benefiting consumers. We shall also explain how economic efficiency and economic welfare may be promoted through this process.

However, when entry barriers are high and monopoly or highly imperfect competition exists in a market, profit may simply reward inefficient producers. This is a form of market failure in which the 'producer is king' rather than the consumer, and in which 'producer sovereignty' rather than 'consumer sovereignty' exists.

The creation of worker incentives

Some companies use profit-related pay and performance-related pay to increase worker motivation, in the hope that workers will work harder and share the objectives of the business's managers and owners. This can, however, be counter-productive, if ordinary workers see higher management and company directors enjoying huge profit-related bonuses, while they receive a pittance.

The creation of shareholder incentives

High profit generally leads to high dividends or distributed profit being paid out to shareholders who own companies. This creates an incentive for more people to want to buy the company's shares. As a result, the company's share price rises, which makes it cheaper and easier for a business to raise finance.

Profits and resource allocation

High profits made by incumbent firms in a market create incentives for new producers to enter the market and for existing firms to supply more of a good or service. Likewise, loss making, or perhaps a failure to make above-normal profits, create incentives for firms to leave markets and to deploy their resources in more profitable markets.

Profit and economic efficiency

Except when monopolies make large profits by exploiting their consumers, profit can be an indicator of economic efficiency. Large profits might mean that firms have succeeded in eliminating unnecessary costs of production and are also using the most efficient production processes.

Profit as a reward for innovation and risk taking

As we explain later in this chapter, innovation is an improvement on something that has already been invented, which thus turns the results of invention into a useful product. If entrepreneurs believe that innovation can result in high profits in the future, the incentive to innovate increases. As we can never be sure of future profits, risks are involved. However, successful risk taking leads to high profits.

Profit as a source of business finance

Instead of being distributed to the business's owners as a form of income, profit can be retained within the business. Retained profits are perhaps the most important source of finance for firms undertaking investment projects. High profits also make it easier and cheaper for firms to use borrowed funds as an important source of business finance.

Profit sends out a signal about the health of the economy

The profit made by businesses throughout the economy can send out an important signal about the health of the economy. Rising profit may reflect improvements in supply-side performance — for example, higher productivity or lower costs resulting from innovation.

SYNOPTIC LINK

The functions of profit in a market economy are closely linked to the functions of prices. Very often, but not always, high prices signal to firms that high profits can be made, and low prices signal the reverse. Book 1, Chapter 5 explains the functions that prices perform in a market economy.

SYNOPTIC LINK

Later in this chapter, in section 2.5, we introduce the concepts of productive efficiency and dynamic efficiency, which we explain in more detail in Chapter 3. (Productive efficiency was also mentioned briefly in Book 1.)

SYNOPTIC LINK

Chapter 8, 'Financial markets and monetary policy', explains how capital markets, including the stock exchange, provide a mechanism through which companies raise finance by selling new share issues and corporate bonds.

Public limited companies (PLCs) publish information about their profits twice a year: in an interim company report midway through the company's financial year, often in October, and in the full company report published at the end of the company's financial year, often in March. Read the business sections of broadsheet newspapers such as *The Times*, the *Daily Telegraph* and the *Guardian* in these months and study the commentaries in which financial journalists analyse company profitability. Occasionally, companies issue profit warnings. Why do they do this, and what might be the effect on the company's share price?

CASE STUDY 2.2

The John Lewis economy

John Lewis PLC is a highly successful retailing company in the UK which not only shares its profits with all its workers, but also makes them part-owners of the John Lewis Partnership. From time to time, leading British politicians climb aboard the John Lewis bandwagon, extolling the virtues of the British retailer and exhorting other companies to introduce co-ownership and profit sharing. Here is an extract from a speech made by Nick Clegg, the then deputy prime minister, on 16 January 2012 at an event hosted by the City of London.

We need more individuals to have a real stake in their firms. More of a John Lewis economy, if you like. What many people don't realise about employee ownership is that it is a hugely underused tool in unlocking growth. I don't value employee ownership because I believe it is somehow 'nicer' — a more pleasant alternative to the rest of the corporate world. Those are lazy stereotypes. Firms that have engaged employees, who own a chunk of their company, are just as dynamic, just as savvy, as their competitors. In fact, they often perform better: lower absenteeism, less staff turnover, lower production costs. In general, they have higher productivity and higher wages. They weathered the economic downturn better than other companies.

Is employee ownership a panacea? No. Does it guarantee a company will thrive? Of course not. But the evidence and success stories cannot be ignored, and we have to tap this well if we are serious about growth. The 1980s was the decade of share ownership. I want this to be the decade of employee share ownership.

Follow-up question

1 Outline one advantage and one disadvantage of profit sharing and co-ownership for the United Kingdom economy.

2.5 Technological change

Most people have a general idea of what technology means, but they nevertheless find it difficult to give the term a precise definition. Internet search engines, being prone to long-winded explanations rather than to short, snappy definitions, often don't help in this respect. Here, however, is one snappy definition: whereas science is concerned with *how* and *why* things happen, technology focuses on *making things happen*. Thus, technology is knowledge put to practical use to solve problems facing human societies.

KEY TERM

technological change a term that is used to describe the overall effect of invention, innovation and the diffusion or spread of technology in the economy.

Technological change, by contrast, involves improving existing technologies and the development of completely new technologies, both to improve existing *products* and the *processes* involved in making the products, and to develop completely new products and processes. In the economic sphere, this leads to the development of completely new markets, to changes in market structure, and also to the destruction of existing markets.

As an aside, the word 'technology' is often associated with technical progress. However, the term 'technical progress' has two rather different meanings. On the one hand, in a normative or value-judgement context, 'technical progress' implies that technological change is fundamentally about increasing economic welfare and making people happier. For example, although the development and use of the motor car has several important drawbacks, such as the harm resulting from road accidents and environmental pollution, for the most part, through making it much easier for most people to travel, cars and buses have significantly improved human welfare. But in a narrower sense, unrelated to welfare considerations, 'technical progress' means applying scientific and engineering knowledge, as it develops, to produce goods which are more efficient and work better, regardless of whether these are good for society. In this narrower meaning, technical progress includes the development of distinctly harmful goods such as chemical weapons, which, when used, have a devastating effect on human welfare.

The difference between invention and innovation

KEY TERMS

invention making something entirely new; something that did not exist before at all.

innovation improves on or makes a significant contribution to something that has already been invented, thereby turning the results of invention into a product.

Invention refers to advancements in pure science, whereas **innovation** is the application of the new knowledge created by invention to production. The American entrepreneur, Tom Grasty, distinguishes between the two concepts in the following way:

> In its purest sense, invention can be defined as the creation of a product or introduction of a process for the first time. Innovation, on the other hand, occurs if someone improves on or makes a significant contribution to an existing product, process or service. Consider the microprocessor. Someone invented the microprocessor. But by itself, the microprocessor was nothing more than another piece on the circuit board. It's what was done with that piece — the hundreds of thousands of products, processes and services that evolved from the invention of the microprocessor — that required innovation.

> If ever there were a poster child for innovation it would be former Apple CEO Steve Jobs. And when people talk about innovation, Jobs' iPod is cited as an example of innovation at its best. But let's take a step back for a minute. The iPod wasn't the first portable music device (Sony popularized the 'music anywhere, anytime' concept 22 years earlier with the Walkman); the iPod wasn't the first device that put hundreds of songs in your pocket (dozens of manufacturers had MP3 devices on the market when the iPod was released in 2001); and Apple was actually late to the party when it came to providing an online music-sharing platform (Napster, Grokster and Kazaa all preceded iTunes).

> So, given those sobering facts, is the iPod's distinction as a defining example of innovation warranted? Absolutely. What made the iPod and the music ecosystem it engendered innovative wasn't that it was the first portable music device. It wasn't that it was the first MP3 player. And it wasn't that it was the first company to make thousands of songs immediately available to millions of users. What

The original iPod, which was launched in 2001 — invention or innovation?

made Apple innovative was that it combined all of these elements — design, ergonomics and ease of use — in a single device, and then tied it directly into a platform that effortlessly kept that device updated with music.

Apple invented nothing. Its innovation was creating an easy-to-use ecosystem that unified music discovery, delivery and device. And, in the process, they revolutionized the music industry.

How technological change affects methods of production, productivity, efficiency and firms' costs of production

Through its diffusion into the economy, technological change affects methods of production, productivity, efficiency and firms' costs of production. We shall now look at each of these in turn.

Methods of production

Throughout human history, technological change has affected methods of production. As far back as the stone age, the bronze age and the iron age, as the names themselves indicate, different materials were used to create early forms of tool used by humankind. These eras covered scores of thousands of years. Moving much closer to the present day, the eighteenth century saw the onset of agricultural and industrial revolutions in which technological change greatly affected methods of agricultural and industrial production. Over the decades and centuries that followed, and right up to the present day, agricultural output greatly increased with the development of new seeds and the breeding of modern farm animals, the mechanisation of production — for example, through the use of combine harvesters — and the application of chemical fertilizers.

At the beginning of the industrial revolution in the eighteenth century, manufacturing moved away from craft and cottage industry, to factory production. Much more energy was now used in the course of production, so manufacturing moved to parts of the country where first water power and then steam power, fired by the burning of coal, was in plentiful supply. In the nineteenth century, the 'new' iron age of the eighteenth century in which cast iron had become perhaps the main industrial raw material, gave way to a 'steel age', when improvements in smelting technology enabled steel, which is strong yet malleable, to replace iron in much of modern manufacturing. The steel age of the mid-nineteenth century was accompanied by a railway-building age, in which railways replaced the rather cumbersome system of eighteenth-century canals to enable the development of a modern transport system necessary for the delivery of goods to markets.

The mid-twentieth century witnessed the growing use of automobiles. The 'automobile age' really got going in the USA in the 1920s, when modern roads were built across the North American continent and mass production allowed affordable cars to be bought by much of the US population. To bring us right up to the present day, we are now living in the 'computer age'. Computers, which were first developed in the 1940s, are now widely used in manufacturing (for example, when computer-controlled robots build cars), in distribution (for example, in the online sale of books by Amazon), and as consumer goods in themselves. And hidden within many goods that are not themselves computers, such as washing machines and cars, are microprocessors that control how the good functions.

Closely allied to the changes in production just described has been the change in recent decades from mechanised to automated production. As a simplification, **mechanisation** means that human beings operate the machines that are used to produce goods. **Automation**, by contrast, means that machines operate other machines — for example, a computer-controlled robot operating a welding tool to weld together the body panels of a car. Both mechanisation and automation have often been accompanied by assembly-line production, allegedly first introduced by Henry Ford in 1908.

Productivity

Earlier in this chapter on page 29, we reminded you of the meaning of *productivity*, a key concept which we explained in some detail in Book 1. We defined productivity as output per unit of input, but, to be more precise, it is 'output per unit of input per time period'. For example, a key measure of labour productivity is 'output per person per hour'. We also said that when economists talk about productivity, they usually mean *labour productivity*, which is output per worker per time period.

Technological change generally increases labour productivity. This has usually been the case following the introduction of both mechanised and automated production methods. However, in the case of automation and the use of computers in production, there have been several well-publicised examples in organisations such as the National Health Service of very expensive computer systems that have failed to work properly and which, in extreme cases, have had to be scrapped. In these cases, labour productivity may fall rather than increase, at least until the system can be made to work properly.

CASE STUDY 2.3

The failure to produce paperless records of patient care in the NHS

On 18 September 2013, the Parliamentary Public Accounts Committee published a report on the Dismantled National Programme for IT in the NHS. Although officially 'dismantled', the National Programme continues in the form of separate component programmes which are still racking up big costs.

Launched in 2002, the National Programme was designed to reform the way that the NHS in England uses information. While some parts of the National Programme were delivered successfully, other important elements encountered significant difficulties. In particular, there were delays in developing and deploying the detailed care records systems. Following three reports on the National Programme by both the National Audit Office and the Public Accounts Committee, and a review by the Major Projects Authority, the government announced in September 2011 that

it would dismantle the National Programme but keep the component parts in place with separate management and accountability structures.

The public purse is continuing to pay the price for failures by the department and its contractors. The department's original contracts totalled £3.1 billion for the delivery of care records systems to 220 trusts in the north, midlands and east. The full cost of the National Programme is still not certain. The department's most recent statement reported a total forecast cost of £9.8 billion. However, this figure did not include potential future costs.

The benefits to date from the National Programme are extremely disappointing. The department's benefits statement reported estimated benefits to March 2012 of £3.7 billion, just half of the costs incurred to this point. The benefits include financial savings, efficiency gains and wider benefits to society (for example, where patients spend less time chasing referrals). However, two-thirds of the £10.7 billion of total forecast benefits were still to be realised in March 2012.

After the sorry history of the National Programme, the Public Accounts Committee was sceptical that the department could deliver its vision of a paperless NHS by 2018. Making the NHS paperless will involve further significant investment in IT and business transformation.

Follow-up questions

1 Research on the internet to find out what has happened to the NHS's plan to introduce paperless patient records in the period since September 2013.
2 Find out about and investigate another example of a 'computer systems disaster' in either the public sector or the private sector.

Efficiency

As we explain in Chapter 3, economists recognise a number of types of economic efficiency. Two of these are productive efficiency and dynamic efficiency. **Productive efficiency** centres on minimising average costs of production. **Dynamic efficiency** measures the extent to which productive efficiency increases over time, in the economic long run. Dynamic efficiency also results from improvements in products and services, innovation and the process of creative destruction.

Technological change generally improves both productive efficiency and dynamic efficiency. As a general rule — though there are exceptions, one of which is illustrated by Case Study 2.3 — technological change leads to improvements in both productive and dynamic efficiency. By increasing productivity, over time technological changes shift downward both short-run and long-run cost curves, thereby improving both productive and dynamic efficiency. Firms that create new products that satisfy people's needs and wants are also dynamically efficient; over time their actions improve social welfare.

Costs of production

It follows from what we have written about technological change generally improving both productivity and efficiency that it also reduces costs of production, in the short run but especially in the long run.

Technological change and the development of new products and new markets, and the destruction of existing markets

A theme running through this section on technological change is that, particularly in recent years, technological change has been highly significant in the development of new products and new markets, and the destruction of existing markets. To explain this further, it is useful to introduce the concepts of *disruptive* innovation and *sustaining* innovation.

A disruptive innovation is an innovation that helps create a new market, but in so doing eventually disrupts an existing market over a few years or decades, thereby displacing an earlier technology. Disruptive innovation often improves a product or service in ways that the market did not initially expect. It creates new goods or services for a different set of consumers in a new market which competes with the established market. By doing so, it eventually lowers prices in the existing market. By contrast, a sustaining innovation does not

KEY TERMS

productive efficiency the level of output at which average costs of production are minimised.

dynamic efficiency occurs in the long run, leading to the development of new products and more efficient processes that improve productive efficiency.

49

create new markets but develops existing markets, enabling firms within them to offer better value and often to compete against each other, sustaining improvements.

According to Harvard University business professors Joseph L. Bower and Clayton M. Christensen, one of the most consistent patterns in business is the failure of leading companies to stay at the top of their industries when technologies or markets change. Writing back in the 1990s, Bower and Christensen gave the example of Xerox, the US company, which at the time had dominated the photocopier market, losing market share to the Japanese company, Canon, in the small photocopier market.

Bower and Christensen ask why it is that companies like Xerox invest aggressively — and successfully — in the technologies necessary to retain their current customers, but then fail to make certain other technological investments that customers of the future will demand? The explanation they offer is that companies that dominate an existing technology are in danger, as disruptive innovation occurs, of remaining too close to their existing body of customers. All too often existing customers reject the goods produced by a new technology because it does not address their needs as effectively as a company's current products. The large photocopying centres that represented the core of Xerox's customer base at first had no use for small, slow table-top copiers produced by Xerox's new technology. Result: Canon stepped in, quickened the speed of the copiers, and took over the market.

CASE STUDY 2.4

Kodak faces an uncertain future

In September 2013, the American camera company Kodak emerged from the bankruptcy it had been in for nearly two years. Since 2000, demand for Kodak's most successful product, camera film, which once ranked among the most profitable consumer products ever invented, had been in rapid decline. To make matters worse, Kodak's management had grossly underestimated the speed of the collapse.

This was all due to the development of digital cameras. Global sales of traditional photographic film and paper had dropped like a stone. Up to that point, the boxes of film that Kodak produced had been highly profitable. New entrants were deterred by the high costs of entry to this capital-intensive market and Kodak enjoyed profit margins that might have been as high as 50%.

But in the first few months of this century, a technology change began that was to wreck one of the most lucrative business models of the last century and threaten Kodak's very existence. In 1999, only 5% of new cameras sold in the USA were digital. By the end of 2000, this had changed dramatically. By 2003, now being accused of ignoring the revolution until it was too late, Kodak cut tens of thousands of jobs at its capital-intensive film factories and announced a new digital strategy.

Disruptive digital technology has caused the crash of many business models since 1999 — but few quite so rapid as the fate that befell Kodak. Within a matter of months, the once hugely profitable camera film market had given way to the surge of digital cameras.

Follow-up questions

1 Research what has happened to Kodak since the company emerged from bankruptcy in 2013.
2 In what way have smartphones, which were first marketed in 2007, affected the market for digital cameras?

The influence of technological change on the structure of markets

The Kodak case study you have just read provides a good example of the influence of technological change on the structure of markets. The case study describes how, when cameras transmitted the images they photographed onto chemical film, very high entry barriers into the chemical film market led to Kodak's domination of the market. By contrast, entry into the digital camera market is relatively easy. Hence the camera film market, dominated by Kodak, was close to a monopoly, whereas the digital camera market is closer to a much more competitive form of market, **monopolistic competition**, which we explain in the next chapter.

Technological change does not always, however, lead to more competitive market structures. In some industries, technological change has led to outcomes in which very large firms dominate. Sometimes technological change leads to capital indivisibilities, which occur when very large quantities of capital equipment are required for one unit of a good to be produced. A good example is the jumbo jet industry. The technological change which enabled very large jet airliners to be produced led to an outcome in which, in the western world, the American Boeing Corporation and the European Airbus consortium are the only two jumbo jet manufacturers. In the next chapter, we shall call this situation a **duopoly**.

How the process of creative destruction is linked to technological change

The term **creative destruction** was first coined in 1942 by the Austrian-American economist Joseph Schumpeter to describe how capitalism, which dominates the economic system in which we live, evolves and renews itself over time. (Capitalism is the name given to the parts of the economy in which the means of production or capital are privately owned. In the UK, public limited companies or PLCs are the dominant form of capitalist business enterprise, but private companies are also important.)

In his famous book *Capitalism, Socialism, and Democracy*, Schumpeter wrote: 'The opening up of new markets, foreign or domestic…incessantly revolutionises the economic structure from within, incessantly destroying the old one, incessantly creating a new one. This process of Creative Destruction is the essential fact about capitalism.' Schumpeter also stated that 'The essential point to grasp is that in dealing with capitalism we are dealing with an evolutionary process.'

Creative destruction is strongly related to the processes through which technological change and innovation affect the ways in which businesses behave. It describes a process in which economic growth occurs in the economy as a result of new innovations creating more economic value than that being destroyed by the decline of the technologies the new innovations replace. Over time, societies that allow creative destruction to operate grow more productive and richer; their citizens benefit from new and better products and higher living standards. Creative destruction is central to the ways in which free market economies and mixed economies develop and change over time.

KEY TERM

creative destruction capitalism evolving and renewing itself over time through new technologies and innovations replacing older technologies and innovations.

ACTIVITY

Cathode-ray television-tube manufacturers, video rental shops, high-street travel agents and bookshops have all in recent years been victims of creative destruction. Research how this has happened in one of these industries (or in an industry of your choice) and explain why you think consumers may or may not have benefited from the process.

51

Apple and creative destruction

On 1 April 1976, Apple Computer Inc. was incorporated by three 'techno-geeks', Steve Jobs, Steve Wozniak and Ron Wayne. Twenty-one years later in 1997, Steve Jobs, having left Apple following disputes about business strategy, rejoined the company and remained in charge until his death in 2011. (In 2007, Jobs had renamed the company Apple Inc. to reflect the fact that Apple had diversified away from computers into the iPod, the iPhone, the iPad and iTunes.)

Over this period, and particularly since 2001 when the iPod was first marketed, Apple had a crushing effect on specific competitors. According to Barry Ritholtz, writing in the *Washington Post* shortly after Job's death from pancreatic cancer, this was creative destruction writ large. Ritholtz argued that Jobs remade entire industries according to his unique vision. From music to film, mobile phones to media publishing and computing, Job's impact has been enormous.

Today, the triple threat of iPod/iPhone/iPad has left behind a wake of overwhelmed business models, confounded managements and bereft shareholders. The businesses which have been destroyed, or left as mere rumps of their former selves, include Hewett-Packard (HP), Nokia and Blackberry. According to Ritholtz, HP's printer business might still have some ink left in its cartridges, but its PC operations are hurting, gutted by sales of the iPad. HP's tablet entry, the TouchPad, was an unmitigated disaster, unable to compete with the iPad.

In 2007, the Finnish company Nokia totally dominated the mobile phone market. Many people thought that Nokia's lead was more or less insurmountable. But what has happened since is a reminder of just how quickly and completely the market power of a previously 'dominant' tech firm can disappear. However, following the introduction of Apple's iPhone in 2007, the previous market leaders Nokia and Blackberry began a rapid decline.

Under a headline 'Once-cool Blackberry fails to keep pace with rivals', China's *Morning Post* described how Blackberry, an early mover in the high-end mobile phone market, lost market share mainly to Apple's iPhone and to smartphones powered by Google's Android operating system. While Blackberry was considered perhaps the hippest if not the largest mobile phone maker several years ago, the company quickly lost momentum as it failed to keep pace with innovations from rivals. Gerry Purdy, an analyst at Compass Intelligence, said that 'The one gigantic issue facing Blackberry was the delay in getting into the smartphone market. And that was three years after the iPhone was released. So that's six years. The market was moving too fast.' Blackberry was too complacent, having become 'blinded' to competitive threats.

Even software giant Microsoft has suffered from Apple's innovation and marketing. Once Apple's main competitor in computer manufacturing and software, Microsoft has become vulnerable on multiple fronts. It has missed nearly every major trend in technology in recent years. Microsoft still has its cash cows Windows and its Office suite of products, but the company could lose out significantly to Apple in the next few years.

Follow-up questions

1 What is meant by 'creative destruction'?
2 This case study was written at the time of Steve Job's death in 2011. Find out what has happened to Nokia's and Blackberry's smartphone businesses in the years since then.

SUMMARY

- The theory of the firm is the main part of business economics.
- The building blocks of the theory of the firm include production theory, cost theory and revenue theory.
- Production and cost theory divide into short-run and long-run theory.
- The key concept in short-run production theory is the law of diminishing returns, also known as the law of diminishing marginal productivity.
- It is vital to understand, and to distinguish between, marginal returns, marginal costs and marginal revenue.
- In the short run, the marginal cost curve and the average variable cost curve are derived from the law of diminishing marginal (and average) returns.
- Assuming that the variable factors of production experience diminishing returns, the short-run marginal cost (MC), average variable cost (AVC) and average total cost (ATC) curves are U-shaped.
- The key concept in long-run production theory is returns to scale.
- The long-run average cost ($LRAC$) curve may be U-shaped, but other shapes are possible.
- Profit is total sales revenue minus total costs of production.
- Perfect competition, monopoly, monopolistic competition and oligopoly are the four market structures you need to know, and you must also be aware of the meaning of imperfect competition.
- Economists usually assume that maximising profit is a firm's main business objective.
- Normal profit is just sufficient to keep incumbent firms in the market but is insufficient to attract new firms into the market.
- Abnormal, or supernormal, profit is any profit over and above normal profit.
- In the long run, capitalism develops through a process known as creative destruction, through new technologies and innovations replacing older technologies and innovations.

Questions

1 Explain the difference between the law of diminishing returns and decreasing returns to scale. How do these affect a firm's cost curves in both the short run and the long run?

2 What is the relationship between returns to scale and economies and diseconomies of scale?

3 Explain why the average and marginal revenue curves of a monopoly slope downward, while those of a perfectly competitive firm are horizontal.

4 Explain the mathematical relationships between the average and marginal values of an economic variable.

5 Evaluate the view that a monopoly can simultaneously increase both the price of the good it produces and the quantity of the good it sells.

6 With two examples of each concept, explain the difference between invention and innovation.

3

Perfect competition, imperfectly competitive markets and monopoly

Chapter 2 has already introduced you to the two market structures of perfect competition and monopoly, and briefly mentioned the imperfectly competitive market structures of monopolistic competition and oligopoly that lie between the two extremes on the market structure spectrum. This chapter draws on the information about cost and revenue curves explained in Chapter 2 to explain profit maximisation in perfect competition and monopoly. After evaluating these two market structures using efficiency and welfare criteria, the chapter then looks at the two intermediate market structures of monopolistic competition and oligopoly. The order in which we cover the different market structures differs from how they are set out in the A-level specification. This is because we believe that it is easier to appreciate the nature of monopolistic competition and oligopoly after first understanding monopoly.

LEARNING OBJECTIVES

This chapter will:

- analyse profit maximisation, first in perfect competition, and then in monopoly
- explain economic efficiency and the different forms of economic efficiency
- relate dynamic efficiency to the process of creative destruction and to how firms compete in real-world markets
- ask whether perfect competition is more efficient than monopoly
- explain how monopolistic competition and oligopoly are forms of imperfect competition
- analyse profit maximisation in monopolistic competition and in oligopoly
- use concentration ratios to define oligopoly in terms of market structure
- define oligopoly in terms of market behaviour or conduct, in the context of interdependence among oligopolists
- distinguish between competitive and collusive oligopoly
- describe price discrimination and explain why firms use this form of pricing
- introduce two welfare criteria of consumer surplus and producer surplus and use these to evaluate perfect competition, monopoly and price discrimination

3.1 Market structures

Market structure can be defined in terms of the organisation and other characteristics of a market. Important features of market structure include:

- the number of firms in the market
- the market share of the largest firms, which as we later explain can be measured with the use of concentration ratios
- the nature of the costs incurred by the firms in the market
- the nature of the sales revenue earned by firms in the market
- the extent to which there are barriers to entry to, and exit from, the market
- ease of access to information about what is going on in the market
- the extent to which firms in the market undertake product differentiation and adopt different price-setting procedures
- the ways, if any, in which firms are affected by buyers' behaviour in the market

The spectrum of competition

In the context of markets, the word 'spectrum' encompasses the range of market structures which lie between the two extremes of perfect competition and monopoly. Figure 3.1 is similar to the lower part of Figure 2.1 in Chapter 2. However, Figure 3.1 contains more information about each of the market structures that we explain in this chapter

Figure 3.1 The spectrum of market structures

Distinguishing between different market structures

The number of firms in a market

Factors such as the number of firms in the market, the degree of product differentiation and ease of entry are used to distinguish between different market structures. A requirement for a market to be perfectly competitive is a large number of buyers and sellers, while at the other extreme pure monopoly is defined by the fact that there is just one firm in the market.

Perfect competition is in fact an abstract theoretical extreme rather than a real-world market structure. It is impossible for markets to display simultaneously all the conditions, listed in Figure 3.1, which are necessary for perfect competition to exist. Since any violation of the conditions of perfect competition immediately renders a market imperfectly competitive, even the most competitive markets in the real economy are examples of imperfect competition rather than perfect competition. The best we can say is that some of the highly competitive markets in the world we live in *approximate* to perfect competition, but nevertheless they are not perfectly competitive.

At the other extreme, pure monopoly does exist, though it is more accurate to say that market structures dominated by one firm are much more common than pure monopoly. In the UK, water companies provide examples of pure monopoly. Depending on where you live, there is only one company supplying tap water to your house or flat. For example, if you live in central London, you must buy your tap water from Thames Water — it is impossible to shop around and buy your water from an alternative supplier. To nit-pick, you could of course buy bottled water instead of tap water, but this would not be a realistic choice for non-drinking uses of water, such as taking a shower or washing a car. And even if a firm appears to be a pure monopoly, the availability of substitute products and foreign competition through which overseas firms compete with the dominant domestic firm weaken the firm's monopoly power.

Almost all real-world firms are therefore better described as imperfectly competitive, located between the two extremes of perfect competition and pure monopoly. As Figure 3.1 indicates, monopolistic competition is often described as *imperfect competition among the many*, which means that, as in perfect competition, there are a large number of firms in such markets. However, unlike perfect competition, many real-world markets display the characteristics of monopolistic competition which we explain later in this chapter. Typical examples are high street coffee shops and newsagents.

We shall also examine oligopoly later in the chapter. In oligopoly, there are only a few firms in the market, at least in terms of large firms, though often the large firms coexist with a number of smaller firms. Figure 3.1 describes oligopoly as *imperfect competition among the few*. As we explain later in the chapter, concentration ratios are used when oligopoly is defined in terms of market structure, while interdependence among the firms that make up the market is a main characteristic when oligopoly is defined in terms of market behaviour.

Market entry barriers

Market structure is also affected by the ease of entry into (and exit from) the market. In the short run, when at least one factor production (usually assumed to be capital) is fixed, firms cannot enter or leave the market, whatever the market structure. In the long run, by contrast, when all the factors of production are variable, firms can enter or leave competitive markets. However, at the other end of the market spectrum, pure monopoly is protected by **entry barriers** in the long run as well as in the short run, while in an oligopolistic market there may also still be significant entry barriers in the long run.

In pure monopoly, entry barriers are permanent in the sense that if they are removed, the entry of new firms, attracted by the monopolist's abnormal profit, immediately means the monopoly is destroyed. (At this point, it is worth noting that an efficient monopolist, making normal profit only,

> **KEY TERM**
> entry barriers obstacles that make it difficult for a new firm to enter a market.

will not attract new entrants into the market.) However, building on the concepts of technological change and creative destruction introduced in Chapter 2, later in this chapter we shall be explaining how the development of competing new products and technologies weakens and often destroys the monopoly power of dominant firms whose power was previously seen as impregnable.

An entry barrier is a cost of production which must be borne by a firm that seeks to enter an industry, but is not borne by businesses already in the industry. Closely related to entry barriers are **exit barriers**, which make it difficult for an established or incumbent firm to leave a market.

> **KEY TERM**
>
> **exit barriers** obstacles that make it difficult for an established firm to leave a market.

> **KEY TERMS**
>
> **natural barriers** barriers that result from inherent features of the industry, such as economies of scale or high research and development costs; *not* barriers that have been erected artificially.
>
> **sunk costs** costs that have already been incurred and cannot be recovered.
>
> **artificial barriers** barriers erected by the firms themselves, such as high levels of advertising expenditure or predatory pricing.

EXTENSION MATERIAL

Types of entry barrier

Monopolies and firms in oligopolistic markets use entry barriers to protect the firm's position and power in the market. There are two main types of entry barrier: natural barriers and artificial (or man-made) barriers.

Natural barriers

Economies of scale form a **natural barrier** to market entry. Economies of scale mean that established large firms produce at a lower long-run average cost, and are more productively efficient, than smaller new entrants, who become stranded on high-cost short-run average cost curves. Indivisibilities, which provide examples of technical economies of scale, prevent certain goods and services being produced in plants below a certain size. Indivisibilities occur in metal smelting and oil refining industries. **Sunk costs** are another natural entry barrier. Sunk costs, which cannot be recovered if a firm decides to leave a market, therefore increase risks and deter entry.

Artificial barriers

In contrast to natural barriers, which are also known as *innocent* barriers, artificial or man-made entry barriers (which are also known as *strategic barriers*) are the result of deliberate action by incumbent firms to prevent new firms from entering the market. Strategic entry barriers include:

- **Patents.** Incumbent firms acquire patents for all the variants of a product that they develop.
- **Product differentiation.** By differentiating their products, which then become protected by intellectual property and trade mark legislation, firms protect themselves from 'copy-cat' market entrants.
- **High levels of expenditure on advertising and marketing.** Established firms can make it difficult for new competitors by spending heavily on advertising and marketing, which are irrecoverable expenditures and a form of sunk cost if the firm decides to leave the market.
- **Benefiting from 'first mover' advantage.** By being first into a market, 'first-movers' such as Apple can establish themselves, build a customer base and make it difficult for later arrivals to compete.
- **Limit pricing and predatory pricing.** These barriers, together with production differentiation, are explained below.

Limit pricing and predatory pricing

When natural barriers to market entry are low or non-existent, incumbent firms (that is, firms already in the market) may set low prices, known as **limit prices**, to deter new firms from entering the market. Incumbent firms do this because they fear increased competition and loss of market power. With limit pricing, firms already in the market sacrifice short-run profit maximisation in order to maximise long-run profits, achieved through deterring the entry of new firms.

Should limit pricing be regarded as an example of a competitive pricing strategy, which reduces prices and the abnormal profits enjoyed by the established firms in the market? Or is limit pricing basically anti-competitive and best regarded as an unjustifiable restrictive practice? The answer probably depends on circumstances, but when limit pricing extends into predatory pricing, there is a much clearer case that such a pricing strategy is anti-competitive and against consumers' interest.

Whereas limit pricing deters market entry, successful use of **predatory prices** removes recent entrants to the market. Predatory pricing occurs when an established or incumbent firm deliberately sets prices below costs to force new market entrants out of business. Once the new entrants have left the market, the established firm may decide to restore prices to their previous levels.

Product differentiation

In Chapter 2, we defined a firm as a productive organisation which sells its output of goods or services commercially. Many decades ago, when economists were first putting together the theory of the firm and developing the model of perfect competition, not only did they regard firms as one-product business organisations, they assumed that within a market, all firms produce a uniform or homogeneous product. (This is one of the conditions of perfect competition listed in Figure 3.1.)

While there are a large number of small firms in the UK economy today, relatively few produce just a single good or service. Most firms — particularly large and medium-sized business enterprises, but also small businesses — undertake varying degrees of **product differentiation**. Firms often produce a range of relatively similar products, some of which compete with each other, but others of which are aimed at differentiated market segments. Mobile phones provide examples of both. Apple is well known for introducing two new smartphones roughly every year: a 'high-end' and a slightly more basic (and cheaper) model. However, Apple continues to manufacture and sell 'last year's model'. As a result, the latest models — at the time of writing, the iPhone 6 models — compete with earlier models which Apple still sells, such as the iPhone 5 and the iPhone 4. Samsung, which is Apple's main rival in the smartphone market, differentiates its phones in a similar way, but launches its new phones more frequently and in a wider variety of options than its American competitor.

3.2 The objectives of firms

Profit maximisation and the profit-maximising rule

We have mentioned on several occasions, both in this book and in Book 1, that traditional economic theory assumes that the owners and entrepreneurs who run firms have only one business objective: to produce the level of output at which profit is maximised.

For all firms, whatever their business objective(s):

total profit = total revenue – total cost

Profit maximisation requires that a firm produces the level of output at which $TR - TC$ is maximised, whatever the market structure in which the firm produces and sells its output. Given the profit-maximising objective, if the firm succeeds in producing and selling the output yielding the biggest possible profit, it has no incentive to change its level of output.

The profit-maximising rule ($MR = MC$)

However, it is generally more useful to state the condition for profit maximisation as:

marginal revenue = marginal cost, or $MR = MC$

$MR = MC$ means that a firm's profits are greatest when the addition to sales revenue received from the last unit sold (marginal revenue) equals exactly the addition to total cost incurred from the production of the last unit of output (marginal cost).

Imagine, for example, a market gardener producing tomatoes for sale in a local market, but unable to influence the ruling market price of 50p per kilo. At any size of sales, average revenue is 50p, which also equals marginal revenue. Suppose that when the horticulturalist markets 300 kilos of tomatoes, the cost of producing and marketing the 300th kilo is 48p. If the tomato grower decides not to market the 300th kilo, 2p of profit is sacrificed. Suppose also that total costs rise by 50p and 52p respectively when a 301st kilo and a 302nd kilo are marketed. The sale of the 302nd kilo causes profits to fall by 2p, but the 301st kilo of tomatoes leaves total profits unchanged: it represents the level of sales at which profits are exactly maximised.

To sum up, when:

$MR > MC$, profits rise when output increases

$MR < MC$, profits rise when output reduces

So only when $MR = MC$, at the level of output Q_1 in Figure 3.2, are profits maximised.

When $MR > MC$ or $MR < MC$ the firm fails to maximise profit. To maximise profit, the firm must change its level of output until it reaches the point at which $MR = MC$. Once this is reached, the firm has no incentive to change output, unless some event disturbs either costs or revenues.

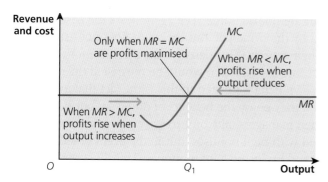

Figure 3.2 A firm's profit-maximising output occurs when $MR = MC$

It is important to understand that firms in *all* market structures (perfect competition, monopoly and imperfectly competitive markets such as monopolistic competition and oligopoly) can only maximise profit when marginal revenue equals marginal cost. $MR = MC$ is a universal condition that must be met for profit maximisation to occur, whatever the market structure.

The divorce of ownership from control

In a firm, the entrepreneur is the decision maker and financial risk-taker, providing answers to such standard economic questions as *what, how, how much, where* and *when* to produce. In many small firms, the owner of the business is the entrepreneur, so ownership and control lie with the same person. But this is generally not true for larger businesses, where there is a **divorce of ownership from control**. Medium-sized and large companies are often owned by thousands of shareholders, though the majority of shares are usually owned by a relatively small number of financial institutions such as pension funds and insurance companies. However, management decisions are made by executive directors, who are members of the company's corporate board and employed by the company, and by other managers or executives who they in turn employ.

In theory, the directors of a public company who exercise the entrepreneurial function are answerable to the shareholders. This means that, in the event of bad performance and a failure to maximise profit, the directors can be voted out of office. In practice, however, this seldom happens.

How divorce of ownership from control may affect firms' objectives and their conduct and performance

Perhaps the most important problem resulting from the divorce between ownership and control is the possibility that directors and managers will pursue an agenda of their own, which is not in the interests of the shareholders as a body. This is an example of what is known as the principal/ agent problem, or agency problem, where shareholders are the principals and managers are the agents. The problem stems from the fact that shareholders, who in a company are the owners of the business, may have an objective (profit maximisation) which differs from the objectives of the managers they employ. Rather than maximise profits, managers or business executives, who possess a monopoly of technical knowledge about the actual running of the company, concentrate on achieving managerial objectives such as maximising managerial career prospects or creature-comforts.

Conflicts of interest arise between agents and principals when the incentives which affect their behaviour are not the same. The agent bears the cost of fulfilling the task delegated by the principal, but the agent does not usually receive the full benefit of their actions. This destroys the incentive for the agent to put the same effort into the task that would be the case if the agent were acting solely on their own behalf. Related to this is the fact that agents may take on excessive risk if they enjoy the benefits of doing so, but not the costs. For example, when managers take on excessive risk in the event of success they are rewarded with high bonuses, but in the event of failure the owners of the business end up losing a lot of money. This illustrates the problem of 'moral hazard', which occurs when one person takes more risks because someone else has agreed to bear the burden of those risks.

There are two important reasons why an agent can get away with not acting in the best interest of the principal. Firstly, the cost to the principal of sacking or punishing the agent may be too high relative to any benefit the principal will enjoy. Secondly, information asymmetry may result from the fact that the agent knows more than the principal about what is going on in the business. It is often difficult or even impossible for shareholders to know whether the directors and managers they employ are acting in their best interests. For example, if a company reports disappointing profits, shareholders may find it difficult to judge whether the blame stems from managerial laziness and incompetence, or whether the poor results are due to adverse economic factors outside management control.

Various methods can be used to realign the incentives facing the owners of a business and the directors and managers they employ. These include profit-related pay and paying managers partly by giving them company shares (executive stock options). These are financial 'carrots', but 'sticks' such as dismissal can also be used. (However, the threat of dismissal is somewhat weakened by the fact that all too often unsuccessful managers are 'rewarded for failure' with large financial pay-offs when they leave the business.)

Possible business objectives other than profit maximisation

In the context of the principal/agent problem, we have already mentioned the pursuit by the managers who run a business of objectives such as maximising management status and power. Another business objective is to provide good customer service and quality of product, both in terms of the product itself and in the provision of good-quality and reliable after-sales service. These objectives, which are particularly important for socially minded owners and managers, are not in themselves inconsistent with the profit-maximising objective. Very often they are best seen as means towards an end, the end being the achievement of some other business objective such as profit maximisation.

Growth maximisation and survival as business objectives

'Growth for growth's sake' is another possible business objective, though usually the continuing growth of a business is best viewed as a means of achieving economies of scale and their associated cost reductions. Growth can also contribute to managerial prestige. It can also be a means of achieving monopoly power by knocking out smaller competitors. In the case of the proprietors of newspapers and TV stations, growth is a means of increasing political influence.

At the other extreme, loss-making businesses, and those that fear their low level of profits might turn into losses, often see survival as a primary business objective. This is most common when the economy is hit by recession. Businesses hope they can ride out the adverse effects of economic downturn, survive and continue to grow once the worst is over.

Sales revenue maximisation

Firms may also try to maximise sales revenue, particularly when managerial pay is linked to revenue rather than profit. Students often confuse profit maximisation with revenue maximisation, but the two concepts are different. As we have explained, profit maximisation occurs at the level of output at which the difference between a firm's total sales revenue (TR) and its total costs of production (TC) is greatest. This is also the level of output at which

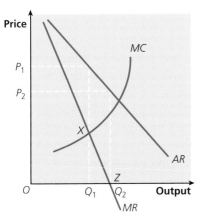

Figure 3.3 Profit maximisation and revenue maximisation when a firm's *AR* curve slopes downward

marginal revenue equals marginal cost (*MR* = *MC*). By contrast, revenue maximisation occurs at the level of output at which marginal revenue is zero. In the context of a monopolist's revenue curves, which we explained in Chapter 2, page 41, the difference between profit maximisation and revenue maximisation is shown in Figure 3.3.

The profit-maximising level of output Q_1 is located below point *X* where *MR* = *MC*. With regard to revenue, whenever marginal revenue is positive (at all levels of output below Q_2), selling an extra unit of output always causes total revenue to rise. But when marginal revenue is negative (at all levels of output above Q_2), selling an extra unit of output always causes total revenue to fall. It follows that the revenue-maximising level of output is Q_2, shown at point *Z*, where *MR* = 0. Provided the *MR* curve slopes downward to the right and marginal cost is greater than zero, the profit-maximising level of output will be below the revenue-maximising level of output.

STUDY TIP

Make sure you don't confuse *profit maximisation* with *revenue maximisation*. Note also that output Q_2 at point *Z* in Figure 3.3 is located immediately below the point on the *AR* curve where price elasticity of demand is neither elastic nor inelastic (i.e. it is unitary elastic). In Figure 3.3, the profit-maximising level of output, Q_1, lies below the elastic section (top half) of the *AR* curve.

QUANTITATIVE SKILLS 3.1

Worked example: profit maximisation

At its present level of output an entrepreneur determines that its marginal cost is £36 (and on the rising portion of the curve), and its marginal revenue is £42 (on a downward-sloping MR curve).

The firm will maximise profits or minimise losses by:

A increasing price while keeping output constant
B decreasing price and increasing output
C decreasing both price and output
D increasing both price and output

The correct answer is B. Since *MR* > *MC* at the firm's *current* level of output, profits rise when the firm increases its level of output. The question tells us that the firm has a downward-sloping *MR* curve. This means that its *AR* curve also slopes downward. Since *AR* is the same as price, whenever the firm increases output, it has to accept a lower price. (If you refer back to Figure 3.3, the firm would initially be producing an output level below and to the left of Q_1. By increasing output up to Q_1, price would fall and profit would increase up to Q_1, but fall thereafter.)

The satisficing principle

As we saw in Chapter 1, behavioural economists argue that it is too crude to view individuals and firms simply as utility and profit maximisers. With regard to the nature of production, behavioural economists see the firm as an organisation comprising coalitions of different groups within the firm, each possessing different group objectives. The different groups, often called *stakeholders* in the business, may each have a different vested interest in terms of how the business performs.

Different stakeholder groups have different views on what the company should be doing. Managers, for example, may seek prestige, power and high salaries. Besides wanting higher wages, workers may be looking for improved job security and working conditions. In their desire to achieve higher profits, shareholders may try to keep down wages and managerial salaries. Differing goals or aspirations can result in group conflict. Management may try to resolve conflict between the different interest groups by replacing the profit-maximising objective with **satisficing**. Satisficing, which means achieving

KEY TERM

satisficing achieving a satisfactory outcome rather than the best possible outcome.

a satisfactory outcome rather than the best possible outcome, may help to resolve the conflict between managers' and shareholders' objectives. While trying to maximise executive creature-comforts such as managerial status, salaries, fringe benefits and career structures, a company's board of directors must keep shareholders happy. According to this theory, managers maximise their own objectives, but subject to the constraint of delivering a satisfactory level of profit for shareholders.

However, attempting to satisfice so as to satisfy the aspirations of as many groups within the firm as possible means compromise and the possible setting of minimum rather than maximum targets. Satisficing is particularly likely for monopolies and firms in imperfectly competitive markets protected by entry barriers. In these circumstances, in seeking an easy life, a firm's managers may content themselves with satisfactory profit, combined with a degree of inefficiency or unnecessary costs, which could in principle be eliminated. In highly competitive markets, by contrast, firms that are initially content with satisfactory profits and a degree of inefficiency might be forced by the entry of new, more competitive firms to eliminate unnecessary costs. In order to survive, firms end up 'as if' they are profit maximisers, even though they may appear, at first sight, to be satisficing or pursuing some other business objective.

TEST YOURSELF 3.1

Explain why one of the five possible answers to the following question is correct and why the other four answers are wrong.

A firm engaged in satisficing behaviour is most likely to:

A maximise profits

B maximise revenue

C produce at an output different from that of a profit-maximising firm

D maximise sales

E minimise costs

3.3 Perfect competition

The meaning of perfect competition

Mention has been made of perfect competition on several occasions both in this chapter and in Chapter 2. To recap, perfect competition does not actually exist in real-world economies because it is impossible to meet simultaneously all the six conditions listed in Figure 3.1. Nevertheless, perfect competition plays a significant role in the traditional theory of the firm because it provides a yardstick against which the desirable and undesirable properties of real-world markets can be measured. For example, we shall use perfect competition as a benchmark against which to judge whether monopoly functions efficiently or inefficiently, and the extent to which resource misallocation occurs in monopoly.

Short-run profit maximisation in perfect competition

At this stage, you should refer back to Chapter 2, page 39 and look again at Figure 2.14. The diagrams illustrate how each firm in a perfectly competitive market passively accepts the ruling market price, which becomes each firm's average revenue (AR) and marginal revenue (MR) curve. The third condition of perfect competition tells us that a perfectly competitive firm can sell as much as it wishes at the market's ruling price. But how much will it actually wish to produce and sell? Providing we assume that each firm's business objective is solely to maximise profit, the answer is shown in Figure 3.4.

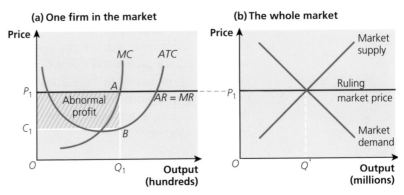

Figure 3.4 Short-run profit maximisation in perfect competition

In Figure 2.14 in Chapter 2, and likewise in Figure 3.4, panel (b) shows how the ruling market price (P_1) is determined at the intersection of the market demand and the market supply curves in the market as a whole. Again, as in Figure 2.14, when beamed horizontally into panel (a) of the diagram, the ruling market price becomes the average revenue (AR) curve and the marginal revenue (MR) curve facing each firm in the market. However, in Figure 3.4, we have added to panel (a) the perfectly competitive firm's average total cost (ATC) curve and its marginal cost (MC) curve. Point A in panel (a) (at which $MR = MC$) locates the profit-maximising level of output Q_1, with the firm's output shown in hundreds of units. At this level of output, total sales revenue is shown by the area OQ_1AP_1 (output multiplied by average revenue or price). Total cost is shown by the rectangular area OQ_1BC_1 (output multiplied by average cost). Abnormal profits (measured by subtracting the total cost rectangle from the total revenue rectangle) are shown by the shaded area C_1BAP_1.

In Figure 3.5, the graph is the same as panel (a) of Figure 3.4, but presented without any information about what is going on in the market as a whole. The diagram enables you to focus on a firm's short-run profits in conditions of perfect competition, especially the positions of the cost and revenue curves and the abnormal profit rectangle.

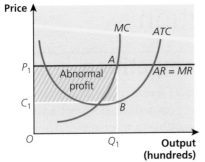

Figure 3.5 A perfectly competitive firm maximising profit in the short run

Long-run profit maximisation in perfect competition

Referring back to the list of the conditions of perfect competition, you will see that although firms cannot enter or leave the market in the short run, they can do so in the long run. Suppose that in the short run, firms make abnormal profit, as we have just illustrated in Figures 3.4 and 3.5. In this situation, the ruling market price signals to firms outside the market that abnormal profits can be made, which provides an incentive for new firms to enter the market.

Figure 3.6 shows what might happen next. Initially, too many new firms enter the market, causing the supply curve to shift to the right to S_2 in panel (b) of the diagram. This causes the price line to fall to P_2, which lies below each firm's ATC curve. When this happens, firms make a loss (or *subnormal profit*). However, just as abnormal profit creates the incentive for new firms to enter the market, subnormal profit has the opposite effect of causing some firms to leave the market.

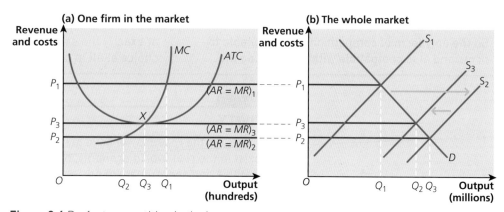

Figure 3.6 Perfect competition in the long run

When the price line lies below the ATC curve in panel (a) of the diagram, and firms start leaving the market, the market supply curve shifts to the left in panel (b). This causes the market price to rise. Eventually, the price settles at P_3, where, as panel (a) shows, surviving firms make normal profit only. In this situation, each firm produces the level of output, measured in hundreds of units, immediately below point X in panel (a) of the diagram.

Figure 3.7 is similar to panel (a) in Figure 3.6, but showing only the price line P_3. In the diagram, a firm's total revenue and also its total cost are shown by the rectangle OQ_3XP_3. The entry of new firms into the market, attracted by short-run abnormal profits, has whittled away these profits to produce a long-run outcome in which surviving firms make normal profit only. (Remember, normal profit is treated as a cost of production, and is not shown explicitly in the diagram.) Since only normal profit is made, there is no incentive for firms to enter or leave the market.

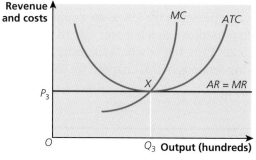

Figure 3.7 A perfectly competitive firm making only normal profit in the long run

65

EXTENSION MATERIAL

How competitive is perfect competition?

Although perfect competition is an abstract and unreal market structure, it is interesting to consider the forms competition might take in a perfectly competitive market economy. The first point to note is that price competition, in the form of price wars or price cutting by individual firms, would not take place. In perfect competition, all firms are passive price-takers, able to sell all the output they produce at the ruling market price determined in the market as a whole. In this situation, firms cannot gain sales or market share by price cutting. Other forms of competition, involving the use of advertising, packaging, brand-imaging or the provision of after-sales service to differentiate a firm's product from those of its competitors, simply destroy the conditions of perfect competition. These are the forms of competition which are prevalent, together with price competition, in the imperfectly competitive markets of the real economy in which we live.

So the only form of competition, both available to firms and also compatible with maintaining the conditions of perfect competition, is cost-cutting competition. Cost-cutting competition is likely in perfect competition because each firm has an incentive to reduce costs in order to make abnormal profit. But even the existence of cost-cutting competition in a perfect market can be questioned. Why should firms finance research into cost-cutting technical progress when they know that other firms have instant access to all market information and that any abnormal profits resulting from successful cost cutting can only be temporary?

Think also of the nature of competition in a perfect market, from the perspective of a typical consumer. The choice is simultaneously very broad and very narrow. The consumer has the doubtful luxury of maximum choice in terms of the number of firms or suppliers from whom to purchase a product. Yet each firm is supplying an identical good or service at exactly the same price. In this sense, there is no choice at all in perfect competition.

ACTIVITY

Although, for the reasons we have given, perfect competition does not exist in the real-world economy, many markets are highly price competitive and *approximate* to perfect competition. Research, and then briefly describe, three such markets.

3.4 Monopoly and monopoly power

The meaning of monopoly

KEY TERM
monopoly one firm only in a market.

As we noted earlier in the chapter, pure **monopoly** means one firm only in a market. We quoted regional water companies in the UK as an example. However, the word 'monopoly' is often used in a much looser way to describe any market in which there is a dominant firm, but in which there are also smaller firms. In this and the following sections of this chapter, we shall be looking solely at pure monopoly.

SYNOPTIC LINK
Chapter 4 compares monopsony in the economy's labour markets with monopoly in the economy's goods markets.

SYNOPTIC LINK
The functions of the Competition and Markets Authority are described in Chapter 6.

ACTIVITY

UK law defines monopoly in a different way to the definition we have given of pure monopoly. How does competition law define monopoly? Access the website of the Competition and Markets Authority (CMA) — the UK government agency which regulates monopoly — and outline details of two recent investigations by the CMA of monopolies or highly concentrated markets.

Short-run and long-run profit maximisation in monopoly

The profit-maximising or equilibrium level of output in monopoly is shown in Figure 3.8. As in perfect competition, the equilibrium output Q_1 is located below point A, where MR = MC. It is worth repeating that providing the firm is a profit maximiser, MR = MC, which is the condition which must be met to maximise profit that applies to any firm, whatever the market structure. However in monopoly, point A does not show the profit-maximising price, which is located at point B on the demand curve or AR curve above point A. P_1 is the maximum price the monopolist can charge and succeed in selling output Q_1.

You will notice that Figure 3.8 does not distinguish between *short-run* and *long-run* profit maximisation in monopoly. This is because a monopoly is protected by barriers to entry, which prevent new firms entering the market to share in the abnormal profit made by the monopolist. Entry barriers enable the monopolist to preserve abnormal profits in the long run as well as in the short run. By contrast, in perfect competition abnormal profits are temporary, being restricted to the short run. Indeed in monopoly, abnormal profit is often called monopoly profit. A monopolist has the market power to preserve profit by keeping competitors out.

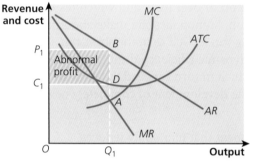

Figure 3.8 Profit maximisation in monopoly

The possible disadvantages and advantages of monopoly

Possible disadvantages

The main disadvantage of monopoly is that it may lead to market failure and resource misallocation. Figure 3.9 illustrates this. If the market were to be perfectly competitive, all the firms in the market would produce output Q_{PC}, which they would sell at the ruling market price P_{PC}, determined where market demand equals market supply below point X in the diagram. Suppose a monopoly now replaces the large number of firms in the competitive market. The monopoly uses its market power to restrict output to Q_M, which is located immediately below point Z on the diagram, where for the monopoly MR = MC. In order to profit maximise, the monopoly raises the price to P_M.

Market failure and resource misallocation occur because, compared to the competitive market, output falls and the price rises, leading to under-consumption of the good that the monopoly produces.

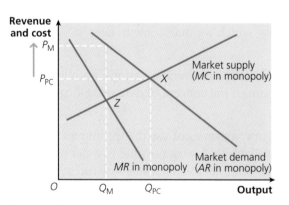

Figure 3.9 A monopoly restricting output and raising the price of a good

Possible advantages

The possible advantages of monopoly result from two sources: economies of scale and dynamic efficiency. When substantial economies of scale are possible in an industry, monopoly may lead to a better outcome than competition. Figure 3.10 illustrates a natural monopoly, which we first explained in Chapter 4 of Book 1, and then in Chapter 2 of this book on page 34. Because of limited market size, there is insufficient room in the market for more than one firm benefiting from full economies of scale.

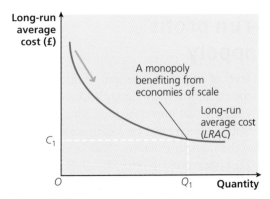

Long-run
average
cost (£)

A monopoly
benefiting from
economies of scale

Long-run
average cost
(*LRAC*)

C_1

O Q_1 **Quantity**

Figure 3.10 How economies of scale may justify monopoly

KEY TERMS

static efficiency efficiency (e.g. productive and allocative efficiency) at a particular point in time.

dynamic efficiency occurs in the long run, leading to the development of new products and more efficient processes that improve productive efficiency.

KEY TERMS

productive efficiency the level of output at which average costs of production are minimised.

allocative efficiency occurs when it is impossible to improve overall economic welfare by reallocating resources between markets. In the whole economy, price must equal marginal cost ($P = MC$) in every market.

In Figure 3.10, economies of scale are shown by the downward-sloping long-run average cost curve. By assumption, a monopoly is able to produce output Q_1 at a long-run average cost (or unit cost) of C_1, whereas competitive firms are unable to produce this output without destroying the competitive market.

So far in this chapter we have analysed perfect competition and monopoly in terms of whether or not they display **static efficiency**, which is efficiency measured at a particular point of time. Monopolies can also benefit from **dynamic efficiency**, which is improvements in other types of efficiency, particularly productive efficiency, that occur over time, and which result from technical progress and innovation. Monopolies can make abnormal profit, or monopoly profit, in the long run as well as in the short run. This profit can achieve improvements in dynamic efficiency through funding research and development (R&D), which in turn can lead to better ways of making existing products and to the development of completely new products.

Nevertheless, there is a counter-argument that monopoly reduces rather than promotes innovation and dynamic efficiency. Protected from competitive pressures, as we noted earlier, a monopoly may *profit-satisfice* rather than *profit-maximise*, content with satisfactory profits and an easy life.

Economic efficiency in perfect competition and monopoly

Economists use two sets of concepts to answer questions such as: is perfect competition preferable to monopoly, or vice versa? First, they apply efficiency concepts, which we briefly mentioned in the previous section, and then they use welfare concepts, which we shall come to later in this chapter.

We have mentioned productive efficiency on several occasions, both in this book and in Book 1, and we introduced the concept of dynamic efficiency in the previous section.

With regard to **productive efficiency**, a firm must use the techniques and factors of production which are available, at lowest possible cost per unit of output. In the short run, the lowest point on the relevant short-run average total cost curve locates the most productively efficient level of output for the particular scale of operation. Short-run productive efficiency is shown in Figure 3.11.

However, *true* productive efficiency occurs at the lowest point of a firm's *LRAC* curve, when the firm has benefited to the full from internal economies of scale. This is shown at output Q_N in Figure 3.12. (Output Q_1 is also productively efficient, but only for the short-run cost curve $SRATC_1$.)

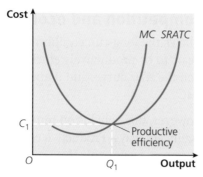

Figure 3.11 Productive efficiency in the short run

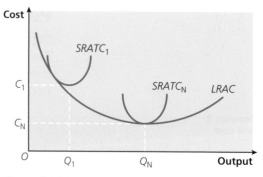

Figure 3.12 Productive efficiency in the long run as well as in the short run

When using efficiency concepts to evaluate perfect competition and monopoly, economists use another key efficiency concept known as **allocative efficiency**. This type of efficiency occurs when it is impossible to improve overall economic welfare by reallocating resources between industries or markets (assuming an initial distribution of income and wealth). As the extension material below explains, for resource allocation in the whole economy to be allocatively efficient, price must equal marginal cost ($P = MC$) in each and every market in the economy.

EXTENSION MATERIAL

Understanding allocative efficiency

This rather abstract type of efficiency occurs when $P = MC$ in all industries and markets in the economy. To explain this further, we must examine closely both P and MC. The price of a good, P, is a measure of the value in consumption placed by buyers on the last unit consumed. P indicates the utility or welfare obtained at the margin in consumption. This is the good's opportunity cost in consumption. For example, a consumer spending £1 on a bar of chocolate cannot spend the pound on other goods. When buying the chocolate bar, other goods or services are sacrificed. At the same time, MC measures the good's opportunity cost in production: that is, the value of the resources which go into the production of the last unit, in their best alternative uses.

Suppose that all the economy's markets divide into two categories: those in which $P > MC$ and those in which $P < MC$. In the markets where $P > MC$, households pay a price for the last unit consumed which is greater than the cost of producing the same unit. The high price discourages consumption, so we conclude that at this price the good is under-produced and under-consumed. Conversely, in the second set of markets, in which $P < MC$, the value (P) placed on the last unit consumed by households is less than the MC of the resources used to produce the last unit. The price is too low, encouraging too much consumption of the good; thus at this price the good is over-produced and over-consumed.

Suppose resources can be taken from the second group of markets where $P < MC$ and reallocated to the former group of markets in which $P > MC$. Arguably, total consumer welfare or utility will increase as reallocation of resources takes place. As the reallocation proceeds, prices tend to fall in those markets *into which* resources are being shifted and prices tend to increase in the markets *from which* resources are being moved. Eventually, as prices adjust, P equals MC in all markets simultaneously. Beyond the point at which $P = MC$ in all markets, no further reallocation of resources between markets can improve consumer welfare (assuming, of course, that all the other factors which influence welfare, such as the distribution of income, remain unchanged). The outcome in which $P = MC$ in all markets is allocatively efficient.

It follows that *allocative inefficiency* occurs when $P > MC$ or $P < MC$. For any given employment of resources and any initial distribution of income and wealth amongst the population, total consumer welfare can increase if resources are reallocated from markets where $P < MC$ into those where $P > MC$, until allocative efficiency is achieved when $P = MC$ in all markets.

Perfect competition and economic efficiency

Figure 3.13 shows the long-run equilibrium of a perfectly competitive firm. The firm appears to be productively efficient because it produces at the lowest point on the *ATC* curve, and it appears to be allocatively efficient because $P = MC$.

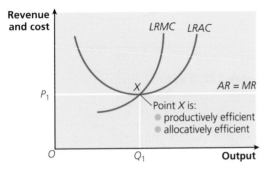

Figure 3.13 In the long run, given certain assumptions, a perfectly competitive firm is productively and allocatively efficient

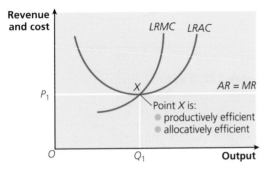

KEY TERMS

private costs and benefits
private costs are costs incurred solely by an individual or firm as a result of their own activities; private benefits are benefits enjoyed solely by an individual or firm as a result of their own activities.

social costs and benefits
social costs are costs which fall on the whole of society: social cost = private cost + external cost; social benefits are benefits enjoyed by the whole of society: social benefit = private benefit + external benefit.

However, this conclusion must be qualified in a number of significant ways. Productive efficiency combined with allocative efficiency occurs only if:

- All the firms in the market benefit from all the available economies of scale at a low level of output, which means that minimum efficient scale (*MES*) has to be small in relation to the total market size. Point *X* in Figure 3.13 shows minimised long-run average costs, and if all the perfectly competitive firms produce at this point, the outcome is indeed both productively and allocatively efficient — but only if we ignore the qualifications made in the next two bullet points. However, given the fact that *MES* is large in many of the markets in the economy, this outcome is not really achievable.
- There are perfectly competitive markets for *all* goods and services, including future markets, and $P = MC$ simultaneously in each and every market. To take this point further, *every* firm in *every* market *throughout the world* must be producing where $P = MC$. This is an impossible outcome to achieve, even if all the conditions of perfect competition could be met.
- There are no externalities, negative or positive. To explain this point, we must reintroduce the distinction between **private costs and benefits** and **social costs and benefits** that was first explained in Book 1.

To achieve allocative efficiency, price must equal the *true* marginal cost of production: that is, the marginal social cost and not just the marginal private cost ($P = MSC$ and not MPC). But in a market situation, profit-maximising firms are assumed only to take account of private costs and benefits. When externalities exist, therefore, the market mechanism fails to achieve an allocatively efficient equilibrium. For example, if negative externalities such as pollution are generated in the course of production, it turns out that $P < MSC$ even when $P = MPC$.

To put it another way, firms evade part of the true or real cost of production by dumping the externality on third parties. The price that the consumer pays for the good reflects only the private cost of production, and not the true cost, which includes the external cost. In a market situation, the firm's output is thus under-priced, encouraging too much consumption. A misallocation of resources results because the wrong price is charged. Too much consumption, and hence too much production, means that too many scarce resources are being used by the industry that is producing the negative externalities.

Monopoly and economic efficiency

In contrast to perfect competition — and once again assuming an absence of economies of scale — monopoly equilibrium is both productively and allocatively inefficient. Figure 3.14 shows that at the profit-maximising level of output Q_1, the monopolist's average costs, indicated at point *D*,

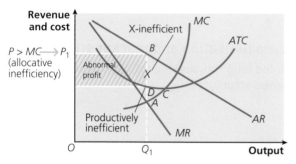

Figure 3.14 Productive and allocative inefficiency in monopoly

are above the minimum level of average costs shown at point *C*. The monopolist's level of output is thus productively inefficient.

However the monopoly is also allocatively inefficient. The monopolist's profit-maximising price, P_1, is considerably above marginal cost, which is shown at point *A*. In monopoly, $P > MC$, which means that compared to the whole of a perfectly competitive market, and once again assuming an absence of economies of scale, the monopoly produces too low an output which it sells at too high a price.

> **EXTENSION MATERIAL**
>
> # Unnecessarily high average costs of production
>
> Another point to note is that, given the absence of competitive pressures which in perfect competition serve to eliminate abnormal profit, a monopoly may be content to incur unnecessary costs. These are costs which, if it wanted to, the monopoly could eliminate. To understand this, take a close look at point *X* in Figure 3.14. If the monopoly produces the level of output Q_1, without incurring unnecessary costs, its average costs are shown at point *D*, which is located on the *ATC* curve. However, if the monopolist's average costs are shown at point *X* rather than at point *D*, unnecessary average production costs are being incurred, equal to the distance between *X* and *D* for a unit of output. A monopoly may be able to survive, perfectly happily and enjoying an 'easy life', and making *satisfactory* rather than *maximum* profits. This is because entry barriers protect monopolies. As a result, the absence or weakness of competitive forces means unnecessary costs very often persist in monopoly and in other imperfectly competitive markets. The technical term, *X-inefficiency*, is used by economists for unnecessarily high average costs of production.

Dynamic efficiency and economies of scale revisited

At the beginning of the discussion of monopoly and economic efficiency, we assumed an absence of economies of scale and we ignored the implications of the concept of dynamic efficiency. This is rather like assuming away the real world. As soon as we bring into our analysis economies of scale and the likelihood of gaining dynamic efficiency improvements over time, it is possible to mount a much stronger case for monopoly, or at least for large rather than small firms. However, as we shall see later in the chapter, this is not always the case. In new technology industries, small and medium-sized firms are often highly innovative and dynamically efficient, with the most successful often growing into large firms, and perhaps eventually exercising a high degree of monopoly power.

QUANTITATIVE SKILLS 3.2

Worked example: profit maximisation and market structure

Firm X is maximising profit in the long run, and the following data are known about its cost and revenue structure:

- **marginal costs = £400**
- **average costs = £450**
- **marginal revenue = £400**
- **average revenue = £500**

Firm X could be operating in all the market structures listed below except one. Which is the exception?

Market structures: perfect competition; monopoly; monopolistic competition; oligopoly.

In the data, $MR = MC$, so we know the firm is making the maximum profit. However, $MC < AC$, so the firm is producing on the downward-sloping section of the AC curve. Also, since $MR < AR$, the AR curve slopes downward. All this is consistent with long-run profit maximisation in monopoly, monopolistic competition and oligopoly, but not with perfect competition, for which the following has to hold: $MR = MC = AC = AR$. Perfect competition is the answer.

KEY TERM

monopoly power firms in market structures other than pure monopoly usually possess significant monopoly power, defined as power over price setting and other aspects of the market such as product differentiation.

Monopoly power in imperfectly competitive market structures

Students often confuse 'monopoly' with '**monopoly power**'. As we shall now see in the following sections of this chapter, firms in monopolistic competition and oligopoly can also exercise a lesser or greater degree of monopoly power.

3.5 Monopolistic competition

The meaning of monopolistic competition

In significant respects, monopolistic competition resembles both perfect competition and monopoly.

Monopolistic competition resembles perfect competition in the following ways:

- As in perfect competition, there are a large number of firms in the market.
- In the long run there are no barriers to entry or exit.
- As a result, the entry of new firms, attracted by short-run abnormal profits, brings down the price each firm can charge until only normal profits are made in the long run.

Monopolistic competition also resembles monopoly in the following ways:

- Each firm faces a downward-sloping demand curve. This results from the fact that each firm produces a slightly different product — differentiated by such features of modern production and marketing as style, design, packaging, branding and advertising. The goods produced by the various firms provide *partial* but *not perfect* substitutes for each other. The resulting 'product differentiation' in the market means that each firm possesses a degree of monopoly power over its product. Unlike in perfect competition, if a firm raises its price, it does not lose *all* its customers because there is brand loyalty.
- Each firm's marginal revenue (MR) curve is below its average revenue (AR) curve, which of course is the demand curve for the firm's output.

STUDY TIP

Students often wrongly believe that monopolistic competition is closer to pure monopoly than it is to perfect competition. In reality, monopolistically competitive markets, characterised by a large number of small to medium-sized firms competing against each other by differentiating the goods or services they produce and sell, are closer to perfect competition.

Short-run and long-run profit maximisation in monopolistic competition

Short-run profit maximisation

Short-run profit maximisation in monopolistic competition is illustrated in Figure 3.15, which is very similar to profit maximisation in monopoly, illustrated earlier in Figure 3.8. However, in monopolistic competition the demand or average revenue curve represents demand for the goods produced by just *one* firm within the market rather than demand for the output of the *whole* market. And because the other firms within the market produce *partial* though *not perfect* substitutes, the demand curve facing the firm is likely to be rather more elastic at the prices each firm may decide to set than would be the case in pure monopoly.

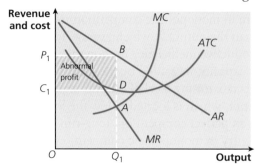

Figure 3.15 Short-run profit maximisation in monopolistic competition

The profit-maximising level of output, Q_1, is located below point A on the diagram, where $MR = MC$, and the abnormal profits made by the firm in the short run are shown by the rectangular area C_1DBP_1.

Long-run profit maximisation

The absence of barriers to entry or exit in the long run is of great importance in the theory of monopolistic competition. Long-run profit maximisation in monopolistic competition is different in an important respect from profit maximisation in monopoly. In the long run, the entry of new firms causes the demand curve or AR curve facing an established firm to shift leftward or inward. The leftward shift may result from the introduction of new substitute products, attracting some customers away from the existing firms. Long-run profit maximisation is achieved when the AR curve just touches (or forms a tangent to) the firm's ATC curve, thereby removing the firm's abnormal profit. This is shown in Figure 3.16, at point B immediately above level of output Q_1. Since only normal profit is made, total sales revenue and total costs of production are both shown by the rectangle OQ_1BP_1. Note also that the point of tangency between the AR and ATC curves occurs immediately above point A, which determines the profit-maximising level of output Q_1 where $MR = MC$.

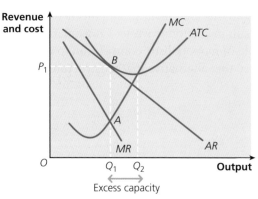

Figure 3.16 Long-run profit maximisation in monopolistic competition

STUDY TIP
It is worth remembering that in all market structures — perfect competition, monopoly and all types of imperfect competition — the profit-maximising level of output occurs where $MR = MC$.

Evaluating monopolistic competition

We have just explained that, as in perfect competition, the market mechanism eliminates abnormal profits in monopolistic competition and brings about a long-run profit-maximising price which equals the average cost of production ($P = ATC$). Nevertheless, in the absence of any economies of scale, monopolistic competition is both allocatively and productively inefficient in comparison with perfect competition. As in monopoly, $P > MC$ and the firm is incurring average costs that are higher than those incurred at the lowest point on its ATC curve.

Indeed, because in the long run a firm in monopolistic competition must be producing a level of output less than the output at which average total costs reach their lowest point, the productive inefficiency in monopolistic competition takes the form of excess capacity, measured by the difference in Figure 3.16 between Q_1 (the profit-maximising level of output) and Q_2, the productively efficient level of output, which is located below the lowest point on the ATC curve. However, as in perfect competition, long-run profit maximisation and freedom of entry in monopolistic competition mean that firms are forced to produce on their average cost curves. They must eliminate any unnecessary costs above average cost; otherwise they will fail to make normal profits.

At the same time, product differentiation increases the range of choice available to the consumer. It can be argued that monopolistic competition can in fact improve economic welfare. The economist Kelvin Lancaster argued that the number of differentiated products increases until the gain to consumers in choice from adding one more product to the market exactly equals the loss resulting from having to produce less of the existing products at a higher cost. According to this argument, monopolistic competition does not necessarily result in economic waste. Consumers may prefer the wider choice available in monopolistic competition to any improvement in productive efficiency that alternative market structures might provide.

QUANTITATIVE SKILLS 3.3

Worked example: profit maximisation in monopolistic competition

Table 3.1 provides information about the price, total revenue, total costs and marginal costs for haircuts on a particular day in a barber's shop operating in monopolistic competition.

Table 3.1 Revenue and costs for a barber's shop

Number of haircuts per day (1)	Price (£) (2)	Total revenue (£) (3)	Marginal revenue (£) (4)	Total costs (£) (5)	Marginal costs (£) (6)
0	11	0		5	–
1	10	10			2
2	9	18			3
3	8	24			6
4	7	28			8
5	6	30			9

From the information in the table:

a fill in the missing information in columns (4) and (5)
b calculate the profit-maximising price of haircuts

a

Number of haircuts per day	Price (£)	Total revenue (£)	Marginal revenue (£)	Total costs (£)	Marginal costs (£)
0	11	0	–	5	–
1	10	10	10	7	2
2	9	18	8	10	3
3	8	24	6	16	6
4	7	28	2	24	8
5	6	30	1	33	9

b Profit maximisation occurs at the level of output 3 haircuts per day, at which $MR = MC$. This is when the price of a haircut is £8 and both MR and MC are £6. (Note that total profit is the same at 2 haircuts per day, with the third haircut having zero effect on total profit.)

TEST YOURSELF 3.2

The price of cotton, a major cost incurred by clothing retailers such as Marks & Spencer, recently increased by 80%. Explain why only one of the five possible outcomes listed below is likely to be correct and why the other four are likely to be wrong.

	Sales of clothing	Profits
A	Constant	Fall
B	Rise	Rise
C	Fall	Constant
D	Constant	Constant
E	Fall	Fall

Non-price competition

In the absence of, or in addition to, price competition — through which firms try to gain market share and/or protect their existing sales by cutting their prices — firms in imperfectly competitive markets, both in monopolistic competition and in oligopoly, are therefore likely to undertake various forms of *non-price competition*. These include:

- marketing competition, including obtaining exclusive outlets such as tied public houses and petrol stations through which breweries and oil companies sell their products
- the use of persuasive advertising, product differentiation, brand imaging, packaging, fashion, style and design
- quality competition, including the provision of point-of-sale service and after-sale service

3.6 Oligopoly

The meaning of oligopoly

The prefix *oligo* attached to a word is taken from the Greek word *oligos*, meaning *few*. In a literal sense, therefore, an oligopoly is a market or industry containing a few firms. This is the way oligopoly is defined as a form of market structure. However, there is a problem with this method of definition. How many or how few firms should there be for oligopoly to exist? Do 10 firms make up an oligopoly but 11 firms do not? And what about a market in which there are, say, seven very large firms, but also scores or even hundreds of small firms or minnows? As we shall see shortly, it is usually more fruitful to define oligopoly in terms of *market conduct* or *market behaviour*, rather than in terms of a precise number of firms. However, before looking at market behaviour and at the interdependence of firms within a market, we shall look at how concentration ratios are used to identify oligopoly in highly concentrated market structures.

Oligopoly, market structure and concentration ratios

A **concentration ratio** can provide a good indicator of an oligopolistic market structure. For example, a five-firm concentration ratio shows the percentage or share of output in an industry produced by the five largest firms in the industry. The five-firm concentration ratio in the UK supermarket industry reported in February 2014, calculated from the market share data shown in Figure 3.17, was 82.7%. This figure tells us that at the time, the five leading supermarket chains accounted for 82.7% of UK supermarket sales. Most economists would conclude that the UK supermarket industry is oligopolistic. With a 30% market share, Tesco was clearly the leading and possibly the dominant firm. However, Tesco suffered significant business problems in 2014, which led to a fall in the company's market share. This was partly the result of the smaller German supermarket firms, Aldi and Lidl, making inroads into the UK supermarket industry.

> **TEST YOURSELF 3.3**
> With the help of a diagram, explain why a firm making normal profit in monopolistic competition is likely to be productively inefficient and also allocatively inefficient.

> **KEY TERM**
> **concentration ratio** measures the market share (percentage of the total market) of the biggest firms in the market. For example, a five-firm concentration measures the aggregate market share of the largest five firms.

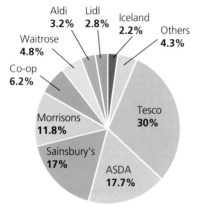

Figure 3.17 Market shares in the UK supermarket industry, February 2014

CASE STUDY 3.1

Competition in the UK supermarket industry

Writing in an October 2014 edition of *Management Today*, Alastair Dryburgh explained why, in his view, Tesco cannot compete with Aldi and Lidl. The management expert argued that if Tesco wanted to return to health, it had to give up the idea that it could win by being the cheapest. Tesco was losing out to 'hard discounter' retailers like Aldi and Lidl.

Some commentators were arguing that Tesco should cut prices by more than it had done in the past in order to compete, but Dryburgh believed that this would be a suicidal move. Aldi had stated publicly that its intention was to remain at least

15% cheaper than Tesco. Aldi has always been well placed to meet this target: its whole business has been designed to be lower cost than the competition.

The hard discounters stock only around 2,000 lines, as against Tesco's 40,000. Around 90% of those lines are own brands. The package sizes are designed to make optimum use of the shelves, and the goods are delivered in shelf-ready packaging. Dryburgh argued that a company cannot compete on price with other firms which have systematically designed their businesses to be lower cost — it would be like British Airways deciding to compete on price with Ryanair.

Follow-up questions

1 Suggest two forms of non-price competition that Tesco might use to regain market share from 'hard discounter' retailers.
2 Research Tesco's business strategy since October 2014 and comment on its success.

QUANTITATIVE SKILLS 3.4

Worked example: calculating the concentration ratio

Table 3.2 shows the usage-based market share of internet web browsers in Europe in a recent year.

Table 3.2 Market share of internet web browsers

Web browser market	Market share (%)
Internet Explorer	62.0
Mozilla Firefox	28.4
Apple Safari	4.3
Google Chrome	2.8
Opera	2.2
Others	0.3

Calculate the four-firm concentration ratio for the web browser market in Europe and comment on the nature of the market structure.

We calculate the four-firm concentration ratio by adding up the percentage market shares of the four leading firms. This is 62.0% + 28.4% + 4.3% + 2.8%, which equals 97.5%. The concentration ratio tells us that the European web browser market is an oligopoly, at least as defined by market structure. The data provide no evidence as to whether or not it is a competitive or collusive oligopoly, though with a lack of evidence discovered by monopoly regulators, such as the Competition and Markets Authority in the UK, it is probably a competitive oligopoly.

KEY TERM

market conduct the price and other market policies pursued by firms. This is also known as market behaviour, but is not to be confused with market performance, which refers to the end results of these policies.

Oligopoly and market behaviour

As already mentioned, oligopoly is best defined, not only by market structure or the number of firms in the market, but also by **market conduct**, or the behaviour of the firms within the market. An oligopolistic firm affects its rivals through its price and output decisions, but its own profit can also be affected by how rivals behave and react to the firm's decisions. Suppose, for example, the firm reduces its price in order to increase market share and boost profit. Whether the price reduction increases or reduces the firm's profit depends on the reactions of the other firms.

ACTIVITY

The household gas and electricity retail markets are often quoted as examples of oligopoly. Research the number of gas and electricity retailers in these markets and collect information about the prices they charge. On the basis of the evidence you collect, do you believe the gas and electricity retailers are acting in the public interest, or are they abusing their market power? Justify your conclusions.

Interdependence and uncertainty in oligopoly

Competitive oligopoly exists when the rival firms are interdependent in the sense that they must take account of each other's reactions when forming a market strategy, but independent in the sense that they decide their market strategies without cooperation or collusion. As a result, uncertainty is a characteristic of competitive oligopoly; a firm can never be completely certain of how rivals will react to its price, marketing and output strategy. If the firm raises its price, will the rivals follow suit or will they hold their prices steady in the hope of gaining sales and market share?

Non-collusive oligopoly, collusive oligopoly and cartels

As we noted in the previous paragraph, in competitive oligopoly, firms act independently in the sense that they do not form agreements with each other. This is also known as non-collusive oligopoly. The uncertainty facing competitive oligopolists can be reduced and perhaps eliminated by the rival firms colluding together — for example, by forming a **cartel** agreement or price ring. In Figure 3.18, five firms jointly agree to charge a price to keep Firm E, which is the least productively efficient firm, in the market. In a competitive market, Firm E would have to reduce costs or go out of business. Cartel agreements enable inefficient firms to stay in business, while other more efficient members of the price ring enjoy abnormal profit. By protecting the inefficient and enabling firms to enjoy an easy life protected from competition, cartels display the disadvantages of monopoly (high prices and restriction of choice). However, this is usually without the benefits that monopoly can sometimes bring, namely economies of scale and improvements in dynamic efficiency.

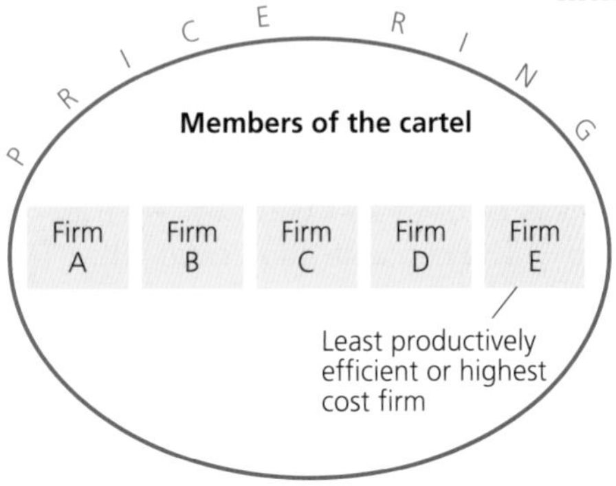

Collusion versus market cooperation

Although forming a cartel can achieve a better outcome than competitive behaviour for oligopolistic firms, the result is unlikely to be good for consumers. For this reason, cartel agreements are usually illegal and judged by governments as being anti-competitive and against the public interest. Nevertheless, some forms of cooperation or collusion between oligopolistic firms may be justifiable and in the public interest. These include joint product development (such as the multi-purpose vehicles, the Ford Galaxy, Seat Alhambra and VW Sharan, jointly developed by Ford and Volkswagen), and cooperation to improve health and safety within the industry or to ensure that product and labour standards are maintained. Such examples of industry collaboration, or overt collusion, which is in the full public view, are normally deemed to be good, in contrast to price collusion, which is regarded as bad. Price collusion and other market-rigging agreements almost always take place

KEY TERM

cartel a collusive agreement by firms, usually to fix prices. Sometimes there is also an agreement to restrict output and to deter the entry of new firms.

Figure 3.18 A cartel or price ring

STUDY TIP

Collusive or cooperative behaviour enables firms to reduce the uncertainty they face in imperfectly competitive markets. However, some forms of collusion — for example, on joint product development or ensuring industry safety standards — are in the public interest.

in secret. This is covert collusion. Tacit collusion, by contrast, occurs when there is 'an understanding' without any explicit agreement between the firms.

CASE STUDY 3.2

Big stores and tobacco firms 'colluded on cigarette prices'

In 2008, eleven big retailers and two tobacco companies faced a government-backed inquiry into allegations that they colluded over the price of cigarettes. Tesco, Sainsbury's and ASDA, as well as Imperial Tobacco and Gallaher, were among those accused by UK competition authorities of increasing profits illegally. The clampdown on alleged anti-competitive practices could have resulted in fines of tens of millions of pounds.

The initial investigation by the competition authorities found that the companies were illegally coordinating the prices of brands to increase their profit margins. Some companies coordinated to link the price of some brands to rival products. Others arranged to swap information on future pricing. The

named companies struck deals that 'restricted the ability of each of these retailers to determine its selling prices independently'.

Companies involved in anti-competitive pricing practices can face fines of up to 10% of the relevant annual turnover. However, penalties can be cut if businesses cooperate with an investigation. By 2008, the largest fine that had been imposed was the £121.5 million levied on British Airways over a conspiracy with Virgin Atlantic to fix passenger fuel surcharges on transatlantic flights. Virgin escaped financial penalty because it had blown the whistle to the competition authorities.

With regard to cigarette pricing, Tesco denied any wrongdoing and Imperial Tobacco said that it takes compliance with competition law very seriously and rejected any suggestion that it has acted in any way contrary to the interests of consumers.

Follow-up questions

1 Why may collusive agreements to raise the price of cigarettes not be in the public interest?
2 Find out what happened to the firms mentioned in the passage after the investigation was completed.

EXTENSION MATERIAL

Joint-profit maximisation in collusive oligopoly

Joint-profit maximisation, which is illustrated in Figure 3.19, occurs when a number of firms decide to act as a single monopolist, yet keep their separate identities. Oligopolistic firms undertake joint-profit maximisation in the belief that it can lead to higher profits for all the firms taking part. The monopoly MC curve depicted in the right-hand side of the diagram is the sum of the identical MC curves of three firms (one of which is shown on the left of the diagram). The three firms share an output of 750 units, determined on the right of the diagram where the industry MR and MC curves intersect. Each firm charges a price of £10, which, as the diagram shows, is the maximum price consumers

are prepared to pay for 750 units of the good. The monopoly output of 750 units is well below 1,000 units, which would be the output if the industry were perfectly competitive. The shaded area in the

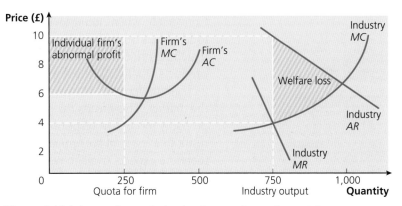

Figure 3.19 Joint-profit maximisation by members of a cartel

right-hand panel shows the efficiency or welfare loss caused by the cartel raising the price to £10 and restricting output to 750 units. In this example, the members of the cartel split the 750 units equally, each firm producing 250 units. The shaded area on the left of the diagram shows the abnormal profit made by each firm.

Although there is an incentive for firms to collude to maximise their joint profits, there is also an incentive for each member of the cartel to cheat on the agreement. The marginal cost of producing the 250th unit of the good is only £4, yet for the firm (but not the whole industry) the marginal revenue received from selling one more unit is £10 (that is, the price set by the cartel). One member of the cartel can increase its profit at the expense of the other firms by secretly selling an output over and above its quota of 250 units at a price less than £10, but greater than the marginal cost incurred (£4). This is an example of a divergence between individual and collective interest. The firms' collective interest is to maintain the cartel so as to keep total sales down and the price up. But each firm can benefit by cheating on the agreement — providing all the others do not cheat.

The kinked demand curve model of competitive oligopoly

The kinked demand curve theory can be used to illustrate how a competitive oligopolist may be affected by rivals' reaction to its price and output decisions. The theory was originally developed to explain alleged price rigidity and an absence of price wars in oligopolistic markets.

Suppose an oligopolist initially produces output Q_1 in Figure 3.20, selling this output at price P_1. In order to anticipate how sales might change following a price change, firms need to know the position and shape of the demand and revenue curves for their products. But in imperfectly competitive markets, firms lack accurate information about these curves, particularly at outputs significantly different from those currently being produced. This means that the demand curve or *AR* curve in Figure 3.20 is not necessarily the correct or *actual* demand curve for the oligopolist's output. Instead, it represents the firm's *estimate* of how demand changes when the firm changes the price it is charging.

When *increasing* price from P_1 to P_2, the oligopolist expects rivals to react by keeping their own prices stable and not following suit. By holding their prices steady, rivals try to gain profit and market share at the firm's expense. This means that the oligopolist expects demand to be *relatively elastic* in response to a price increase. The rise in price from P_1 to P_2 is likely to result in a *more than proportionate fall in demand* from Q_1 to Q_2.

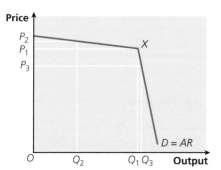

Figure 3.20 The kinked demand curve

Conversely, when *cutting* its price from P_1 to P_3, the oligopolist expects rivals to react in a very different way, namely by following suit immediately with a matching price cut. In this situation, because the market demand curve for the products of all the firms slopes downward, each firm will benefit from *some* increase in demand. However, the oligopolist fails to gain sales from rivals *within* the market. This means the oligopolist expects demand to be less elastic, and probably *inelastic* in response to a price cut. The fall in price from P_1 to P_3 may result in a *less than proportionate increase in demand* from Q_1 to Q_3. The oligopolist therefore expects rivals to react *asymmetrically* when price is raised or lowered.

In Figure 3.20, the oligopolist's initial price and output of P_1 and Q_1 intersect at point X, or at the kink at the junction of two demand curves of different elasticity, each reflecting a different assumption about how rivals may react to a change in price. If when price is raised, demand is elastic, and when price is cut, demand is inelastic, any change in price will reduce the oligopolist's total revenue. In this situation, the oligopolist fears that both a price increase and a price cut are likely to reduce total profit. Given this fear, the best policy may be to leave price unchanged.

EXTENSION MATERIAL

Developing the kinked demand curve theory

By developing the theory a little more, we can explain a second reason why prices may tend to be stable in oligopoly. As Figure 3.21 below illustrates, a mathematical discontinuity exists along the vertical line drawn above output Q_1. For the demand and average revenue curves, the discontinuity occurs at the 'kink' where the curves intersect. But for the marginal revenue curves, which are twice as steep as the AR curves with which they are associated, the discontinuity is the 'gap' between the two MR curves, shown by the distance B to C.

Suppose initially the firm's marginal cost curve is MC_1, intersecting the MR curve at point A, which is positioned in the middle of the vertical section. The diagram shows that the MC curve can rise or fall within the vertical section of the MR curve, without altering the profit-maximising output Q_1 or price P_1. But if marginal costs rise above MC_2 at point B or fall below MC_3 at point C, the profit-maximising output changes. In either of these circumstances, the oligopolist would have to set a different price to maximise profits, providing of course that the AR curve accurately measures demand for the firm's product at different prices. Nevertheless, the oligopolist's selling price remains stable at P_1 as long as the marginal cost curve lies between MC_2 and MC_3, despite quite considerable changes in marginal costs.

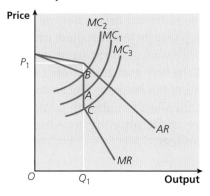

Figure 3.21
Developing the theory of the kinked demand curve

Criticisms of the kinked demand curve theory

There are a number of weaknesses in the theory we have just described. Although at first sight it is attractive as a neat and apparently plausible explanation of price stability in conditions of oligopoly, few economists now accept the kinked demand theory of oligopoly pricing.

First, it is an incomplete theory, since it does not explain how and why a firm chooses in the first place to be at point X in Figure 3.20. Second, the evidence provided by the pricing decisions of real-world firms gives little support to the theory. Competitive oligopolists seldom respond to price changes in the manner assumed in the kinked demand curve theory. It is more reasonable to expect a firm to test the market — that is, to raise or lower its selling price to see if rivals react in the manner expected. If rivals do not, then the firm must surely revise its estimate of the shape of the demand curve facing it. Research has shown fairly conclusively that oligopoly prices tend to be stable or sticky when demand conditions change in a predictable or cyclical way, but that oligopolists usually raise or lower prices quickly and by significant amounts, both when production costs change substantially, and when unexpected shifts in demand occur.

STUDY TIP
Students often wrongly believe that the kinked demand curve provides a complete theory of oligopoly. It is actually a very doubtful theory, but it does illustrate how oligopolists are interdependent and affected by uncertainty.

Price leadership, price agreements and price wars

Price leadership

Because overt collusive agreements to fix the market price, such as cartel agreements, are usually illegal, imperfectly competitive firms often use less formal or tacit ways to coordinate their pricing decisions. An example of covert collusion is **price leadership**, which occurs when one firm becomes the market leader and other firms in the industry follow its pricing example.

Price agreements

We have already seen earlier in the chapter how members of a cartel often fix the prices that all the members of the cartel charge by forming a price ring. **Price agreements** can also be made between firms and their suppliers, and between firms and their customers. In both these cases, a price agreement is usually good for a specified period of time, such as 6 months.

Price wars

Price wars, which take place both in monopolistic competition and in oligopoly, may be started accidently or may be instigated deliberately to damage competitors. Whereas price leadership usually involves quite friendly relations between the companies involved, price wars — as the name indicates — centre on price cutting aimed at the very least at increasing market share, and in the extreme at forcing rival firms out of business. Consumers may of course benefit from a price war, at least in the short run, though if firms are driven out of the market, the monopoly power of the surviving firms increases, which is likely to be to the detriment of consumers.

CASE STUDY 3.3

Discounting in the book market

Many years ago, UK law allowed manufacturers to decide the prices at which retailers sold their goods. If a shop tried to undercut or discount a set price, the manufacturer could stop supplying the good to the retailer. As a result, price competition between firms selling similar goods hardly existed and manufacturers made excessive profits. This was a restrictive practice known as *retail price maintenance*.

Eventually the law was changed in an effort to promote more competition. However, manufacturers then set recommended retail prices (RRPs), which they hoped shops would abide by. Selling at recommended retail prices became especially important in book publishing, where very little price discounting took place. Paperback books were generally sold at the prices printed by the publishers on the covers. Small bookshops justified the lack of price competition on the ground that consumers benefited, both from bookshops

surviving in small towns and from a much wider selection of books being on display.

However, in the 1980s this changed. Large book chain stores such as Waterstones sold books at prices well below the publishers' recommended prices. Small bookshops could not compete and many closed down. However, large stores themselves now face increasing competition from the growth of the online retailer, Amazon. Many people now pop into bookshops, not to buy books, but to browse, before going home to order the books they want online.

The picture is different in France. In 1981 French law fixed book prices with the result that readers pay the same whether they buy online, from a big high-street chain, or from a small bookseller. Extensive discounting is banned, although 5% discounts are allowed. Result: there are between 2,500 and 3,000 independent bookshops in

Independent bookshops are more common in France than in the UK

France, compared with fewer than 1,000 in the UK. Most small French towns have at least two bookshops and there is a wide choice of books on display.

The French government says that the banning of discounts of more than 5% has saved its independent bookstores from the ravages of free-market capitalism that hit the UK when it abandoned fixed prices. Nevertheless, the owners of French bookshops still argue they cannot compete with Amazon, even with Amazon's discounts limited to 5%, because the online retailer provides free postage and free fast delivery deals on top of the discount. Consumers can also bypass French law by ordering books online in countries such as Belgium.

The French culture minister recently said: 'Everyone has had enough of Amazon, which by dumping practices, slashes prices to get a foothold in markets, only to raise them as soon as they have established a virtual monopoly...the book and reading sector is facing competition from certain sites using every possible means to enter the French and European book market...it is destroying bookshops.'

Follow-up questions

1 Explain how the changing nature of competition in the book market illustrates the process of creative destruction.
2 Do you agree that the growth of Amazon has been good for consumers? Justify your answer.

3.7 Price discrimination

The meaning of price discrimination

> **KEY TERM**
>
> **price discrimination** charging different prices to different customers for the same product or service, with the prices based on different willingness to pay.

Price discrimination involves firms charging different prices to different customers for the same product or service, based on differences in the customers' ability and willingness to pay. Those customers who are prepared to pay more are charged a higher price than those who are only willing to pay a lower price. In the main form of price discrimination, the different prices charged are not based on any differences in costs of production or supply. However, in one form of price discrimination, bulk buying, consumers buying larger quantities are charged lower prices than consumers purchasing smaller quantities of the good. When this happens, different costs of supply may be involved. Bulk purchases generally have lower average costs of production than smaller purchases.

In Figure 3.22 a night club divides its market into male and female customers, each with a different elasticity of demand at each price of admission. At all the prices that could be charged for entry into the club, female demand is more elastic than male demand. For both men and women, the downward-sloping demand curves in Figure 3.22 show average revenue, but not marginal revenue. In each case, the *MR* curve is twice as steep as the *AR* curve. The diagrams also assume that the marginal cost incurred when an extra person enters the club is always the same. This is shown by the horizontal *MC* curve.

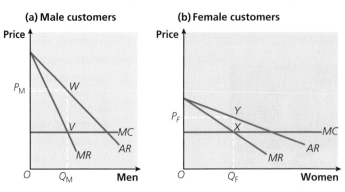

Figure 3.22 Price discrimination when a firm charges different prices to two groups of customers

To maximise profit, *MR* must equal *MC* in both male and female sub-markets. As the diagrams show, this means that men pay a higher price for admission than women, namely P_M, with women paying the lower entry price of P_F. With the different prices being charged, Q_M males and Q_F females are allowed into the club. The point to note is that the different prices charged result from the different male and female price elasticities of demand. Profit is maximised when more price-sensitive female customers pay less to enter the club than the less price-sensitive males. Note that when profit maximising, the *MR* received from the last man and woman admitted are the same. If this were not the case, the club could increase profit by changing the numbers of men and women admitted.

KEY TERMS

consumer surplus a measure of the economic welfare enjoyed by consumers: surplus utility received over and above the price paid for a good.

producer surplus a measure of the economic welfare enjoyed by firms or producers: the difference between the price a firm succeeds in charging and the minimum price it would be prepared to accept.

STUDY TIP

It is important to understand consumer surplus and producer surplus in order to analyse how economic welfare may be affected by events that raise or lower the price of a good.

EXTENSION MATERIAL

Developing the analysis of price discrimination

In order to analyse price discrimination in greater depth, we must introduce the key welfare concepts of consumer surplus and producer surplus, which we will revisit in the final section of this chapter.

Consumer surplus is the difference between the *maximum price* a consumer is prepared to pay and the *actual price* he or she has to pay. In a competitive market such as Figure 3.23, the total consumer surplus enjoyed by all the consumers in the market is measured by the triangular area P_1EA. Consumer welfare increases whenever consumer surplus increases — for example, when market prices fall. Conversely, however, higher prices reduce consumer surplus and welfare.

Producer surplus, which is a measure of producers' welfare, is the difference between the *minimum price* a firm is prepared to charge for a good and the *actual price* charged. In Figure 3.23, the producer surplus enjoyed by all the firms in the market is measured by the triangular area FP_1A.

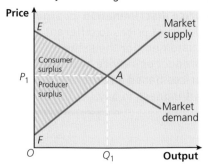

Figure 3.23 Consumer surplus and producer surplus

The conditions necessary for price discrimination

Successful price discrimination requires that the following conditions are met:

- It must be possible to identify different groups of customers or sub-markets for the product. This is possible when customers differ in their knowledge of the market or in their ability to shop around. Some customers may have special needs for a product and competition among oligopolists may vary in different parts of the market. In some geographical areas and for some products, a firm may face many competitors, whereas in other parts of the market the firm may be the sole supplier.
- At any particular price, the different groups of customers must have different price elasticities of demand. In these circumstances, total profits are maximised by charging a higher price in a market in which demand is less elastic.
- The markets must be separated to prevent seepage. Seepage takes place when customers buying at the lower price in one sub-market resell in another sub-market at a price which undercuts the oligopolist's own selling price in that market. In the European car market, car manufacturers have often charged higher prices for a vehicle in the UK market than in mainland Europe. One reason for this has been the fact that UK motorists demand right-hand drive cars in contrast to cars in mainland Europe which are left-hand drive. However, seepage occurred when specialist car importers bought cars on the Continent to resell in the UK market, thereby undercutting the prices the car manufacturers' recommended for the UK market.

The advantages and disadvantages of price discrimination

The firms undertaking price discrimination benefit from the practice, but their customers generally suffer. What is an advantage to firms or producers is a disadvantage for consumers. Figure 3.24 shows how consumer surplus falls when different prices are charged to different customers. Consumer surplus is a measure of consumer welfare, so consumers end up being worse off. By contrast, the firms undertaking the price discrimination benefit. Their profits and producer surplus increase as a result of the transfer of consumer surplus away from their customers.

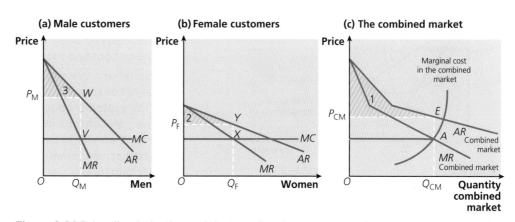

Figure 3.24 Price discrimination and the transfer of consumer surplus

As Figure 3.24 illustrates, price discrimination allows firms to increase profit by taking consumer surplus away from consumers and converting it into additional abnormal profit. Panels (a) and (b) of Figure 3.24 are the same as the two panels in Figure 3.22 on page 84. However, panel (c) has been added to show the combined market with the male and female average revenue curves added together. The male and female marginal revenue curves have also been added together. Note that for the combined market (but *not* the male and female sub-markets considered separately), the marginal cost curve slopes upward, depicting the impact of the law of diminishing returns.

In the absence of price discrimination, all consumers pay the same price, namely P_{CM} shown in panel (c) of the diagram. Without price discrimination, consumer surplus is shown by the shaded area (labelled 1) above P_{CM} in panel (c). But with price discrimination, when male customers are charged price P_M and female customers P_F, consumer surplus falls to equal the shaded areas labelled 3 and 2 in panels (a) and (b). The firm's profit has increased by transferring consumer surplus from consumers to the producer. Producer welfare (or producer surplus) has increased at the expense of consumer welfare (or consumer surplus).

EXTENSION MATERIAL

Price discrimination: the limiting case

So far we have explained price discrimination where discriminating firms divide the market into a number of different market segments. This is also called 'third degree' price discrimination. We shall now look at 'first degree' price discrimination, which is also called 'perfect' price discrimination. It is the limiting case of price discrimination. (There is also another type of price discrimination called 'second degree' price discrimination. This occurs when the price charged varies according to quantity demanded. With 'bulk buying', larger quantities are available at a lower price per unit — a 'bulk-buying' discounted price.)

'Perfect' or 'first degree' price discrimination is illustrated in Figure 3.25.

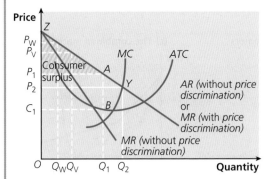

Figure 3.25 Price discrimination: the limiting case, when each customer is charged the maximum price he or she is prepared to pay

Figure 3.25 illustrates a situation in which *all* the consumer surplus is transferred into producer surplus or producer welfare. Every customer is charged the maximum price he or she is prepared to pay. Figure 3.25 is basically the same as Figure 3.8 on page 67, which shows monopoly equilibrium. In the absence of price discrimination, the firm produces the level of output Q_1 where $MR = MC$ and all customers are charged the price P_1. Abnormal profit is shown by the rectangle C_1BAP_1, and consumer surplus by the triangular area P_1AZ.

Now consider what happens when the firm charges each customer the maximum price he or she is prepared to pay. Customer Q_V depicted in the diagram is charged price P_V, customer Q_W is charged P_W, and so on. In this situation, there may be as many prices as there are customers. Because each customer is paying the maximum price he or she is prepared to pay, all the consumer surplus is transferred away from consumers to the firm, thereby boosting monopoly profit.

In summary, price discrimination leads to a loss of consumer surplus or consumer welfare. Firms exploit producer sovereignty and monopoly power, and charge most consumers higher prices than would be charged in the absence of price discrimination. For these reasons, price discrimination is usually regarded as undesirable.

However, Figure 3.25 also shows how *some* consumers at least, often the poorest consumers, can benefit from price discrimination. Each time the firm sells to one more customer, total sales revenue rises by the extra units sold multiplied by the price the customer pays. Because different customers are charged different prices, charging a high (or low) price to one customer does not affect the prices charged to other customers. In the absence of price discrimination, the firm's *AR* curve continues to be the demand curve the firm faces, with the firm's *MR* curve located below the demand (and *AR*) curve. But when each customer is charged the maximum price he or she is prepared to pay, the demand curve is now the same as the firm's *MR* curve. The profit-maximising level of output, where *MR* = *MC*, shifts to Q_2, located at point *Y* in Figure 3.25. Customers who would refuse to buy the good at price P_1 buy the extra output because the prices they are charged are lower than P_1. As a result, most consumers end up paying a price which is higher than P_1 (the profit-maximising

price in the absence of price discrimination), but some consumers pay a lower price. The lowest of all the prices charged is P_2, which is the price charged to the marginal, and perhaps the poorest, customer.

Consider also a situation in which a firm cannot make enough profit to stay in business unless some consumer surplus is taken from consumers and transferred to the producer. Market provision of healthcare by a doctor in an isolated village or very small town is an example. When charging the same price to all her patients, a doctor cannot earn enough income to continue to provide the service. Without an increase in income, the doctor will move to a larger city and local medical care will no longer be available in the village. But with price discrimination, the rich pay a higher price than the poor. Everybody gets some benefit, and a needed service is provided.

3.8 The dynamics of competition and competitive market processes

On a number of occasions in this chapter, we have distinguished between price competition, in which firms try to increase market share and profits by cutting prices, and various forms of non-price competition that firms pursue. The traditional view has been that price competition is the main form of competition in markets in which there are a large number of firms, but that markets become less competitive, at least in the form of price competition, as large firms become more dominant and market concentration increases.

However, many economists now argue that all market structures in a capitalist economy can be highly competitive, although business decisions which on first sight may appear to be competitive are in fact 'anti-competitive' in the sense that they aim to increase the market power of already dominant firms. This view of competition is closely linked to the process of creative destruction (mentioned in Chapter 2 and also earlier in this chapter), an idea developed by the Austrian-American economist Joseph Schumpeter to explain the dynamic process through which capitalist economies change over time. It has been said that creative destruction has become the centrepiece for modern thinking on how economies evolve.

Pro-free-market economists such as Michael Cox, the chief economist at the Federal Reserve Bank of Dallas, believe that societies that allow creative destruction to operate grow more productive and richer, with their citizens benefiting from new and better products and higher living standards.

Drawing on Schumpeter's work, Cox argues that entrepreneurs compete through the introduction of new products and technologies in order to increase their profits:

> New goods and services, new firms, and new industries compete with existing ones in the marketplace, taking customers by offering lower prices, better performance, new features, catchier styling, faster service, more convenient locations, higher status, more aggressive marketing, or more attractive packaging. In another seemingly contradictory aspect of creative destruction, the pursuit of self-interest ignites the progress that makes others better off. The market's 'invisible hand' — a phrase owing not to Schumpeter but to Adam Smith — shifts resources from declining sectors to more valuable uses as workers, inputs, and financial capital seek their highest returns.

CASE STUDY 3.4

How Apple competes

Over 30 years ago, when the Apple Macintosh personal computer was launched, all rival computers were square boxes and most of them were battleship grey. Not much thought was given to design. But the introduction of the Apple Mac changed things completely.

The first way in which Apple separated itself from the crowd was to 'think different'. Apple's main method of competition is to create new products, and new categories of products, which did not exist before. Examples which have taken place over the years include innovation in the markets for MP3 players, smartphones, tablets and, of course, computers. By not being much bothered about what its competitors do, Apple has broken the mould with all these products and has set industry standards.

Apple also competes through the management style the company has had since its first inception.

In rival companies, competitive decisions take a very long time to make because they have to be approved by a plethora of committees, all of which feed into the decision-making process. Apple is not like this. All decisions are made by a single executive committee. This leads to an almost seamless roll-out of new products, and the ability to launch a new product which nobody else had thought of almost every other year.

The third way in which Apple sets itself aside from its competitors is design. It is said that 'great design principles are pervasive in the Apple DNA'.

Unless Apple's competitors start innovating on their own, Apple will continue to have at least a 2-year lead over them. Tim Bajarin, the president of Creative Strategies Inc., believes that thanks to Apple's ability to 'think different', its management style and its design DNA, the company will keep its competitors following it instead of leading the market forward themselves.

Follow-up questions

1 Explain how Apple's success illustrates the dynamics of competition and competitive market processes.
2 Research how Apple has marketed new products in the years between when this book was published and your reading of the case study.

3.9 Contestable and non-contestable markets

The significance of market contestability for the performance of an industry

Much of the debate about the best way to deal with the problems posed by market concentration and monopoly power now centres upon the need to deregulate and remove barriers to market entry. This debate reflects the growing influence of **contestable market** theory. Until about 40 years ago, government approaches to the abuse of monopoly power involved an ever-increasing extension of government regulation into the activities of private sector firms. Increased intervention was justified by the belief that regulatory powers must be strong enough, first, to countervail the growing power of large business organisations and, second, to make monopolies behave in a more competitive fashion.

At the time, monopoly was normally defined by the number of firms in the market and by the share of the leading firms, measured by a concentration ratio. The basic dilemma facing the policy-makers centred on how to reconcile the potential gains of large-scale productive efficiency with the fact that lack of competitive pressure can lead to monopoly abuse and consumer exploitation.

However, in contestable market theory, monopoly power is not dependent on the number of firms in the market or on concentration ratios, but rather on the ease or difficulty with which new firms may enter the market. Industrial concentration is not a problem, provided that an absence of barriers to entry and exit creates the ability for new firms to enter and contest the market. *Actual* competition in a market is not essential. The threat of entry by new firms or *potential* competition is quite enough, according to contestable market theory, to ensure efficient and non-exploitative behaviour by existing firms within the market.

In recent years, contestable market theory has had a major impact upon UK monopoly policy. The theory implies that, provided there is adequate potential for competition, a conventional regulatory policy is superfluous. Instead of interfering with firms' pricing and output policies, the government should restrict the role of monopoly policy to discovering which industries and markets are potentially contestable. Deregulatory policies should be used to develop conditions in which barriers to entry and exit are minimised, to ensure that reasonable contestability is possible. Appropriate policies suggested by the theory of contestable markets include removal of:

● licensing regimes for public transport and television and radio transmissions
● controls over ownership, such as exclusive public ownership
● price controls that act as a barrier to entry, such as those which used to be practised in the aviation industry

Sunk costs and hit-and-run competition

For a market to be perfectly contestable, there must be no barriers to entry or exit and hence no sunk costs. Sunk costs, as described earlier, are costs incurred when entering a market that are irrecoverable should the firm decide to leave the market. *Sunk costs* must not be confused with *fixed costs*, although some sunk costs are also fixed costs. Suppose a firm invests in new machinery when it enters the market. This is a fixed cost, but if the machinery can be sold at a good price to another firm, it is not a sunk cost. In this situation, the cost can be recovered if the firm decides to leave the market. By contrast, if the machinery has no alternative use and a cost of disposal rather than a second-hand value, investment in the fixed capital is a sunk cost. Another sunk cost might be expenditure on advertising to establish the firm in the market. If market entry is unsuccessful and the firm decides to leave, the expenditure cannot be recovered.

Because sunk costs are unrecoverable and therefore make exit from a market costly, they discourage **hit-and-run competition**. Hit-and-run competition

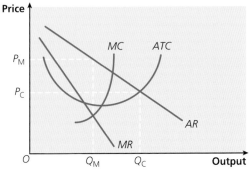

Figure 3.26 A monopoly setting a contestable price P_C to prevent the market being contested

occurs when a firm temporarily enters a market to share in the abnormal profit being made by firms already in the market, and then leaves when abnormal profits have been competed away. As such, it is a feature of a contestable market. And just as *potential* ease of entry makes a market contestable, so the threat of hit-and-run competition can be sufficient to keep prices and profits at their lowest possible levels, thereby increasing consumer surplus. This situation is shown in Figure 3.26, which illustrates how a monopolist facing the threat of potential market entrants reacts by reducing the selling price from P_M to P_C, with the result that only normal profits are made. (This pricing policy is basically the same as limit pricing.)

3.10 Consumer and producer surplus

Evaluating perfect competition and monopoly using welfare criteria

The important welfare concepts of consumer surplus and producer surplus were defined and explained on page 84. Figure 3.27 shows how consumer surplus falls, and producer surplus increases, when the perfectly competitive industry is transformed into a monopoly —provided we assume that neither economies of scale nor dynamic efficiency improvements result from the transformation. That is assuming that the marginal costs under monopoly and perfect competition are the same.

As Figure 3.27 shows, industry output in perfect competition is determined at point A, with output at Q_1 and price at P_1. However, monopoly equilibrium is determined at point B where $MR = MC$. (Note that the *marginal cost curve* in *monopoly* is the same curve as the *market supply curve* in *perfect competition*.) As explained earlier in the chapter, the diagram illustrates the standard case against monopoly, namely that compared to perfect competition, monopoly restricts output (to Q_2) and raises price (to P_2).

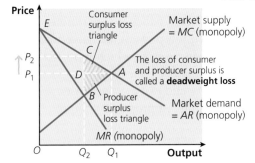

Figure 3.27 Consumer surplus and producer surplus in monopoly

We can use Figure 3.27 to illustrate how consumer surplus and producer surplus (and hence economic welfare) are affected by a monopoly replacing perfect competition. By raising the price from P_1 to P_2 the monopoly gains some of the consumer surplus that would have existed under perfect competition. The reduction in consumer surplus is equal to the rectangular area P_1P_2CD. This means that producer surplus (in the form of monopoly profit) increases at the expense of consumer surplus. Over and above this transfer, however, there is a net loss of economic welfare caused by the fact that the amount bought and sold falls to Q_2. The welfare loss or **deadweight loss** is shown by the two shaded triangular areas in Figure 3.27, which depict the loss of consumer surplus (the top triangle) and the loss of producer surplus (the bottom triangle). (The deadweight loss is evidence of market failure in monopoly.)

KEY TERM

deadweight loss the name given to the loss of economic welfare when the maximum attainable level of total welfare is not achieved.

SYNOPTIC LINK

You will come across consumer surplus and producer surplus in Chapter 10 when analysing the effect of an import duty or tariff on economic welfare.

SUMMARY

● Market structures provide the framework in which businesses exist.
● Different market structures display different degrees of competitiveness.
● In all market structures, profit maximisation occurs at the level of output at which $MR = MC$.
● Economists evaluate perfect competition and monopoly using efficiency and welfare criteria.
● Provided we ignore dynamic efficiency considerations, perfect competition wins over monopoly in terms of being statically efficient (productively and allocatively efficient).
● However, monopoly can be justified by dynamic considerations.
● Imperfect competition covers the range of market structures between perfect competition and pure monopoly. Monopolistic competition and oligopoly are two imperfectly competitive market structures.
● Oligopoly, which is 'imperfect competition among the few', can be defined in terms of market concentration and in terms of market behaviour or conduct. For the former, concentration ratios are used.
● An important distinction can be made between collusive and competitive oligopoly.
● The theory of the kinked demand curve, which is often used to model competitive oligopoly, illustrates the effects of uncertainty and interdependence in oligopoly, but the theory has a number of weaknesses.
● By restricting output and raising prices, monopolies and also oligopolies transfer consumer surplus into producer surplus.

Questions

1 Explain why profit is maximised when $MR = MC$ both in perfect competition and in monopoly.

2 Explain why firms in real-world markets use methods of competition other than price competition.

3 Explain the main efficiency concepts economists use when analysing and evaluating perfect competition and monopoly.

4 'Increasing consumer surplus is always good but increasing producer surplus is always bad.' Evaluate this statement.

5 Do you agree that perfect competition, if it existed, would always be preferable to monopoly? Justify your answer.

The labour market

Much of the theory we explain in this chapter is really just the price theory you have already studied in the goods markets (or product markets) of an economy, operating in the labour market. A labour market is an example of a factor market — that is, a market in which the services of a factor of production are bought and sold. Markets for land, capital goods and entrepreneurial skill are the other factor markets.

As Figure 4.1 shows, households and firms function simultaneously in both sets of markets, but their roles are reversed. Whereas firms are the source of supply in a goods market, in a factor market firms exercise demand for factor services supplied by households. The incomes received by households from the sale and supply of factor services contribute in large measure to households' ability to demand the output supplied by firms in the goods market. To exercise demand, which requires an ability to pay as well as a willingness to pay, households need an income, and for most people this requires the sale of their labour services in a labour market.

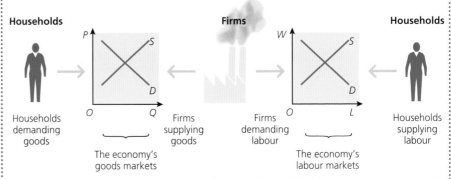

Figure 4.1 The goods market and the labour market, which is one of the economy's factor markets

Indeed, as we explained in the context of the circular flow of income in Book 1, pages 163–65, the relationship between households and firms in the two markets is essentially circular. In goods markets, finished goods and services flow from firms to households, who spend their incomes on the goods. In labour markets, members of households earn the incomes they spend on goods by selling labour to their employers.

SYNOPTIC LINK

The relationship between households and firms in the economy's labour markets is central to the circular flow of income explained in Book 1.

4.1 The demand for labour — marginal productivity theory

The derived demand for labour

A firm demands labour only if profits can be increased by employing more workers. But this assumes that households in goods markets demand the goods and services that workers are employed to produce. This means that a firm's demand for labour is a **derived demand** — it is derived from the demand for goods. Assuming a profit-maximising objective on the part of firms, there can be no demand for labour in the long run unless the firms employing labour sell the outputs produced for at least normal profit in the goods market.

Marginal productivity theory and the demand for labour

The marginal physical product of labour

To understand a firm's demand curve for labour, we begin by explaining the **marginal physical product of labour** (MPP_L). Rather confusingly, this term is just another name for the marginal returns (or marginal product) of labour, which we explained in Chapter 1. MPP_L measures the amount by which a firm's total output rises in the short run (holding capital fixed), as a result of employing one more worker. In Chapter 1, we explained how the law of diminishing returns or diminishing marginal productivity operates as a firm employs more labour when capital is held fixed.

The law of diminishing returns is illustrated in Figure 4.2, which shows the marginal product of labour falling as additional workers are hired by the firm.

KEY TERMS

derived demand demand for a good or factor of production, not wanted for its own sake, which is a consequence of the demand for something else.

marginal physical product of labour the addition to a firm's total output brought about by employing one more worker.

93

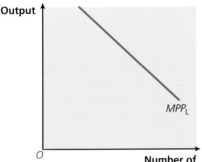

Output

MPP_L

O   Number of
                workers

Figure 4.2 The marginal physical product of labour

SYNOPTIC LINK

In Figure 4.2, we have not shown the likelihood of increasing marginal returns at low levels of employment. Instead, we have assumed that the marginal product of labour falls when an additional worker is taken on. Compare this diagram to Figure 2.2 in Chapter 2.

QUANTITATIVE SKILLS 4.1

Worked example: calculating the marginal physical product of labour

Using the total physical product data in Table 4.1, calculate the marginal physical product of labour of workers employed assembling wheel barrows in a particular week.

Table 4.1 Total physical product of labour

Size of labour force	Total physical product of labour (wheel barrows per week)
0	0
1	5
2	12
3	21
4	31
5	40
6	46
7	50
8	51
9	51
10	49

The marginal physical product of labour measures the change in the total physical product of labour when an additional worker is added to the labour force. For the first worker employed, the answer is calculated by subtracting the total physical output when no workers are employed from the total physical product of labour when one worker is employed. This is 5 minus 0, which is 5. For the second worker, the answer is 12 minus 5, which is 7. Likewise, for the 3rd, 4th, 5th, 6th, 7th, 8th, 9th and 10th workers, their marginal physical productivities are respectively: 9, 10, 9, 6, 4, 1, 0 and −2.

(If you were to plot this information on a graph, the slope of the marginal physical productivity curve would resemble the marginal returns curve drawn in the lower panel of Figure 2.2 in Chapter 2. This is because the total physical product schedule in Table 4.1 assumes that the wheel barrow manufacturing business initially benefits from the increasing marginal productivity of labour before diminishing marginal returns sets in.)

KEY TERM

marginal revenue product of labour the money value of the addition to a firm's total output brought about by employing one more worker.

The marginal revenue product of labour

The falling MPP_L curve in Figure 4.2, which is also drawn in panel (a) of Figure 4.3 below, shows the *physical* output produced by an extra worker — measured, for example, in automobiles or loaves of bread, or whatever goods or services the firm produces. To convert the marginal *physical* product of labour into the **marginal revenue product of labour** (MRP_L), the *MPP* of labour has to be multiplied by marginal revenue (*MR*), which is the addition to the firm's total sales revenue resulting from the sale of each of the extra products in the goods market. Assuming a perfectly competitive goods market (as well as a perfectly competitive labour market), *MR* is identical to the good's price, and is shown by the horizontal *MR* curve in panel (b) of Figure 4.3.

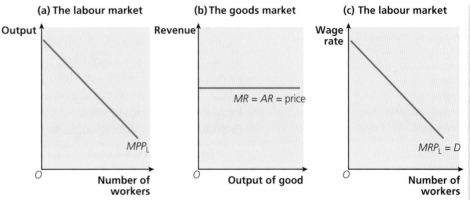

Figure 4.3 Deriving the MRP_L curve from the MPP_L curve

The marginal revenue product curve of labour, which is shown in panel (c) of Figure 4.3, can be explained with the use of the following equation:

$$\text{marginal physical product} \times \text{marginal revenue} = \text{marginal revenue product of labour}$$

or:

$$MPP_L \times MR = MRP_L$$

Under perfect competition, since $MR = AR$ in the goods market where a firm sells its output, then in the labour market:

$$MRP_L = MPP_L \times \text{price}$$

To summarise, the equation shows that when the labour market and the goods market are both perfectly competitive, the MRP of labour is calculated by multiplying the MPP of labour in panel (a) of the diagram by the constant value of MR, which is the same as the price of the product, as shown in panel (b).

EXTENSION MATERIAL

Deriving the *MRP* curve of labour when the goods market is imperfectly competitive

Assuming perfect competition in the goods market in which the firm sells its output, the slope of the *MRP* curve in panel (c) of Figure 4.3 is explained solely by the diminishing marginal physical product of labour: that is, by the law of diminishing returns.

However, if output is sold in an imperfectly competitive goods market, marginal revenue product of labour declines faster than in a perfectly competitive goods market. This is because in

imperfectly competitive goods markets, the marginal revenue earned from selling an extra worker's output also falls as output increases. This is because the firm faces a downward-sloping demand curve for its products and, therefore, it has to reduce the price of the product in order to sell the extra output the worker produces. In this situation, there are *two* reasons for the MRP_L curve to fall as employment increases.

TEST YOURSELF 4.1
Using the answers to Quantitative Skills 4.1, calculate the marginal revenue productivity of each of the ten workers, given the assumption that, however many wheel barrows are produced, their price is always £60.

What a demand curve for labour shows

Figure 4.4(a) shows a *firm's* demand curve for labour in a perfectly competitive labour market. In such a market, the *market* demand curve for labour, which is shown in Figure 4.4(b), would simply be the addition of the demand curves for labour of each of the firms that make up the market. Since each firm's demand for labour would be shown by the MRP_L curve facing the firm, the market demand curve for labour would be the horizontal sum of all the MRP_L curves.

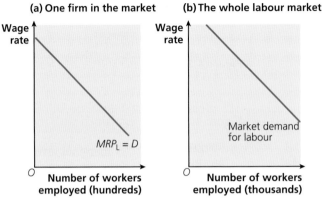

Figure 4.4 The *market* demand curve for labour in panel (b) is the sum of each *firm's* demand curve for labour in panel (a)

Shifts of the market demand curve for labour in different labour markets

The market demand curve for labour can shift to the right or left for a number of reasons. (A rightward shift is called an increase in demand for labour and a leftward shift is a decrease in demand for labour.) The reasons include:

- **A change in labour productivity.** As explained, a firm's demand curve for labour is the *MRP* curve of labour facing the firm. It follows from this that if labour productivity increases, more labour is demanded at each wage rate and the firm's demand curve for labour shifts to the right. The same is the case when marginal revenue increases. (Remember, the demand for labour is a *derived demand*. If demand increases for the good that labour produces, raising the price of the product, the demand for labour curve shifts to the right.) And if a firm's demand curve for labour shifts to the right, the market demand curve for labour, which is the sum of each firm's demand curve for labour, must also shift to the right.

- **A change in technology.** Changes in technology can cause the demand curve for labour to shift, in some cases to the right, but in other cases to left. If technical progress makes labour more productive relative to other factors of production, firms are likely to substitute labour for other factors of production, in which case the demand curve for labour shifts to the right. Technical progress is also likely to improve productive and dynamic efficiency, which reduce the cost of making the product; if this leads to lower prices and higher demand for the product, it is also likely to increase the demand for labour.

  However, technical progress can also have the opposite effect by causing firms to substitute capital for labour. For example, a switch to automated methods of production, which increases the productivity of capital relative to labour, may reduce the demand for labour, thereby causing the demand

STUDY TIP
Don't confuse a *movement* or *adjustment along* a demand curve for labour with a *shift* of the demand curve for labour. In the former case, a fall in the wage rate relative to the price of capital causes more labour to be demanded because workers become relatively cheaper than capital to employ. Factor substitution occurs with labour replacing capital in the production process. In the latter case, an increase in the derived demand for labour leads to more labour being demanded at all wage rates, causing a rightward shift in the demand curve for labour.

curve for labour to shift to the left. Technical progress can also increase the demand for certain types of labour at the expense of workers with other skills, who may lose their jobs. The technological unemployment which results is a part of the process of creative destruction which we described in Chapter 2, page 52.

The elasticity of demand for labour

KEY TERM
elasticity of demand for labour proportionate change in demand for labour following a change in the wage rate.

If the wage rate increases, but nothing else that might affect the demand for labour changes, by how much will employment fall? The answer is affected by firms' **elasticity of demand for labour**. The demand for a particular type of labour is likely to be relatively inelastic:

- when the relevant wage cost forms only a small part of total production costs (this has been called 'the importance of being unimportant')
- when the demand for the good or service being produced by the labour is inelastic
- when it is difficult to substitute other factors of production, or other types of labour, for the labour currently employed
- in the short run, rather than the long run, since it often takes time for employers to adjust the method of production

QUANTITATIVE SKILLS 4.2

Worked example: calculating the effect of a wage increase on employment

You are a labour market analyst providing advice to a trade union, whose members are unskilled workers currently being paid £10 an hour for their work. The union, which is pushing for a wage increase of 50p per hour, wants to know what will happen to the employment of its 20,000 members who currently have jobs. Your research tells you that the employer's wage elasticity of demand for unskilled workers is −10. Assuming that everything else in the economy remains unchanged, calculate the effect of an increase in the wage rate by 50p per hour on the employment of the union members.

Given that the wage rate initially is £10 an hour, the proposed wage rate increase of 50p pence an hour is a 5% increase. The formula for the employers' wage elasticity of demand for labour is:

$$\text{wage elasticity of demand for labour} = \frac{\% \text{ change in quantity of labour demanded}}{\% \text{ change in the wage rate}}$$

The equation can be rewritten as:

$$\% \text{ change in quantity of labour demanded} = \% \text{ change in the wage rate} \times \text{wage elasticity of demand for labour}$$

Given the data in the question, the equation becomes:

% change in quantity of labour demanded = 5% × −10 = −50%

Given that 20,000 unskilled union members currently have jobs, the data indicate that half of them (10,000 union members) may lose their jobs.

4.2 The supply of labour

What a supply curve of labour shows

Just as a firm's demand curve for labour shows how much labour a firm or employer plans to demand at different wage rates, so a worker's supply curve of labour shows how much labour a particular worker plans to supply at different wage rates.

An individual worker's supply of labour

An individual worker's supply curve of labour shows how many hours of labour the worker plans to supply — for example, at different hourly wage rates. Figure 4.5 illustrates such a curve. The diagram depicts a situation in which a worker responds to an increase in the hourly wage rate from £7 to £15 by increasing the number hours she is prepared to work by 12 hours, from 28 hours a week to 40 hours a week.

The supply curve of labour shown in Figure 4.5 illustrates the **substitution effect** of a change in the wage rate. A higher wage rate makes work more attractive than leisure, so workers substitute labour for leisure. (A second effect called the **income effect** also operates. An increase in the hourly wage rate means higher real income. If leisure is a normal good, the quantity of leisure goes up, which means a reduction in the quantity of labour supplied. Usually the substitution effect is more powerful than the income effect.)

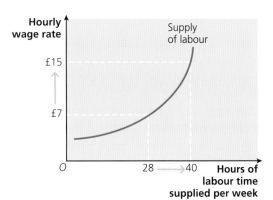

Figure 4.5 A worker's supply curve of labour in a particular week

KEY TERMS

substitution effect a higher hourly wage rate makes work more attractive than leisure, so workers substitute labour for leisure.

income effect an increase in the hourly wage rate means higher real income, and if leisure is a normal good, the quantity of leisure demanded goes up which means a reduction in the quantity of labour supplied.

A worker trying to maximise net advantage

Supplying labour to earn a wage and buy goods

Enjoying leisure time

Figure 4.6 The choice between supplying labour and enjoying leisure time

Figure 4.6 shows a worker who is free to choose how many hours to work each day or each week, choosing between supplying more labour or enjoying more leisure time. But both the money wage and leisure time yield less and less extra welfare, the greater the quantity that a person has. As more labour time is supplied at a particular hourly wage rate, the extra income yields less and less extra satisfaction. However, the decision to supply more labour simultaneously means the decision to enjoy less leisure time. In this situation, each extra hour of leisure sacrificed is accompanied by an increasing loss of economic welfare. At the margin, to maximise personal welfare, a worker must supply labour up to the point at which:

$$\text{utility of welfare from the last unit of money earned} = \text{utility or welfare from the last unit of leisure time sacrificed}$$

In this situation, the marginal private benefit received by a worker from supplying labour equals the marginal private cost incurred from giving up leisure time. Provided personal preferences remain stable, there is no incentive for the worker to supply more labour at the *going* hourly wage rate.

However, a *higher* hourly wage will provide an incentive to work more hours. With a higher wage rate, at the margin, the welfare derived from the wage becomes greater than the welfare derived from the last unit of leisure time enjoyed. To maximise personal welfare at the higher wage rate, the worker would be expected to supply more labour and enjoy less leisure time. The result is the upward-sloping labour supply curve shown earlier in Figure 4.5. An increase in the wage rate from £7 an hour £15 an hour means that the worker increases the hours of labour time supplied from 28 to 40 hours a week.

Monetary and non-monetary considerations

Our starting point for explaining the shape of the labour supply curve shown in Figure 4.5 was the assumption we made that a worker supplies more labour to increase personal economic welfare: that is, to maximise private benefit. The welfare that a worker derives from the supply of labour divides into two parts, which taken together are sometimes called **net advantage**.

An individual worker's job choice depends on the net advantage they expect to derive from different occupations. However, given that the non-monetary advantages usually change slowly, a rise in the wage in an occupation should lead to an increase in the supply of labour because it increases the net advantage of that occupation compared to others.

Net advantage includes:

- utility or welfare derived from the wage (or strictly speaking, from the goods and services bought with the money wage)
- utility or welfare derived from other aspects of working, sometimes called the non-monetary benefits (these include what is popularly known as job satisfaction, or if negative, job dissatisfaction)

net advantage = utility derived from the wage + utility derived from working

Different types of work yield different amounts of positive or negative utility or welfare (job satisfaction and dissatisfaction). When a worker enjoys the job, the net advantage of work is greater than the welfare yielded by the wage. In this situation, the worker is willing to work for a money wage lower than the wage that would be acceptable if there were no satisfaction from the work itself. But for some workers, work such as routine assembly-line work in factories and heavy manual labour is unpleasant, yielding job dissatisfaction. The supply of labour for this type of employment reflects the fact that the hourly wage rate must be high enough to compensate for the unpleasantness (or sometimes the danger) of the job.

Net advantage includes the benefits of job security, promotion prospects, good working conditions, holiday entitlement, and other psychological benefits of work. Improvements in these benefits will shift the supply curve of labour to the right. A deterioration of these benefits shifts the supply curve of labour to the left. Non-monetary benefits can be negative (in other words, non-monetary costs) — for example, job dissatisfaction experienced when working.

ACTIVITY

Assume that you work as a 'bouncer' outside a public house in central Liverpool. You work from 7 p.m. to 1 a.m. the next morning, including at weekends. Make a list of various possible factors, positive and negative, that might affect the net advantage you gain from your work.

SYNOPTIC LINK

Book 1, page 263 discusses possible links between the shape of the microeconomic supply curve of labour and supply-side economic policy.

The market supply of labour

Just as it is important in demand theory to distinguish between a particular firm's demand for labour and the market demand for labour, so, in the case of supply theory, we must distinguish between an individual worker's supply of labour and the market supply of labour. However, as is the case with the

99

demand for labour, the market supply curve of labour is simply the sum or addition of the supply curves of all the individual workers in the labour market. If the individual supply curves of labour, on average, slope upward, the market supply curve of labour also slopes upward, showing that at a higher real wage rate more labour is supplied in the labour market. (The market supply curve of labour will also slope upward even if *some* workers respond to increases in the hourly wage rate by choosing to supply less labour — provided *most* of the workers in the labour market have upward-sloping supply curves of labour.)

CASE STUDY 4.1

Who should be paid more, MPs or newsreaders?

Economics teachers often ask their students to ponder on whether workers employed in pleasant occupations, such as television celebrities, should be paid more than those in disagreeable occupations, such as road sweepers. If job satisfaction or dissatisfaction were to be the only factor determining wages, the road sweeper would be paid more. However, more often than not, other factors, related to supply and demand, productivity, learned skills and innate ability, tend to override the job satisfaction factor and explain why television celebrities are paid more than road sweepers.

A few years ago, a government minister asked 'should MPs be paid more than television newsreaders?' In a follow-up poll, 45% of the general public said 'yes' and 55% voted 'no'. Former Conservative MP Michael Portillo, now a TV presenter, argued that:

Low pay will discourage good people from becoming MPs, especially if we are now going to denigrate their outside earnings too, even though that's how TV presenters boost their salaries. The present exchange rate is approximately one Jonathan Ross equals 100 MPs. It is a topsy-turvy world where we pay top journalists more to comment occasionally on what the prime minister does than we pay him to do his job 24/7.

Replying 'no', Ken Livingstone, the Labour ex-mayor of London, said:

Far too many people are paid too much for what they do. In 1979, Britain's top 10% of earners were paid four times as much as the bottom 10%. By 2015 that figure had doubled to at least ten times as much. Is Britain more than twice as well run as it was nearly 40 years ago? Is the output of television twice as good as in the 1970s? Are our politicians and bankers twice as honest? It's time for a dramatic reduction in top salaries across the board, not just those of TV presenters.

Follow-up question

1 Do you believe that both MPs and TV newsreaders are paid too much? Use economic theory to justify your argument.

Shifts of the market supply curve of labour

We have already mentioned one reason why an individual worker's supply curve of labour shifts to the right or left: improvements in any of the non-monetary benefits of working, such as holiday entitlement, shift the supply curve to the right. Conversely, a deterioration of any of these benefits shifts the curve to the left. A change in attitudes toward work and leisure is therefore likely to shift the supply curve for labour, both for a particular worker and for the labour market as a whole. If people decide they value leisure more highly, they will work fewer hours at each wage rate, and the supply curve for labour will shift to the left. If they decide they want more goods and services rather than leisure time, the supply curve is likely to shift to the right.

Other factors that can shift the supply curve of labour include:

- **Changes in income.** It is reasonable to assume that leisure time is a normal good for most people, so a rise in income increases the demand for leisure time, which in turn causes the supply curve of labour to shift to the left. However, for a few people, leisure time might be an inferior good. For them, higher income reduces their demand for leisure time and they end up supplying more labour.
- **Changes in population.** A rise in population, perhaps caused by immigration, increases the supply of labour; a reduction lowers it. A fall in the number of people of working age causes the labour supply curve to shift to the left, except perhaps when this is offset by those who have reached retirement age deciding to work longer in order to finance their eventual retirement.
- **Changes in expectations.** Likewise, if older people expect to live longer yet become less optimistic about their future pensions, this could increase the labour supply. A rise in the proportion of people staying on in further and higher education will tend to reduce the supply of labour.

SYNOPTIC LINK

At this point you might refer back to Book 1, page 23 and refresh your understanding of normal goods and inferior goods.

The elasticity of supply of labour

The factors which determine the wage **elasticity of supply of labour** include the following:

KEY TERM

elasticity of supply of labour proportionate change in the supply of labour following a change in the wage rate.

- The supply of unskilled labour is usually more elastic than the supply of a particular type of skilled labour. This is because the training period of unskilled labour is usually very short, and any innate abilities required are unlikely to be restricted to a small proportion of the total population.
- Factors which reduce the occupational and geographical mobility of labour tend to reduce the elasticity of labour supply.
- The supply of labour is also likely to be more elastic in the long run than in the short run.
- The availability of a pool of unemployed labour increases the elasticity of supply of labour, while full employment has the opposite effect.

QUANTITATIVE SKILLS 4.3

Worked example: calculating the wage elasticity of supply

Fearing a shortage of labour, a firm which wants to expand, and currently employs 1,000 workers, increases the wage it pays to all its workers from £10 per hour to £15 per hour. As a result, 500 workers apply for jobs at the firm. What is the wage elasticity of supply of labour with respect to the stated wage rate increase?

The formula needed to calculate the correct answer is:

$$\text{wage elasticity of supply of labour} = \frac{\%\text{ change in labour supply}}{\%\text{ change in the wage rate}}$$

$$= \frac{+50\%}{+50\%} = +1$$

Thus, between these two hourly wage rates the wage elasticity of supply of labour is unitary: that is, equal to 1.

4.3 Perfectly competitive labour markets

So far in this chapter we have made several references to perfectly competitive labour markets, mainly in the contexts of explaining the demand for and supply of labour. In this section, we bring demand and supply together and explain the determination of relative wage rates and levels of employment in perfectly competitive labour markets. In the next section we shall look at imperfectly competitive labour markets.

A perfectly competitive labour market, if it were to exist, would have to meet all of the following conditions at the same time. As would be the case in a perfectly competitive goods market, a perfectly competitive labour market would have to contain a large number of buyers and sellers, each unable to influence the ruling market price (in this case, the ruling market wage), and operating in conditions of perfect market information. Employers and workers would be free to enter the labour market in the long run, but an individual employer or firm could not influence the ruling market wage through its independent action.

Just as in a perfectly competitive goods market, it is impossible for all these requirements to be met simultaneously. It follows that perfectly competitive labour markets do not exist in the real world. Some labour markets, such as the market for fruit-pickers in a region or district where there are a very large number of orchards, *approximate* to perfect competition, but nevertheless they are not perfectly competitive.

SYNOPTIC LINK
Refer back to Figure 3.1 in Chapter 3, which lists the six conditions which would have to be met for a goods market to be perfectly competitive.

In Chapter 3, we explained how a firm in a perfectly competitive goods market would be able to sell as much as it wanted at the ruling market price, meaning that the firm faces a perfectly elastic demand curve which is also the firm's average and marginal revenue curve. Each firm is a passive price-taker at the ruling price determined in the market as a whole, choosing the quantity to sell, but not the price.

A very similar situation would exist for a firm employing workers in a perfectly competitive labour market, except that now the firm could buy as much labour as it wanted to employ at the ruling market wage. To state this another way, each employer would face a perfectly elastic supply of labour curve in a perfectly competitive labour market. Figure 4.7 illustrates why. This diagram is similar to Figure 4.4(a), except that we now show the market supply curve of labour and the ruling market wage rate in panel (b).

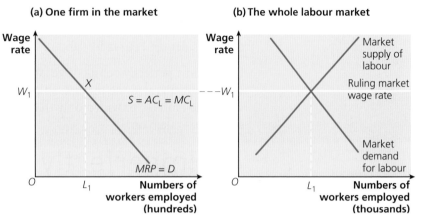

(a) One firm in the market

(b) The whole labour market

Figure 4.7 A perfectly competitive labour market

In a perfectly competitive labour market, each employer would have to passively accept the ruling market wage. The ruling wage, determined in Figure 4.7(b), is also the perfectly elastic supply curve of labour facing each of the firms in the labour market. This means it would also be the **average cost of labour** (AC_L) curve and the **marginal cost of labour** (MC_L) curve facing each firm in the labour market. This is shown in the left-hand panel (a) of the diagram. At the ruling market wage, each firm would be a passive price-taker, able to hire as many workers as it wished to hire at the ruling market wage, but unable to influence the ruling wage by its own actions.

To maximise profit when selling the output produced by labour, each firm would have to demand labour up to the point at which:

| the addition to sales revenue resulting from employment of an extra worker | = | the addition to production costs resulting from the employment of an extra worker |

or:

$$MRP_L = MC_L$$

The marginal revenue product of labour would be the marginal benefit accruing to the employer when hiring an extra worker. Likewise, the marginal cost of labour or MC_L would be the marginal private cost incurred by each firm. Since, in a perfectly competitive labour market, the marginal cost of labour would always equal the wage paid to the workers, the perfectly competitive firm's level of employment or demand for labour at each wage rate would be where:

$$MRP_L = W$$

Point X in Figure 4.7(a) shows the number of workers that a firm would be willing to employ at a ruling wage rate W_1. Consider what would happen if the firm were to employ a labour force larger than L_1. Additional workers would add more to total costs of production than to total revenue, and so total profit would fall. Conversely, with a workforce below L_1, the MRP of the last worker is greater than the wage, and the total profit would increase if more workers were employed.

Summarising:

- If $MRP > W$, more workers should be hired.
- If $MRP < W$, fewer workers should be employed.
- If $MRP = W$, the firm is employing the number of workers consistent with profit maximisation.

As the *MRP* curve shows each firm's demand for labour at each possible wage rate, including wage rate W_1, the *MRP* curve facing each firm would in fact be the firm's demand curve for labour.

Indeed, in a perfectly competitive labour market, each employer would be just one among many in the market, able to hire whatever number of workers it wished to employ, provided only that the ruling market wage was offered to all employees taken on.

4.4 Imperfectly competitive labour markets

Since perfectly competitive labour markets do not exist, all real-world labour markets are imperfectly competitive to a lesser or greater degree. As we have seen, some labour markets approximate to perfect competition, but at the other extreme are monopsonistic labour markets.

Monopsony means a single buyer, just as monopoly means a single seller. In a pure monopsonistic labour market, workers cannot choose between alternative employers, since there is only one firm or employer available to hire their services. However, pure monopsonistic labour markets are extremely rare — the NHS as a monopsony buyer of the services of midwives is about the closest example. Nevertheless, many large firms exercise a high degree of **monopsony power** in the labour market in which they hire their workers. The market for firefighters in the public sector is a good example.

The determination of relative wage rates and levels of employment in a monopsony labour market

Although in some ways a monopsonistic labour market resembles a monopolistic goods market, there are also significant differences. In much the same way that the market demand curve facing a monopoly supplier of a good is the monopolist's average revenue curve, so in a monopsonistic labour market, the market supply curve of labour is the firm's average cost of labour curve. The AC_L curve shows the different wage rates that the monopsony must pay to attract labour forces of different sizes. For example, Figure 4.8 shows a monopsonistic employer hiring five workers at an hourly wage rate or AC_L of £10. As the diagram shows, the hourly wage per week must rise to £11 to attract a sixth worker into the firm's labour force.

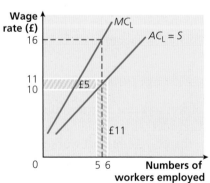

Figure 4.8 In a monopsony labour market, the MC_L curve lies *above* the AC_L or supply curve

The supply or AC_L curve facing the monopsony shows the wage that has to be paid to *all* workers at each size of the labour force, to persuade the workers to supply their services. However, in a monopsony labour market, the AC_L curve is *not* the marginal cost of labour curve (MC_L). To attract an extra worker, the monopsony must raise the hourly wage rate and pay the higher wage to all the workers. In this situation, the marginal cost of labour incurred by employing an extra worker is the change in total amount by which the wage bill rises, and not just the wage rate paid to the additional worker hired. The MC_L curve of labour illustrated in Figure 4.8 is positioned *above* the AC_L (or supply) curve.

In Figure 4.8, the MC_L incurred per hour by employing the sixth worker is £16, made up of the £11 wage rate paid to the sixth worker, plus the £1 extra that now has to be paid to each of the five workers already employed before the sixth worker joined the labour force.

> ### SYNOPTIC LINK
> If you refer back to Chapter 2, page 41, you will see that for a similar reason, in the goods market, a monopolist's *MR* curve is *below* its *AR* curve.

Figure 4.9 shows how the equilibrium wage and the equilibrium level of employment are determined in a monopsonistic labour market. As in the case of a perfectly competitive employer in the labour market, the monopsonist's level of employment is determined by the point where $MRP_L = MC_L$. This occurs at point A in Figure 4.9, with L_1 workers being hired.

However, the wage rate is determined at point B on the supply curve (and AC_L curve), which lies below point A. The monopsony wage rate (W_1 in Figure 4.9) is therefore less than the marginal revenue product of labour. At point B, L_1 workers are willing to work for an hourly wage rate of W_1. Although the monopsony could pay a wage rate higher than W_1, it has no need to do so. Why pay more, when W_1 attracts all the workers the monopsony wants to hire? Indeed, if the monopsony were to pay a wage higher than W_1, it would inevitably incur unnecessary production costs and fail to maximise profits when selling its output in the goods market. Profit maximisation requires that L_1 workers are employed and a wage of W_1 is paid.

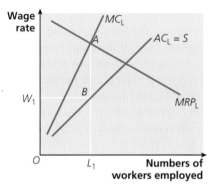

Figure 4.9 The determination of the wage rate and the level of employment in a monopsony labour market

> ### EXTENSION MATERIAL
> # Why wage differences occur in different labour markets
>
> If all labour markets in the economy were perfectly competitive, there would be an absence of barriers which prevent workers moving between labour markets. In this situation, the forces of competition would reduce many of the differences in wages between different occupations. Some differences would probably remain because different types of work have different skill requirements, and innate abilities and skills would still vary between workers. Nevertheless, higher wages in one occupation would attract workers from other labour markets, causing the supply curve of labour to shift to the right in the high-wage labour market and to the left in the low-wage market.
>
> At the same time, wage differentials would create incentives for firms in the high-wage market to reduce their demand for labour by substituting capital for labour, and for firms in the low-wage labour markets to adopt more labour-intensive methods of production. Demand and supply curves and wages would continue to adjust until there was no further incentive for firms to change their method of production or for workers to shift between labour markets. Wage differentials would diminish throughout the economy, but would not completely disappear.
>
> Also, as we explained earlier in the chapter, different jobs have different non-monetary characteristics. Other things being equal, a firm must pay workers a higher wage rate to compensate for any relative unpleasantness in the job. An equalising wage differential is the payment that must be made to

compensate a worker for the different non-monetary characteristics of jobs.

In imperfectly competitive labour markets, wage differences in different labour markets are often substantial. Five reasons for this are:

- **Disequilibrium trading.** Economies are subject to constant change, such as the development of new goods and services and improved methods of production or technical progress. Patterns of demand also change. Because market conditions are always changing, labour markets — like other markets — are usually in disequilibrium rather than in equilibrium. Although market forces tend to equalise wages in competitive labour markets, at any point in time disparities exist, reflecting the disequilibrium conditions existent at the time.

- **Imperfect market information.** As the name implies, imperfectly competitive labour markets are characterised by imperfect market information. Workers sometimes lack accurate information on rates of pay, not only in other labour markets, but also within the industry in which they are selling their labour. Likewise, employers lack information about wage rates in other labour markets and also, on occasion, within their own industries. Imperfect market information also contributes to the immobility of labour which is described below.

- Occupational immobility of labour. In Book 1, page 115, we explained that occupational immobility of labour occurs when workers are prevented, by either natural or artificial barriers, from moving between different types of job. Workers are obviously not homogeneous or uniform, so differences in natural ability may prevent or restrict movement between jobs. Artificial or 'man-made' barriers also prevent workers from moving between labour markets. These barriers include membership qualifications imposed by professional bodies such as accountancy associations, and trade union restrictive practices such as closed shops, which restrict employment to union members. Non-members may find it difficult or impossible to join the trade union, though such practices are now illegal in the UK.

- Geographical immobility of labour. As Book 1 also explained, geographical immobility occurs when factors, such as ignorance of job opportunities, family and cultural ties, and the financial costs of moving or travel, prevent a worker from filling a job vacancy located at a distance from his or her present place of residence. Perhaps the most significant cause of geographical immobility in the UK in recent years has been the state of the housing market, which itself reflects imperfections in other factor markets. During house price booms, low-paid and unemployed workers in the northern half of the UK have found it difficult or impossible to move south to fill job vacancies in the more prosperous southeast of England. The prices of owner-occupied housing have soared and there has been very little housing available at affordable rents in either the private or the public sector. At the same time, workers living in their own houses in the southeast may be reluctant to apply for jobs elsewhere in the country, for fear that they will never be able to afford to move back to southern England.

- **Discrimination.** Various forms of racial, religious, age and gender discrimination affect both the demand for and the supply of labour. On the demand side, employers may be unwilling to employ certain types of labour, while on the supply side, workers may refuse to work alongside other workers they perceive to be different.

KEY TERMS

occupational immobility of labour when workers are unwilling or unable to move from one type of job to another, e.g. because different skills are needed.

geographical immobility of labour when workers are unwilling or unable to move from one area to another in search of work.

ACTIVITY

Find out the hourly rates of pay earned by other students in your school or college who have part-time jobs, such as baby-sitting, delivering newspapers, waiting or waitressing employment. Can you think of any factors which explain the differences in the rates of pay your fellow-students have reported? How much bargaining power do you think students have when trying to sell their labour in the market for casual labour?

A **trade union** is an association of workers formed to protect and promote the interests of its members. A major function of a union is to bargain with employers to improve wages and other conditions of work. In the analysis which follows, we shall regard a trade union as a monopoly supplier of labour, which is able to keep non-members out of the labour market and also to prevent its members from supplying labour at below the union wage rate. Of course, in real life a union may not necessarily have the objectives specified above, and even if it does, it may not be able to achieve them.

In labour markets where trade unions are strong and possess significant bargaining power, wage rates are usually determined through a process known as **collective bargaining**. This term refers to a situation in which unions bargain with employers, with the unions negotiating collectively on behalf of their members. Sometimes bargaining takes place with a single employer, while on other occasions it may be with a number of employers in the labour market. The market wage rate is determined through the bargaining process, with the employers then deciding how many workers to employ at this wage rate.

However, many UK employers are now reluctant to recognise and bargain with the unions to which their employees belong. A number of factors are responsible for the shift in the balance of power in the labour market away from trade unions and toward employers. Two of the factors are a series of Employment Acts which have restricted the legal rights of trade unions, and the impact of globalisation and international competition upon British labour markets. UK trade unions remain powerful only in industries which are protected from international competition, such as London Transport, the rail industry and other areas of public sector employment.

The decline of collective bargaining in the UK means that more and more rates of pay, including those of teachers, are now 'employer determined' on a 'take-it-or-leave-it' basis.

The effect of introducing a trade union into a previously perfectly competitive labour market

Figure 4.10 shows the possible effects which may result from workers organising a trade union in a labour market that had previously been perfectly competitive. Without a trade union, the competitive wage rate is W_1. The workers join a trade union, which through collective bargaining negotiates a rise in the minimum wage rate acceptable to union members to W_2. Without the union, the market supply of labour curve is the upward-sloping line labelled $S = AC_L$. With the union, the market supply of labour curve is the

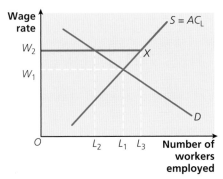

Figure 4.10 The effect of introducing a trade union into a previously competitive labour market

kinked line W_2XS. For all sizes of labour force to the left of, or below, L_3, the supply curve of labour is horizontal or perfectly elastic, lying along the wage W_2 set by the trade union. If employers wish to hire a labour force larger than L_3 (and to the right of point X), a wage higher than W_2 has to be offered. Beyond L_3, the supply curve of labour slopes upward because higher wage rates are needed to attract more workers.

At the wage level set by the union, employers only wish to hire L_2 workers. However, L_3 workers are willing to work at this wage rate. This means there is excess supply of labour and unemployment in the labour market. More workers wish to work than there are jobs available. The resulting unemployment is shown by the distance $L_3 - L_2$. However, the fall in employment compared to the competitive equilibrium is $L_1 - L_2$.

SYNOPTIC LINK
In Chapter 7, the type of unemployment shown in Figure 4.10 is called classical, or real-wage, unemployment.

STUDY TIP
The effects shown in Figure 4.10 can also be used to explain the effect of a national minimum wage imposed above the wage rate that would be determined by market forces.

The effect described above is sometimes used to justify the argument that any attempt by a union to raise wages must inevitably be at the expense of jobs, and that if unions are really interested in reducing unemployment, they should accept wage cuts. However, many economists — especially those of a Keynesian and left-of-centre persuasion — dispute this conclusion. They argue, first, that it is unrealistic to assume that conditions of demand for labour are unchanged. By agreeing to accept technical progress, by working with new capital equipment and new methods of organising work and by improving the skills of their members, a union can ensure (with the cooperation of management) that the *MRP* curve of labour shifts to the right. In these circumstances, increased productivity creates scope for both increased wages and increased employment. Higher wages may encourage firms to adopt improvements in productivity to pay for the higher wages but, on the other hand, some unions may resist the changes in working practices that lead to increased productivity.

Second, both wages and employment can rise when a union negotiates for higher wages in firms producing in an expanding goods market. In these conditions, increased demand for output creates increased demand for labour to produce the output. Indeed, rising real wages throughout the economy are likely to increase the aggregate demand for the output of all firms producing consumer goods because wages are the most important source of consumption expenditure in the economy.

So far, we have assumed that trade unions try to increase pay by preventing union members supplying labour at wage rates below the rate set by the union. Figure 4.11 illustrates a second way in which much the same result can be achieved. In this case, the trade union establishes a closed shop, which keeps non-union workers out of the labour market. The union-controlled entry barrier shifts the supply curve of labour leftward, and increases the inelasticity of the curve. A similar effect can be achieved by unions and professional associations

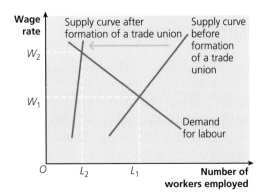

Figure 4.11 A trade union shifting the market supply curve of labour

that insist on long periods of training before the worker is formally qualified, during which time only very low wages are paid. Employment falls from L_1 to L_2, and the wage rate rises to W_2. The advantage to the union, and its members who are employed, is that there is no pool of unemployed workers who would be willing to work for lower wages — that is, there is not an excess supply of labour.

The effect of introducing a trade union into a monopsony labour market

The assertion that unions raise wages at the expense of jobs is heavily dependent on the assumption that, before the union was formed, the labour market was perfectly competitive (it is worth remembering that *no* real-world labour market can meet all the conditions of perfect competition). In the case of a monopsonistic labour market, it is possible for a union to raise *both* the wage rate and employment, even without the *MRP* curve shifting rightward. This is illustrated in Figure 4.12. If the monopsonistic labour market is non-unionised, the equilibrium wage rate is W_1 and the level of employment is L_1.

The introduction of a trade union into a monopsonistic labour market has the same effect on the labour supply curve as would be the case if the labour market were to be perfectly competitive. In Figure 4.12, when the union sets the wage rate at W_2, the kinked line W_2XS becomes the labour supply curve (and also the AC_L curve). But in monopsony, W_2XS is *not* the marginal cost of labour curve. The MC_L curve is the double-kinked line W_2XZV. The double kink is explained in the following way.

Provided the monopsony employs a labour force smaller than or equal to L_2, the MC_L of employing an extra worker equals both the AC_L and the union-determined wage of W_2. But beyond L_2 and point X, the monopsony must offer a higher wage in order to persuade the members of an enlarged labour force to supply their labour. In this situation, with all the workers now being paid the higher wage, the marginal cost of labour increases significantly and there is a discontinuity, X to Z, in the MC_L curve; to the right of L_2 the MC_L curve lies above the AC_L curve. The upward-sloping line ZV drawn in Figure 4.12 shows the MC_L of increasing employment above the level L_2.

This means there is a discontinuity, shown by the vertical distance from point X to point Z, between the horizontal section of the MC_L curve (for levels of employment at or below L_2 and point X) and the upward-sloping section of the curve (ZV) to the right of point X. In the absence of a union, the level of employment is L_1, determined at point A (with point B determining the wage rate W_1). But when the union sets the wage rate at W_2, employment rises to L_2, which is the level of employment at which the *MRP* curve intersects the gap or discontinuity in the MC_L curve at point C, between X and Z. The union has managed to increase both the wage rate and the level of employment.

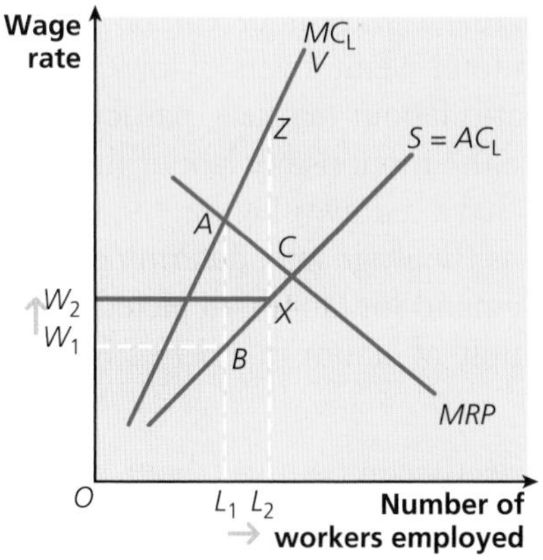

Figure 4.12 The effect of introducing a trade union into a monopsony labour market

4.6 The national minimum wage

The explanation in the previous section, of how a trade union can increase both the wage rate and the level of employment, can also be used to analyse the effect of a **national minimum wage** (NMW) set by the government. Assuming a perfectly competitive labour market, Figure 4.10 can be adapted to show how a national minimum wage set above the market-clearing wage

KEY TERM

national minimum wage a minimum wage or wage rate that must by law be paid to employees, though in many labour markets the wage rate paid by employers is above the national minimum wage.

rate leads to a loss of jobs and unemployment. The same may be true if labour markets are highly competitive without being perfectly competitive. But if labour markets are monopsonistic, Figure 4.12, which can be adapted to show how a national minimum wage can increase both the wage rate and the level of employment, might be more appropriate. However, this does not mean that the imposition of a minimum wage will never lead to a fall in employment. To repeat, some labour markets are very competitive even if they do not satisfy all the conditions of a perfectly competitive labour market.

The advantages and disadvantages of a national minimum wage

A national minimum wage only really affects labour markets where, before its introduction, the market-determined wage rate is below the NMW rate. This, of course, includes markets where wages are depressed through monopsony power. When the national minimum wage rate is set below wage rates determined by free market forces, then, just like any other minimum price law, it has no effect on the market.

SYNOPTIC LINK
See Book 1, Chapter 5, page 121.

Supporters of a national minimum wage argue that a 'wage floor' can be justified on the ground that it reduces exploitation by employers of low-paid workers. As we have mentioned, many real-world labour markets, particularly those for low-paid unskilled workers, resemble the monopsony labour market shown earlier in Figure 4.9. In Figure 4.13 we have redrawn Figure 4.9, but with wage rate W_2 added to the diagram. This is the wage rate, determined at point C in the diagram, where the market demand for labour, depicted by the MRP curve, would equal the market supply of labour in a perfectly competitive labour market.

Figure 4.13 illustrates the fact that in an imperfectly competitive labour market, the employer or employers use their market power to drive down the wage rate below the competitive rate of W_2 to the lower rate of W_1. Trade unions might, of course, create a situation in which the monopsony power of the buyers of labour (the employers) is matched by the monopoly power of the sellers of labour (the unions). This might restore the wage rate to W_2. But if this does not happen, a national minimum wage is deemed necessary, according to its supporters, to eliminate or reduce labour market exploitation of low-paid workers.

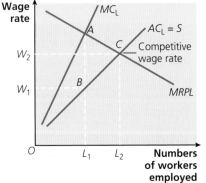

Figure 4.13 Comparing market wage rates in perfect competition and monopsony

Exploitation of low-paid workers also increases poverty. Supporters of the national minimum wage believe that an NMW, set at a 'fair' level, should be a vital part of government policy which aims to reduce poverty. (See the section on low wages and poverty on p. 131 of Chapter 5.) By redistributing income from employers toward low-wage workers, a national minimum wage reduces income inequality as well as poverty.

Most of the evidence collected since national minimum wages were first introduced suggests that 'wage floors' either slightly increase or slightly decrease employment. Either way they do not result in mass unemployment. Recent studies generally conclude that, although there probably are unemployment effects, such effects are extremely slight. By raising the incomes of low-paid workers with only a slight impact on employment, according to this view, the benefits of national minimum wages far outweigh the costs.

Economists who believe in the virtues of a free-market economy, subject to the minimum possible level of government intervention, argue that the disadvantages of a national minimum wage exceed any possible advantages. In a briefing paper, 'The minimum wage: silver bullet or poisoned chalice?', published in 2014 by the Institute of Economic Affairs (IEA), a pro-free-market 'think tank', Ryan Bourne and J. R. Shackleton argued that:

> There is evidence of reduced working hours in response to NMW increases. International research suggests many of the negative effects operate after a long time period through reducing new job creation.

> Employment impacts of increases in the minimum wage are likely to disproportionately affect the young, the unskilled, the long-term unemployed and those in lower productivity regions. There is evidence that minimum wages lead firms to replace lower-skilled and less experienced younger workers with older workers. The 18–24 year old unemployment rate has risen from 11.5 per cent in April 1999 (when the NMW was introduced) to 17.9 per cent today. And of those unemployed within this age group, the proportion out of work for more than 12 months has risen from 14.4 per cent in 1999 to 31.8 per cent in 2013.

> Claims employers are 'subsidised' by in-work benefits in the form of tax credits have some truth, but are exaggerated. Nearly a third of all tax credit recipient households do not have an adult in paid employment and a further million households work fewer than 30 hours per week. Reforming tax credits would be a better means (than raising the NMW) of eliminating the degree to which tax credits subsidise the employers of the remaining full-time workers in receipt of credits.

(It is well worth reading the whole of Bourne and Shackleton's briefing paper, which you can access on the IEA website.)

EXTENSION MATERIAL

The national living wage replaces the national minimum wage

Between 1999, when it was introduced by a Labour government, and 2016 when the Conservative government largely phased it out and replaced it with the **national living wage** (NLW), the national minimum wage (NMW) was increased in most years by an amount more or less in line with the inflation rate measured by the CPI. Each year, the UK government decided the level of the NMW, taking advice from the Low Pay Commission. The government did not guarantee to increase the NMW each year, although in recent years, before it was phased out in 2016, the NMW was raised annually. When it was first introduced in April 1999, the NMW rate was £3.60 per hour (£3.00 for 18- to 21-year-olds). In July 2015, the adult NMW rate was £6.50 per hour. The final increase in the adult NMW took place in October 2015, with the rate rising to £6.70 per hour.

At the time of its introduction, the national *living* wage was set at £7.20 per hour, for both full-time and part-time workers. Although the NLW rate was higher than the NMW rate it replaced, the national living wage rate only applies to workers aged 25 or older. (NMW rates still apply for workers under the age of 25.) Figure 4.14 compares the proposed increases in the NLW between 2016 and 2020 with the likely increases in the NMW adult rate, had the adult national minimum wage rate been kept.

Students have often confused the official *national minimum wage* with the concept of a *living wage*. The July 2015 budget introduced an extra source of confusion, namely that between the *national living wage* and the *living wage*. Back in 2001 a campaign group which eventually became known as Citizens UK advocated the introduction of a living

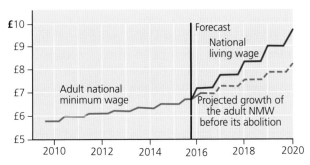

Figure 4.14 The national living wage and the national minimum wage in the UK

Source: HM Treasury

By announcing an official national living wage in the 2015 summer budget, George Osborne essentially hijacked the 'living wage' campaign. NLW rates are below *living wage* rates, only rising to £9.00 an hour in 2019, which will almost certainly be below *living wage* rates. Alison Garnham, chief executive of the Child Poverty Action Group, has described the NLW as a 'higher minimum wage' rather than a true living wage. It is also worth noting that, at the time of the announcement of the abolition of the adult national minimum wage rate, the government also planned a reduction in the levels at which working tax credits are paid. (Working tax credits are benefits paid by the government to low income families.) The Institute for Fiscal Studies (IFS), a respected 'think tank', said after the budget that low-income families would immediately lose more from the reduction in tax credits than they would eventually gain from the new NLW. The overall effect would be significantly regressive. In December 2015 the government abandoned this plan.

wage. Citizens UK, which began life as a rag-tag assortment of charities and churches in east London, calls for every worker in the country to earn enough to provide their family with the essentials of life. The Living Wage Foundation (LWF) was set up in 2011. In 2015, the campaign argued that the living wage should be set at £9.15 per hour for London, and at £7.85 per hour for the rest of the country.

4.7 Discrimination in the labour market

The nature of wage discrimination

In imperfectly competitive labour markets, employers often possess sufficient market power to reduce the total wage bill through undertaking **wage discrimination**, which involves paying different workers different wages for doing the same job. Figure 4.15 illustrates the effect of wage discrimination introduced into a previously competitive labour market. We shall assume that in the absence of wage discrimination, all workers are paid the same wage, W_1, determined by supply and demand. Employers' total wage costs are shown by the rectangle OW_1AL_1.

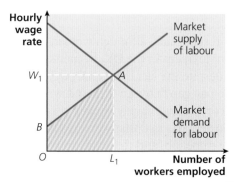

Figure 4.15 Wage discrimination

But if, instead of paying W_1 to all workers, employers pay each worker the minimum he or she is prepared to work for, the total wage bill falls to equal the shaded area $OBAL_1$. Employers thus gain at the expense of workers, which is one reason why firms pay, and trade unions resist, discriminatory wages whenever possible.

Wage discrimination can also occur when a group of workers is systematically paid a wage that is below their *MRP*. This occurs when employers successfully exploit their monopsony power in the labour market, as illustrated in Figures 4.9 and 4.13.

> **STUDY TIP**
> You should understand the similarity between *wage discrimination* in the labour market where a firm hires its labour and *price discrimination* in the goods market where the firm sells its output.

> **EXTENSION MATERIAL**
>
> ## Bringing together wage discrimination and price discrimination
>
> In the case of perfect price discrimination (often called first-degree price discrimination), a firm charges different prices to different customers for the same good, with the same marginal cost of production, so that each customer pays the maximum price he or she is prepared to pay. The entire consumer surplus that customers would otherwise enjoy is transferred to the firm, enlarging the firm's profit.
>
> With perfect wage discrimination, the firm pays each worker the minimum wage the worker is prepared to accept, without changing jobs. The part of the wage that workers would otherwise get is transferred to the firm, once again boosting profit.
>
> Wage discrimination occurs in imperfectly competitive labour markets. From an imperfectly competitive firm's point of view, the best possible outcome is simultaneous price discrimination in the goods market where it sells its output and wage discrimination in the labour markets where it hires its workers. Profit is boosted from two directions at once.
>
> Can you think of reasons why such simultaneous exploitation seldom takes place?

A condition necessary for wage discrimination

Successful wage discrimination, through which employers pay different wage rates to different groups of workers, requires employers to be able to identify and separate different groups of workers supplying the same type of labour. This is possible when workers differ in their knowledge of the labour market and in their ability to shop around among employers.

Types of wage discrimination

So far we have defined wage discrimination in terms of employers paying workers the minimum they are prepared to work for, without focusing on issues of gender, ethnicity and other aspects of discrimination. Different ethnic and religious groups may be paid less than other groups for a variety of reasons, which include the prejudice of employers who try not to hire members of racial minorities or particular religious groups, and also lower educational levels among certain groups in society. Both demand and supply factors contribute to lower wages among certain ethnic and religious groups.

Gender discrimination

Gender discrimination is also significant. In recent years, although women have accounted for an increasing share of total employment in the UK, women's pay often continues to be lower than men's pay, despite the fact that equal pay legislation has been in place since 1972. The pay gap between men and women is at risk of widening for the first time on record, a leading pay equality campaign group has warned. The Fawcett Society has said that women still earn 14.9% less on average than men for the same job, and that this gap could widen as public sector cuts push women into the private sector, where the gap is wider. A second survey, the 2012 Gender Salary Survey, undertaken by the Chartered Management Institute (CMI) found that the average annual pay gap between men and women stood at £10,060. Women also lose out when it comes to bonuses, receiving less than half the average that men receive.

There are two main reasons why women earn less than men:

● Women work predominantly in low-paid industries and occupations.
● Within many occupational groups, women are paid less than men. This is often because women are under-represented in the higher-paid posts within an occupation, rather than because women are paid less for doing the same job.

Discrimination against women in labour markets may contribute to both these sets of circumstances. In addition, women are disproportionately highly represented in industries where the average size of firm and plant is small. These industries tend to pay lower wages and offer fewer promotion prospects than large firms and large industries. Such industries are also seldom unionised. Indeed, within all industries, women workers traditionally have been less unionised than men, but this is now changing.

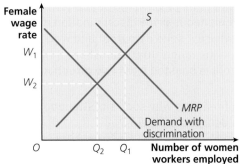

Figure 4.16 How gender discrimination may affect a labour market

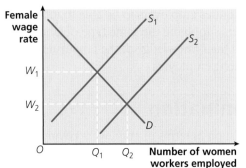

Figure 4.17 The effect of gender discrimination in one market upon female employment and wage rates in other labour markets

This relates to another reason why women earn less than men: on average, their attachment to the labour force is weaker. Each year of work experience raises the pay of both men and women by an average 3%. Yet when women leave the labour force, usually to look after young children, their potential pay falls by 3% for each year involved. For example, a man and woman enter employment with equal potential and after 8 years the woman leaves the workforce in order to raise a family. If she re-enters the labour force 8 years later, she will be 16 years, in pay terms, behind the man.

The higher labour turnover of women also imposes costs on the employer — for example, the costs of training replacement workers. This may reduce the incentive for employers to train female workers. Similarly, women may have less incentive to spend time and money on their own education and training if they expect the benefits that they will eventually receive to be less than the costs initially incurred.

Figures 4.16 and 4.17 illustrate how gender discrimination may affect labour markets. In Figure 4.16 the demand curve for female workers, shown as 'Demand with discrimination', lies to the left of their marginal revenue product curve. This results in Q_2 women being employed, with each being paid an hourly wage rate of W_2. Without gender discrimination, female employment would be Q_1, with the wage rate at W_1.

If gender discrimination takes place in one labour market, other labour markets in which no discrimination is taking place will also be affected.

In these markets, as Figure 4.17 shows, the supply curve of female workers increases as a direct result of discrimination taking place in the first labour market. Female employment increases from Q_1 to Q_2, and the female wage rate falls from W_1 to W_2.

CASE STUDY 4.2

A real-world example of wage discrimination: Ford car workers in 1968 and after

In 2010 the film Made in Dagenham *was released, to be followed in 2014 by a West End musical with the same name. The two events drew to popular attention the important story of how UK law was changed by the action of women employed at Ford's Dagenham car plant in the East End of London in 1968 and in the years thereafter. Here is part of the real story of* Made in Dagenham.

Back in 1968, the idea of a male breadwinner bringing in a 'family wage' legitimised lower pay for women. However, in that year, women sewing machinists in Ford's car plant in Dagenham took a stand for equal pay in a strike that stopped production for 3 weeks. The Ford strike, which captured the attention of Barbara Castle, the secretary of state for labour, led to the 1970 Equal Pay Act.

The demand of the Ford women had originally been to re-grade their jobs from unskilled B grade to semi-skilled grade C. At the time, Ford graded its workers according to a skilled male rate, a semi-skilled male rate, an unskilled male rate and a women's rate. The women's rate of pay was only 87% of the unskilled male rate. However, a grade C rating was only achieved in 1984, following a second strike. Even then, given the fact that Ford's seamstresses were skilled rather than semi-skilled workers, they continued to be underpaid.

Follow-up questions

1 What is the difference between skilled, semi-skilled and unskilled work? Give an example of each of these types of work.
2 Research details about the extent to which women workers remain underpaid today.

SUMMARY

- The price mechanism operates in the labour market in a similar way to how it operates in the goods market, but the roles of firms and households are reversed.
- In their role as employers, firms demand labour in the labour market.
- The demand for labour is a derived demand.
- In a perfectly competitive labour market, the marginal revenue product (*MRP*) curve facing an employer is the employer's demand curve for labour.
- The opportunity cost of working is the leisure time forgone.
- A monopsony is the only buyer of labour in a labour market.
- In monopsony, the wage rate and the level of employment are likely to be lower than in a perfectly competitive labour market.
- In monopsony, a trade union may be able to increase both the wage rate and the level of employment toward the perfectly competitive levels. A national minimum wage can have the same effect.
- From 2016 onward, for adults the national living wage (NLW) replaced the national minimum wage (NMW).
- Gender discrimination means that women often earn less than men.

Questions

1 Explain three factors that are significant in determining a firm's demand for labour.

2 Explain the shape of a market supply curve of labour.

3 Explain how the wage rate would be determined in a perfectly competitive labour market, both for the market as a whole and for one employer within the market.

4 Evaluate the view that when trade unions raise wages they inevitably reduce levels of employment.

5 Why are women often paid less than men?

5

The distribution of income and wealth: poverty and inequality

As the experience of many poor countries shows, unregulated market forces tend to produce highly unequal distributions of income and wealth, which many economists believe to be an important form of market failure. However, a minority of economists disagree. Extreme pro-free-market economists sometimes argue that people who end up poor deserve to be poor. According to this view, the market does not fail; it simply creates incentives that cause people to generate income and wealth which end up benefiting most of the population. They also argue that attempts by governments to redistribute income and wealth from the rich to the poor usually end up, through the distortion of personal incentives, in government failure which harms national economic performance. Nevertheless, the mainstream economic view is that some form of intervention to moderate the extreme inequalities that would occur in a completely free-market economy is desirable. The arguments are about the *extent* to which governments should intervene to reduce inequality, and the methods of intervention.

For households at the bottom of the income distribution, severe income inequalities are an important cause of poverty (although, as mentioned above, pro-free market economists argue that the resulting incentives provide a route out of poverty). However, poverty has causes other than those associated with income inequality, and we shall examine these later in the chapter.

LEARNING OBJECTIVES
This chapter will:

- examine the nature and causes of inequalities in the distribution of income and wealth in the UK
- summarise how government policies such as progressive taxation, transfers and the national minimum wage attempt to make the distribution of income more equal
- discuss the meaning of poverty
- distinguish between absolute poverty and relative poverty
- explain the main causes of poverty in the UK
- relate progressive taxation to fiscal drag and to the poverty and unemployment traps

5.1 The distribution of income and wealth

KEY TERMS

distribution of income how income is divided between rich and poor, or between different groups in society, e.g. on a regional, age or gender basis.

distribution of wealth how wealth is divided between rich and poor, or between different groups in society, e.g. on a regional, age or gender basis.

income personal or household income is the flow of money a person or household receives in a particular time period.

wealth personal wealth is the stock of everything which has value that a person or household owns at a particular point in time.

The **distribution of income** measures how personal or household income is distributed among different income groups in society, such as between rich and poor. The term is also used to measure other forms of distribution — for example, between people living in different parts or regions of the economy, between different generations (such as the old and the young), and between men and women. Measures of income distribution can also be extended to the international distribution of income between countries — with countries at different stages of economic development having not only different total levels of income, but also different distributions between rich and poor — and also between different regions, age groups and gender.

Likewise, the **distribution of wealth** measures how personal or household wealth is distributed among different groups in society. Again, the distribution between rich and poor (and the intermediate groups which separate rich and poor) is most often considered, though economists sometimes focus on differences in regional, age group and gender distributions of wealth.

Together with other members of the general public, economics students often confuse the two words, **income** and **wealth**. The main difference between them is that income is a *flow* whereas wealth is a *stock*. Personal wealth is the stock, or historical accumulation, of everything you own that has value. For those households with at least one working member, wage and salary payments into the household's bank account are an inward flow of income, whereas, for an owner-occupying household, the house they live in, minus any outstanding mortgage debt, usually forms a large part of their household wealth.

To recap, your personal income is the *flow* of money you receive hourly, weekly, monthly or annually, some of which (the part that you *save*) can add to your personal wealth. As we shall see, this is one of the links between income and wealth. A second link operates in the opposite direction — the wealthier you are, the more investment income or unearned income you are likely to earn, which adds to your total income. Indeed, the rich benefit from a virtuous circle: wealth increases income, which allows the wealthy to save, and saving adds to wealth, and so on. By contrast, many of the poor suffer a vicious circle: low income means the poor have to borrow, borrowing adds to personal debt, income is then spent on debt repayment, consumption falls, and any wealth the poor possess disappears.

SYNOPTIC LINK

Book 1, Figure 7.1 illustrates national income and national wealth in a macroeconomic context.

EXTENSION MATERIAL

How the World Bank classifies world countries according to income per capita

The World Bank divides countries into four income groupings: low, lower-middle, upper-middle and high income. Income is measured using gross national income (GNI) per capita, in US dollars. For 2016, low-income economies were defined by the World Bank as those with a GNI per capita of $1,045 or less in 2014; middle-income economies as those with a GNI per capita of more than $1,045 but less than $12,736; high-income economies as those with a GNI per capita of $12,736 or more. The World Bank further subdivided middle-income countries into two groups: lower-middle-income countries with a GNI per capita extending to $4,125 and upper-middle-income countries with a GNI per capita lying between $4,126 and $12,735. The UK is, of course, a high-income country with GNI per capita (according to the World Bank) of $42,690. Turkey is an upper-middle-income country (GNI per capita $10,850 in 2014); Bolivia is a lower-middle-income country (GNI per capita of $2,830 in 2014); while in sub-Saharan Africa the Democratic Republic of Congo is a low-income country (GNI per capita of $410 in 2014).

SYNOPTIC LINK

See Chapter 10, section 10.5 for further information about the construction of the United Nation's Human Development Index (HDI).

The various factors which influence the distribution of income and wealth

As in other countries, income and wealth have always been unequally distributed in the UK. Even when economic growth creates full employment, the incomes of the rich tend to increase faster than those of the poor. For this reason, fast economic growth may actually widen income differences, though those at the bottom of the pile can still end up *absolutely* better off.

The distribution of income in the UK

Figure 5.1 shows how the distribution of income in the UK has changed over the years between 1977/78 and 2011/12, both before and after taxation and welfare benefits have altered the distribution. Each line colour represents a different quintile, or 20%, of the population. The red line is the poorest 20%, the blue line the next poorest 20%, the green line the middle 20%, the purple line the second richest 20%, and the orange line the richest 20%.

The dotted line of each colour shows what percentage of the total income that 20% earned from employment, private pensions and investment before any government intervention. The solid line shows what proportion of the total income they received after paying direct and indirect taxes, and receiving any cash benefits.

Figure 5.1 shows that the gap between the top and bottom quintiles peaked toward the end of the twentieth century, but income inequality after tax and the receipt of government benefits fell in 2011/12 back to its 1987 level.

This was mostly due to changes in the tax and benefit system, as original income inequality remained about the same over the period. Without the tax and benefit system being used to redistribute income, the bottom 20% of the population would have received just 3% of the total income, and the second poorest 20% would have received the same as the poorest 20% do today. In contrast, the richest 20% would have received over 50% of the national income.

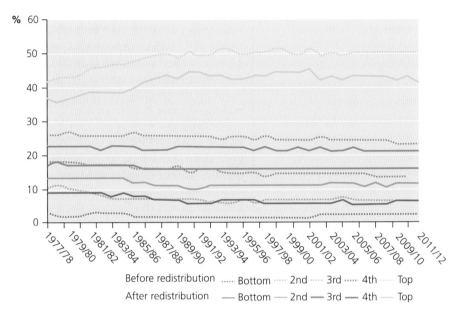

Figure 5.1 UK income distribution, 1977/78 to 2011/12 (% of total, by quintile, before and after redistribution)

Source: ONS

QUANTITATIVE SKILLS 5.1

Worked example: quintiles and quantiles

Explain what is meant by a quintile. Describe two other quantiles economists often use when they present data.

As the second part of the question implies, a quintile is an example of a quantile. A quantile is a portion of a total amount divided into sub-groups. Total income in Figure 5.1 has been divided five equal-sized groups, or fifths. These are quintiles. Other commonly used quantiles are quartiles (the total is divided into four groups, or quarters); deciles (the total is divided into ten groups, or tenths); vigintiles (the total is divided into 20 groups, or twentieths); and finally percentiles (the total is divided into 100 groups, or hundredths).

Factors influencing the distribution of income

A large number of factors influence the distribution of income. These include:

- **Factors of production.** An important factor is the distribution of national income between the different factors of production: land, labour, capital and entrepreneurs. The owners of large land holdings, such as country estates or large parts of the West End of London, receive large incomes in the form of rent. This puts large landowners in the top income quintiles shown in Figure 5.1. The share of national income of landlords and owners of capital has grown, whereas labour's share has fallen. The OECD has calculated that, across the world, labour's share of worldwide incomes was 62% in the early 2000s, down from over 66% in the early 1990s. One reason for this is that wages have not been rising as fast as productivity and hence labour's share of national income has fallen. Many of the owners of capital, including entrepreneurs, receive their income in the form of dividend payments on the shares they own. Profits and entrepreneurial incomes have risen at the expense of wages and salaries, although the salaries received by top business executives have also grown much faster than wages.

● **The distinction between earned and unearned income.** Earned income includes wages, salaries, other forms of employee compensation, and self-employment income. Unearned income is income derived from sources other than employment, including interest and investment income (such as dividend income paid to shareholders). The various determinants of wages discussed in Chapter 4 can be used to explain differences in earned incomes. By contrast, differences in unearned income depend primarily on inequalities in the distribution of wealth.

● **Wage and salary differentials.** Within the labour market, the difference between the wages and salaries of those at the top and those at the bottom have widened. To an extent this can be explained by standard supply and demand theory. The two panels of Figure 5.2 show a high hourly wage rate in the left-hand panel depicting the market for airline pilots, and a much lower wage rate in the right-hand panel which shows the market for aircraft cleaners. Two of the main factors contributing to this difference in hourly wage rates are the differences in labour productivity, which determine the relative positions of the demand curves for pilots and for cleaners, and the different slopes and positions of the supply curves. The labour productivity of an airline pilot is significantly higher than that of an aircraft cleaner. Because of factors such as long training periods, the supply of airline pilots is lower and more inelastic with respect to changes in their salaries. By contrast, the supply of airline cleaners is higher at any given wage and more wage-rate elastic. The cleaners are unskilled and do not require much training. As a result, an increase in the wage paid to airline cleaners greatly increases the number of workers willing to clean aircraft. Because of these factors, and others we have not considered, pilots' salaries end up being much higher than the wages received by the workers who clean their aircraft. In Figure 5.2, pilots are paid £300 an hour, whereas cleaners earn £10 an hour, which is just above the National Living Wage.

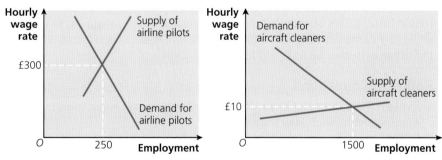

Figure 5.2 Differences in rates of pay in different jobs

● **Globalisation and the international migration of workers**. These factors have also widened the differences between the wages and salaries paid to different groups of workers. Within the UK, low-paid workers are in competition, both with incoming migrants from poorer parts of the world, and with overseas-based workers employed in developing countries, to which UK employers have outsourced jobs. A call-centre worker, serving the UK market but employed in India, earns a much lower wage than a similar worker employed in Britain. International competition has led to falling wages in UK labour markets where workers are competing for jobs against similar workers in other countries. Similar competition does exist at the high end of labour markets too, but in this case, well-paid UK business executives often succeed in raising their pay on the ground that their employers must match the 'rate for the job' established in richer countries such as the USA. If their pay does not rise, they argue, they will move to better-paid jobs in other countries.

STUDY TIP

This theoretical explanation for different rates of pay draws on the analysis provided in Chapter 4 on the determination of pay and levels of employment in different labour markets. You should be aware that the same body of theory can help in your explanations of inequalities in the distribution of income and the causes of poverty (see later in this chapter).

CASE STUDY 5.1

UK income inequality in 2012

A study published in March 2013 by the High Pay Centre, a think-tank set up in the wake of an inquiry into escalating executive pay, shows that there are now 26,000 Britons taking home more in a month than those on average salaries earn in a year. According to the study, the UK has returned to levels of income inequality last seen in the 1930s, with the share of the national income going to the top 1% more than doubling since 1979, to 14.5%. In 2013, the 26,000 top-earning UK residents, who have salaries of more than half-a-million pounds a year, receive at least £21,500 per month after tax — more than the average annual wage of £20,500. At the other end of the spectrum, there are 6.75 million workers earning less than £800 a month. Figure 5.3 shows that in 2012, 4.21% of people in receipt of income enjoyed incomes of £75,000 or more a year, while at the other extreme, 48.45% had to live on incomes of £25,000 or less. The richest 1%, of course, received much more than £75,000 while the very poor made do with much less than £25,000.

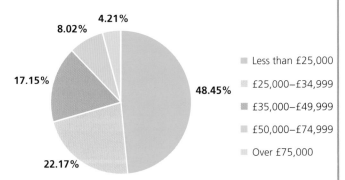

Figure 5.3 Percentages of UK adults in different income groups, 2012

Follow-up questions

1 Explain the sentence: 'The richest 1%, of course, received much more than £75,000 while the very poor made do with much less than £25,000.'
2 Outline your view on whether governments should attempt to redistribute income.

The distribution of wealth

Figure 5.1 showed that the distribution of income in the UK is unequal, but as Figure 5.4 indicates, the distribution of wealth is significantly more unequal than the distribution of income. In 2010–12, the least wealthy half of all households owned just 9% of all the wealth between them. The top fifth owned 62% of all the wealth.

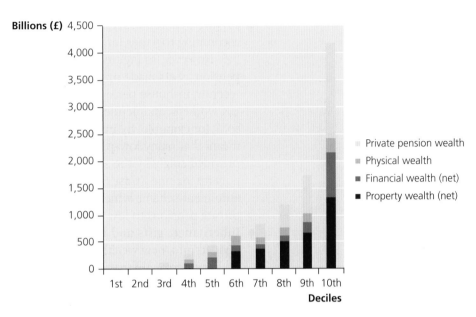

Figure 5.4 The distribution of wealth in the UK, 2010–12

Source: ONS

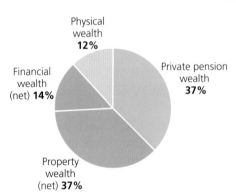

Figure 5.5 Breakdown of the types of wealth owned by UK households in 2010–12

Source: ONS

The Office for National Statistics (ONS) defines total net wealth as the sum of four components: net property wealth, physical wealth, net financial wealth and private pension wealth, although it does not include rights to state pensions. As we mentioned earlier, wealth is a 'stock' concept rather than a 'flow'; it is measured at a particular point in time. Income, which refers to the flow of resources received over a period of time, allows wealth to be accumulated, but similarly, wealth is capable of producing flows of income either in the present or — as in the case of pension wealth — in the future.

Figure 5.5 shows the relative contribution of each of the four wealth components to aggregate total wealth. In 2010–12, the two components making the largest contribution to aggregate total wealth were private pension wealth and net property wealth (each accounting for 37%). Financial wealth made up 14% of the total wealth in 2010–12 and physical wealth (other than property wealth, e.g. cars) made the smallest contribution of the four components (12%).

Factors influencing the distribution of wealth

The factors influencing the distribution of wealth are closely linked to the factors which influence the distribution of income. Indeed, as we have already mentioned, high incomes lead both to a large amount of saving taking place, and to spending on items such as expensive houses, both of which add to household wealth. By contrast, households living on small incomes can afford neither to save nor to purchase houses, which appreciate rather than depreciate in value.

Among the other factors which influence the distribution of wealth are:

● **The ability to benefit from capital gains.** A capital gain occurs when the value of an asset such as a house increases. Most consumer durable goods, such as cars and TV sets, depreciate in value over the years after they are purchased. By contrast, the value of land and property generally increases, at least in the UK. Share prices also tend to rise in the long run, though they can also fall in value. On the whole, the already wealthy own the most expensive houses, often also owning more than one house, and they are the main owners of shares. The least wealthy often rent rather than own the houses they live in, and seldom own shares.

- **Private pension assets.** Houses and shares are forms of marketable wealth, accounting together for 51% of the household wealth shown in Figure 5.5. However, as Figure 5.5 shows, in 2010–12 non-marketable private pension assets made up 38% of total household wealth. However, until very recently, in-house pension schemes were not available for many low-paid UK workers, and neither did they contribute to private pension schemes sold, for example, by insurance companies such as Standard Life. This has meant that many low-paid workers expect their retirement income to be provided solely by the state pension, which on its own is little more than a poverty income. (Case Study 5.4 on page 137 explains the new automatic enrolment scheme which the UK government has introduced to extend private pensions to low-paid workers.)

- **Inheritance, gifts and luck.** In popular parlance, wealthy families are often divided into 'new wealth' and 'old wealth'. Entrepreneurs who have built up large personal fortunes, often starting from scratch, through founding their own businesses and successful risk taking, fall into the category of 'new wealth'. By contrast, 'old wealth' includes people who inherit wealth through the luck of having been born into very rich families, rather than through exercising entrepreneurial skills. Members of the landed aristocracy who pass wealth-holdings from generation to generation are 'old wealth'. 'Old wealth' can, of course, lead to 'new wealth' — for example, when the sons and daughters of rich families use their expensively acquired education and inherited wealth as the platform on which to develop entrepreneurial skills. Likewise, 'new wealth' can create 'old wealth', when for example the fortunes of the newly rich are passed on to the next generation.

- **Wealth taxation versus taxation of income.** In the UK, a much larger fraction of the government's tax revenue comes from taxation of income than from the taxation of wealth. Wealth is lightly taxed and there are many loopholes through which the already wealthy can legally avoid paying wealth taxes such as inheritance tax. The wealthy can also afford to employ accountants and financial advisers who minimise the tax they are liable to pay, and in this way the wealthy become even wealthier.

The difference between equality and equity in relation to the distribution of income and wealth

The general public often use the terms **equality** and **equity** interchangeably, which can be confusing. Although the concepts are related, they are not the same. Complete equality in the distribution of income is achieved when each person receives exactly the same amount of income. The degree of inequality is indicated by the extent to which people's incomes differ. Equity is when people are treated fairly, but differently, having taken into account their different circumstances. Very few people would argue that it would be equitable if everyone received the same income, irrespective of their efforts and the contribution they make to society. It is when people start to discuss how much inequality is fair that the arguments usually begin.

Equity, which means fairness or justness, is a *normative* concept, which cannot be measured. Different people form different value judgements on what is

> **KEY TERMS**
>
> **equality** means that everyone is treated exactly the same. A completely equal distribution of income means that everybody has the same income.
>
> **equity** means that everybody is treated fairly.

equitable or inequitable. By contrast, equality is a *positive* concept. A positive statement, such as the view that the incomes received by everyone in the economy are the same, can be tested against the evidence to see if it is true or untrue. As we shall shortly explain, it is possible to measure the degrees of equality and inequality in the distributions of income and wealth.

TEST YOURSELF 5.1

In a highly competitive market economy, the price mechanism serves to allocate resources

A efficiently, but not necessarily fairly

B fairly and efficiently

C fairly, but not necessarily efficiently

D efficiently and equally

Explain why statement A probably provides the best answer and why the other statements are wrong.

SYNOPTIC LINK
We first described positive and normative statements in Book 1, pages 4–5.

EXTENSION MATERIAL

Horizontal and vertical equity

Government intervention in the economy, which treats people in the same circumstances equally, obeys the principle of *horizontal equity*. Horizontal equity occurs when households with the same income and personal circumstances (for example, number of children) pay the same income tax and are eligible for the same welfare benefits. *Vertical equity* is much more controversial, since it justifies taking income from the rich (on the grounds that they do not need it) and redistributing it to the poor (on the grounds that they do need it). The distribution of income after taxation and receipt of transfers is judged by many to be more equitable than the distribution of income before taxes have been paid

and transfer payments received. (In this context, a *transfer* or *transfer payment* is a payment of money for which goods or services are not received in exchange. Governments use transfer payments, such as pensions, as means of income redistribution by giving out money as a part of their social welfare programmes.)

However, achieving greater vertical equity can conflict with another principle of intervention, the *benefit principle*, which argues that those who receive most benefit from government spending (for example, motorists benefiting from roads) should pay the most in taxes.

The Lorenz curve and Gini coefficient

KEY TERM
Lorenz curve a graph on which the cumulative percentage of total national income or wealth is plotted against the cumulative percentage of population (ranked in increasing size of share). The extent to which the curve dips below a straight diagonal line indicates the degree of inequality of distribution.

Economists use **Lorenz curves** and the **Gini coefficient** to measure inequality. A Lorenz curve measures *the extent* to which the distribution of income (or wealth) is equal or unequal. The degree of inequality is measured by a Gini coefficient statistic.

The Lorenz curve in Figure 5.6 shows population on the horizontal axis, measured in cumulative percentages from 0% to 100%. The vertical axis shows the cumulative percentage of income received by the population. If incomes were distributed equally, the Lorenz curve would lie along the diagonal line in the diagram. The nearer the Lorenz curve is to the diagonal, the more equal is the distribution of income.

The Gini coefficient measures the area between the Lorenz curve and the diagonal as a ratio of the total area under the diagonal. In terms of the diagram, the Gini coefficient is calculated using the following formula:

$$\text{Gini coefficient} = \frac{\text{area } A}{\text{area } A + \text{area } B}$$

The lower the value of the Gini coefficient, the more equally household income is distributed. If the Lorenz curve were to lie along the 45-degree line in Figure 5.6, every household would have exactly the same income and the Gini coefficient would be zero. At the other extreme, if one person received all the income and everybody else no income, the Lorenz curve would be the reverse L-shape lying along first, the horizontal axis, and then the right-hand vertical axis in the diagram. Between these two extremes, Lorenz curves closer to the line of complete equality show greater equality (and Gini coefficients approaching zero), while Lorenz curves further away from the diagonal display greater inequality (and Gini coefficients approaching 1).

Figure 5.7 shows how the Gini coefficient for equivalised disposable income changed in the UK between 1978 and 2013. Inequality of disposable income increased in the 1980s, and then grew only slightly. The Gini coefficient was around 10 percentage points higher in 2010 than it had been in 1980. Both real disposable incomes and inequality, measured by the Gini coefficient, rose over this period. By contrast, both real disposable incomes and inequality fell between 2011 and 2013.

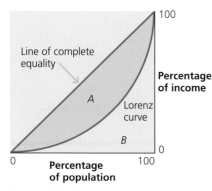

Figure 5.6 A Lorenz curve

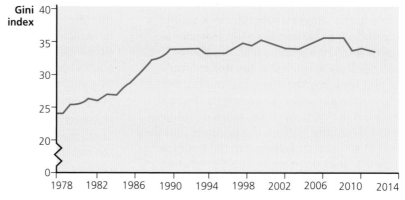

Figure 5.7 Gini coefficient for equivalised disposable income, UK, 1978–2013

TEST YOURSELF 5.2
Table 5.1 shows the distribution of income (by quintile) in country X and country Y. Plot Lorenz curves for the two countries.

Table 5.1 Income distributions by quintile

Quintile	Percentage of total disposable income	
	Country X	**Country Y**
1st	5	4
2nd	10	6
3rd	15	25
4th	20	30
5th	50	4
Total	100	35

EXTENSION MATERIAL

Comparing different Lorenz curves

Figure 5.8 shows a case of two Lorenz curves crossing. In this case, Y is more equal than X for low levels of income, but X is more equal than Y for high levels of income. In this situation, it is not possible to make a definite statement about which represents the more equal distribution of income but the Gini coefficient would help.

Whereas Figures 5.6 and 5.8 show income Lorenz curves, Figure 5.9 provides an example of a wealth Lorenz curve. To repeat, the closer the Lorenz curve is to the diagonal line, the more equal the distribution becomes. Figure 5.9 shows that in 2010–12, the most inequality was in net financial wealth, whilst physical wealth shows the greatest equality. The curve for net financial wealth shows negative values of cumulative wealth, up to about the 68th percentile of cumulative wealth. This is because households with large debts and few if any financial assets have negative net financial wealth.

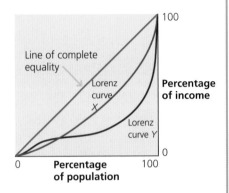

Figure 5.8 Lorenz curves that cross

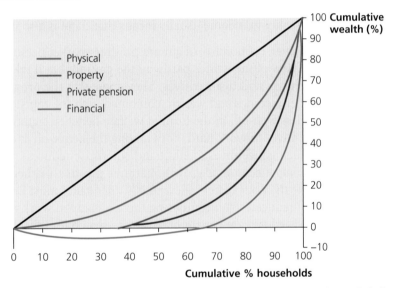

Figure 5.9 Lorenz curves for individual wealth components: Great Britain, 2010–12

Source: ONS

TEST YOURSELF 5.3

Which **two** of the following are most likely to reflect a move towards a more equal distribution of income? Explain your answer.

A The share of total income going to the bottom 50% of income earners rises from 30% to 40%.

B The share of total income going to the top 15% of income earners rises from 60% to 62%.

C The Gini coefficient rises towards 1.

D The Gini coefficient falls towards 0.

The likely benefits and costs of more equitable distributions of income and wealth

It is sometimes argued, particularly by economists who favour government intervention in markets, that a more equitable or fair distribution of income and wealth can lead to faster economic growth. The fruits of faster growth can then be used to improve living standards and the economic welfare of most or all of the population. The logic behind this argument is that people on low incomes and who possess little wealth generally spend all or most of their incomes on consumption and save very little, or nothing at all. Increased spending on consumer goods and services increases aggregate demand in the economy, which promotes economic growth. By contrast, the better-off spend a smaller fraction of their incomes on consumption, which leads to slower growth. Inequality can also mean that the talents of some people in society are wasted or, at least, not fully exploited. For example, children from families on low incomes are likely to do less well than children with affluent parents. Inequality in income usually means that there is also inequality of opportunity.

However, economists of a more pro-free-market persuasion generally reject this view of the world, partly on the ground that it takes no account of incentives and disincentives. They argue that the **progressive taxation** of higher incomes and wealth, combined with the transfer of taxed income to the less well-off, in the form of welfare benefits, significantly reduces the incentives to work hard, both among the better-off and among the poor. Reducing incentives to effort and enterprise reduces, rather than increases, the rate of economic growth. Extreme pro-free-market analysts argue that to make the poor better off *eventually*, inequality must first be increased rather than reduced. By incentivising those already in work to work harder, and the unwaged welfare benefit claimants to search for jobs, faster economic growth can be achieved. In the long run, the low-waged benefit even though in the short run their incomes fall.

Taken to the extreme, however, widening income and wealth inequalities undoubtedly increases poverty, at least in the short run. Most people in the UK seem to subscribe to a consensus view that there should be a certain amount of redistribution, compared to the outcome that would be achieved in a complete free-market situation. This redistribution is necessary for moral reasons and also to maintain social cohesion within society. The debating issues are, first, where to draw the line when redistributing income and wealth, and second, what methods should be used to achieve the degree of redistribution desired.

> **KEY TERM**
>
> **progressive taxation** a tax is progressive when, as income rises, a greater proportion of income is paid in taxation. The term can be applied to a particular tax such as income tax or to taxation in general.

> **SYNOPTIC LINK**
>
> The difference between progressive, proportional and regressive taxes is explained more fully in section 9.2 of Chapter 9.

> **ACTIVITY**
>
> Taxation is not always progressive. Find out the meanings of a *regressive tax* and a *proportional tax* and identify UK taxes which are regressive.

5.2 The problem of poverty

KEY TERMS

poverty the state of being extremely poor and not having enough money or income to meet basic needs.

absolute poverty a condition characterised by severe deprivation of basic human needs, including food, safe drinking water, sanitation facilities, health, shelter, education and information. It depends not only on income but also on access to services.

relative poverty occurs when income is below a specified proportion of average income, e.g. below 60% of median income.

Poverty is the state of being extremely poor and not having enough money or income to meet basic needs including food, clothing and shelter. The World Bank describes poverty in the following way:

> Poverty is hunger. Poverty is lack of shelter. Poverty is being sick and not being able to see a doctor. Poverty is not having access to school and not knowing how to read. Poverty is not having a job, is fear for the future, living one day at a time.

Poverty is caused both by a low real national income relative to a country's total population size and by inequalities in the distributions of income and wealth. The former leads to **absolute poverty** for many if not most of a country's inhabitants, whereas the latter causes **relative poverty**.

The gap between rich and poor is an issue in the UK

The difference between relative and absolute poverty

Absolute poverty

The Joseph Rowntree Foundation defines absolute poverty in the following way:

> A poverty level that does not change over time, in terms of the living standard that it refers to. It stays the same even if society is becoming more prosperous. An absolute poverty line thus represents a certain basic level of goods and services, and only rises with inflation to show how much it would cost to buy those goods and services.

Relative poverty

Relative poverty is suffered by a household if its income is below a specified proportion of the average income for all households For example, in the UK, the 'poverty line' has usually been set at 60% of median income. The charity Barnardo's says:

> Relative poverty defines 'poverty' as being below a relative poverty threshold. It classifies individuals or families as 'poor' not by comparing them to a fixed cut-off point, but by comparing them to others in the population under study.

TEST YOURSELF 5.4

The inability to satisfy basic food needs is part of the definition of:

A relative poverty

B obesity

C absolute poverty

D idleness

Explain why statement C provides the correct answer and why the other statements are wrong.

CASE STUDY 5.2

The Conservatives aim to redefine child poverty

On 1 July 2015, Iain Duncan Smith, the secretary of state for work and pensions, announced that he intended to repeal the 2010 Child Poverty Act, which committed the government to a target of eradicating child poverty in the UK by 2020. In so doing, the work and pensions secretary dispensed with the current relative definition of poverty (anyone in a household beneath 60% of median income), abandoned all targets and introduced a new (although still rather unclear) definition, embracing work and education levels in the family.

According to the *Guardian*, although Duncan Smith did not spell it out, there will be a moral, judgmental dimension to the new definition. The government says it plans to develop a 'range of other measures and indicators of root causes of poverty, including family breakdown, debt and addiction', which it will put together in a 'children's life chances strategy'.

Follow-up questions

1 Find out what has happened to Duncan Smith's proposals since 2015.
2 Explain why you agree or disagree with the proposed new definition of child poverty.

The causes and effects of poverty

The causes of poverty in the UK

For the most part, UK poverty is relative rather than absolute, although many homeless people living in cardboard boxes in town centres are absolutely as well as relatively poor. Three of the main causes of relative poverty in the UK are old age, unemployment and the low wages of many of those in work.

Old age and poverty

Old age causes relative poverty largely because, as we have seen, many old people rely on the state pension and lack a private pension. Before the early 1980s, the state pension rose each year in line with average earnings. This meant that pensioners, albeit from a lower base, shared in the increase in national prosperity delivered by economic growth and higher real earnings.

However, pensions then moved away from being index-linked to average earnings, to be linked instead to the rate of inflation, measured at first by changes in the retail prices index (RPI). Pensions no longer rose in line with the general increase in the standard of living and pensioners' living standards were in effect kept at their 1980 level. Old people who were reliant solely on the state for their income became increasingly worse off compared to people in work.

In 2011, the Coalition government introduced what is known as the 'triple lock'. The government said that the state pension would now rise in line with either earnings, or CPI inflation, or a 2.5% increase, whichever is the greatest. Shortly afterwards, the government considered switching back to linking pension increases solely to rises in average earnings, thus ending the annual inflation-linked rise in benefits. In contrast to earlier decades when the rate of increase in average earnings exceeded the rate of inflation, by 2013 earnings were rising by around 1% a year, which was lower than the rate of inflation — which, at the time, was nearer to 2%. By 2015, average earnings were rising by slightly more than the then low rate of inflation. Whatever is likely to happen in the future, unless supplemented from other sources of income, the state pension will continue to be very much a poverty income.

ACTIVITY

Find out about any changes in government pensions policy since the election of the Conservative government in May 2015. Find out also what has happened to changes in average earnings and the rate of inflation since 2015.

Unemployment and poverty

Unemployment benefits are generally lower than the pay workers received before losing their jobs. An increase in unemployment therefore increases poverty. In 2013, as part of the policy of cutting public spending, the Coalition government introduced a limit on the total amount of benefit that most people aged 16 to 64 can claim. The limit may further increase poverty, though this effect could be offset by a continuing rapid fall in unemployment. Absolute poverty can best be reduced by fast and sustained economic growth and by creating jobs. This may also reduce relative poverty. Economic growth can also create the wherewithal, if the electorate and state are so minded, to increase the real value of the state pension and unemployment benefits. Possibly in part due to the political power of the so-called 'grey vote', the government may be more minded to increase the real value of the state pension than of unemployment benefits.

ACTIVITY

Find out about how recent changes in welfare benefits and the national living wage have been affecting poverty.

Low wages and poverty

When discussing the nature of both absolute and relative poverty in the UK, we must distinguish between the low-waged and the unwaged, who are unemployed. The low-waged, unlike the unwaged, are workers with jobs, albeit jobs in which their hourly and weekly earnings are low. The low-waged include many unskilled workers, together with skilled workers who have lost their jobs in industrial sectors such as manufacturing and coal mining, and who have had to accept employment in low-waged, unskilled jobs. The low-waged poor are almost always relatively poor rather than absolutely poor. In contrast, some of the unwaged, including homeless people living on the street, fall into the category of the absolutely poor. The national minimum wage which we explained in Chapter 4 was an attempt to reduce the poverty of the low-waged. The national living wage is now taking on this mantle.

The effects of poverty in the UK

According to the anti-poverty pressure group, the Child Poverty Action Group (CPAG), poverty damages childhoods, life chances and eventually all in society. It is a direct cost to government resulting from additional demands placed on services and benefits for the poor, as well as reduced tax receipts.

Educational deprivation

In terms of education deprivation, the CAPG argues that children from poorer backgrounds lag at all stages of education. For example, by the age of three, poorer children are estimated to be, on average, nine months behind children from more wealthy backgrounds. By the end of primary school, pupils receiving free school meals are estimated to be almost three terms behind their more affluent peers. This gap grows to over five terms by the age of 14, and by 16, children receiving free school meals achieve 1.7 grades lower at GCSE.

Health deprivation

The CAPG says that poverty is also associated with a higher risk of both illness and premature death. Children born in the poorest areas of the UK weigh, on average, 200 grams less at birth than those born in the richest areas. Children from low-income families are also more likely to die at birth or in infancy than children born into richer families. They are more likely to suffer chronic illness during childhood or to have a disability. Poorer health over the course of a lifetime has an impact on life expectancy: professionals live, on average, 8 years longer than unskilled workers.

The effect of poverty on communities

Children living in poverty are almost twice as likely to live in bad housing. This has significant effects on both their physical and mental health, as well as their educational achievement. Fuel poverty also affects children detrimentally as they grow up. Low-income families sometimes have to make a choice between food and heating. Children from low-income families often forgo activities that most children would take for granted. They miss school trips; can't invite friends round for tea; and can't afford a one-week holiday away from home.

Besides having serious effects on children, poverty adversely affects other groups in society, particularly pensioners whose sole income is the state pension. The elderly are the main group in society suffering from fuel poverty, though in 2016 falling energy prices may have been alleviating this problem. However, falling energy prices may turn out to be a short-term 'blip', soon to be replaced by the 'normal service' of rising prices in response to global resource depletion. Old-age poverty and the fact that the old are living for longer lead to other adverse effects on society — for example, elderly 'bed-blockers' continuing to occupy hospital wards after they have been successfully treated, simply because they have nowhere else to go.

ACTIVITY

Access the Child Poverty Action Group's website on **www.cpag.org.uk** and find out about CPAG's policies and campaigns aimed at reducing poverty, particularly child poverty.

5.3 Government policies to alleviate poverty and to influence the distribution of income and wealth

Poverty and the tax and benefits system

Poverty is seldom caused directly and immediately by taxation and the benefits system. However, through a process known as fiscal drag (which will be explained shortly) and through cuts in welfare benefits, poverty can increase. Making taxation more progressive and increasing welfare benefits reduces poverty and inequalities in the distribution of income, at least in the short run. However, as we have already mentioned, pro-free-market economists believe that, in the drive to reduce inequality, these changes worsen labour market incentives, competitiveness and economic growth. They may lead to a culture of welfare dependency where some people are long-term unemployed and are reluctant to look for work. According to this view, in the long run, low incomes may fail to grow and poverty may increase. If true, government intervention in labour markets in an attempt to reduce poverty results in government failure.

The effects of taxes and benefits on household income, 2012/13

A household is a group of people, such as a family, who are living together in a house or flat. Before taxes and benefits, the richest fifth of UK households had an average income of £81,300 in 2012/13, almost 15 times greater than the poorest fifth, who had an average income of £5,500. Overall, taxes and benefits lead to income being shared more equally between households. After all taxes and benefits are taken into account, the ratio between the average incomes of the top and the bottom fifth of households (£59,900 and £15,600 per year respectively) is reduced to four-to-one.

Fifty-two per cent of households received more in benefits (including benefits in kind, such as free education and healthcare) than they paid in taxes in 2012/13. This is equivalent to 13.8 million households.

The average disposable income in 2012/13 remained lower than at the start of the economic downturn or recession in 2008, with average equivalised disposable income falling by £1,200 since 2007/08 in real terms. The fall in income has been largest for the richest fifth of households.

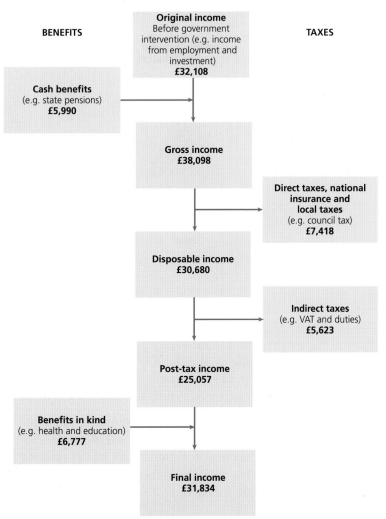

Figure 5.10 Average household income, cash benefits received, including benefits in kind, and taxes paid, 2012/13

Source: ONS

There are five stages through which taxes and benefits affect the distribution of income. These are:

1   Household members begin with income from employment, private pensions, investments such as the shares they own, and other non-government sources. This is referred to as 'original income'.
2   Households then receive income from cash benefits. The sum of cash benefits and original income is referred to as 'gross income'.
3   Households then pay direct taxes. Income after direct taxes have been subtracted from gross income and cash benefits are added is called 'disposable income'.
4   Indirect taxes are then paid on spending on goods and services. Disposable income minus indirect taxes is referred to as 'post-tax income'.
5   Households finally receive a benefit from services provided by the government (benefits in kind). Post-tax income plus benefits in kind is referred to as 'final income'.

Fiscal drag, poverty and low pay

The UK tax system has affected poverty partly through a process known as fiscal drag. Fiscal drag occurs in a progressive income tax system when the government fails to raise tax thresholds (or personal tax allowances) to keep pace with inflation. The left-hand panel of Figure 5.11 shows an income pyramid with the rich at the top and the poor at the bottom, and with the tax threshold fixed at an income of £10,000. In this example, a person with an income of £9,900 is just below the threshold and pays no income tax.

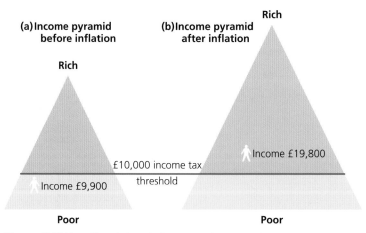

Figure 5.11 How fiscal drag brings people on low income into the tax net

Suppose that over the next few years both prices and all money incomes exactly double. In the absence of taxation, real incomes would remain unchanged, with households no better or worse off. But if the government fails to increase personal tax allowances in line with inflation (that is, to raise the tax threshold to £20,000), a doubling of the person's money income to £19,800 means that £9,800 of income is now taxable. The individual concerned is now worse off in real terms.

The new situation is shown in the right-hand panel of Figure 5.11. Inflation has dragged the low-paid worker across the basic tax threshold and into the tax net. In a similar way, higher-paid workers are dragged deeper into the tax net if the higher 40% and 45% **marginal tax rates** remain unadjusted for inflation.

KEY TERM

marginal tax rates the tax rate levied on the last pound of income received. The term can be applied solely to income taxes or to all the taxes a person or business pays.

In the UK, between 2010 and May 2015, the Coalition government tried to reduce relative poverty among the low-paid by raising income tax thresholds by more than the rate of inflation, taking the basic tax threshold to £10,600 in 2015. This policy has been continued by the Conservative government elected in 2015. The government announced that the tax-free personal allowance would increase to £11,000 in 2016/17, with the ambition to raise it to £12,500 by 2020. The increases in the personal tax allowance, or tax threshold, have taken a significant number of the low-paid out of the income tax net and 'clawed back' some of the fiscal drag that had taken place in earlier years.

The earnings trap or poverty trap

Fiscal drag is one of the causes of the poverty trap. As there are a number of ways in which the poor can be trapped in poverty, this particular trap, which traps the *low-waged* in relative poverty, is perhaps better called the earnings trap. It affects people in employment on low rates of pay, rather than the unemployed who are *unwaged*. Another cause of poverty affecting the homeless stems from the fact that to get a job they need a home, but to get a home they first need a job.

The immediate cause of the earnings trap is the overlap, illustrated in Figure 5.12, between the income tax threshold (the level of income at which income tax starts to be paid) and the means-tested welfare benefits ceiling (the level of income at which **means-tested benefits** cease to be paid). When welfare benefits are means-tested, a person's right to claim the benefit is reduced and eventually tapers away or disappears completely, as income rises. By contrast, **universal benefits** claimed as of right and is not dependent on income, although the state can claw back universal benefits that are taxable.

> ### KEY TERMS
> **means-tested benefits** the ability to claim these benefits depends on a person's income or 'means'.
>
> **universal benefits** benefits claimable of right and not dependent on a person's income.

> ### STUDY TIP
> Make sure you understand the difference, and also the relationship, between the poverty trap (or earnings trap) and the unemployment trap.

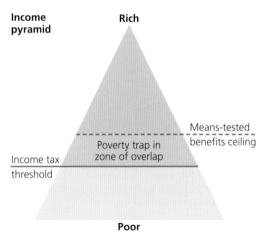

Figure 5.12 The earnings trap or poverty trap

A low-paid worker caught within the zone of overlap in Figure 5.12 not only pays income tax and national insurance contributions on each extra pound earned; he or she also loses part or all of the right to claim benefits. Thus low-paid workers and their families whose income falls within this zone of overlap become trapped in relative poverty, since any increase in their pay results in little or no increase (and in extreme cases a fall) in their disposable income.

The effective marginal rate of taxation of workers in poorly paid occupations is high when the loss of means-tested benefits is added to deductions through income tax and national insurance contributions. Calculated in this way, the marginal tax rates of the low-paid can be much higher (often around 70% and in extreme cases over 100%) than the top 45% rate currently paid by the better-off. Moreover, since the low-paid are generally employed in occupations yielding little job satisfaction or scope for legal tax avoidance, it can be argued that disincentives to work imposed by the UK tax and benefits system affect the poor at the lower end of the income pyramid much more than they affect the better-off.

The poverty trap can be eliminated by getting rid of the zone of overlap in the income pyramid illustrated in Figure 5.12. The income tax threshold could be raised to take low-waged households out of the tax net. Means-tested benefits could be replaced by universal benefits, though this is unlikely to happen. The national living wage rate might also reduce poverty by being raised to a higher rate than is currently planned in an attempt to prevent employers paying 'poverty wages'. However, raising the NLW could be counterproductive if unemployment increases as a result. At the time of its introduction, the Conservative government said that the NLW might lead to a loss of 60,000 jobs, which implies that a higher NLW rate would lead to even more job losses. However, the government also said that continuing economic growth would create many more jobs.

CASE STUDY 5.3

The introduction of Universal Credit may place more families in the poverty trap

When Universal Credit was announced in 2013, the UK government at the time (the Coalition government) stood accused that its changes to the tax and benefits system risked penalising almost 2 million low earners. A report by the anti-poverty campaigning group, the Joseph Rowntree Foundation, suggested that Universal Credit could see people worse off in work and struggling to manage their finances, with many left to deal with a more complex benefits system than before. The report stated that, while making work pay is the key aim of Universal Credit, many households are set to be worse off, or only marginally better off.

The report also raised serious concerns about a 'one-size-fits-all' IT-based delivery system and about potential IT failures which could quickly lead to backlogs, poor service and complaints.

However, in February 2015, the Coalition government claimed that in monetary terms, 3.1 million households would be entitled to more benefits as a result of the introduction of Universal Credit, while 2.8 million households would be entitled to less. The government also claimed that nobody would lose out during the initial transition — assuming their circumstances stayed the same. Iain Duncan Smith, the secretary of state for work and pensions, said that across all households, there would be an average household gain of £16 per month.

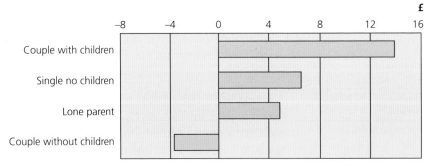

Figure 5.13 Average net change in family income for benefit recipients, by family type, £ per month, following the introduction of Universal Credit

Source: Department of Work and Pensions

Follow-up questions

1 Figure 5.7 on page 126 showed the changes in the UK's Gini index over the years between 1978 and 2013. How can the changes in income inequality between 2006 and 2010 be explained?

2 Research whether Universal Credit has reduced the poverty trap, or increased poverty and drawn more families into the poverty trap.

The unemployment trap

The poverty trap, described earlier, affects the low-waged in jobs rather than the unemployed who are unwaged. It is important not to confuse the poverty trap or earnings trap with the unemployment trap. The unemployment trap is closely related to the earnings trap, since both affect the poor and result from the nature of the tax and benefits systems. But people caught in the unemployment trap are out of work — at least in terms of officially declared employment. The unemployment trap contains unwaged social security claimants who choose unemployment. This is because they decide they are better off out of work, living on benefits, than in low-paid jobs paying income tax and NICs, and losing some or all of their right to claim means-tested benefits.

One link between the earnings trap and the unemployment trap is the underground economy — the hidden or informal economy in which people work, usually for cash payments, while failing to declare income and sometimes fraudulently claiming social security benefits. Low-paid workers in employment can escape the earnings trap by giving up declared work in order to claim unemployment benefits, while receiving income from undeclared work in the underground economy. The underground economy is sometimes called the 'black economy'.

CASE STUDY 5.4

Enrolling low-paid workers into workplace pension schemes

As they approach retirement, some workers wrongly believe that their entitlement to a state pension will provide them with more than just a 'poverty income'. As a result, too many have chosen not to opt into private pension plans. Two further factors have contributed to under-enrolment. In the first place, many low-paid and often young workers saw that contributing to a private pension scheme would leave them with even less of their already meagre incomes to spend on everyday living. Better to adopt a 'live-now, pay-later' approach to life and to spend now and not bother to save.

In the second place, private pension schemes were until recently often based on the 'opt-in' principle. Lethargy and inertia meant that too few workers bothered to join a private pension scheme.

Drawing on the insights of behavioural theory which we explained in Chapter 1, this is now changing. The UK government has introduced, since 2012, a system of automatic workplace pension contributions, in which a slice of workers' pay packets is diverted to savings pots to pay for their eventual pensions. Employers are obliged to pay in as well, and the government also adds a little extra through tax relief.

The new system, called automatic enrolment, is an important example of 'nudge' theory being taken on board in government policy. Unless employers already provide 'in-house' workplace pension schemes

(which have traditionally been available mostly for the better-paid professional workers), workers are now being automatically enrolled in workplace pension schemes — unless they choose to 'opt out'.

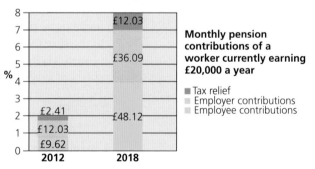

Monthly pension contributions of a worker currently earning £20,000 a year

- Tax relief
- Employer contributions
- Employee contributions

Figure 5.14 Example of employee and employer contributions to a typical workplace pension, together with tax relief, 2012 and 2018

The 'opt-in default' scheme is being introduced gradually over a 6-year period, extending to 2018. It is expected that relatively few eligible workers will decide to opt out. Once again, this is partly due to lethargy, but workers also know opting out will lead to the loss of employers' contributions. Workers below the age of 22 will still have to opt in, as will part-time workers. Since the pension contributions of low-paid workers are generally small, the value of their eventual pension will usually be less than £5,000 (at 2016 prices). When the private pensions have been added to the state pension, the retirement incomes of previously low-paid workers will still be relatively low compared to the more fortunate pensioners.

Automatic enrolment may also have the unintended consequence of hastening the introduction by so-called rogue employers of more casual part-time employment and zero-hours employment contracts.

Follow-up questions

1 Explain the phrase 'the value of their eventual pension will usually be less than £5,000 (at 2016 prices)'.
2 What is a zero-hours employment contract?

The consequences of government policies which affect poverty and the distribution of income and wealth

We have made passing reference to some of these consequences in earlier sections of this chapter. Among the points we have made are:

- Redistributive policies can make the distributions of income and wealth more equal and reduce relative poverty. Many would argue that such policies are equitable. However, by reducing incentives to work hard and to be entrepreneurial, redistributive polices may have adverse unintended consequences, such as slower economic growth and loss of international competitiveness.
- Redistributive policies can alleviate child poverty, old-age poverty and fuel poverty, but these aims have been only partially achieved.
- Arguably, faster economic growth provides the main avenue for reducing absolute poverty, and perhaps also relative poverty, but according to pro-free-market economists, wider inequalities in the distributions of income and wealth may be necessary if fast growth is to be achieved and sustained.
- Some fiscal measures, used to try to reduce poverty and narrow inequalities in the distribution of income, have resulted in the development of the poverty and unemployment traps.

SUMMARY

- Inequalities in the distribution of UK income and wealth have widened over recent decades but have narrowed slightly since 2010.
- Inequalities in the distribution of wealth have always been wider than those in the distribution of income.
- Equality must not be confused with equity or fairness.
- In the past, governments have used progressive taxation and transfers to the poor as the main methods of making the distribution of post-tax income more equal.
- Fiscal drag in the tax system has contributed to the existence of a poverty trap or earnings trap, and also to an unemployment trap.
- It is important to distinguish between absolute and relative poverty.
- Absolute poverty is a condition characterised by severe deprivation of basic human needs.
- A household is relatively poor if its income is below a specified proportion of average income for all households.

- Old age, unemployment and low wages are important causes of poverty in the UK.
- Government intervention to reduce poverty may lead to government failures that may make matters worse.
- Pro-free-market economists focus on the disincentive effects of progressive taxation and transfers, whereas interventionist economists argue that the policies are necessary if post-tax income inequalities and poverty are to be reduced.

Questions

1 Describe how inequalities in the distribution of income and wealth have widened in recent years.

2 Evaluate the view that progressive taxation and transfers should not be used to reduce income inequalities and poverty.

3 Evaluate the view that the government should rely on market forces to determine the distribution of income and wealth in the UK, and should reduce direct intervention in the economy which has aimed at making the UK more equal.

4 Explain the difference between absolute and relative poverty.

5 Do you agree that faster economic growth which is needed to reduce poverty necessarily requires that the distribution of income becomes less equal? Justify your answer.

6

Revisiting market failure and government intervention in markets

In Chapter 5 of Book 1, we introduced you to the circumstances in which markets can fail and then went on to explain examples of market failure such as public goods, positive and negative externalities and merit and demerit goods. In this chapter, having briefly revisited these examples of market failures, we look in more detail at externalities and merit and demerit goods by introducing, and then applying, the concepts of marginal private and external cost and benefit. The chapter then focuses on environmental externalities, property rights and information problems associated with market failure.

The second half of the chapter introduces some 'industrial policy' issues. These are government competition policy, public ownership versus the privatisation of industries and services, and the regulation and deregulation of markets

LEARNING OBJECTIVES
This chapter will:

- remind you of some of the main types of market failure described in Chapter 5 of Book 1
- introduce the concepts of marginal private, external and social cost and benefit
- use these concepts in the analysis of negative and positive externalities, and merit and demerit goods
- apply the concept of allocative efficiency to market failure
- consider a number of environmental market failures
- explain the importance of property rights in the public policy response to externalities
- analyse merit and demerit goods in the context of information problems
- explain how governments use competition policy to try to reduce or eliminate the market failures associated with monopoly and imperfectly competitive markets for goods and services
- compare the reasons for public ownership and privatisation of firms and industries
- assess the track record of the UK's privatised industries
- explain how governments use both regulation and deregulation in contexts such as dealing with market failures and in competition policy

6.1 Marginal analysis and market failure

Market failure revisited

Market failure occurs whenever the market mechanism or price mechanism performs unsatisfactorily, with the result that resource misallocation occurs.

Resource allocation and misallocation

Resource allocation is about how factors of production or inputs into the production process are allocated between competing uses. Within an economy, the best possible resource allocation occurs when factors of production are employed in a productively efficient way and also in a way which maximises social welfare or the happiness of the population. It follows from this that resource misallocation occurs when inputs are employed in such a way that productive inefficiency results, and the economy fails to maximise social welfare.

Two types of market failure

There are two main ways in which markets fail. Markets can function inefficiently or they can function inequitably. It is also useful to distinguish between **complete market failure**, when the market simply does not exist, and **partial market failure**, when the market functions but produces the 'wrong' quantity of a good or service. In the former case, there is a **missing market**. In the latter case, the good or service may be provided too cheaply, in which case it is over-produced and over-consumed. Alternatively, as in monopoly, the good may be too expensive, in which case under-production and under-consumption result.

Public and private goods

Private goods

Most goods are **private goods**, possessing two important characteristics. The owners can exercise private **property rights**, preventing other people from using the good or consuming its benefits. This is called excludability. The second characteristic possessed by a private good is rivalry or diminishability. When one person consumes a private good, less of its benefits are available for other people. Private goods also have a third characteristic: rejectability. People can opt out and refuse to purchase private goods.

Public goods

Public goods such as national defence exhibit the opposite characteristics to those of a private good, namely **non-excludability** and **non-rivalry**, together with a third characteristic of **non-rejectability**.

Non-excludability means that it is impossible to provide a good to one person while preventing others from enjoying it. If the good is provided to one person, it is provided to all.

KEY TERMS

market failure occurs when the price mechanism fails to allocate scarce resources in a productively efficient way and when the operation of market forces leads to an allocatively inefficient outcome.

complete market failure a market fails to function at all and a 'missing market' results.

partial market failure a market does function, but it delivers the 'wrong' quantity of a good or service, which results in resource misallocation.

missing market the absence of a market for a good or service, most commonly in the case of public goods and externalities.

KEY TERMS

private good a good which exhibits the characteristics of excludability and rivalry.

property rights the exclusive authority to determine how a resource is used. In the case of a private property right, the owner of private property such as a bar of chocolate in a sweet shop has the right to prevent other people from consuming the bar unless they are prepared to pay a price to the owner.

141

KEY TERMS

public good a good which exhibits the characteristics of non-excludability and non-rivalry.

non-excludability a property of a public good which means that if it is provided for one person it is provided for all.

non-rivalry a property of a public good which means that when a good is consumed by one person, it does not reduce the amount available for others.

non-rejectability a property of a public good which means that if the good is provided, it is impossible for a person to 'opt out' and not gain its benefits.

free-rider problem occurs when non-excludability leads to a situation in which not enough customers choose to pay for a good, preferring instead to free ride, with the result that the incentive to provide the good through the market disappears and a missing market may result. (A free rider is someone who benefits without paying.)

quasi-public good a good which has characteristics of both a public and private good, e.g. it might be non-excludable but rival, or excludable but non-rival.

Non-rivalry means that when a good is consumed by one person, it does not reduce the amount available for others. For example, when a person benefits from nuclear defence, it does not prevent other people from experiencing similar benefits. By contrast, an item of food such as a strawberry is rival because when one person eats the strawberry, nobody else can consume it.

As mentioned, nuclear defence is an example of a public good. If prices were to be charged for the benefits provided by the ring of nuclear missiles protecting the UK, then, without coercion, people could refuse to pay but still enjoy the benefits. Any attempt by the private provider to retaliate, by preventing those who do not pay from receiving the service, will not work. If the benefits are withdrawn from one person, they are withdrawn from everyone. By the same token, as is the case with nuclear defence, if the benefits are provided for one person, they are provided for everybody.

Nevertheless, all individuals face the temptation to consume without paying, or to free ride. If enough people choose to free ride, market provision of nuclear defence breaks down. The incentive to provide the service through the market disappears. There is a missing market. Assuming that the majority of the country's inhabitants believe nuclear defence to be necessary (that is, a 'good' rather than a 'bad'), the market fails because it fails to provide a service for which there is a need.

Public goods are also associated with the **free-rider problem**. Free riding occurs when people decide to gain the benefits of a good or service while refusing to pay for it. In the case of private goods, the property of excludability prevents people from free riding. However, with pure public goods, non-excludability leads to free riding.

STUDY TIP
Make sure you understand the difference between a private good and a public good, and can give examples of both.

Quasi-public goods or non-pure public goods

Most public goods are **quasi-public goods** (or non-pure public goods) rather than pure public goods. This is often because various methods can be used to exclude free riders. Non-pure public goods include roads, television and radio broadcasts, street lighting and lighthouses. In principle, roads can be converted into private goods, provided for profit through the market. This could be done by limiting points of access, by constructing toll gates or by introducing a scheme of electronic road pricing. However, the cost of making the good excludable may be very high, as in the case of road-pricing schemes on minor roads. (Read Case Study 6.1 to find out more about the case for road pricing on congested roads.)

TV broadcasting is a prime example of a product that was a pure public good before the introduction of cable and satellite technology. But, with these relatively new methods of broadcasting, it has become a quasi-public good, in that it is now excludable but non-rival.

STUDY TIP
Make sure you understand the difference between a public good and a quasi-public good, and can give examples of both.

Public goods and allocative efficiency

In Chapter 3 we explained that the allocatively efficient or 'correct' quantity of any good produced and consumed is the quantity that people choose to consume when $P = MC$. However, in the case of a public good, assuming it is already being provided, the MC of providing the good to an extra consumer is zero. Allocative efficiency therefore occurs when $P = 0$ and the good is free for consumers. But private entrepreneurs only willingly provide goods if profits can be made, and for this to happen the price must be above zero ($P > 0$). In the case of a quasi-public good such as a road, this means that markets can only provide a road if the price of road use is set above the marginal cost of supply ($P > MC$). This reduces road use to below the allocatively efficient level. Hence, to achieve an allocatively efficient level of road use, motorists should not be charged for driving on the road, at least until the road becomes congested (again, see Case Study 6.1).

As we have already explained, non-rivalry means that when an extra person benefits from a public good, the benefits available to other people are not reduced. In turn, this means that the marginal cost incurred by the provider of the public good when an extra person benefits from the good is zero ($MC = 0$). For example, when a person switches on a television set, the availability and benefits of the broadcast programme are not diminished for people viewing the programme on other television sets. Equally, the broadcasting company incurs no extra cost.

Public goods and government-provided goods

Students often wrongly define a public good as a good that is provided by the government. The word 'public' in 'public good' refers to the fact that members of the general public cannot be excluded from enjoying the good's benefits. It is this that *causes* market failure. To correct the market failure, governments often provide public goods. Government-provided goods include public goods such as defence, police and roads, but they also include merit goods such as education and healthcare.

Education and healthcare are both private goods and merit goods. They are both excludable and rival. Although it does not generally happen in the NHS, it is perfectly possible to deny someone access to a doctor if they refuse to pay — the service is excludable. Also, if an individual has a consultation with a doctor, this reduces the time the doctor has available to see other patients — the marginal cost is not zero and the service is rival. Both education and healthcare can be and are provided through the market mechanism.

Public 'bads'

A 'bad' is the opposite of a good. People are prepared to pay a price to gain the benefits of a good such as a TV set. Equally, they are prepared to pay a price to avoid consuming a 'bad', such as the household rubbish they produce. But in the case of many 'bads', known as public 'bads', people can free ride by dumping the 'bads' they produce on others. Examples are the emission of pollution into the atmosphere and fly tipping rubbish in public parks or in other people's gardens. If a private sector company tries to charge a price for rubbish removal, households may avoid paying the price by dumping their garbage. This is why local authorities empty dustbins without charging, financing rubbish removal through local taxation.

ACTIVITY

Get together with two or three fellow students. Each of you should list as many situations as possible in which you 'free ride'. Also list and briefly describe five goods that you own, over which you can exercise private property rights. Compare your answers.

143

Externalities

An **externality** is a special type of public good or public bad, which is dumped by those who produce it on to other people who receive or consume it, whether or not they choose to. (These people are known as third parties, and the externality is sometimes called a spin-off effect.) Because externalities are generated and received outside the market, they also provide examples of missing markets.

Externalities are classified in two main ways:

● as negative externalities or positive externalities, also known as external costs and external benefits
● as production externalities or consumption externalities

A **negative externality** is generated when a firm or an individual making a decision to produce or consume a good or service does not have to pay the full cost of the decision. If the production of a good generates a negative externality, then the cost to society is greater than the cost incurred by the firm itself. Road congestion is a negative externality.

Likewise, a **positive externality** is generated when an individual or firm making a decision does not receive the full benefit of the decision. The benefit to the individual or firm is less than the benefit to society. The pollination of fruit trees on neighbouring farms is a positive externality resulting from bee-keeping.

As is the case with public goods, the production and consumption of externalities leads to the free-rider problem. The provider of an external benefit such as a beautiful view cannot charge a market price to any willing free riders who enjoy it. Conversely, the unwilling free riders who receive or consume external costs such as pollution and noise cannot charge a price to the polluter for the bad that they reluctantly consume.

The concepts of marginal private, external and social costs and benefits

At the heart of traditional microeconomic theory lies the assumption that, in a market situation, an economic agent considers only the private costs and benefits resulting from its market actions, ignoring any costs and benefits imposed on others. For the agent, private benefit maximisation occurs when:

marginal private benefit (MPB) = marginal private cost (MPC)

However, social benefit maximisation, which maximises the public interest or the welfare of the whole community, occurs when:

marginal social benefit (MSB) = marginal social cost (MSC)

Orthodox or traditional economic theory usually assumes that households and firms seek to maximise their private benefit or self-interest, net of costs, and not the wider social interest of the whole community. They ignore the effects of their actions on other people. However, when externalities are generated, costs and benefits are inevitably imposed on others, so maximising net private benefit no longer coincides with the maximisation of net social benefit.

Social benefit is defined as private benefit plus external benefit. As a result:

marginal social benefit = marginal private benefit + marginal external benefit

($MSB = MPB + MEB$)

Likewise, social cost is defined as private cost plus external cost, which means that:

marginal social cost = marginal private cost + marginal external cost

$(MSC = MPC + MEC)$

Negative externalities and allocative inefficiency

In Chapter 3, we explained how a perfectly competitive economy can, in theory at least, achieve a state of allocative efficiency when it brings about an outcome in which $P = MC$ in all the markets that make up the economy. However, allocative efficiency could only occur if:

- there were competitive markets for all goods and services, including future markets
- there were no economies of scale
- markets were simultaneously in equilibrium

However, it is impossible for markets throughout the economy — or indeed throughout the world economy — to meet all these conditions, so allocative efficiency is an abstract rather than a real-life concept. And in the context of market failure, we can now add a fourth requirement for allocative efficiency to be achieved:

- when $P = MC$ there would have to be no externalities, negative or positive

If we ignore the four bullet points set out above, in the long run, profit maximisation occurs in a perfect market at the price at which $P = MPC$. In the absence of externalities, this also means that the price equals the marginal social cost (MSC) of production: $P = MSC$. But as we have seen, when the production of a good causes pollution, external costs are generated, with the result that $MSC > MPC$. This means that when $P = MPC$, $P < MSC$.

To achieve allocative efficiency, price must equal the *true* marginal cost of production: that is, the marginal social cost and not just the marginal private cost. But in a market situation, profit-maximising firms are assumed only to take account of private costs and benefits. When externalities exist, therefore, the market mechanism fails to achieve an allocatively efficient outcome.

To put it another way, firms evade part of the true or real cost of production by dumping the externality on third parties. The price that the consumer pays for the good reflects only the private cost of production, and not the true cost, which includes the external cost. The firm's output is thus under-priced, encouraging too much consumption. A misallocation of resources results: too much consumption, and hence too much production, means that too many scarce resources are being used by the industry that is producing the negative externalities.

Production and consumption externalities

In this section, we go one stage further than we did in our coverage of externalities in Book 1 by explaining production and consumption externalities with the use of marginal analysis.

> **STUDY TIP**
> Before reading any further, go back to Book 1 and read through the coverage of externalities in Chapter 5, section 5.4 (pages 104–08).

A **production externality** is generated, usually by firms, in the course of producing a good or service. By contrast, a **consumption externality** is generated by households and individuals in the course of consuming a good or service.

Using marginal analysis to show how negative production externalities cause market failure

In this section we return to the example of pollution emitted by a fossil-fuel burning power station which we used in Book 1, pages 104–5. We initially assumed that when a coal-burning power station generates electricity, only negative externalities are discharged and there are no positive externalities. Given this simplification, the marginal private benefit accruing to the power station from the production of electricity, and the marginal social benefit received by the whole community, are the same and shown by the downward-sloping curve in Figure 6.1. But, because pollution is discharged in the course of production, the marginal social cost of electricity production exceeds the marginal private cost incurred by the power station.

In the diagram, the MSC curve is positioned above the MPC curve. The vertical distance between two curves shows the marginal external cost (MEC) at each level of electricity production.

The power station maximises private benefit by producing output Q_1, where $MPC = MPB$. Q_1 is immediately below point A in Figure 6.1. However, the socially optimal level of output is Q_2, where $MSC = MSB$. Q_2 is immediately below point B in Figure 6.1. The privately optimal level of output is thus greater than the socially optimal level of production. To put it another way, market forces over-produce electricity by the amount Q_1 minus Q_2. The market fails because the power station produces the wrong quantity of the good: namely, too much electricity. At the free-market price of P_1, electricity is too cheap. The price would have to rise to P_2 to bring about the socially optimal level of consumption.

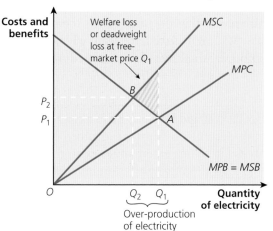

Figure 6.1 A coal-burning power station generating pollution (a negative production externality)

The shaded area in Figure 6.1 illustrates the 'loss' of welfare or deadweight loss (DWL), which exists at the free market output, Q_1 (where $MPC = MPB$), all the way back to the socially optimum output, Q_2. This is because for units Q_2 to Q_1, the social cost of producing each unit of electricity is greater than the benefit society derives from each unit produced — that is, $MSC > MSB$. Society would be better off if these units, Q_2 to Q_1, were not produced and the resources were transferred to the production of other products. When production takes place at the socially optimal output (where $MSB = MSC$), the DWL is eliminated.

QUANTITATIVE SKILLS 6.1

Worked example: calculating private, social and external costs

Table 6.1 shows the costs incurred when producing different quantities of a chemical. Some of the cells in the table are blank.

Table 6.1 Costs incurred in chemical production

Output of chemicals (tonnes per week)	Marginal private cost (£000)	Marginal social cost (£000)	Marginal external costs (£000)
500	100		20
600		160	30
700	160	200	

Copy the table and insert the correct numbers in the blank spaces.

The complete table is shown below:

Output of chemicals (tonnes per week)	Marginal private cost (£000)	Marginal social cost (£000)	Marginal external costs (£000)
500	100	**120**	20
600	**130**	160	30
700	160	200	**40**

The correct numbers to insert in the three blank spaces should be calculated by using the following equation:

$$MSC = MPC + MEC$$

In the top row: **£120,000** = £100,000 + £20,000
In the middle row: £160,000 = **£130,000** + £30,000
In the bottom row: £200,000 = £160,000 + **£40,000**

(Note: remember to include the thousands and the £ sign in your answers.)

Using marginal analysis to show how positive production externalities cause market failure

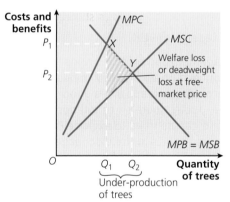

Figure 6.2 A commercial forestry company generating positive production externalities

Whereas *negative* production externalities (illustrated in Figure 6.1) lead to the marginal social costs of production exceeding marginal private costs of production, when *positive* production externalities are generated, the marginal social costs of production lie *below* the marginal private costs incurred by the producers of the good or service. This is illustrated in Figure 6.2, which shows the costs incurred when a commercial forestry company plants trees.

The positive production externalities generated by tree planting include improved water retention in the soil and a carbon sink effect, whereby trees absorb greenhouse or global-warming gases from the atmosphere. As stated, positive production externalities such as these mean that the *MSC* curve is positioned below the *MPC* curve. The vertical distance between the two curves shows a *negative* marginal external cost (*MEC*) at each level of tree planting. (A *negative* marginal external cost is exactly the same as a *positive* marginal external benefit enjoyed by society as a whole.)

The shaded area in Figure 6.2 illustrates the 'loss' of welfare or deadweight loss (*DWL*), which exists at the free market output, Q_1 at point *X* (where *MPC* = *MPB*), all the way forward to the socially optimal output, Q_2. When production takes place at the socially optimal output (where *MSB* = *MSC*) at point *Y*, the *DWL* is eliminated. This is sometimes referred to as a 'welfare gain'. There is a net gain in social welfare if the trees between Q_1 and Q_2 are planted because the *MSB* is greater than the *MSC* for each of these trees.

In order to maximise its private benefit, the commercial forestry plants Q_1 trees. (This is the free-market level of output.) Q_1 is immediately below point *X*, where *MPC* = *MPB*. However, Q_1 is less than the socially optimal level of output Q_2, located below point *Y*, where *MSC* = *MSB*. Figure 6.2

STUDY TIP

Note that in Figure 6.2 the 'spillover' benefits generated by production (positive external benefits) are depicted as a 'negative external cost'. The planting of trees reduces the costs imposed on society by pollution and hence the total cost to society of planting the trees is less than the cost to the firm.

illustrates the fact that, when positive production externalities are generated, the market fails because too little of the good is produced and consumed. Under-production and under-consumption are depicted by the distance Q_2 minus Q_1.

QUANTITATIVE SKILLS 6.2

Worked example: marginal costs and benefits of vaccination

Table 6.2 shows some of the costs a consumer incurs and the benefits received by her family and also by society when her young child receives a measles vaccination.

Table 6.2 Costs and benefits of a vaccination

Marginal private cost of the vaccination (£)	Marginal private benefit resulting from the vaccination (£)	Marginal social benefit resulting from the vaccination (£)
20	100	1,000

1 **What is the marginal external benefit resulting from the vaccination?**

2 **Suppose evidence shows that a fraction of children who are vaccinated suffer brain damage as a result of receiving the treatment. This creates a marginal social cost for society of £1,200 per vaccination. On the basis of these figures, should the health service recommend that children be vaccinated?**

1 Using the equation $MSB = MPB + MEB$, the marginal external benefit received by society from the vaccination of a child is £900.

2 Given the extra information, the marginal social cost of each vaccination exceeds the marginal social benefit by £200. Marginal social benefit is £1,000, but marginal social cost is £1,200. On the basis of these figures alone, the health service should not recommend that children are vaccinated.

CASE STUDY 6.1

Road pricing

In recent years the issue of whether or not to charge motorists for the use of roads has entered public debate. The issue centres largely on road *congestion*, rather than on pollution, because fuel taxes are a better way of reducing the environmental pollution caused by vehicles burning fossil fuels. Motorists are now charged for driving in central London during business hours, and a private sector firm owns and runs a section of toll motorway north of Birmingham. Electronic pricing has become technically possible and is likely *eventually* to be used in future road-charging schemes. However, in the short term, the power of the motoring lobby, which argues that motorists should enjoy the freedom to use of the public highway without charge, is likely to delay the widespread introduction of road pricing, at least in the UK.

The case for and against road pricing brings together issues concerning both public goods and negative externalities. Roads are a good example of a quasi-public good, since toll booths or electronic pricing can be used to exclude free riders. Road use also results in the discharge of negative externalities. The extent to which negative externalities are produced depends in part upon whether the road is congested or uncongested. During peak periods, a rise in the number of road users increases the journey time of other road users. A negative externality is generated.

Toll booths are used to exclude free riders in road-charging schemes

In the following analysis, we shall assume that commercial vehicles but not private cars use the road. This means that all the negative externalities unleashed by road users are negative production externalities. However, road congestion could also legitimately be treated as a negative consumption externality — if generated by the use of private cars.

Given our simplifying assumption, Figure 6.3 illustrates the benefits and costs resulting from an extra commercial vehicle using the road, first when the road is uncongested, and then when road congestion has set in. The diagram shows the flow of traffic (for example, the number of commercial vehicles travelling on the road per hour) on the horizontal axis and the cost per journey on the vertical axis.

When the traffic flow is less than F_1, an extra vehicle on the road does not impose any negative externalities or external costs upon other road users — provided we ignore the pollution emitted by the vehicles. In this situation, road use should be free, to encourage the allocatively efficient or socially optimal level of use. For levels of traffic flow between zero and F_1, the marginal social cost of road use equals the marginal private cost borne by vehicles and their owners ($MSC = MPC$). But once the road becomes congested (at flows of traffic greater than F_1), this is no longer the case, and there is a case for road pricing to provide the incentive to reduce road use.

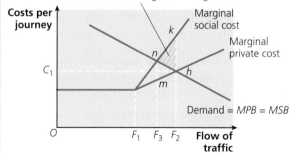

Shaded area shows welfare loss to society if road users are not charged for congestion

Figure 6.3 The benefits and costs of driving on an uncongested and a congested road

For traffic flows above F_1, each commercial vehicle driven on the road adds to traffic congestion, and all road users then suffer from increased journey times and the frustration of being stuck on a congested road. Beyond F_1, the marginal social cost of motoring is greater than the marginal private cost incurred by the last commercial vehicle to drive on the road ($MSC > MPC$). But in the absence of road pricing, when deciding whether or not to drive on the road, road users consider only the private cost of motoring and not the external cost dumped on others. Providing there is no charge for road use, commercial vehicles are driven up to traffic flow F_2 (at point h). At F_2, the marginal private benefit of driving the vehicle equals the marginal private cost ($MPB = MPC$). At this point, the private cost incurred by the marginal vehicle to use the road is C_1, but this is less than the social cost of the marginal journey, which includes the marginal cost of congestion caused by the marginal vehicle but suffered by other road users. At traffic flow F_2, the marginal external cost of congestion imposed on other road users is shown by the distance $(k - h)$.

A misallocation of resources is the result. Commercial vehicles make more journeys than they would, had their owners or drivers borne the full social cost of using their vehicles. The shaded triangle bounded by the points n, k and h measures the welfare loss suffered by society at the privately optimal traffic flow F_2, where $MPB = MPC$.

Arguably, there is a case for road pricing when roads become congested. Allocative efficiency is improved when a motorist is charged a price equal to the marginal external cost imposed on other road users, as a result of the journey. The optimal congestion charge would be $(n - m)$, which measures the marginal external cost of a journey at the socially optimal level of road use, F_3. Some congestion still occurs at F_3, but it is less than at F_2, and the owners or drivers of commercial vehicles pay for the congestion they generate. The congestion charge or road price internalises the externality. Journeys that are worth undertaking in the absence of a congestion charge are not worthwhile once the appropriate charge is imposed.

149

Follow-up questions

1 Do you agree that fuel taxes are the best way of reducing the environmental pollution caused by vehicles burning fossil fuels? Justify your answer.
2 The passage states that electronic pricing has become technically possible. If this is the case, why have hardly any road-pricing schemes been introduced in the UK?

Demerit goods and merit goods

We first explained demerit goods and merit goods in Book 1, section 5.5 (pages 108–14). You might wish to go back to these pages and refresh your memory of the meaning of demerit and merit goods.

There are two main characteristics of a **demerit good**, the first centring on negative externalities, and the second on *information problems* that affect the good's consumption. With the first characteristic, the benefit the smoker or drinker derives from consumption is greater than the benefits to society. The second characteristic is based on the distinction between the short-term and long-term net benefit derived by the person consuming a demerit good.

- **Demerit goods and negative externalities.** When a person consumes a demerit good such as tobacco, negative externalities are generated which are unpleasant or harmful for other people. People unwillingly breathe in the fumes the smoker discharges, with eventual harmful effects on their health. (This is the problem of passive smoking.) Smelly clothing is a more trivial example of a negative externality in consumption that is caused by smoking. Hence, the marginal social benefit is less than the marginal private benefit.
- **Demerit goods and information problems.** When teenagers first get the 'habit' of smoking, drinking or drug taking, they may either ignore the long-term private costs they may suffer later in life, or downplay the significance of these costs. Either way, young people tend to be short-sighted with respect to the costs of consuming demerit goods. A person who started drinking as a teenager may regret the decision later in life when suffering an alcohol-related illness. Hence, the long-run net benefit of consuming a demerit good is less than the short-run benefit.

These characteristics of demerit goods mean that free-market provision leads to market failure. Left to themselves, markets over-provide demerit goods. If this argument is accepted, there is a case for government intervention to reduce or even to eliminate production and consumption of a good such as tobacco, through taxation and/or regulation. Indeed, at the extreme, production and/or consumption of a demerit good can be banned, though since these goods yield utility to their users, at least in the short run, banning may simply drive production and consumption into an illegal and criminalised black market.

It should be noted that not all products that generate negative externalities in consumption and whose consumption is affected by imperfect information are regarded as demerit goods. A value judgement is also involved. For example, there is general, but not universal, agreement in our society that smoking, recreational drugs and alcohol are undesirable products and that their consumption should be controlled.

In a similar way to a demerit good, a **merit good** has two important characteristics: positive externalities in consumption and information problems which distort a consumer's choice on what is the privately optimal level of consumption.

- **Merit goods and positive externalities.** When a person consumes a merit good such as healthcare, the resulting positive externalities benefit other people. An obvious example is that healthy people seldom spread diseases. The social benefit enjoyed by the wider community is greater than the private benefit enjoyed by the healthy person.
- **Merit goods and information problems.** For a merit good such as healthcare, the long-term private benefit of consumption exceeds the

ACTIVITY

If the eventual long-term private cost of smoking is £200,000 while the short-run private cost of buying cigarettes over future decades is only £30,000, why do people still smoke? Discuss this question with your fellow students.

short-term private benefit of consumption. But when deciding how much to consume, individuals take account of short-term costs and benefits, ignoring or undervaluing the long-term private costs and benefits. In the UK, Open University students, whose ages range from 22 to well over 70, have been known to say: 'If only I had got my qualifications when I was younger; unfortunately I did not value education when I was at school.'

Whereas free-market provision leads to over-provision of a demerit good such as alcoholic drink, it leads to under-provision of merit goods such as education and healthcare. As a result, there is an argument for governments to provide these goods, or to subsidise market provision. Regulation, in the form of compulsory consumption of education and healthcare services such as vaccination, can also be used.

However, not all products that generate positive externalities in consumption and whose long-term benefits are greater that the short-term benefits are judged to be merit goods. In the case of merit goods, a value judgement is made that these products are more important than most other products — for example, in the UK it is generally agreed that children should not be denied access to education and people who are ill should not be denied access to healthcare.

EXTENSION MATERIAL

Merit goods and uncertainty, moral hazard and adverse selection

Uncertainty about future long-term benefits and costs contributes to under-consumption of merit goods. For example, a person does not know in advance when, if ever, the services of a specialist surgeon might be needed. Sudden illness may lead to a situation in which a person cannot afford to pay for costly surgery, if provided solely through a conventional market.

One market-orientated solution is for private medical insurance to pay for the cost of treatment at the time when it is needed. However, private medical insurance often fails to pay for treatment for the chronically ill or for the poor. Private insurance may also fail to provide medical care for risk-takers in society who decide not to buy insurance, as distinct from risk-averters, who are always the most ready customers for insurance.

Like all private insurance schemes, healthcare insurance suffers from two further problems, both of which lead to market failure. These are the problems of **moral hazard** and **adverse selection**. Moral hazard is demonstrated by the tendency of people covered by health insurance to be less careful about their health because they know that, in the event of accident or illness, the insurance company will pick up the bill. Adverse selection relates to the fact that people whose health risks are greatest are also the people most likely to try to buy insurance policies. Insurance companies react by refusing to sell health policies to those who most need private health insurance. For those to whom they do sell policies, premium levels are set sufficiently high to enable the companies to remain profitable when settling the claims of customers facing moral hazard or who have been adversely selected.

Public collective provision, perhaps organised by private sector companies but guaranteed by the state and funded by compulsory insurance, may be a better solution. Both private and public collective-provision schemes are a response to the fact that the demand or need for medical care is much more predictable for a large group of people than for an individual.

KEY TERMS

moral hazard the tendency of individuals and firms, once insured against some contingency, to behave so as to make that contingency more likely.

adverse selection a situation in which people who buy insurance often have a better idea of the risks they face than do the sellers of insurance. People who know they face large risks are more likely to buy insurance than people who face small risks.

Using marginal analysis to show how negative consumption externalities cause over-consumption of demerit goods

According to the first characteristic of a demerit good given in the previous section, the consumption of goods such as tobacco and alcohol by an individual leads to the dumping of negative externalities on other individuals or third parties. Figure 6.4 shows that too much tobacco is consumed when bought at market prices unadjusted by taxes or by a minimum price law. At least in the short term, the privately optimal level of consumption is Q_1, where $MPC = MPB$. This is greater than the socially optimal level of consumption, Q_2, located where $MSC = MSB$. Free-market provision of demerit goods therefore leads to over-consumption, and hence over-production of tobacco.

Because the negative externalities in this example are generated when people smoke (for example, the smoke breathed in by passive smokers who do not enjoy the fumes they inhale), the externalities are *consumption* externalities rather than *production* externalities. As a result, the marginal social benefit (MSB) curve of the whole community lies below the marginal private benefit (MPB) curve of the smokers themselves, with the distance between the two curves showing the negative externality.

To bring about the socially optimal level of consumption at Q_2, an indirect tax equal to the distance between points B and C in Figure 6.4 could be imposed, which would increase the price of tobacco to P_2. The tax needs to set equal to the marginal external cost (MEC) of consumption at the socially optimal level of consumption (Q_2).

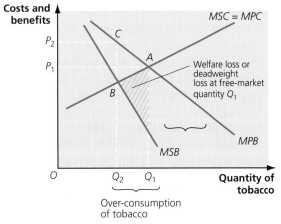

Figure 6.4 How over-consumption of a demerit good occurs in a free market

STUDY TIP

It is important to understand that the costs imposed by consumers on society (the negative externalities) are depicted in Figure 6.4 as negative benefits. Thus the distance between points B and C on the graph can be interpreted either as the marginal external cost of smoking or as the *negative* external benefit of smoking at the socially optimal level of smoking, Q_2. The two are the same. For example, if someone is smoking at a party, the pleasure derived from the event by non-smokers is reduced; hence the cumulative benefit to all the party-goers is less than the pleasure derived by the smoker.

Note also that, for the socially optimal level of smoking to be zero (in which case a ban might be imposed on smoking, the MSB curve in Figure 6.4 would need to positioned well to the left of the curve in the diagram, intersecting the MSC curve at zero quantity.

TEST YOURSELF 6.1

Table 6.3 shows the marginal private and external benefits and the marginal private and external costs of two products at their free-market equilibrium level of output.

Table 6.3 Private and external costs and benefits of products W and Z

	Product W (£)	Product Z (£)
Marginal private benefit	400	140
Marginal external benefit	100	80
Marginal private cost	400	140
Marginal external cost	180	60

Taking into account the information provided in the table, for each of the products W and Z, is there a case for increasing the level of output above the free-market output, or is there a case for reducing the level of output so that it is below the free-market output?

EXTENSION MATERIAL

Are there such things as demerit goods and merit goods?

Some economists, usually of a pro-free-market persuasion, question whether any goods are demerit goods or merit goods. These economists are libertarians who believe that individuals are the best judges of what is bad or good for them. People should be free, within the law, to smoke or drink themselves to death, or to prevent their children being vaccinated against measles. According to this view, it is not the state's role to intervene in individual behaviour, except when the pursuit of self-interest harms other people. For example, the state should prevent motorists from exercising the freedom to drive on the wrong side of the road.

Anti-libertarians, however, do not accept this view of individual freedom of choice. They argue that over-consumption of demerit goods and under-consumption of merit goods invariably leads to other people being harmed and that the libertarian argument is specious. Taxation, subsidy and regulation are fully justified as means of altering individual behaviour.

Lying somewhat in between these two approaches are the insights of behavioural economists, who argue that individuals should be given as much choice as possible in deciding what is good for them, but that governments should use appropriate policies to 'nudge' them in the direction deemed socially optimal.

Using marginal analysis to show how positive consumption externalities cause under-consumption of merit goods

If we consider the first characteristic of a merit good that we gave earlier, the consumption of goods such as education or healthcare benefits the individual consumer but also leads to the wider community benefiting from the positive externalities generated. The community gains the advantages of an educated (and civilised) population, and in the case of healthcare, a healthy population means there are fewer people to spread diseases.

Taking education as an example, when schooling is available only through the market, at prices unadjusted by subsidy, too little of the merit good ends up being consumed. Many people (especially the poor) end up uneducated, or at least relatively uneducated. In Figure 6.5, the privately optimal level of consumption is Q_1, determined at point A,

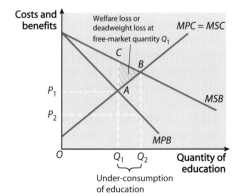

Figure 6.5 Under-consumption of a merit good in a free market

153

where $MPC = MPB$. This is below the socially optimal level of consumption, Q_2. The socially optimal level of education lies below point B on the diagram, located where $MSC = MSB$. According to this analysis, free-market provision of merit goods leads to under-consumption. The welfare loss at output Q_1 is the triangular area bounded by points A, B and C.

Suppose that the government reacts by providing a subsidy which reduces the price of education to P_2. At the subsidised price, consumption of education rises to the socially optimal level of Q_2. The market failure has now been corrected.

KEY TERM

government failure occurs when government intervention in the economy makes the allocation of resources worse. The intervention may be ineffective, wasteful and/or damaging.

STUDY TIP

Government failure often results from the unintended consequences of interventionist policies that were introduced in an attempt to correct market failure.

EXTENSION MATERIAL

How policies to correct market failure may lead to government failure

Students often confuse market failure with government failure. Whereas market failure occurs when markets function inefficiently or inequitably, government failure can occur when government intervention to try to reduce or eliminate a market failure has the unintended consequence of creating a new problem or problems. If the government failure is greater than the market failure that the government intervention was intended to correct, it is better to leave the market failure uncorrected and to live with it. This is broadly the view of some pro-free-market economists who dislike government intervention in the economy.

Taking the example illustrated in Figure 6.5, the higher taxes needed to pay for the subsidy introduced to encourage more consumption of education may distort economic activity in the rest of the economy. Higher rates of income tax, for example, may reduce personal incentives and have a detrimental effect on economic growth, while higher indirect taxes imposed on some goods but not on others may distort spending patterns in undesirable directions.

EXTENSION MATERIAL

Public choice theory, public interest theory and government failure

Economists of a free-market persuasion argue that governments should be wary of intervening to try to correct any alleged market failures, including those related to the environment. This approach to markets and market failure is associated with a wider body of theory about the role of government in the economy, known as *public choice theory*.

The free-market advocates of public choice theory regard a market economy as a calm and orderly place in which the price mechanism, working through the incentives signalled by price changes in competitive markets, achieves a more optimal and efficient outcome than would result from a policy of government intervention. They believe that risk-taking entrepreneurs, who lose or gain through the correctness of their decisions in the market place, know better what to produce than civil servants and planners employed by the government on risk-free salaries with secured pensions. Provided that markets are sufficiently competitive, what is produced is ultimately determined by consumer sovereignty, with consumers knowing better than governments what is good for them.

According to the free-market philosophy, the correct function of government is to reduce to a minimum its economic activities and interference with private economic agents. Thus government should be restricted to a night-watchman role, maintaining law and order, providing public goods and possibly offering other minor corrections when markets fail. Generally, government is there to ensure a suitable environment in which wealth-creating entrepreneurship can function in competitive markets subject to minimum regulation. This philosophy leads free-market economists to reject government intervention in the economy, including policies that aim to correct alleged market failures. They believe that, at best, such intervention will be ineffective; at worst, it will be damaging, destabilising and inefficient.

Public interest theory is very different from the public choice theory we have just explained. Public interest theory is favoured by Keynesian economists who generally support government intervention in a market economy. They believe that governments intervene in a benevolent fashion in the economy in order to eliminate waste and to achieve an efficient and socially desirable resource allocation. Public interest theory, applied at the microeconomic level to correct market failure, is matched at the macroeconomic level by Keynesian economic management. Keynesians believe that government intervention at the macro level can anticipate and counter the destabilising forces existent in the market economy, achieving a better outcome than could be achieved in an economy subject to unregulated market forces. Keynesians justify discretionary government intervention in the economy on the ground that, provided the intervention is 'smart' and sensible, government activity stabilises an otherwise inherently unstable market economy.

6.2 Environmental market failures

Several of the market failures we have discussed, both in this chapter and in Book 1, Chapter 5, result from the discharge of negative externalities into the environment. Such environmental externalities may involve pollution of land, sea, rivers and air, and the externalities associated with road use and congestion. On page 104 in Book 1 we described, and illustrated in Figure 5.3, how coal-burning power stations discharge sulphur dioxide pollution into the atmosphere, and also the 'eyesore' pollution caused by unsightly buildings and electricity transmission lines. We then went on to explain how governments could attempt to correct such market failures through taxation, regulation including outright bans, or a combination of the two policy approaches.

However, these days, governments are increasingly making use of behavioural 'nudges' of the type we explained in Chapter 1, section 1.3 of this book.

QUANTITATIVE SKILLS 6.3

Worked example: calculating an allocatively efficient price

The marginal private cost of producing an extra unit of a good is £15 and the marginal external cost resulting from the pollution incurred in the course of production is £3 for each extra unit.

Assuming no other externalities in consumption or production, all other things being equal, what price should achieve an allocatively efficient level of production and consumption of the good?

All other things being equal, the allocatively efficient level of production and consumption requires that price equals marginal social cost ($P = MSC$), with $MSC = MPC + MEC$. For this good, the MSC of producing an extra unit is £18 (£15 + £3), so a price of £18 is needed to ensure that the level of production and consumption of the good is allocatively efficient.

Note: In this example, since there are no externalities in consumption, the price of the product reflects the marginal social benefit (MSB) derived from the last unit of the product that is produced and consumed. Hence $P = MSC$ is equivalent to $MSB = MSC$.

CASE STUDY 6.2

The economics of climate change

In 2006 the economist Sir Nicholas Stern (now Lord Stern) published a highly influential report on the economics of climate change. A year later in 2007, when delivering the Royal Economic Society (RES) public lecture in Manchester, Stern said:

> The problem of climate change involves a fundamental failure of markets: those who damage others by emitting greenhouse gases generally do not pay.

> Climate change is a result of the greatest market failure the world has seen. The evidence on the

seriousness of the risks from inaction or delayed action is now overwhelming. We risk damages on a scale larger than the two world wars of the last century. The problem is global and the response must be collaboration on a global scale.

Rich countries must lead the way in taking action. That means adopting ambitious emissions reduction targets; encouraging effective market mechanisms; supporting programmes to combat deforestation; promoting rapid technological progress to mitigate the effects of climate change; and honouring their aid commitments to the developing world.

Follow-up question

1 Lord Stern obviously believes that rich countries are more responsible than poorer developing countries for global warming. Explain why you agree or disagree with him.

6.3 Property rights

Earlier in the chapter, when summarising the difference between *private goods* and *public goods*, we made brief mention of the important economic concept of property rights. Most goods in the economy are private goods, over which the owners can exercise private property rights that prevent other people from using the good or enjoying its benefits. By contrast, with pure public goods, the ownership of property rights cannot be exercised, and this leads to their characteristic of non-excludability and the free-rider problem. (With quasi-public goods this is not always so, as they might be excludable but not non-rival.)

EXTENSION MATERIAL

Establishing markets for trading private property rights

In 1960, Professor Ronald Coase argued that if markets can be created for private property rights, government intervention to correct market failures may not be necessary. Coase used the example of wood-burning locomotives, which in nineteenth-century America frequently set fire to farmers' fields. If farmers possess the property right to prevent crops being destroyed, they can sell the rights to the railway companies. By contrast, if the railway companies possess the property right to emit sparks, farmers could pay the companies to reduce emissions.

Coase argued that in both cases the outcome might be the same. If farmers have a right to stop the sparks, but emitting sparks is worth more to the railway than stopping

the sparks is worth to the farmers, the railway will buy the right to emit sparks from the farmers, and the damage continues. But if the railway companies have the right to emit sparks, and this right is worth more to them than to the farmers, the right will not be sold, and the damage again continues. In this example, initial ownership of property rights has no effect on the amount of resources devoted to suppressing sparks. The ability to trade property rights ensures the same outcome in either case.

This theory, which is known as the Coase theorem, has greatly influenced the free-market approach to market failures. Indeed, most economists now accept that governments should try to work *with the market* rather than *against the market* through regulation.

The tragedy of the commons

Critics of the private ownership of property rights do not generally want to abolish those rights. Instead, they wish to transfer property rights from private ownership to government ownership. However, the worst-case scenario is when private property rights are abolished and replaced by 'common ownership', but without any form of government control that aims to achieve the 'common good'.

In 1968, in a famous article titled 'The tragedy of the commons', Garrett Hardin told the following story. (We have adapted Hardin's story into our own words.)

> In Britain before the eighteenth century, much farmland was open common land on which farmers could graze as many animals as they wished, for free.
>
> As long as poaching and disease keep the numbers of animals below the carrying capacity of the land, common land grazing works well. However, it was in a herdsman's self-interest to graze more and more animals, since his gain, the money earned from selling slaughtered additional animals, would exceed any loss incurred from the gradual deterioration of the common. The herdsman would receive all the proceeds from the sale of an additional animal, but the effects of over-grazing would be shared by all the herdsmen.

> A rational herdsman would therefore conclude that the only sensible course for him to pursue was to add another animal to his herd. But each herdsman would then be locked into a system that compelled him to increase his herd without limit — in a world that is limited. Another animal would be added to the grazing land, and then another, and then another...But this would be the conclusion reached by each and every rational herdsman sharing a commons. Therein is the tragedy. Freedom of the commons brings ruin to all.

A few years later in 1974, Hardin used the following example to illustrate the tragedy of the commons. Satellite photos of northern Africa showed an irregular dark patch 390 square miles in area. Ground-level investigation revealed a fenced area inside of which there was plenty of grass. Outside, the ground cover had been devastated. Hardin argued that the explanation was simple. The fenced area was private property, subdivided into sections. Each year, the owners moved their animals to a new section. Fallow periods of 4 years gave the pastures time to recover from the grazing. The owners did this because they had an incentive to take care of their land. But no one owned the now barren land outside the fenced-off area. This land being open to nomads and their herds, the tragedy of the commons was taking its toll.

6.4 Competition policy

The theoretical background to competition policy

Before proceeding further, refer back to Chapter 3 and read through the sections that describe and compare perfect competition and monopoly (pages 63–72). To recap, if we ignore the fact that perfect competition does not actually exist in real-world economies, two important points are:

- In the absence of economies of scale, perfect competition is more productively and allocatively efficient than monopoly.
- In perfect competition, the 'consumer is king' and consumer sovereignty rules, whereas monopoly leads to the manipulation of consumers and the exploitation of producer sovereignty. By restricting output and raising prices, monopoly results in a net welfare loss as well as a transfer of consumer surplus into producer surplus and monopoly profit.

Even though perfect competition does not exist, when firms operate in markets where a high degree of competition prevails, many economists believe that this helps to prevent the abuses that can occur when firms possess a significant degree of monopoly power.

As its name implies, **competition policy** is the part of government economic policy which tries to make the imperfectly competitive and monopolistic

> **KEY TERM**
>
> **competition policy** the part of the government's microeconomic policy and industrial policy which aims to make goods markets more competitive. It comprises policy toward monopoly, mergers and restrictive trading practices.

markets of the real world more competitive. The aims of competition policy include preventing the exploitation of monopoly power, reducing costs of production, improving efficiency, getting rid of excessive profit so that prices reflect costs of production, and removing entry and exit barriers which separate markets.

Competition policy does recognise, however, that there are two main circumstances in which monopoly may be preferable to small firms producing in a competitive market.

First, when the size of the market is limited but economies of scale are possible, monopolies can produce at a lower average cost than smaller, more competitive firms.

Second, under certain circumstances, firms with monopoly power may be more innovative than firms that are not protected by entry barriers. When this is the case, monopoly may be more dynamically efficient than a more competitive market.

The three different parts of UK competition policy

As noted in the key term above, competition policy in the UK comprises policy toward monopoly, mergers and restrictive trading practices.

Monopoly policy

Since there are few, if any, pure monopolies in the UK, monopoly policy might better be called 'oligopoly policy' or policy toward highly concentrated markets dominated by just a few firms. Of the three main elements of competition policy we examine in this chapter, monopoly policy is the one with the longest history, dating back well over half a century to the establishment of the Monopolies Commission in 1948. The Monopolies Commission later became the Competition Commission, which in turn in 2013 was rebranded as the **Competition and Markets Authority** (CMA). The CMA is not restricted solely to the investigation of pure monopoly. It also investigates mergers that might create a new monopoly or a highly concentrated market structure.

> **KEY TERM**
> **Competition and Markets Authority** government agency responsible for advising on and implementing UK competition policy.

> **STUDY TIP**
> The label 'monopoly policy' is slightly misleading as very often the policy is aimed at oligopolies or concentrated markets rather than at pure monopoly.

A cost–benefit approach to monopoly policy

Because economists recognise that monopoly can be either good or bad depending upon circumstances, UK policy has always been based on the view that each case must be judged on its merits. If the likely costs resulting from the reduction of competition exceed the benefits, monopoly should be prevented, but if the likely benefits exceed the costs, monopoly should be permitted. Ongoing regulation is needed to make sure that firms, particularly large firms, continue to act in the public interest.

The Competition and Markets Authority

As already noted, since 2014 UK monopoly policy has been implemented by the Competition and Markets Authority (CMA). The CMA was formed through the merger of two older government agencies, the Office of Fair Trading (OFT) and the Competition Commission (CC). The CMA is responsible to a government ministry, the Department for Business, Innovation and Skills (BIS).

The CMA uses market structure, conduct and performance indicators to scan or screen the UK economy on a systematic basis for evidence of monopoly abuse. Concentration ratios provide evidence of monopolistic market structures. Market conduct indicators such as consumer and trade complaints allow the CMA to monitor anti-competitive business behaviour. When the CMA discovers evidence of monopoly that it believes is likely to be against the public interest, it investigates further. Until recently, the main issue to be decided was the relatively narrow one of whether particular trading practices undertaken by the investigated firm(s) were in the public interest. The 'public interest' was fairly vaguely defined. The 2002 Enterprise Act changed this, introducing competition-based tests to replace the public interest test. The tests centre on whether any features of the market (which include structural features and conduct by firms or customers in the market) prevent, restrict or distort competition.

Alternative approaches to the problem of monopoly

Ever since the start of competition policy over 60 years ago, the UK has adopted a regulatory and investigatory approach to the problem of monopoly. Relatively few firms and takeover bids are actually investigated. The policy rationale is that the possibility of a CMA investigation creates sufficient incentive for most large firms to behave well and to resist the temptation to exploit monopoly power in ways which are against the public interest.

However, although the CMA has adopted a 'watchdog investigatory/regulatory' role, a number of other strategic approaches could, in principle, be used to deal with the problem of monopoly. These include:

- **Compulsory breaking up of all monopolies ('monopoly busting').** Many free-market economists believe that the advantages of competitive and free markets, namely economic efficiency and consumer sovereignty, can be achieved only when the economy is as close as possible to perfect competition. In itself, monopoly is bad and impossible to justify. The government should adopt an automatic policy rule to break up monopolies wherever they are found to exist.
  UK policy-makers have seldom if ever adopted a monopoly-busting approach, although, as we have explained, powers do exist that allow the government to order the break-up of an established monopoly. Two examples have been the break-up of the gas and electricity industries so that no one company generates, transports and sells energy, and in 2011 the break-up of the British Airports Authority (BAA) into separately owned airports. In 2009 Ferrovial, a Spanish company which owned BAA, had been ordered to sell Stansted, Gatwick and either Glasgow or Edinburgh, on the basis that the group had a monopoly.
- **Use of price controls to restrict monopoly abuse.** Although price controls have been used by UK governments at various times to restrict the freedom of UK firms to set their own prices, this policy has only been used in a

limited way in recent years. Under the influence of free-market economic theory, price controls have fallen out of favour.

- **Taxing monopoly profits.** As well as controlling prices directly, the government can tax monopoly profit to punish firms for exploiting their monopoly power and making excessive profit. Monopoly taxes have not generally been used in the UK, except on a few occasions — for example, on the 'windfall' gain that landlords receive when the land they own is made available for property development. Similarly, windfall profits received by banks from high interest rates have been subject to a special tax. Also, in the late 1990s, the incoming Labour government imposed a windfall profit tax on the privatised utilities.

- **Rate of return regulation.** In the USA, the regulators have imposed maximum rates of return on the capital that the utility companies employ. In principle, these act as a price cap, as the utilities are fined if they set prices too high and earn excessive rates of return. However, in practice, instead of increasing productive efficiency, rate of return regulation often has the opposite effect. This type of intervention has the unintended consequence of encouraging utility companies to raise costs so that raising prices does not lead to higher profits and hence they comply with the rate of return regulation. The higher costs, which are the result of the productively inefficient use of resources, may allow the managers of the business to have an easier life. Monopolies are especially likely to allow costs to rise when protected by high entry barriers.

- **State ownership of monopoly.** In the past, UK Labour governments have sometimes regarded the problem of monopoly as resulting solely from private ownership and the pursuit of private profit. At its most simplistic, this view leads to the conclusion that the problem of monopoly disappears when the firms are nationalised or taken into public ownership. Once in public ownership, the monopolies are assumed to act solely in the public interest.

- **Privatising monopolies.** Opposing state ownership, past Conservative governments argued that state ownership produces particular forms of abuse that would not be experienced if the industries were privately owned. These include a general inefficiency and resistance to change, which stem from the belief by workers and management in the state-run monopolies that they will always be bailed out by government in the event of a loss. According to the Conservative view, monopoly abuse occurs in nationalised industries, not from the pursuit of private profit, but because the industries are run in the interest of a feather-bedded workforce that is protected from any form of market discipline. It is also alleged that interference by governments for social and political reasons made it difficult for nationalised industries to operate efficiently. The Conservatives believe that the privatisation of state-owned monopolies should improve efficiency and commercial performance, because privatisation exposes the industry to the threat of takeover and the discipline of the capital market. In some cases, privatisation has also subjected previously state-owned monopolies to competition.

- **Deregulation and the removal of barriers to entry.** Most economists believe that privatisation alone cannot eliminate the problem of monopoly abuse; it merely changes the nature of the problem to private monopoly and the commercial exploitation of a monopoly position. In recognition of this problem, the privatisation of the telecommunication, gas and electricity monopolies was accompanied by the setting up of the regulatory bodies Ofcom and Ofgem, operating in addition to the CMA. One method of exposing monopolies — including the privatised utility industries — to increased competition is to use deregulatory policies to remove artificial barriers to entry. We explain deregulation in greater detail later in the chapter.

Contestable market theory revisited

In Chapter 3, section 3.9 we explained that in recent years, contestable market theory has had a major impact on UK monopoly policy. We described how the theory implies that, provided there is adequate potential for competition, a conventional regulatory policy is superfluous. The government's main role should be to discover which industries and markets are potentially contestable. The growing influence of contestable market theory has been accompanied by the introduction of deregulatory policies that are meant to develop conditions in which there are reduced barriers to entry and exit or a complete absence of such barriers.

For a market to be perfectly contestable, barriers to entry must disappear and there must be no sunk costs. As we explained in Chapter 3, sunk costs are costs incurred, when entering a market, that are irrecoverable should the firm decide to leave the market.

Merger policy

Whereas a government's monopoly policy deals with established monopoly, or markets already dominated by large firms, merger policy is concerned with takeovers and mergers that might create a new monopoly. Strictly, a merger involves the voluntary coming together of two or more firms, whereas a takeover is usually involuntary, at least for the victim being acquired through a hostile takeover. However, the term 'merger policy' is used to cover all types of acquisition of firms, friendly or hostile, willing or unwilling.

Until quite recently, the government itself decided whether to make merger references. This laid the government open to the criticism that, when deciding against a merger reference, it was bending to the lobbying power of big business and engaging in political opportunism. However, the CMA now makes virtually all merger references. The CMA keeps itself informed of all merger situations that might be eligible for investigation on public interest grounds. Currently, a takeover or merger is eligible for investigation if it is expected to lead to a substantial lessening of competition (SLC).

SYNOPTIC LINK
Sunk costs must not be confused with fixed costs. In Chapter 2, we explained the nature of fixed costs, while sunk costs are explained in Chapter 3 and in this chapter. As we noted in Chapter 3, some costs are both fixed and sunk.

EXTENSION MATERIAL

Have UK governments been serious about merger policy?

In the 1990s, barely 100 mergers (out of a total of over 3,000) were in fact referred for investigation. Of these, only a minority were found to be against the public interest and banned. These figures give some support to the argument that UK governments were not serious in their attitude to mergers and the problem of growing industrial concentration. Governments tended to assume that all mergers were beneficial unless it could clearly be shown that the effects were likely to be adverse. In recent years even fewer eligible mergers have been investigated.

CASE STUDY 6.3

Overruling merger policy? Lloyds TSB's takeover of HBOS

In October 2008 the UK's banking system was in deep trouble in the financial meltdown triggered by the credit crunch. Halifax Bank of Scotland (HBOS) nearly went bankrupt. To rescue HBOS, the government waived through a takeover by another large bank, Lloyds TSB, without referring the takeover to the competition authorities as had been expected.

Sir John Vickers, the former chairman of the OFT wrote:

> It would appear to have been a mistake to waive normal merger law to address the HBOS problem once it was clear, as it was by early October 2008, that a systemic solvency problem existed. Relaxation of competition law was not a good way to help financial stability in this case, and as the subsequent problems of Lloyds have shown, it may have worsened it.

Vickers believed that nationalising HBOS instead of allowing Lloyds to take over the ailing lender 'would have had important economic advantages'.

By any measure, the takeover by Lloyds TSB of HBOS created a bank with substantial monopoly power. With 30% of current accounts and much the same share of the domestic mortgage market, the new 'super bank' had the potential to exploit customers. It was said that the competition authorities would struggle to contain the super bank's ability to misuse its monopoly power.

Recognising this problem, in 2013 the Coalition government complied with a European Commission decision to force the super bank to sell off the TSB, which now functions, as it did before merger with Lloyds in 1995, as a separate bank (from 1999 to 2013, the two banks traded as Lloyds TSB Bank plc). Having had their fingers burnt in the financial crisis, both banks have been reducing their exposure to the risks of investment banking and are now largely high-street banks dealing with the general public rather than trading in exotic financial securities.

Follow-up questions

1 What was 'the credit crunch'?
2 Why might Lloyds TSB's takeover of HBOS be deemed anti-competitive?
3 Do you agree that the takeover should have been investigated by the government's competition authorities? Justify your answer.

European Union merger policy

The European Commission, which is the executive body of the EU, has long had powers to prevent and control mergers in member countries, but before 1990 the commission did not apply these powers systematically. In 1990 a new EU merger policy came into operation to control the growing number of mergers involving companies active in more than one member country. The EU merger policy, which is the main part of EU competition policy, is based on the principle of *subsidiarity*, which delegates policy as much as possible to national governments. Member countries continue to use national policy to deal with smaller mergers, but the European Commission adjudicates on larger mergers with a community dimension. As with UK merger policy, nearly all the commission's criteria for assessing whether a merger is justified are competition-related, showing again the influence of contestable market theory.

The European Commission justifies its policy as providing a 'one-stop regulatory system' for mergers, in which the borderline between national and EU jurisdiction is clear-cut. However, many commentators believe that the opposite is the case. They criticise EU merger policy as an unclear, time-consuming lawyers' paradise. UK firms contemplating a merger or takeover bid have to register their plans with both UK and EU authorities to minimise the chance of falling foul of either.

Restrictive trading practice policy

Restrictive trading practices undertaken by firms in imperfect product markets can be divided into two broad kinds: those undertaken independently by a single firm, and collective restrictive practices that involve either a written or an implied agreement among two or more firms.

Independently undertaken restrictive practices include:

- decisions to charge discriminatory prices (see Chapter 3)
- the refusal to supply a particular resale outlet
- full-line forcing, whereby a supplier forces a distributor that wishes to sell one of its products to stock its full range of products

A cartel agreement, in which firms come together to fix or rig the price of a good, is the most commonly known example of a collective restrictive trading practice.

Both independently undertaken and collective restrictive trading practices are now dealt with by the Competition and Markets Authority. The CMA usually asks the firm or firms involved to drop the practice voluntarily on the ground that it is anti-competitive. A cartel agreement is usually banned, unless the firms involved persuade the CMA that the agreement is in the public interest — for example, to protect the public from injury.

> **ACTIVITY**
>
> Google the Competition and Markets Authority website and, together with a group of your classmates, find out about two or more cases that the CMA has investigated. Report your findings.

6.5 Public ownership

Publicly owned or state-owned industries are also known as *nationalised industries*. Although there were nationalised industries in the UK in the nineteenth and early twentieth centuries, the main period of nationalisation occurred in the years after the Second World War. From 1945 until 1951 and then intermittently from 1964 until 1979, whenever Labour governments had control of the UK economy, industries such as coal mining, the railways and the steel industry were taken into **public ownership**. Labour governments justified nationalisation on the ground that effective state planning required public ownership of the 'commanding heights' of the economy. Public ownership was essential for efficient operation of key industries which were regarded as too important to be left to the vagaries of private ownership and market forces.

> **KEY TERM**
>
> **public ownership** ownership of industries, firms and other assets such as social housing by central government or local government. The state's acquisition of such assets is called nationalisation.

As well as being an instrument of socialist planning and control of the economy, public ownership was used (as we explained in the previous section) as a method of regulating the problem of monopoly — in particular, the problem of natural monopoly in the utility industries.

Since 1979 very few new industries have been taken into public ownership in the UK. However, there have been two examples of *temporary* nationalisation. The first of these was the complete or partial nationalisation of the Northern Rock, Lloyds, RBS and HBOS banks. This was a response to the financial crisis which hit the UK economy (and also the wider world economy) in 2007 and 2008. Because of the extreme adverse effects that bank collapses would have on other industries and consumers, banks were regarded as 'too important to fail'. Those that were in danger of failing were either nationalised or merged. The decision to take banks into public ownership was made for pragmatic rather than ideological reasons. The intention was always, particularly under the Conservative-led Coalition government, to sell the nationalised banks back to the private sector as soon as they became financially viable.

The other industry taken into temporary public ownership was the east coast railway service. The nationalisation of this service and its eventual return to the private sector are discussed in Case Study 6.4.

CASE STUDY 6.4

East Coast Rail returns to private hands

In March 2015, the *Guardian* newspaper reported that train services on the mainline between London and Edinburgh were once again being operated by a private firm after more than five years under state control, reigniting the row over ownership of the railway.

East Coast trains have been rebranded as Virgin Trains East Coast. Under the management of a joint venture between two private sector companies, Stagecoach and Sir Richard Branson's Virgin, a private sector organisation has taken over the running of the railway on an 8-year franchise.

The previous private operators of the east coast railway line failed to meet their financial commitments. A small government-owned company, Directly Operated Railways, stepped in to run trains on the mainline in late 2009 after the last franchisee, National Express, walked away when revenues fell during the financial crisis.

In its 5 years as East Coast, the state-run firm gave several millions of pounds in profits to the Treasury. In the last 2 years in which it operated, East Coast was one of two state-owned firms to make a net contribution to government coffers, paying in more to the government than it received in subsidy or indirect grants.

The success of the nationalised East Coast trains led to calls to keep the line in state hands. The TUC general secretary, Frances O'Grady, said the sale to the private sector would be a 'costly mistake'. She said: 'By taking East Coast out of public ownership the government is passing the profits to Stagecoach and Virgin shareholders, instead of using the cash to reduce rail fares and improve services for passengers.'

Follow-up questions

1 Why was National Express replaced as franchisee of the east coast railway service?
2 Do you agree that the publicly owned East Coast trains should still operate the east coast railway service? Justify your answer.

6.6 Privatisation

KEY TERM

privatisation the transfer of assets from the public sector to the private sector.

Privatisation involves the transfer of publicly owned assets to the private sector. In the UK, this has usually involved the sale to private ownership of nationalised industries and businesses that were previously owned by the state and accountable to central government. Between 1981 and 2015 more than 16 major industries were privatised and state ownership of industries was transformed from the ownership of major parts of the British economy to becoming a mere rump. Although the main privatisations involved the sale of nationalised firms and industries, other state-owned assets such as land and socially owned housing have also been privatised.

Before privatisation, some state-owned industries, such as electricity, gas and the railways, were vertically integrated. (Vertical integration means that all production activities, ranging from the extraction of raw materials from the earth's crust to the final sale of finished goods or services, are undertaken by a single firm.) When these industries were sold to the private sector, their privatisation involved significant vertical disintegration or the breaking up of the nationalised industry or firm into separate firms, each undertaking activities at different stages of production. The industries were split into horizontal layers, with different companies in each layer buying or selling from companies above or below them in the supply or distribution chain. However, the gas industry was initially privatised in fully, vertically integrated form, with British Gas owning all the stages of production from purchasing natural gas to selling through regional marketing boards to the customer. The industry was split into separate layers a few years later in order to weaken natural monopoly and promote competition.

For gas and electricity, this strategy has generally been successful. Consumers now choose between competing electricity and gas marketing companies, and the prices of electricity and gas fell in real terms, at least for a number of years. However, by 2008 energy prices were rising faster than the general rate of inflation and there were calls for the reintroduction of controls on gas and electricity prices.

EXTENSION MATERIAL

Privatisation and the free-market revival

The general case for privatisation can only be properly understood when seen as part of the revolution (or counter-revolution) in economic thinking known as the free-market revival. In the past, socialists often regarded nationalisation as an end in itself, apparently believing that by taking an industry into public ownership, efficiency and equity would automatically improve and the public interest would be served. In much the same way, supporters of the free-market revival at the opposite end of the political and economic spectrum believe that private ownership and capitalism are always superior to public ownership. Whatever the circumstances, they believe that the privatisation of state-run industries will inevitably improve economic performance.

The advantages of privatisation

Specific arguments used to justify privatisation include:

- **Revenue raising.** Privatisation, or the sale of state-owned assets, provides the government with a short-term source of revenue, which at the height of privatisation was at least £3–4 billion a year. But obviously an asset cannot be sold off twice.
- **Reducing public spending and the government's borrowing requirement.** After 1979, Conservative governments aimed to reduce public spending and government borrowing. When the state successfully sold loss-making industries such as the Rover Group, public spending on subsidies fell. Government borrowing also falls if private ownership returns the industries to profitability, since corporation tax revenue is boosted and the state earns dividend income from any shares that it retains in the privatised company.
- **The promotion of competition.** Privatisation has been justified on the ground that it promotes competition through the break-up of monopoly. At the time of their privatisation, industries such as gas and electricity were natural monopolies. But the growth of technology-driven competition, together with the removal of barriers to entry by regulating agencies such as Ofgem, has significantly increased competition.
- **The promotion of efficiency.** For free-market economists, this is perhaps the most important justification for privatisation. Supporters of privatisation believe that public ownership gives rise to special forms of inefficiency

which disappear once an industry moves into the private sector. The culture of public ownership makes nationalised industries resistant to change. Through exposure to the threat of takeover and the discipline of the capital market, the privatisation of a state-owned monopoly should improve the business's efficiency and commercial performance.

- **Popular capitalism.** The promotion of an enterprise culture was an important reason for privatisation in the UK. Privatisation extended share ownership to employees and other individuals who had not previously owned shares, and thus added to the incentive for the electorate to support the private enterprise economy. Privatisation has generally proved popular with voters, so governments, both Conservative and then Labour, saw no point in abandoning a winning programme.

The disadvantages of privatisation

Privatisation has the following possible disadvantages:

- **Monopoly abuse.** Opponents of privatisation have argued that, far from promoting competition and efficiency, privatisation increases monopoly abuse by transferring socially owned and accountable public monopolies into weakly regulated and less accountable private monopolies.

- **Short-termism wins over long-termism.** Many of the investments that need to be undertaken by the previously nationalised industries can only be profitable in the long term. There is a danger that under private ownership, such investments will not be made because company boards concentrate on the short-termism of delivering dividends to keep shareholders and financial institutions happy. Under-investment in maintaining the rail track and in technically advanced trains by the privatised railway companies is said to provide an example. However, there is a counter-argument: that under public ownership, the government starved the nationalised industries of investment funds in order to keep government borrowing down.

- **Selling the family silver.** Opponents of privatisation argue that if a private sector business were to sell its capital assets simply in order to raise revenue to pay for current expenditure, it would rightly incur the wrath of its shareholders. The same should be true of the government and the sale of state-owned assets. Taxpayers should not sanction the sale of capital assets owned on their behalf by the UK government to raise revenue to finance current spending on items such as wages and salaries. In reply, supporters of the privatisation programme argue that, far from selling the family silver, privatisation merely returns the family's assets to the family: that is, from the custody of the state to direct ownership by private individuals.

- **The free-lunch syndrome.** Opponents of privatisation claim that state-owned assets have been sold too cheaply, encouraging the belief among first-time share buyers that there is such a thing as a free lunch. This is because the offer price of shares in newly privatised industries was normally pitched at a level which guaranteed a risk-free capital gain or one-way bet at the taxpayer's expense. Arguably, this encourages the very opposite of an enterprise economy.

ACTIVITY

Choose at least one privatised industry and research its track record since it was privatised. Has it performed better or worse than under state ownership?

CASE STUDY 6.5

The UK government agrees to sell its Eurostar stake to Canadian and British institutional investors

In March 2015, the UK government announced that it would sell its 40% stake in the Eurostar rail link to two institutional investors: a Canadian public sector pension fund and the British asset management firm, Hermes Investment Management. The rest of Eurostar is owned by nationalised French rail operator SNCF, which has a 55% stake, and Belgian national rail operator SNCB, which has 5%.

The sale of the UK government's 40% stake in the Eurostar rail service follows a competitive process begun by the chancellor of the exchequer in October 2014

The deal is part of a trend for institutional investors such as pension funds and insurance companies, squeezed by low interest rates globally, to buy into infrastructure projects. Such assets are high yielding and match the long-term liabilities of pension funds and insurance companies. The UK government is hoping that pension and infrastructure funds will be willing bidders in future infrastructure privatisations. Singapore, Kuwait and Qatar have made it clear that their sovereign wealth funds are interested in European projects where there is the potential for long-term, sustainable gains. Chinese banks are also interested, keen as they are to gain a foothold in Western-facing businesses.

The sale, worth £585 million, is part of a government plan to raise £20 billion by selling off publicly owned assets to reduce the UK's national debt and help balance the country's books. However, £585 million additional government revenue will have little impact on the state of government finances — it will simply slow the increase in the stock of national debt, rather than actually cut it. The UK government is still running a deficit — that is, its receipts are lower than its spending.

The Eurostar sell-off deal requires regulatory approval by the CMA and also the French and Belgian owners of the remaining 60% agreeing not to exercise their option to acquire the British stake at a 15% premium.

Follow-up questions

1 What is an institutional investor?
2 Explain why, despite its receiving £585 million extra revenue, the UK government is still faced with a growing national debt.

Economic liberalisation

So far, we have defined privatisation in a strictly narrow sense, as the transfer of assets from the public sector to the private sector. Some commentators extend the definition of privatisation to include other aspects of the programme of economic liberalisation pursued by UK governments since 1979. Economic liberalisation means opening up markets to private ownership and competition, and reducing government intervention in the economy.

Policies that are closely related to privatisation include:

- contractualisation
- marketisation
- public–private partnerships (PPP) and the private finance initiative (PFI)
- deregulation

Contractualisation, marketisation, PPP and PFI

Contractualisation or contracting out takes place when services, previously provided by the public sector, such as road cleaning and refuse collection are put to private sector tender, although the taxpayer still ultimately pays for the service. To try to get value for money for the taxpayer, services that were previously provided in house by public sector workers are provided out of house through competitive tendering.

Whereas privatisation (narrowly defined) involves transferring assets from the public sector to the private sector, **marketisation** (or commercialisation) shifts the provision of services from the non-market sector into the market sector. A price is charged for a service that consumers previously enjoyed 'free'. Governments have also experimented in creating internal markets, whereby one part of a state-owned enterprise charges a price to another part of the same enterprise for the service it provides within the organisation.

As its name suggests, a **public–private partnership** (PPP) is a partnership between the private and public sectors to provide public services. PPPs include the contractualisation of services that we have already described, but also cover activities such as the transfer of council homes to housing associations using private loans. PPP has been particularly important in the provision of health services, but private sector providers are running prisons, local authority revenue and benefit services, the majority of residential homes for the elderly, and some schools.

The **private finance initiative** (PFI), which was introduced by the Conservative government in 1993 and enthusiastically taken up by the subsequent Labour government, is closely related to PPP. Before PFI, the government was involved in all stages of planning, building and then running a public investment project such as a new school. Under PFI, the government's role is restricted to deciding the service it requires and then seeking tenders from the private sector for designing, building, financing and running the project. The government becomes an *enabler* rather than a *provider*.

Recent governments have favoured PFI because public sector services can be provided, but government borrowing (or at least on-balance sheet borrowing) does not increase, at least in the short run. The capital costs of the project are paid for by the private sector provider, but the taxpayer subsidises the project if it is not self-financing. Taxpayers also contribute towards the profit made by the private provider. The government hopes, however, that efficiency gains resulting from private sector provision will more than offset the payment of taxpayers' funds into private sector profits. Public service trade unions oppose PPPs, and especially PFIs, because they see them as the creeping privatisation of public services. By contrast, governments argue that PPPs can provide the public sector with the commercial values of the private sector, injecting a fresh, innovative and entrepreneurial 'can-do' approach. They believe that, without PPP and PFI, public services have a tendency to be entrenched, reactive and conservative.

STUDY TIP
Avoid confusing privatisation with other policies that have reduced the role of the state in the economy, such as marketisation and deregulation. However, note how the policies are linked.

KEY TERMS
contractualisation services which were previously provided by the public sector, such as road cleaning and refuse collection, are put to private sector tender and then provided by private sector firms.

marketisation the provision of goods and service is shifted from the non-market sector into the market sector of the economy. Also known as commercialisation.

public–private partnership partnership between the private and public sectors to provide public services.

private finance initiative the government seeks tenders from the private sector for designing, building, financing and running infrastructure projects.

6.7 Regulation and deregulation of markets

Regulation

Economic **regulation** involves the imposition of rules, controls and constraints which restrict freedom of economic action in the market place. There are two types of regulation: external regulation and self-regulation. Both types of regulation can be imposed by law. When this is the case, a failure to comply with a regulation means breaking the law. Court cases may follow which could lead to the imposition of fines or even imprisonment.

- External regulation, as the name suggests, involves an external agency laying down and enforcing rules and restraints. The external agency may be a government department such as the Department for Business, Innovation and Skills, or a special regulatory body or agency set up by government, such the Competition and Markets Authority.
- By contrast, self-regulation or voluntary regulation involves a group of individuals or firms regulating themselves — for example, through a professional association such as the Law Society or the British Medical Association.

Regulation and market failure

Competition can sometimes bring about a situation in which social costs and benefits are not the same as the private costs and benefits incurred and received by the people actually undertaking the market activity. As explained earlier in the chapter, the over-production of externalities such as environmental pollution, and the under-consumption of education, healthcare and other merit goods provide familiar examples of divergence between private and social costs and benefits. Governments use regulation to try to correct such market failures and to achieve a socially optimal level of production and consumption. Monopoly is also a form of market failure, and regulation is used to limit and deter monopoly exploitation of consumers.

Deregulation

Deregulation involves the removal of any previously imposed regulations that have adversely restricted competition and freedom of market activity. During the last 30 years, significant deregulation has taken place in the UK and the USA. Systems of regulation built up during the early post-1945 period have on occasion been completely abandoned, while in other cases they have been watered down or modified. The UK government has removed the protected legal monopoly status enjoyed, for example, by bus companies, airlines and commercial television and radio companies. Access to BT's distribution network of land lines has been given to competitors in the telecommunications industry, and private power companies have been allowed to rent the services of the national electricity and gas distribution grids.

There are two main justifications of deregulation:

- the promotion of competition and market contestability through the removal of artificial barriers to market entry
- the removal of red tape and bureaucracy which imposes unnecessary costs on economic agents, particularly businesses

Deregulation and the free-market revival

The switch away from the imposition of ever-more stringent rules and regulations upon private sector economic activity, and towards the opposite policy of deregulation, reflects the resurgence of free-market economics. Deregulation should be regarded as a part of an overall policy of economic liberalisation, which, as already explained, also involved the policies of privatisation, contractualisation and marketisation (or commercialisation). In recent years, governments in most industrialised countries, including most recently those in the formerly planned economies of central Europe, such as Poland, have begun this process of economic liberalisation and rolling back the economic functions of the state. However, as the recent history of the financial services and banking industries shows, 'light-touch' regulation was arguably a major cause of the financial melt-down that began in 2007. Since then, there have been calls for much tougher regulation of banking and financial services.

Deregulation and the theory of contestable markets

Much of the justification for the policies of deregulation and economic liberalisation that have been pursued in recent years has been provided by the theory of contestable markets, which was explained earlier in the chapter. Contestable market theory argues that the most effective way to promote competitive behaviour within markets is not to impose ever-more regulation upon firms and industries, but to carry out the opposite process of deregulation.

According to this view, the main function of deregulation is to remove barriers to entry, thereby creating incentives both for new firms to enter and contest the market and for established firms to behave in a more competitive way. Under the influence of the theory of contestable markets, governments have sought to remove or loosen all regulations whose main effect has been to reduce competition and to create unnecessary barriers to market entry.

Regulatory capture

Another theory that has had some influence upon the trend towards deregulation is the theory of **regulatory capture**. This theory argues that regulatory agencies created by government can be 'captured' by the industries or firms they are intended to oversee and regulate. Following capture, the regulatory agencies begin to operate in the industry's interest rather than on behalf of the consumers whom they are supposed to protect. A classic case of regulatory capture occurred when the director general of Oflot, the agency which regulates the national lottery, was caught accepting free air tickets and other 'sweeteners' from one of the lottery companies he was supposed to regulate.

Regulatory capture can also occur without the regulator behaving inappropriately. For example, the inevitable close contacts between the

KEY TERM

regulatory capture occurs when regulatory agencies act in the interest of regulated firms rather on behalf of the consumers they are supposed to protect.

regulator and the regulated may mean that the regulator becomes predisposed to accepting the views of the organisations being regulated rather than those of the consumer. Also, the regulator often relies on the regulated organisations to provide much of the information which it uses to make its judgements; the information supplied may be biased.

Even if regulatory capture does not take place, the supporters of deregulation argue that much regulatory activity is unnecessary and ultimately burdensome upon industry and consumers. Once established, the regulators have an incentive to extend their role by introducing ever-more rules and regulations, since it is in this way that they justify their pay and their jobs. Regulation acts both as an informal 'tax' upon the regulated, raising production costs and consumer prices, and also as an extra barrier to market entry, restricting competition.

EXTENSION MATERIAL

The regulation of the privatised utility industries

As we have explained, deregulatory policies have been implemented alongside privatisation in liberalising the UK economy. In the 1980s and 1990s, UK governments realised that once industries such as telecommunications, gas, water and electricity were privatised, there was a danger they might abuse their monopoly position and exploit the consumer. For this reason, special regulatory agencies such as Ofgem, which now regulates the gas and electricity industries, were set up at the time of privatisation to act as watchdogs over the performance of the utilities in the private sector. Initially, industry-specific regulatory bodies were created, but some of these agencies have recently been merged and now cover more than one industry.

The establishment of regulatory agencies such as Ofgem at a time when governments have actively been pursuing a policy of deregulation and economic liberalisation created a rather strange paradox and a source of possible conflict. On the one hand, by setting markets free, deregulation reduces the role of the state; on the other hand, new watchdog bodies such as Ofgem have extended the regulatory role of government and its agencies.

However, successive governments have argued that there need be no conflict between regulation and deregulation. This is because the regulatory bodies are themselves actively involved in deregulating the industries they oversee — for example, by

enforcing the removal of barriers that prevent the entry of new firms. Recent technological progress has made it increasingly possible for new firms to enter the utility industries, particularly in the telecommunications industry. By introducing competition into markets that were previously dominated by established companies such as BT and British Gas, new market entrants have eroded the natural monopoly position previously enjoyed by the privatised utilities.

Supporters of the liberalisation programme hope that the watchdog agencies will prove so successful that eventually these regulatory bodies can wither away, when the markets they oversee have become sufficiently competitive. However, at best this is likely to be a long process. Although new firms are beginning to compete in the markets previously completely dominated by state-owned utilities, established companies like British Gas are still dominant. Their continuing market power means that, certainly for the next few years, the regulatory bodies set up at the time of privatisation must continue as a surrogate for competition. Some commentators argue that, far from withering away, the new regulatory agencies may gradually extend their powers and functions. Free-market critics of economic regulation believe that the UK regulatory system provides a classic example of a growing bureaucracy.

Technology-driven competition

Regulatory agencies have been able to lower and sometimes to remove barriers to market entry by promoting technology-driven competition. This type of competition occurs when technical progress enables new firms to enter markets that were previously natural monopolies. In the telecommunications industry, developments such as mobile telephony, satellite technology and the falling real cost of laying fibre-optic land lines have meant that new market entrants such as Vodafone and the cable television companies can invest in their own distribution networks. Although BT generally owns the land lines through which mobile phone calls are transmitted into people's homes, Ofcom regulates the prices BT can charge the mobile phone companies for this service. It is now many years since BT was able to exercise monopoly power over the whole of the telecommunications distribution network.

In the gas, water and electricity industries, new firms have entered the market by renting the services of the existing distribution network or grid. New electronic information and recording systems allow customers living, for example, in Manchester to buy electricity from a distribution company located in another region. These developments make it possible for customers to shop around and find the distributor that offers the most attractive price.

Technology-driven competition can be thwarted if the distribution network through which the service is delivered into people's homes is owned by an established utility company, which is a major producer of the good or service transported through the system. In this situation, there is an obvious danger that the vertically integrated company owning the network might prevent new market entrants from using the distribution grid. For example, a vertically integrated British Gas Corporation could charge new gas suppliers artificially high prices for using its distribution grid, to prevent the new firms gaining market share.

This explains why government and the regulators have forced previously vertically integrated utility companies to split and become separate companies. Different companies now own the different layers of the gas and electricity industries. This means that the distribution layer (owned by National Grid Gas plc) is free to carry the electricity or gas of as many suppliers as it wishes, and not just the energy supplied by British Gas. In 2015, there were 22 energy marketing companies, including Sainsbury's Energy and M&S Energy, which supplied gas and electricity to different parts of the United Kingdom.

Yardstick competition

The telecommunications industry offers the greatest scope for technology-driven competition, with new market entrants able to bypass BT's distribution network or pay fair rents for its use. However, at the other end of the spectrum, the water industry possesses the least scope for technology-driven competition to remove barriers to entry and break up the natural monopoly.

For this reason, the Office of Water Services (Ofwat) uses yardstick competition as the main regulatory device to promote efficient and competitive behaviour by the water companies. After comparing the performance and costs of all the water companies, Ofwat requires the water companies to have to match the standards achieved by the best in the industry. If and when the other utility watchdogs run up against the realistic limits to technology-driven competition in the industries they regulate, they may turn to yardstick competition to assess the efficiency of the companies they oversee.

SUMMARY

- Markets can fail because they function inequitably or because they function inefficiently.
- Free markets, without government intervention, are likely to result in great inequalities in income and wealth. Most people would regard such extreme inequalities as inequitable.
- Allocative inefficiency occurs when the *MSB* of a good or service does not equate with *MSC*.
- Monopoly, public goods (and public bads), externalities, merit goods and demerit goods all lead to market failure and a misallocation of resources.
- Extending the legal entitlement to property rights is a method of reducing negative externalities and encouraging the production of goods and services that create positive externalities.
- Uncertainty, moral hazard and adverse selection all contribute to under-consumption of merit goods.
- Government failure occurs when governments intervene in markets, often when attempting to cure market failure, but actually making matters worse.
- The three main elements of competition policy are monopoly policy, merger policy and policy toward restrictive trading practices.
- UK monopoly policy is based on a cost–benefit approach to large firms.
- Mergers are most likely to be prevented if they are viewed as potentially anti-competitive.
- Collusive trading practices such as cartel agreements are deemed against the public interest and are generally illegal.
- Governments have established regulatory agencies, such as Ofcom, to regulate the privatised industries.
- Regulatory agencies also try to deregulate. If successful, the agencies, in theory, can wither away because the competition they are set up to create should mean that regulation is no longer needed.

Questions

1 Using examples, explain the difference between market failures resulting from inefficiency and those resulting from inequity.

2 Evaluate the case for using taxes and subsidies to promote the allocatively efficient level of consumption of merit goods and demerit goods.

3 Do you agree that markets can be relied upon to reduce the problems of environmental pollution? Justify your answer.

4 Assess the view that, in the light of the possibility of government failure, the state should not intervene in markets to try to correct market failures.

5 Explain three ways in which a government can try to deal with the problems posed by monopoly.

6 Evaluate the advantages and disadvantages of privatisation.

Microeconomics key terms

abnormal profit profit over and above normal profit. Also known as supernormal profit and above-normal profit.

absolute poverty a condition characterised by severe deprivation of basic human needs, including food, safe drinking water, sanitation facilities, health, shelter, education and information. It depends not only on income but also on access to services.

adverse selection a situation in which people who buy insurance often have a better idea of the risks they face than do the sellers of insurance. People who know they face large risks are more likely to buy insurance than people who face small risks.

allocative efficiency occurs when it is impossible to improve overall economic welfare by reallocating resources between markets. In the whole economy, price must equal marginal cost $(P = MC)$ in every market.

altruism concern for the welfare of others.

anchoring a cognitive bias describing the human tendency when making decisions to rely too heavily on the first piece of information offered (the so-called 'anchor'). Individuals use an initial piece of information when making subsequent judgements.

artificial barriers barriers erected by the firms themselves, such as high levels of advertising expenditure or predatory pricing.

asymmetric information when one party to a market transaction possesses less information relevant to the exchange than the other.

automation automatic control where machines operate other machines.

availability bias occurs when individuals make judgements about the likelihood of future events according to how easy it is to recall examples of similar events.

average cost of labour total wage costs divided by the number of workers employed

average fixed cost total cost of employing the fixed factors of production to produce a particular level of output, divided by the size of output: $AFC = TFC \div Q$.

average returns of labour total output divided by the total number of workers employed.

average revenue total revenue divided by output.

average total cost total cost of producing a particular level of output, divided by the size of output; often called average cost: $ATC = AFC + AVC$.

average variable cost total cost of employing the variable factors of production to produce a particular level of output, divided by the size of output: $AVC = TVC \div Q$.

behavioural economics a method of economic analysis that applies psychological insights into human behaviour to explain how individuals make choices and decisions.

bounded rationality when making decisions, an individual's rationality is limited by the information they have, the limitations of their minds, and the finite amount of time available in which to make decisions.

bounded self-control limited self-control in which individuals lack the self-control to act in what they see as their self-interest.

cartel a collusive agreement by firms, usually to fix prices. Sometimes there is also an agreement to restrict output and to deter the entry of new firms.

choice architecture a framework setting out different ways in which choices can be presented to consumers, and the impact of that presentation on consumer decision making.

cognitive bias a mistake in reasoning or in some other mental thought process occurring as a result of, for example, using rules-of-thumb or holding onto one's preferences and beliefs, regardless of contrary information.

collective bargaining a process by which wage rates and other conditions of work are negotiated and agreed upon by a union or unions with an employer or employers.

Competition and Markets Authority government agency responsible for advising on and implementing UK competition policy.

competition policy the part of the government's microeconomic policy and industrial policy which aims to make goods markets more competitive. It comprises policy toward monopoly, mergers and restrictive trading practices.

complete market failure a market fails to function at all and a 'missing market' results.

concentration ratio measures the market share (percentage of the total market) of the biggest firms in the market. For example, a five-firm concentration measures the aggregate market share of the largest five firms.

condition of demand a determinant of demand, other than the good's own price, that fixes the position of the demand curve. A change in one or more of the conditions of demand leads to a shift of demand.

constant returns to scale when the scale of all the factors of production employed increases, output increases at the same rate.

consumer surplus a measure of the economic welfare enjoyed by consumers: surplus utility received over and above the price paid for a good.

consumption externality when consumption of a good or a service imposes external costs or benefits on third parties outside of the market without these being reflected in market prices.

contestable market a market in which the potential exists for new firms to enter the market. A perfectly contestable market has no entry or exit barriers and no sunk costs, and both incumbent firms and new entrants have access to the same level of technology.

contraction of demand an adjustment or movement up a demand curve following an increase in the good's price.

contractualisation services which were previously provided by the public sector, such as road cleaning and refuse collection, are put to private sector tender and then provided by private sector firms.

creative destruction capitalism evolving and renewing itself over time through new technologies and innovations replacing older technologies and innovations.

deadweight loss the name given to the loss of economic welfare when the maximum attainable level of total welfare is not achieved.

decrease in demand a leftward shift of the demand curve.

decreasing returns to scale when the scale of all the factors of production employed increases, output increases at a slower rate.

default choice an option that is selected automatically unless an alternative is specified.

demerit good a good for which the private benefits of consumption are greater than the social benefits and for which the long-term private benefits are less than the short-term benefits.

deregulation the removal of previously imposed regulations.

derived demand demand for a good or factor of production, not wanted for its own sake, which is a consequence of the demand for something else.

diseconomy of scale as output increases, long-run average cost rises.

distribution of income how income is divided between rich and poor, or between different groups in society, e.g. on a regional, age or gender basis.

distribution of wealth how wealth is divided between rich and poor, or between different groups in society, e.g. on a regional, age or gender basis.

divorce of ownership from control the owners and those who manage the firm are different groups with different objectives.

duopoly two firms only in a market.

dynamic efficiency occurs in the long run, leading to the development of new products and more efficient processes that improve productive efficiency.

economic sanctions restrictions imposed by regulations and/or laws that restrict an individual's freedom to behave in certain ways. Breaking a sanction can lead to punishment.

economy of scale as output increases, long-run average cost falls.

elasticity of demand for labour proportionate change in demand for labour following a change in the wage rate.

elasticity of supply of labour proportionate change in the supply of labour following a change in the wage rate.

entry barriers obstacles that make it difficult for a new firm to enter a market.

equality means that everyone is treated exactly the same. A completely equal distribution of income means that everybody has the same income.

equity means that everybody is treated fairly.

exit barriers obstacles that make it difficult for an established firm to leave a market.

extension of demand an adjustment or movement down a demand curve following a fall in the good's price.

external diseconomy of scale an increase in long-run average costs of production resulting from the growth of the market or industry of which the firm is a part.

external economy of scale a fall in long-run average costs of production resulting from the growth of the market or industry of which the firm is a part.

externality occurs when production or consumption of goods or services imposes external costs or benefits on third parties outside of the market without these being reflected in market prices. When an externality is generated, there is a divergence between private and social costs and benefits.

fairness the quality of being impartial, just, or free of favouritism. It can mean treating everyone the same. Fairness involves treating people equally, sharing with others, giving others respect and time, and not taking advantage of them.

firm a productive organisation which sells its output of goods or services commercially.

framing how something is presented (the 'frame') influences the choices people make.

free-rider problem occurs when non-excludability leads to a situation in which not enough customers choose to pay for a good, preferring instead to free ride, with the result that the incentive to provide the good through the market disappears and a missing market may result. (A free rider is someone who benefits without paying.)

geographical immobility of labour when workers are unwilling or unable to move from one area to another in search of work.

Gini coefficient measures the extent to which the distribution of income or wealth among individuals or households within an economy deviates from a perfectly equal distribution.

government failure occurs when government intervention in the economy makes the allocation of resources worse. The intervention may be ineffective, wasteful and/or damaging.

hit-and-run competition occurs when a new entrant can 'hit' the market, make profits and then 'run', given that there are no or low barriers to exit.

hypothesis of diminishing marginal utility for a single consumer the marginal utility derived from a good or service diminishes for each additional unit consumed.

income personal or household income is the flow of money a person or household receives in a particular time period.

income effect an increase in the hourly wage rate means higher real income, and if leisure is a normal good, the quantity of leisure demanded goes up which means a reduction in the quantity of labour supplied.

increase in demand a rightward shift of the demand curve.

increasing returns to scale when the scale of all the factors of production employed increases, output increases at a faster rate.

individual demand curve shows how much of a good or service the consumer plans to demand at different possible prices.

innovation improves on or makes a significant contribution to something that has already been invented, thereby turning the results of invention into a product.

internal economies and diseconomies of scale changes in long-run average costs of production resulting from changes in the size or scale of a firm or plant.

invention making something entirely new; something that did not exist before at all.

labour productivity output per worker.

law of demand as a good's price falls, more is demanded.

law of diminishing returns a *short-term* law which states that as a variable factor of production is added to a fixed factor of production, eventually both the marginal and average returns to the variable factor will begin to fall. It is also known as the law of diminishing marginal (and average) productivity.

limit prices prices set low enough to make it unprofitable for other firms to enter the market.

long-run average cost cost per unit of output incurred when all factors of production or inputs can be varied.

long-run marginal cost addition to total cost resulting from producing one additional unit of output when all the factors of production are variable.

Lorenz curve a graph on which the cumulative percentage of total national income or wealth is plotted against the cumulative percentage of population (ranked in increasing size of share). The extent to which the curve dips below a straight diagonal line indicates the degree of inequality of distribution.

mandated choice people are required by law to make a decision.

marginal cost addition to total cost resulting from producing one additional unit of output.

marginal cost of labour the addition to a firm's total cost of production resulting from employing one more worker.

marginal physical product of labour the addition to a firm's total output brought about by employing one more worker.

marginal returns of labour the change in the quantity of total output resulting from the employment of one more worker, holding all the other factors of production fixed.

marginal revenue addition to total revenue resulting from the sale of one more unit of the product.

marginal revenue product of labour the money value of the addition to a firm's total output brought about by employing one more worker.

marginal tax rates the tax rate levied on the last pound of income received. The term can be applied solely to income taxes or to all the taxes a person or business pays.

marginal utility the additional welfare, satisfaction or pleasure gained from consuming one extra unit of a good.

market conduct the price and other market policies pursued by firms. This is also known as market behaviour, but is not to be confused with market performance, which refers to the end results of these policies.

market failure occurs when the price mechanism fails to allocate scarce resources in a productively efficient way and when the operation of market forces leads to an allocatively inefficient outcome.

market structure the organisational and other characteristics of a market.

marketisation the provision of goods and service is shifted from the non-market sector into the market sector of the economy. Also known as commercialisation.

means-tested benefits the ability to claim these benefits depends on a person's income or 'means'.

mechanisation process of moving from a labour-intensive to a more capital-intensive method of production, employing more machines and fewer workers.

merit good a good for which the social benefits of consumption exceed the private benefits and for which the long-term private benefits of consumption are greater than the short-term private benefits.

minimum efficient scale the lowest output at which the firm is able produce at the minimum achievable *LRAC*.

missing market the absence of a market for a good or service, most commonly in the case of public goods and externalities.

monopolistic competition a market structure in which firms have many competitors, but each one sells a slightly different product.

monopoly one firm only in a market.

monopoly power firms in market structures other than pure monopoly usually possess significant monopoly power, defined as power over price setting and other aspects of the market such as product differentiation.

monopsony there is only one buyer in a market.

monopsony power the market power exercised in a market by the buyer of a good or the services of a factor production such as labour, even though the firm is not a pure monopsonist.

moral hazard the tendency of individuals and firms, once insured against some contingency, to behave so as to make that contingency more likely.

national living wage an adult wage rate, set by the UK government, which all employers must pay from 2016 onward, and which has replaced the adult national minimum wage rate.

national minimum wage a minimum wage or wage rate that must by law be paid to employees, though in many labour markets the wage rate paid by employers is above the national minimum wage.

natural barriers barriers that result from features of the industry, such as economies of scale or high research and development costs; *not* barriers that have been erected artificially.

negative externality a cost that is suffered by a third party as a result of an economic transaction. In the transaction, the producer and consumer are the first and second parties, and third parties include any other people or firms that are affected by the transaction. Pollution is a negative externality when unwillingly consumed by third parties.

net advantage the sum of the monetary and non-monetary benefits of working.

non-excludability a property of a public good which means that if it is provided for one person it is provided for all.

non-rejectability a property of a public good which means that if the good is provided, it is impossible for a person to 'opt out' and not gain its benefits.

non-rivalry a property of a public good which means that when a good is consumed by one person, it does not reduce the amount available for others.

normal profit the minimum profit a firm must make to stay in business, which is, however, insufficient to attract new firms into the market.

nudges factors which encourage people to think and act in particular ways. Nudges try to shift group and individual behaviour in ways which comply with desirable social norms.

occupational immobility of labour when workers are unwilling or unable to move from one type of job to another, e.g. because different skills are needed.

optimum firm size the size of firm capable of producing at the lowest average cost and thus being productively efficient.

partial market failure a market does function, but it delivers the 'wrong' quantity of a good or service, which results in resource misallocation.

plant an establishment, such as a factory, a workshop or a retail outlet, owned and operated by a firm.

positive externality a benefit that is enjoyed by a third party as a result of an economic transaction, e.g. a beautiful garden, visible to third parties.

poverty the state of being extremely poor and not having enough money or income to meet basic needs.

predatory prices prices set below average cost (or very cheaply) with the aim of forcing rival firms out of business.

price agreement an agreement between a firm, similar firms, suppliers or customers regarding the pricing of a good or service.

price discrimination charging different prices to different customers for the same product or service, with the prices based on different willingness to pay.

price leadership the setting of prices in a market, usually by a dominant firm, which is then followed by other firms in the same market. In barometric price leadership, one firm acts as a 'barometer' or a benchmark, whose prices other firms follow.

price-maker when a firm faces a downward-sloping demand curve for its product, it possesses the market power to set the price at which it sells the product.

price-taker a firm which is so small that it has to accept the ruling market price. If the firm raises its price, it loses all its sales; if it cuts its price, it gains no advantage.

price war occurs when rival firms continuously lower prices to undercut each other.

private costs and benefits private costs are costs incurred solely by an individual or firm as a result of their own activities; private benefits are benefits enjoyed solely by an individual or firm as a result of their own activities.

private finance initiative the government seeks tenders from the private sector for designing, building, financing and running infrastructure projects.

private good a good which exhibits the characteristics of excludability and rivalry.

privatisation the transfer of assets from the public sector to the private sector.

producer surplus a measure of the economic welfare enjoyed by firms or producers: the difference between the price a firm succeeds in charging and the minimum price it would be prepared to accept.

product differentiation the marketing of generally similar products with minor variations or the marketing of a range of different products.

production externality when production of a good or a service imposes external costs or benefits on third parties outside of the market without these being reflected in market prices.

productive efficiency the level of output at which average costs of production are minimised.

productivity output per unit of input.

profit the difference between total sales revenue and total cost of production.

profit maximisation occurs at the level of output at which total profit is greatest.

progressive taxation a tax is progressive when, as income rises, a greater proportion of income is paid in taxation. The term can be applied to a particular tax such as income tax or to taxation in general.

property rights the exclusive authority to determine how a resource is used. In the case of a private property right, the owner of private property such as a bar of chocolate in a sweet shop has the right to prevent other people from consuming the bar unless they are prepared to pay a price to the owner.

public good a good which exhibits the characteristics of non-excludability and non-rivalry.

public ownership ownership of industries, firms and other assets such as social housing by central government or local government. The state's acquisition of such assets is called nationalisation.

public–private partnership partnership between the private and public sectors to provide public services.

quantity-setter when a firm faces a downward-sloping demand curve for its product, it possesses the market power to set the quantity of the good it wishes to sell.

quasi-public good a good which has characteristics of both a public and private good, e.g. it might be non-excludable but rival, or excludable but non-rival.

rational behaviour acting in pursuit of self-interest, which for a consumer means attempting to maximise the welfare, satisfaction or utility gained from the goods and services consumed.

regulation the imposition of rules and other constraints which restrict freedom of economic action.

regulatory capture occurs when regulatory agencies act in the interest of regulated firms rather on behalf of the consumers they are supposed to protect.

relative poverty occurs when income is below a specified proportion of average income, e.g. below 60% of median income.

restricted choice offering people a limited number of options so that they are not overwhelmed by the complexity of the situation. If there are too many choices, people may make a poorly thought-out decision or not make any decision.

returns to scale the rate by which output changes if the scale of all the factors of production is changed.

rule-of-thumb a rough and practical method or procedure that can be easily applied when making decisions.

satisficing achieving a satisfactory outcome rather than the best possible outcome.

shift of a demand curve the movement of a demand curve to a new position.

social costs and benefits social costs are costs which fall on the whole of society: social cost = private cost + external cost; social benefits are benefits enjoyed by the whole of society: social benefit = private benefit + external benefit.

social norms forms or patterns of behaviour considered acceptable by a society or group within that society.

static efficiency efficiency (e.g. productive and allocative efficiency) at a particular point in time.

substitution effect a higher hourly wage rate makes work more attractive than leisure, so workers substitute labour for leisure.

sunk costs costs that have already been incurred and cannot be recovered.

technological change a term that is used to describe the overall effect of invention, innovation and the diffusion or spread of technology in the economy.

total returns of labour total output produced by all the workers employed by a firm.

total revenue all the money received by a firm from selling its total output, $TR = P \times Q$.

trade union a group of workers who join together to maintain and improve their conditions of employment, including their pay.

universal benefits benefits claimable of right and not dependent on a person's income.

utility the satisfaction or economic welfare an individual gains from consuming a good or service.

wage discrimination paying different workers different wage rates for doing the same job.

wealth personal wealth is the stock of everything which has value that a person or household owns at a particular point in time.

Microeconomics practice questions

In this section you will find a set of multiple-choice questions, followed first by a context question for A-level and then by three essay questions for A-level Paper 1.

Multiple-choice questions

1 Which one of the following is an example of the factor of production capital?

   A an acre of farmland

   B a TV set used for family entertainment

   C the purchase of shares issued by a public company

   D a photocopier used by a private company

2 In the study of economics, the term *utility* refers to:

   A single-use goods

   B the satisfaction derived from a good

   C rational economic behaviour by producers and consumers

   D the alternate use of resources by firms

3 A firm has a fixed amount of land and capital, and increases output by employing additional labour according to the schedule below:

Labour	Output
1	10
2	64
3	100
4	125
5	140
6	130

The law of diminishing marginal returns begins to operate after how many units of labour have been employed?

   A 2

   B 4

   C 5

   D 6

4 The following diagram shows the cost and revenue curves for a firm operating in an imperfectly competitive market.

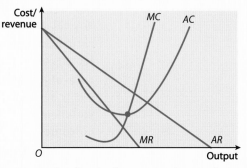

The firm's objectives change from sales maximisation to profit maximisation. As a result there would be:

   A a higher output and a higher price

   B a lower output and a lower price

   C a lower output and a higher price

   D a higher output at a lower price

5 The following diagram illustrates the costs of production of a firm.

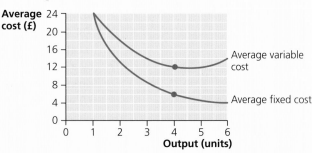

The total cost of producing 4 units is:

   A £12

   B £24

   C £48

   D £72

6 Firm Z is maximising profits in the long run and the following information is known about its cost and revenue structure:

marginal cost = £400

average cost = £500

marginal revenue = £400

average revenue = £500

Firm Z could be operating under each of the following market conditions *except*:

A monopoly

B oligopoly

C monopolistic competition

D perfect competition

7 The diagram below depicts the market for a good in which negative externalities are generated in the course of production.

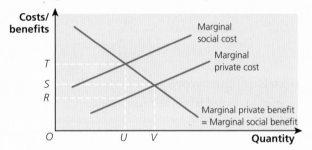

Which of the following might achieve an optimum allocation of resources from society's point of view?

A a tax per unit of *RT*

B a subsidy per unit of *RT*

C a tax per unit of *ST*

D a subsidy per unit of *ST*

8 The table below shows the costs and benefits from producing different quantities of a pesticide.

Output of pesticides (tons per week)	Marginal private cost (£000)	Marginal social cost (£000)	Marginal social benefits (£000)
500	100	130	165
600	130	160	160
700	160	170	150
800	180	190	150

In order to achieve the best outcome from society's point of view:

A the firm should produce at its profit-maximising output

B marginal social benefit should be maximised by producing 500 tons per week

C 600 tons of pesticides should be produced each week

D output of pesticides should be banned completely

9 The diagram below shows the labour market for a particular country in which a minimum wage rate is introduced at W_M.

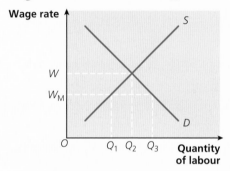

The effect of the minimum wage rate will be:

A unemployment equal to Q_3 minus Q_1

B a labour shortage equal to Q_2 minus Q_1

C employment remaining unchanged at Q_2

D an excess demand for labour

10 Which **one** of the following is a necessary condition for a firm to practise price discrimination between two markets?

A There must be no barriers between the markets.

B Costs of production in each market must be different.

C Consumers must be aware of price differences between the two markets.

D Price elasticities of demand must be different in each market.

A-level Paper 1 context question

Context 1

Total for this context: 40 marks

The insurance industry and price comparison websites

Study **Extracts A**, **B** and **C** and then answer **all** parts of Context 1 which follow.

Extract A: Current financial reserves and UK employees of selected leading UK insurance companies, 2013

Company	Current UK reserves	Number of employees
Aviva	£8.1 billion	8,950
Direct Line	£8.0 billion	14,400
AGEAS	£360.4 million	2,000
AIG	£2.9 billion	1,300
Aspen	£4.4 billion	533
Allianz Insurance	£1.6 billion	4,500
NFU Mutual	£3.2 billion	3,841
Liverpool Victoria (LV)	£2.0 billion	5,700
Tesco Underwriting	£186.9 million	400

Source: *Post Magazine*, 23 July 2015

Extract B: How price comparison sites work

Price comparison sites are designed to do just what their name implies: compare the price of goods and services supplied by a large number of firms. This allows the consumer to make an informed decision about which provider to choose in order to save money.

The best-known price comparison websites tend to specialise in financial products such as insurance policies. The appeal of comparison websites that specialise in products such as life, motoring and travel insurance is that they allow consumers to get quotes from a variety of insurance firms at a single stroke, thus avoiding the need to fill in multiple sets of forms and make enquiries about what is on offer from the market's vast array of insurers — 976 general insurers in 2013.

Price comparison sites generally allow users to search for the products that might suit them via simple 'best buy' tables. Because they largely get rid of the need to troop around from shop to shop or, in the case of insurance, to phone up a large number of insurance companies, price comparison websites increase the amount of information available to consumers. In theory, price comparison websites should make markets become closer to the economist's model of perfect competition.

Source: news reports

Extract C: We could all be worse off because of price comparison websites

The existence of price comparison websites may be bad for consumers, research by the University of Warwick's Department of Economics has found.

Writing in June 2015, analyst David Ronayne argues that price comparison websites may push prices up, not down, and that increasing the number of competing comparison sites may make the problem worse.   5

'The common belief is that these sites benefit consumers by increasing competition among firms selling goods and services. But these websites are not charities; they charge fees to the firms whose products they recommend, which in turn have to be passed on to consumers through increased prices. Since most firms now have their own websites, you can find out about their   10
prices in a few clicks, without having to access a commercially run price comparison website. We found that only in the unlikely case where people who use price comparison websites check every single site that is available, is it guaranteed that consumers will benefit from the existence of the price comparison website industry.'   15

The Consumer Association's *Which?* magazine research has shown that using a price comparison website isn't always straightforward. No two price comparison websites for insurance policies are likely to yield exactly the same results. The websites also provide quotations from only a limited set of insurance companies, namely those that are prepared to pay comparison   20
companies a substantial fee for quoting their services. Companies which refuse to do this, such as Direct Line, never appear on price comparison websites.

The fact that price comparison websites charge hefty fees to companies that appear on their sites raises costs of production in the insurance   25
industry. Customers end up paying higher prices than they would pay if the comparison websites did not exist. Hence Ronayne's conclusion that price comparison websites may be bad for consumers.

01 Calculate the median value of the current UK reserves of the selected UK insurance companies shown in **Extract A**, in 2013 and name the median company.   *(2 marks)*

02 Assuming that current UK reserves indicate the amount of capital employed in each of the selected insurance companies shown in **Extract A**, explain how the data in the extract might be used to conclude that Aviva is a more capital-intensive insurance business than Direct Line.   *(4 marks)*

03 **Extract B** (lines 16–18) states 'price comparison websites should make markets become closer to the economist's model of perfect competition'.

With the help of a diagram, explain why perfectly competitive markets are both productively and allocatively efficient?   *(9 marks)*

04 **Extract C** (line 1) states that 'price comparison websites may be bad for consumers'.

Using the data in the extracts and your knowledge of economics, assess the view that price comparison websites are bad for consumers.   *(25 marks)*

A-level Paper 1 essay questions

Either

Essay 1

Traditionally, most economists have assumed that, when buying goods and services, consumers aim to maximise the utility they expect to derive from their purchases. Behavioural economists dispute this assumption.

09 Explain the meaning of the term 'utility' and, with the aid of a diagram, explain how utility is likely to change as more of a good or service is consumed. *(15 marks)*

10 From 2013 to 2015, the UK government used the 'Green Deal', a policy introduced on the advice of behavioural economists, to nudge people into using home heating systems more efficiently.

   Evaluate the benefits and costs of trying to alter people's behaviour through the use of 'nudge' policies such as the 'Green Deal'. *(25 marks)*

or

Essay 2

Some economists believe that employers hold too much market power in UK labour markets and that workers have too little market power.

11 Explain how the demand for labour is determined in a competitive labour market. *(15 marks)*

12 To what extent, if at all, should governments intervene in labour markets? Justify your answer with the help of examples of government intervention in labour markets. *(25 marks)*

or

Essay 3

Sports events, cultural activities such as opera and the theatre, art galleries and museums have attracted thousands of foreign visitors to the UK, all of whom have contributed to the country's economic success.

13 Explain the economic reasons why organisers of cultural activities such as plays, ballet and opera charge people different prices for tickets to watch the shows they provide. *(15 marks)*

14 Evaluate the economic case for and against the government subsidising cultural activities. *(25 marks)*

2

Macroeconomics

7 Revisiting and developing macroeconomic theory

This is the first of four chapters which revisit and further develop the macroeconomics covered previously in Book 1, Part 2.

Book 1 introduced you to two related macroeconomic models which try to explain how the macroeconomy works, namely the circular flow and the aggregate demand/aggregate supply (*AD/AS*) models. This chapter revisits these models, while Chapters 8 and 9 focus on their implications for monetary, fiscal and supply-side policies. Chapter 10 covers international economics.

You should appreciate that different economic models provide insights into different aspects of the behaviour of the macroeconomy. Exam questions may ask you to assess the impact and effectiveness of government policies to deal with recent and current macroeconomic problems, and also to consider alternative approaches to economic policy.

Your knowledge and understanding of macroeconomics will be assessed in Papers 2 and 3 of the A-level examination. To remind you, Paper 2 is similar to the microeconomic Paper 1 in that it requires you to answer one Context data-response question from a choice of two, and one essay question from a choice of three. Paper 3, by contrast, comprises questions which are both microeconomic and macroeconomic, namely 30 multiple-choice questions and an extended Case study/Investigation question. You will find examples of questions written in the style of Papers 2 and 3 at the end of the book.

LEARNING OBJECTIVES
This chapter will:

- outline how macroeconomic theory and policy have changed over the years
- revisit the circular flow of income and expenditure
- remind you of the meaning of aggregate demand and aggregate supply
- develop the aggregate demand/aggregate supply (*AD/AS*) macroeconomic model
- refresh and develop your knowledge and understanding of employment and unemployment issues
- revisit inflation theory and explain the Phillips curve relationship

7.1 Introducing the national and international economy

When using macroeconomic models, you should be critically aware of the assumptions upon which the models are based and their limitations when they are used to make sense of real-world phenomena. You may be asked to propose, analyse and evaluate possible solutions to macroeconomic problems.

You are not required to have specific knowledge of economic developments in any individual country, other than the UK. If such information is needed, it will be presented to you in the extracts of the Context or Investigation question you are answering. The introduction to the AQA A-level economics specification includes the following advice: 'It is expected that students will acquire a good knowledge of trends and developments in the economy which have taken place over the past fifteen years and also have an awareness of earlier events where this helps to give recent developments a longer term perspective.'

To understand important aspects of macroeconomic behaviour, you must have a firm grasp of related microeconomic principles — for example, understanding price elasticity of demand is essential when analysing the impact of changes in the exchange rate on an economy. Sound knowledge of microeconomic principles will also aid your understanding of much of macroeconomic theory — for example, microeconomic supply and demand analysis of individual markets for goods and services underpins the *AD/AS* explanation of how these markets function in aggregate at the level of the whole economy.

A brief history of modern macroeconomics

Although the A-level specification only requires you to know about trends and developments in the economy which have taken place over the 15 years before you sit the examination, in order to understand the nature of modern macroeconomics, it is useful to go back to what was happening in the UK and world economies in the 1920s and 1930s. Most economists at the time, especially those in British and American universities, were free-market economists who believed that in a competitive market economy market forces would automatically deliver full employment and economic growth. In so far as governments needed to have a macroeconomic policy, it was generally believed that the policy should be restricted to maintaining the 'sound money' deemed necessary for a stable price level, and possibly to maintaining a fixed exchange rate.

KEY TERMS

full employment occurs when the number of people wishing to work equals the number of workers whom employers wish to hire.

economic growth the rate of increase in the potential output of an economy.

STUDY TIP

Free-market economics is sometimes called *neoclassical economics* but there are also other groups of economists who believe that the free workings of the market economy deliver the best results — the Austrian School of economists is one example.

189

However, the problem was that in the UK economy of the 1920s, and in the wider world economy (especially the USA) in the 1930s, free-market forces did *not* deliver **full employment** and **economic growth**. Instead, unregulated

John Maynard Keynes, whose book *The General Theory of Employment, Interest and Money* marked the beginning of modern macroeconomics

KEY TERMS

aggregate demand total planned spending on the goods and services produced within the economy in a particular time period.

aggregate supply the aggregate level of real output that all the firms in the economy plan to produce at different average price levels.

fiscal policy the use of government spending, taxation and the government's budgetary position to achieve the government's policy objectives.

unemployment occurs when people who are actively searching for employment are unable to find work.

inflation a continuous and persistent rise in the price level and a fall in the value of money.

market forces seemed to have produced economic stagnation and mass unemployment. The most seminal event of the time was the Great Depression, which began around 1929–30 and lasted on and off for much of the following decade. Unemployment rose in 1933 to almost 25% in the USA, and in 1931 to 24% in the UK. Regional unemployment in towns such as Jarrow in northeast England rose to as high as 70%, though London, the southeast and the midlands fared much better.

Free-market economists responded to the Great Depression by arguing that markets were not to blame for persistent large-scale unemployment. Instead, they believed that mass unemployment was caused by institutional factors, such as the power exercised by trade unions, which prevented markets from operating freely. In the free-market view, wage cuts were necessary to 'price the unemployed into jobs', but trade unions resisting wage cuts prevented this from happening.

In the late 1920s, John Maynard Keynes, who started his academic career as an economist in the neoclassical tradition, began to change his view on the main cause of unemployment. In response to an accusation of inconsistency, Keynes is reported to have said, 'When the facts change, I change my mind — what do you do, sir?'

Keynes believed that orthodox free-market economic theory failed to explain how the whole economy works, and that a better and more general theory was needed to explain mass unemployment. Keynes completed his new theory in 1936 with the publication of his great book *The General Theory of Employment, Interest and Money*, commonly referred to as Keynes's *General Theory*.

Keynes's *General Theory* marks the beginning of modern macroeconomics. For over a generation until about 1979, Keynesian economics was macroeconomics, and macroeconomics was Keynesian economics. In the three decades after the Second World War, Keynesianism became the new economic orthodoxy in the UK, the Netherlands and the Scandinavian countries. Economic policy in the USA also eventually became Keynesian, with the Republican president, Richard Nixon, famously stating in 1971 that 'we are all Keynesians now'.

Macroeconomics in the Keynesian era

The Keynesian era covered the three decades after Keynes's death in 1946, when economists and politicians who claimed to have inherited his mantle implemented policies they believed he would have supported. We shall explain more about Keynesian economics later in this chapter, and also in Chapters 8 and 9. For the moment, we shall restrict ourselves to saying that Keynesian economic policy mainly centred on managing the level of **aggregate demand** in the economy, primarily through the use of **fiscal policy**, in order to prevent both large-scale **unemployment** and also **inflation**. Aggregate demand is the total planned spending on domestically produced real output in the economy by all the economic agents in the economy, whereas **aggregate supply** shows the aggregate level of real output that all the firms in the economy plan to produce.

The free-market counter-revolution

An economic orthodoxy can remain dominant and resistant to being replaced, as long as its theories appear to explain how the economy operates or functions, and the policies based on those theories appear to work. But if its

KEY TERMS

macroeconomic policy
government policy aimed at achieving macroeconomic objectives such as a satisfactory and sustainable rate of economic growth, full employment or low unemployment, control of inflation and a satisfactory balance of payments.

monetarist an economist who argues that a prior increase in the money supply is always the cause of inflation.

money supply the stock of money (coins, notes and bank deposits) in the economy at a particular point of time.

SYNOPTIC LINK
We mentioned monetarism in Book 1, Chapter 8 and the term is explained in more detail in Chapters 8 and 9 of this book.

KEY TERM

supply-side policies
government economic policies which aim to make markets more competitive and efficient, increase production potential, and shift the *LRAS* curve to the right. Supply-side fiscal policy is arguably the most important type of supply-side policy, but there are also non-fiscal supply-side policies.

theories fail adequately to explain events taking place in the real economy, and if the policies based on those theories are ineffective or don't work at all, the orthodoxy becomes vulnerable to attack.

Just as free-market economic theories were attacked by Keynes's new theories in the 1930s, so, more than a generation later in the 1970s, Keynesian theories were attacked through a revival of free-market economics. After the Second World War, Keynesianism had dominated as long as Keynesian demand-management policies delivered full employment and economic growth, combined with low inflation. But in the 1970s, in the UK there was simultaneous failure to achieve any of the standard objectives of **macroeconomic policy**, including full employment and control of inflation. The 1970s became the decade of the crisis in Keynesian economics, characterised by zero, negative or very low economic growth accompanied by accelerating inflation.

Perhaps not surprisingly therefore, the failure of Keynesianism led to the free-market counter-revolution or revival. To begin with, in the 1970s and 1980s, an important part of the free-market revival was known as monetarism. A **monetarist** is an economist who believes that inflation (a persistent rise in the price level) is always caused by a prior increase in the **money supply**. (The money supply is usually defined as comprising: coins, notes and bank deposits. See Chapter 8 for more information.) It follows that if a government wishes to control inflation, it must first control the rate of growth of the money supply.

Supply-side economics

To begin with, monetarism was perhaps the most important part of the free-market revival. However, in 1985 the UK government, which at first had enthusiastically tried to control the rate of growth of the money supply so as to control inflation, largely abandoned monetarist policies. It did this because monetarist policies had not worked. But this did not mean that free-market economists immediately switched to becoming 'born-again Keynesians'. Instead, free-market theories continued to dominate the macroeconomic agenda, but were now 'rebranded' under the label 'supply-side theory'.

STUDY TIP
These days, Keynesian demand-management policies are often called demand-side policies, so as to separate them from the supply-side policies advocated by free-market economists. (Some supply-side policies, such as government labour training schemes, are interventionist, but free-market supply-side policies are anti-interventionist and part of a programme to reduce the role of the state in the economy.)

Supply-side policies aim to improve national economic performance by creating competitive and more efficient markets. Arguably, for this reason, supply-side policies are more microeconomic than macroeconomic. Indeed, in the early days of supply-side economics, the UK government argued that a redefinition was needed of the respective roles of macro- and microeconomic policies. The government argued that macro-policy would be restricted to the limited role of controlling inflation, while micro-policy would be used to promote growth and employment. This would be the new orthodoxy.

Where are we now?

Until the onset of **recession** in 2008, conflicts between free-market and Keynesian economists to some extent disappeared, or at least were downplayed. Members of both schools agreed about the importance of supply-side economics and about the need at the macro level to control inflation — a need that to some extent was ignored during the Keynesian era. In the other direction, many free-market economists accepted the Keynesian argument that governments should manage the level of aggregate demand, though with the use of **monetary policy** rather than fiscal policy. **Bank Rate** continues to be the main instrument of modern monetary policy, though in recent years various 'unconventional' monetary policy instruments, such as **quantitative easing** (QE), have been introduced. We explain the reasons for recent changes in monetary policy in Chapter 8. In the 2008/09 recession, and in the period of economic recovery since 2009, Bank Rate has been kept unchanged at the historic low of 0.5% (at least up to the time of writing in January 2016), in order to promote economic recovery. However, for reasons we also explain, 'unconventional' monetary policy instruments have been introduced because lowering Bank Rate becomes less effective in promoting economic recovery, the closer Bank Rate gets to zero.

SYNOPTIC LINK

Go to Chapter 8, pages 248–57 and Chapter 9, pages 265–90 to find out more about modern monetary policy and fiscal policy.

For several years before the 2008/09 recession, fiscal policy was mostly being used to achieve supply-side objectives, and to promote the macroeconomic stability deemed necessary for markets to be competitive and efficient. However, from 2008 until the 2010 general election, fiscal policy was used to manage aggregate demand. Government spending increased, some taxes were cut and the **budget deficit** widened, as the Labour government injected demand into the economy in an attempt to 'spend the economy out of recession'. Indeed, by the time of the 2010 general election, the Labour government's 'fiscal stimulus' seemed to be producing the 'green shoots' of economic recovery.

However, for reasons we explain in Chapter 9, the burgeoning budget deficit caused by the increase in government spending led to the sovereign debt problem. Free-market economists have since argued that it would have been impossible for the fiscal stimulus to be maintained. Keynesian economists disagree, and also argue that the austerity programme introduced in 2010 unnecessarily led to a loss of output that can never be recovered. Be that as it may, the appointment in May 2010 of George Osborne as chancellor of the exchequer in the Conservative–Liberal Democrat Coalition government meant that a minister ideologically opposed to Keynesian-style fiscal policy took over the management of the British economy.

Thus, fiscal austerity (fiscal restraint or fiscal consolidation), in which government spending is cut or taxes are raised in a bid to reduce the size of the budget deficit, with the eventual aim of creating a **budget surplus** so as to reduce the size of the **national debt**, replaced the short-lived fiscal stimulus. (**Balancing the budget** occurs when there is neither a budget deficit nor a budget surplus.) In the UK, the main emphasis has been on cutting public spending.

In other respects, fiscal policy resumed its earlier role of trying to achieve supply-side objectives through the lowering of income tax rates and the raising of income tax thresholds, so that fewer low-paid earners now pay income tax. Corporation tax was also cut but the standard rate of VAT was increased. The Coalition relied on expansionary monetary policy to try to boost aggregate demand.

7.2 Circular flow and *AD/AS* revisited

Circular flow theory

In Book 1, on pages 163 and 165, we drew three diagrams which show the **circular flow of income** around the economy. We then used the circular flow diagrams to explain the important macroeconomic concepts of **macroeconomic equilibrium** and **injections** into, and **withdrawals** from, the flow of income as expenditure circulates around the economy. Later in Book 1, we linked injections and withdrawals to shifts of the aggregate demand (*AD*) curve, to **cyclical unemployment**, and to **multiplier** effects. When injections increase and exceed withdrawals, there is a multiplier effect which leads to an increase in national income that is larger than the increase in injections. When withdrawals exceed injections, the multiplier effect leads to a larger fall in national income.

SYNOPTIC LINK

At this stage, to make sure you fully understand the multiplier, you should re-read Book 1, pages 178–80.

The circular flow diagrams which we drew in Book 1 are quite simple and are enough to build up a basic understanding of circular flow theory. The basic circular flow diagram illustrates the financial flows between households and firms in the aggregate market for goods and services (the goods market) and the market for the services supplied in aggregate by the owners of factors of production (the factor market). Both markets feed on each other. Firms pay workers for goods and services the workers produce. The workers simultaneously act as consumers to purchase these goods and services. The sales revenue then received by the firms is in turn used to purchase additional services provided by the owners of factors of production, and so the circular process continues.

KEY TERMS

macroeconomic equilibrium occurs in a circular flow diagram when injections into the circular flow of income equal withdrawals from the circular flow. It can also be shown in an *AD/AS* diagram as the level of real national income at which *AD* = *AS*. Also known as the equilibrium level of national income.

injections investment spending by firms on capital goods (*I*), government spending (*G*) and overseas spending on the economy's exports (*X*) are injections into the circular flow of income.

withdrawals saving (*S*), tax revenues (*T*) and spending on imports (*M*) are withdrawals from the circular flow of income. They are also known as leakages from the circular flow.

cyclical unemployment unemployment occurring in the downswing of the economic cycle or business cycle, caused by a lack of aggregate demand in the economy. Also known as Keynesian or demand-deficient unemployment.

multiplier the relationship between an initial change in aggregate demand and the resulting usually larger change in national income.

KEY TERM

gross domestic product the sum of all goods and services, or the value of output, produced in the economy over a period of time, e.g. 1 year.

CASE STUDY 7.1

Circular flow and the Phillips machine

In the Meade Room in the Department of Applied Economics of Cambridge University stands a Phillips machine — a device so cunning and ingenious that it can predict the running of the national economy to within 4% accuracy. The prototype was an odd assortment of tanks, pipes, sluices and valves, with water pumped around the machine by a motor cannibalised from the windscreen wiper of a Lancaster bomber. Bits of filed-down Perspex and fishing line were used to channel the coloured dyes that mimicked the flow of income round the economy into consumer spending, taxes, investment and exports. Bill Phillips and Walter Newlyn, who helped piece the machine together at the London School of Economics toward the end of the 1940s, experimented with treacle and methylated spirits before deciding that coloured water was the best way of displaying the way money circulates around the economy.

Water flows through a series of clear pipes, mimicking the way that money flows through the economy. The machine lets you see (literally) what happens if you lower tax rates or increase the money supply or whatever; just open a valve here or pull a lever there and the machine sloshes away, showing in real time how the water levels rise and fall in various tanks representing the growth in personal savings, tax revenue and so on. This device was state of the art in the 1950s, but it looks hilarious now, with all its plumbing and noisy pumps.

One early demonstration of the machine displayed the difficulties that can arise when monetary and fiscal policy are not synchronised. Phillips asked one of his students to be chancellor of the exchequer and control taxes and spending; another to be governor of the Bank of England and control interest rates. Predictably, the policies were uncoordinated and the upshot was that water overflowed on to the floor.

ACTIVITY

Read more about the Phillips machine in Tim Harford's book, *The Undercover Economist Strikes Back*, which is also available on a BBC radio podcast, and at **http://opinionator.blogs.nytimes.com/2009/06/02/ guest-column-like-water-for-money/?_r=0** and **www.theguardian.com/ business/2008/may/08/bankofenglandgovernor.economics**.

Developing the circular flow model

The circular flow of income illustrates the interdependent links between the various sectors which make up the economy and how the flows of money between sectors are continuous in nature.

The Office for National Statistics (ONS) states that the circular flow of income shows how financial payments flow between firms and households within the economy. It also shows the interaction between different sectors of the economy and the rest of the world. **Gross domestic product** (GDP) measures the total output of the UK economy in a particular time period, and the quarterly national accounts build this into a complete picture of all the transactions in the UK economy.

If you access the ONS website on **www.ons.gov.uk**, you can locate a circular flow graphic. (Alternatively, google 'How ONS statistics explain the UK economy'.) The circular flow graphic is an interactive diagram which, by clicking on the numbered icons, can be used to research up-to-date data about the quarterly economic activity of households, firms, the government and the rest of the world. For example, when we clicked the green icon 9 on 27 July 2015, we were informed that consumer price inflation in the UK was 0.1% in the 12 months up to May 2015, compared with a 0.1% fall in the 12 months up to April 2015. (Along with the other data which can be accessed from the graphic, the percentage annual rate of consumer price inflation will, of course, have changed by the time you access the interactive graphic yourself. However, the data we have quoted homes in on a very brief period of price deflation which occurred in May 2015.)

The aggregate demand/aggregate supply model: the essentials

In the last 35 years or so, the *AD/AS* model has become the preferred theoretical framework that many economists use for explaining macroeconomic issues. For example, the model is useful for analysing the effect of an increase in aggregate demand upon the economy. This addresses a key issue: will expansionary fiscal policy and/or monetary policy increase real output and jobs (i.e. will they be *reflationary*), or will the price level increase instead (i.e. will they be *inflationary*)? As this chapter explains, the answer to this key macroeconomic question depends to a large extent on supply-side factors as represented by the shape of the *AS* curve, in both the short run and the long run.

Aggregate demand, which must not be confused with the national income concept of national expenditure, is the total planned spending on the goods and services produced within the economy in a particular time period, such as a year. Aggregate demand measures *planned* spending, whereas national expenditure measures *realised* or *actual* spending, which has already taken place — for example, UK national expenditure in 2014.

The four sources of spending included in aggregate demand, each originating in a different sector of the economy (households, firms, the government sector and the overseas sector), are shown in the equation:

$$AD = C + I + G + (X - M)$$

where *C*, *I*, *G*, *X* and *M* are the symbols used respectively for planned consumption, investment, government spending, exports and imports.

STUDY TIP

Make sure you understand and can apply the aggregate demand equation:

$$AD = C + I + G + (X - M)$$

It is useful in a number of different contexts, such as explaining some of the effects of changes in monetary and fiscal policy.

QUANTITATIVE SKILLS 7.1

Worked example: components of aggregate demand

Table 7.1 shows the components of aggregate demand for an economy in 2015 and 2016.

Table 7.1 Components of aggregate demand, 2015 and 2016 (£bn)

Year	Government and private consumption expenditure	Government and private investment expenditure	Exports	Imports
2015	1,000	150	300	200
2016	1,200	170	250	220

1 **What was the change in the level of aggregate demand between 2015 and 2016?**
2 **What was the change in net export demand between 2015 and 2016?**

The information in Table 7.1 relates to the aggregate demand equation:

$$AD = C + I + G + (X - M)$$

1 Adding together the information in the columns, in 2015:

$AD = £1,000bn + £150bn + £300bn - £200bn = £1,250bn$

In 2016:

$AD = £1,200bn + £170bn + £250bn - £220bn = £1,400bn$

This means that between 2015 and 2016 aggregate demand increased by £150bn.

2 In 2015 net export demand $(X - M)$ was £300bn - £200bn, which was £100bn.
In 2016 net export demand $(X - M)$ was £250bn - £220bn, which was £30bn.
There was a balance of trade surplus in both years. The trade surplus fell by £70bn between 2015 and 2016.

The *AD* curve

The aggregate demand curve is illustrated along with a **short-run aggregate supply** (*SRAS*) curve in Figure 7.1. The aggregate demand curve shows the total quantities of real output that all economic agents plan to purchase at different price levels within the economy, when all the factors influencing aggregate demand other than the price level are held constant. If any of the determinants of aggregate demand change (apart from the price level), the *AD* curve shifts to the right or left, depending on whether there has been an increase or a decrease in aggregate demand. For example, an increase in consumer or business confidence shifts the *AD* curve to the right, via the effect of consumption or investment. An increase in net export demand $(X - M)$ has a similar effect, as does expansionary monetary policy and expansionary fiscal policy. By contrast, an increase in imports, contractionary monetary or fiscal policy, or a collapse in consumer or business confidence shifts the *AD* curve to the left.

In Figure 7.1 the equilibrium level of national income, y_1, is determined at point X, which is located where the *AD* curve intersects the *SRAS* curve. (The equilibrium level of national income can also be called *macroeconomic equilibrium*, a concept introduced earlier in this chapter in the context of circular flow theory.)

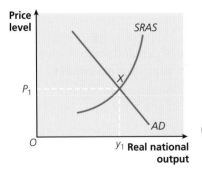

Figure 7.1 A downward-sloping *AD* curve and an upward-sloping *SRAS* curve

STUDY TIP
The *slope* of the *AD* curve tells us what happens to aggregate demand when the price level changes. Don't make the mistake of asserting that a change in the price level *shifts* the *AD* curve.

Explaining the shape of the aggregate demand (AD) curve

The *AD* curve slopes downward to the right, showing that as the price level falls, aggregate demand expands. A number of factors explain the *slope* of the *AD* curve, as distinct from a *shift* of the curve.

- One explanation lies in a *wealth effect* or *real balance effect*. Assuming a given nominal stock of money in the economy, a decrease in the price level increases people's real money balances: that is, the same amount of money buys more goods and services. An increase in real money balances makes people wealthier because money is a part of people's wealth.

- The increase in real money balances we have just described also means that the real money supply has increased, relative to the demand to hold real money balances. Basic supply and demand analysis tells us that when the supply of any commodity increases relative to demand for the commodity, its price tends to fall. Now, the rate of interest is the price of money. The increase in the supply of real money balances relative to demand reduces real interest rates, which in turn leads to higher levels of consumption and investment.

- A third factor relates to exports and imports. Other things remaining equal, including the **exchange rate** and the price levels in overseas economies, if the domestic price level falls, demand increases for the country's exports. At the same time, consumers buy domestically produced goods instead of relatively more expensive imports. Aggregate demand thus increases as the price level falls.

KEY TERM

exchange rate the external price of a currency, usually measured against another currency such as the US dollar or the euro.

The *SRAS* curve

Just as the *AD* curve shows the total quantities of real output that all the consumers, firms, the government and the overseas sector plan to purchase at different levels of domestic prices, so the *SRAS* curve shows the quantities of real output that producers plan to sell at different price levels.

The position of the *SRAS* curve is determined by a number of factors, which include firms' costs of production, including money wage rates and raw material costs, the taxes firms have to pay and changes in labour productivity.

If any of these factors change, the *SRAS* curve shifts to a new position. For example, an increase in business costs shifts the *SRAS* curve upward and to the left, while a reduction in business costs would have the opposite effect, shifting the *SRAS* curve downward and to the right.

Explaining the shape of the short-run aggregate supply curve

Whereas the *AD* curve is almost always drawn sloping downward, different assumptions about the nature of aggregate supply lead to different shapes and slopes of the *SRAS* curve. We shall first consider the *SRAS* curve illustrated in Figure 7.2, which is similar to the curve drawn earlier in Figure 7.1.

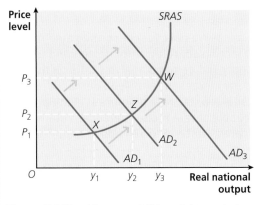

Figure 7.2 The *AD* curve shifting rightward along an upward-sloping *SRAS* curve

Figure 7.2 shows what happens in the economy when the *AD* curve shifts rightward up a *non-linear SRAS* curve whose slope becomes steeper moving from point to point up the curve. Following an increase in aggregate demand from AD_1 to AD_2 in Figure 7.2, which disturbs an initial macroeconomic equilibrium at point *X*, the price level rises to P_2, determined at point *Z*, to create conditions in which profit-maximising firms are happy to supply more output (real national output has increased from y_1 to y_2). However, when the *AD* curve shifts rightward again to AD_3, the adjustment to a new equilibrium is more of a price level adjustment than an output adjustment, reflecting the fact that the *SRAS* curve becomes steeper, moving from point to point up the curve. At the new equilibrium, determined at point *W*, the price level and output have risen respectively to P_3 and y_3. (Figure 7.2 reflects the fact that the *SRAS* curve is often shown as horizontal at low

levels of output, when there is lots of spare capacity, and vertical at high levels of output as full capacity is reached. Between the horizontal and vertical sections of the curve, the upward-sloping part of the *SRAS* curve represents the economy producing under 'normal' circumstances.)

The shape of the upward-sloping *SRAS* curve drawn in Figures 7.1 and 7.2 is explained by two assumptions which we made in Chapter 1 of this book. The assumptions, which are central to traditional economic theory, are that:

- all firms aim to maximise profits
- in the short run, the law of diminishing returns or diminishing marginal productivity operates

Taken together, these assumptions mean that if firms cannot charge higher prices, it is not profitable for them to supply more output. To explain this further, we assume that at current prices, firms are already producing the profit-maximising level of output, which occurs when $MR = MC$. If firms increase output beyond this point, marginal costs rise, which leads to falling total profit unless they are able to charge higher prices. Marginal costs rise because of the impact of the law of diminishing returns, explained in Chapter 2.

For profit-maximising firms to produce and supply more output in the face of rising marginal costs, marginal revenues must also rise. This requires higher prices. Without higher average prices, profit-maximising firms would not be willing to increase output.

It is also important to emphasise that, because each *SRAS* curve is drawn under the assumption that the money wage rate remains unchanged, there is a different *SRAS* curve for each and every money wage rate. When the money wage rate rises, production costs increase and firms reduce the quantity of output they are willing to supply at any given price level. As a result, the *SRAS* curve shifts to the left. Conversely, a fall in the money wage rate shifts the *SRAS* curve to the right.

STUDY TIP
Make sure you don't confuse short-run aggregate supply curves and long-run aggregate supply curves.

Long-run aggregate supply

So far in this chapter, we have been looking at an economy's short-run aggregate supply curve. We now turn to the economy's vertical **long-run aggregate supply** (*LRAS*) curve, which shows the maximum level of real output the economy can produce at its production potential, when all the available factors of production are employed and producing at their 'normal capacity' level of output.

The *LRAS* curve in Figure 7.3 is located at the 'normal capacity' level of real output y_N, with production taking place on the economy's production possibility frontier. In the long run, firms cannot produce more output to meet the increase in aggregate demand depicted by the shift of the *AD* curve from AD_1 to AD_2. In the short run, firms may be able to produce beyond their long-run sustainable level of output, but the emerging positive output gap will generate inflationary pressures. In this situation, the excess demand for real output is met by an increase in the price level, with the point of macroeconomic equilibrium moving from point X to point Z.

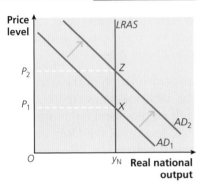

Figure 7.3 The economy's long-run aggregate supply (*LRAS*) curve, located at the 'normal capacity' level of real output

EXTENSION MATERIAL

A closer look at the 'normal capacity' level of output

'Normal capacity' is not quite the same as 'full capacity'. Even when producing at 'normal capacity', the economy may still be capable of temporarily producing a *higher* level of real output. This possibility is shown in Figure 7.4.

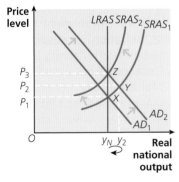

Figure 7.4 The economy can *temporarily* produce a level of real output higher than the 'normal capacity' level of output, y_N

We shall assume that the economy is initially in macroeconomic equilibrium at point X in the diagram, where curve AD_1 intersects both the $SRAS_1$ and the *LRAS* curves. Since the economy is producing on the *LRAS* curve, real output is at its 'normal capacity' level y_N. An increase in aggregate demand, caused perhaps by an expansionary monetary policy,

shifts the *AD* curve rightward to AD_2, which brings about a new short-run macroeconomic equilibrium at point Y. In the new equilibrium, the level of real output has risen to y_2, which is above the 'normal capacity' level of output.

However, this level of output, in which the economy is producing above its production potential, cannot be sustained, unless of course the *LRAS* curve itself shifts rightward. To understand why this is the case, we must remember that one of the determinants of the position of an *SRAS* curve is the level of money wages in the economy. A higher level of money wages shifts the *SRAS* curve upward or leftward, whereas lower money wages would shift the curve rightward. At y_2 there are shortages of labour and other factors of production and so excess demand in the labour market and other factor markets leads to rising factor prices. To persuade workers to supply the extra labour needed for y_2 to be produced, given the fact that the price level has risen to P_2, money wages must also rise. As soon as this happens, the *SRAS* curve shifts to $SRAS_2$. As the backward-bending curved arrow lying along the horizontal axis shows, real output falls back from y_2 to the 'normal capacity' level of real output at y_N, located below point Z on the diagram.

Revisiting the Keynesian long-run aggregate supply curve

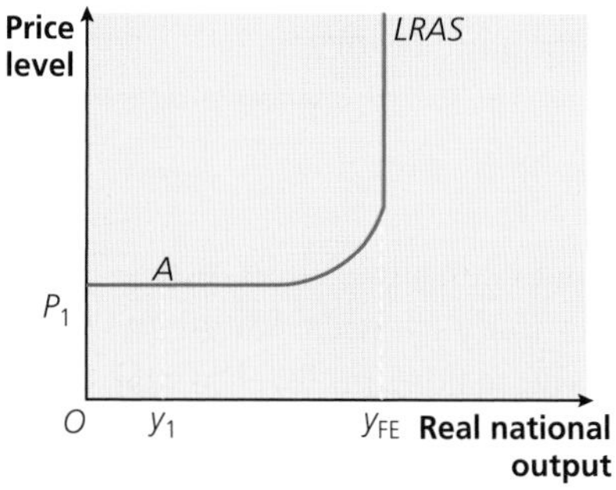

Figure 7.5 The Keynesian *LRAS* curve

The vertical *LRAS* curve we have described is often called the *free-market* or *neoclassical LRAS* curve. This label reflects the view commonly expressed by free-market economists that, provided markets function competitively and efficiently, the economy always operates at or close to 'normal capacity'. As we have explained, in the short run real output is influenced by the average price level, but in the long run aggregate supply is determined by the economy's maximum production capacity.

Most modern Keynesians (who are often called New Keynesians) agree that the *LRAS* curve is vertical. However, in the past some Keynesians were associated with the rather different *LRAS* curve illustrated in Figure 7.5.

The Keynesian *LRAS* curve is based on Keynes's explanation of the Great Depression in the UK and US economies in the 1930s. Keynes argued that a depressed economy can settle into an under-full employment equilibrium, shown for example by point *A* on the horizontal section of the *LRAS* curve in Figure 7.5. At point *A*, the level of real national output is y_1. Keynes argued that without purposeful intervention by the government, an economy could display more or less permanent demand deficiency. Market forces would fail to adjust automatically and achieve full employment. But if the government is able to shift the *AD* curve to the right along the horizontal section of the *LRAS* curve (mainly through expansionary fiscal policy), the existence of significant amounts of spare capacity would lead, in Keynes's view, to a growth in real output (and employment), without an increase in the price level.

KEY TERM

disinflation a fall in the rate of inflation, but inflation remains positive.

EXTENSION MATERIAL

AD/AS analysis and the rate of inflation

Students are often puzzled by a particular feature of the *AD/AS* model as taught and learnt at A-level. If you look carefully at conventional *AD/AS* diagrams such as Figure 7.6, you will see that a leftward movement of the *AD* curve results in a *fall* in the price level: that is, deflation. However, we all know that except in a deep recession or immediately after a very large fall in world commodity prices, contractionary fiscal or monetary policy that shifts the *AD* curve to the left results not in falling prices, but in a slowdown in the rate of inflation, or **disinflation**. Average prices still rise, but at a slower annual rate of increase.

In Figure 7.7, by contrast, contractionary fiscal or monetary policy, and indeed a fall in any of the components of aggregate demand, reduces the rate of inflation (shown in Figure 7.7 by the symbol $\dot{P}$), but not necessarily the price level.

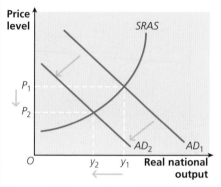

Figure 7.6 The traditional *AD/AS* model

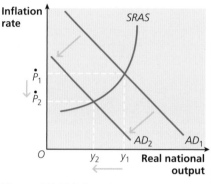

Figure 7.7 *AD/AS* analysis and the rate of inflation

TEST YOURSELF 7.1

Table 7.2 shows selected macroeconomic indicators for an economy in 2015 and 2016.

Table 7.2 Macroeconomic indicators, 2015 and 2016

	% change in real GDP	% change in prices	% change in earnings	Unemployment rate (%)
2015	4.2	4.6	9.4	8.4
2016	6.0	4.2	9.2	7.2

Explain why statement B of the following statements is correct, and also why the other three statements are incorrect.

A The price level fell between 2015 and 2016.

B Economic growth was accompanied by a falling unemployment rate.

C A fall in the rate of unemployment was accompanied by a falling price level.

D Earnings fell by 0.2% between 2015 and 2016.

Revisiting output gaps

Output gaps and the economic cycle

You first came across **output gaps** in Book 1 when learning, in the context of the economic cycle, how the economy's actual output usually differs from trend output and how the actual growth rate differs from the trend growth rate. Any point on the trend output line represents the economy's normal capacity level of output at that time. A **negative output gap** and a **positive output gap** are illustrated in Figure 7.8. The economy experiences negative and positive output gaps when actual output (shown by the economic cycle line in Figure 7.8) is respectively below and above the trend output line. For example, between points *A* and *B* there is a negative output gap. By contrast, the output gap is positive between points *C* and *D*.

KEY TERMS

output gap the difference between the current level of real GDP and the potential output of the economy.

positive output gap occurs when the current level of real GDP is above the potential output of the economy.

negative output gap occurs when the current level of real GDP is below the potential output of the economy.

STUDY TIP

Actual growth is another name for short-run growth whereas trend growth is another name for long-run growth.

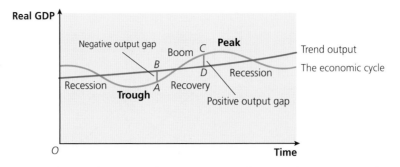

Figure 7.8 Negative and positive output gaps illustrated on an economic cycle diagram

---

Output gaps and the upswings and downswings of the economic cycle

Figure 7.8 seems to indicate that downswings of economic cycles always involve recessions — that is, falling real GDP for two quarters or more. But as Figure 7.9 illustrates, this is not necessarily the case. During the period of almost continuous positive economic growth that occurred in the UK between 1993 and 2007, it was certainly possible to identify economic cycles and both positive and negative output gaps. However, in the downswing of the cycle, the rate of short-run economic growth slowed down, but it did not become negative — at least until the 'great recession' of 2008–09 kicked in. Figure 7.9 also shows that economic cycles begin and end when output gaps disappear. A single economic cycle extends from point X to point Z on the graph, or, if we prefer, from point A to point B.

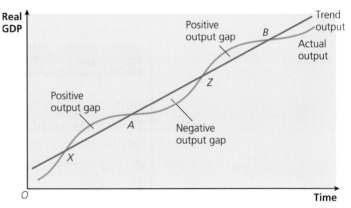

Figure 7.9 Positive and negative output gaps when short-run growth remains positive

Output gaps and *AD/AS*

Figure 7.10 shows negative and positive gaps on an *AD/AS* diagram. The economy suffers a **negative output gap** whenever the level of output is to the left of the *LRAS* curve and *below* the 'normal capacity' level of output y_N.

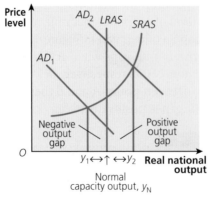

Figure 7.10 Negative and positive output gaps illustrated on an *AD/AS* diagram

Positive output gaps occur when the economy temporarily produces at a point outside its current production possibility frontier. However, because this represents overuse of capacity, such a point cannot be sustained for long. In the context of the *AD/AS* model, this means that the economy temporarily produces a level of output to the right of the *LRAS* curve, and above 'normal capacity' level of output y_N.

EXTENSION MATERIAL

Did hysteresis occur in the 'great recession'?

Arguably, the 'great recession' which began in the UK in the third quarter of 2008 and ended in the last quarter of 2009 led to a phenomenon which economists call 'hysteresis'. Hysteresis in an economy occurs when a significant amount of productive capacity is destroyed in an economic downturn and therefore is not available to meet any increase in demand when the economic recovery eventually takes place. In a rather similar way, workers who lose their jobs in the recession become deskilled and/or possess the wrong sort of skills

when employers are once again thinking of hiring more workers.

If hysteresis did indeed occur, it could mean that UK real GDP will be unable to make up lost ground and recover to the level of output that would have been achieved, had there been no recession. Figure 7.11 shows that by the third quarter of 2014, real output had recovered to its quarter 1 2008 level, but this is not the same as recovering to the level shown by the 'dotted' line immediately above the year 2015 in Figure 7.11.

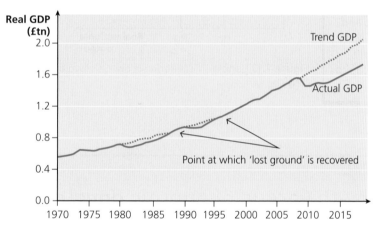

Figure 7.11 Recovering 'lost ground' after a recession

Source: ONS

7.3 Economic growth revisited

KEY TERMS

short-run economic growth occurs when an increase in aggregate demand brings spare capacity into production.

long-run economic growth occurs when the productive capacity of the economy is increasing. It is used to refer to the trend rate of growth of real national output in an economy over time.

We first explained the meaning of economic growth in Book 1, Chapter 6, distinguishing between **short-run economic growth** and **long-run economic growth**. Figure 7.12 uses the economy's production possibility frontier to illustrate and distinguish between these two forms of growth. Suppose that, initially, the economy is producing at point *A*, which is located well inside production possibility frontier *PPF₁*. This means that there is plenty of spare capacity, including unemployed labour, in the economy, together with a state of deficient aggregate demand. In this situation, short-run economic growth, which brings spare capacity into production, can be brought about by an increase in aggregate demand. Short-run economic growth, or economic recovery, can continue until full capacity (or 'normal capacity') is reached at a point such as *B* located on production possibility frontier *PPF₁*. The economy is now producing at its production potential.

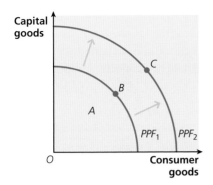

Figure 7.12 Economic growth shown in the context of the economy's production possibility frontier and a shift of the *LRAS* curve

For long-term economic growth to occur, the economy's production potential must increase and the production possibility frontier must shift outward, for example to production possibility frontier *PPF*₂. Whereas the movement from point *A* to point *B* shows short-run economic growth, the movement from point *B* to point *C* illustrates long-run economic growth.

Long-run economic growth can also be shown by a rightward shift of the *LRAS* curve from *LRAS*₁ to *LRAS*₂ in Figure 7.13. Note that the diagram also shows aggregate demand increasing from *AD*₁ to *AD*₂. In this situation aggregate demand increases just sufficiently to *absorb* the increase in aggregate supply without the price level rising or falling. Although output has increased to y_{N2}, the price level has remained at P_1. If aggregate demand were to remain at *AD*₂, or if the *AD* curve were to shift by either more or less than is shown in Figure 7.13, the price level would change.

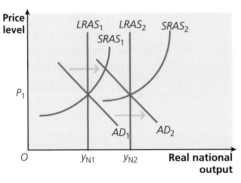

Figure 7.13 Long-run economic growth shown by a rightward shift of the economy's *LRAS* curve

TEST YOURSELF 7.2
An economy had nominal GDP growth of 8% in the last year, an inflation rate of 5.5%, and population growth of 2.5%. What was the approximate change in real GDP per capita over the year?

EXTENSION MATERIAL
Economic growth versus economic development

Economic growth does not necessarily improve the economic welfare of all or most of the people living in a country. On occasions, in some countries, the fruits of economic growth have allowed a rich elite to enjoy a champagne lifestyle, while the vast bulk of the population lives in poverty. In such a society, growth also helps to maintain a military and police system used primarily to protect the rich and subdue the poor. Even when the benefits of economic growth are spread to all or most of the population, growth may not be sustainable. In this situation, future generations as yet unborn may eventually suffer from the profligacy of people living today and their quest for ever-faster economic growth.

Economic development is a better indicator of improved human welfare, and the ability to continue to improve welfare, than economic growth. Economic development, which includes the *quality* and not just the *quantity* of growth, is measured by:

- general improvement in living standards which reduces poverty and human suffering
- access to resources such as food and housing that are required to satisfy basic human needs
- access to opportunities for human development (for example, through education and training)
- sustainability and regeneration, through reducing resource depletion and degradation
- access to decent healthcare

Resource depletion occurs when finite resources such as oil are used up, and when soil fertility or fish stocks irreversibly decline. By contrast, *resource degradation* is best illustrated by pollution of air, water and land. To benefit people in the long run, growth (and development) must be sustainable. Sustainable economic growth requires the use of:

- renewable rather than non-renewable resources
- resources that minimise pollution and other forms of resource degradation

The causes of long-run economic growth

Long-run economic growth is explained almost exclusively by supply-side factors. However, sufficient aggregate demand has to be generated to absorb the extra output produced by the growth process. The immediate supply-side cause of long-run growth is *increased labour productivity*, which itself results from investment in, and accumulation of, capital goods and human capital, and from technological progress.

There are two main theories of long-term economic growth: neoclassical growth theory and new growth theory.

Neoclassical growth theory

The older theory, known as neoclassical growth theory, which was developed by Professor Robert Solow in the 1950s, argues that a sustained increase in investment increases the economy's growth rate, but only temporarily. The ratio of capital to labour goes up, the marginal product of capital declines and the economy moves back to a long-term path, which is determined by output growing at the same rate as the workforce, plus a factor to reflect improving labour productivity.

In neoclassical growth theory, the rate at which labour productivity improves is determined by technological progress. But the theory does not explain why technological progress occurs. Technological progress is assumed to fall on the economy 'like manna from heaven'. This is the theory's weakness. The causes or determinants of the ultimate engine of economic growth, namely technological progress, are exogenous to the theory (exogenous means 'outside'). Neoclassical growth theory therefore fails to provide a complete explanation of economic growth.

New growth theory

In recent years, neoclassical growth theory has been replaced to a significant extent by new growth theory. New growth theory is also called *endogenous growth theory*, reflecting the fact that, unlike in neoclassical growth theory, the determinants of technological progress are brought inside the theory. The three main sources of technological progress explained by new growth theory are profit-seeking research, openness to foreign ideas and accumulation of human capital:

- **Profit-seeking research.** The rate at which technological progress occurs depends on the stock of ideas. The flow of new ideas thought up by current researchers adds to the 'capital stock' of existing ideas. How many new ideas there are

depends on the number of researchers, but the extent to which new ideas improve technological progress depends on whether or not 'over-fishing' occurs. 'Over-fishing' means that the discovery of new ideas makes it harder to find further new ideas. But conversely, the opposite may be true, as accumulating ideas may make researchers more rather than less productive. This is the so-called 'standing on the shoulders' effect. Paul Romer, one of the most influential developers of new growth theory, assumes that the this effect is dominant, which means that countries with more researchers can have higher growth rates.

- **Openness to foreign ideas.** Economic growth can derive either from domestic innovation or from technological transfer from other countries. In 1999, Cameron, Proudman and Redding argued that the rate at which technological progress occurs in a country depends on three factors: the domestic rate of growth of technology in the absence of technology transfer; the rate at which technology can be adopted from abroad; and the proportion of foreign technologies that can be adopted. This means that for a technology follower, technology grows at its own domestic rate of technology growth, plus some extra 'catch-up' generated by technology-leading countries.

- **Accumulation of human capital.** Human capital accumulates through educating and training a skilled workforce from among a country's indigenous population, and through migration from other countries. Migration adds to human capital provided migrants possess appropriate education and skills, or are willing and able to attain them. A high level of human capital is best regarded as a necessary but not a sufficient condition for successful economic growth. This is because technological change requires workers to possess the skills and aptitudes required for adapting to new technologies, rather than those that used to be necessary for old, declining technologies.

New growth theory suggests that appropriate government intervention can create the supply-side conditions which favour growth. These include:

- conditions that encourage profit-seeking research and appropriate accumulation of human capital
- externalities or external economies provided by the state which benefit private sector businesses
- patent legislation and a judicial system that enforces the law of contract and intellectual property rights, which create the incentive for firms to innovate

Worked example: calculating percentage changes

Table 7.3 shows, for a particular country, GDP measured at current prices and the price index used to measure inflation.

Table 7.3 GDP at current prices and the index of average prices, 2005 and 2015

Year	GDP at current prices (£ billion)	Index of average prices (2005 = 100)
2005	70	100
2015	125	115

1 Calculate to two decimal places the percentage change in GDP at current prices over the period shown by the data.
2 Calculate to one decimal place the value of real GDP in 2015, measured at 2005 constant prices.

1 GDP at current prices, or nominal GDP, increased by £55 billion from £70 billion in 2005 to £125 billion in 2015. The percentage increase is 55/70 × 100, which is 78.57%.
2 Multiply GDP at 2015 prices by the 2005 index of average prices and then divide by the 2015 index of average prices. Real GDP in 2015 prices measured at 2005 constant prices is £108.7 billion.

7.4 A further look at employment and unemployment issues

Along with promoting economic growth and controlling inflation, achieving full employment — or at least reducing unemployment to an acceptable level and keeping it there — is one of any government's most important economic policy objectives. In Book 1 we defined full employment as a situation in which the number of people wishing to work at the going market real wage rate equals the number of workers whom employers wish to hire at this real wage rate. We called this the 'free-market' definition of full employment. We also looked briefly at the definition of full employment suggested by William Beveridge in 1944. Beveridge's definition is explored in a little more detail in Case Study 7.2.

Beveridge and full employment

In his famous 1944 book, *Full Employment in a Free Society*, the British economist William Beveridge said that full employment 'means having always more vacant jobs than unemployed men, not slightly fewer jobs. It means that the jobs are at fair wages, of such a kind, and so located that the unemployed men can reasonably be expected to take them; it means, by consequence, that the normal lag between losing one job and finding another will be very short.'

Beveridge went on to say that full employment does not mean literally no unemployment: that is to say, it does not mean that every man and woman in this country who is fit and free for work is employed productively on every day of his or her working life. He argued that full employment would allow for no more than 3% unemployment due to frictions but there always had to be more vacancies than unemployed workers.

In terms of the categories of unemployment explained in Book 1, Beveridge split his 3% unemployment into 1% seasonal, 1% frictional and 1% structural unemployment. In Beveridge's view, these frictions would never mean that an unemployed worker was in that state for anything other than a very short period.

Beveridge also asked who is responsible for maintaining full employment. He believed that 'the ultimate responsibility for seeing that outlay as a whole, taking public and private outlay together, is sufficient to set up a demand for all the labour seeking employment, must be taken by the State'. Full employment required active government

support to ensure that aggregate demand was sufficient to maintain employment opportunities for all those who desired to work.

Follow-up questions

1 Which of the two definitions of full employment, the free-market definition or the Beveridge definition, has most influenced UK governments since 2010? Justify your answer.

2 At the time you are reading this book, is the UK labour force now fully employed? Explain your answer.

Revisiting frictional and structural unemployment

> **KEY TERMS**
>
> **frictional unemployment** short-term transitional unemployment or 'between jobs' unemployment.
>
> **structural unemployment** occurs when certain industries decline because of long-term changes in market conditions. It is joblessness caused not by lack of aggregate demand, but by changes in the pattern of demand or technological change.

As we explained in Book 1, pages 200–01, **frictional unemployment** occurs when it takes time for the labour market to match the available jobs with those people seeking work. Also known as transitional unemployment, it is caused by people moving between jobs. Redundant workers, who have been laid off by their previous employers because they are no longer needed, may take time to find the types of work they want at wage rates they are prepared to accept. They remain unemployed whilst involved in job search. Likewise, young workers joining the labour market for the first time, such as university graduates, may be frictionally unemployed for a short time.

Imperfect information in the labour market, through which the jobless are unaware of jobs that are in fact available, tends to worsen frictional unemployment, as do incentive problems resulting from the fact that people may believe their pay will be swallowed up in taxes and loss of benefits.

Structural unemployment, by contrast, occurs when there is a long-run decline in demand for the goods or services produced by an industry, caused by competition either from new industries located within the country, or from similar firms located in other countries. The growth of international competition in an increasingly globalised economy is an important cause of structural unemployment, as is the impact of technological change on the economy. During the Keynesian era from the 1950s to the 1970s, structural unemployment in the UK was concentrated in regions where nineteenth-century staple industries, such as textiles and shipbuilding, were suffering structural decline.

Regional unemployment caused by the decline of such 'sunset' industries was more than offset by the growth of employment elsewhere in the UK in the 'sunrise' industries that replaced them. However, in the severe recessions of the early 1980s, the early 1990s and 2008–09, structural unemployment affected almost all regions in the UK, as deindustrialisation spread across the manufacturing base. In the 2008–09 recession, service industries such as banking and other financial services suffered a greater decline than manufacturing.

The growth of structural unemployment in the service sector has partly been caused by the increasing use of information and communication technology (ICT) and automated services. Call centre employment has grown significantly in the service sector in recent years, though to some extent call centres have moved overseas to lower-waged countries such as India. Moreover, some companies which used to employ call centre workers now use automated communication software rather than humans to provide customer services.

It is not easy to separate changes in structural unemployment from other causes of unemployment, particularly changes in aggregate demand. Manufacturing output grew in many of the years between 1993 and 2008, but manufacturing employment fell. However, during these years, there was a danger of exaggerating the growth of unemployment in manufacturing industries because many activities, ranging from cleaning to information technology maintenance, previously undertaken 'in-house' by manufacturing firms, were out-sourced to external service-sector providers.

Technological unemployment is a special case of structural unemployment, resulting from the successful growth of new industries using labour-saving technology. In contrast to mechanisation (workers operating machines), which has usually increased the overall demand for labour, automation (machines operating other machines) reduces the demand for labour. Whereas the growth of mechanised industry increases employment, automation of production can lead to the shedding of labour, even when industry output is expanding.

Changes in technology can also lead to changes in the pattern of demand. Solar panels have been replacing electricity generated by coal, which leads to structural unemployment in the coal industry, when fossil-fuel burning power stations close down.

EXTENSION MATERIAL

Equilibrium and disequilibrium unemployment

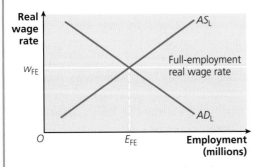

Figure 7.14 The equilibrium level of employment in the economy's aggregate labour market

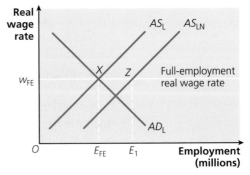

Figure 7.15 Equilibrium unemployment shown by the distance from X to Z

Figure 7.14 shows the economy's aggregate labour market in a state of balance or rest — that is, in *equilibrium* — with the level of employment at E_{FE}. It appears from this free-market diagram that there is *no* unemployment at all when the labour market is in equilibrium because the demand for labour at W_{FE} equals the supply of labour — firms are creating enough jobs for those who are willing to work at the equilibrium wage rate. But as Figure 7.15 now shows, this is not the case.

For free-market economists, full employment does not necessarily mean that every single member of the working population is in work. Instead, it means a situation in which the number of people wishing to work at the going market real wage rate equals the number of workers whom employers wish to hire at this real wage rate.

But even this definition needs qualifying, since in a dynamic economy change is constantly taking place, with some industries declining and others growing. Workers moving between jobs may decide to take a break between the two employments. This is the *frictional* unemployment we have already explained. As new products are developed and demand and cost conditions change, firms demand more of some labour skills while the demand for other types of labour declines. This leads to the *structural* unemployment we have again described. Frictional and structural unemployment make up what is called *equilibrium unemployment*, which exists even with the real wage rate at its market-clearing level. Imperfect information, occupational and geographical immobility of labour, and a tax and benefits system that discourages people from seeking work are seen as important causes of equilibrium unemployment.

By contrast, as the name indicates, disequilibrium unemployment results from the labour market being out of equilibrium. This occurs when:

- the aggregate supply of labour exceeds the aggregate demand for labour
- labour market imperfections prevent the real wage rate falling to restore labour market equilibrium (wage stickiness)

There are two main types of disequilibrium unemployment. These are:

- real-wage unemployment
- cyclical, demand-deficient or Keynesian unemployment

Real-wage unemployment

Nearly a century ago, large-scale persistent unemployment occurred in the United Kingdom, preceding the spread of unemployment worldwide in the Great Depression of the 1930s. Much of British unemployment in the 1920s probably resulted from the lack of competitiveness and decline of nineteenth-century staple industries such as shipbuilding and textiles. This problem was made worse by an overvalued exchange rate. However, free-market economists blamed a substantial part of the unemployment on excessively high real wages.

Unemployment caused by excessively high wage rates is called **classical unemployment** or **real-wage unemployment**. This type of disequilibrium unemployment is illustrated in Figure 7.16. In the diagram, full employment (equilibrium employment) is determined where the aggregate demand for labour equals the aggregate supply of labour, shown at point X, at the real wage rate w_{FE}. However, suppose wages are fixed at a higher real rate, at w_1 rather than w_{FE}. At this real wage rate, employers wish to hire E_1 workers, but E_2 workers wish to supply their labour. There is excess supply of labour in the labour market, equal to the horizontal distance between points Z and W, i.e. $(OE_2 - OE_1)$. (Although Figure 7.16 is a macroeconomic diagram, depicting the economy's aggregate labour market, real-wage unemployment can also be thought of as a microeconomic phenomenon, related to individual labour markets that are in decline.)

Free-market economists argue that, as long as labour markets remain competitive, the resulting real-wage unemployment should be temporary. Competitive forces in the labour market should cure the problem, bidding down the real wage rate to w_{FE} and thereby eliminating the excess supply of labour. Full employment should quickly be restored when the number of workers willing to work once again equals the number of people that firms wish to hire.

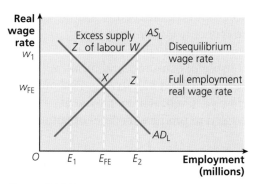

Figure 7.16 Real-wage unemployment in the economy's aggregate labour market

But suppose labour market rigidity or 'stickiness', perhaps caused by trade unions, prevents the real wage rate falling below w_1. In this situation, the market mechanism fails to work properly, the excess supply of labour persists, and real-wage unemployment occurs. Pre-Keynesian free-market economists blamed trade unions and other causes of labour market imperfection for the mass unemployment that occurred between the First and Second World Wars. In their view, responsibility for unemployment lay with the workers in work and their trade unions who, by refusing to accept lower wages, prevented the unemployed from pricing themselves into jobs.

Cyclical unemployment

In the inter-war years of the 1920s and 1930s, John Maynard Keynes argued that deficient aggregate demand was the main cause of persistent mass unemployment in the UK economy. Pro-free-market or pre-Keynesian economists did not accept this explanation. They believed that although deficient demand can occur temporarily in the economy, the resulting cyclical unemployment (as they called it) would quickly be eliminated by the self-regulating nature of market forces.

EXTENSION MATERIAL

Say's Law

To explain the difference between the pre-Keynesian (free-market) and Keynesian views on the existence of deficient demand in the economy, we must introduce Say's Law, named after an early nineteenth-century French economist, Jean-Baptiste Say. In popular form, Say's Law states that supply creates its own demand. Whenever an output, or supply, is produced, factor incomes such as wages and profits are generated that are just sufficient, *if spent*, to purchase the output at the existing price level, thereby creating a demand for the output produced. Stated thus, there is nothing controversial about Say's Law, it is really a statement that is true by definition.

The controversial and critical issue concerns whether the *potential* demand or incomes generated are *actually* spent on the output produced. The pre-Keynesians believed that if households save more than firms wish to borrow to finance investment spending, the rate of interest falls to equate savings with investment. This adjustment mechanism means that Say's Law holds. Keynes disputed this, arguing that in recessionary conditions when business and consumer confidence is low, savings will exceed investment, and there is a glut or excess of savings. Say's Law breaks down and the resulting deficient demand causes unemployment.

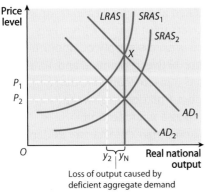

Figure 7.17 A leftward shift of the AD curve may cause cyclical unemployment, but a rightward shift of the SRAS curve may then correct it

In the context of an *AD/AS* diagram, Figure 7.17 shows how cyclical unemployment occurs — and also how, according to the anti-Keynesian view, it might be corrected by the operation of free-market forces. In the diagram, the economy is initially producing at point X, where the aggregate demand curve AD_1 intersects both the *SRAS* curve, $SRAS_1$, and the *LRAS* curve. This means that the economy is producing the 'normal capacity' level of output y_N. A significant fall in aggregate demand, caused for example by a collapse of consumer and business confidence, then shifts the *AD* curve inward from AD_1 to AD_2. Real output falls to y_2, which is considerably below y_N. Cyclical unemployment occurs because fewer workers are needed to produce the level of output y_2 than y_N.

In the Keynesian view, a 'sticky' wage rate means that the level of real output remains at y_2 (an under-full employment equilibrium), and cyclical or demand-deficient unemployment persists. Pro-free-market economists disagree. In their view, flexible prices and wage rates, which quickly adjust to market conditions, fall, which in turn means that lower wages and other factor prices reduce firms' costs of production and shift the *SRAS* curve rightward to $SRAS_2$. Output moves back to its 'normal capacity' level and the cyclical unemployment has been eliminated.

SYNOPTIC LINK
See Chapter 9, pages 280–82 for an explanation of the role of automatic stabilisers in the economy.

CASE STUDY 7.3

The credit crunch and aggregate demand

There is little doubt that the main cause of the massive increase in unemployment in the recession that hit the world economy around 2008 was a collapse of aggregate demand on a global scale. The key event that triggered the collapse of demand was the credit crunch, which originated in the USA in August 2007, but then quickly spread to reduce aggregate demand in other countries, including the United Kingdom.

Virtually all firms, large and small, require a reliable supply of credit or bank lending in order to remain in business. In normal circumstances, the banking system provides this liquidity, which businesses, consumers and governments usually take for granted.

When a massive financial crisis and 'credit crunch' hit the world economy in 2007 and 2008, banks throughout the world, but particularly in America, were raising the funds they lent to customers by borrowing from each other rather than from households. The funds were borrowed on the inter-bank market. In the USA, much of the borrowed funds were lent in the form of mortgages to low-income customers who were bad credit risks. These loans became known as *sub-prime* mortgages (in contrast to *prime* mortgages, which are secured loans granted to low-risk home owners).

From a bank's point of view, a mortgage granted to a customer is an *asset*. For the borrower, it is a *liability*, since the house owner must eventually pay back the loan and pay interest in the intervening months and years. By definition, a sub-prime mortgage is a risky asset since there is a danger of the loan turning into a bad debt, which the bank owning the loan cannot recover. In 2007, the credit crunch developed because the banks that had created sub-prime mortgages repackaged the risky assets and sold them on to other banks as if they were prime mortgages. In essence, banks were buying 'toxic debt' from each other, without realising the repackaged assets were extremely risky. As banks realised that many of their so-called 'assets' were more or less worthless, the situation quickly deteriorated and the supply of liquidity began to freeze. Banks became unwilling to lend to each other because they distrusted each other's creditworthiness. At the next stage, the credit crunch triggered a financial meltdown when banks either collapsed (Lehman Brothers in the USA) or were nationalised by governments (Northern Rock in the UK).

Follow-up questions

1 Why is a supply of liquidity so important for an economy to function properly?
2 How did the credit crunch affect business and consumer confidence and hence aggregate demand?

EXTENSION MATERIAL

Labour's fiscal stimulus gives way to Coalition fiscal restraint

In 2008, when the 'great recession' began, Keynesian fiscal policy suddenly came back into fashion. Barack Obama in the USA and the then Labour government in the UK justified the use of an expansionary fiscal policy, which became known as the *fiscal stimulus*. For a time, both monetary policy and fiscal policy were used in conjunction in the demand-side management of aggregate demand to try to reduce the 'cyclical element' of the budget deficit. The Labour government implemented tax cuts (the rate of VAT was cut temporarily to 15%) and public spending increases, and the automatic stabilisers also kicked in, supporting the discretionary action of governments. This led to a burgeoning budget deficit designed to 'spend the economy out of recession'

For a few months, the rebirth of Keynesian fiscal policy seemed to work, helping the economy to recover from a deep recession. Labour politicians claimed that the fragile recovery in economic growth which began in the fourth quarter of 2009 was largely the result of the fiscal stimulus, combined with an expansionary monetary policy; Bank Rate was cut to an all-time low of 0.5%, the exchange rate fell by almost 25% and quantitative easing was implemented.

However, as in other EU countries such as Greece and Ireland, the massive increase in government borrowing and the national debt that resulted from the fiscal stimulus, led to a new problem: the sovereign debt problem. Put simply, there was a risk that the rest of the world would not be prepared to lend to the UK government to help it finance its budget deficit, except at ever-higher interest rates which the country could not afford. As in other countries, Britain's 'Triple A' credit rating was threatened.

In May 2010, however, a new Coalition government, dominated by the Conservatives, was elected that was ideologically opposed to Keynesian economic policies. Under chancellor George Osborne, the Conservatives immediately abandoned the fiscal stimulus and introduced a new fiscal policy based on public spending cuts and higher taxes (VAT was increased to 20% on 4 January 2011). The Labour government's Keynesian-inspired fiscal stimulus was replaced by a policy of fiscal austerity (or fiscal restraint or fiscal consolidation, the preferred bland terms used by George Osborne).

In the event, the cuts in public spending and tax rises failed to eliminate the budget deficit as quickly as originally planned. It is not now expected that the deficit will disappear until 2019–20. It should also be noted that, although reducing the budget deficit contributes to a fall in aggregate demand compared to the previous year, the continued existence of the deficit still represents a net injection of demand into the circular flow of income.

The Coalition government's critics believed that the public spending cuts, tax increases and the attempt to cut the budget deficit would trigger a severe negative multiplier effect that would plunge the UK economy into the second dip of a double-dip recession. The government, by contrast, hoped that the fiscal contraction would be offset by a loose and lax monetary policy so that the overall effect on aggregate demand of the two policies taken together would be neutral, or even slightly expansionary. It was also hoped that the resources (especially the newly unemployed labour) created by the fiscal contraction would quickly be put to use in a resurgent private sector, set free by the public spending cuts.

CASE STUDY 7.4

Under-employment and zero-hours employment contracts

In 2014 the UK prime minister announced: 'We have reached an important milestone, with more people in work than ever before in our history.' However, while unemployment had fallen by over 400,000 since early 2012, during these years under-employment rose by 93,000. At 3.4 million in 2014, under-employment was over a million higher (46%) than it had been before the 2008 recession.

Most of the rise in under-employment took place between 2008 and 2009, and most of the under-employment has been concentrated among part-time workers. During the recession many workers moved from full-time to part-time roles and many of those returning to work after a period of unemployment could only find part-time jobs. Of the extra 1 million under-employed workers in 2012 compared with 2008, three-quarters were in part-time posts.

Across the UK the number of people who count as under-employed — people working part time because they can't get a full-time job, or wanting more hours in their current job, has increased for both employees and the self-employed.

While there was a small fall in 2014 in involuntarily part-time work (people working part time because they can't get a full-time job), there was a rise in the numbers who wanted more hours in their existing jobs. Overall, under-employment was still increasing.

Despite the economic recovery, continual real wage falls in 2014 meant that more people than ever were looking for extra hours to make ends meet. However, by 2015, real wages had begun to rise, and at the time of writing in January 2016, it seems likely that they will continue to rise — unless the UK economy is hit by an adverse economic 'shock' emanating, for example, from the eurozone or from China.

The problem of under-employment is exacerbated by zero-hours employment contracts. Zero-hours contracts do not guarantee a minimum number of hours of employment. In the summer of 2014, 1.8 million mostly low-paid workers were on zero-hours contracts, but this figure was probably bloated by the growth of summer-time seasonal employment in tourist trades. On average, someone on a zero-hours contract usually worked 25 hours a week. The majority were women and students, often aged under 25, or 65 and over. About a third of them wanted more hours, primarily in their current job, compared with 10% of other people in employment.

Protesters against zero-hours contracts outside a fast-food restaurant in central London

TUC general secretary Frances O'Grady has said: 'Zero-hours contracts sum up what has gone wrong in the modern workplace. They shift almost all power from the worker and give it to their boss.' But the government's business secretary has argued that 'Zero-hours contracts are valued by many employers and individuals who want flexibility in the hours they work, such as students, people with caring responsibilities and those who want to partially retire.' The shadow business secretary responded by saying: 'Ministers have watered down every person's rights at work and zero-hours contracts have gone from being a niche concept to becoming the norm in parts of our economy. Workers are unhappy that staff can simply be sent home if there is no work to be done.'

Follow-up questions

1 Why are women more likely than men to be under-employed?
2 Assess the advantages and disadvantages of zero-hours employment contracts.

7.5 Inflation, the Phillips curve and the quantity theory of money revisited

Forty-five or so years ago in the 1970s, accelerating and highly variable rates of inflation caused acute problems in the UK economy. As a result, in the monetarist decade of the 1980s, the control of inflation was elevated to pole position among government macroeconomic policy objectives. Eventually, after 1980 when inflation touched 20%, the rate of inflation came down, though it increased again to 10% in 1990. Whether the fall in the rate of inflation was related to 'monetarist' monetary policy is debatable. Nevertheless, from 1993 until 2007, the UK inflation rate remained within 1% above or below the 2% inflation rate target set by the government, apart from on one occasion when it nudged over the 3% upper limit.

Until 2008, control of inflation was accompanied by arguably the longest period of continuous economic growth the UK has ever experienced, at least in modern times. Many other economies around the world, including the USA, experienced similar conditions of low inflation and steady growth; this period has become known as 'The Great Moderation'. However, in 2007 things started to go wrong. Along with other economies, the UK was hit by a sudden burst of cost-push inflation, mostly imported from the rest of the world via escalating oil, gas, commodity and food prices. Together with the credit crunch that began in the USA, severe cost-push inflation undermined business and consumer confidence. Then, in 2008, the problems in financial markets caused aggregate demand to collapse and the UK economy entered the deepest recession it has experienced since the Second World War. The rate of inflation began to fall and some economists believed that deflation would replace inflation.

213

ACTIVITY

Track what has happened to the UK rate of inflation since this book was published and explain your findings.

Although, at the time of writing in January 2016, the price level had fallen in a couple of months, this did not really constitute 'deflation' — defined as a persistent fall in the price level. Sharp, but probably temporary, falls in oil, gas and commodity prices were mainly responsible for the inflation rate dipping below zero, but most commentators were expecting positive inflation to return sooner rather than later.

Inflation, deflation, disinflation and reflation

KEY TERM

deflation a persistent tendency for the price level to fall and for the value of money to rise.

As we mentioned earlier in the chapter, *inflation* is best defined as a persistent or continuous rise in the price level, or as a continuing fall in the value of money. **Deflation** is the opposite, namely a persistent tendency for the price level to fall or for the value of money to rise. However, the overall price level has seldom fallen in western industrialised countries since the 1930s. Since the Keynesian revolution, the phrase 'to deflate the economy' has been applied in a rather looser way to describe a reduction in aggregate demand and levels of economic activity, output and employment. A deflationary policy uses fiscal and/or monetary policy to reduce aggregate demand, in order to take excess demand out of the system. In this situation, the rate of inflation is likely to fall, but remain positive. (Earlier in the chapter, we used the word *disinflation* to describe this circumstance.) By contrast, *reflation* refers to an increase in economic activity and output, and a reflationary policy stimulates aggregate demand. Often, inflation is 'reflation gone wrong', stimulating the price level rather than real output and employment.

ACTIVITY

Check the price of a litre of unleaded petrol at a petrol station near to where you live. Check the price again at monthly intervals over the next 4 months. Calculate the percentage change in price over the 4-month period. What factors might have caused any price changes you have noted?

QUANTITATIVE SKILLS 7.3

Worked example: calculating the rate of inflation and price level changes

Table 7.4 shows monthly measures of the UK consumer prices index for January and February 2014, and for January and February 2015.

Table 7.4 UK consumer price index, selected months

Month	Monthly CPI (January 2005 = 100)
January 2014	126.7
February 2014	127.4
January 2015	127.1
February 2015	127.4

1 **To one decimal place, calculate the annual rate of inflation in January 2015 and February 2015.**

2 **What was the percentage change in the average price level between January 2005 and February 2015?**

1 Between January 2014 and January 2015 the CPI increased by 0.4 index points, from 126.7 to 127.1 index points. Measured as a percentage of the January 2014 index number, this is 0.4/126.7 × 100, which is a 0.316% annual rate of inflation. Measured to one decimal place, the annual rate of inflation was 0.3%. A month later in February 2015, the annual rate of inflation had fallen to 0% (0/127.4 × 100, which is 0%).

2 Between January 2005 and February 2015, the CPI increased from a base year index number of 100 to 127.4. Because we are comparing 127.4 to the base index number of 100, the change in index points (27.4) is exactly the same as the percentage change in the average price level, which is therefore 27.4%.

How theories of the causes of inflation have changed over the years

Table 7.5 provides a summary of how theories of inflation have developed over the years, and of how the rate of inflation has changed in the UK in recent decades.

Table 7.5 Theories of inflation and details of recent UK inflation

Eighteenth century to the 1930s	The old quantity theory of money is dominant.
1930s	The problem of inflation disappears. Keynes's *General Theory* explains deflation in terms of deficient aggregate demand.
1940 and 1950s	Keynesians develop Keynes's ideas to explain how, in conditions of full employment, excess demand can pull up the price level through demand-pull inflation.
1950s	The early monetarist theory of inflation begins to develop when Milton Friedman revives the quantity theory of money (the modern quantity theory).
1950s–1960s	Many Keynesians switch away from the demand-pull to the cost-push theory of inflation.
1960s	The Phillips curve is introduced into the Keynesian demand-pull versus cost-push debate.
1968	The role of expectations in the inflationary process is incorporated into the monetarist theory of inflation. The theory of adaptive expectations is built into Milton Friedman's theory of the long-run Phillips curve.
1970s	The Phillips curve relationship appears to breaks down with the emergence of stagflation.
1980s onward	There is controversy once again between cost-push and demand-pull explanations of inflation, with New Keynesian explanations versus monetarist and free-market explanations, and the latter incorporating rational expectations into their models of the economy.
2008 onward	For a short period the problem of inflation largely disappeared, being replaced by the fear of deflation or a falling price level. However, there were two imported cost-push price spikes in 2008 and 2011.
2014 and 2015	The inflation rate fell once again, becoming negative in April 2015 and then hovering around 0%. Deflation threatened to emerge, though some economists regarded this as a good thing. Most thought that a falling price level would be a temporary phenomenon.

The old quantity theory of money

quantity theory of money theory that assumes inflation is caused by a prior increase in the money supply.

demand-pull inflation a rising price level caused by an increase in aggregate demand, shown by a shift of the *AD* curve to the right. Also known as demand inflation.

The **quantity theory of money** is the oldest theory of inflation, dating back at least to the eighteenth century. For two centuries until the 1930s, when it went out of fashion with the Keynesian revolution, the quantity theory was *the* theory of inflation. However, Milton Friedman's revival of the quantity theory in its modern form in the 1950s is usually regarded as marking the beginning of the monetarist counter-revolution. In recent years, the quantity theory has once again occupied a central place in debate and controversy about the causes of both inflation and deflation.

All versions of the quantity theory, old and new, are a special case of **demand-pull inflation**, in which rising prices are caused by excess aggregate demand. In the quantity theory, the source of excess demand is located in *monetary* rather than *real* forces, in an excess supply of money created or condoned by the government. At its simplest, the quantity theory is sometimes described as too much money chasing too few goods. A starting point for developing

KEY TERM

Fisher equation of exchange
the stock of money in the economy multiplied by the velocity of circulation of money equals the price level multiplied by the quantity of real output in the economy: $MV = PQ$.

the theory is the **Fisher equation of exchange**, devised by an American economist, Irving Fisher, early in the twentieth century:

$$\text{money supply (stock of money)} \times \text{the velocity of circulation of money} = \text{price level} \times \text{quantity of output}$$

or:

$$MV = PQ$$

As we explained in Book 1, for a particular time period, say a year, the stock of money in the economy (M) multiplied by the velocity of circulation of money (V) equals the price level (P) multiplied by the quantity of real output (Q) in the economy. You should note that PQ is in fact nominal or money national income. PQ can increase, either because real output increases or because inflation is taking place, in which case the price level increases. Because monetarists, along with other pro-free-market economists, argue that market forces ensure that real output is generally at or near its 'normal capacity' level, they believe that the effect of excess monetary growth falls mainly on the price level. Keynesian economists disagree, believing that a monetary expansion can *reflate* real output rather *inflate* the price level.

To convert the equation of exchange ($MV = PQ$) into a theory of inflation, it is necessary to take into account these factors:

- The velocity of circulation or speed at which money is spent is fixed, or at least stable.
- Total transactions, which are determined by the level of real national output in the economy, are also fixed in the short run.
- In the old quantity theory, money was regarded as a *medium of exchange* (means of payment) rather than as a store of value. This meant that people would quickly spend any money they received. (However, when Milton Friedman reformulated the quantity theory in the 1950s, he did treat money as a store of value as well as a medium of exchange.)

Suppose the government allows the money supply to expand faster than the rate at which real national output increases. As a result, households and firms possess money balances that are greater than those they wish to hold. According to the quantity theory, these excess money balances will quickly be spent or, according to the 'new' quantity theory, converted into other assets, bidding up asset prices and pushing down interest rates.

According to monetarists, changes in the money supply are assumed to bring about changes in the price level (rather than vice versa), whereas most Keynesians believe that in a sophisticated, global financial system, changes in the money supply respond to increases in aggregate demand and the resulting increase in the demand for money and credit.

In summary, the main elements of the quantity theory that you need to know are:

- Initially the government creates or condones an expansion of the money supply greater than the increase in real national output.
- As a result, households and firms hold excess money balances which, when spent, pull up the price level.

Keynesian rejection of the quantity theory

Keynesians generally reject the quantity theory of money as an explanation of inflation, or claim that it only provides an explanation of rising prices when a number of highly restrictive assumptions hold. There are three ways in which Keynesians have attacked the quantity theory.

1 **The velocity of circulation is not constant.** Much of the debate between Keynesians and monetarists about the quantity theory has centred on the issue of whether the velocity of circulation of money (V) is constant. In ordinary language, V represents how often money is spent. Monetarists believe that, because money earns little or no interest, it is generally rational to spend quickly any extra money holdings, either on goods or on non-money financial assets such as shares, and not to hold idle money balances for any length of time. By contrast, Keynesians take the opposite view, arguing that under certain circumstances (particularly when share and bond prices are expected to fall), it is perfectly sensible to hold idle money balances. In this situation, to avoid capital losses they expect to suffer from falling financial asset prices, people decide to hold money instead as an idle wealth asset. They hang on to, rather than spend, their extra money holdings.

2 **Under-full employment equilibrium.** Keynesians also attack the quantity theory by arguing that if there is spare capacity and unemployment in the economy, an increase of the money supply may increase real income and output (y and Q) rather than the price level P. In the Keynesian view, market forces are too weak and take too long to return the economy to its normal capacity output. This means that the economy can get stuck in an under-full employment equilibrium.

3 **Reverse causation.** The two Keynesian attacks on the quantity theory we have so far examined accept the monetarist argument that changes in MV can cause changes in PQ, but they argue that an increase in the money supply (M) does not *necessarily* result in inflation (an increase in P). Instead an increase in the money supply may be absorbed in a slowing down of the velocity of circulation of money (V), or in a reflation of real income or output, which is a good thing. The third Keynesian attack on the quantity theory is more deep seated, since it is based on the idea of *reverse causation*. Instead of changes in the money supply causing changes in the price level, the true relationship is the opposite: changes in the price level cause the money supply to change. In this interpretation, inflation is caused by cost-push institutional factors in the real economy. The money supply then passively adapts, expanding to the level required to finance the level of desired transactions that the general public undertake at the new higher price level. In essence, the money supply accommodates itself to (rather than determines) the price level. Keynesians agree with the monetarists over what they consider to be the rather trivial point that an increase in the money supply is needed to finance a higher price level and allow inflation to continue. However, the reverse causation argument rejects the view that an increase in the money supply is the cause of inflation. The monetarist response is that if the central bank were to exert control over the money supply, a temporary rise in the price level caused by rising costs could not persist.

Keynesians argue that if a government tightly restricts the growth of money to try to stem inflation, the main effect might be that the current level of transactions cannot be financed, so real activity will fall, resulting in higher unemployment. This effect occurred in the credit crunch that started in 2007, though the cause of the credit crunch lay not in tight control of the money supply by the government, but in a sudden collapse in the supply of money or liquidity emanating from the banking system itself.

The Keynesian demand-pull theory of inflation

The quantity theory of money and the Keynesian demand-pull theory are both *demand* theories of inflation, which locate the cause of inflation in excess demand for goods and services. After the Second World War, Keynesian economists accepted the argument that inflation results from excess demand pulling up the price level, but they rejected the quantity theory view that the source of the excess demand lies solely in excess monetary growth. Instead,

Keynesians located the cause of inflation firmly in the real economy, in behavioural factors that cause the planned expenditure of economic agents (households, firms, the government and the overseas sectors) to exceed the quantity of output that the economy was capable of producing. In Keynesian theory, inflation is explained by real forces determining how people behave and not by money.

In the Keynesian era, from the 1950s to the 1970s, governments were committed to achieving full employment. Arguably, this caused people to behave in an inflationary way, both as workers and as voters. Workers and their unions bargained for money wage increases in excess of any productivity increase without fear of unemployment. At the same time in the political arena, the electorate added to the pressure of demand by voting for increased public spending and budget deficits. As a result of these pressures, excess demand for output emerged.

Nonetheless, the Keynesian demand-pull theory and the quantity theory of inflation may not really be very different. In both theories, the ultimate cause of inflation may lie with the government. In the quantity theory of money, the government's budget deficit and borrowing requirement cause monetary expansion, which first triggers and then sustains demand-pull inflation. In the Keynesian demand-pull theory, a budget deficit leads to an injection of spending into the circular flow of income that, with the economy operating at full or near-full capacity, results in excess aggregate demand.

In Figure 7.18, demand-pull inflation is caused by a rightward shift of the AD curve from AD_1 to AD_2, with the shift itself caused by an increase in one or more of the components of aggregate demand (C, I, G or net export demand, $X - M$). Macroeconomic equilibrium moves from point X to point Z on the diagram. Note that the rightward shift of the AD curve has created a positive output gap, equal to the horizontal distance between the normal capacity level of output y_N and y_2. This might be a response to the fact that the government has been attempting to keep the economy producing beyond its normal capacity level of output, which leads to demand-pull inflation.

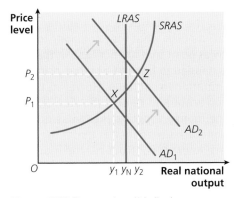

Figure 7.18 Demand-pull inflation illustrated on an AD/AS diagram

The Keynesian cost-push theory of inflation

As the Keynesian era progressed, many Keynesian economists switched away from the demand-pull theory of inflation to a new theory: the theory of **cost-push inflation**. Cost theories of inflation locate the cause of inflation in structural and institutional conditions on the supply side of the economy, particularly in the labour market and the wage-bargaining process. Most cost-push theories are essentially wage-push theories, although other variants include profits-push and import cost-push theories. The rapid but temporary cost-push inflation that occurred in the UK in 2008 and 2011 was caused by rises in the price of imported oil, gas, commodities such as copper, and food.

Wage-push theories generally argue that the growth of monopoly power in both the labour market and the goods market is responsible for inflation. They usually assume that wages are determined in the labour market through the process of collective bargaining, while in the goods market, prices are formed by a cost-plus pricing rule in which imperfectly competitive firms add a standard profit margin to average cost when setting prices. In labour markets, growing trade union strength in the Keynesian era enabled trade unions to bargain for money wage increases in excess of any rise in labour productivity. Monopoly firms were prepared to pay these wage increases, partly because of the costs of disrupting production and partly because they believed that they could pass cost increases on to consumers through higher prices when output was sold.

The question then arises as to why trade union militancy and power grew in the Keynesian era. The guarantee of full employment by the state and the provision of a safety net of labour protection legislation and welfare benefits may have sustained the inflationary process. In the cost-push theory, this created the conditions in which trade unions were more militant and were able to achieve substantial increases in money wage rates.

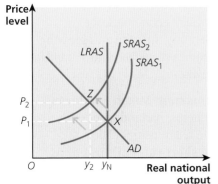

Figure 7.19 Cost-push inflation illustrated on an *AD/AS* diagram

Cost-push inflation is illustrated on an aggregate demand and supply diagram in Figure 7.19. Initially, macroeconomic equilibrium is at point *X*, with real output and the price level respectively at y_N and P_1. Firms' money costs of production rise, for example, because money wages or the price of imported raw materials increases. This causes the *SRAS* curve to move upward and to the left from $SRAS_1$ to $SRAS_2$. The cost-push inflationary process increases the price level to P_2, but higher production costs have reduced the equilibrium level of output that firms are willing to produce to y_2. The new macroeconomic equilibrium is at point *Z*.

The rise of the Phillips curve

KEY TERM

Phillips curve based on evidence from the economy, a curve showing the apparent relationship between the rate of inflation (originally the rate of increase in money wages) and the rate of unemployment.

We first described the **Phillips curve** in Book 1, pages 230–31. In this and the following sections of this chapter, we explore the Phillips curve in greater depth and explain its role in the monetarist theory of inflation.

Before the revival of free-market economics in the 1970s and 1980s, Keynesian economists who then formed the macroeconomic orthodoxy could be divided into demand-pull and cost-push schools in terms of their views on the causes of inflation. After 1958, the debate between demand-pull and cost-push Keynesians was conducted with the aid of a statistical relationship, the **Phillips curve**, which is illustrated in Figure 7.20.

When developing the Phillips curve from his analysis of the labour market, the economist A.W. Phillips argued that a stable inverse statistical relationship existed between the rate of change of wages (the rate of *wage* inflation) and the percentage of the labour force unemployed. Later versions of the Phillips curve, such as the one illustrated in Figure 7.20, measure the inverse relationship between unemployment and the rate of *price* inflation.

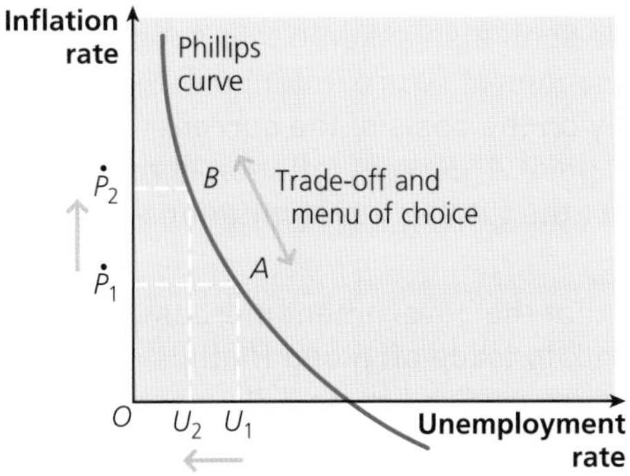

Figure 7.20 The Phillips curve

The Phillips curve is *not* a theory of inflation, but it does give support to both Keynesian theories of inflation. In the demand-pull theory, falling unemployment is associated with excess demand, which pulls up money wages in the labour market. In the cost-push theory, falling unemployment means that trade union power increases, enabling unions to use their monopoly power to push for higher wages.

Although the Phillips curve illustrates the conflict between full employment and control of inflation as policy objectives, it also illustrates the choices available to a government. Suppose unemployment initially is U_1 and the rate of inflation is $\dot{P}_1$ with the economy at point *A* on the Phillips curve. (Note that we are using the symbol $\dot{P}$ to show the rate of price inflation.)

By increasing aggregate demand, the government can move the economy to point B. Unemployment falls to U_2, but at the cost of a higher rate of inflation at $\dot{P}_2$. By using demand management policies, it appears possible for governments to trade off between increasing the number of jobs in the economy and reducing inflation. Points such as A and B on the Phillips curve represent a menu of choice for governments when deciding upon the combination of unemployment and inflation they are willing to accept.

KEY TERMS

short-run Phillips curve the original downward-sloping Phillips curve, developed by A.W. Phillips.

long-run Phillips curve a vertical Phillips curve, developed by Milton Friedman and Edmund Phelps, along which trade-offs between reducing inflation and reducing unemployment are not possible. Also called the L-shaped Phillips curve.

The breakdown of the Phillips relationship

In the 1970s, at the time of the crisis in Keynesian economics, the Phillips relationship broke down when accelerating inflation and growing unemployment occurred together. The nicknames *stagflation* and *slumpflation* were given to the combination of these two evils.

A few years earlier, the famous monetarist economist, Milton Friedman, and another American economist, Edmund Phelps, had independently predicted the breakdown of the Phillips curve relationship. (The original Phillips curve is now often called the **short-run Phillips curve**.) In 1968, Milton Friedman had developed the theory of the **long-run Phillips curve**.

EXTENSION MATERIAL

Friedman's theory of the long-run Phillips curve, and the natural rate of unemployment

To explain Milton Friedman's theory of the long-run Phillips curve, we must introduce the role of expectations into the inflationary process, and we also introduce and explain Milton Friedman's concept of the **natural rate of unemployment** (NRU). We start by explaining that the original Keynesian explanation of the (short-run) Phillips curve wrongly took into account only the *current* rate of inflation and ignored the important influence of the *expected* rate of inflation.

In Figure 7.21, the natural rate of unemployment is located where the *LRAS* curve intersects the unemployment axis on a Phillips curve diagram.

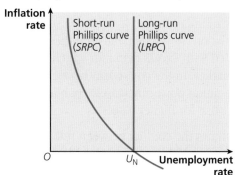

Figure 7.21 The long-run Phillips curve and the natural rate of unemployment

To explain the natural rate of unemployment (NRU, shown at U_N in Figures 7.21 and 7.22), we shall start by assuming, as a simplification, that the rate of growth of labour productivity is zero and that the rate of increase of prices (price inflation) equals the rate of increase of wages (wage inflation). In Figure 7.22, the economy is initially at point A, with unemployment at the natural rate U_N. At point A, the rate of inflation is zero, as is the rate of increase of money wages. We shall also assume that people form their expectations of future inflation in the next time period solely on the basis of the current rate of inflation. Thus at point A, current inflation is zero, so workers expect the future rate of inflation also to be zero.

We now assume that the government increases aggregate demand, to trade off along Phillips curve $SRPC_1$ to a point such as B in Figure 7.22, where unemployment at U_1 is below the natural rate, U_N. Inflation initially rises to $\dot{P}_1$ (say, 5%). But a point such as B is unsustainable. For workers to be willing to supply more labour, the real wage must rise, yet a rising real wage causes employers to demand less labour. In the short run, more workers may indeed enter the labour market in the false belief that a

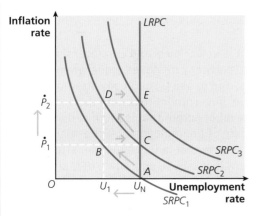

Figure 7.22 Long-run and short-run Phillips curves

5% increase in money wages is also a real wage increase. (This false belief is an example of *money illusion*.) Similarly, firms may be willing to employ more labour if they also suffer money illusion, falsely believing that rising prices mean that sales revenues are rising faster than labour costs.

This means that, to sustain an increase in employment above the natural rate, workers and employers must suffer money illusion in equal but opposite directions, thereby keeping expectations of inflation, formed in the previous time period, consistently below the actual rate to which inflation has risen. However, as workers continuously adjust their expectations of future inflation to the rising actual rate and bargain for ever-higher money wages, the short-run Phillips curve shifts outward

from $SRPC_1$ to $SRPC_2$ and so on. There is indeed a separate short-run Phillips curve for each expected rate of inflation. 'Further-out' short-run Phillips curves such as $SRPC_2$ and $SRPC_3$ are associated with higher expected rates of future inflation. Conversely, the short-run Phillips curve shifts inward when the expected rate of inflation falls.

Free-market economists argue that, in the long run, the only way to keep unemployment below the NRU is to permit the money supply to expand and finance an ever-accelerating rate of inflation. Actual inflation always has to be above the expected rate for workers and firms to be willing respectively to supply and to demand more labour. But if this happens, accelerating inflation will eventually create a hyperinflation, which, in the resulting breakdown of economic activity, is likely to increase the NRU. Any attempt to reduce unemployment below the NRU is therefore foolhardy and irresponsible. In the short run it leads to accelerating inflation, while in the long run it perversely increases the NRU to an unnecessarily high level.

If the government realises it made a mistake when expanding the economy to point B, it can stabilise the rate of inflation at 5%. Workers and employers 'see through' their money illusion and realise that they have confused money quantities with real quantities. As soon as this happens, they refuse respectively to supply and to demand the labour necessary to keep unemployment below the NRU. The economy now moves to point C.

KEY TERM

natural rate of unemployment the rate of unemployment when the aggregate labour market is in equilibrium, i.e. the demand for labour equals the supply of labour. All unemployment is therefore voluntary.

EXTENSION MATERIAL

Rational expectations

The theory of expectations formation described in the previous extension material box is called the theory of *adaptive expectations*. According to this theory, workers and firms form expectations of what will happen in the future solely on the basis of what is happening currently and what has happened in the recent past. However, pro-free-market economists often favour an alternative theory of how expectations are formed, called the theory of *rational expectations*. The theory stems from the assumption that it is unrealistic to assume that workers and firms, acting rationally in their self-interest, form

expectations of future inflation solely on the basis of current or recent inflation.

To understand the difference between the theories of adaptive and rational expectations, consider the situation of a gambler deciding whether to place a bet on a particular horse winning a race. Three races ago, the horse ended the race in fourth position, improving to third place two races ago and to second place recently. Forming her expectations adaptively, the gambler decides to bet on the horse, expecting it now to win. But gambling on the basis of recent form alone could be less successful than a strategy that makes use of all the information available, including past form. Information about the quality of the jockey, and about other matters such as the qualities of the other horses and their jockeys, the length of the race, the state of the track, and perhaps 'inside information' provided by a stable boy, might lead to a more rational gambling decision.

This story does not mean that a gambler who forms expectations rationally always wins her bets. She may win or lose, just as bets made on decisions formed adaptively or by picking a name out of a hat may be right or wrong. However, over a long sequence of races, it is likely that gambling decisions formed on the basis of rational expectations will produce better outcomes than decisions formed adaptively or randomly. The more 'perfect' the information on which rational expectations are formed, the more likely it is that the expectations will prove correct. It is less sensible to gamble on the basis of limited information when more up-to-date and relevant information is available.

Returning to the causes of inflation, modern free-market economists argue that it is unrealistic to assume that a rational economic agent, acting on self-interest, forms expectations of future inflation solely on the basis of past or experienced inflation. Self-interest requires quick modification of economic behaviour in line with expectations formed on the basis of the most up-to-date information available. This means that it is less likely that people will suffer from money illusion.

As a result, free-market economists now tend to reject the idea that economic agents suffer money illusion for quite long periods. If expectations are formed rationally rather than adaptively, people don't suffer from money illusion and any attempt by a government to reduce unemployment below its natural rate fails, since 'artificially' stimulating aggregate demand leads solely to accelerating inflation. The correct way to reduce unemployment is to reduce the natural rate itself, rather than to increase demand to try to reduce unemployment below the NRU. To do this, the government should use appropriate free-market supply-side policies.

To conclude, modern free-market economists continue to accept the Friedmanite concept of the natural rate of unemployment. But whereas Milton Friedman believed that, in the short run at least, governments can trade off along a short-run Phillips curve and reduce unemployment below the natural

rate, the theory of rational expectations rejects this possibility.

As a result, it is in workers' and employers' interests to realise instantly any mistakes made when forming expectations, and to see through any attempt by an 'irresponsible' government to reflate the economy beyond the level of output that is produced at the natural rate of unemployment. Free-market economists believe that in this situation, attempts by government to increase aggregate demand to stimulate output and employment are anticipated fully by private economic agents. Workers and firms modify their behaviour to offset or neutralise the effects intended by the government, so the increase in aggregate demand has no effect upon real economic activity and employment. For extreme neoclassical economists, this is the case in both the short run and the long run because they believe that market forces will ensure that output and employment are always at their natural or equilibrium levels.

Another important difference separating the adaptive and rational expectations of free-market economics is the length of time unemployment must remain above its natural rate as the cost or penalty of an attempt to reduce unemployment below the natural rate. In Friedmanite theory, the economy experiences a lengthy period of unemployment above its natural rate, to 'bleed' the system of inflationary expectations built up during the period of fiscal or monetary expansion.

In contrast to this 'gradualist' theory, rational expectations theory assumes that economic agents immediately reduce expectations of future inflation, provided they believe in the credibility of a tough free-market government's commitment to reducing inflation. Believing that the government means business in pursuing tight fiscal and monetary policies to control inflation, workers and firms immediately build a lower expected rate of inflation into their wage-bargaining and price-setting behaviour. Inflation falls quickly and fairly painlessly, without the need for a lengthy period of unemployment above its natural level. In effect, a firmly free-market government reduces inflation by 'talking down' inflation. However, if credibility in government policy were to disappear, its ability to control inflation would also be diminished. People would now expect higher prices, and would alter behaviour accordingly. Expectations of higher prices would become self-fulfilling.

Inflation psychology

Until the recent rapid fall in the rate of inflation and the appearance of zero inflation and actual deflation, it was widely agreed by Keynesians as well as by free-market economists that what made inflation particularly difficult to control in the UK has been the existence, built up over decades, of an *inflation psychology*. Over the years, many groups in UK society, including house owners and wage earners in strong bargaining positions, did extremely well out of inflation. For example, house owners with large mortgages had a vested interest in allowing inflation to continue, in order to reduce the real value of their personal debt. Indeed, house owners did even better when house price inflation exceeded the general rate of inflation. In this situation, the real value of houses increased while the real value of mortgages fell.

In most of the years between the late 1990s and 2015, the UK government and the Bank of England succeeded in reducing people's expectations of inflation (except with regard to house price inflation). Therefore, because of the benign effect on people's behaviour, it became much easier to control inflation. The authorities had successfully 'talked down' the rate of inflation. However, as recent bursts of cost-push inflation have shown, circumstances can quickly change for the worse and, while inflation can be dormant, it is never dead.

SYNOPTIC LINK
Refer back to Book 1, pages 215–16, and read the section 'The consequences of inflation for the performance of the economy and for individuals'. Then read the following section on 'The consequences of deflation for the performance of the economy and for individuals', which distinguishes between a 'good' and a 'bad' deflation.

SUMMARY

- Aggregate demand is the total planned spending on the goods and services produced within the economy, per period of time.
- The aggregate demand curve slopes downward from left to right, showing that at a lower price level, more real goods and services are demanded.
- The short-run aggregate supply (*SRAS*) curve shows the quantities of real output that businesses plan to produce and sell at different price levels when the economy's total productive capacity is fixed.
- *SRAS* curves slope upward from left to right, showing that at a higher price level firms are willing to supply more real goods and services.
- The vertical slope of the *LRAS* curve results from the fact that the curve is located at the 'normal capacity' level of output. At this level of output, firms cannot increase output, except temporarily in the short run, following an increase in aggregate demand.
- Expansionary fiscal and monetary policies shift the *AD* curve to the right. Contractionary fiscal and monetary policies shift the *AD* curve to the left.
- Supply-side policies attempt to shift the *LRAS* curve to the right.
- There is still some unemployment, often known as the equilibrium level of unemployment, when the economy is 'fully employed'.
- Equilibrium unemployment, which is also known as the natural rate of unemployment, comprises frictional, seasonal and structural unemployment.
- Disequilibrium unemployment occurs when the economy's aggregate labour market fails to clear.
- There are two main types of disequilibrium unemployment: classical or real-wage unemployment and demand-deficient, cyclical or Keynesian unemployment.
- Real-wage unemployment is caused by real wage rates being too high in individual labour markets.
- Cyclical or Keynesian unemployment is caused by deficient aggregate demand. The policy solution is to use fiscal and/or monetary policy to increase aggregate demand.

- Theories of inflation can be divided into demand-pull and cost-push theories.
- The quantity theory of money, which is the oldest theory of inflation, is a demand-based theory of inflation.
- A short-run Phillips curve illustrates the conflict between controlling inflation and reducing unemployment, but is not itself a theory of inflation.
- Monetarist and free-market economists argue that the long-run Phillips curve is vertical, located at the economy's natural rate, or level, of unemployment.
- Around 2009 and again in 2015 some economists feared that the problems of deflation might replace the problems of inflation.

Questions

1 With the help of a *PPF* diagram, explain the difference between short-term and long-term economic growth.

2 Evaluate different policies a government might use to try to shift the *LRAS* curve to the right.

3 Do you agree that it is supply-side, rather than demand-side, factors which have been the more important cause of UK unemployment in recent years? Justify your answer.

4 Explain the differences between inflation, deflation, disinflation and reflation.

5 Explain why the relationship between unemployment and inflation is likely to be different in the short run from the long run.

6 Evaluate the view that the avoidance of inflation should always be the major macroeconomic objective.

8

Financial markets and monetary policy

Like all the economies of nation states in the world today, the UK's economy is a monetary economy, in which most of the goods and services produced are traded or exchanged via the intermediary of money. This chapter begins by describing the nature and functions of money in the UK economy and then explains the structure of UK financial markets and the characteristics of some of the important financial assets that are traded in these markets. The chapter goes on to explain how bank deposits, which form the largest part of the money supply in modern economies, are created by the free enterprise banking system. It then surveys the changes that have recently taken place in UK monetary policy, showing how current monetary policy has developed out of the monetary policies implemented by UK governments and the Bank of England over the last 20–35 years.

LEARNING OBJECTIVES

This chapter will:

- explore the characteristics and functions of money
- describe the financial assets which have functioned as money, both in the present day and in the past
- outline the structure and functions of UK financial markets: money markets, capital markets and foreign exchange markets
- explain the relationship between asset prices and interest rates
- outline the roles of different types of bank: commercial banks, investment banks and central banks
- explain how a commercial bank creates credit and new bank deposits
- examine how the Bank of England, the UK's central bank, implements monetary policy
- examine the regulation of the UK's financial markets

8.1 The structure of financial markets and financial assets

The characteristics and functions of money

Money is best defined by focusing on the two principal functions it performs in the economy. Money functions as:

- **A medium of exchange or means of payment.** The economy we live in is a monetary economy in which most of the goods and services produced are traded or exchanged via the intermediary of money, rather than through barter (that is, swapping goods). Whenever money is used to pay for goods or services, or for the purpose of settling transactions and the payment of debts, it performs this function.
- **A store of value or store of wealth.** Money is also an asset, something people own which has value. Most people store some of their wealth in the form of money in preference to holding other *financial assets*, such as stocks and shares, or *physical assets*, such as a house or car. When stored rather than spent, money's purchasing power is transferred to the future, although over time inflation may erode money's purchasing power.

EXTENSION MATERIAL

Money's other functions

Money has two other functions which are less important for you to know. Money serves as:

- a measure of value
- a standard of deferred payment

Combined together, these are often called the 'unit of account' function. Money is the unit in which the prices of goods are quoted and in which accounts are kept. This allows us to compare the relative values of goods even when we have no intention of actually spending money and buying goods — for example, when we 'window-shop'. This is the measure of value function. Money's function as a standard of deferred payment allows people to delay paying for goods or settling a debt, even though goods or services are being provided immediately. Money acts as a standard of deferred payment whenever firms sell goods on credit or draw up contracts specifying a money payment due at a later date.

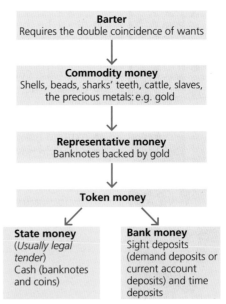

Figure 8.1 Barter and different forms of money

CASE STUDY 8.1

The development of modern money

Before the development of money, exchange and trade took place in simple and primitive village economies, where the exchange of goods and services was initially based on *barter* — the swapping of goods and services. However, barter is inefficient and impractical in a more complex economic system characterised by specialisation and trade. Successful barter requires a *double coincidence of wants*, which means that a person wishing to trade a television set for a refrigerator must not only establish contact with someone with equal but opposite wants (that is, an individual possessing a refrigerator who wishes to exchange it for a television set); they must also agree that the television set and refrigerator are of equal value (or how many TV sets equal one fridge — or vice versa).

The people of Paraja and Mali in Orissa in India hold a weekly barter market

Barter is inefficient because the time and energy spent searching the market to establish the double coincidence of wants results in unnecessary search costs (involving shoe-leather costs) and transaction costs. If trading products is inefficient, it inhibits the development of specialisation, division of labour and large-scale production. All of these contribute to the productive efficiency and range of consumer choice available in modern and sophisticated monetary economies.

Commodity money

Figure 8.1 shows the three main forms of money that have developed since money replaced barter. The earliest form of money was commodity money. Commodities that functioned as money had an intrinsic value of their own: they yielded utility and consumer services to their owners. Beads, shells, sharks' teeth and other commodities could be used for decorative purposes while being stored as wealth. Some commodities used as money, such as cattle, could be slaughtered and eaten.

Representative money

As money evolved, gold and silver gradually replaced other forms of commodity money because they possessed, to a greater degree, the desirable characteristics necessary for a commodity to function as money: *relative scarcity*, *uniformity*, *durability*, *portability* and *divisibility*. All of these help to create confidence in money, which is necessary for its *acceptability*. Nevertheless, gold and silver are vulnerable to theft and are difficult to store safely. Eventually, wealthy individuals deposited the precious metals they owned with goldsmiths for safekeeping.

At the next stage, the goldsmiths developed into banks, and the receipts they issued in return for deposits of gold became the first banknotes or paper money. These notes were *representative money*, representing ownership of silver or gold. Early banknotes were acceptable as a means of

227

payment because they could be exchanged for silver or gold on demand. They were issued on the whole by privately owned banks rather than by the state, although the state continued to issue gold and silver coinage. Although worthless in themselves, banknotes functioned as money because people were willing to accept them as long as there was confidence that notes could be changed into gold, which does have an intrinsic value.

Token money

Modern money is almost all token money with no intrinsic value of its own. It takes two main forms:

cash and *bank deposits*. In England and Wales, the state, or rather its agent, the Bank of England, has a monopoly over the issue of cash (although in other parts of the UK, Scottish and Northern Ireland banks also have a limited ability to issue banknotes). However, cash is best thought of as the 'small change' of the monetary system — bank deposits form by far the largest part of modern money. Most modern money takes the form of bank deposits created by the private enterprise banking system.

Follow-up questions

1 Why does money provide a more efficient means of payment than barter?
2 What are the advantages and disadvantages of using cash as the main form of personal wealth?

ACTIVITY

Find out the meaning of search costs, shoe-leather costs and transaction costs.

SYNOPTIC LINK

At this stage, it might be a good idea to go to section 8.3, pages 246–57, which explains how, through their ability to create credit, private enterprise banks such as Barclays create bank deposits, which make up the lion's share of modern money.

TEST YOURSELF 8.2

Only **one** of the following has increased the need to hold money on one's person:

A inflation

B increased use of credit cards

C increased use of automatic transfers between deposits

D increased use of ATM machines

Explain why only statement A provides the correct answer.

The money supply

Fifty or so years ago, before the advent of *monetarism*, few economists gave much attention to the precise definition of the money supply or stock of money in the economy. This reflected the Keynesian view that money did not matter in the macroeconomic management of the economy. However, when monetarism replaced Keynesianism as the prevailing orthodoxy in the 1970s, money did begin to matter — particularly in the years before monetarism itself drifted from favour after around 1985. For a few years from the mid-1970s to the mid-1980s, during the 'monetarist era', control of the money supply became an important part of monetarist economic management in general and monetary policy in particular. During this period, monetarist economists devoted considerable attention to the problem of deciding which assets to include and exclude when defining the money supply.

SYNOPTIC LINK

At this stage, re-read Chapter 7, page 191, which introduced you to the term *monetarism*.

EXTENSION MATERIAL

Goodhart's Law

A significant problem that contributed to the decline of monetarism as a major force influencing UK governments stemmed from what has become known as Goodhart's Law. This 'law' is named after Charles Goodhart, formerly a professor at the London School of Economics and a member of the Bank of England's Monetary Policy Committee (MPC). Goodhart argued that, as soon as a government tries to control the growth of a particular measure of the money supply, any previously stable relationship between the targeted measure of money and the economy breaks down. The more successful the Bank of England appears to be in controlling the rate of growth of the financial assets defined as the money supply, the more likely it is that other financial assets, regarded previously as *near money* outside the existing definition and system of control, will take on the function of a medium of exchange and become money.

In this way, attempting to control the money supply is rather like a man trying to catch his own shadow. As soon as he moves, his shadow also moves. Although what is defined as money may be controlled, when other financial assets become money, this becomes irrelevant. The difficulties of, first, defining the money supply and, second, exerting control over its rate of growth contributed to the downfall of monetarism after 1985.

Narrow money and broad money

KEY TERMS

narrow money the part of the stock of money (or money supply) made of cash and liquid bank and building society deposits.

broad money the part of the stock of money (or money supply) made of cash, other liquid assets such as bank and building society deposits, but also some less liquid assets. The measure of broad money used by the Bank of England is called M4.

liquidity measures the ease with which an asset can be converted into cash without loss of value. Cash is the most liquid of all assets.

Narrow money and broad money

Over the years, the Bank of England has used more than one definition of the money supply. These divide into measures of **narrow money** and **broad money**. Narrow money, which restricts the measure of money to cash and bank and building society sight deposits, reflects the medium of exchange function of money, namely money functioning as a means of payment. Broad money also includes other financial assets, which although stores of value, are too illiquid, at least for the time being, to function as media of exchange.

STUDY TIP

It is important to understand the meaning of the word 'liquidity' in the context of money, financial markets and monetary policy. **Liquidity** measures the ease with which an asset can be converted into cash without loss of value; cash is itself the most liquid of all assets. Assets that generally can only be sold after a long exhaustive search for a buyer are known as illiquid. Liquidity is also affected by whether or not the conversion can take place at a pre-known value. A share issued by a public company (PLC) is highly liquid in that it can quickly be sold on the stock exchange, but less liquid in the sense that the seller does not know the price the asset will fetch, in advance of the sale.

TEST YOURSELF 8.3

Which of the following statements is true about a highly liquid asset?

A It generally has a very limited market for its resale.

B It cannot be sold on a market.

C It can be converted into a means of payment easily without loss of value.

D It has high transaction costs associated with its sale.

Explain why statement C provides the correct answer, and why statements A, B and D are wrong.

Assets and liabilities

To understand fully the nature of both money and the monetary system, it is important first to understand the two words: *assets* and *liabilities*. Banknotes and coins function as both financial assets and financial liabilities. A £10 note is an asset to the person owning it, since it gives the person £10 worth of spending power. However, it is a liability for the Bank of England which issued it. Many years ago, Bank of England notes were convertible into gold. The Bank had to meet this liability and, if asked by note owners, convert banknotes into gold on demand. These days and more innocuously, the Bank's liability is to replace an old and dirty note, or a note mangled in a washing machine, with a brand-new note.

From a commercial bank's point of view, a loan (or credit) granted to a customer is an interest-earning asset, which the borrower is liable to repay. But the act of creating credit or a loan simultaneously creates a bank deposit owned by the customer to whom the loan is made. The bank deposit is the customer's asset, but it is a liability for the bank itself. The bank must honour cash withdrawals and cheques or debit card payments drawn on the deposit, which transfer ownership of part of the deposit to other people. The key point to remember is that the loan-creating process increases the bank's assets (i.e. the credit it creates) and its liabilities (i.e. customers' deposits) by equal amounts. The creation of credit (an asset from a bank's point of view) simultaneously increases by the same amount customers' deposits held in the bank (a liability from the bank's point of view).

In summary, when a bank creates an interest-earning asset (the credit it extends to its customers), it is simultaneously adding to its deposit liabilities, since it must now honour customers' withdrawals from their deposits of cash or payments they make to other people. The act of creating an asset simultaneously creates a liability. (It is worth remembering that liabilities and capital represent a bank's 'source of funds' whereas the assets show its 'use of funds'.)

KEY TERMS

equity is wealth; shares are known as equities. However, equity can also mean fairness or justness; it depends on the context in which the term is used.

debt money people owe.

CASE STUDY 8.2

Positive and negative equity

The word **equity** has two very different economic meanings. On the one hand, in the context of topics such as fiscal policy, poverty and the distributions of income and wealth, equity means fairness or justness. However, in the context of this chapter, equity means wealth. Consider the following situation.

Many of the parents of the students reading this book will have taken out a mortgage to finance the purchase of their house. The house is the parents' asset. However, the mortgage, or the money they have borrowed to finance house purchase, is the parents' liability. (Assets are everything you *own* that possesses value, while liabilities are everything that you *owe* to other people.)

In much of recent history, the value of mortgages has remained unchanged (or even fallen when part of the mortgages are paid off each year), but house prices have risen, at least in most parts of the UK. This means that owner-occupiers of houses have benefited from *positive equity* (what they own is greater than what they owe.)

However, in the financial crisis which hit the UK in 2007, house prices fell rapidly. This created the problem of *negative equity*, which occurs when what is owed exceeds the value of what is owned: that is, the amount owed on the mortgage is more than the value of the house. People in the negative equity trap often have crippling **debt** from which it is very difficult to escape.

Follow-up questions

1 What is the negative equity trap?
2 In the years after 2007, young house buyers who got onto the property ladder just before the financial crisis were the main victims of the negative equity problem. Explain why this was so.

Portfolio balance decisions

In old-fashioned English, a portfolio is a bag or piece of luggage in which people store things and transport them from one place to another. An art portfolio is the collection of drawings and paintings a student submits in order to gain an Art A-level pass. In financial jargon, a wealth portfolio contains the different wealth assets that an individual owns and holds at a particular point in time.

Everyone, except the completely destitute, makes decisions, consciously or subconsciously, on the form of asset in which to keep their wealth. In the first instance, people choose between holding physical assets (or non-financial assets), such as houses, and holding financial assets. (Physical assets such as property, fine art, classic cars and antiques can be attractive because they tend to go up in value or appreciate, thus providing a hedge against inflation.)

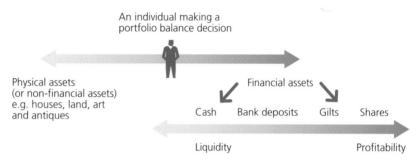

Figure 8.2 A spectrum of assets over which a portfolio balance decision may be made

When choosing the assets to hold, people make *portfolio balance decisions*. A portfolio balance decision is illustrated in Figure 8.2, which, besides making the distinction between physical and financial assets, arranges financial assets according to *liquidity* and *profitability*. As we have noted, liquidity measures the ease with which an asset can be converted into cash, and the certainty of what it will be worth when converted. We have seen that, provided it is generally accepted and can be used as a means of payment, cash is the most liquid of all assets. For the most part, bank deposits are not quite as liquid as cash, but they are sufficiently liquid to be treated as money. The other financial assets shown in Figure 8.2 are examples of non-money financial assets, in some cases being near-money. Shares and government **bonds** (gilt-edged securities, or gilts) are marketable (they can be sold second-hand on the stock exchange), but they are less liquid than money. In contrast to money, which earns little or no interest, shares and gilts generally hold out the prospect of providing a profit for their owners.

> **KEY TERM**
>
> **bonds** financial securities sold by companies (corporate bonds) or by governments (government bonds) which are a form of long-term borrowing. Bonds usually have a maturity date on which they are redeemed, with the borrower usually making a fixed interest payment each year until the bond matures.

Financial markets

In Book 1, page 20, we defined a market as a voluntary meeting of buyers and sellers. We went on to stress that markets do not have to exist in a particular geographical location, and in recent years, 24/7 global markets have grown up, facilitated by the development of the internet. This has enabled many markets to become truly global and to function on a worldwide basis.

This is certainly the case for some of the **financial markets** functioning in the UK — for example, the capital and foreign exchange markets and Lloyds insurance market. However, at the other extreme, some of the smaller financial markets, such as the market for Treasury bills and commercial bills, are restricted largely to trading in the City of London, the hub of UK financial markets.

> **KEY TERM**
>
> **financial markets** markets in which financial assets or securities are traded.

Some of the main financial markets in the UK and global economies

A financial market is a market in financial assets or securities. (A security is so called because it secures a claim against a person or institution — for example, a share secures ownership of a fraction of the company which initially sold the share to the general public.) Financial markets can be classified in a number of ways, but one of the most fruitful is into markets for short-dated financial assets (often called **money markets**) and long-dated and undated financial assets (often called **capital markets**). There are also **foreign exchange markets**.

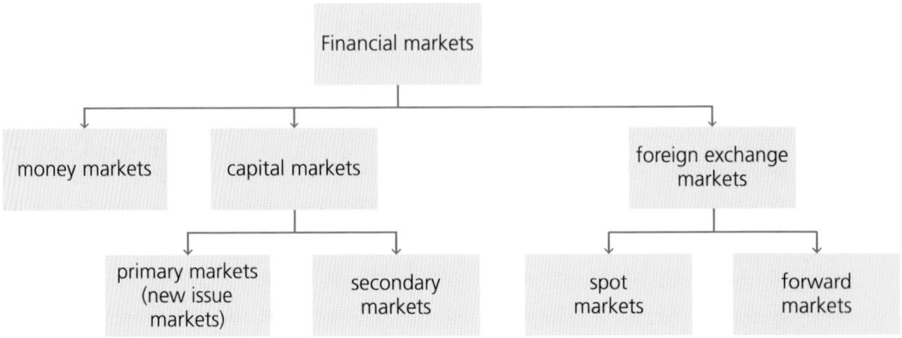

Figure 8.3 Some of the main financial markets in the UK and global economies

> **KEY TERMS**
>
> **money markets** provide a means for lenders and borrowers to satisfy their short-term financial needs. Assets that are bought and sold on money markets are short term, with maturities ranging from a day to a year, and are normally easily convertible into cash. The term 'money market' is an umbrella that covers several markets, including the markets for Treasury bills and commercial bills.
>
> **capital markets** where securities such as shares and bonds are issued to raise medium- to long-term financing, and where shares and bonds are then traded on the 'second-hand' part of the market, e.g. the London Stock Exchange.
>
> **foreign exchange markets** (forex, FX, or currency markets) global, decentralised markets for the trading of currencies. The main participants in this market are large international commercial banks. Collectively, foreign exchange markets are the largest markets in the global economy.

> **STUDY TIP**
> You should be aware of other financial markets beside those shown in Figure 8.3. These include markets for commodity futures and insurance products.

UK money markets

As we explain shortly, money markets provide mechanisms for banks to arrange their assets in terms of their liquidity and profitability, with highly liquid assets such as Treasury bills and commercial bills at the liquid end of the spectrum. Organising their assets in this way enables commercial banks to perform perhaps the most important banking function, namely that of a financial intermediary linking savers to borrowers.

A money market which has recently become extremely important in the operation of monetary policy is the London interbank market, in which the LIBOR interest rate is charged. (LIBOR is the London Interbank Offered Rate, which is a rate of interest charged when banks lend to each other, usually for very short periods of time.) We shall explain the role of the London interbank market later in the chapter, in the context of monetary policy.

UK capital markets

In contrast to money markets, capital markets, which include the London Stock Exchange, provide the mechanism through which public limited companies (PLCs), which are arguably the most important form of business organisation in the UK, can raise the funds to finance their long-term growth. In addition, the part of the capital market known as the bond market performs a critical role in government finance — for example, by enabling a government to finance a budget deficit.

Comparing money markets and capital markets

Table 8.1 enables us to compare the important similarities of, and also the important differences between, two of the most important money markets (the markets for commercial bills and Treasury bills) and the capital market.

Table 8.1 Money markets and capital markets

	Money markets (markets for short-dated financial assets or securities)	Capital markets (markets for undated and long-dated financial assets or securities)
The private sector raising finance	Sale of commercial bills	Sale of new issues of shares Sale of new issues of corporate bonds
Central government raising finance	Sale of Treasury bills	Sale of new issues of government bonds (in the UK also known as gilt-edged securities or gilts)

The function of money markets is to supply both private sector commercial firms and the government with a source of short-term finance. For a firm, bill finance is an alternative to a conventional bank loan. Bills are short-dated financial assets or securities, which mature within a year (and often within 3 months) of their date of issue. There are two main types of bill, or bills of exchange as they are known: *commercial bills* and *Treasury bills*. Commercial bills are sold by investment banks on behalf of client firms. Treasury bills, which are sold as new issues by the Bank of England on behalf of the government, provide the government with a method of financing the differences that emerge at certain times in the financial year between tax revenues and government spending.

Treasury bills are in fact short-dated government loans. (The word *bill* is used for a short-dated loan raised on a money market, whereas the word *bond* is used for a long-dated loan raised on a capital market.) The role of capital markets will be explained in the next section. **Shares, corporate bonds** and **government bonds** (gilt-edged securities or gilts) are the main securities traded on capital markets.

The inverse relationship between bond prices and interest rates

Economics students are often confused by the relationship between the prices of bonds and long-run interest rates. To understand the relationship, consider Figure 8.4, which depicts the main characteristics of government bonds (in the UK, gilt-edged securities, or gilts) and the long-run rate of interest.

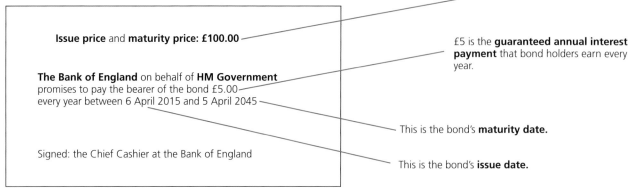

£100 is the price at which the bond was first sold on 6 April 2015 (the bond's **issue price**) and it is also the **maturity price** at which the bond can be **redeemed** 30 years later on 5 April 2045. However, it is not the second-hand price at which the bond can be bought or sold on the capital market (the stock exchange) on any day during the 30-year life of the bond. The second-hand price is determined by supply and demand, and can vary daily.

Issue price and **maturity price: £100.00**

The Bank of England on behalf of **HM Government** promises to pay the bearer of the bond £5.00 every year between 6 April 2015 and 5 April 2045

Signed: the Chief Cashier at the Bank of England

£5 is the **guaranteed annual interest payment** that bond holders earn every year.

This is the bond's **maturity date**.

This is the bond's **issue date**.

Figure 8.4 The key characteristics of a bond (in this case a UK government bond or gilt)

KEY TERMS

coupon the guaranteed fixed annual interest payment, often divided into two 6-month payments, paid by the issuer of a bond to the owner of the bond.

maturity date the date on which the issuer of a dated security, such as a gilt-edged security (long-dated) or a Treasury bill (short-dated), pays the face value of the security to the security's owner.

Gilts (and also corporate bonds issued by private sector companies) are *fixed-interest securities* sold by the government (or by companies) when they borrow in the long term. The bond in Figure 8.4 is a 30-year bond with a face value of £100 carrying a guaranteed annual interest payment, known as the coupon, of £5. Simple arithmetic will tell you that £5 is 5% of £100. Suppose, however, that after the bond has been sold on its day of issue for £100, its second-hand price on the London Stock Exchange or bond market *rises* to £200. This means that the bond's *yield* falls to 2.5% (£5 as a percentage of £200). (A bond's *yield* is in effect *the long-run rate of interest* earned by holder of the bond. It is determined primarily by the coupon and the price the holder paid for the bond.)

Suppose, by contrast, the bond's price falls to £50. This means that the bond's yield rises to 10% (£5 as a percentage of £50). Both these simple calculations illustrate the inverse relationship between bond prices and *long-run* interest rates. If bond prices rise, yields or long-term interest rates fall, and if bond prices fall, yields of long-term interest rates rise.

The guaranteed interest (or **coupon**) earned each year by gilt holders is paid in two instalments at 6-month intervals. Gilts and other bonds usually have a specific **maturity date**.

QUANTITATIVE SKILLS 8.1

Worked example: calculating the yield on a bond

The government sells a new issue of 50-year gilt-edged securities, each with a nominal value, or maturity value, of £100 and a guaranteed yearly interest payment (or coupon) of £2.50. Five years after the gilt was issued, its second-hand or market price on the stock exchange falls to £50.

Calculate the yield on the gilt-edged security at this date.

$$\text{Yield} = \frac{\text{Annual coupon payment}}{\text{Gilt's current market price}} \times 100$$

$$= \frac{£2.50}{£50} \times 100$$

$$= \frac{1}{20} \times 100$$

$$= 5\%$$

EXTENSION MATERIAL

Capital gains and losses and bond and share prices

In Quantitative Skills 8.1, the fact that the gilt does not mature until 50 years after the date of issue means that an approaching maturity date has no noticeable effect on the gilt's current market price or on its yield. If, by contrast, the maturity date were next week, the market price would be very close to its maturity value (£50), and its yield would have converged to be very close to 2.5%.

For a gilt or a corporate bond with many years to go until maturity, another factor affecting changes in its market price is the expectation of making a capital gain (and the fear of suffering a capital loss). Suppose the current bond price is £100, but speculators *expect* the price to rise shortly to £150. If the bond can be bought now at or near its current price of £100, and its price does indeed shortly rise, speculators who buy the bond make a capital gain when selling the bond later — for example, for £150. If a sufficiently large number of speculators decide to buy the bond at or near the price of £100, increased demand for the bond pulls up the market price, until eventually it may indeed reach £150.

Conversely, a fear that the bond price will fall, say to £50, will induce speculative selling of the bond, which in turn causes the bond's price to fall. Provided a sufficiently large number of speculators behave in the same way, speculative buying and selling, in the hope of making a capital gain — or avoiding a capital loss — is an important determinant of short-run changes in bond prices. (Share prices are also affected in a similar way.)

There are some government bonds in existence (Consolidated Stock) which will never mature. Because there are no complications brought about by an approaching maturity date, the yield on Consolidated Stock, at any point of time, is the best indicator there is of the long-run interest rate on relatively risk-free assets at that time. Long-term interest rates on risky assets such as corporate bonds and on even riskier assets, such as Greek government bonds, will be higher.

QUANTITATIVE SKILLS 8.2

Worked example: calculating a bond's current market price

The annual coupon payment on a 40-year bond issued last year is £8. When the bond was first sold, the long-run interest rate was 8%. The bond's maturity value is £100. Within the last year, long-run interest rates have fallen to 4%.

Calculate the approximate current market price of this bond on the stock exchange.

$$\text{Yield} = \frac{\text{Annual coupon payment}}{\text{Bond's current market price}} \times 100$$

$$4 = \frac{£8}{\text{Bond's current market price}} \times 100$$

$$\text{Bond's current market price} = \frac{£8}{4} \times 100$$

$$= £200$$

TEST YOURSELF 8.4

A £100 bond paying a nominal rate of interest of 10% with 30 years to maturity has just paid this year's annual coupon. Long-term interest rates are currently 6%. Assuming that other factors such as expectations of capital gains are not involved, which one of the following is the best approximation of the bond's current market price?

A £105.62

B £106.00

C £110.00

D £100.00

E £166.00

Explain your answer.

A closer look at capital markets

Capital markets are made up of two parts: the *new-issues market* (or *primary market*) and the *second-hand market* (or *secondary market*). In the UK, the London Stock Exchange (LSE) functions as the main secondary market. There are, however, other secondary markets. These include the Alternative Investment Market (AIM), which is run by the London Stock Exchange, mainly for small PLCs, and second-hand trading, which takes place online and is outside the LSE's control. Many students confuse the capital market with the stock exchange. The LSE is indeed an important part of the capital market, but it is only a part, and the terms 'capital market' and 'stock exchange' are not interchangeable. On stock exchanges, previously issued shares and bonds are sold second-hand.

The relationship between the primary and the secondary parts of the main capital market is illustrated in Figure 8.5. The actual raising of new capital or long-term finance takes place in the primary market when public companies (in the private sector of the economy) or the government (in the public sector) decide to issue and sell new marketable securities. Companies can borrow long-term by selling corporate bonds, or they may sell an ownership stake in the company by issuing shares or equity. When selling corporate bonds, the company extends its debt, and the purchaser of the bond becomes a creditor of the company.

STUDY TIP

Remember, equity has two very different meanings: fairness or justness, and wealth. With the latter meaning, shares are often called equities, and the market in shares is often called the equity market.

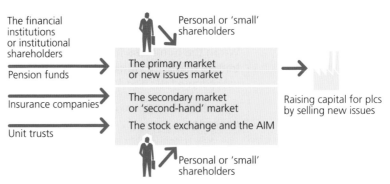

Figure 8.5 The role of capital markets in financing investment in British industry

By contrast, new issues of shares are sold when a company 'goes public' for the first time, or when an existing public company decides to raise extra capital with a new equity issue. In the latter case, the new share issue is most often a rights issue, in which the company's existing shareholders are given the right to buy the new issue of shares at a discount.

New issues of shares are seldom sold directly on the stock exchange. Instead, the direct sale of new issues to the general public takes place in the primary market, usually being arranged by investment banks (whose functions are explained in section 8.2), via newspaper advertisements and the post. Though sometimes accused of being a mere casino devoted to the speculative buying and selling of second-hand shares, the secondary part of the capital market does perform an important economic role. Without the existence of a second-hand market, public companies or PLCs would find it difficult, if not impossible, to sell new share issues. The shares issued by private companies, which don't have a stock market listing, are generally illiquid and difficult to sell. But shares issued by listed public companies can be sold second-hand on the stock exchange. The stock exchange enables shares to be converted quickly into cash. Without the stock exchange, the general public would be reluctant to buy shares that could not easily be resold. An important source of funds necessary to finance the growth of a firm would be denied to public companies.

The principal function of the London stock exchange and other secondary capital markets is to increase the liquidity of second-hand securities (bonds and shares), making it easier for buyers to manage their investments and sell these securities when required. This in turn makes it more likely that those with surplus funds will be willing to buy new issues of shares and bonds, thus facilitating expansion in the economic activities of PLCs and government.

Foreign exchange markets

Over the last 60 years or so, foreign exchange markets have become more and more important in facilitating the growth of international trade and capital movements between countries. Arguably, the growth of international trade has been the main driver of economic growth, both in the world as a whole, and in trading nations such as the United Kingdom.

Foreign exchange markets are financial markets in which different currencies are bought and sold. International trade means that exporters and importers need to convert the funds they use to finance trade from one currency to another — for example, the UK pound sterling into euros or dollars. Foreign exchange can be traded on either the *spot market* or the *forward market*. Spot transactions involve the immediate exchange of foreign currency whereas forward markets involve the exchange of foreign currencies at some specified time in the future. Forward markets are used by, for example, exporters and importers to protect themselves against exchange rate risks.

SYNOPTIC LINK
Chapter 10 explains how foreign exchange markets work. We will see how, in the modern globalised economy, the vast majority of foreign exchange deals finance international capital investment rather than payments for exports and imports, though international trade has itself grown significantly.

8.2 Commercial banks and investment banks

The difference between a commercial bank and an investment bank

The main aim of almost all banks is to make profits for their owners. The Bank of England, the country's **central bank**, though highly profitable, is an exception, since its aims are primarily to oversee the financial system and to implement the country's monetary policy. The most commonly used way of classifying banks other than the central bank is into commercial banks and investment banks.

Commercial banks

A **commercial bank** is often also known as a *retail bank* or a *'high street' bank*. UK examples include Barclays and HSBC. Commercial banks' customers are ordinary members of the general public and businesses. To make themselves attractive to customers, commercial banks have built up networks of branch banks, located in high streets and other shopping centres. However, with the development of electronic banking conducted over the internet and accessed on customers' computers and smartphones, most of the large commercial banks have been closing many of their branch banks.

In summary, commercial banks are commercially run financial institutions that:

- accept deposits from the general public that can be transferred by cheque, by debit card or through an online transfer of funds undertaken on the internet
- create deposits which are lent to customers who wish to borrow from their bank

Investment banks

Until fairly recently, **investment banks** were commonly known as merchant banks. Before the development of the internet, investment banks were clustered in the square mile of the City of London. This was partly because investment banks don't generally deal directly with ordinary members of the general public, so unlike commercial banks they do not need expensive branch networks.

Investment banks help companies, other financial institutions and other organisations (such as the government and its agencies) to raise finance by selling shares or bonds to investors and to hedge against risks. They do this by underwriting share issues. In return for substantial fees, investment banks guarantee to buy up all unsold shares in the event of the unsuccessful launch of a new share issue. Over recent decades, investment banks have earned large amounts of money, paid ultimately by taxpayers, through underwriting the privatisation of previously state-owned businesses, including recently the Royal Mail in 2013.

In addition, investment banks trade on their own behalf in shares, bonds and other financial assets. This trade also takes place with other investment banks and with other financial institutions such as insurance companies and pension funds.

Investment banks are essentially global banks, the largest of which trade in financial assets which are greater in size than the GDPs of most of the world's

KEY TERMS

central bank a national bank that provides financial and banking services for its country's government and banking system, as well as implementing the government's monetary policy and issuing currency. The Bank of England is the UK's central bank.

commercial bank a financial institution which aims to make profits by selling banking services to its customers. Also known as a retail bank and a 'high-street' bank.

investment bank a bank which does not generally accept deposits from ordinary members of the general public. Traditional 'investment banking' refers to financial advisory work, such as advising private companies on how to become a public company by floating on the stock market, or advising public companies on how to buy up another company. Investment banks also deal directly in financial markets for their own account.

countries. Many of the largest investment banks have been formed through the merger of a retail bank and a previously smaller independent investment bank. A good example is provided by S.G. Warburg & Co., a London-based investment bank. Warburg was listed on the London Stock Exchange and was once a constituent of the FTSE 100 Index. The bank was acquired by the Swiss Bank Corporation in 1995 and ultimately became a part of the renamed Swiss investment bank, UBS.

Only the 'big two' US investment banks, J.P. Morgan and Goldman Sachs, have at all times remained independent of the retail banking sector. They head the world-wide list of investment banks shown in Table 8.2.

Table 8.2 Banking groups with largest global investment bank activities at December 2013

Banking group	Trading assets (£bn)
J.P. Morgan	895
Goldman Sachs	683
Bank of America Merrill Lynch	665
Citigroup	625
Deutsche Bank	595
Morgan Stanley	564
Credit Suisse	511
Barclays	481
BNP Paribas	386
Société Générale	369
HSBC	351
Royal Bank of Scotland	347
UBS	256
Crédit Agricole	163
Mitsubishi UFJ	144

Source: *Bank of England Quarterly Bulletin*, Q1 2015

Although investment banks have headquarters in a range of countries which include the USA, the UK, France, Germany, Switzerland and Japan, they also have offices in all the world's financial centres, including the City of London and 'City-East' — that is, Canary Wharf to the east of the City proper. Indeed, all of the large global investment banks have a presence in London. These banks therefore contribute to UK economic activity, and help support the efficient functioning of the financial system. But investment banks also bring risks to the United Kingdom's financial system.

Investment banks and the problems of systemic risk

As we have noted, many banks carry out both retail and investment banking activities. However, this led to some of the difficulties and problems which appeared in the financial crisis that hit the global financial system in 2007. Perhaps the major problem results from the appearance of **systemic risk**. Systemic risk refers to the risk of a breakdown of the entire banking system rather than simply the failure of individual banks. This is a cascading failure caused by inter-linkages in the financial system, which may result in a severe downturn within the whole economy.

It is important to distinguish between systemic and one-off risks. In contrast to a one-off shock which affects only a single bank without rippling into the rest of the banking system, systemic risk affects the entire banking system and

KEY TERM
systemic risk in a financial context, this refers to the risk of a breakdown of the entire financial system, caused by inter-linkages within the financial system, rather than simply the failure of an individual bank or financial institution within the system.

other financial institutions as well. The consequences of a systemic financial crisis can be devastating because of the role that banks and finance play in the wider economy.

Largely in response to these difficulties, national banking authorities are in the process of introducing regulations designed to separate 'high-street' and investment banking activities. Following the publication of the final version of the Vickers Report in September 2011, the retail banking activities of banks operating in the UK must be *ring fenced* from their investment banking activities by 2019.

Without ring fencing, an investment bank's mergers and acquisitions (M&A) department may acquire 'inside knowledge' about a company it is advising. This 'inside knowledge' could be very useful to the bank's own trading in the company's shares. An effective ring fence, which is also known as a firewall and a 'Chinese wall', is an internal device erected by the bank to separate different parts of a bank's activities.

SYNOPTIC LINK

Chapter 6, section 6.6 investigates privatisation in considerable detail.

How banks create credit and bank deposits

In contrast to cash, which is tangible and can be seen and touched, bank deposits are intangible. Customers only 'see' a bank deposit when reading the statement of a bank account, or when viewing the electronic display in a cash-dispensing machine. Bank deposits are the main form of money, and most transactions are paid for by transferring bank deposits from one account to another. Banks possess the ability to create new deposits, almost out of thin air, where none previously existed.

STUDY TIP

You should understand that bank deposits are the main form of money and that cash is a relatively small part of the total stock of money. If you read the book *Where Does Money Come From?*, published by the New Economics Foundation in 2011, you will see that, at the time, 97.4% of the broad money measure M4 took the form of bank and building society deposits, together with other liquid assets, which means that only 2.6% of M4 was cash.

Many students are completely mystified as to how bank deposits are created. A good starting point for developing an understanding is provided by the following story.

Suppose we write our signatures on a scrap of paper, together with the words: 'We promise to pay the bearer £100'. We then give you the scrap of paper (a *promissory note* or 'I owe you'), and ask you to go to a shop and buy £100 worth of goods. Then, when the time comes to pay, you must give the scrap of paper to the shop assistant. Now we all know that, in real life, shops almost always refuse to accept such an 'I owe you'. But just suppose the shop did accept our scrap of paper, believing it could then use the note to buy goods from its suppliers. Our 'I owe you' note would have become money!

Now, while ordinary individuals cannot generally create money in the manner in which we have described, banks can. If the promissory note were to be headed 'Lloyds Bank promises to pay the bearer £100', as long as people believe that Lloyds will honour its promise, the 'I owe you' can function as money.

KEY TERM

credit when a bank makes a loan it creates credit. The loan results in the creation of an advance, which is an asset on the bank's balance sheet, and a deposit, which is a liability of the bank.

STUDY TIP

Economics students often confuse **credit** with bank *deposits*. While the two terms are linked, they are not exactly the same thing. When a bank makes a loan, it gives the customer an 'advance', which is shown as an asset on the bank's balance sheet. It is an asset to the bank because the bank has a call on its client to repay the loan. But the loan is also shown as a deposit on the liabilities side of the bank's balance sheet. The loan extended to its customers creates both an asset and a liability. The deposits, which are the bank's liabilities because the bank must honour any cash withdrawals or payments from a deposit, are the most important part of the money supply. The essential point to note is that whenever a bank gives a loan it simultaneously creates an equivalent bank deposit. This is known as the process of credit creation or deposit creation.

We explain the process through which banks create credit and new bank deposits in the following extension material, first (rather unrealistically) in the context of a 'monopoly bank', and then, more realistically, in the context of the real-world 'multi-bank' banking system.

EXTENSION MATERIAL

Creation of credit and bank deposits in different banking systems

A 'monopoly' banking system

To illustrate the credit and bank deposit creating process, we are first going to assume:

- There is only one commercial bank in the economy (a monopoly bank).
- The bank possesses only one reserve asset, namely cash, which it uses to meet any cash withdrawals (and running down of deposits) by customers.
- The bank decides that, to maintain confidence and always to be able to meet its customers' desire to withdraw cash out of their accounts, it must always possess cash equal to 10% of total customer deposits.

Although the first assumption is unrealistic, the retail banking system taken as a whole behaves as if there is just one bank. In the second section of this box, we explain how the end result of credit and deposit creation in the 'multi-bank' system in which we live is much the same as in the 'monopoly bank' system.

The assumption that there is only one retail bank means that, unlike in a system in which there are many banks, customers cannot withdraw and transfer cash from one bank to another. The second and third assumptions taken together mean that, for prudential reasons, the bank chooses to operate a cash ratio in which 10% of customers' deposits in the bank are backed by cash. Remember that most transactions are settled without any withdrawal of cash and, on most days, whilst some customers are withdrawing cash, other customers are depositing cash with the bank. This means that the bank does not need to back all its deposits with cash.

Suppose now that a member of the general public deposits £1,000 cash in the bank. From the bank's point of view, both its assets and its liabilities increase by £1,000. The cash is the bank's asset, but the £1,000 deposit credited in the customer's name is the bank's liability, since the bank is liable to honour any cash withdrawals made by the customer. The £1,000 is recorded in the bank's balance sheet in the following way:

Assets	Liabilities
Cash: £1,000	Deposit: £1,000
Total assets: £1,000	**Total liabilities: £1,000**

As things stand, all the bank's deposit liabilities are backed with cash (that is, the bank's *cash ratio* is 100%). If this remained the position, the 'bank' would not be a bank at all, but a safe-deposit institution, guarding, for a fee, the cash deposited by customers. The difference between a retail bank and a safe-deposit institution is that a bank uses the cash deposited with it as a *monetary base*, from which to launch the profitable loans it grants to customers.

Unlike the customer depositing cash, other customers may need to borrow from the bank. Provided they are creditworthy, the 10% cash ratio the bank has chosen to work with means that the bank is in a position to lend exactly £9,000 to these customers. This may take the form of an interest-earning advance on the assets side of the bank's balance sheet, which is matched by a £9,000 created deposit on the liabilities side of the balance sheet:

Assets	Liabilities
Cash: £1,000	Deposit: £1,000
Advances: £9,000	Created deposits: £9,000
Total assets: £10,000	**Total liabilities: £10,000**

Both the customers who made the initial deposit of £1,000 and the customers in receipt of the advances can draw cheques or make payments equal to £10,000 in total on their deposits. The initial £1,000 cash deposit has enabled total deposits to be increased to £10,000.

Although our assumption of a monopoly bank is completely unrealistic, it has allowed us to illustrate in a simplified way that the banking system *as a whole* can expand credit, bank deposits and hence the money supply to a multiple of the reserve assets (in this case, cash) that back the created deposits. The 'single-stage' creation of credit and deposits is possible in a 'monopoly bank' model because there is no danger that customers who have been granted loans will draw cheques on their deposits payable to customers of other banks. The main constraint on deposit creation is the need for the bank to hold sufficient cash to meet likely customer withdrawals. (A further constraint is the existence of customers who actually want to borrow from the bank. If no one is willing to borrow, the bank cannot expand its deposits by giving loans.)

A 'multi-bank' banking system

However, the real-world banking system contains more than one bank. Some of the biggest are HSBC, Barclays, Lloyds and the Nationwide. We call this a 'multi-bank' banking system. When we drop the simplification of a 'monopoly bank' and assume a 'multi-bank' system similar to that in the United Kingdom, the general conclusions of our simple 'monopoly' model still hold. If the increase in cash deposits is spread over all the banks, deposits can expand to £10,000, provided every bank in the system is prepared to lend to the full extent that its chosen reserve ratio allows. But if only one bank is prepared to create deposits to the full, it will begin to face demands for cash that it cannot meet, losing some of its cash reserves to other banks. This will happen when the bank's customers make payments into the accounts of customers of the other banks. However, if all banks are prepared to expand deposits to the full, payments to customers of other banks will tend to cancel out. The banking system as a whole can expand deposits to £10,000, though some banks may gain business at the expense of others.

The above models illustrate how the supply of reserve assets, such as cash, available to the banks can limit their ability to create deposits. However, the banks' ability to create credit is also limited by their need to have sufficient capital. Since the financial crisis, central banks have imposed larger minimum required capital ratios on the banks and this has restricted their ability to lend.

If banks hold more capital, they are less likely to become insolvent if there is a fall in the value of their assets — for example, as a result of customers being unable to repay the money they have borrowed. This is the main reason why capital ratios are imposed.

> **STUDY TIP**
> In the real-world banking system, the cash ratio is much lower than 10% — for example, 5%. However, for illustrative purposes, we shall stick with the assumption of a 10% cash ratio as it makes the arithmetic in the calculations simpler. See Quantitative Skills 8.3 for a calculation involving a 5% cash ratio.

> **STUDY TIP**
> In section 8.3, when examining the functions of a central bank (in the UK, the Bank of England), we explain how the central bank acts as a 'lender of last resort' to the banking system. To maintain confidence in the banks and to prevent a 'run' on an individual bank, the central bank is always prepared to supply cash at a price to a bank threatened by a sudden deposit withdrawal. However, this does not mean that the central bank will bail out a bank which has made bad investments and is making losses.

Worked example: calculating an increase in bank deposits

A customer makes a cash deposit of £100,000 in her bank. All the retail banks in the economy choose to keep 5% of their total assets in cash.

Calculate the maximum level of total bank deposits resulting from the deposit of £100,000 into the banking system.

A 5% cash ratio means that cash equals 0.05 of total deposits.

$$\text{Total bank deposits} = \frac{\text{Initial deposit}}{0.05}$$

$$= \frac{£100,000}{0.05}$$

$$= £2,000,000$$

The answer is £2,000,000. As all banks in the banking system have chosen to operate a 5% cash ratio, assuming that the banking system retains the extra cash, total bank deposits can increase to £2,000,000, following a deposit of £100,000 into the system. Notice that £100,000 is 5% of £2,000,000.

The structure of a retail bank's balance sheet

So far we have assumed that retail banks possess just two assets: cash and advances to customers. The left-hand column of Table 8.3 shows that, in fact, banks possess a range of other assets.

Table 8.3 The structure of a retail bank's balance sheet

Assets	Liabilities
Cash (notes and coins)	Share capital
Balances at the Bank of England	Reserves (retained profit)
Money at short and call notice (money lent to other banks via the interbank market)	Long-term borrowing (e.g. bonds issued by the bank)
Bills (commercial bills and Treasury bills)	Short-term borrowing from money markets
Investments (e.g. holdings of government bonds (gilts) and corporate bonds)	Customers' deposits (sight deposits and time deposits)
Advances (e.g. credit or loans and mortgages extended to the bank's customers)	
Fixed assets (e.g. bank buildings and other premises)	

In fact, banks possess *reserve assets* or *liquid assets* other than the cash we have already discussed. Two of these are items two to four in the left-hand column of Table 8.3. Nevertheless, cash is the most important reserve asset and source of liquidity in the banking system. The purpose of reserve assets is to allow banks to maintain liquidity and confidence and to meet any likely demands by customers for cash. In the event of a withdrawal of cash by customers, a bank must be able to turn reserve assets into cash without suffering a capital loss. To be as profitable as possible, a greedy or imprudent bank might be tempted to reduce cash and other liquid assets to a minimum, but this would run the risk of illiquidity and a loss of confidence among customers in the bank's ability to meet its liabilities.

The liquidity–profitability trade-off and potential conflicts between liquidity, profitability and security

As we mentioned earlier, if a bank kept all its assets in the form of cash, it would not really be a bank at all, but a safe-deposit institution. The bank's profits, if it earned any, would come solely from the fees it charged customers for guarding their valuables. The bank's cash would be completely liquid, but not very profitable.

To make a profit, a bank has to make its cash go to work — in other words, be a monetary base upon which advances to customers are launched. Essentially, cash acts as 'high-powered' money which allows the banks to make advances to customers, creating deposits and increasing the total stock of money. The rates of interest that retail banks charge their customers on the advances granted to them are a major source of the banks' profits. Imprudent or greedy banks could be tempted to create far too many profitable advances — imprudent in the sense that the banks possess insufficient cash to meet customers' possible cash withdrawals. These banks would be operating on too low a ratio of cash and other liquid assets to the advances they have created. If a run on the banks occurred, the banks would crash.

Prudent retail banking requires banks to operate on ratios of cash and other liquid assets to advances that maintain customers' confidence in the bank, while generating acceptable profits for the bank. In other words, prudent banking involves trading off liquidity against **profitability**. But taking the UK retail banking system as a whole, over the years, cash ratios fell below 5%. Some would say that this was a major contributing factor to the failure in the 2007/08 financial crisis of the Northern Rock and Bradford and Bingley banks and to the government's need to rescue much larger banks such as Lloyds TSB (as it then was called). Since the financial crisis, cash ratios have risen again toward 5%.

Besides trading off between profitability and liquidity, banks also have to make choices with regard to the **security** of their assets. The profitability for banks of loans granted to customers depends to a significant extent on the degree of risk attached to the loans. Non-secured loans are risky because if a customer defaults on the loan, the bank cannot recover any money. Because of the risk of non-repayment of unsecured loans, banks charge higher interest rates, and hence make more profit than is the case with secured loans. Mortgage loans granted to house purchasers are secured loans. If the borrower is unable to repay the loan or interest on the loan, the bank or building society which provided the mortgage can repossess the property which secures the loan. This reduces the risk in granting long-term mortgage loans.

Table 8.4 shows a slightly simplified version of the left-hand column of Table 8.3, with a vertical arrow added to depict the liquidity–profitability trade-off.

KEY TERMS

profitability the state or condition of yielding a financial profit or gain.

security secured loans, such as mortgage loans secured against the value of property, are less risky for banks than unsecured loans.

Table 8.4 The liquidity–profitability trade-off

Liquidity / Profitability	Assets
	Cash (notes and coins)
	Balances at the Bank of England
	Money at short and call notice (money lent to other banks via the interbank market)
	Bills (commercial bills and Treasury bills)
	Investments (e.g. holdings of government bonds (gilts) and corporate bonds)
	Advances (e.g. credit or loans and mortgages extended to the bank's customers)

We have already explained why cash (sometimes called 'till money' because it is held in the tills and the cash machines that banks own) is the most liquid asset of all. We have also explained why, at the other end of the spectrum, advances to customers are highly profitable, but illiquid. The other items in Table 8.4 deserve a brief explanation. The first of these is balances at the Bank of England. Just as members of the general public make payments to each other by shifting ownership of bank deposits from the person making the payment (the payer) to the person receiving the payment (the payee), so the retail banks settle debts between themselves in the same way. To do this, all the banks keep balances at the Bank of England. As a bank can instantly withdraw funds by running down its balance at the Bank of England, the balance is as liquid as cash.

If a retail bank is temporarily short of cash, which it needs to meet customers' demand for cash over the counter or via a cash machine, it can borrow cash from other banks. The old-fashioned name for this is money borrowed at call and short notice. Money borrowed in this way which must be paid back tomorrow (overnight money) is an example of money at call. Money borrowed for a rather long period, say a month, is money at short notice. These days, the market on which money is lent and borrowed in this way is called the inter-bank money market. The money *lent* in this way is the third asset in Table 8.4, but since banks borrow from, as well as lend to, other banks, money at call and short notice figures on both sides of a bank's balance sheet — as a *liability* (money borrowed) as well as an *asset* (money lent). Since the money lent can quickly be turned into cash, money at call and short notice is a highly liquid asset for the bank making the loan to other banks.

Retail banks also like to hold a portfolio of commercial bills and Treasury bills as a liquid asset (the fourth item in Table 8.4). When first issued and sold to the retail banks (by investment banks on behalf of businesses in the case of commercial bills, and by the Debt Management Office (DMO), an executive agency of the Treasury, on behalf of the government (in the case of Treasury bills) bills typically have a life of 3 months before they mature. This means that for the bank purchasing a newly issued bill, the bank makes a profit because it buys the bill at a discount — the purchase price is lower than the bill's maturity value. The bank earns the bill's discount rate which is, in effect, the interest rate on the bill, and the money market on which commercial and Treasury bills are bought and sold is called the *discount market*. At any point in time, retail banks possess a portfolio of bills, some of which mature today or tomorrow, some in a week's time, and some in 3 months' time. From the bank's point of view, its bill portfolio provides it with liquid assets which are nevertheless profitable.

This is even more evident for the fifth set of assets in Table 8.4, namely investments. Because of a risk factor related to the fact that shares never mature and might have to be sold second-hand on a falling capital market, retail banks don't generally invest in company shares or equities. However, they do invest in corporate bonds issued by private sector PLCs, and even more so in government bonds (gilt-edged securities or gilts). When first issued, most gilts have a life of anything up to 50 years before they mature. However, because gilts are issued by the 'ship of state' and their maturity value and yearly interest payment (the gilt's coupon) are guaranteed by the government, banks usually regard gilts as being absolutely safe and profitable investments. For the banks which own them, gilts are profitable, but illiquid in the sense that the banks may suffer capital losses if they decide to sell the gilts on a falling second-hand market. From the banks' point of view, the risk of capital loss is greater than for bills.

8.3 Central banks and monetary policy

The main functions of a central bank

We have already mentioned that most banks are either commercial or investment banks, or both, whose main aim is to make a profit for their owners. Although it makes a considerable profit, the most significant exception is the Bank of England, which is the UK's central bank. For most of the period since its formation in 1694, the Bank of England was a private enterprise company. However, the Bank was nationalised in 1946 and its surplus profit goes to the state.

A central bank has two key functions: to help the government maintain macroeconomic stability and to bring about financial stability in the monetary system. With regard to macroeconomic stability, the Bank of England's remit is to deliver price stability and, subject to that, to support the government's economic objectives including those for growth and employment. The price stability remit is defined, not in terms of zero inflation, but by the government's inflation target, currently 2% on the consumer prices index (CPI). The remit emphasises the importance of price stability in achieving macroeconomic stability, and in providing the right conditions for sustainable growth in output and employment.

> **STUDY TIP**
> It is extremely important to understand the meaning of 'macroeconomic stability', and also of a related term, 'macroeconomic performance'. 'Macroeconomic stability' can be thought of as stable growth, stable employment, a stable price level, and stability in the current account of the balance of payments. 'Macroeconomic performance' can be assessed by considering the extent to which these desirable objectives are being achieved.

Financial stability can be achieved, in part, through the central bank acting as lender of last resort to the banking system, and also, in part, by the central bank's monitoring and regulation of the financial system. The lender of last resort function is a standard function of central banks worldwide. It is commonly defined as the readiness of the central bank to extend loans to banks that are solvent but have short-term liquidity problems. By providing these funds, though at a price, the central bank aims to protect depositors and in the extreme case to prevent a systemic crisis in the financial system.

Central banks also carry out other related functions such as: controlling the note issue, acting as the bankers' bank, acting as the government's bank, buying and selling currencies to influence the exchange rate, and liaising with overseas central banks and international organisations.

We explained on pages 245–46 how and why banks keep balances at the Bank of England, just as members of the general public keep balances in the retail banks themselves. This is the 'bankers' bank' function of the Bank of England. The government also has bank accounts at the Bank of England. However, the Bank's role as banker to the government has been significantly reduced; since May 1998 the Debt Management Office (DMO) has issued gilts on behalf of the Treasury, and in 2000 the DMO took over responsibility for issuing Treasury bills and managing the government's short-term cash needs.

Monetary policy

Complementing the central bank functions we have just explained is the Bank of England's function of implementing monetary policy on behalf of the UK government.

Monetary policy is the part of economic policy that attempts to achieve the government's macroeconomic objectives using monetary instruments, such as controls over bank lending and the rate of interest. Before 1997, monetary policy was implemented by the Bank of England on a day-to-day basis but the Bank 'consulted' with the Treasury and in the end the Treasury had a veto over Bank Rate decisions (though the veto was never exercised). The Treasury, which is a part of central government, and the Bank of England were then known as the monetary authorities. But the Treasury abandoned its hands-on role in implementing monetary policy in 1997 when the government made the Bank of England operationally independent. Unless the Bank is put under pressure by the Treasury, there is now only one monetary authority: the Bank of England.

Objectives and instruments of monetary policy

To understand monetary policy, it is useful to distinguish between policy objectives and policy instruments. A policy objective is the target that the Bank of England aims to hit. By contrast, a policy instrument is the tool of control used to try to achieve the objective.

Monetary policy objectives and instruments can be classified in different ways. Policy objectives can be divided into ultimate and intermediate objectives. Policy instruments separate into those that directly affect the supply of new deposits that the commercial banks can create and those that influence the creation of bank deposits by affecting the demand for loans or credit.

Monetary policy objectives

For over 30 years, control of inflation has been the main objective of UK monetary policy. The government needs to control inflation in order to create conditions in which the ultimate policy objective of improved economic welfare can be attained. With this in mind, the government, in the person of the chancellor of the exchequer, sets the inflation rate target, which since 2003 has been 2% CPI inflation, and instructs the Bank of England's MPC to operate monetary policy so as to 'hit' this target. The MPC is given a leeway of 1% above and 1% below the 2% CPI inflation rate, but if the inflation rate moves outside this band of flexibility, the governor of the Bank of England must write an open letter to the chancellor explaining why this has happened.

However, in the 2008/09 recession negative economic growth and growing unemployment led to a situation in which controlling inflation as the main monetary policy objective was temporarily placed on the back-burner, with monetary policy being used instead to try and increase aggregate demand and bring about recovery from recession.

For several years before this, the objectives of monetary policy had been symmetrical in the sense that the Bank of England must stimulate aggregate demand, which will generally raise the rate of inflation, whenever inflation is expected to fall below the target rate, just as the Bank will try to increase aggregate demand to reduce inflation whenever inflation is expected to exceed the target rate. Although the Bank's primary objective is price stability, it must also support the government's economic policy objectives, including those for growth and employment.

In his 2013 Budget, while still paying lip service to the 2% inflation rate target, George Osborne, the chancellor of the exchequer, said it may be 'necessary to deploy new unconventional policy instruments or approaches in future', in an effort to bring about sustained recovery from recession. The Bank had already introduced the Asset Purchase Scheme (QE) and the Funding for Lending Scheme, and Mark Carney, the new governor of the Bank of England, immediately indicated that he would continue to employ unconventional measures such as these for as long as necessary.

Monetary policy instruments

Monetary policy instruments are the tools used to achieve the objectives of monetary policy. In the UK, they can involve the Bank of England taking action to influence interest rates, the supply of money and credit, and the exchange rate.

There are two categories of monetary policy instrument: those that affect the general public's *demand* for bank loans and those that affect the retail banks' ability to *supply* credit and to create bank deposits. Before 2009, UK monetary policy relied almost exclusively on the use of **Bank Rate**, which is the Bank of England's key interest rate, to manage the demand for bank loans. In 2009, however, the Bank of England began to use **quantitative easing** (QE) to influence commercial banks' ability to supply new loans to their customers. We shall now look at each of these in turn.

KEY TERMS

Bank Rate the interest rate set by the Bank of England which it uses as a benchmark for setting the interest rates that it charges when lending to commercial banks and other financial institutions.

quantitative easing (QE) an unconventional form of monetary policy through which a central bank, such as the Bank of England, creates new money electronically which it then uses to buy financial assets, such as government bonds, on the country's financial markets. Also known as the Asset Purchase Scheme.

ACTIVITIES

1 Bank Rate is just one of a very wide range of interest rates in the UK. Undertake a search, either by visiting a number of branch banks in your neighbourhood, or using the internet, of the different rates of interest that banks offer to customers who save with them. Why do banks offer these different rates?

2 The very wide range of interest rates in financial markets can be organised in a spectrum. For example, the rates paid to savers differ significantly from the rates charged to borrowers. Find out what is meant by 'the spectrum of interest rates' and explain how time and risk are reflected in the spectrum.

Managing the demand for credit through the use of Bank Rate

As mentioned, Bank Rate is a key interest rate used by the Bank of England in the operation of monetary policy. Bank Rate is the minimum rate of interest charged when the Bank of England lends money to the commercial banks to enable the banks to maintain their liquidity. However, the rate charged is usually above Bank Rate and the banks also have to deposit securities, such as government bonds, with the Bank of England as collateral. An increase in Bank Rate makes it more expensive for banks to borrow from the Bank of England and the banks will usually have to increase the interest rates they charge when lending to the general public. Likewise, a cut in Bank Rate usually leads to a fall in the interest rates charged by the banks. In this way, changes in Bank Rate cause changes in other short-term interest rates (though less so in long-term interest rates such as the yield on government bonds or gilts).

Two factors affecting interest rates are time and risk. As a general rule, long-term interest rates are higher than short-term interest rates because lenders are sacrificing their ability to spend their own money for longer periods. However, there are exceptions to this rule, partly explained by the second factor: risk. The riskier the loan, the higher the rate of interest because, for example, the lender has to be compensated for those who fail to repay the loan. Thus short-term risky and unsecured credit card loans carry much higher rates than long-term mortgage loans, secured by the value of the house being purchased.

For several decades before 2009, modern UK monetary policy operated almost solely through changes in Bank Rate (that is, through interest rate policy). To influence the quantity of bank deposits being created (and also the level of aggregate demand in the economy), the Bank of England rationed demand for credit by raising or lowering Bank Rate. If interest rates rise, other things being equal, fewer people will want to borrow money and hence bank lending will fall and fewer bank deposits will be created. To explain how this affects the economy, a good starting point is the aggregate demand equation which we revisited in Chapter 7:

$$AD = C + I + G + (X - M)$$

Whereas fiscal policy can affect aggregate demand by changing the level of government spending (G), monetary policy affects the other components of aggregate demand, C, I and $(X - M)$. A fall in interest rates causes the AD curve illustrated in Figure 8.6 to shift to the right from AD_1 to AD_2.

There are three main ways in which a cut in interest rates, brought about by a change in Bank Rate, increases aggregate demand. These are as follows:

- **Lower interest rates increase household consumption (C).** This happens in four ways. First, lower interest rates discourage saving, which means that more income is available for consumption. Second, the cost of household borrowing falls, which cuts the cost of servicing a mortgage and credit card debt. Borrowers have more money to spend on consumption because less of their income is used for interest payments. Third, lower interest rates may cause asset prices, such as the prices of houses and shares, to increase. Higher house and share prices increase personal wealth, which in turn increases consumption because people feel wealthier. Fourth, rising house and share prices lead to an increase in consumer confidence, which further boosts consumption.

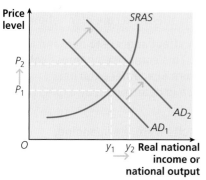

Figure 8.6 How a decrease in interest rates causes the *AD* curve to shift to the right

- **Lower interest rates increase business investment (*I*).** Investment is the purchase of capital goods such as machines by firms. Businesses bring forward investment projects they would have cancelled or postponed at a higher cost of borrowing, believing that new capital goods can now be profitably used. A rise in business confidence will also boost investment.
- **Lower interest rates increase net export demand (*X* – *M*).** Lower UK interest rates lead to the selling of the pound sterling, as owners of international capital decide to hold other currencies instead. This causes the pound's exchange rate to fall, which increases the price competitiveness of UK exports in world markets. At the same time, the prices of imports rise and they become less competitive in the UK market. The UK's balance of payments on current account improves, with the increase in net export demand shifting the *AD* curve to the right.

By contrast, a rise in interest rates makes it more attractive for overseas residents to 'save' with UK financial institutions, triggering a short-term capital inflow on the balance of payments, which increases the exchange rate. Exports lose their competitiveness, and the current account of the balance of payments deteriorates. Aggregate demand falls and the *AD* curve shifts to the left.

CASE STUDY 8.3

The transmission mechanism of interest rate policy

The Bank of England believes that interest rate policy affects aggregate demand and inflation through a number of channels, which form the transmission mechanism of monetary policy. The flow chart in Figure 8.7 shows the routes through which changes in Bank Rate (the instrument of monetary policy), shown at point 1 in the diagram, eventually affect inflation (the objective of monetary policy), shown at point 11.

Official Bank Rate decisions (point 1 in Figure 8.7) affect market interest rates (point 2), such as mortgage rates and bank deposit rates set by commercial banks and other financial institutions. At the same time, policy actions and announcements affect expectations about the future course of the economy and the confidence with which these expectations are held (point 4).

They also affect asset prices (point 3) and the exchange rate (point 5). (A rise or fall in the exchange rate also changes the prices of imports (point 10), which in turn affect the rate of inflation.)

These changes in turn affect aggregate demand in the economy (point 8). This comprises domestically generated demand (point 6) and net external demand (point 7), which is determined by export and import demand.

Domestic demand results from the spending, saving and investment behaviour of individuals and firms within the economy. Lower market interest rates increase domestic demand by encouraging consumption rather than saving by households and investment spending by firms. Conversely, higher market interest rates depress domestic spending. If Bank Rate falls, asset prices rise and people feel wealthier and generally more confident about the future. As a result, consumption increases.

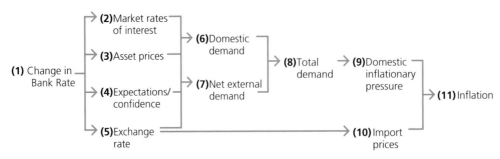

Figure 8.7 The transmission mechanism of interest rate policy

Changes in aggregate demand affect domestic inflationary pressures (point 9). An increase in aggregate demand that exceeds the economy's ability to increase the supply of output creates demand-pull inflationary pressures.

The relationship between changes in interest rates and the exchange rate

A fall in UK interest rates causes financial capital to flow out of the pound and into other currencies in search of better rates of return. This reduces the demand for pounds and increases the supply of pounds on the foreign exchange market, which in turn causes the pound's exchange rate to fall. Changes in export and import prices brought about by a fall in the exchange rate affect inflation in two ways.

First, a falling exchange rate increases the prices of imported food and consumer goods. This increases the rate of inflation in the UK. At the same time, increased prices of imported raw materials and energy create cost-push inflationary pressures in the UK (import-cost-push inflation).

Second, a falling exchange rate reduces UK export prices, while raising the price of imports. This feeds into the inflationary process described above, by increasing the demand for UK exports and persuading some UK residents to buy more home-produced goods and fewer imports. This adds to demand-pull inflationary pressures. It is also likely to improve the UK's balance of payments on current account.

Time lags in the transmission mechanism of monetary policy

The Bank of England estimates a time lag of up to 2 years between an initial change in Bank Rate (point 1) and the resulting change in the rate of inflation (point 11). Output is affected within 1 year, but the fullest effect on inflation occurs after a lag of 2 years. In terms of the size of the effect, the Bank believes a 1% change in its official interest rate affects output by about 0.2–0.35% after about a year and inflation by around 0.2–0.4% per year after 2 years.

Follow-up questions

1 What is meant by 'asset prices'? Explain, using examples, how an increase in interest rates affects asset prices.
2 Why might a fall in interest rates affect import prices in the UK?

CASE STUDY 8.4

LIBOR and Bank Rate

Until quite recently, high-street banking was a boring form of business. For each borrower, a bank had to have around ten savers to provide the funds being lent. The need to attract savers was a significant constraint on the banks' ability to provide new loans or credit.

All this changed in the deregulated and liberalised financial world created in the 1980s and 1990s. The traditional business of 'boring' banking went out of the window as high-street banks moved onto a much more interesting business plan. Out went household savings as the banks' principal source of liquidity and in came the borrowing of funds on the London interbank wholesale money market.

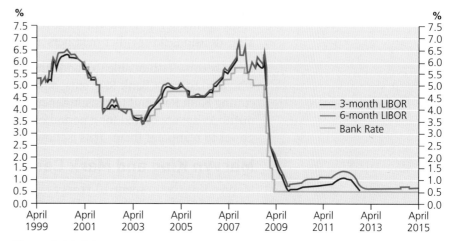

Figure 8.8 LIBOR and Bank Rate, April 1999 to April 2015

The rate of interest at which banks lend to each other is called LIBOR, which is the acronym for the London Interbank Offered Rate of Interest. Unlike Bank Rate, which is set monthly by the Bank of England, LIBOR is determined on a daily basis by the demand and supply for funds as banks lend to each other to balance their books.

In normal times, the 3-month LIBOR trades at a small premium of around 0.15% above where the market thinks Bank Rate will be in 3 months' time. However, when the credit crunch spread from America in 2007, LIBOR shot up to around 1.5% above Bank Rate. As Figure 8.8 shows, for most of the time, the 3-month LIBOR remained well above Bank Rate during the period from 2007 to 2015, especially in 2008. By April 2015, the 3-month LIBOR had converged with the 0.5% Bank Rate set by the Bank of England. This was partly the result of the revelations that LIBOR had been rigged and the break-up of a 'LIBOR-fixing' scam operated by the banks.

Divergence between Bank Rate and LIBOR makes it difficult for the Bank of England to operate monetary policy effectively. When LIBOR is significantly above Bank Rate, a cut in Bank Rate aimed at reducing the interest rates that the general public have to pay when borrowing from high-street banks is ineffective if the rates the banks charge is determined by LIBOR rather than by Bank Rate.

In March 2015 the Bank of England said it aimed to introduce in 2016 an alternative to the discredited LIBOR interest rate at the centre of the recent rate of interest-rigging scandal. In the wake of this scandal, which resulted in banks paying billions of dollars in fines over allegations that they manipulated LIBOR, the Group of Twenty (G20) recommended in July 2014 that alternatives to LIBOR should be developed.

Follow-up questions

1 How might changes in Bank Rate affect mortgage interest rates?
2 What has happened to Bank Rate and LIBOR since April 2015?

The Bank of England's Monetary Policy Committee

Each month the Monetary Policy Committee (MPC) at the Bank of England decides the level at which Bank Rate is set. (As we shall see shortly, the MPC has also been responsible for introducing and later suspending quantitative easing.) The MPC has eight members, comprising four Bank of England 'insiders' and four 'outsiders' or external members appointed by the chancellor of the exchequer, plus the Bank's governor who exercises a casting vote on MPC decisions if the other members are split fifty-fifty.

It has become fashionable to divide the members of the MPC into 'hawks', who tend to resist Bank Rate cuts, and 'doves', who are much more prone to cutting Bank Rate and to resisting increases in Bank Rate. The four external members are appointed for a period of 3 years, though the chancellor has the power to reappoint them. This is, however, unusual.

Mervyn King and Mark Carney

Mervyn King, who spent 10 years as governor of the Bank of England until 2013, was described as 'having been "hawkish" but becoming "dovish" at the end of his period of office'. It is yet to be seen which camp Mark Carney, Mervyn King's successor, will fall into, or indeed whether he will pragmatically change his stance to meet new circumstances. In a speech in the City of London in March 2014, Carney criticised the narrow view of the central bank as a guardian of stable inflation. He said that in the late 1970s and 1980s it had made sense for monetary policy to focus on controlling inflation. Over time, however, this became a 'dangerous distraction'. Carney went on to argue that a new range of 'unconventional' monetary policy tools at the Bank's disposal meant that in future the Bank will be able to control overheating markets without having to raise interest rates. Orthodox inflation targeting

Mark Carney became governor of Bank of England in July 2013

had caused policymakers to miss the rapid accumulation of dangerous risk in the financial system. Mr Carney said his objective up to 2018 was to make the Bank work seamlessly towards its twin objectives of creating monetary and financial stability for the UK. (The Bank of England achieves monetary stability by controlling the rate of inflation, and financial stability by ensuring that financial institutions are stable and robust, and that the financial system is not prone to speculative bubbles.)

Asked whether the reforms he proposed to introduce could have prevented the UK's financial crisis if implemented a decade earlier, Mr Carney said the financial crisis had been a 'powerful reminder' that price stability alone was not enough to guarantee wider macroeconomic stability.

'Conventional' monetary policy

'Conventional' monetary policy involves the Bank of England raising or lowering Bank Rate (or leaving the rate unchanged) so as to manage the level of aggregate demand in an attempt to control the rate of inflation.

'Unconventional' monetary policy

Since 2009, the Bank of England has introduced a number of 'unconventional' monetary policy instruments to support Bank Rate policy in an attempt to bring about and sustain economic recovery.

The first 'unconventional' policy instrument was introduced toward the end of the recession in 2009. This was quantitative easing, which we mentioned earlier and will explain in the extension material which follows. In another new policy, known as **forward guidance**, the MPC said in August 2013 that it would leave interest rates unchanged at 0.5% until the unemployment rate had fallen to 7%, provided there weren't any risks to inflation or financial stability. When unemployment fell much more quickly than expected, the guidance was amended. According to the MPC, 'there remained room for growth in the economy before raising interest rates. And, when they come, increases in interest rates are likely to be gradual and limited.' Along with QE, we will now explain forward guidance and other 'unconventional' monetary policies.

> **KEY TERM**
>
> **forward guidance** attempts to send signals to financial markets, businesses and individuals, about the Bank of England's interest rate policy in the months and years ahead, so that economic agents are not surprised by a sudden and unexpected change in policy.

EXTENSION MATERIAL

Quantitative easing, forward guidance and other 'unconventional' monetary policies

What is quantitative easing?

As we explained earlier in this chapter, monetary policy can operate in two contrasting ways: on the demand for money, or on the supply of money. Unlike changes in Bank Rate, which attempt to influence the demand for money and thence aggregate demand, quantitative easing (QE) is primarily meant to increase the money supply directly — though it also affects long-term interest rates and hence does impact on the demand for loans. When QE was started in 2009, the Bank of England hoped that it would help to revive consumer and investment spending and economic growth.

People often think that QE involves increasing the money supply by printing new banknotes. Indeed, when QE started in 2009, the metaphor was used of a central bank filling a helicopter with newly printed banknotes, before dropping the 'helicopter money' on the general public.

However, QE is not as simple as this. The various stages of QE, illustrated in Figure 8.9, which is based on an illustration from a Bank of England pamphlet, stem from the Bank of England buying financial assets, mostly long-dated government bonds (gilts) and some corporate bonds, from the banks but mainly from other financial institutions

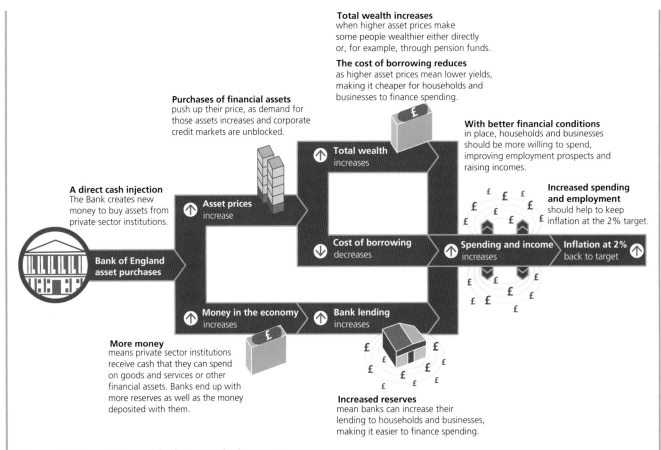

Figure 8.9 Quantitative easing's transmission route

Source: Bank of England, 'Quantitative easing explained'

such as insurance companies and pension funds. (The pamphlet, 'Quantitative easing explained', can be accessed at: **www.bankofengland.co.uk/ monetarypolicy/Documents/pdf/qe-pamphlet.pdf**.)

In the pamphlet, under the heading, 'Supplying more money: how it works', the Bank of England describes QE's transmission route in the following way:

> Direct injections of money into the economy, primarily by buying gilts, can have a number of effects. The sellers of the assets have more money so may go out and spend it. That will help to boost growth. Or they may buy other assets instead, such as shares or company bonds. That will push up the prices of those assets, making the people who own them, either directly or through their pension funds, better off. So they may go out and spend more. And higher asset prices mean lower yields, which brings down the cost of borrowing for businesses and households. That should provide a further boost to spending.
>
> In addition, banks will find themselves holding more reserves. That might lead them to boost their lending to consumers and businesses. So, once again, borrowing increases and so does spending. That said,

if banks are concerned about their financial health, they may prefer to hold the extra reserves without expanding lending. For this reason, the Bank of England is buying most of the assets from the wider economy rather than the banks.

Normally, central banks do not intervene in private sector asset markets by buying or selling private sector debt. But in exceptional circumstances, such intervention may be warranted — for example, when corporate credit markets became blocked as the financial crisis intensified towards the end of 2008. Bank of England purchases of private sector debt can help to unblock corporate credit markets, by reassuring market participants that there is a ready buyer should they wish to sell. That should help bring down the cost of borrowing, making it easier and cheaper for companies to raise finance which they can then invest in their business.

QE1, QE2 and QE3

Quantitative easing was first used by the Bank of England in March 2009, though the USA had begun QE a few months earlier. In the UK there have so far been three 'bouts' of quantitative easing, first in March 2009 (QE1), then in October 2011 (QE2) and finally in February and July 2012 (QE3), ending in November 2012. In the three bouts, first £200 billion, then £125 billion and finally £50 billion of 'new money' was unleashed into the banking system. By July 2012, therefore, a total of £50 billion of 'new money' had been released into the British economy (see Table 8.5).

It can be argued that QE1 worked in the sense that it prevented the recession from developing — as a result of collapsing aggregate demand — into a full-blown depression. It is debateable, however, whether the later bouts of quantitative easing had much effect in bringing about recovery from recession. From 2010 onward, the growth rate in the UK economy 'flat-lined', remaining very close to zero. When in 2013 a more substantial recovery did occur, further rounds of QE were not implemented in the UK, though the Bank is continuing to purchase bonds so as to maintain the stock it holds at £375 billion, given that some of the bonds it originally purchased have matured.

It has also been the case that, until early 2015, the continuation of QE in America stimulated growth in other countries, including the UK. (It is worth noting that QE was also started by the European Central Bank (ECB) in 2015 to try to offset the danger of negative growth returning to the eurozone economy.)

It could be argued that QE was partly responsible, along with the 0.5% Bank Rate, for the fact that, until quite recently, the UK inflation rate was persistently above the government's 2% target. This was mainly through its effect on the exchange rate. However, from late 2013 onward, the CPI inflation rate fell dramatically, reaching 0% in February 2015. (Some commentators have called this 'noflation' or 'flatflation'). And if deflation does occur, it is likely to be a 'good' deflation, caused by falling world commodity prices — for example, a fall in the price of oil — rather than a 'bad' deflation caused by a collapse of aggregate demand. If this is the case, with GDP continuing to grow, there are unlikely to be many calls for a reintroduction of QE in order to increase aggregate demand further.

In the end, many believe that the increased bank lending made possible by quantitative easing went, not into cheap loans to small businesses and households, but into speculative activities undertaken by the banks themselves and by the big corporations which have most benefited from the cheap money sloshing around the British and American economies.

By reducing long-term interest rates and raising bond prices, QE also benefited the UK government. This was because QE made it much cheaper for central government to borrow to finance its large budget deficit and to pay interest on the national debt. House buyers have also benefited from the cheap mortgage loans made possible by the 0.5% Bank Rate and quantitative easing. On the other hand, savers and workers contributing to private pension schemes have suffered, although recent government policy has tried to counter this.

The *Bank of England Quarterly Bulletin* published in Quarter 4, 2012 estimated that the £375 billion of QE had increased the supply of broad money in the UK by about £220 billion, or 15%, which in turn increased nominal GDP by nearly 6%. If this is true, then quantitative easing was indeed a factor causing recovery from recession. However, in an article titled 'Monetary impact of UK QE much smaller than claimed by BoE', which was published in January 2013, Simon Ward, the chief economist at Henderson Global Investors, argued that £375 billion of QE had delivered a monetary boost of only £78 billion.

Table 8.5 The three periods of quantitative easing in the UK

QE1: £200 billion between March 2009 and January 2010
QE2: £125 billion between October 2011 and May 2012
QE3: £50 billion between July 2012 and October 2012
Total amount: £375 billion
The cumulative impact of QE on the money supply has been estimated to be £222 billion

The decision not to extend QE and the introduction of 'forward guidance'

In the UK at least, the period of expansionary quantitative easing did not last very long. QE was introduced in the depths of recession in 2009, but eventually, late in 2012, was not extended.

When it began, QE was sold to the general public as an example of 'unconventional' monetary policy. As we have explained, 'conventional' monetary policy involves raising or lowering Bank Rate so as to manage the level of aggregate demand. However, the zero bound and liquidity trap problems reduced the effectiveness of conventional monetary policy in stimulating aggregate demand.

Three and a half years of expansionary quantitative easing came to an end because the UK economy appeared to be performing significantly better in the autumn of 2012 than had been the case in previous months. Following the decision not to extend quantitative easing, Stephen King, senior economist at UK bank HSBC, argued that QE 'certainly served a purpose. Without it, the world might well have ended up facing a downward economic and financial spiral not dissimilar to the terrible traumas of the 1930s'.

The decision to halt expansionary quantitative easing was also a result of the Bank of England prioritising its **Funding for Lending** (FLS) scheme over the bond purchases in financial markets which had been the central feature of QE. Launched in 2012, Funding for Lending allowed banks and other lenders to borrow money cheaply from the Bank of England. The scheme was designed to make it easier for financial institutions to provide loans at a time when they might otherwise be reducing lending, because of their need — following the 2007/08 financial crisis — to shore up their battered balance sheets.

Although the rules were changed in January 2014 so that FLS became no longer available for mortgage lending, by initially helping cut mortgage rates for house buyers the scheme helped to bring about recovery in UK housing markets, though at the potential cost of creating another speculative house price bubble, particularly in London and the southeast. This is why the rules were changed. However, FLS has not been very successful in financing business investment. The scheme had aimed to bolster the economy, by halting a downward spiral of lending and borrowing that the UK had experienced since the onset of the credit crunch and international banking crisis.

Quantitative easing and the Funding for Lending Scheme were the first and second 'unconventional' monetary policies to be used by the Bank of England. More recently, they were followed in 2013 by the 'Help to Buy' Scheme and by forward guidance. 'Help to Buy' was a government-promoted scheme to provide loans to first-time buyers and home owners moving house up to a purchase price up to £600,000. To qualify for a government loan of up to 20%, the house purchaser must contribute at least 5% of the property price and arrange a mortgage of up to 75% to cover the rest.

As we noted earlier, forward guidance, introduced by Mark Carney shortly after taking up his appointment as governor of the Bank of England, attempts to send signals to financial markets, businesses and individuals about the Bank of England's interest rate policy in the months and years ahead.

Is forward guidance credible?

Forward guidance should be seen as a policy which tries to increase the credibility of monetary policy. By using forward guidance, the Bank of England aims to calm uncertainty in otherwise jittery financial markets. If, for example, markets fear that low interest rates will move higher, interest rates on bonds and other credit instruments and agreements will rise and begin to discourage people and companies from taking out loans or spending money. But if the Bank of England signals that it intends to keep rates low, the Bank can engineer an outcome in which interest rates are indeed kept low.

However, forward guidance is not just for financial markets. By altering expectations favourably, forward guidance aims to improve the credibility of monetary policy, thereby enabling households and businesses to feel calmer about their future economic prospects. According to the Bank, forward guidance means companies and mortgage borrowers can estimate for how long low interest rates will be around. If this is achieved, forward guidance is a way of converting low short-term interest rates into lower long-term interest rates.

When first announcing forward guidance in August 2013, Mark Carney said that the Bank would not consider raising Bank Rate from its low of 0.5% until the unemployment rate fell to 7% or below, which, drawing on the Bank of England's forecast shown in Figure 8.10, Carney expected to be in 2016. The green line in the graph shows the actual unemployment rate, from 2008 to late 2013, while the purple line shows the forecast or predicted unemployment rate from then until the end of 2016. The interesting part of the graph is where the green and purple lines cross, late in 2013. The intersection occurred at a time when actual unemployment began to fall much faster than the Bank of England was predicting. This meant that forward guidance, which was based on the prediction that unemployment would fall fairly slowly, had to be quickly revised to take account of this inaccurate prediction.

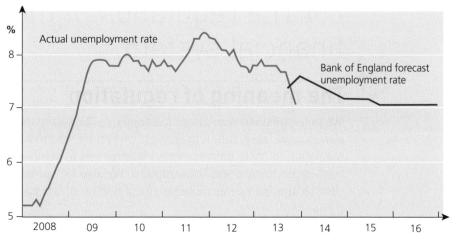

Figure 8.10 Actual unemployment falling faster than the forecast rate of unemployment in 2013

Sources: ONS, Bank of England

If financial markets believed what Carney and the MPC were saying, the hope was that the markets would remain calm and orderly, and behave in a way which was consistent with the forward guidance strategy. There were, however, two dangers. First, the strategy could be knocked off course by an event such as a house price bubble hitting the UK economy (or, as happened, a faster than expected fall in unemployment). Second, and related to this, financial markets might form their own expectations of what they thought was going to happen in the future. If markets believed that a bubble was going to occur, then, whatever the Bank of England's official policy, market operators might ignore the forward guidance strategy and raise interest rates anyway. Either way, if traders in financial markets perceive the strategy to be 'wishful thinking', forward guidance could damage rather than increase the credibility of the Bank of England in its management of the UK economy.

Forward guidance also loses credibility if the Bank of England repeatedly 'moves the goal posts' — that is, changes policy every few months in the light of unexpected events hitting the economy. This happened for the first time in January 2014, when UK borrowing costs shot up in expectation of a rise in Bank Rate, after the fall in unemployment had proved larger than Carney had expected. A few days later, Carney signalled the end of his forward guidance of linking interest rates to the unemployment rate, adding that the British economy was in a different place from where it had been in the previous summer. Thus, the Bank of England had overhauled its forward guidance strategy less than 6 months after it was first implemented.

Carney said that, instead of just the unemployment rate, the next phase of forward guidance would be determined by a range of 18 different indicators, which include productivity and the size of the output gap — the gap between potential and actual output. The Bank argued that a lack of inflationary pressure, spare capacity, and 'headwinds' at home and abroad, meant that 'Bank Rate may need to remain at low levels for some time to come'. Seeking to reassure businesses and households, the Bank's Monetary Policy Committee said that when rates did eventually go up, they would do so only gradually, settling around 2–3% — below the pre-crisis norm of around 5%.

Economists employed in the financial services industry were less than convinced. For example, Schroder's UK economist branded the new guidance as a 'bamboozling cluster bomb' which, on the one hand, highlights the degree of complexity in setting monetary policy, while, on the other hand, thoroughly confuses the average person. For cynics, forward guidance has introduced a new uncertainty for expectations on the future path of interest rates.

257

KEY TERM

Funding for Lending Scheme incentivises banks and building societies to boost their lending to the UK real economy. FLS is skewed towards small and medium-sized enterprises (SMEs).

8.4 The regulation of the financial system

The meaning of regulation

We first explained regulation in Chapter 6, 'Revisiting market failure and government intervention in markets', when we said that governments use regulation to try to correct market failures and to achieve a socially optimal level of production and consumption. We also explained how regulation is used to limit and deter monopoly exploitation of consumers.

Regulation means imposing rules and sometimes laws which limit the freedom of individuals and businesses to make decisions of their own free will. *Financial regulation* involves limiting the freedom of banks and other financial institutions, and of the people they employ, to behave as they otherwise might wish to do.

Financial regulation in the UK

The recent history of financial regulation in the UK

Before 2001 the Bank of England largely controlled financial regulation in the UK. However, back in 1985 a self-regulatory board, the Securities and Investments Board, was created with a limited number of regulatory powers. But after a series of scandals in the 1990s, culminating in the collapse of Barings Bank, there was a desire to bring to an end the self-regulation of the financial services industry and to consolidate regulatory responsibilities which previously had been split amongst multiple regulators.

In 1997, the name of the Securities and Investments Board was changed to the Financial Services Authority (FSA), an external regulator with a range of regulatory powers. The 1998 Bank of England Act, which also formally established the MPC and thereby radically changed the role of the Bank of England, transferred the responsibility for the supervision of deposit-taking institutions from the Bank to the FSA. However, the FSA didn't start to exercise these powers until 2001 when the Bank of England was instructed to concentrate on banking, with its regulatory function taken away and given to the FSA.

But due to perceived regulatory failure of the banks during the financial crisis of 2007–08, the Treasury decided to abolish the FSA. It had been criticised for failing to spot the lending boom before 2007 and the subsequent bust, and for not curbing risky trading by banks, the end result of which was to see the collapse of banks such as Northern Rock and the Royal Bank of Scotland. The regulatory function of the FSA had lasted from 2001 until 2013, when the authority was eventually wound up.

With effect from 1 April 2013, some of the FSA's responsibilities were given to a new committee, the **Financial Policy Committee** (FPC) at the Bank of England, with the others being split between two new agencies, the **Prudential Regulation Authority** (PRA) — itself a part of the Bank of England — and the **Financial Conduct Authority** (FCA), which is not part of the Bank.

KEY TERMS

Financial Policy Committee the part of the Bank of England charged with the primary objective of identifying, monitoring and taking action to remove or reduce systemic risks with a view to protecting and enhancing the resilience of the UK financial system. The committee's secondary objective is to support the economic policy of the government.

Prudential Regulation Authority the part of the Bank of England responsible for the microprudential regulation and supervision of banks, building societies, credit unions, insurers and major investment firms.

Financial Conduct Authority primarily responsible for macroprudential regulation, the FCA aims to make sure that financial markets work well so that consumers get a fair deal, by ensuring that the financial industry is run with integrity and that consumers can trust that firms have their best interests at heart, and by providing consumers with appropriate financial products and services.

The Bank of England's Financial Policy Committee

Through the FPC, the Bank of England once again has responsibility for the Bank's second key function: maintaining financial stability. The FPC is primarily responsible for *macro*prudential regulation whereas the PRA and FCA are mainly responsible for *micro*prudential regulation. Macroprudential regulation is concerned with identifying, monitoring and acting to remove risks that affect the stability of the financial system as a whole. Microprudential regulation focuses on ensuring the stability of individual banks and other financial institutions; it involves identifying, monitoring and managing risks that relate to individual firms.

CASE STUDY 8.5

Macroprudential policy at the Bank of England

A vital element of recent reforms to the architecture of UK financial regulation is the creation of a macroprudential authority at the Bank of England — the Financial Policy Committee (FPC). In the 2008/09 recession, policy-makers around the world recognised that focusing separately on price stability and on microprudential regulation of individual firms and markets was not enough. A broader approach — macroprudential policy — was needed to ensure the resilience and stability of the financial system.

In the period leading up to the 2007–08 financial crisis, insufficient attention was paid to tackling risks and vulnerabilities across the financial system as a whole. The FPC fills that gap by identifying, monitoring and, crucially, taking action to remove or reduce systemic risks to the resilience of the financial system.

Under the Bank of England Act 1998, as amended by the Financial Services Act 2012, the Bank has a statutory objective to protect and enhance the stability of the financial system of the United Kingdom. The FPC is tasked with helping the Bank meet that objective and, subject to that, also supporting the government's economic policy, including its objectives for growth and employment.

The FPC has a statutory responsibility to identify, monitor and take action to remove or reduce risks that threaten the resilience of the UK financial system as a whole. This is supported by the objectives of the microprudential regulator, the

Prudential Regulation Authority (PRA), which is part of the Bank of England. The PRA is responsible for the microprudential regulation of individual deposit-takers, insurers and major investment banks. The Financial Conduct Authority (FCA) is a separate institution responsible for ensuring that relevant markets function well, for conduct regulation and for microprudential regulation of financial services firms not supervised by the PRA, such as asset managers, hedge funds, many smaller broker-dealers and independent financial advisers.

One way in which the FPC can mitigate threats to the resilience of the financial system is by raising awareness of systemic risks among financial market participants. The FPC is required to publish a Financial Stability Report twice a year, which must identify key threats to the stability of the UK financial system.

At times, simply warning about risks may be sufficient to catalyse action within the private sector to reduce vulnerabilities. But experience from before the crisis showed that warnings alone are not always enough. The new legislation gives the FPC two main types of power: Recommendations and Directions.

Source: *Bank of England Quarterly Bulletin*, Quarter 3, 2013

Follow-up questions

1 What is the difference between macroprudential and microprudential regulation?
2 Explain the differences between the Bank of England's Monetary Policy Committee (MPC) and the Bank's Financial Policy Committee (FPC).

ACTIVITY

Find out the names of the current members of both the Bank of England's Financial Policy Committee and its Monetary Policy Committee. Why are some people members of both committees?

The Prudential Regulation Authority

The Prudential Regulation Authority (PRA) is responsible for the microprudential supervision of banks, building societies, credit unions, insurers and major investment firms. It sets standards and supervises financial institutions at the level of the individual firm. The authority regulates by setting standards which financial institutions are required to follow and supervises by assessing the risks posed by individual financial firms and taking action to make sure they are managed properly. It aims to promote the soundness of banks and other firms providing financial services so that the stability of the UK financial system is enhanced.

The PRA may require individual institutions to maintain specified capital and liquidity ratios so as to try to ensure that, if a financial firm fails, it does so in a way that avoids significant disruption to essential financial services.

The Financial Conduct Authority

The aim of the Financial Conduct Authority (FCA) is to regulate the financial services industry in order to:

- *protect consumers* by securing an appropriate degree of protection for them
- *protect financial markets* so as to enhance the integrity of the UK financial system
- *promote effective competition* in the interests of consumers

However, the FCA is not without its critics and stands accused of being its own worst enemy, obsessed with media management rather than regulating markets. In March 2015 the authority was accused, in its search for flattering newspaper headlines, of creating a false market in insurance company shares — the very sin it is meant to prevent others committing.

Bank failures, liquidity assurance and moral hazard

If banks do not have sufficient capital, they are at risk from a fall in the value of their assets. If the value of a bank's assets falls below the value of its liabilities, it is insolvent. A bank's capital is equal to the value of its assets minus the value of its liabilities and if the value of its assets falls so that it runs out of capital, it is insolvent or bankrupt. A bank can also fail because it does not have sufficient liquidity. Insufficient liquidity makes a bank vulnerable to a run on the bank which can cause the bank to fail, even if its assets are greater than its liabilities. However, the willingness of the central bank to act as lender of last resort and provide liquidity insurance increases confidence in the stability of the banks. It is necessary because the banks borrow short term (for example, overnight money borrowed on the inter-bank market), but lend long term (for example, mortgage loans which finance house purchase).

As the 2007–08 financial crisis showed, banks are sometimes tempted to take too many risks in pursuing the huge profits that lending long allows. They do this because they believe that the Bank of England, in its role as lender of last resort, and the government through its bailouts, will not allow banks to fail.

This illustrates the problem of moral hazard. Moral hazard exists when a firm or individual pursues profit and takes on too much risk in the knowledge that, if things go wrong, someone else will bear a significant portion of the cost.

Investing in high-risk assets can lead to high profits, but unless there is the possibility that financial institutions will be allowed to fail, there is insufficient incentive to act prudently.

When the Northern Rock bank got into financial difficulty in 2007, the Bank of England's initial reaction was to allow the bank to fail, as a way of teaching a lesson to other banks that might be taking excessive financial risks. However, the Bank soon realised that instead of promoting less risky behaviour, allowing a relatively small bank to fail could trigger a crisis within the whole commercial banking system, the effects of which would dwarf those of bailing out a reckless bank. The Bank of England quickly changed its policy and in effect nationalised the bank. Instead of allowing banks to go under, the Bank and the government started to bail out banks such as RBS, which failed in October 2008 and was then part-nationalised. Rescuing banks deemed 'too big to fail' had replaced the policy of allowing banks to fail to teach others about the dangers of excessive risk taking.

However, the Bank of England's recognition of the problem of moral hazard did lead to other more robust measures being introduced, such as imposing 'firewalls' between the retail and the investment banking activities of the banks. In principle, such measures are meant to allow the riskier parts of the banks to fail without impairing the provision of their retail banking services.

Liquidity and capital ratios

Over time, banks have failed or required government assistance either because they lacked liquidity, or because they had inadequate capital, or through a combination of both of these contributory factors. Liquidity and capital are *distinct* but *related* concepts. Each plays an essential role in understanding a bank's viability and solvency.

We can use a family's finances to illustrate the differences between liquidity and capital. On the liquidity side, money in a family's bank account and any cash the family has on hand that can be used quickly and easily to pay its bills are measures of the family's liquidity position. On the capital side, the family's assets include not just the money in its bank account, but also its home, savings accounts and other investments. The family debts, or money it owes, such as a mortgage, are its liabilities. So the difference between the family's debts and its assets would provide a measure of the family's capital position.

> **KEY TERM**
> **liquidity ratio** the ratio of a bank's cash and other liquid assets to its deposits.

We have already looked at a retail bank's **liquidity ratio** in the context of explaining how banks create credit and money. A bank's liquidity ratio is the ratio of cash and other liquid assets owned by the bank to its deposit liabilities. Liquidity is a measure of the ability and ease with which assets can be converted to cash. Liquid assets are those that can be converted into cash quickly, if needed to meet financial obligations. Examples of liquid assets are cash itself, balances held at the central bank, and holdings of short-dated government debt. To remain viable, a financial institution must have enough liquid assets to meet its near-term obligations, such as withdrawals of cash by depositors. Liquidity problems arise when a bank does not hold sufficient cash (or assets that can easily be converted into cash) to repay depositors and other creditors.

A bank's capital, which is the difference between the value of the bank's assets and its liabilities, represents the net worth of the bank or its value to those who own the bank. Alternatively, assuming the bank is a company, the bank's capital can be thought of as the shareholders' stake in the bank. Capital, which acts as a financial cushion that allows a bank to absorb unexpected losses, protects creditors in case the bank's assets fall in value. A bank's **capital ratio** is the amount of capital on a bank's balance sheet as a proportion of its loans. The ratio can be used as an indicator of a bank's financial health. Bank regulators are likely to require the capital ratio to be above a prescribed minimum level.

If banks do not have sufficient capital, they are at risk if the value of their assets falls. While *insufficient liquidity* makes a bank vulnerable to a run on the bank, *insufficient capital* exposes the bank to the risk of a fall in the value of its assets. If a bank invests in assets which fall in value because, for example, some customers default on their loans, this will result in losses and reduce the bank's capital. If the reduction in the value of a bank's assets is so large that it wipes out the whole of the bank's capital, the bank is technically bankrupt and cannot continue trading.

In 2010 and 2011 the Basel III agreement was signed by the members of the Basel Committee on Banking Supervision, which include the Bank of England. The agreement, which is voluntary, is supposed to strengthen bank capital requirements by increasing bank liquidity and decreasing borrowing by banks. At the time of writing in August 2015, it is likely that the changes to capital ratios agreed in Basle III will be introduced by 31 March 2019.

Systemic risk and the impact of problems that arise in financial markets upon the real economy

We defined and briefly explained systemic risk earlier in the chapter. We stated that financial systemic risk refers to the risk of a breakdown of the entire financial system, caused by inter-linkages within the financial system, rather than simply the failure of an individual bank or financial institution within the system.

The largest and most dramatic recent example of financial systems being threatened by systemic failure occurred in the so-called 'credit crunch', which began in 2007 and extended into 2009. The credit crunch, defined as 'a severe shortage of money or credit', began on 9 August 2007 when the French bank BNP Paribas told its depositors that they would not be able to take money out of two of the bank's funds because BNP Paribas could not value the assets in them, owing to a 'complete evaporation of liquidity' in the market.

BNP Paribas's failure to honour its financial obligations started the credit crunch and the financial crisis that followed eventually destabilised the real economies of many countries, including the USA and the UK. The financial crisis caused a collapse of aggregate demand, which in turn led to rising unemployment and recession. The credit crunch paralysed financial markets, threatening affected countries with the problem of systemic failure in their financial systems. Systemic failure was eventually largely averted through government and central bank intervention to rescue financial systems, but by this time much real economic damage had been done.

SUMMARY

- Money is best defined by its two principal functions, as a medium of exchange and a store of value or wealth.
- Banks can be divided into commercial banks and investment banks. Commercial banks are also known as retail banks or 'high-street' banks.
- By creating credit, giving loans, banks also create deposits, which are the main constituent of the money supply.
- The amount of credit a bank can create is affected by its liquidity and its capital.
- The main functions of the Bank of England are to implement the government's monetary policy and maintain the stability of financial markets.
- In recent decades, Bank Rate has been the main monetary policy instrument, aimed primarily at targeting the rate of inflation — that is, hitting a target of a 2% CPI rate of inflation. The target is set by the government and not the Bank.
- In 2009, monetary policy switched away from relying solely on Bank Rate changes to a policy of quantitative easing (QE), through which the Bank of England buys bonds, reducing long-term interest rates and increasing the liquidity of financial markets.
- In the UK, following the Bank of England's decision not to extend QE, other 'unconventional' monetary policy instruments were introduced, including the Finance for Lending scheme and forward guidance.
- In the light of what happened in the financial crisis and credit crunch after 2007, new financial regulatory authorities have been set up in the UK to try to prevent systemic risk and moral hazard problems.

Questions

1 What is money? Explain how both the Bank of England and privately owned banks create money.

2 Explain how changes in Bank Rate may affect bank lending and the economy.

3 How has quantitative easing operated in the UK? Evaluate the case for and against the Bank of England extending quantitative easing.

4 Do you agree that monetary policy has been highly effective in the UK in recent years? Justify your answer.

5 Distinguish between capital markets and money markets. Explain how UK capital markets help both public limited companies (PLCs) and the government to undertake their functions.

9

Revisiting fiscal policy and supply-side policies

Fiscal policy is the part of economic policy in which the government attempts to achieve policy objectives using the fiscal instruments of government spending, taxation and the government's budgetary position (balanced budget, budget deficit or budget surplus). Supply-side economic policy is the set of government policies that aim to change the underlying structure of the economy and improve the economic performance of markets and industries, and also of individual firms and workers within markets. Supply-side fiscal policy is an important supply-side policy, but supply-side policies encompass more than just fiscal policy measures.

We start section 9.1 with a précis of the topics included in Book 1's coverage of fiscal policy. This is followed by a more in-depth explanation of certain key aspects of fiscal policy. Section 9.2, which makes up the second half of the chapter, provides a similar coverage of supply-side policies.

LEARNING OBJECTIVES

This chapter will:

- remind you of the key elements of fiscal policy introduced in Book 1, Chapter 9
- describe the main features and composition of UK taxation and public expenditure
- explain and compare demand-side and supply-side fiscal policies
- use *AD/AS* diagrams to analyse how fiscal policy affects the economy
- relate progressive, regressive and proportionate taxation to marginal and average tax rates
- compare discretionary fiscal policy with the use of automatic stabilisers
- discuss the role of the Office for Budget Responsibility in analysing and reporting on the UK's public finances
- provide an in-depth examination of the national debt
- discuss the consequences of budget deficits and surpluses for macroeconomic performance
- undertake a detailed analysis of UK fiscal policy from 1997 to 2015
- remind you of the key elements of supply-side policies introduced in Book 1, Chapter 9
- further develop the analysis and evaluation of supply-side policies

9.1 Fiscal policy

Revisiting the key elements of fiscal policy

What is fiscal policy?

As stated in the introduction to this chapter, **fiscal policy** is the part of a government's overall economic policy that aims to achieve the government's economic objectives through the use of the fiscal instruments of taxation, public spending and the government's budgetary position. As an economic term, fiscal policy is often associated with Keynesian economic theory and policy, and the management of aggregate demand. However, it is also used to influence the supply-side performance of the economy and we shall examine the supply-side nature of fiscal policy later in the chapter.

STUDY TIP

Students often assume wrongly that fiscal policy is only used to manage aggregate demand. During a brief period between 2008 and May 2010, in response to recession, fiscal policy was indeed used to stimulate aggregate demand in an attempt to bring about economic recovery. However, in recent years supply-side fiscal policy has been dominant.

Taxation and other sources of government revenue

Taxation is the principal source of government revenue for most economies. In the UK about 89% of total taxation is levied by central government, with local government taxation (currently the council tax and business rates) accounting for the remaining 11%. In the financial year 2015/16, all but £62 billion of the total expected revenue of £667 billion was expected to come from taxation. The non-tax income was expected to come from other sources, such as interest and dividends which the government receives. UK governments have also received revenue from privatising state-owned firms and industries. However, in order to keep down the figure for public spending, UK governments perform the accounting trick of classifying these receipts as 'negative public expenditure' rather than as a source of government revenue.

Figure 9.1, which has been taken from an Institute of Fiscal Studies (IFS) briefing note, 'A Survey of the UK Tax System', shows how the structure of UK taxation changed between the fiscal years 1978/79 and 2012/13.

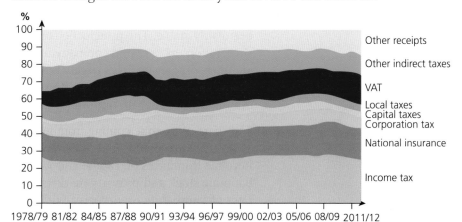

Figure 9.1 Changes in the composition of UK government receipts, 1978/79 to 2011/12

Source: IFS

What the diagram does not show is that the income tax rate structure was transformed during these years, the taxation of savings was repeatedly adjusted, the national insurance contributions system was overhauled, the VAT rate more than doubled, some excise duty rates rose sharply while others fell, the corporate income tax system was subject to numerous reforms, and local taxation today is unrecognisable compared to the situation in 1978/79.

Worked example: calculating the mean and median

Table 9.1 shows the weekly incomes of the 20 members of an economics class at an adult education college.

Table 9.1 Weekly incomes of an economics class

Class member	Weekly income (£)	Class member	Weekly income (£)
Student 1	220	Student 11	500
Student 2	1,000	Student 12	370
Student 3	800	Student 13	80
Student 4	340	Student 14	1,200
Student 5	620	Student 15	50
Student 6	800	Student 16	570
Student 7	400	Student 17	920
Student 8	680	Student 18	30
Student 9	730	Student 19	250
Student 10	690	Student 20	820

Calculate the mean and median weekly incomes for the class.

As we explained in Chapter 5, the mean and the median are two kinds of 'average'. The mean class income can be calculated by adding up the incomes of all the members of the class (in this case £11,070) and dividing this number by 20 (the total number of class members). The mean value for all the members of the economics class is £553.50.

The 'median' is the 'middle' value in the list of numbers. To find the median, you should list the numbers in numerical order (£30; £50; £80; £220; £250; £340; £370; £400; £500; £570; £620; £680; £690; £730; £800; £800; £820; £920; £1,000 and £1,200), and then locate the middle value. In this example, because there is an even number of students in the class (20), there are two middle values, £570 and £620. The median is midway between the two: £595.

TEST YOURSELF 9.1

Chloé wants to achieve a mean score of at least 90% on her six economics multiple-choice tests. Her first five multiple-choice test scores are:

95%, 88%, 97%, 82%, 91%

What is the minimum score that Chloé needs to get on her last multiple-choice test in order to reach her target?

ACTIVITY

Find out the main features of national insurance contributions, and consider whether they should be regarded as a tax.

Since the mid-1990s, the shares of revenue provided by different taxes have been fairly stable. The principal change has been in the contribution of corporation tax (a tax on company income or profits), which has risen, fallen and then risen again. This largely reflects the changing fortunes of firms in the financial sector, whose profits were strong in the late 1990s, weaker thereafter, but then stronger again until the recession of 2008–09.

The share of revenue coming from indirect taxes has fallen since the late 1990s, mainly because fuel duties have been cut substantially in real terms. Revenue from taxes on capital and wealth increased during the period of booming stock and property markets, helped by the introduction of higher rates of stamp duty on property, but it still only accounted for 4.25% of total revenue in 2007/08 before falling again during the slump in the markets for shares and property that began in late 2007. Since 2011/12 changes to the stamp duty system have reduced the amount of duty received by the government when lower-priced houses are sold.

Overall, the share of revenue from income tax has remained virtually unchanged, despite radical structural changes, and the most dramatic shift over the decade has been a doubling of the share of revenue flowing from VAT and a substantial reduction in revenue from other indirect taxes, mainly excise duties.

Figure 9.2, again taken from the IFS briefing note, shows changes between 1978 and 2014 in the real value of excise duties levied on cigarettes, fuel and alcoholic drinks. Unlike VAT, which is a percentage or *ad valorem* tax, excise duties are specific or unit taxes levied, not on the price of a good, but on a physical quantity of the good, such as a litre of petrol or a bottle of wine. (Both VAT and excise duty are levied on the goods shown in Figure 9.2, though the diagram shows only the effect of excise duties.)

1978 = 100

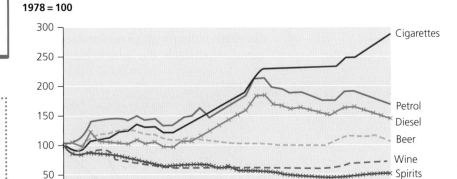

Figure 9.2 The real level of UK excise duties, 1978–2014

Source: IFS

Progressive taxation revisited

Many people believe that the UK has a **progressive tax** system, in which the proportion of a person's income paid in tax increases as income rises. However, as we stated in Book 1, page 257, overall the UK tax system is at best only slightly progressive, and it may even be regressive. Cigarette duty is an example of a **regressive tax**. The low-paid lose a greater proportion of their incomes in tax than rich people when buying cigarettes and alcohol. VAT is another example of a regressive tax.

To understand why the tax on cigarettes is regressive, compare two smokers, one with an income of £100 a week and the other with an income of £1,000 a week. Both smoke 20 cigarettes a week, which in 2014 cost £7.98, of which £6.17 was tax — both excise duty and VAT. This is 6.17% of the poor smoker's income, compared to 0.617% of the rich smoker's income. Additionally, because they recognise the health hazards of tobacco consumption, richer people, who may be better educated, have often given up or never started smoking.

The regressive nature of taxes such as these partially offsets the fact that income tax is generally progressive. Some economists have argued for a 'flat' 10% income tax which, if it were to be introduced, would be a **proportional tax**.

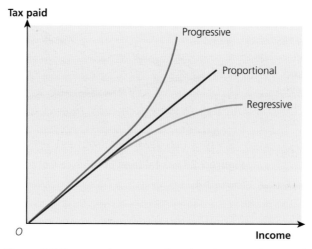

Figure 9.3 Progressive, proportional and regressive taxation

The principles or canons of taxation revisited

Before reading any further, it would be useful to read once again our explanation of the canons or **principles of taxation**, which you will find in Book 1, page 252. As stated there, a 'good' tax meets as many of these principles as possible, although because of conflicts and trade-offs, it is usually impossible for a tax to meet them all at the same time. By contrast, a 'bad' tax meets few, if any, of the principles. To remind you, the main principles are:

- Economy: a tax should be cheap to collect in relation to the revenue it yields.
- Equity: a tax system should be seen to be fair and based on taxpayers' ability to pay.
- Efficiency: a tax should achieve its desired objective(s) with minimum undesired side-effects or unintended consequences.
- Flexibility: a tax must be easy to change to meet new circumstances.
- Convenience: a tax should be convenient for taxpayers to pay.
- Certainty: taxpayers should be reasonably certain of the amount of tax they will be required to pay.

CASE STUDY 9.1

The main taxes levied in the UK

A large proportion of people's income goes in paying taxes. Tax accounts for around a third of the money people earn. Direct taxes such as income tax and national insurance account for 20%. The rest goes mainly on VAT, duty on alcohol and petrol, council tax and other indirect taxes. (Before reading any further, you should refer back to the section 'How taxation affects the pattern of economic activity' in Book 1, pages 256–58. Remember also that changes in income taxes shift the positions of demand curves for goods, whereas changes in expenditure taxes such as VAT and excise duties shift the positions of goods' supply curves.)

Some of the main taxes levied in the UK are:

- **Income tax.** This is the UK's main direct tax, which is paid on earnings, pensions, benefits, savings and investment income, and rents. For most people, the first slice of income is untaxed. In the tax year 2015/16, the personal tax allowance (untaxed income) for people with an income of £100,000 or less was £10,600, but for higher income earners the personal tax allowance tapered away, falling to zero for incomes above £121,200. In the same year, the standard rate of income tax (20%) was levied on individual income above the personal tax allowance but below £42,385. Higher rates of tax were levied on personal incomes above £42,385, namely 40% on the slice of income between £42,386 and £150,000, and 45% on income above £150,000.

- **National insurance.** Whereas personal income tax has a history in the UK going back to 1799, when it was used to help pay for the Napoleonic Wars, national insurance has a much shorter history. National insurance contributions (NICs), first started in 1911, were initially introduced to finance a government safety-net for workers who fell on hard times. Anyone needing cash for medical treatment, or because they had lost their job, could claim from the fund. Over the years, the system has changed. The national insurance fund is now used to help finance the NHS and welfare benefits, including unemployment benefit and the state pension. However, NICs are insufficient for this purpose and have to be supplemented from general taxation.

  In strict legal terms, NICs are not a tax. Consequently, on a number of occasions UK governments have increased NICs, while leaving personal income tax rates and allowances unchanged, and then claimed that they have not

Taxes are used to finance the provision of public goods, such as defence, police and roads

increased income tax! Most people, however, regard NICs as a supplementary form of income tax. Over the years, NICs have generally been regressive, and this has reduced the progressivity of the direct tax system, provided we regard NICs as a form of tax.

In the future, income tax and national insurance could be merged by the Conservative government under plans to simplify the tax system. If this happens, it will be the biggest shake-up in the UK tax system, certainly since the introduction of VAT in 1973, when it replaced an older percentage sales tax called purchase tax.

- **Corporation tax.** This is a tax on company profits. It is levied at a lower rate than personal income tax. In its summer 2015 budget, the newly elected Conservative government set the main rate of corporation tax at 19% for the years starting 1 April 2017, 2018 and 2019, and at 18% for the year starting 1 April 2020.

- **Value added tax (VAT).** Unlike income tax and NICs, which are direct taxes, VAT is an indirect tax, currently paid at a standard percentage rate of 20% on spending on most goods and services. VAT is set at a lower rate of 5% on gas and electricity. It is not currently levied on books, children's clothes and food.

- **Excise duties.** These are another form of expenditure tax (and indirect tax) paid on tobacco, alcohol, petrol and diesel fuel. Unlike VAT, which is an *ad valorem* percentage tax, these so-called 'sin taxes' are specific taxes or unit taxes levied on physical quantities of a good. For example, in 2015 an excise duty of £273.31 was levied on each hectolitre of wine with an alcohol content between 5% and 15%. With motor fuels, the excise duty levied on petrol is lower than that on diesel fuel. As inflation erodes the real value of excise duties, the government usually increases excise duties in the annual budget. Excise duties are generally regressive because they take a larger percentage of the income of the low paid.

- **Stamp duty.** Stamp duty land tax (SDLT) is paid on residential property purchases above £125,000. In 2015/16, the starting rate, for properties worth between £125,001 and £250,000, was 2%. House buyers pay 5% on the portion between £250,000 and £925,000. Between that point and £1.5 million, the rate is 10% — then 12% on anything over £1.5 million. Stamp duty is also payable on purchases of shares and some other securities at a flat rate of 0.5%.
- **Inheritance tax.** When a person dies, inheritance tax, which is a tax on wealth, is paid on their estate if it is worth more than £325,000 during 2015/16 (or potentially up to £650,000 if the person is married or in a civil partnership). Inheritance tax may also be due on some gifts made during a person's lifetime, depending on the overall value of the estate. The Conservative government would like to reduce inheritance tax, and many of its supporters want the tax to be abolished.
- **Capital gains tax.** This is levied on the profit a person makes when selling possessions or investments. The tax is paid on the increase in value from the date the assets were acquired to the date when they are sold or given away. Some forms of wealth are exempt from capital gains tax — for example, a main home or personal assets with a value of less than £6,000, or if the gain is less than £11,100 during the tax year. For standard rate taxpayers, capital gains realised in 2015 were taxed at a standard rate of 18%. For those who pay income tax at 40%, the rate was 28%.
- **Council tax.** This is a tax charged by local authorities on the value of houses and flats to the people who live in the properties. Council tax rates are 'banded' with the lowest rate charged on Band A properties with a value of up to £40,000 (in 1993 when the tax was introduced), while the highest rate is paid on Band H properties with a value above £320,000 in 1993. Since they have never been revised, these bands are now hopelessly out of date. One result is that people living in £10 million-priced mansions pay the same council tax each year as households living in modest £350,000 properties. As a result, council tax has become a highly regressive tax.

Follow-up questions

1 Check out any changes that have occurred since 2015 in the rates at which the UK's main taxes have been levied, and whether or not new taxes have been introduced or old taxes abolished.

2 In the 2015 general election campaign, the Labour Party announced that it wanted to introduce a so-called mansion tax. What is a 'mansion tax'? Explain **one** advantage and **one** disadvantage of such a tax.

The role and merits of different UK taxes

An obvious role of taxation is to raise the revenue required to finance government spending. Also, as you learnt when reading Book 1, Chapter 9, taxes and subsidies can be used to alter the relative prices of goods and services in order to change consumption patterns. Summarising, many of the aims or objectives of public spending and taxation can be divided into the categories of *allocation* and *distribution*.

For a reminder of how taxes (and their opposite, subsidies) can affect resource allocation, refer back to the coverage of merit goods, demerit goods, public goods and externalities in Chapter 6 of this book. Consider also how you might apply the concept of allocative efficiency (equating a good's price with its marginal social cost of production) in your analysis of how taxes and subsidies can be used to correct market failure through improving resource allocation.

With regard to the distributions of income and wealth, in past decades UK governments used taxation and public spending to try to reduce inequality between rich and poor. More recently, although governments have been less concerned about reducing inequality, the combined effects of taxes and public spending have made the distribution of income much more equal than if governments did not intervene. Under the influence of supply-side thinking, government policy has been affected by the conflict between two of the principles of taxation mentioned previously: *efficiency* and *equity*. Efficiency requires greater incentives for work and enterprise in order to increase the UK's growth rate. However, progressive taxation and transfers to the poor used on the ground of equity meant that people had less incentive to work hard and to take risks by engaging in entrepreneurial activity. Moreover, the ease with which the poor could claim welfare benefits and the level at which they were available created a situation in which the poor rationally chose unemployment and state benefits in preference to low wages and work. In this so-called *dependency culture*, the unwaged were effectively 'married to the state', but some of the poor, obviously not enjoying this marriage, drifted into antisocial behaviour, attacking bus shelters and other public property, as well as privately owned property.

Many supply-side economists and politicians have argued that income tax rates and benefit rates should both be reduced. They believe that tax and benefit cuts would alter the work/leisure choice in favour of supplying labour, particularly for benefit claimants who lack the skills necessary for high-paid jobs. They believe that to make everyone eventually better off, it is necessary to increase the gap between the amount people earn when they are in work and what they receive when they are out of work. This means making those who are poor, because they are unemployed, worse off. According to this view, increased inequality is necessary to create incentives to facilitate economic growth, from which all will eventually benefit. Through a 'trickle-down' effect, the poor would end up better off in absolute terms but, because inequalities had widened, they would still be relatively worse off compared to the rich.

According to the Institute for Fiscal Studies, a range of summary measures of inequality, including the Gini coefficient, show that inequality rose significantly between 1996/97 and 2008/09. However, this increase in inequality is much smaller in magnitude than the rise in inequality that occurred during the earlier period of supply-side fiscal policy in the 1980s. Since 2009–10, according to the OECD, inequality has been constant, albeit at a high level.

As we stated in our coverage of the canons of taxation in Book 1 and also earlier in this chapter, taxpayers often consider all taxes as 'bad', in the sense that they do not enjoy paying them. Nevertheless, most people realise that taxation is necessary in order to obtain the useful goods and services provided by the government. When considering the merits and demerits of different types of taxation, a starting point is to consider the extent to which a particular tax satisfies the various principles of taxation. We explained that a 'good' tax meets as many of these principles as possible, whereas a 'bad' tax meets few, if any, of the guiding principles.

271

A closer look at taxes on income, indirect taxes and taxes on capital and wealth

Taxes on income

As Case Study 9.1 explains, taxes on income, which include corporation tax and national insurance contributions as well as personal income tax, are direct taxes. This means that the person or organisation being paid the income is directly liable to pay the tax to the government. Failure to declare income is tax *evasion*. Tax evasion is illegal.

With regard to some of the principles of taxation outlined earlier, for most wage and salary earners, income tax is cheap to collect, it is convenient and certain for the taxpayer, and, if progressive, it is equitable in the sense that it reflects taxpayers' ability to pay. In addition, when the basic tax threshold is set at a relatively high level, people who receive very low incomes can be taken out of the 'tax net', thereby paying zero income tax. (For most wage and salary earners, income tax is collected by the government through 'pay as you earn' (PAYE). This makes personal income tax cheap to collect, as employers bear most of the costs.)

Nevertheless, for some in society, income tax has been relatively easy to *avoid* and *evade*. By providing services such as plumbing and home-hairdressing, 'strictly for cash', those on relatively low incomes may successfully evade tax. Meanwhile, those at the top of the income pyramid find it relatively easy to avoid tax legally through signing up to 'tax-efficient' schemes provided by their financial advisers. Tax avoidance is not illegal but may allow some taxpayers to exploit unintended loopholes in the tax system.

The opportunities for avoiding and/or evading paying tax are, of course, among the disadvantages of income tax. Additionally, a highly progressive income tax may lead to undesirable 'unintended consequence' — for example, the disincentivising of hard work, risk taking and entrepreneurial effort. We return to this in the second half of the chapter, in our discussion of supply-side economic policies.

However, as Figure 9.1 clearly shows, personal income tax has long been the main source of government tax revenue in the UK. In part, this reflects the fact that for personal income tax, the 'tax base' is extremely wide in the sense that millions of people receive income that can be taxed. Total government revenue from the taxation of income is actually much higher than the revenue collected from personal income tax. Companies pay corporation tax on their income or profits and most of their employees pay national insurance contributions (NICs) as well as personal income tax to the government.(In a strict legal sense, NICs are a charge for services to be received, such as sickness benefit and the old-age pension, and are not a tax. Nevertheless, employees certainly feel that the contributions they are forced to pay are a tax. Again, as Case Study 9.1 explains, NICs are also quite regressive, a fact which offsets the general progressivity of the UK income tax system.)

Indirect taxes

As Figure 9.1 also shows, after income taxes, VAT and 'other indirect taxes' make up the second most important group of taxes in the UK. The 'other indirect taxes' are mostly excise duties, which were looked at in the context of Figure 9.2. Whereas VAT is an *ad valorem tax*, excise duties are almost always *specific* or *unit taxes*, levied not on a good's price, but on the physical quantity of the good.

An advantage of excise duties is that they can be used to encourage people to switch their spending away from goods deemed to be undesirable to those regarded as 'good' for consumers — for example, away from demerit goods and toward merit goods. Some economists, mainly of a free-market persuasion, believe this to be a disadvantage rather than an advantage. They dislike governments exercising paternalism — that is, claiming to know better than ordinary individuals what is good for those whom they govern. VAT, by

STUDY TIP
Make sure you understand the difference between tax avoidance and tax evasion, and that you can provide examples of both.

contrast, is a generally neutral tax, in that it is levied on spending on most goods and services, with the result that a change in the VAT rate has little effect on patterns of expenditure.

Many economists believe that, unless there is a good reason to affect people's choices through the tax system, the taxation of goods should conform to the principle of neutrality. Reasons for taxing some products at a higher rate than others could relate to demerit goods and externalities. Another reason could be to influence the distribution of income, imposing zero tax on basic necessities and high taxes on frivolous luxuries.

In any case, using indirect taxes to encourage people to alter their expenditure patterns becomes less effective if more and more goods are taxed at the same rate. Although this widens the 'tax base', which allows the government to collect more tax revenue, the tax becomes less useful as a tool for influencing the pattern of consumer spending.

Indirect taxes can also be evaded: for example, when a builder says he will not include VAT in the price he is quoting to a householder, as long as the householder pays in cash. However, it is generally less easy to evade and avoid indirect taxes than direct taxes.

Taxes on capital and wealth

Taxes on capital and wealth are also direct taxes. Some taxes on capital and wealth can be avoided and evaded, but with others it is less easy to do so. Wealth in the form of cash can be 'money laundered' when given from one person to another, but on the other hand, wealth in the form of property is less easily hidden. If the taxman were to be given the authority, he could use a helicopter and data stored on the land registry to find out information about property values, and who owns the property. Having said that, successive British governments have shown little interest in updating property values. The last time houses were valued for the purpose of collecting council tax, which is the main UK tax on property, was back in 1991, since when house prices have soared.

In the run-up to the 2015 general election, the Labour Party announced that if elected into government, it would introduce a so-called mansion tax on all properties valued at more than £2 million. The Liberal Democratic Party, which originally proposed the idea, has favoured staggering the introduction of a high-value property levy to ease the burden on owners of homes over the £2 million threshold.

ACTIVITY

Find out about any changes which have occurred in recent years to the following taxes on capital: council tax, capital gains tax and inheritance tax.

273

Public expenditure revisited

According to the IFS briefing note 'Survey of Public Spending in the UK', published in 2014, over the second half of the twentieth century, government spending fluctuated between around 35% and 45% of national income. Before the financial crisis which began in 2007, and in the so-called 'great recession' that followed, UK government spending was at around 40% of GDP. This level

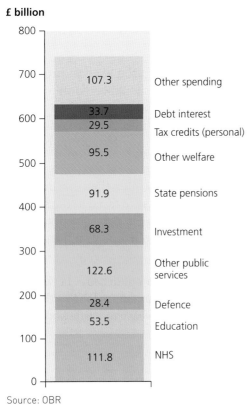

£ billion

Source: OBR

Figure 9.4 Expected public sector spending, 2015/16

TEST YOURSELF 9.2
Using the data in Figure 9.4, calculate the percentage contribution of each category of public expenditure in 2015/16.

was not particularly high, either by the UK's own historical standards or by international standards. However, during the financial crisis, the UK government experienced a particularly large increase in spending as a share of GDP: in the fiscal year 2009/10 it rose to approximately 47% of GDP. Without government policy intervention actively to reduce the level of government spending, according to some, the public finances might have got out of control.

Figure 9.4 shows the pattern of UK public spending, estimated in 2014 for 2015/16. (See also Book 1, Figure 9.10.)

In recent years, the largest areas of public spending in the UK have been social security (state pensions and other welfare in Figure 9.4), which by 2013/14 had reached 29.3% of the total, the NHS (18.1%) and education (12.6%). Prior to 2016 at least, growth of the state pension has been protected by a so-called 'triple lock' which guarantees that the state pension rises with whatever is highest out of wages increases, inflation or 2.5%. If this protection continues, the shares in total public spending of social security, the NHS and state education are likely to continue to rise. Robert Chote, the chairman of the Office for Budget Responsibility, recently said the pensions 'triple lock' was pushing up government spending at a time when the population was ageing rapidly.

Spending on social security increased after 2007 partly because the recession reduced incomes and, for a time, increased the number of unemployed. It is also worth noting that pensioners now receive over half of all social security spending, with, as noted, spending on the elderly forecast to continue to increase rapidly. This increase has been driven by steady growth in the number of pensioners, and by the 'triple lock' which protects pensioners from the effect of spending cuts.

Health spending has also experienced significant growth over recent decades. From 2002 onward, Labour governments increased spending on the NHS, to around 7% of national income prior to the recession, but this is still below the OECD average. While other departments have experienced budget cuts as part of the government's austerity programme, spending on the NHS has effectively been frozen in real terms since 2010. However, given increased population, longer life spans, and the cost of new drugs and medical technology, NHS spending levels are likely to lag behind demographics-driven demand.

The education budget also grew substantially under Labour governments from 2002 onward. As with the NHS and state pensions, spending on schools has been protected, but other areas of education spending have not. Higher education has seen the largest cuts in public spending, though this has been more than offset by an increase in fees paid by students.

Spending on defence has been unprotected, and before the 2015 general election the defence budget was facing sharp cuts. Whether further cuts will be implemented will depend significantly on the changing state of world security and perceived 'threats from outside'. In 2015, the Conservative government made a commitment to maintain defence spending at a minimum of 2% of GDP.

The pattern of public spending, and also the extent to which certain types of public spending increase while others fall, depends in part on the extent to which spending is *demand-led*. Demand-led spending, for example on unemployment benefits, is literally led by demand, increasing when unemployment grows and falling when unemployment drops. Although the rates at which unemployment benefits and pensions are paid, and the ages at which people qualify, can be changed, demand-led spending changes according to the phases of the economic cycle and, in the case of demand-led spending on the state pension, according to how long elderly people live.

The total amount that the government spends is known as Total Managed Expenditure (TME). This is split up into:

● Departmental budgets — the amount that government departments have been allocated to spend. This is known as Departmental Expenditure Limits, or DEL.
● Money spent in areas outside budgetary control — spending that is not controlled by a government department, including welfare, pensions and things such as debt interest payments. This is known as Annually Managed Expenditure, or AME. (Demand-led spending falls mostly into AME.)

Keynesian or demand-side fiscal policy

In the Keynesian era, fiscal policy came to mean the use of the overall levels of public spending, taxation and the budget deficit to manage the level of aggregate demand in the economy. The aim was to achieve full employment and to stabilise the economic cycle, without at the same time creating excessive inflationary pressures. Keynesian fiscal policy was implemented with varying degrees of success in the decades before 1979. Some of the Keynesian views which strongly influenced the use of fiscal policy at the time were as follows:

● Left to itself, an unregulated market economy results in unnecessarily low economic growth, high unemployment and volatile business cycles.
● A lack of aggregate demand, caused by a tendency for the private sector to save too much and invest too little, can mean that the economy settles into an under-full employment equilibrium characterised by demand-deficient unemployment.
● By deliberate deficit financing, the government can, using fiscal policy as a demand management instrument, inject demand and spending power into the economy to eliminate deficient aggregate demand and achieve full employment.
● Having achieved full employment, the government can then use fiscal policy in a discretionary way (that is, changing tax rates and levels of public spending to meet new circumstances) to fine-tune the level of aggregate demand. For much of the Keynesian era, governments believed that fiscal policy could achieve full employment and stabilise the economic cycle, while avoiding an unacceptable rate of inflation.
● The overall stance of fiscal policy and, indeed, of economic policy in general, was orientated towards the demand side of the economy. The more microeconomic elements of fiscal policy, such as transfers to industry, were aimed at improving economic performance on the supply side. But on the whole, supply-side fiscal policy was treated as subordinate to the macroeconomic management of aggregate demand and to the assumption that output would respond to demand stimulation. In any case, the microeconomic elements of Keynesian fiscal policy were generally interventionist rather than non-interventionist, extending rather than reducing the state's role in the mixed economy.

ACTIVITY

Carefully read the OBR publication 'A brief guide to the UK public finances', which can be accessed on **http://budgetresponsibility. org.uk/wordpress/docs/Brief- guide-to-the-public-finances- July-2015.pdf**.

275

● Central to Keynesian fiscal policy was the assumption that the government spending multiplier has a high value. At this stage you could refer back to Book 1, Chapter 7 and refresh your knowledge of the national income multiplier in the context of shifts of the economy's aggregate demand curve. If the national income multiplier is quite large with respect to real output — for example, 3 — an increase in government spending of £10 billion increases aggregate demand and money national income by £30 billion. A relatively large multiplier means that changing the levels of government spending, taxation and the budget deficit (or surplus) can be quite effective in managing aggregate demand. However, real-world government spending multipliers are generally thought to be small, and in most cases are not significantly different from unity (1).

The government's budgetary position

Using the symbols G for government spending and T for taxation and other sources of revenue, the three possible budgetary positions a government can have are:

- $G = T$: balanced budget
- $G > T$: budget deficit
- $G < T$: budget surplus

A government can *eliminate* a budget deficit by cutting public spending or by raising taxation, both of which can balance the budget or move it into surplus. Assuming a budget deficit persists, the extent to which spending exceeds revenue must be *financed* by public sector borrowing.

Over the years, UK governments have used a number of technical terms as labels for public sector borrowing. These have included the *public sector net cash requirement* (PSNCR), public sector net borrowing, and the *public sector net borrowing requirement* (PSBR), which is mentioned in Case Study 9.2. However, because the Treasury frequently changes its official terminology, the most important thing to appreciate is that public sector borrowing represents 'the other side of the coin' to the budget deficit. Whenever there is a budget deficit there is a positive borrowing requirement. Conversely, a budget surplus means that the government can use the tax revenues that it is not spending to repay previous borrowing. In this case, the borrowing requirement is negative.

KEY TERMS

balancing the budget setting government spending equal to government revenue ($G = T$).

budget deficit the amount by which government spending exceeds government revenue in a particular time period ($G > T$, assuming that taxation is the only source of government revenue).

budget surplus the amount by which government spending is less than government revenue in a particular time period ($G < T$).

CASE STUDY 9.2

Sound finance and balanced budgets

The passage below is an extract from a budget speech delivered by Conservative chancellor Nigel Lawson during a period known as the 'Lawson boom'. The budget followed nearly 6 years of economic growth. During these years the public finances moved from deficit into surplus. Margaret Thatcher, the prime minister, hoped that the budget would remain in balance or in surplus and that budget deficits were a thing of the past. This was not to be. The severe recession that followed the Lawson boom in the early 1990s led to the return of a budget deficit.

At one time, it was regarded as the hallmark of good government to maintain a balanced budget; to ensure that government spending was fully financed by revenues from taxation, with no need for government borrowing.

Over the years, this simple and beneficent rule was increasingly disregarded. Profligacy not only brought economic disaster and the national humiliation of a bail out by the IMF; it also added massively to the burden of debt interest, not merely now but for a generation to come.

Thus, one of our main objectives, when we first took office in 1979, was to bring down government borrowing. In 1987/88, the year now ending, we are set to secure something previously achieved only on one isolated occasion since the beginning of the 1950s: a balanced budget.

Indeed, we have gone even further. It looks as if the final outturn for 1987/88 will be a budget surplus of £3 billion. Instead of a PSBR, a PSDR: not a public sector borrowing requirement, but a public sector debt repayment.

Some two-thirds of this substantial undershoot of the PSBR I set at the time of last year's Budget is the result of the increased tax revenues that have flowed from a buoyant economy; while the remaining third is due to lower than expected public expenditure, again the outcome of a buoyant economy: less in benefits for the unemployed.

A balanced budget is a valuable discipline for the medium term. It represents security for the present and an investment for the future. Having achieved it, I intend to stick to it. In other words, henceforth a zero PSBR will be the norm. This provides a clear and simple rule, with a good historical pedigree.

Nigel Lawson's budget speech, 15 March 1988

Follow-up questions

1 Explain the meaning of a balanced budget.
2 Research the changes that have taken place in the state of the public finances from 1988 to the present day. In which years was there a budget surplus? How have the 2008 recession and subsequent recovery affected the public finances?
3 What is the view of the current chancellor of the exchequer on the desirability of balancing the budget and possibly then achieving a budget surplus?

KEY TERMS

cyclical budget deficit the part of the budget deficit which rises in the downswing of the economic cycle and falls in the upswing of the cycle.

structural budget deficit the part of the budget deficit which is not affected by the economic cycle but results from structural change in the economy affecting the government's finances.

Cyclical and structural budget deficits and surpluses

We compared the cyclical and the structural components of a budget deficit in Book 1, pages 250–51. There we said that the **cyclical budget deficit** is the part of an overall budget deficit that rises and falls with the upswings and downswings of the economic cycle. The cyclical deficit falls in the recovery and boom phases of the economic cycle — perhaps moving into surplus in the boom — but it increases when growth slows down and the economy is threatened with recession. In the upswing of the economic cycle, tax revenues rise and spending on welfare benefits falls. By contrast in the downswing, tax revenues fall but public spending on unemployment and poverty-related welfare benefits increases. As a result, the government's finances deteriorate.

By contrast, the **structural budget deficit**, or surplus, is the portion of a country's budget deficit that is not the result of changes in the economic cycle. The structural deficit will exist even when the economy is at the peak of the cycle. The structural deficit results from fundamental imbalance in government tax revenues and public spending, and is not caused by short-term fluctuations in tax revenues and expenditures. Examples of factors that can cause a change in the structural deficit are an ageing population, the desire to increase spending on defence perhaps in times of global political instability, and the desire to reduce taxes to create incentives combined with an unwillingness to reduce public expenditure.

The term *cyclical deficit* should not be confused with the similar-sounding *cyclically adjusted deficit*. The latter is in fact the *structural deficit*. The two are interchangeable terms. According to the OBR, the structural or cyclically adjusted deficit is what you would expect to see if economic activity was at its sustainable 'potential' or trend level, which would be consistent with maintaining stable inflation.

Figure 9.5 shows how a hypothetical country's budget deficit or surplus (labelled the 'headline' budget deficit or surplus) is made up of the structural deficit (or

277

surplus) and the cyclical deficit (or surplus). On the two occasions on the graph when the headline deficit is zero (in approximately mid-1997 and mid-2007), the structural, or cyclically adjusted, surplus is just sufficient to offset the cyclical deficit in mid-1997, with the reverse relationship holding in mid-2007.

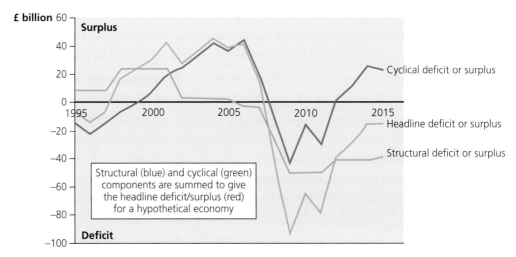

Figure 9.5 Changes in the cyclical deficit budget deficit (or surplus), the structural deficit (or surplus), and the 'headline' deficit (or surplus) in a hypothetical economy

Using an *AD/AS* diagram to illustrate Keynesian or demand-side fiscal policy

Before applying *AD/AS* analysis to Keynesian fiscal policy and its effects on the economy, it is worth reminding ourselves of the aggregate demand equation:

$$AD = C + I + G + (X - M)$$

Government spending (*G*) is one of the components of aggregate demand. An increase in government spending and/or a cut in taxation increases the size of the budget deficit (or reduces the size of the budget surplus). Either way, an injection into the circular flow of income occurs and the effect on aggregate demand is expansionary.

Figure 9.6 illustrates the effect of such a reflationary or expansionary demand-side fiscal policy. Initially, with the aggregate demand curve in position AD_1, macroeconomic equilibrium occurs at point *X*. Real national income or output is y_1, and the price level is P_1.

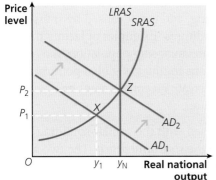

Figure 9.6 Expansionary demand-side fiscal policy

However, the extent to which expansionary fiscal policy reflates real output (in this case from y_1 to y_N), or creates excess demand that leads to demand-pull inflation (in this case an increase in the price level from P_1 to P_2), depends on the shape of the *AS* curve, which in turn depends on how close the economy initially was to the 'normal capacity' level of output. The nearer the economy gets to normal capacity, the greater the inflationary effect of expansionary fiscal policy and the smaller the reflationary effect. Once normal capacity is reached on the long-run aggregate supply curve at y_N, a further increase in government spending or a tax cut inflates the price level. In this situation, real output cannot grow (except possibly temporarily) because there is no spare capacity. The economy is producing on its production possibility frontier.

Figure 9.6 can be adapted to illustrate the effect of a **contractionary** (deflationary) **fiscal policy**. In this case a cut in government spending and/or an increase in taxation shifts the *AD* curve to the left. The extent to which the demand deflation results in the price level or real income falling depen(on the shape and slope of the *SRAS* curve. (However, if the economy is experiencing inflation at point *X*, it is unlikely that reducing *AD* will redu the price level. Instead, disinflation will occur — inflation will fall and there is also likely to be some reduction in real national output.)

Supply-side fiscal policy revisited

In the Keynesian era, the management of aggregate demand and deficit financing became respectable and fiscal policy was used to fine-tune the economy by manipulating aggregate demand. However, under prime minister Margaret Thatcher in the 1980s, demand management was generally rejected and there was a return to the principles of 'sound finance' and balanced budgets. Fiscal policy remained an important part of macroeconomic policy, but with the exception of the short-lived 'fiscal stimulus' between 2008 and 2010 when demand-side fiscal policy was used to 'try to spend the UK economy out of recession', fiscal policy was used primarily, then and now, in a supply-side way to try to improve the economy's productive capacity by, for example, increasing incentives and productivity. Now when income tax rates are cut, and personal tax thresholds increased, the aim is not to stimulate aggregate demand, but to improve personal incentives to work harder, save, invest and be entrepreneurial.

Using an *AD/AS* diagram to illustrate supply-side fiscal policy

Along with other **supply-side policies**, which we examine in some detail later in this chapter, supply-side fiscal policy was and is used to try and shift the economy's long-run aggregate supply (*LRAS*) curve to the right, thereby increasing the economy's potential level of output. The effect of successful supply-side fiscal policy on the *LRAS* curve is shown in Figure 9.7. The economy's *LRAS* curve shifts rightward from $LRAS_1$ to $LRAS_2$, which means that the 'normal capacity' level of output has increased (due to long-run economic growth) from y_{N1} to y_{N2}. (Note that the diagram also shows a rightward shift of the *SRAS* curve, reflecting the improvement in productivity and falling unit costs. You could also develop the diagram a stage further, by depicting the resulting fall in the price level, to show a 'good deflation', in which the price level falls because of the benign effects of successful supply-side policies and supply-side reform in the economy's private sector.) However, in normal circumstances, the improvements in the supply-side performance of the economy are accompanied by rising aggregate demand, which means that the effect is to moderate inflation rather than lead to deflation.

> ### KEY TERM
>
> **supply-side policies**
> government economic policies which aim to make markets more competitive and efficient, increase production potential, and shift the *LRAS* curve to the right. Supply-side fiscal policy is arguably the most important type of supply-side policy, but there are also non-fiscal supply-side policies.

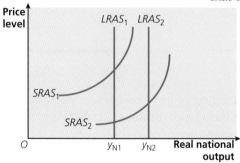

Figure 9.7 Supply-side fiscal policy shifting the *LRAS* curve to the right

Developing your knowledge and understanding of fiscal policy

Relating progressive, regressive and proportional taxation to marginal and average tax rates

For particular taxes such as income tax or inheritance tax, we can identify whether the tax is progressive, regressive or proportional by examining the relationship between the *average* rate at which the tax is levied and the *marginal rate*. In a progressive income tax system, the marginal tax rate is higher than the average tax rate, which means that the average rate, which measures the proportion of income paid in tax, rises as income increases. Conversely, in a regressive income tax system, the marginal rate of tax is less than the average rate, while the two are equal in the case of a proportionate tax.

For income tax, the average tax rate is calculated as total tax paid divided by total income. By contrast, the marginal tax rate is the tax paid on the last pound of income earned, calculated as the change in tax paid divided by the change in income.

$$\text{average tax rate} = \frac{\text{tax paid}}{\text{income}} \text{ or } \frac{T}{Y}$$

$$\text{marginal tax rate} = \frac{\Delta \text{ tax paid}}{\Delta \text{ income}} \text{ or } \frac{\Delta T}{\Delta Y}$$

As a general rule, the average tax rate indicates the overall burden of the tax on the taxpayer, but the marginal rate may significantly affect economic choices and decision making. In the case of income tax, the marginal tax rate influences the choice between work and leisure when deciding how much labour to supply. It also influences decisions on whether to spend income on consumption or to save.

QUANTITATIVE SKILLS 9.3

Worked example: calculating the marginal tax rate

Assuming that all income between £30,000 and £38,000 is taxed at the same rate, if total tax paid is £4,000 when total income is £30,000 and £6,000 when income is £38,000, what is the marginal tax rate?

Income rises by £8,000 and the tax paid rises by £2,000. The marginal tax rate is:

$$\frac{\Delta T}{\Delta Y} \text{ or } \frac{£2,000}{£8,000}$$

which is 25%.

Automatic stabilisers

Reading through the first half of our coverage of fiscal policy, you might have concluded that the fiscal policy choice facing a government lies between Keynesian-style discretionary demand management and the 'balancing the budget' approach advocated by many supply-side economists. But in reality, there is an alternative approach that lies between these extremes, in which a government bases fiscal policy on the operation of automatic stabilisers. These dampen or reduce the multiplier effects resulting from any change in aggregate demand within the economy, thereby reducing the volatility of the 'ups' and 'downs' in the economic cycle. (The 'ups' and 'downs' in the economic cycle are illustrated in Figure 9.8. The upper panel of the diagram shows economic cycles in an economy in which there are no automatic stabilisers. The lower panel depicts less volatile cycles brought about by the operation of automatic stabilisers.)

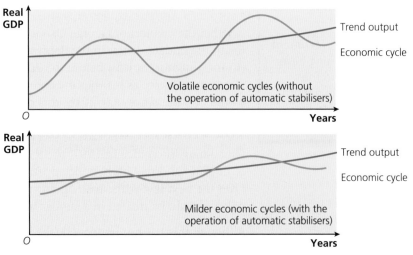

Figure 9.8 The shape of the economic cycle before and after the operation of effective automatic stabilisers

Suppose, for example, that a collapse of confidence or export orders causes aggregate demand to fall. National income then also begins to fall, declining by the initial fall in demand. But as national income falls and unemployment rises, *demand-led* public spending on unemployment pay and welfare benefits also rises. If the income tax system is progressive, the government's tax revenues fall faster than national income. In this way, increased public spending on transfers and declining tax revenues inject demand back into the economy, thereby stabilising and dampening the deflationary impact of the initial fall in aggregate demand, and reducing the overall size of the contractionary multiplier effect.

Automatic stabilisers also operate in the opposite direction to dampen the expansionary effect of an increase in aggregate demand. As incomes and employment rise, the take-up of means-tested welfare benefits and unemployment-related benefits automatically falls, while at the same time tax revenues rise faster than income. By taking demand out of the economy and reducing the size of the expansionary multiplier, automatic stabilisers reduce overheating in the boom phase of the economic cycle.

It is now widely agreed that automatic stabilisers such as progressive taxation and income-related transfers contributed to milder economic cycles experienced by the UK, prior to 2008 at least. Before 1939, economic cycles — or trade cycles, as they were then known — were much more volatile, displaying greater fluctuations between boom and slump than in the years between the Second World War and 1973. Keynesians claimed that the relatively mild economic cycles prior to 1973 are evidence of the success of Keynesian demand management policies in stabilising cyclical fluctuations.

However, the economic cycle was relatively mild both in the UK and in countries such as West Germany, which did not use fiscal policy to manage aggregate demand in a discretionary way. This could suggest that the automatic stabilisers of progressive taxation and the safety net provided by welfare benefits for the poor — both of which were introduced widely in western industrialised economies after 1945 — were more significant than discretionary fiscal policy in reducing fluctuations in the economic cycle. Either way, most economists now agree that a deficit should grow in the downswing of the economic cycle, provided the deficit is matched by

KEY TERMS

Office for Budget Responsibility advisory public body that provides independent economic forecasts and analysis of the public finances as background to the preparation of the UK budget.

national debt the amount of accumulated debt, resulting from past government borrowing, that is owed by the UK government. It is the stock of debt owed by the UK government both to UK residents and financial institutions, and also to overseas-based individuals and financial institutions. It has built up over many years as many UK governments have run budget deficits.

a surplus in the subsequent upswing. There is some doubt, however, as to whether the chancellor George Osborne accepted this view when taking action to cut the budget deficit in the depressed UK economy in 2010 and 2011. (In the outcome, at least before the 2015 general election, Osborne's cuts were not as severe as his rhetoric and government pronouncements said they would be.) But since May 2015, this might have changed.

The Office for Budget Responsibility

On coming into office in 1997, the then Labour government made the Bank of England and monetary policy operationally independent from the Treasury. Over the next few years, many politicians and economists argued that fiscal policy should be treated in a similar way.

Although this has not happened (the Treasury remains firmly in control of fiscal policy), in 2010 George Osborne, the incoming Conservative chancellor, created the **Office for Budget Responsibility** (OBR) to provide independent analysis of the UK's public sector finances.

The OBR produces medium-term forecasts of the UK economy twice a year in its *Economic and Fiscal Outlook*. By contrast, the Treasury compiles a monthly list of external economic forecasts, comparing them to those of the OBR. And instead of the chancellor making judgements based on Treasury forecasts, the OBR rules on whether the government's policy has a better than 50% chance of meeting the Treasury's fiscal targets.

Rule-based fiscal policy

In 2010 chancellor George Osborne had abandoned demand-side fiscal policy and reverted to supply-side fiscal policy. Before 2008, the Labour government had also introduced a rule-based fiscal policy, though this policy largely disintegrated with the onset of recession and the adoption of the demand-based fiscal stimulus. In 2010 the Coalition government introduced two new fiscal rules to replace those of Labour — the *deficit rule* and the *debt rule*. The OBR judges whether progress is being made toward achieving these two fiscal rules, which the government aims to meet in the medium term (that is, over a period of about 5 years).

- **The deficit rule**. According to the OBR, the deficit rule is to: 'Balance the cyclically-adjusted current budget (CACB) by the end of a rolling, five-year period.' This means taking action to get rid of the structural part of the budget deficit within 5 years, but without stating when the 5 years begin. Osborne's opponents interpreted this as meaning eliminating the structural deficit before the end of the 5-year 2010 parliament, i.e. by May 2015, but in fact the rule was adjusted as it soon became obvious that this was not going to be achieved. The definition of the deficit rule is in fact so woolly that it became impossible for Osborne to break it. But by the same token, as the rule did not bind the chancellor to a definite deficit-reduction programme, this largely reduced the rule's usefulness.
- **The debt rule**. This is more straightforward than the deficit rule, since the debt rule does not involve rolling forecast horizons and tricky definitions. The debt rule (relating to the **national debt** or debt of central government) was to 'Ensure that debt is falling as a share of GDP by 2015/16'. However, as this was not achieved, the debt rule has also been adjusted.

In 2011, the government published a *Charter for Budget Responsibility* which set out the main duties of the Office for Budget Responsibility. Each year in the annual budget, the chancellor republishes these duties. The 2015 summer budget, which outlined the fiscal policy of the newly elected Conservative government, stated the duties as follows:

1   The main duty of the OBR is to examine and report on the sustainability of the public finances.
2   The scope of this duty means the OBR has a broad remit. The remit provides for the OBR to investigate the impact of trends and policies on the public finances from a multitude of angles, including through forecasting, long-term projections and balance sheet analysis.
3   The duty feeds directly into the Treasury's fiscal objective to deliver sound and sustainable public finances.

CASE STUDY 9.3

The OBR as a fiscal watchdog

In 2012, Robert Chote, the OBR's chairman, explained the OBR's role as a 'fiscal watchdog':

The OBR is one of a new wave of independent fiscal watchdogs created in recent years. Academics have for some time thought that such bodies could help take some of the politics out of tax and spending policy in the same way that independent central banks had taken much of the politics out of monetary policy.

The core analytical argument for fiscal watchdogs is that, left to their own devices, democratic governments are prone to **'deficit bias'** and **'pro-cyclicality'** in their management of the public finances.

There are many possible reasons for such bias. Ministers may be seduced by their own rhetoric. Governments may be less forward-looking than voters, driven by elections and impatience. Finance ministries may be weaker than the large spending departments they are meant to control. You might expect outside scrutiny by unofficial bodies (such as the IFS) to be sufficient to counteract these tendencies. But governments can all too easily dismiss the scepticism of outside bodies by pointing out that government ministers have access to privileged information on the behaviour of tax revenues and public spending that outsiders lack.

The creation of the OBR was designed to breach that line of defence. We have been given a statutory entitlement to all the relevant information available within government necessary to fulfil our core duty — 'to examine and report on the sustainability of the public finances'.

In 2011 the OBR published the following list of other countries with longstanding, recent or forthcoming independent fiscal watchdogs:

● longstanding — Netherlands, Denmark, USA, Belgium
● recent — Sweden, Hungary, Canada, Slovenia, UK
● forthcoming — Ireland, Portugal, Slovakia

Since 2011, the list has extended to include about 25 countries. The three conditions that, in the OBR's view, must be met for a government agency or organisation to qualify or function as a fiscal watchdog are:

● clear fiscal watchdog function
● macroeconomic competence
● a high degree of independence from the political system

In a high-profile speech in 2013, prime minister David Cameron said that, according to the OBR, there is 'no alternative' to the government's fiscal austerity programme. But the next day, the OBR published a letter sent to the prime minister taking exception to his claims. A spokesperson at the OBR said that this shows that the OBR is truly independent and a fiscal watchdog rather than a fiscal lapdog.

Follow-up questions

1   Find out the meaning of the two bold terms: 'deficit bias' and 'pro-cyclicality'.
2   The OBR has claimed that it is a 'fiscal watchdog' rather than a 'fiscal lapdog'. What do these terms mean?

CASE STUDY 9.4

George Osborne and 'normal times'

In normal economic times governments should run an overall budget surplus, so our country is better prepared for whatever storms lie ahead. In short we should always fix the roof while the sun is shining.

Today I publish the new Fiscal Charter that commits our country to that path of budget responsibility. While we move from deficit to surplus, this Charter commits us to keeping debt falling as a share of GDP each and every year — and to achieving that budget surplus by 2019/20.

Thereafter, governments will be required to maintain that surplus in normal times — in other words, when there isn't a recession or a marked slowdown.

Only when the OBR judge that we have real GDP growth of less than 1% a year, will that surplus no longer be required.

Extracted from Chancellor George Osborne's Mansion House speech in the City of London, 11 June 2015

But what are 'normal times?

Commenting on Osborne's speech, Ben Brettell, senior economist at Hargreaves Lansdown, said: 'in practice the definition of normal is pretty arbitrary and subject to error'. And according to Ross Campbell, director of public sector at the Institute of Chartered Accountants in England and Wales: 'It seems an extraordinary proposal to legislate to constrain the fiscal policy choices of future elected governments, and one which looks more

like a political manoeuvre than being about sound management of the public finances.'

Robert Peston, the BBC's economics editor at the time, questioned whether:

'normal' growth is GDP growing at about 2.6% or so — the average rate of growth since 1945? Or in the wake of the productivity-smashing disaster of 2008, is underlying growth now nearer 2%? And would the de facto target for growth be a point, say 2%, or a range — a bit like the inflation target — of 2% plus or minus one percentage point?

Before the 2015 election the chancellor said that he would expect the Office for Budget Responsibility to be the arbiter of 'normal' times. Presumably the OBR will determine the UK's 'normal' rate of growth, every few years or so. But will it then decide at any particular moment whether current growth is sub-normal or supra-normal? And how often would it judge whether growth is normal and expected to remain so? Just twice a year, at the time of the autumn statement and in the Budget? Or would it be expected to make snap judgements as and when there is a big shock to the economy?

Would the OBR make the judgement about whether times are normal in retrospect, over the course of the most recent economic cycle, or would it do this in a forward-looking way that could be prescriptive of the chancellor's actions?

So although the idea of generating a surplus in normal times may seem to have the virtue of simplicity, in practice it may be fiendishly complicated.

Follow-up questions

1 In economic terms, what is meant by the expression 'we should always fix the roof while the sun is shining'?
2 Find out what has happened to the concept of 'normal times' since George Osborne first used the term in 2015.

The national debt

To remind you, the government's budget deficit is an example of an economic *flow* (and is the difference between the two much larger flows of government or public sector spending and government revenue) and must not be confused with the national debt, which is a *stock* concept. The budget deficit is measured over a period of time, usually one year, whereas the national debt is measured at a particular point in time.

STUDY TIP
Make sure you understand the difference between a *flow* and a *stock*, and can provide other examples of economic flows and stocks.

The national debt is a rather misleading term. It is *not* the debt of the whole nation, or even of the whole of the public sector (the public sector debt), with which it is often confused.

Rather, the national debt is the total stock of central government debt — the accumulated stock of central government borrowing which has built up over the years and which the government has not yet paid back.

In the Keynesian era, when almost continuous deficit financing led to a steadily rising nominal national debt in the UK, the national debt was not regarded as a burden on the population and reduction of the national debt was not really a fiscal policy objective. However, during this period the national debt as a proportion of nominal GDP was falling because the economy was growing and experiencing inflation. By contrast, in more recent years — and related to the aim of trying to reduce the levels of both public spending and public sector borrowing as proportions of national output — national debt reduction has become an important part of supply-side fiscal policy. Free-market supply-side economists are in favour of low levels of government spending and low levels of taxation, and are also, usually, in favour of the government running a balanced budget.

As we explained earlier in the chapter, whenever there is a central government budget deficit, the *nominal* national debt increases. (The size of the nominal national debt is the national debt measured in 'cash' or money terms for the year in question). A more useful measure of national debt is nominal debt as a percentage of nominal GDP. This ratio falls whenever nominal GDP grows at a faster rate than the nominal national debt, which itself can be explained either by fast economic growth, or by inflation, or by both.

From the mid-1990s until the first 2 years of the 2000s, the national debt as a percentage of GDP fell, bottoming out at 29% in 2002. However, from 2002 to 2007, the national debt increased to 37% of GDP. Despite the boom years in this period, this increase occurred as a result of the Labour government's decision to increase spending on health, education and social security.

If the rate of inflation is greater than the rate at which the budget deficit and borrowing requirement add to the nominal national debt, the money value of the debt as a proportion of money or nominal GDP falls. And if the rate of inflation is greater than the nominal interest rate the government pays to debt-holders, the government gains and debt-holders lose. This is an example of inflation redistributing wealth from lenders (holders of the national debt) to borrowers (the government), thereby reducing the real burden of the debt to the government. But if holders of the national debt catch on to this, they will try to demand much higher nominal interest payments as a condition for continuing to lend to the government.

Each year, part of the national debt matures and, unless there is a budget surplus, the government must also sell new debt in order to raise the funds with which to repay the maturing debt. This is called renewing or 'rolling over' the national debt. If the government is forced to pay higher nominal interest rates to provide lenders with a real return on their savings, this can lead to financial 'crowding out', a process we shall shortly explain.

The cost of *servicing* the national debt — represented by the interest payments to debt-holders — would not be a problem, first if the national debt were small, and second if all the debt were held *internally* by people living in the country. When the debt is internally held, servicing costs, apart from management costs, are really just a transfer from taxpayers (whose taxes are higher than they would be in the absence of debt interest payments) to debt-holders who have lent to the government. But when the debt is externally held by people living in other countries, the servicing burden of the national debt becomes significant for the country. We shall shortly examine this further in the context of the *sovereign debt problem*.

The national debt can also be divided into the *reproductive debt* and the *deadweight debt*. Suppose that the government sells gilts in order to finance the building of a motorway or some other capital investment or infrastructure project. Although the government is borrowing for a period of many years, the resulting liability is matched by a wealth-producing asset, the motorway. This type of 'reproductive' borrowing is not such a burden on future generations, since interest payments on the debt are in essence 'paid for' out of the motorway's contribution to future national output. (However, some capital assets such as schools and hospitals do not last 'for ever', whereas the debt incurred when they were built often does.) In contrast, any long-term borrowing to finance *current* spending (for example, on wars, the salaries of public sector employees or cash welfare benefits) can be regarded as a burden on future generations, whose taxes will be required to pay interest on the deadweight spending indulged in by the government today. Since the deadweight debt does not cover any real asset, interest payments end up being a burden on both current and future generations of taxpayers.

QUANTITATIVE SKILLS 9.4

Worked example: interpreting national debt statistics

In an economy, the cash value of the national debt increased from £1,000 billion in 2015 to £1,200 billion in 2016, while the nominal value of the country's GDP increased by 10% over the same period from its £1,600 billion value in 2015.

a What was the nominal national debt as a ratio of nominal GDP in 2015?
b What happened to this ratio over the year in question?
c What can we conclude about any change in the burden of the national debt over the year in question?

a In 2015 the ratio was £1,000bn/£1,600bn, which is 0.625 or 62.5%.
b In 2016, the ratio increased, calculated from £1,200bn/£1,760bn, which is 0.6818 or 68.18%.
c The burden of the national debt, measured by the nominal (or cash) value of the debt as a ratio of nominal national income, increased from 62.5% to 68.18%.

CASE STUDY 9.5

'We're paying down Britain's debts'

So said prime minister David Cameron, on 24 January 2013. It's not just the politicians who are in a muddle about the economy. Only a tiny proportion of Britons understand the difference between debt and deficit — or know which one the government is trying to reduce. According to a Centre for Policy Studies (CPS) report, *A Distorted Debate*, only 10% of Britons know that even after the government's cuts package the national debt was projected to increase by around £600 billion by 2015. Many more (47%) assumed — incorrectly — that the government wanted to reduce the debt by this amount. The think-tank report showed that the prime minister, his deputy and the chancellor all fed this confusion by making 'misleading' claims about their financial plans.

The confusion stems from 'debt' and 'deficit' being used interchangeably. In fact, the CPS report itself introduced another point of confusion, being unclear about the difference between the 'debt of the whole of the nation' and the national debt.

The CPS report went on to say: 'The Government has often said that it wants to pay off the debt on the nation's credit card. But if it wants to use that analogy correctly, it should be saying that it wants to reduce the amount that is added to the credit card debt each year — that is, reduce the amount of new borrowing.'

Follow-up questions

1 Explain why the national debt rises when there is a budget deficit.
2 Find out what has happened to the budget deficit and the national debt in both money terms and as a percentage of nominal GDP since 2015. Has the government met its fiscal rules?

EXTENSION MATERIAL

The sovereign debt problem

While you are not required to know about sovereign debt, your understanding of current economic problems will be weak and superficial if you don't know what sovereign debt is, and its implications for economic policy. Sovereign debt, which we described briefly in Book 1, does not refer to the amount of money the queen owes (though when the queen mother died at the age of 101 in 1992, she allegedly left debts of £7 million for UK taxpayers to pay!). Instead, sovereign debt is simply another name for public sector debt (which includes the national debt). Think of sovereign debt as the debt of the 'sovereign ship of state'.

Very often, however, the term 'sovereign debt' is used more narrowly to refer to the debt issued by a national government in a foreign currency and sold abroad, in order to finance public spending in the country issuing the debt. The UK's sovereign debt is owned by overseas financial institutions.

The sovereign debt problem emerges when countries are unable to pay back the debt, and very often the annual interest they are obliged to pay on the debt. In this situation, governments find it impossible to sell new debt overseas, unless they are prepared to pay exorbitantly high interest rates, which of course make the problem worse. Developing countries are most likely to be hit by the sovereign debt problem, though as the euro crisis has shown, developed countries such as Greece have also been badly affected. The UK has never really suffered the sovereign debt problem. However, during the financial crisis of 2007 and 2008, overseas financial institutions *feared* that the UK government might not be able to repay its debts, so UK interest rates rose to an extent.

So why does the size of overseas-owned debt create problems for UK economic policy? Several decades ago, UK governments financed budget deficits largely by borrowing from their own citizens. This is no longer the case. These days, much UK government borrowing takes place on international financial markets. Large UK budget deficits and borrowing requirements, together with the additional borrowing that has to take place to renew or 'roll over' public sector debt, require the rest of the world to lend huge amounts of money to the UK government. In this situation, international financiers may be reluctant to lend to Britain, except at ever-higher interest rates which the country cannot afford.

Overseas lenders are also influenced by the credit rating granted to UK government borrowing by credit-rating agencies such as Moody's, Fitch, and Standard and Poor. Before 2013, the UK government enjoyed a 'Triple A' rating with Standard and Poor and

Fitch, and the equivalent Aaa rating with Moody's. These ratings indicated that overseas investors had a high degree of confidence in the government's ability to repay its debt. However, in February 2013, Moody's cut the UK's rating from Aaa to Aa1, on the ground that UK growth would 'remain sluggish over the next few years'. Similarly, Fitch reduced the UK government's credit rating from AAA to AA+. Despite the UK economic recovery, by 2014 neither Moody's nor Fitch had restored the UK's top rating. Standard and Poor is the only one of the three credit rating agencies that has kept the UK government's rating at AAA, indeed upgrading the rating from AAA negative to AAA stable in June 2014.

The consequences of budget deficits and surpluses for macroeconomic performance

From the early 1950s to 1979, in the UK and in some other countries, mainly in western Europe and also the USA, Keynesian-inspired governments used discretionary macroeconomic policy, in the manner we described earlier, to manage the level of aggregate demand in the economy.

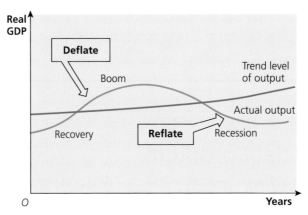

Figure 9.9 Deflating and reflating to 'smooth' the economic cycle

They did this by using contractionary fiscal and/or monetary policy to deflate aggregate demand in the boom phase of the economic cycle (see Figure 9.9), following this with expansionary fiscal and/or monetary policy to reflate (increase) aggregate demand to counter the downswing of the cycle. If successful, the economic cycle would be smoother and less volatile than would be the case had discretionary demand management not been used. And through better utilisation of labour and other resources throughout the cycle, the long-run trend rate of growth might improve. This is known as counter-cyclical demand management policy.

Pro-free-market or anti-Keynesian economists are against the use of Keynesian counter-cyclical demand management policies. They argue, in the first place, that with discretionary demand management, governments may get their timing wrong — deflating when they should be reflating, and vice versa. This outcome might be especially likely if governments reflate aggregate demand to win votes in a general election, when economic conditions suggest that they should resist this temptation. The time lags between the change in the state of the economy and when the policy becomes effective also cause problems for policy-makers wishing to fine-tune the economy. Free-market economists believe that our knowledge of the economy is imperfect and that in the medium term market forces will drive the economy towards its normal

SYNOPTIC LINK
At this point, you might like to read again our description of the 'political business cycle' in Book 1, page 194.

capacity level of output, without government intervention. They believe that government intervention is likely to contribute to greater cyclical instability rather than reduce it.

In the second place, whether or not governments get their timing wrong, pro-free-market economists argue that when discretionary fiscal policy is used to try to 'smooth' the economic cycle, the long-run trend rate of growth is likely to fall.

Anti-Keynesian economists also believe that deliberate use of deficit financing promotes a harmful crowding-out process. There are two types of crowding out: *resource crowding out* and *financial crowding out*. In Book 1, page 248, we explained the crowding out of resources which occurs when resources used by the government cannot simultaneously be employed in the private sector. However, in the context of the possible harmful effects of large budget deficits, financial crowding out is more relevant.

Financial crowding out results from the method of financing an increase in public spending. Public spending can be financed by taxation or borrowing. Taxation obviously reduces the spending power of the private individuals and firms paying the taxes. Suppose, however, that the government increases public spending by £40 billion, financing the resulting budget deficit with a sale of new gilt-edged securities (gilts) on the capital market. In order to persuade insurance companies, pension funds and the other financial institutions in the market for gilts to buy the extra debt, the guaranteed annual interest rate offered on new gilt issues must increase. But the resulting general rise in interest rates makes it more expensive for firms to borrow and to raise capital. Private sector investment thus falls and financial crowding out takes place. Higher interest rates are also likely to reduce household consumption.

When analysing the benefits and costs of budget deficits, Megan McArdle, a free-market economist, believes that we must again distinguish between the effects of cyclical and structural deficits. According to McArdle, Keynesian economists focus on cyclical deficits, which are not a big problem, whereas pro-free-market economists are more concerned about structural deficits, which can be a big problem.

When correcting cyclical fluctuation in the economy, government intervention may be effective, whether the intervention is based on discretionary demand management, or on the automatic fiscal stabilisers we explained earlier in the chapter. McArdle argues that this intervention can be thought of as 'Great Depression insurance'. In addition, the resulting debt is likely to be eaten away by inflation, so it will cost even less in real than nominal terms. Also, cyclical deficits should disappear as the economy recovers and in a boom a cyclical surplus should emerge, allowing some of the debt to be paid off.

The problem is the structural deficit: the mismatch between government spending and tax revenues that is unaffected by the phase of the economic cycle. The mismatch is manageable as long as the resulting growth of the national debt is roughly the same or less than the rate of GDP growth. In this situation, even persistent structural deficits can be tolerated because the debt to GDP ratio will not increase. But when the structural deficit begins to exceed the rate at which the economy is growing, the economy rapidly runs into trouble. Interest payments begin to grow as a proportion of the overall budget, and as they get bigger, the size of the tax increases or spending cuts needed to close the budget deficit starts to grow. Higher taxes may reduce incentives and cuts in spending will often harm the most vulnerable.

So what about budget surpluses? On the plus side, budget surpluses may reduce inflationary pressures by taking demand out of the economy, and, as we have explained, they enable the national debt to fall. However, persistent budget surpluses may induce harmful deflation caused by excessive depression of aggregate demand. They can also mean that taxes are higher than necessary, reducing potential growth by damaging the supply-side performance of the economy.

CASE STUDY 9.6

The following passage has been extracted, with the author's permission, from the 'Mainly Macro' web page published by the Oxford University professor of economic policy, Simon Wren-Lewis, on 18 April 2015. You can access the 'Mainly Macro' website on: **http://mainlymacro.blogspot.co.uk**.

Comparing two chancellors

There are three similarities between how the former Labour chancellor, Gordon Brown, and the Conservative chancellor George Osborne started their time in office. First, they both made important and progressive institutional changes: Brown established the Monetary Policy Committee and Osborne set up the Office for Budget Responsibility. Second, they both established fiscal rules that improved on past practice. Third, they both started with significant fiscal contractions.

So why will history judge Osborne so much more harshly than Brown? Why did Osborne's policy cost each UK household on average at least £4,000, while Brown's (inherited) contraction had no similar cost in terms of lost resources?

The answer, of course, is that the macro contexts were very different. Brown's fiscal contraction happened when the economy was relatively strong, and interest rates were above 6%. Osborne's austerity happened when the economy was just starting a recovery from a deep recession, and interest rates were at their then Zero Lower Bound (ZLB) of 0.5%. Mainstream macroeconomic theory says that these different contexts make all the difference: when interest rates are at the ZLB, monetary policy cannot counteract the negative impact of fiscal austerity on output.

Why did Osborne ignore this basic piece of macroeconomics? Was his policy based on an alternative macro theory? A remarkable speech he gave at the RSA [Royal Society for the encouragement of Arts, Manufactures and Commerce] in April 2009 suggests not. In that speech he said that his macro framework was based on New Keynesian theory, because that theory implied monetary policy should look after macro stabilisation and fiscal policy should focus on debt control. Yet New Keynesian theory also says that monetary policy becomes ineffective at the ZLB, and cutting government spending in that situation reduces output. Incredibly the speech makes no mention of the ZLB problem, even though UK interest rates had just hit 0.5%!

Osborne's proposals for more austerity after the 2015 election, if the Conservatives are part of the new government, risks making exactly the same mistake again, with interest rates still at or near their ZLB.

Follow-up questions

1 When were the Monetary Policy Committee (MPC) and the Office for Budgetary Responsibility (OBR) established?
2 Do you agree with Simon Wren-Lewis's view that history will 'judge Osborne so much more harshly than Brown'? Justify your answer.

9.2 Supply-side policies

Revisiting supply-side policies

Earlier in the chapter, in the section 'Using an *AD/AS* diagram to illustrate supply-side fiscal policy' (page 279), we described briefly, with the help of Figure 9.7, how supply-side fiscal policy can be used to try to increase the potential output of an economy and hence its long-run rate of economic growth. At this point you should go back and read this section again.

Go back also to Book 1, Chapter 9, which explains the main features of supply-side economics and supply-side policies. There, supply-side economics was defined as a branch of free-market economics arguing that government policy should be used to improve the competitiveness and efficiency of markets. Supply-side policies were defined as the set of government policies, micro as well as macro, which aim to improve national economic performance by creating competitive and more efficient markets. The important point was made there that supply-side *reform* or **supply-side improvements** can take place within the economy's private sector without being brought about explicitly by government policy. Nevertheless, a major aim of supply-side policies should be to encourage the reform of markets and the ways in which the economy's supply side operates.

Fiscal policy is a major element, perhaps even the dominant element, of supply-side policy. In the Keynesian era, fiscal policy played a central role in the UK in the creation of a mixed economy, based on the political consensus that the British economy should contain a mix of market and non-market economic activity, and of public and private ownership. However, the more supply-side and pro-free-market fiscal policy pursued in recent years has been very different. Along with more microeconomic supply-side policies such as privatisation and deregulation, fiscal policy has been used to change the mixed economy by increasing the role of markets and of private sector economic activity, and by reducing the economic role of the state, so as to create incentives among private individuals and firms for work, entrepreneurship, saving and investment.

To recap, the main features of supply-side fiscal policy implemented by recent British governments have included:

- Ceasing to use taxation and public spending as discretionary instruments of demand management. Under supply-side influence, recent governments have argued that a policy of using fiscal policy to stimulate or reflate aggregate demand to achieve growth and full employment is, in the long run, at best ineffective, and at worst damaging. They have argued that any growth of output and employment resulting from an expansionary fiscal policy is short-lived and that, in the long term, the main effect of such a policy is inflation, which quickly destroys the conditions necessary for satisfactory market performance and wealth creation.
- The adoption of a medium-term policy 'rule' (in place of short-term discretionary fiscal changes) to reduce public spending, taxation and government borrowing as proportions of national output. Besides wishing to reduce what they see as the inflationary effects of 'big government spending', many supply-side economists believe that the high levels of

government spending, taxation and borrowing of the Keynesian era led to the 'crowding out' of the private sector which we explained earlier in the chapter.

- A greater emphasis on microeconomic fiscal policy than on macroeconomic fiscal policy. Governments have subordinated the more macroeconomic elements of fiscal policy, which were dominant during the Keynesian era, to a much more microeconomic fiscal policy, combining an overall reduction in the levels of taxation and public spending with the intention of increasing incentives to effort and enterprise, aimed at improving economic performance on the supply side of the economy.

- Subordinating the overall stance of fiscal policy to the needs of monetary policy. As well as focusing on the microeconomic supply-side effects of fiscal policy, the macroeconomic elements of fiscal policy have also become subservient to the needs of monetary policy. Control over public spending and the borrowing needed to finance state spending is now regarded as a precondition for successful control of the conditions needed for monetary policy to control inflation.

Supply-side policies other than supply-side fiscal policy

We concluded our coverage of supply-side policies in Book 1 with a brief explanation of supply-side policies other than supply-side fiscal policy that have been used, or at least considered, by UK policy-makers. These included:

- Industrial policy measures such as privatisation, marketisation (or commercialisation), deregulation and the creation of internal markets.

- Labour market measures such as changing employment law to reduce the power of trade unions, removing trade unions' legal protection and reducing their power to bargain over pay, replacing collective bargaining with individual wage negotiation and employer determination of pay, restricting the right to strike and to undertake industrial action, introducing short-term employment contracts, including 'zero-hours' contracts, to replace 'jobs for life', and making it easier for employers to 'hire and fire' workers. (Labour-market-orientated supply-side policies also include reducing both marginal rates of income tax and state welfare benefits relative to average earnings, though these can also be classified as fiscal policy measures.)

- Financial and capital market measures involving deregulating financial markets and promoting competition in financial markets.

- Encouraging saving by giving individual shareholders first preference in the market for shares issued when former nationalised industries such as British Gas were privatised. However, most individual shareholders quickly sold their shares to institutional shareholders, which negated one of the main reasons for privatisation. It is also worth noting that in recent years, very low interest rates, brought about by the government's monetary policy, have discouraged saving. (Supply-side policies also include encouraging saving through the creation of tax privileges for saving, though once again this can be classified as a fiscal policy measure.)

- Promoting entrepreneurship. Governments have encouraged the growth of popular capitalism and an enterprise culture. Markets have been deregulated to encourage risk taking and company taxation has been reduced (again a fiscal policy measure).

To find out more about supply-side policies other than supply-side fiscal policy, you should revisit Book 1, Chapter 9, pages 264–65. Likewise, to understand the important role that creating incentives has in supply-side economics, go back and read the explanation of the Laffer curve on page 261 of the same chapter.

Non-interventionist versus interventionist supply-side policies

The supply-side policies that we have described so far in this chapter have generally been non-interventionist, in the sense that they have been used to 'free up' markets, to 'roll back' the economic functions of the state, and to replace public sector economic activity with that of the private sector. This view of the supply side of the economy stems also from the original use of the term 'supply-side economics' in the free-market revival 40 years ago.

However, interventionist policies can also be supply-side, provided that they aim to improve the efficiency and economic performance of individual firms, industries and markets. Interventionist supply-side policies include measures such as government spending on education and training, industrial and regional policy, spending on infrastructure such as motorways, and subsidising spending on research and development (R&D). Interventionist supply-side policies are based on the view that government intervention in the economy is needed to correct market failure and short-termism, which may reduce investment and growth, whereas more recent pro-free-market supply-side policies have generally aimed to correct and reduce government failure.

Some of the supply-side policies introduced and implemented by the Conservative/Lib-Dem coalition government between 2010 and 2015 were interventionist rather than non-interventionist. These included proposed public sector investment in high-speed rail links between London, Birmingham and the north, together with George Osborne's plan, announced in 2014, to transform the north of England into an economic 'powerhouse' with investment of up to £15 billion to finance the building of infrastructure, besides the already announced investment in High Speed 2 (HS2).

Developing further knowledge of supply-side economics and supply-side policies

Monetary policy and supply-side policies

When supply-side policies were first implemented nearly 40 years ago, extreme supply-side economists argued that *neither* monetary policy *nor* fiscal policy should be used to manage aggregate demand. Instead, government activity should be restricted to creating the supply-side conditions (and 'sound' money) in which markets function competitively and efficiently. Most free-market economists now accept that monetary policy should be used to manage demand, but that it should be supportive, both of the supply-side reforms introduced over the years, and of any further supply-side changes to be made in the future. The essential tasks of monetary policy are to make sure there is just enough demand to absorb the extra output produced by the supply side of the economy, and to maintain the general public's confidence in 'sound' money by achieving a low, stable inflation rate.

UK governments (and the Bank of England) now realise that, because monetary and fiscal policy are interdependent rather than independent of each other, the success of monetary policy depends on the fiscal policy implemented by the Treasury. As we have seen, whenever it runs a budget deficit, the government has to borrow to finance the difference between spending and revenue. Conversely, a budget surplus enables repayment of past borrowing and a fall in the national debt. As we explained in Chapter 8, governments borrow in two main ways, by selling short-dated debt or Treasury bills, and by borrowing long term by selling government bonds or gilts. Treasury bills are sold by the government to the banks, which create new bank deposits when they buy the bills. Because bank deposits are a form of money, this type of government borrowing increases the money supply and makes it difficult for monetary policy to control monetary growth.

By contrast, new issues of gilts are largely sold to non-bank financial institutions such as pension funds and insurance companies. To persuade these institutions to finance a growing budget deficit, the government may have to raise the rate of interest offered on new gilt issues. But higher interest rates discourage investment in capital goods by private sector firms. (This is the financial crowding-out process referred to earlier in this chapter.)

Either way, government spending financed by borrowing has implications for monetary policy and produces an arguably undesirable result. Either the borrowing increases the money supply (which may be inflationary), or it raises interest rates (which may crowd out private sector investment). The undesirable monetary consequences resulting from budget deficits and government borrowing explain why UK governments now try to make fiscal policy consistent with, and subordinate to, the needs of monetary policy.

Supply-side policies, the rate of inflation and the balance of payments

Supporters of the use of pro-free-market supply-side policies argue that by reducing business's costs of production and by reducing monopoly profits through making markets more price competitive, supply-side policies reduce cost-push inflationary pressures. Also, by enabling productive capacity to grow in line with aggregate demand, successful supply-side policies help to reduce demand-pull inflation pressures.

By creating 'lean and fit' firms, successful supply-side policies and supply-side reforms are also likely to improve the country's quality competitiveness. Highly competitive firms, which invest in product design and 'state-of-the-art' technology and methods of production, end up producing high-quality goods which customers demand. Taken together, increased price and quality competitiveness give the country a competitive edge, both in domestic and in overseas markets. With domestic customers switching to high-quality home-produced goods and overseas residents buying more of the country's exports, the country's balance of payments on current account should improve.

Expansionary fiscal contractionism

Figure 9.10 illustrates how chancellor George Osborne implemented fiscal policy in the period immediately after May 2010. Osborne believed that severe cuts in government spending would free resources for the private sector to use, and that the private sector would make better use of these resources than the government. If this was the case, workers who lose their jobs in the public sector would soon be employed more productively in the private sector. This view of how fiscal policy should operate has been called 'expansionary fiscal contractionism' (EFC) or 'expansionary austerity'. The expansionary fiscal contractionism hypothesis predicts that, given certain assumptions about how people behave, a major reduction in government spending that changes future expectations about taxes and government spending can expand private sector spending, resulting in overall economic expansion.

Not all economists accept the EFC hypothesis. Christina Romer at the University of California commented:

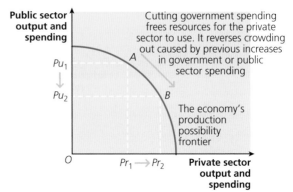

Figure 9.10 Expansionary fiscal contractionism

Despite what I feel is overwhelming and compelling evidence that fiscal stimulus is expansionary, and fiscal contraction is, well, contractionary, many politicians claim the opposite is true...But even more striking are the number who assert forcefully that fiscal austerity — getting the budget deficit down immediately — would be good for unemployment and growth.

ACTIVITY

Christina Romer expressed this view late in 2011, at a time when there was little evidence of economic recovery in the UK. Find out what has happened to economic growth in the UK since then. Do you think that George Osborne was right or wrong with regard to expansionary fiscal contractionism back in 2010? Justify your conclusion.

Bringing together three elements of supply-side macroeconomic theory

There can be no doubt that the transformation of Britain's economic performance...is above all due to the supply-side policies we have introduced to allow markets of all kinds to work better.

Nigel Lawson, Conservative chancellor of the exchequer, July 1988

The three panels of Figure 9.11 bring together three of the main elements of supply-side macroeconomics. The upper panel of the diagram depicts the economy's aggregate labour market, while the middle and lower panels respectively show the long-run vertical Phillips curve and long-run *AS* curve.

The upper and lower panels of Figure 9.11 respectively show equilibrium in the economy's aggregate labour market and in the economy's aggregate goods or product market. As the upper panel shows, the natural or 'equilibrium' level of employment E_{N1} is determined in the economy's aggregate labour market at real wage rate w_{FE}. When the labour market is in equilibrium, the number of workers willing to work equals the number of workers whom firms wish to hire.

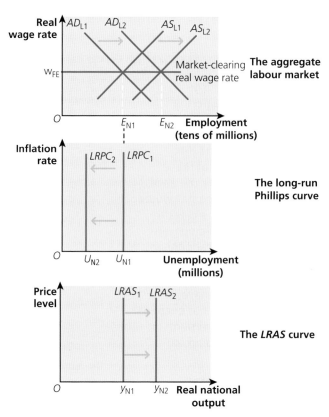

Figure 9.11 Bringing together the natural levels of employment and unemployment and *AD/AS* analysis in supply-side analysis

The middle panel of the diagram shows the natural *level* of unemployment U_{N1} (or natural *rate* if stated as a percentage of the labour force) immediately below E_{N1} in the upper panel. Likewise, the natural level of real output (y_{N1}), which is the same as the 'normal capacity' level of real output, is shown in the lower panel of the diagram, where the long-run aggregate supply curve ($LRAS_1$) is positioned immediately below U_{N1} (in the middle panel) and E_{N1} (in the top panel).

Having set up the three panels of the diagram in Figure 9.11, we can now analyse how, according to the supply-side view, tax cuts can affect employment, unemployment and the 'normal capacity' level of real output in the economy. Suppose the government cuts *employers'* national insurance contributions. Employment costs fall and it becomes more attractive for firms to employ labour. As a result, in the upper panel of Figure 9.11, the aggregate demand for labour curve shifts *rightward* from AD_{L1} to AD_{L2}. Likewise, if income tax is cut, this will increase workers' disposable income and thus the incentive to work, shifting the aggregate supply curve of labour *rightward* from AS_{L1} to AS_{L2}. Both these changes increase the economy's natural level of *employment*, which rises from E_{N1} to E_{N2}.

In the middle panel of Figure 9.11, the long-run Phillips curve shifts *leftward* from $LRPC_1$ to $LRPC_2$, which means that the economy's natural level of *unemployment* falls from U_{N1} to U_{N2}. Finally, the *increase* in the natural level of *employment* and the *fall* in the natural level of *unemployment*, depicted in the top two panels of the diagram, lead to a *rightward* shift of the long-run aggregate supply (*LRAS*) curve in the lower panel of the diagram. The curve shifts rightward from $LRAS_1$ to $LRAS_2$, which means the economy can produce more output without running into the wall of inflation.

SYNOPTIC LINK
At this point go back to Chapter 7 and read again the explanations on pages 220–21 and 199 respectively of the natural rate of unemployment (NRU) and the 'normal capacity' level of real output or GDP.

SUMMARY

- Over decades, UK fiscal policy developed from balanced budgets and 'sound finance' to Keynesian demand management, to supply-side fiscal policy, back to Keynesian demand management in 2008, and then back again to achieving supply-side improvements and macroeconomic stability in 2010.
- Taxes can be progressive, regressive or proportionate, and direct or indirect.
- The principles or canons of taxation are used to judge whether a tax is good or bad.
- Public spending is used to provide economic services, to transfer income from rich to poor and to pay interest on past government borrowing.
- Taxation and public spending have allocative, distributional and economic management aims.
- Keynesian fiscal policy centred on using discretionary changes in the budget deficit to manage aggregate demand, illustrated through shifts of the aggregate demand (AD) curve, and also on the use of automatic stabilisers.
- Progressive taxation and means-tested welfare benefits function as automatic stabilisers.
- Free-market supply-side fiscal policy focuses on shifting the long-run aggregate supply (LRAS) curve to the right by attempting to increase incentives to effort and enterprise.
- Interventionist supply-side policies also attempt to shift the long-run aggregate supply (LRAS) curve to the right, but they are based on the view that free markets are imperfect and may fail to deliver long-run growth unless the government intervenes.

Questions

1 Distinguish between the principles of taxation and the aims or objectives of taxation.

2 Explain the difference between the cyclical and the structural components of a budget deficit.

3 Explain how automatic stabilisers operate.

4 Evaluate the view that budget deficits and government borrowing are a cause for concern.

5 Evaluate the impact of measures undertaken by governments to reduce the budget deficit.

6 Do you agree that supply-side policies on their own are sufficient to help the economy achieve a stable, sustainable and satisfactory rate of economic growth? Justify your answer.

10 The international economy

10.1 Globalisation

The meaning of globalisation

Globalisation is the name given to the processes that integrate all or most of the world's economies, making countries increasingly dependent upon each other. Some economists argue that globalisation has occurred over centuries, going back at least as far as the creation of a system of relatively free worldwide trade in the nineteenth century. Perhaps it extends even further back to the Spanish and Portuguese occupation of much of South America.

KEY TERM

globalisation the process of growing economic integration of the world's economies.

In the late nineteenth century and the period before 1914, communication and transport networks expanded throughout much of the world and international trade grew significantly. At the same time, older industrial countries, and particularly the UK, began to invest their surplus savings in capital projects located overseas rather than in their domestic economies.

However, these changes are better described as aspects of *internationalisation* rather than *globalisation*. Globalisation, which has come to mean rather more than mere internationalisation of economic relationships, began to feature in the economics literature of the mid-1980s. The use of the term has increased dramatically ever since.

Recent globalisation has been made possible by improvements in information and communication technology (ICT), as well as by developments in transport and other more traditional forms of technology. Examples of globalisation include service industries in the UK dealing with customers through call centres in India, and fashion companies designing their products in Europe, making them in southeast Asia and finally selling most of them in North America.

Indeed, this textbook illustrates globalisation. The text on page ii of this book states that it is typeset in India, printed in Italy, while being written and published in England.

The main characteristics of globalisation

Some of the main characteristics of globalisation are:

- the growth of international trade and the reduction of trade barriers, known as trade liberalisation — a process encouraged by the **World Trade Organization** (WTO)
- greater international mobility of capital
- greater international mobility of labour
- a significant increase in the power of international capitalism and **multinational corporations** (MNCs) or transnational companies
- the deindustrialisation of older industrial regions and countries, and the movement of manufacturing industries to newly industrialising countries (NICs)
- more recently, the movement of internationally mobile service industries, such as call centres and accounts offices, to NICs
- a decrease in governmental power to influence decisions made by MNCs to shift economic activity between countries

A Thai Coca-Cola advert

Figure 10.1 depicts some of these characteristics or features of globalisation in the form of a 'mind map'.

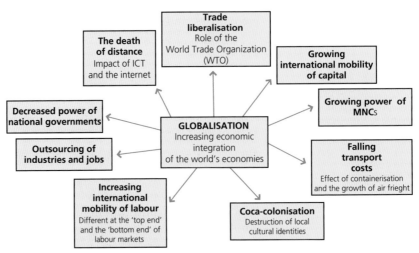

Figure 10.1 Some of the main characteristics or features of globalisation

The consequences of globalisation for less developed countries

KEY TERM

less developed countries countries considered behind in terms of their economy, human capital, infrastructure and industrial base.

Less developed countries are countries whose state of economic development is characterised by low national income per head, a high rate of population growth, low levels of human capital, high unemployment, poor infrastructure and overdependence on the export of a few primary commodities. Many nations in Asia, Africa and Latin America fit this model.

For the critics of globalisation, low-paid workers in sweatshops, farmers in the developing world being forced to grow genetically modified crops, the privatisation of state-owned industry in order to qualify for IMF and World Bank loans, and the growing dominance of US corporate culture and multinational companies symbolise what is wrong with globalisation in its effects on less developed countries.

According to this view, globalisation has led to a 'McDonaldisation' or 'Coca-Colonisation' of significant parts of the world's economy, which involves the destruction of local and national products, identities and cultures by US world brands. This process is to some extent offset by a process known as 'glocalisation'. This word, which is a combination of the words 'globalisation' and 'localisation', reflects the idea that a global product or service is more likely to succeed if it is adapted to local practices and cultural expectations. An example of glocalisation is McDonald's restaurants offering menus to satisfy local tastes in different countries. In this sense, glocalisation is an extension of globalisation, being another way of extending the reach of global brands.

Closely related to the 'world brand' process, there has been controversy concerning the treatment of local labour by multinational corporations. On the one hand, companies such as Nike are accused of selling trainers and footballs in developed countries such as the UK, at prices far above the cost of raw materials and the low wages paid to workers in developing countries who make the goods. On the other hand, the multinationals argue that the 'low wages' they pay far exceed the local wages paid by indigenous firms. They believe this encourages local wages to rise. MNCs also claim to improve labour productivity, health and safety and other labour market conditions in the poor countries in which they operate.

The consequences of globalisation for more developed countries

The anti-globalisation argument that 'Coca-colonisation' of significant parts of the world's economy has had a harmful effect on the economies of less developed economies is not accepted by supporters of globalisation, who believe that people in the rest of the world demand the products supplied by global corporations because they consider them superior to traditional local produce.

The anti-globalisation lobby also believe that, by threatening to close down factories and offices in **more developed countries** and to move production to poor countries, MNCs may reduce wages and living standards in developed countries. The significance of this depends on the type of jobs that emerge in developed countries to replace those lost through deindustrialisation and globalisation. Are the new jobs being created in the highly skilled service sector, or are they menial, low-paid, unskilled 'McJobs'?

The arguments used so far in this and the previous section have been cast somewhat in a 'lose/win' or 'win/lose' format, implying that winners gain at the expense of losers. However, supporters of globalisation who believe that the world as a whole is a net winner from the globalisation process argue that globalisation stems in part from the massive increase in world trade that has taken place since the Second World War. This itself has only been possible because of increased trade liberalisation and the reduction of import controls and other forms of protectionism. They believe that free trade leads to a better allocation of resources and that additional benefits have been derived from international competition and the spread of technology making most people better off.

The belief that globalisation benefits most countries — less developed countries as well as more developed countries — has been attacked by supporters of the *dependency theory* of trade and development. Dependency theorists argue that many developing countries possess little capital because the system of world trade and payments has been organised by developed industrial economies to their own advantage. The terms of trade — the ratio of a country's export prices to its import prices — have generally moved in favour of industrialised countries and against primary producers. This means that, by exporting the same amount of manufactured goods to the developing world, a developed economy can import a greater quantity of raw materials or foodstuffs in exchange. By the same token, the developing country must export more in order to buy the same quantity of capital goods or energy vital for development. Globally, the movement of the terms of trade in favour of developed nations has raised levels of income and standards of living in the richer countries at the expense of poorer developing countries. However, there have been exceptions, such as the oil-producing non-industrial countries, which, until 2014 at least, benefited from substantial increases in the price of oil during recent decades.

Economists of the dependency school argue that the transfer of wealth and resources to the richer countries is further promoted by profit flows and interest payments. On an international scale, dividends and profits flow to multinational corporations with headquarters in North America, western Europe and Japan from their subsidiaries in the developing world. Similarly, there is a flow of interest payments to western banks from loans originally

---

SYNOPTIC LINK
See page 314 for an explanation of 'North–North' and 'North–South' patterns of world trade.

made to finance development in developing countries. In most years, flows of dividends and interest payments from 'South' to 'North' exceed aid flows in the opposite direction. (The countries of the 'North' include the USA, the UK, Germany, France and Japan, and all other countries benefiting from a high degree of economic development. The 'North' gets its name from the fact that most of the countries which comprise the 'North' are geographically located to the north of most of the countries of the 'South'. The latter are poorer developing countries located in parts of the world such as sub-Saharan Africa.)

Free-market economists generally support globalisation and regard its growth as inevitable. They argue that the benefits of further global economic integration, which include the extension of political freedom and democracy as well as the economic benefits of more production and higher living standards, significantly exceed the disadvantages, such as the destruction of local cultures. However, opponents argue that globalisation is a respectable name for the growing exploitation of the poor, mostly in developing countries, by international capitalism and US economic and cultural imperialism.

Globalisation in the service sector

Until quite recently, it was said that manufacturing was much more internationally mobile than service sector employment, but this is now disputed. Call centres became one of the fastest-growing sources of employment in the UK in the 1980s and 1990s. At that time, UK-based companies favoured locating call centres in regions of high unemployment (and relatively low wages) within the UK. To some extent this has now changed. Many call centres and back-office activities of firms in industries such as financial services have been moved to less developed countries, notably on the Indian subcontinent, and also to the eastern member countries of the **European Union** (EU), such as the Czech Republic. These movements result from the death of distance, which is an important part of the globalisation process. The rapid development of electronic methods of communication means that many service activities can now be located anywhere in the world, with little or no effect on a company's ability to provide the service efficiently to its customers.

Four factors encouraging the overseas location of call centres have been:

- relatively low wages in developing countries and in eastern and central Europe
- highly reliable and cheap telecommunications
- 24-hour shift employment to overcome the problem of time zones
- workers fluent in English, which is now the world's business language

However, for call centres, a fifth factor is often lacking: many overseas workers are insufficiently familiar with UK culture and habits, which leads to a communication problem. This has recently led to some call centres being relocated back to the UK. This disadvantage is much less significant for back-office employment: for example, employing people in India to administer a UK company's accounts.

Global labour and capital mobility

As the previous paragraphs indicate, globalisation involves moving capital to lower-cost labour much more than it involves allowing low-paid workers born in poor countries to enter rich countries in North America and Europe. However, since the late nineteenth century there has been a much greater

KEY TERM
European Union an economic and partially political union established in 1993 after the ratification of the Maastricht Treaty by members of the European Community and since expanded to include numerous central and eastern European nations.

movement of poor people into rich countries than ever before. To some extent, immigration controls introduced by countries such as the USA and Australia, which replaced an earlier completely free movement of labour, have slowed this process. But this has been offset by illegal immigration and the fact that rich countries informally encourage migration to fill the relatively low-paid jobs that their own citizens do not wish to do. MNCs recruit skilled labour from other countries and governments also encouraging highly trained and talented individuals to migrate to fill skill shortages.

Enlargement of the EU is increasing both labour and capital mobility on a regional basis. Western European firms have been moving eastward, but this is balanced by workers from countries such as Poland and Hungary migrating westward. Nonetheless, it is still much easier in a globalised world for a brain surgeon or a highly paid business executive to move between countries than it is for a Chinese or Indian peasant.

Globalisation and the power of national governments

In recent decades, globalisation has considerably reduced the power of national governments, certainly in smaller countries, to control multinational firms operating within their boundaries. National governments have also lost much of the freedom to undertake the economic policies of their choice with respect to managing domestic economies. Governments enjoy less freedom to introduce tariffs and other import controls. At the same time, capital flows into and out of currencies severely constrain a government's ability to implement an independent monetary policy, even when the country's exchange rate is freely floating.

The World Trade Organization's role in promoting globalisation

Economists and politicians who believe that the benefits of globalisation far exceed any disadvantages involved claim there has been too little rather than too much international integration of countries' economies. In their view, if countries get rid of all protectionist measures, then Adam Smith's 'invisible hand' of the market will promote international trade, which then benefits poor countries as well as rich ones. This view of the world lies behind the creation of the World Trade Organization (WTO), the international organisation established to remove trade barriers and liberalise world trade.

CASE STUDY 10.1

Has globalisation given way to de-globalisation?

Robert J. Samuelson of Investors.com recently asked: 'What has happened to globalisation?' Samuelson argued that for decades, growing volumes of cross-border trade and money flows have fuelled strong economic growth. But something remarkable is happening — trade and money flows are slowing and, in some cases, declining. Samuelson pondered whether these changes herald prolonged economic stagnation and rising nationalism or, optimistically, whether they make the world economy more stable and politically acceptable.

For workers employed or previously employed in US manufacturing industries, some aspects of de-globalisation are very attractive. Globalisation has sucked factory jobs out of North America. But now, the tide may be turning. Apple has announced a $100 million investment to return some Mac computer manufacturing back to the USA. Though small, the decision may reflect a new trend.

General Electric's sprawling Appliance Park in Kentucky once symbolised America's manufacturing prowess, with employment peaking at 23,000 in 1973. Since then, jobs have shifted abroad or succumbed to automation. However, now GE is moving production of water heaters, refrigerators and other appliances back to Appliance Park from China and Mexico. Nor is GE alone. Otis is moving some elevator output from Mexico to South Carolina.

China's labour cost advantage has eroded. In 2000, Chinese factory wages averaged 52 cents an hour; but annual double-digit percentage increases will

have brought that to $6 an hour in high-skilled industries by 2015.

Although wages of US production workers average $19 an hour, other non-wage factors favour the USA. American workers are more productive; automation has cut labour costs, and cheap natural gas further lowers costs; finally, until 2014 at least, higher oil prices boosted freight rates for imports. According to some estimates, by 2015 China's overall cost advantage had shrunk to 7%.

As important for the USA is the likelihood that the USA will maintain significant cost advantages over other developed-country manufacturers: 15% over France and Germany; 21% over Japan; and 8% over the UK. The USA will be a more attractive production platform. In America, imports will weaken; exports will strengthen.

Follow-up questions

1 Has there been any evidence of manufacturing jobs being attracted back to the UK in recent years?
2 How might the slowing down of globalisation processes be linked to the recession which hit the global economy in 2008–09? Since that time, has there been a recovery in the globalisation process?

10.2 Trade

In Book 1, page 217, we described a small closed economy (we used the example of Iceland) whose production possibilities are limited to the goods and services that its narrow resource base can produce. This means that its average costs of production are likely to be high because the small population and the absence of export markets mean that economies of scale and long production runs cannot be achieved. At the same time, the consumption possibilities of the people living within the country are restricted to the goods that the country can produce.

We then compared this to the opportunities the country could face in a world completely open to international trade. In an open world economy, the country's ability to import raw materials and energy would greatly boost its production possibilities. In theory at least, the country could now produce a much wider range of goods and services. In practice, however, the country might specialise in the production of the relatively few goods and services that it produces most efficiently, and import all the rest. By gaining access to the much larger world market, the country's industries would benefit from economies of scale and long production runs. Likewise, imports of food and other consumer goods would present the country's inhabitants with a vast array of choice and the possibility of a much higher standard of living and level of economic welfare than could be achieved in a world without trade.

The model of comparative advantage

We shall follow this rather 'common sense' justification of the benefits of international specialisation and trade with a more rigorous explanation provided by the principle of comparative advantage.

To show how the principle of *comparative advantage* explains some of the benefits of international specialisation and free trade, it is helpful to look first at a related concept: *absolute advantage*.

Absolute advantage

A country has an **absolute advantage** if it can produce more of a good with a given amount of resources than another country. (Alternatively, we may say that it can produce the same amount of the product with fewer resources.)

To explain absolute advantage, we shall assume just two countries in the world economy, Atlantis and Pacifica. Each country has only 2 units of resource. Only two goods can be produced: guns and butter. Each unit of resource, or indeed a fraction of each unit (because we shall assume that resources or inputs are divisible), can be switched from one industry to another, if so desired, in each country. Table 10.1 shows each country's production possibilities from 1 unit of resource.

Table 10.1 Production with 1 unit of resource

	Guns		Butter
Atlantis	4	or	2 tonnes
Pacifica	1	or	6 tonnes

Quite clearly, Atlantis has an absolute advantage in producing guns. It is four times better in gun production than Pacifica. However, this is not the case for butter production. Pacifica is three times better in butter production and so possesses an absolute advantage in this good.

Suppose that both countries devote half their total resources to each activity (that is, 1 unit of resource out of the 2 units available for each country). We shall call this *production without specialisation*. Without specialisation, Atlantis produces 4 guns and Pacifica produces 1 gun, which means that 5 guns are produced in total. Likewise, without specialisation, total butter production is 8 tonnes. Atlantis produces 2 tonnes and Pacifica produces 6 tonnes. Table 10.2 shows the outcome.

Table 10.2 Production without specialisation

	Guns		Butter
Atlantis	4	and	2 tonnes
Pacifica	1	and	6 tonnes
Total output without specialisation	5	and	8 tonnes

Now let's see what happens when each country produces only the good in which it has an absolute advantage. Table 10.3 shows that if Atlantis devotes both its resource units to guns, it produces 8 guns. Likewise, if Pacifica completely specialises, the country produces 12 tonnes of butter with its 2 units of resource.

Table 10.3 Production with complete specialisation

	Guns		Butter
Atlantis	8	and	0 tonnes
Pacifica	0	and	12 tonnes
Total output with complete specialisation	8	and	12 tonnes

The final table in this series, Table 10.4, shows how, when each country enjoys an absolute advantage in a different good, complete specialisation results in more of both goods being produced.

Table 10.4 Output gain from complete specialisation

	Guns		Butter
Atlantis	8	and	0 tonnes
Pacifica	0	and	12 tonnes
Total output without specialisation	5	and	8 tonnes
Total output with complete specialisation	8	and	12 tonnes
Output gains from specialisation	3	and	4 tonnes

In this example, specialisation produces a net output gain of 3 guns and 4 tonnes of butter. Since more has been produced, more can be consumed and it is possible to make people better off.

However, for *output* gains to translate into gains from *trade*, two further factors have to be taken into account. First, administration and transport costs occur whenever trade takes place. As a result, the net gains from trade are:

(3 guns + 4 tonnes of butter) – transport and administration costs

Clearly, specialisation and trade are not worthwhile if transport and administration costs exceed the output gains resulting from specialisation.

Second, assuming that only two countries trade with each other, for output gains to transfer into *welfare* gains for the inhabitants of both countries, the goods being traded must be in demand in each of the importing countries. Given this assumption about demand, we shall further assume that each country exports its surplus to the other country once it has satisfied its own inhabitants' demand for the good in which it specialises. (This *double coincidence of wants* is not necessary when more than two countries trade together.)

But suppose Atlantis's inhabitants are vegans who refuse to eat animal products, while Pacifica's inhabitants are pacifists who hate guns. For Atlantis's inhabitants, butter is a 'bad' rather than a good. Likewise, guns are a 'bad' for Pacifica's residents. (A good yields utility or economic welfare to consumers, but a bad yields disutility or negative welfare.) Atlantis refuses to import butter, and Pacifica refuses to buy guns. Specialisation and trade do not take place. Without suitable demand conditions, the case for specialisation and trade disappears.

Comparative advantage

Absolute advantage must not be confused with the rather more subtle concept of **comparative advantage**. However, understanding absolute advantage is a stepping-stone to understanding comparative advantage. To explain comparative advantage, we shall change the production possibilities of both countries so that Atlantis possesses the absolute advantage for both guns and butter (which means that Pacifica has an absolute disadvantage in both goods). Table 10.5 shows how much 1 unit of resource can produce in each country.

Table 10.5 Production with 1 unit of resource

	Guns		Butter
Atlantis	4	or	2 tonnes
Pacifica	1	or	1 tonne

Although Atlantis is 'best at' — or has an absolute advantage in — producing both guns and butter, the country possesses a comparative advantage in the production of guns but has a comparative disadvantage in the production of butter. *This is because comparative advantage is measured in terms of opportunity cost, or what a country gives up when it increases the output of a product by 1 unit.* The country that gives up least of the other commodity when increasing output of a particular commodity by 1 unit possesses a comparative advantage in that good. Ask yourself how many guns Atlantis has to give up in order to increase its output of butter by 1 tonne. The answer is 2 guns. But Pacifica only has to give up 1 gun to produce an extra tonne of butter. Thus Pacifica possesses a comparative advantage in butter production even though it has an absolute disadvantage in both products.

Table 10.6 shows the total output of guns and butter, if each country devotes 1 unit of resource to each industry.

Table 10.6 Production without specialisation

	Guns		Butter
Atlantis	4	and	2 tonnes
Pacifica	1	and	1 tonne
Total output without specialisation	5	and	3 tonnes

When one country possesses an absolute advantage in both products, as in the example above, its comparative advantage always lies in producing the good in which its absolute advantage is greater. Similarly, the country that has an absolute disadvantage in both activities possesses a comparative advantage in the product in which its absolute disadvantage is less. The table shows that Atlantis has a comparative advantage in gun production, while Pacifica's comparative advantage lies in butter production.

In this example, as Table 10.7 shows, complete specialisation results in more guns but less butter being produced, compared to a situation in which each country devotes half its total resources to each activity. Without specialisation, the combined output of both countries is 5 guns and 3 tonnes of butter. With complete specialisation, this changes to 8 guns and 2 tonnes of butter. While production of guns has increased, production of butter has fallen.

Table 10.7 Output gain from complete specialisation

	Guns		Butter
Atlantis	8	and	2 tonnes
Pacifica	0	and	1 tonne
Total output without specialisation	5	and	3 tonnes
Total output with complete specialisation	8	and	2 tonnes
Output gains from specialisation	3		–1 tonne

When one country has an absolute advantage in both goods, complete specialisation in accordance with the principle of comparative advantage does not result in a net output gain. The output of one good rises, but the output of the other good falls.

Students are puzzled by this, thinking (wrongly) that because of the loss of output of one of the two goods, specialisation cannot lead to gains from trade. However, *partial* specialisation can produce a net output gain. For example, suppose Pacifica (which suffers an absolute disadvantage in both goods) specialises completely and produces 2 tonnes of butter. By contrast, Atlantis (which has the absolute advantage in both goods) devotes just enough resource (half a unit) to top up world production of butter to

3 tonnes. This means that Atlantis can still produce 6 guns using 1.5 units of resource. Total production in both countries is therefore 6 guns and 3 tonnes of butter. At least as much butter and more guns are now produced compared with the 'no specialisation' outcome. This example shows that specialisation can produce a net output gain, even though one country is absolutely better at both activities.

Another way of stating this is that for both countries to benefit from trade, the terms of trade must lie between the two countries' opportunity cost ratios. The terms of trade is the rate at which two products are exchanged for each other. In our example, a terms of trade where 1 gun is exchanged for 0.75 tonnes of butter would be beneficial for both countries. Atlantis would benefit because, by producing and exporting 1 gun, it would gain 0.75 tonnes of butter, whereas if it had produced its own butter, it would have gained only 0.5 tonnes of butter for each gun it gave up producing. Pacifica benefits because, through trade, it can get a gun by producing and exporting 0.75 tonnes of butter. If it had produced its own guns, it would have had to sacrifice 1 tonne of butter.

STUDY TIP
Make sure you don't confuse the 'terms of trade' with the 'balance of trade'. The balance of trade is a major part of the balance of payments on current account, which is explained later in this chapter. The balance of trade is the difference in value between a country's imports and exports. If the value of exports exceeds the value of imports, there is a balance of trade surplus. Conversely, if the value of exports is less than the value of imports, there is a balance of trade deficit.

EXTENSION MATERIAL

Adam Smith, David Ricardo and absolute and comparative advantage

Although he did not use the precise term, Adam Smith is credited with introducing the concept of absolute advantage in his great eighteenth-century book, *The Wealth of Nations*. Some years later, in the early nineteenth century, another distinguished classical economist, David Ricardo, developed Adam Smith's ideas into the principle of comparative advantage. Neither Smith nor Ricardo was interested solely in abstract economic theory. Instead, like many great economists, they wished to change society for the better by influencing the politicians of their day.

The assumptions underlying the principle of comparative advantage

When arguing that definite benefits result when countries specialise and trade in accordance with the principle of comparative advantage, we made a number of rather strong but not necessarily realistic assumptions. Indeed, the case for trade — and hence the case *against* import controls and other forms of protectionism — is heavily dependent upon these assumptions. Likewise, some of the arguments in favour of import controls and against free trade, which we shall explain shortly, depend on showing that the assumptions necessary for the benefits of specialisation and trade to occur are simply not met in real life.

The assumptions underlying the principles of comparative advantage are as follows:

- Each country's endowment of factors of production, including capital and labour, is fixed and immobile between countries, although factors can be switched between industries within a country. In the course of international trade, finished goods rather than factors of production or inputs are assumed to be mobile between countries.
- There are *constant returns to scale*. In our example, 1 unit of resource is assumed to produce 4 guns or 2 tonnes of butter in Atlantis, whether it is the first unit of resource employed or the millionth unit. But in the

real world, increasing or decreasing returns to scale are both possible and indeed likely. In a world of increasing returns to scale, the more a country specialises in an activity in which it initially has an absolute advantage, the more its productive efficiency and advantage increases. Countries that are 'best' to start with become even 'better'. But if decreasing returns to scale occur, specialisation erodes efficiency and destroys a country's initial advantage. A good example occurs in agriculture, where over-specialisation can result in monoculture or the growing of a single cash crop for export. Monoculture often leads to soil erosion, vulnerability to pests and falling future agricultural yields.

● Demand and cost conditions are relatively stable. Over-specialisation can cause a country to become particularly vulnerable to sudden changes in demand or to changes in the cost and availability of imported raw materials or energy. Changes in costs, and new inventions and technical progress, can quickly eliminate a country's earlier comparative advantage. The greater the uncertainty about the future, the weaker the case for a country specialising in a narrow range of products.

STUDY TIP

There are other justifications of specialisation and free trade beside the argument that global economic welfare increases if countries specialise and trade in accordance with the principle of comparative advantage. We mentioned a justification earlier in our discussion of widening production possibilities and consumption possibilities. A further justification, also mentioned briefly, is the ability to enjoy the benefits of economies of scale that lead to greater efficiency and lower average costs. (If you remember from Chapter 2, economies and diseconomies of scale are closely linked to increasing returns to scale and decreasing returns to scale.)

EXTENSION MATERIAL

Comparative advantage and competitive advantage

Comparative advantage must not be confused with *competitive* advantage. A country, or a firm within a country, enjoys a competitive advantage when it produces better-quality goods at lower costs and better prices than its rivals. Competitive advantage is more similar to absolute advantage than to comparative advantage.

Dynamic factors that promote the growth of firms can create competitive advantage. Successful investment undertaken over many years equips a country with modern, 'state-of-the-art' production capacity, capable of producing high-quality goods that people want to buy. Properly funded and organised research and development (R&D) contributes in a similar way, while the stock of human capital resulting from investment in education and training adds to competitive advantage.

Factors that create competitive advantage can trigger a virtuous spiral of larger profits, higher investment, better products and greater sales, which in turn leads to even higher profits, and so on. Conversely, countries and firms that are not competitive may enter a vicious spiral of decline. Inability to compete causes profits to fall, which in turn reduces investment. The quality of goods declines and sales are lost to more competitive countries or firms. Profits again fall (maybe disappearing altogether), and a further round in the vicious circle of decline is unleashed.

Supporters of free trade argue that the increased competition between countries which an absence of import duties and other forms of protectionism creates are exactly the circumstances needed to foster the growth of competitive advantage. However, as we shall see in the next section, in our coverage of strategic trade theory, others argue that, if used *strategically*, protectionism is better at providing selected industries with a competitive advantage against the rest of the world.

The case for import controls and protectionism

Import controls can be divided into quantity controls such as import **quotas**, which put a maximum limit on imports, and **tariffs** or import duties (and their opposite, **export subsidies**), which raise the price of imports (or reduce the price of exports).

Supporters of free trade believe that import controls prevent countries from specialising in activities in which they have a comparative advantage and from trading their surpluses. As a result, production takes place inefficiently and economic welfare is reduced. However, as already noted, the case for free trade depends to a large extent upon some of the assumptions underlying the principle of comparative advantage. Relax these assumptions and the case for free trade is weakened. Nevertheless, it should be remembered that the proponents of free trade also emphasise the dynamic benefits that result from opening up an economy to competition from abroad.

Below are some of the contexts in which import controls have been justified.

- **Infant industries.** As already explained, many economic activities benefit from increasing returns to scale, which mean that the more a country specialises in a particular industry, the more productively efficient it becomes. This increases its competitive advantage. Developing countries justify the use of import controls to protect infant industries from established rivals in advanced economies. It is argued that protectionism is needed while newly established industries develop and achieve full economies of scale.

- **Sunset industries.** A rather similar case to the infant industry argument is sometimes made in advanced industrial economies such as the UK to protect older industries from the competition of infant industries in developing countries. Some economists advocate the selective use of import controls as a potentially effective supply-side policy instrument to prevent unnecessary deindustrialisation and to allow orderly rather than disruptive structural change in the manufacturing base of the economy. According to this view, import controls are justified, at least on a temporary basis, to minimise the social and economic cost of the painful adjustment process, as the structure of an economy alters in response either to changing demand or to changing technology and comparative and competitive advantage. Labour is not perfectly mobile and import controls may help to reduce the incidence of structural unemployment.

- **Strategic trade theory.** The infant and sunset industry arguments are closely related to strategic trade theory, a relatively new theory that has grown in influence in recent years. Strategic trade theory argues that comparative and competitive advantage are often not 'natural' or 'God-given'. Rather, governments try to create competitive advantage by nurturing strategically selected industries or economic sectors. This justifies protecting the industries while competitive advantage is being built up. The skills that are gained will then spill over to help other sectors in the economy. Strategic trade theory also argues that protectionism can prevent exploitation by a foreign-based monopoly.

   More developed countries use two types of strategic trade policy to help declining industries such as textiles and shipbuilding. Their governments provide trade adjustment assistance and other aid to workers and firms in these industries. They also use subsidies on exports or taxes on imports and investment or adjustment assistance subsidies to protect the industries from foreign competition. However, export subsidies, with few exceptions, such as agricultural products, violate World Trade Organization rules. By contrast, less developed countries use strategic trade policies to protect and promote the growth of their infant industries.

- **Agricultural efficiency.** As noted earlier, monoculture, which might result from specialisation and trade, erodes efficiency and destroys comparative advantage that existed before specialisation took place. Decreasing returns to scale weaken the case for complete specialisation.

- **Changes in demand or cost conditions.** Over-specialisation may cause a country to become particularly vulnerable to sudden changes in demand or to changes in the cost and availability of imported raw materials or energy. Specialisation can lead to a lack of diversity in a country's economy. In this situation, countries could benefit from diversifying their economies, and import controls might lead to this outcome.

- **Anti-dumping.** When a country produces too much of a good for its own domestic market, the surplus may then be 'dumped' and sold at a price below cost in overseas markets. Import controls are often justified as a means to prevent this supposedly 'unfair' competition. Article 6 of the General Agreement on Tariffs and Trade allows countries to protect themselves against dumping where there is a material injury to the competing domestic industry.

- **Self-sufficiency.** Politically, it is often argued that protection is necessary for military and strategic reasons to ensure that a country is relatively self-sufficient in vital foodstuffs, energy and raw materials in a time of war.

- **Employment.** Trade unions argue that import controls are necessary to prevent multinational firms shifting capital to low-wage developing countries and exporting their output back to the countries from which the capital was moved. They further argue the case for employing labour, however inefficiently, in protected industries rather than allowing labour to suffer the greatest inefficiency of all: mass unemployment. This is an example of *second-best theory*. The second-best argument stems from the fact that the 'first best' (free trade in a world of fully employed economies and perfect markets) is unattainable. Therefore, a country can settle legitimately for the second best. Employing resources perhaps inefficiently, protected by tariffs, is better than leaving resources, such as labour, unemployed. This justification for protecting domestic industries and maintaining employment returned to prominence after the financial crisis, at around the time that Barack Obama took over the US presidency in 2009.

STUDY TIP
When considering the case for free trade (or the case for import controls) it is best to avoid a 'shopping list' approach. Instead, select, develop, analyse and evaluate three or four arguments or counter-arguments. Also consider the likelihood of retaliation and its implications.

STUDY TIP
The case for free trade, or trade liberalisation, is the case against import controls and other forms of protectionism. Likewise the case for import controls is the case against free trade. However, remember that it is not unreasonable to argue that trade liberalisation is generally desirable but to accept that there are circumstances when protectionism may be justified. There is a wide spectrum of opinion amongst economists about the extent to which protectionist measures are economically justifiable.

CASE STUDY 10.2

Paul Krugman and strategic trade theory

In 2008, Paul Krugman, professor of economics at Princeton University, USA, was awarded the Nobel Prize in Economics, in part for his pioneering work in developing strategic trade theory in the 1980s and 1990s. In contrast to the orthodox free-market approach to international trade, firmly grounded in the principle of comparative advantage, strategic trade theory argues that import controls can sometimes be justified. Krugman argued that rich, developed countries benefited from protectionism while they established their national wealth. However, they now put pressure on poor countries to abandon import controls and to allow overseas-based multinational corporations unlimited access to their economies. And as we mentioned earlier in the chapter, opponents of globalisation argue that free trade theory is used to justify first-world economic imperialism.

Below is an extract from the beginning of a paper Krugman wrote in 1987:

> If there were an Economist's Creed, it would surely contain the affirmations 'I understand the principle of comparative advantage' and 'I advocate free trade'. For 170 years, the appreciation that international trade benefits a country whether it is 'fair' or not has been one of the touchstones of professionalism in economics.

> Yet the case for free trade is currently more in doubt than at any time since the 1817 publication of Ricardo's *Principles of Political Economy*. This is not because of the political pressures for protection, which have triumphed in the past without shaking the intellectual foundation of comparative advantage

theory. Rather, it is because of the changes that have recently taken place in the theory of international trade itself.

In the last 10 years the traditional *constant returns*, *perfect competition* models of international trade have been supplemented and to some extent supplanted by a new breed of models that emphasise *increasing returns* and *imperfect competition*. These new models call into doubt the extent to which actual trade can be explained by comparative advantage.

Showing that free trade is better than no trade is not the same thing as showing that free trade is better than sophisticated government intervention. The view that free trade is the best of all possible policies is part of the general case for laissez-faire in a market economy and rests on the proposition that markets are efficient. If increasing returns and imperfect competition are necessary parts of the explanation of international trade, we are living in a *second-best* world where government intervention can in principle improve on market outcomes.

Source: Paul Krugman, 'Is free trade passé?', *Journal of Economic Perspectives*, 1987. The full article can be found online at: **www.aeaweb.org/articles.php?doi=10.1257/jep.1.2.131**.

Follow-up questions

1 Briefly define each of the terms underlined in the extract.
2 Do you agree that increasing returns to scale and imperfect competition weaken the case for unlimited free trade based on the principle of comparative advantage? Justify your answer.

Welfare losses and welfare gains

In this and the next two sections of the chapter, we bypass the justifications for tariffs put forward by economists such as Paul Krugman and return to the free-market case for free trade. Analysis of the welfare gains from free trade and the welfare losses caused by import controls centres on the concepts of consumer surplus and producer surplus that you learnt when studying Chapter 3.

SYNOPTIC LINK
Chapter 3 on perfect competition, imperfectly competitive markets and oligopoly explains the key welfare concepts of consumer surplus and producer surplus.

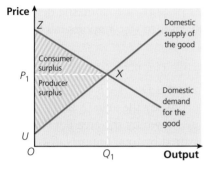

Figure 10.2 Consumer and producer surplus in a market closed to international trade

If a country does not enter into international trade, which means its economy is *closed*, domestic demand for a good within a country can only be met by domestic supply (that is, by firms producing *within* the country). Such a situation is shown in Figure 10.2, where market equilibrium for the good occurs at point X. Consumers pay price P_1 for the good, and the quantity bought and sold is Q_1. Consumer surplus, which is a measure of consumer welfare, is shown by the triangular area bounded by points XZP_1. Likewise, producer welfare (producer surplus) is the triangular area bounded by points XP_1U.

But consider what happens in a world of completely free trade, in which domestically produced goods have to compete with cheaper imports. In Figure 10.3, imports are priced at the ruling world price of P_W, which is lower than P_1. In this situation, equilibrium now occurs in the domestic market at point V. Although domestic demand has increased to Q_{D1}, domestic supply (located where the domestic supply curve cuts the horizontal price line at P_W) falls to Q_{S1}. Imports (equal to $Q_{D1} - Q_{S1}$) fill the gap between domestic demand and supply.

To understand how imports affect economic welfare within the country, it is important to understand how consumer surplus and producer surplus change after the price of the good falls to the world price P_W. Consumer surplus increases by the wedge-shaped area bounded by the points P_WVXP_1. This divides into two parts, shown on the diagram by areas B and C. Look closely at area B. This shows a welfare transfer away from domestic firms to domestic consumers. The fall in the price from P_1 to P_W, brought about by lower import prices, means that part of the producer surplus that domestic firms previously enjoyed now becomes consumer surplus. The consumers 'win' and the domestic producers 'lose'.

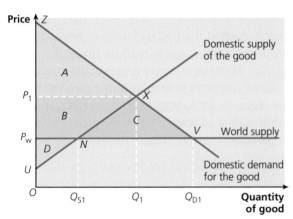

Figure 10.3 The welfare gains and losses resulting from the introduction of a tariff

But this is not the end of the story. Consumers enjoy a further increase in consumer surplus, which is brought about by receipt of area C. As a result, the total increase in consumer surplus exceeds the size of the welfare transfer from producer surplus to consumer surplus. A net welfare gain thus results, equal to area C, which makes up part of the consumer surplus that households now enjoy.

> ## STUDY TIP
> You should practise drawing and explaining Figure 10.3 and the diagrams that follow to show the welfare gains and losses resulting from trade and import controls. Remember, however, the assumptions that underpin free-trade theory which we explained earlier. Question these assumptions and the case for free trade weakens.

How a tariff or import duty affects economic welfare

We shall now assume that domestic firms pressure the government to introduce a tariff to protect the home market. If the tariff equals or exceeds the distance between P_1 and P_W, the domestic market for the good reverts to the original equilibrium position that existed before imports entered the country. But suppose the government imposes a smaller tariff, which is just sufficient to raise the price of imports (also allowing domestic producers to charge higher

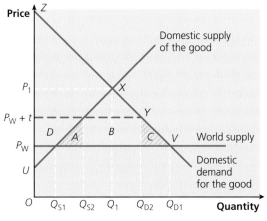

Figure 10.4 The effect of imposing a tariff

prices) to $P_W + t$ in Figure 10.4. At price $P_W + t$, domestic demand falls to Q_{D2}, while domestic supply rises to Q_{S2}. Imports fall from $Q_{D1} - Q_{S1}$ to $Q_{D2} - Q_{S2}$.

At the higher price, consumer surplus *falls* by the wedge-shaped area $P_W VY P_W + t$, which equals the areas $D + A + B + C$. The higher price increases producer surplus by the area D, and the government gains tariff revenue shown by the area B. (The government's tariff revenue is measured by total imports, $Q_{D2} - Q_{S2}$, multiplied by the tariff per unit of imports, $P_W + t - P_W$.) The areas D and B are *transfers* of welfare away from consumers to domestic producers and the government respectively. The *net welfare loss* resulting from the tariff, which is the sum of triangles A and C in the diagram, is:

$(D + A + B + C) - (D + B)$, which equals $A + C$

Changing comparative advantage and the pattern of world trade

To many people living in industrial countries during the nineteenth century and the first half of the twentieth century, it must have seemed almost natural that the earliest countries to industrialise, such as the UK, had done so because they possessed a competitive and comparative advantage in manufacturing. It probably seemed equally natural that a pattern of world trade should have developed in which the industrialised countries in what is now called the North exported manufactured goods in exchange for foodstuffs and raw materials produced by countries whose comparative advantage lay in the production of primary products — in modern parlance, the countries of the South.

However, in recent years, the pattern of world trade has become quite different from the North–South exchange of manufactured goods for primary products that characterised the nineteenth century. In a North–North pattern of trade, which is illustrated in Figure 10.5, the developed industrial economies now exchange goods and services mostly with each other. However, a growing fraction of their trade, particularly in the case of imports, is with newly industrialising countries (NICs) or emerging markets, particularly India, China and South Korea. A group of countries known as the BRIC countries (Brazil, Russia, India and China) are responsible for exporting large quantities of goods and services to the North. India, China and South Korea now export manufactured goods to countries in the North such as the UK and the USA, and import raw materials or commodities such as copper from developing countries such as Zambia. Before 2014 they also imported a growing fraction of the crude oil produced by oil-exporting developing countries such as Saudi Arabia and Venezuela.

The shift of manufacturing to China and other NICs reflects changing competitive and comparative advantage and the deindustrialisation of the UK, North America and some of the major European economies. Only a relatively small proportion of the trade of North countries is with poorer countries in the non-oil-producing developing world.

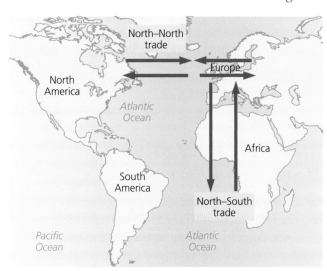

Figure 10.5 North–North and North–South patterns of trade

The pattern of the UK's international trade

Table 10.8 shows that over the 56-year period from 1955 to 2011 (which was the last year for which the ONS published data in this form), the pattern of the UK's international trade changed from a 'North–South' to a 'North–North' pattern. The UK now trades mainly with other developed countries in the North, and especially with other EU countries. In 1955, only 15% of UK exports and 12.6% of UK imports were with countries that eventually formed the EU. By contrast, 32.9% of UK exports and 31.4% of UK imports were with developing countries.

By 2011, this situation was reversed: respectively 47.4% and 50.6% of UK exports and imports were with EU countries, while exports to other developing countries had fallen to 25.1% of total exports, with imports marginally higher at 25.2% of total imports. However, 'other developing countries' include emerging-market 'giants' such as India and China, the latter having become the world's largest exporter of manufactured goods to developed economies such as the UK. Indeed, while China's agricultural sector remains characteristic of a developing country, the same is not true for manufacturing and, increasingly, transport. The growing importance of emerging market countries, particularly China, in international trade explains why the share of their trade in UK imports and exports has been creeping upwards, compared, for example, to the 2002 figures in Table 10.8. By contrast, slippage in the percentages of UK trade with other EU countries has occurred, partly as a result of the depth of recession in many **eurozone** countries.

> **KEY TERM**
>
> **eurozone** the name used for the group of EU countries that have replaced their national currencies with the euro. In 2015, 19 of the 28 EU countries were in the eurozone, though this may change in future years. The eurozone is also known as the euro area.

Table 10.8 North–North and North–South patterns of UK trade, percentages of total UK trade in goods

UK trade with	1955 Exports (%)	1955 Imports (%)	2002 Exports (%)	2002 Imports (%)	2007 Exports (%)	2007 Imports (%)	2011 Exports (%)	2011 Imports (%)
EU	15.0	12.6	54.6	57.3	50.2	54.0	47.4	50.6
Other west European countries (EFTA)	13.9	13.1	3.8	4.4	4.3	5.7	4.3	7.2
North America	12.0	19.5	19.7	14.0	19.8	12.2	17.9	11.0
Other developed countries (OECD except 1955)	21.1	14.2	2.7	4.2	2.3	3.3	2.5	2.8
Oil-exporting developed countries	5.1	9.2	2.2	1.2	2.5	1.6	2.8	3.2
Other developing countries	32.9	31.4	17.0	18.9	20.9	22.2	25.1	25.2

Sources: *Annual Abstract of Statistics, Monthly Review of External Trade Statistics,* 2012

As we stated at the beginning of this section on the pattern of UK trade, the ONS no longer publishes data in the way shown in Table 10.8. For this reason we have not been able to update the table to cover the years since 2011. However, the ONS does now publish details of UK trade in goods with EU and non-EU countries, and trade with eurozone member countries. Table 10.9 shows the pattern of the UK's trade with these three areas, together with trade with the whole world in 2014.

Table 10.9 The pattern of the UK's trade in goods with eurozone countries, the whole of the EU, non-EU countries and the whole of the world, 2014 (£m)

Eurozone members		Total EU		Non-EU		All world countries	
Exports	Imports	Exports	Imports	Exports	Imports	Exports	Imports
130,639	195,488	147,926	224,904	144,941	187,568	292,867	412,472

Worked example: calculating the balance of trade in goods

1 **Calculate the UK's balances of trade in goods with: eurozone member states; the whole of the EU; non-EU countries; and the whole of the world.**

2 **Calculate, to two decimal places, the UK's exports and imports to and from: the eurozone; the whole of the EU; and non-EU countries, as percentages of total UK exports and imports.**

1 To calculate the balances of trade in goods, for each group of countries subtract the total imports from total exports. The answers are:

UK's balance of trade with eurozone member states: –£64,849 million

UK's balance of trade with EU member states: –£76,978 million

UK's balance of trade with non-EU countries: –£42,627 million

UK's balance of trade with the whole of the world: –£119,605 million

Note: the UK was running a deficit on the balance of trade in goods with all four groups of countries. The last item (–£119,605 million) also appears later in the chapter in Table 10.11, which shows the UK's balance of payments in 2014.

2 UK exports to the eurozone as a % of the whole of UK exports: £130,639/£292,867 = 44.61%

UK exports to the EU as a % of the whole of UK exports: £147,926/£292,867 = 50.51%

UK exports to non-EU countries as a % of the whole of UK exports: £144,941/£292,867 = 49.49%

UK imports from the eurozone as a % of the whole of UK imports: £195,488/£412,472 = 47.39%

UK imports from the EU as a % of the whole of UK imports: £224,904/£412,472 = 54.53%

UK imports from non-EU countries as a % of the whole of UK imports: £187,568/£412,472 = 45.47%

In contrast to Tables 10.8 and 10.9, which show changes in the global pattern of UK trade, Table 10.10 focuses on changes in the commodities traded over the period 2002–14. The table shows that, despite the impact of deindustrialisation, which has reduced manufacturing output to less than 15% of GDP, the UK's trade in goods is still dominated by the export and import of manufactured goods, though with the country importing significantly more than it exports. We shall take up this story again in section 10.3, in the context of the UK's balance of payments.

Table 10.10 Changes in items in UK trade in goods by type of commodity, 2002–14 (£m), with percentages of total trade in goods shown in brackets

	2002		2005		2007		2014	
	Exports	Imports	Exports	Imports	Exports	Imports	Exports	Imports
Food, beverages and tobacco	10,010	19,389	10,673	23,713	11,753	26,708	18,943	38,575
	(5.4%)	(8.3%)	(5.0%)	(8.5%)	(5.3%)	(8.6%)	(?%)	(?%)
Raw materials	2,858	5,966	3,990	6,778	5,517	9,558	6,997	11,745
	(1.5%)	(2.6%)	(1.9%)	(2.4%)	(2.5%)	(3.1%)	(?%)	(?%)
Fuels and energy	16,031	10,288	21,613	26,002	24,393	32,307	36,568	51,789
	(8.6%)	(4.4%)	(10.2%)	(9.3%)	(11.1%)	(10.4%)	(?%)	(?%)
Manufactured goods	156,642	196,845	174,260	221,956	177,496	240,057	224,272	305,584
	(84.0%)	(84.1%)	(82.3%)	(79.2%)	(80.5%)	(77.2%)	(?%)	(?%)
Total exports (excluding miscellaneous items)	186,574		211,606		220,525		?	
Total imports (excluding miscellaneous items)		233,934		280,292		311,003		?

Sources: *Monthly Review of External Trade Statistics* (various) and *ONS Statistical Bulletin* (February 2015)

Worked example: calculating percentages from raw data

The figures for total UK exports and imports in 2014 have not been included in Table 10.10; nor have the percentage contributions of each category in 2014. Calculate, to one decimal place, the total value of UK exports and imports in 2014, and also the percentage contribution of each category of exports and imports.

Add up all the export items (£18,943m + £6,997m + £36,568m + £224,272m) to arrive at total exports of £286,780 million.

Likewise, add up all the import items (£38,575m + £11,745m + £51,789m + £305,584m) to arrive at total imports of £407,693 million.

Then calculate the percentage of each export item as a ratio of £286,780 million. The percentages, to one decimal place, are:

Food, beverages and tobacco: 6.6%

Raw materials: 2.4%

Fuels and energy: 12.8%

Manufactured goods: 78.2%

Then calculate the percentage of each import item as a ratio of £407,693 million. The percentages, to one decimal place, are:

Food, beverages and tobacco: 9.5%

Raw materials: 2.9%

Fuels and energy: 12.7%

Manufactured goods: 75.0%

Degrees of international economic integration

The main types of international economic integration are:

- **Preference areas.** Countries agree to levy reduced, or preferential, tariffs on certain trade — for example, the EU's Association Agreements with certain developing countries.
- **Free trade areas.** Member countries abolish tariffs on mutual trade, but each partner determines its own tariffs on trade with non-member countries. A potential problem here is that traders try to import goods into the partner with the lowest external tariff and then re-export them to others tariff-free from there. To avoid this, complex rules of origin and border controls tend to govern intra-area trade to ensure that free trade refers only to the partners' produce and not to their imports.
- **Customs unions.** These involve intra-union free trade but also a common external tariff on all members' trade with non-members.
- **Common markets.** These are customs unions with additional provisions to encourage trade and integration through the free mobility of factors of production and the harmonisation of trading standards and practices.
- **Economic unions.** These add further harmonisation in the areas of general economic, legal and social policies, and the development of union-wide policies. Economic union may be supplemented by monetary union, which entails a common currency and monetary policy.
- **Political unions.** These are the ultimate form of economic integration. They involve the submersion of separate national institutions. Even within this category, however, several degrees of integration exist. For example, in the USA the states have substantial powers of taxation, whereas at the moment UK local government has few such powers (though Scotland now has some ability to raise its own taxes).

KEY TERMS

free trade area member countries abolish tariffs on mutual trade, but each partner determines its own tariffs on trade with non-member countries.

customs union a trading bloc in which member countries enjoy internal free trade in goods and possibly services, with all the member countries protected by a common external tariff barrier.

Free trade areas versus customs unions

Figure 10.6 illustrates the main difference between a customs union and a free trade area, and also the way in which the two forms of trading bloc are similar. The similarity lies in the fact that both organisations have internal free trade, at

317

least in goods though not necessarily in services. However, the difference lies in the way tariffs are set against imports from non-member states. Members of a free trade area are free to set their own tariffs against non-members, but members of a customs union lose this freedom and have to abide by an external tariff common to all member states.

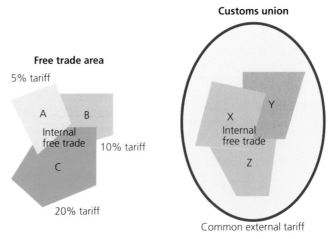

Figure 10.6 The difference between a free trade area and a customs union

A brief history of the European Union

The European Union (as it is now called) started life as a customs union, but since 1993 has developed one stage further into a more or less full common market. Prior to entering the EU's predecessor, the European Economic Community (EEC), in 1973, the UK had been a member of a free trade area (the European Free Trade Association or EFTA), and also of a preference area (the Commonwealth).

The Treaty of Rome, which created the EEC in the late 1950s, envisaged that free movement of goods between member countries would be followed over a period of 12 years by free trade in services and free movement of capital and labour. When all this was accomplished, the trading area would be a full common market. However, these events did not happen, at least in the period before the signing of a new community treaty, the 1986 Single European Act (SEA).

There were a number of reasons why member countries dragged their feet in creating a full common market. To take one example, Germany feared that its financial service firms would be unable to compete in a community-wide financial market with the accession of the UK in 1973. But having established agreement between member countries, the SEA set out a 6-year timetable, to be completed by 1993, after which a *more or less full* common market, the **Single European Market** (SEM), would operate. The words *more or less full* are actually quite significant. Although, there is supposed to be internal free trade in both goods and services within the EU, these freedoms are not complete. An inability to decide on, and then to impose, uniform standards relating to goods, and distortions created by member governments favouring local suppliers, are two reasons why this is so. National governments still prevent foreign arms suppliers from competing in the supply of weapons, and the EU lacks a community-wide energy market. Competition is discouraged in protected national energy markets from gas and electricity supply companies located in other member countries.

318

KEY TERM
Single European Market the SEM was intended to establish the 'four freedoms' — free movement of goods, services, workers and capital between the EU member states — from 1993 onward. However, the SEM is only partially complete.

The extent to which membership of a trading bloc is advantageous, both for the country involved and for the welfare of people throughout the world, depends partly on whether the trading bloc is *trade creating* or *trade diverting*. Trade creation increases the total volume of international trade because the growth of internal free trade among members exceeds any loss of trade with non-members brought about by tariffs protecting the trading bloc.

For example, after the formation of a customs union, member states can import lower-cost products from other member states, rather than producing the products themselves at a higher cost. Trade creation shifts consumption away from buying goods and services produced by high-cost firms toward buying from lower-cost producers within the trading bloc. This leads to efficiency gains.

Trade diversion, by contrast, refers to changes in the pattern of international trade which occur when trade that used to take place with non-member states diverts into trade between member states. If, after the formation of a customs union, a member country replaces imported goods from lower-cost countries in the rest of the world with goods produced by higher-cost member countries, efficiency losses occur.

If the trade-creating benefits of joining a customs union such as the EU exceed any loss of trade resulting from trade diversion, there is a net efficiency and welfare gain. However, countries within the union receive most of the gain, whereas countries outside the union suffer an efficiency and welfare loss. In the case of the European Union, this means that already-rich countries grow wealthier whereas already-poor developing countries suffer the effect of the common external tariff and agricultural levies protecting EU members. To some extent, special access given to trade from developing countries can reduce this adverse effect.

Defenders of the European Union's trade policies argue that customs unions are a 'second-best' solution to the need to create international trade, given the fact that the 'first-best' solution (completely free trade between all the world's nations) has proved impossible to achieve in the modern world. For the EU, the extent to which this argument is true depends on whether the union is outward-looking or inward-looking, which in turn depends on the extent to which the EU is protectionist. A low common external tariff supports the pro-free trade case, but a high tariff wall provides evidence of a 'beggar-my-neighbour' desire to gain at the expense of others. (At this stage, you should refer back to our coverage earlier in this section of the welfare gains and losses that result from tariffs.)

The defenders of the European Union's trade policies also argue that the union has led to *dynamic benefits* additional to the benefits resulting from trade creation. In the absence of a customs union, domestic producers, especially those in monopolistic and oligopolistic markets, are likely to be sluggish and complacent in their sheltered position protected behind trade barriers. However, when exposed to competition from tariff-free imports from within the trading bloc, producers in each member state must become more efficient to meet the competition of other producers within the bloc. The increased level of competition is also likely to stimulate the development and utilisation of new technology, reducing the cost of production to the eventual benefit of consumers.

The European Union as an example of international economic integration

The organisation which became the EU in 1993 was originally called the European Economic Community (EEC). The reasons why it was formed almost 60 years ago were partly economic and partly political. The economic reasons for the formation of the EEC stemmed from the benefits that all the member countries believed they could achieve from creating a large area of internal free trade.

On the political front, West Germany (as it was then called), which was one of the original six members of the new organisation, hoped that EEC membership would help to protect Germans from the military threat of Russian invasion. By contrast, France hoped that a stable and economically successful Germany would reduce the chance of another major war in Europe. This could best be achieved if EEC member states traded freely with each other.

On the economic front, France was willing to create free trade in manufactured goods (which would mostly benefit Germany), provided small French farms could be protected by a common external tariff from the competition of more efficient New World farmers in countries outside the EEC. Germany readily agreed to the creation of a protectionist common agricultural policy (CAP) as the *quid pro quo* of free trade in manufactured goods within the EEC.

Trade creation, trade diversion and the UK's membership of the European Union

There is some evidence that, as far as manufactured goods such as automobiles are concerned, the UK has benefited from the trade-creating advantages of EU membership. But this is not true of many agricultural products, for which the UK has suffered the trade-diverting disadvantages of membership. This has involved a shift from a low-cost source outside the EU, such as Jamaican sugar cane, to a high-cost source within the EU, such as sugar beet grown in countries such as the UK and the Netherlands. Since joining the original EEC in 1973, and taking out the distorting effects of inflation, the British consumer has often had to pay higher prices for food than was the case before entry.

However, whether or not, for the UK, the trade-diverting disadvantages of EU membership exceed the trade-creating benefits, the UK could lose tariff-free access to the huge EU market, if it decides to leave. Supporters of leaving the EU claim that the UK could negotiate tariff-free access in the same way that non-members such as Switzerland and Norway have done. However, these are small countries and they have never been members of the EU. Will Germany, France and other EU countries be prepared to grant the UK similar privileged access if it decides to leave the EU? Perhaps not, but it should be remembered that the UK imports more from the EU than it exports and this may make it easier for the UK to persuade other EU countries to negotiate a free trade agreement.

The EU as an economic union

In the early 1970s, the United Kingdom's decision to join the EEC meant leaving a free trade area and joining a customs union which already possessed a number of common economic policies. Indeed, the fact that the word 'economic' is central to the European Union's original name clearly indicates that the union's founding fathers intended to develop the economic nature of the organisation well beyond a mere trading bloc.

British residents who support the UK's continued membership of the European Union are often known as Europhiles, while those who want the country to withdraw membership are often known as Eurosceptics. Some, but not all, Eurosceptics would be happy for the UK to remain an EU member, but only if the union were to restrict its role to that of a glorified free trade area. However, for Europhiles, rolling back the clock in this way is completely unrealistic. To gain the benefits of free trade which the EU's huge internal market provides, their view is that the UK must accept the common economic policies. For a Europhile, the British government should work actively within the EU to make the common economic policies work better.

Since the creation of the EEC nearly 60 years ago, the EU has introduced a number of common economic policies. Of these, the common agricultural policy, or CAP, which began in 1962 is by far the most important (and expensive). Other common policies include the common fisheries policy, the EU competition policy and the EU regional policy. There was also an early attempt to introduce a common tax policy, centring on the introduction of VAT as the EEC's main expenditure tax. But member countries continue to levy their own national rates of VAT and tax harmonisation has not been developed much further.

Nonetheless, the creation in the late 1990s of the Stability and Growth Pact to constrain or limit government spending and borrowing in eurozone countries was an attempt to impose some elements of a common fiscal policy. In very recent years, the European Commission (the EU's executive body) and the European Central Bank (ECB) have imposed stiff conditions on countries in the eurozone, particularly Greece, when lending to them to bail out the huge national debts these countries incurred in the so-called eurozone crisis.

SYNOPTIC LINK
In section 10.4, we link the topic of economic union to that of monetary union, looking in particular at the role of the common currency, the euro, which has replaced national currencies in eurozone countries.

The European Central Bank in Frankfurt

321

The World Trade Organization

To understand how the World Trade Organization (WTO) came into existence and its role today, it is useful to go back to events occurring in the 1930s and 1940s. In the 1940s, during the Second World War, it was widely believed (especially in the UK and the USA) that the worldwide Depression and mass unemployment of the 1930s had been made worse, and were possibly caused, by a collapse of international trade. 'Beggar my neighbour' protectionist policies, introduced by countries desperately trying to save local jobs, were blamed.

By 1945 the USA and the UK had decided to try to create a postwar world of free trade. Because this required international agreement, the General Agreement on Tariffs and Trade (GATT) was established as a multilateral agreement to try to liberalise world trade. To begin with, GATT was supposed to be a temporary organisation, to be replaced with a 'world trade organization' as soon as member countries could agree. However, because member countries were unable to agree, the 'temporary' organisation lasted much longer than intended. Indeed, GATT still exists today, though its functions have largely been taken over by the WTO.

Throughout their history, GATT and later the WTO organised rounds of talks among member countries to reduce import controls. The rounds, which took place at roughly 5-year intervals, were often named after the city or country in which the talks were initiated: for example, the Tokyo Round, the Uruguay Round and, more recently, the Doha Round. Out of respect, the Kennedy Round in the mid-1960s was named after the then recently assassinated American president. Each round of talks ends with an agreement to reduce import controls. GATT, and latterly the WTO, have then tried to get member countries to implement the tariff cuts they have agreed.

GATT and WTO agreements have been successful in reducing import controls on manufactured goods. There has been much less success in securing agreement to reduce tariffs and quotas on trade in services and agricultural goods. Recently, the WTO has tried to persuade the developed countries of the EU and the USA to open their markets to cheap food imports from the developing world. However, the most recent rounds of talks organised by the WTO at Cancún (in Mexico) and Doha (in Qatar) were not successful. Economists and politicians in many developing countries claim that this lack of success provides further evidence of globalisation and international organisations serving the interests of rich countries at the expense of the poor.

10.3 The balance of payments

In Book 1, Chapters 6 and 8, we explained in some depth the **current account** of the **balance of payments**, and the impact of current account deficits and surpluses on macroeconomic performance. In Book 2, except for a short recap, we are not going to cover the same ground. Instead the focus of this section is, first, on the policies available for a government to correct fundamental imbalances (deficits or surpluses) in the current account, and second, on the significance of capital flows in the financial account of the balance of payments.

KEY TERMS

current account measures all the currency flows into and out of a country in a particular time period in payment for exports and imports of goods and services, together with primary and secondary income flows (previously known as income flows and transfers).

balance of payments the record of all money flows or transactions between the residents of a country and the rest of the world in a particular period, usually monthly, quarterly or annually.

The difference between the current, capital and financial accounts of the balance of payments

The current account of the balance of payments: a brief recap

For the most part, the balance of payments on the current account measures the flow of expenditure on goods and services, and shows the difference between the amount received from exports and the amount paid for imports. The current account is usually regarded as the most important part of the balance of payments because it reflects the economy's international competitiveness and the extent to which the country may or may not be living within its means.

To measure the balance of payments on current account, we first add together the balance of **trade in goods** and the balance of **trade in services**. If receipts from exports of goods and services are less than payments for imports of goods and services, there is generally a trade deficit. Conversely, a trade surplus occurs when receipts from trade exceed payments for trade. However, because there are other items in the current account besides trade flows, a deficit on the balance of trade in goods and services does not necessarily mean that the current account is in deficit. The other items are now officially called primary income flows and secondary income flows.

Primary income flows are net income flows made up mostly of investment income generated from profits, dividends and interest payments flowing between countries. When we look later at the financial account of the balance of payments, we explain how UK-based multinational companies (MNCs) invest in capital assets located in other countries. The profit income generated from overseas investment flows back to the parent company and its UK shareholders. The investment itself is an outward capital flow, but the income it generates is current income, figuring in the current account of the balance of payments.

KEY TERMS

trade in goods exports and imports of visible, or tangible, items such as cars, oil and tea.

trade in services exports and imports of services such as financial services, tourism and shipping.

primary income flows inward primary income flows comprise income flowing into the economy in the current year, which is generated by UK-owned capital assets located overseas. Outward primary income flows comprise income flowing out of the economy in the current year, which is generated by overseas-owned capital assets located in the UK.

ACTIVITY

Changes in the size and direction of primary flows (net investment income flows) have been the major cause of the deterioration in the UK's balance of payments in recent years. Find out details of these changes and the reasons for them.

Profits also flow out of the UK to the overseas owners of assets located in the UK — for example, to Japanese or US multinational companies owning subsidiary companies in the UK. In Table 10.11, the item 'primary income flows' is largely determined by the difference between these inward and outward profit flows resulting from capital investment undertaken in the past. The fact that the UK's net income flows (primary income flows) were −£33,108 million in 2014 indicates that in that year, UK companies owned less profitable assets in the rest of the world than overseas-based MNCs owned in the UK. In many previous years, inward primary income flows had far exceeded outward flows. The collapse of foreign investment earnings was a main factor contributing to the current account deficit rising to over £90 billion, up from over £22 billion 3 years earlier.

Table 10.11 Selected items from the UK balance of payments (£m), 2014

The current account (mostly trade flows)	
Balance of trade in goods	−123,672
Balance of trade in services	+ 89,140
Primary income flows *(Net income flows)*	−33,108
Secondary income flows *(Net current transfers)*	−25,249
Balance of payments on the current account	**−92,889**
The capital account	**−762**
The financial account Net direct investment	−81,600
Net portfolio investment	−81,958
Other capital flows *(including many short-term 'hot money' flows)*	+80,992
Drawings on reserves	+7,113
Net financial transactions *(This is the overall balance for the financial account.)*	**−89,408**
Net errors and omissions *(The financial account balance minus the current and capital account balances. It is required to compensate for inevitable mistakes.)*	**+4,243**

Source: *United Kingdom Quarterly Accounts*, Q2, 2015

(Note that the ONS has changed how it presents figures in the Financial account. Figures that used to be shown as a plus are now shown as a minus and vice versa. Consequently, mathematically, the balances for the account as a whole no longer sum to zero.)

Finally, it is worth remembering that not all primary income flows are profit payments generated by multinational companies on their direct investments abroad. A significant proportion of the income flows are generated from portfolio investment, which is investment in financial assets such as shares and bonds. Interest and dividend payments within the international financial system contribute significantly to net primary income flows. By the time you read this book, further significant changes may have taken place in the UK current account. Make sure you keep up to date with these changes.

Secondary income flows are current transfers of income arising from such items as gifts between residents of different countries, donations to charities abroad, and overseas aid. The UK's net contribution to the EU budget is another example of a current transfer of income between countries.

KEY TERM

secondary income flows current transfers, such as gifts of money, international aid and transfers between the UK and the EU, flowing into or out of the UK economy in a particular year.

SYNOPTIC LINK

At this point you should revisit Book 1, pages 218–23, to remind yourself of items in the current account of the UK's balance of payments.

The capital account of the balance of payments

Several years ago, a change was made to the way the UK balance of payments is presented. The items in the capital account, a long-standing part of the balance of payments, were changed. Capital flows were moved out of the capital account and listed under a new heading: the financial account. The capital account now comprises various transfers of income that were part of the current account before the new method of classification was adopted. It is now a very small, and usually insignificant, part of the overall balance of payments account.

The financial account of the balance of payments

As our discussion of primary income flows in the current account indicates, it is important to avoid confusing capital flows, which figure in the **financial account** of the balance of payments, with investment income, which is lion's share of the primary income flows in the current account. As explained, outward capital flows generate inward flows of investment income in subsequent years. The capital outflow enlarges the stock of capital assets located in other countries, owned by residents and MNCs based in the country exporting the capital. Net capital flows are the difference between inward and outward capital movements. Positive net outward capital flows, over a period of years, mean that the country acquires capital assets located in other countries that are greater in value than the country's own assets bought by overseas companies.

The positive net investment income flow (in the current account) which occurred in years prior to 2012 suggests that, in these years, UK residents and MNCs had invested in a larger and more profitable stock of capital assets in the rest of the world than that acquired by overseas residents and MNCs in the UK. Following the UK's abolition of virtually all foreign exchange controls in 1979, the UK became a large net exporter of capital, presumably because owners of UK MNCs believed that investment abroad would be more profitable than investment within the UK. During the 1980s, the positive net capital outflow meant that the UK became a large owner of overseas capital assets. However, by 2010 the UK had once again become a net debtor nation. The difference between foreign assets that domestic UK residents own and domestic assets held by residents of other countries was a liability of £354.7 billion late in 2014.

Within the financial account of the balance of payments, we shall distinguish between long-term direct capital flows, long-term portfolio capital flows, and short-term speculative 'hot money' capital flows.

Long-term direct capital flows

Direct overseas investment involves acquisition of real productive assets, such as factories, oil refineries, offices and shopping malls, located in other countries. On the one hand, a UK-based MNC may decide to establish a new subsidiary company — for example, in the USA. Direct investment can also involve acquisition, through merger or takeover, of an overseas-based company. These are examples of outward direct investment. Conversely, the decisions in the 1980s and 1990s by the Japanese vehicle manufacturers Nissan, Toyota and Honda to invest in automobile factories in the UK led to inward direct investment, or inward **foreign direct investment** (FDI).

Long-term direct capital flows can partly be explained by competitive advantage. The flows are a response to people's decisions to invest in economic activities and industries located in countries that have a competitive advantage. Comparative advantage may also rest in the same country. But since changes in competitive and/or comparative advantage usually take place quite slowly, long-term direct capital flows tend to be relatively stable and predictable.

> **KEY TERM**
> **financial account** the part of the balance of payments which records capital flows into and out of the economy.

> **KEY TERM**
> **foreign direct investment** investment in capital assets, such as manufacturing and service industry capacity, in a foreign country by a business with headquarters in another country. Very often the overseas company establishes subsidiary companies in the countries in which it is investing.

Portfolio capital flows

These involve the purchase of financial assets (that is, pieces of paper laying claim to the ownership of real assets) rather than physical or directly productive assets. Typically, **portfolio investment** occurs when fund managers employed by financial institutions such as insurance companies and pension funds purchase shares issued by overseas companies, or securities issued by foreign governments.

The globalisation of world security markets or capital markets and the abolition of exchange controls between virtually all developed countries have made it easy for UK residents to purchase shares or bonds that are listed on overseas capital markets. This has led to a massive increase in portfolio investment. UK residents can now buy shares and corporate bonds that were previously only available on the capital market of the company's country of origin. Securities issued by foreign governments, such as US Treasury bonds, can also be bought.

The credit crunch that began in the USA in 2007, and the so-called 'financial meltdown' that followed, had a significant adverse effect on portfolio investment both within and between countries. Many financial assets, particularly those bought and sold by banks, became known as 'toxic assets'. This term arose from the fact that a potential purchaser of a package of financial assets offered for sale by a bank could not know in advance whether assets in the package were of high risk and potentially little value, or a sound investment (even the bank trying to make the sale might not know). In such conditions of imperfect information, trading in many types of financial asset collapsed.

Short-term speculative 'hot money' capital flows

Short-term capital movements, which are also called 'hot money' flows, are largely speculative. The flows occur because the owners of funds, which include companies and banks as well as wealthy private individuals, believe that a quick speculative profit can be made by moving funds between currencies. Speculating that a currency's exchange rate is about to rise, owners of funds move money into that currency and out of other currencies whose exchange rates are expected to fall. 'Hot money' movements are also triggered by differences in interest rates. Funds flow into currencies with high interest rates and out of currencies with lower interest rates. International crises, such as the outbreak of a war in the Middle East, also cause funds to move into the currency of a 'safe-haven' country, which is regarded as politically stable.

If the pool of hot money shifting between currencies were small, few problems would result. However, short-term capital flows have grown significantly over the last 60 or so years. A large-scale movement of funds from one currency to another creates an excess supply in the former currency and an excess demand for the second currency. To eliminate excess supply and demand, the exchange rates of the two currencies respectively fall and rise. As a result, the movement of funds between currencies produces the changes in exchange rates that speculators were expecting.

More importantly, a large-scale hot money flow of funds between currencies destabilises exchange rates, the current accounts of balance of payments and, indeed, domestic economies. Such destabilisation occurred late in 2008 and early in 2009 when owners of hot money shifted their funds out of the pound on a massive scale. However, in the next few years, market sentiment changed with the result that hot money flowed into the pound, at least until the middle of 2015. At the time of writing in 2015, the main 'hot money' flow is into the US dollar, forcing up its value. Things might, of course, have changed by the time you read this chapter.

Speculative capital flows between currencies such as the dollar, the pound and the euro, which occupy a central place in the finance of international trade, can destabilise the international monetary system. The most recent examples of destabilisation followed the credit crunch and the financial meltdown that were referred to earlier. Banks and other financial institutions, and also governments, within a range of countries (which included the UK) saw their international credit ratings downgraded. To fight the recession that was hitting their economies, governments built up massive budget deficits, which they tried to finance in part by borrowing overseas.

QUANTITATIVE SKILLS 10.3

Worked example: calculating missing statistics in a balance of payments table

Table 10.12 shows some of the items in the balance of payments for a country in 2015.

Table 10.12 Balance of payments, 2015

Item	£ million
Balance of trade in goods	+1,000
Balance of trade in services	?
Balance of trade in goods and services	+600
Primary income	−75
Secondary income	+30
Balance of payments on current account	?
Net direct investment	+300
Net portfolio investment	−400
Other items in the financial account	+655
Financial account balance	?

Assuming that 'net errors and omissions' and the 'capital account balance' are zero in the balance of payments, fill in the missing numbers in the table indicated by question marks, in each case with a plus or minus sign.

The missing numbers are shown in bold in the full table below.

Item	£ million
Balance of trade in goods	+1,000
Balance of trade in services	**−400**
Balance of trade in goods and services	+600
Primary income	−75
Secondary income	+30
Balance of payments on current account	**+555**
Net direct investment	+300
Net portfolio investment	−400
Other items in the financial account	+655
Financial account balance	**+555**

Policies to cure or reduce a balance of payments deficit

The rest of our coverage of the balance of payments returns to the current account. Before reading further, it will be useful to remind yourself of our coverage of whether or not current account deficits and surpluses pose problems, which you will find in Book 1, Chapter 8, pages 226–27.

Traditionally, it was thought that a government (or its central bank) can use three different policies to try to cure a persistent deficit caused by an overvalued exchange rate. These are the '3 Ds' of deflation, direct controls, and devaluation or currency depreciation, which are shown in Figure 10.7.

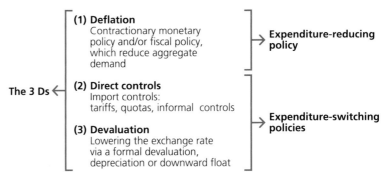

Figure 10.7 The '3 Ds' of deflation, direct controls and devaluation

A deflationary policy, which in this context refers to a reduction in the level of aggregate demand in the economy, reduces a current account deficit because for the most part it is an example of an **expenditure-reducing policy**. As aggregate demand falls, people's incomes fall and hence spending on imports is reduced. By contrast, import controls and devaluation are for the most part examples of **expenditure-switching policies** and affect the balance of payments by changing the relative price of home-produced and foreign goods.

Deflation as an expenditure-reducing policy

Deflationary policy involves using contractionary monetary and/or fiscal policy to reduce the demand for imports. For example, if the marginal propensity to import in the economy is 0.4, reducing aggregate demand by £10 billion should cause spending on imports to fall by £4 billion. This is an expenditure-reducing policy.

Although deflation is primarily an expenditure-reducing policy, it also has an expenditure-switching element. By reducing the rate of domestic price inflation relative to inflation rates in other countries, deflation improves the price competitiveness of exports and reduces that of imports.

However, in modern economies this is usually quite a small effect, and the main effect of deflationary policies, at least in the short run, is to reduce aggregate demand and depress economic activity in the domestic economy. Output, incomes and employment tend to fall rather than the price level. Falling demand for domestic output may force firms to seek export orders, so as to use spare production capacity. However, because exports are generally less profitable than domestic sales, a sound and expanding home market may be necessary for a successful export drive.

In summary, when deflating aggregate demand to achieve the external objectives of supporting the exchange rate and reducing a current account deficit, a government sacrifices the domestic economic objectives of full employment and economic growth. For this reason, governments may choose to use expenditure-switching policies of import controls and devaluation, in preference to expenditure-reducing deflationary policies. However, when an economy is overheating, expenditure-reducing measures are more appropriate than expenditure-switching policies. Reducing aggregate demand will help to control domestic inflationary pressures as well as to correct a balance of payments deficit.

Direct controls as expenditure-switching policies

Direct controls involve imposing quotas or even outright bans (embargoes) on imports. These directly cut or prevent expenditure on imports and, as a result, people switch their spending from foreign to home-produced goods. Together with import duties or tariffs, which make imports less price competitive, direct controls do not, however, cure the underlying cause of a current account deficit, namely the uncompetitiveness of a country's goods and services. Moreover, because a country essentially gains a 'beggar my neighbour' advantage at the expense of other countries, import controls tend to provoke retaliation.

Free-market economists believe that protectionism reduces specialisation and causes world trade, world output and economic welfare to fall. Because of this, international organisations such as the EU and the World Trade Organization have reduced the freedom of individual countries to impose import controls unilaterally to improve their current accounts. However, the EU does use its common external tariff to provide protection for *all* its member states. As a member of the WTO and the EU, the UK government is extremely unlikely to be able to use import controls to reduce a current account deficit.

Devaluation or currency depreciation as an expenditure-switching policy

The exchange rate is the value of one currency in terms of another currency. The word *devaluation* is used in a number of different ways. In a narrow sense, a country devalues by reducing the value of a fixed exchange rate or an adjustable peg exchange rate. (Fixed exchange rates and adjustable peg exchange rates are explained in section 10.4.) However, the term is sometimes used in a looser way to describe a *downward float* or *depreciation* of a floating exchange rate. In a floating exchange rate system, the term 'depreciation' is the correct term to describe a fall in the external value of a currency.

The word 'depreciation' can also confuse. Devaluation or a downward float causes an *external* depreciation of the currency; more units of the currency are needed to buy a unit of *another* currency. This should not be confused with an *internal* depreciation of the currency, occurring when there is inflation *within* the economy and the internal purchasing power of the currency falls as the price level rises.

In a fixed exchange rate system, an increase in the external value of a currency is known as a *revaluation*, whereas in a floating rate system it is known as an *appreciation* in the exchange rate.

Unavailability of import controls means that a country must generally choose between *deflation* and *devaluation*, or *currency depreciation*, if it wishes to reduce a current account deficit. As with tariffs and export subsidies, a fall in the external value of the currency has a mainly expenditure-switching effect. By increasing the price of imports relative to the price of exports, a successful devaluation switches domestic demand away from imports and towards home-produced goods. Similarly, overseas demand for the country's exports increases in response to the fall in export prices.

Price elasticity of demand and devaluation

The effectiveness of a fall in the exchange rate in reducing a balance of payments deficit depends to a significant extent upon the price elasticities of demand for exports and imports.

As Figure 10.8 shows for the UK, when the demand for exports and the demand for imports are both highly price elastic, a fall in the exchange rate *is likely to* reduce a current account deficit.

Following a devaluation, the domestic price of imports into the UK rises from P_1 to P_2, while the overseas price of UK's exports falls from P_3 to P_4. As a result, UK residents spend less on imported goods following an increase in their relative prices. At the same time, residents of overseas countries spend more on the UK's exports, whose relative prices have fallen.

SYNOPTIC LINK

Make sure you can apply the microeconomic concept of elasticity to macroeconomic analysis of the expenditure-switching policy of devaluation

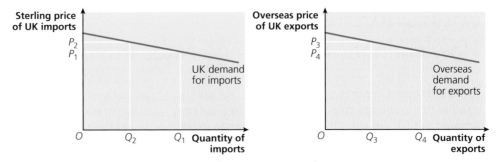

Figure 10.8 The effect of a devaluation (or downward float) of the pound's exchange rate on the current account of the UK balance of payments

On the import side, in Figure 10.8, spending falls from the rectangular area bounded by P_1 and Q_1 to the area bounded by P_2 and Q_2. Higher import prices mean that consumers switch to the now cheaper domestically produced substitutes.

In a similar way, expenditure on the country's exports increases from the rectangular area bounded by P_3 and Q_3 to the area bounded by P_4 and Q_4. Overall, the current account improves, assuming the demand for imports and the demand for exports are both price elastic.

EXTENSION MATERIAL

The Marshall–Lerner condition

It is more difficult to see what may happen to the current account when, for example, the demand for exports is price inelastic but the demand for imports is price elastic. Fortunately, the *Marshall–Lerner condition* provides a simple rule to assess whether a change in the exchange rate can improve the current account. The condition states that when the *sum* of the export and import price elasticities is greater than unity (ignoring the minus sign), a fall in the exchange rate can reduce a deficit and a rise in the exchange rate can reduce a surplus. When, however, the export and import price elasticities of demand are both highly inelastic, summing to less than unity, a fall in the exchange rate can have the perverse effect of worsening a deficit (while a revaluation might increase a surplus).

The Marshall–Lerner condition is a *necessary*, but not *sufficient* condition for a fall in the exchange rate to reduce a payments deficit. For a devaluation or currency depreciation to be successful, firms in the domestic economy must have spare capacity with which they can meet the surge in demand brought about by the fall in the exchange rate. This means that if the economy is working at, or close to, full capacity, expenditure-reducing deflation and expenditure-switching devaluation should best be regarded as complementary policies rather than as substitute policies for reducing a current account deficit. Deflation *alone* may be unnecessarily costly in terms of lost domestic employment and output, yet may be necessary to provide the spare capacity and conditions in which a falling exchange rate can successfully cure a payments deficit. It may also be needed to offset the potential inflationary consequences of a fall in the exchange rate, which will erode the improvement in competitiveness resulting from the initial fall in the external value of the currency.

How changes in exchange rates affect the prices of imports

To understand why, when the demand for exports and the demand imports are both highly price elastic, a fall in the exchange rate *is likely to* reduce a current account deficit, consider the effect of a change in the exchange rate upon the UK prices of imports.

The UK firm, Quidsin supermarkets, buys 500 tonnes of Californian apples each month. The dollar price of the apples is $100 per tonne. The total amount that Quidsin has to pay for the apples, therefore, is $50,000. If the exchange rate in January is £1 = $1.50, then Quidsin will have to give up around £33,333 to acquire $50,000 (50,000 ÷ 1.50).

When the exchange rate changes a year later to £1 = $2.00, Quidsin now has to give up £25,000 to get the $50,000 that the supermarket chain needs

to pay its suppliers. The strengthening of the pound's exchange rate has benefited Quidsin. The supermarket chain now has to give up fewer pounds to get the same amount of dollars. Quidsin's costs have fallen by around £8,333 a month.

However, 2 years later the situation changes again, with the exchange rate falling back to £1 = $1.50. This means that, once again, Quidsin has to give up £33,333 to acquire $50,000 (50,000 ÷ 1.50). Compared to a year earlier, Quidsin's costs have now risen by approximately £8,333.

The position for a UK business which *exports* rather than *imports* goods or services would be the exact opposite of the above.

The J-curve effect

Even if domestic demand for imports and overseas demand for exports are both price elastic and spare capacity exists in the economy, in the short run the balance of payments may deteriorate. It takes time for demand to respond to the price changes, and firms within the country may still be unable immediately to increase supply following a fall in the exchange rate. In the short run, the Marshall–Lerner condition (explained in the extension material) may not hold because elasticities of demand are lower in the short run than in the long run. In these circumstances, the balance of payments may worsen before it improves. This is known as the *J-curve* effect, which is illustrated in Figure 10.9.

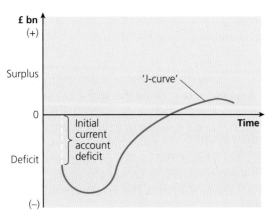

Figure 10.9 The J-curve effect

The initial worsening of the balance of payments that follows the fall in the exchange rate may reduce confidence in the idea that changing the exchange rate is the most appropriate method for reducing a deficit in the current account of the balance of payments. Falling confidence may, in turn, cause capital outflows to occur that destabilise both the balance of payments and the exchange rate. The J-curve effect thus reduces the attractiveness of exchange rate adjustment as an instrument to correct payments disequilibrium. Even when the benefits of a falling exchange rate are realised, they may be short-lived. The increased price competitiveness produced by the devaluation is likely to be eroded as increased import prices raise the country's inflation rate.

Nevertheless, if conditions are right, devaluation can reduce a current account deficit. Despite occurring on 'Black Wednesday', the pound's devaluation in September 1992 was extremely successful, at least for a number of years. There were two main reasons for this. First, expenditure reduction in the severe recession of the early 1990s created the spare capacity that enabled successful expenditure switching following the pound's devaluation. Second, the adoption and achievement of a low inflation target helped to prevent the benefits of the fall in the exchange rate being eroded by accelerating inflation.

In addition, the factories built in the UK by Japanese companies such as Honda and Toyota had just come on stream, producing goods of a quality that people wanted, in the UK and overseas. Some economists believe that the supply-side reforms that were introduced in the 1980s and 1990s also helped.

Supply-side policies and the current account

Deflation, devaluation and direct controls (the '3 Ds') may be effective *short-term* policies for reducing current account deficits. However, it is now increasingly recognised that *long-term* improvement in trade flows requires appropriate and successful supply-side policies and supply-side reforms undertaken by firms within the economy.

The ability of the UK economy to deliver sustained growth of exports and meet the challenge of imported goods and services depends on making UK exports *quality competitive* as well as *price competitive*. A low exchange rate, low interest rates at which British firms can borrow and low domestic inflation all contribute to increased export price competitiveness. However, price competitiveness on its own is not enough. UK goods and services must also be quality competitive. This involves good design and well-made products.

Improved quality competitiveness may only be achievable in the long run if helped by appropriate government supply-side policies together with supply-side reforms undertaken by the private sector. Supply-side policies which promote greater investment in research and development and improved marketing strategies can have powerful long-term effects in improving quality competitiveness. Supply-side reforms, followed by an outward shift of the *LRAS* curve, provide the economy with an increased capacity — enabling a reallocation of resources towards exporting. Successful supply-side policies can also improve exports and lead to import substitution, by increasing labour productivity, which in turn is likely to improve the price competitiveness of UK exports.

Export-led growth and the UK economy

Export-led growth is a term first introduced about 45 years ago, in the context of speeding up the rate of economic growth in developing countries. The term is still widely used with regard to growth strategies in the developing world, but in recent years in the UK, together with the concept of investment-led growth, export-led growth has been more narrowly focused on how best to increase the competitiveness of UK exports and achieve sustained economic growth, without the UK economy slipping into recession. Perhaps not surprisingly, debate in the UK about how to achieve export-led growth became prominent when the economy appeared to be mired in recession in 2008 and 2009, and there seemed to be little hope of speedy economic recovery.

To remind you, short-term economic growth occurs whenever one or more of the components of aggregate demand increases. The components of aggregate demand are consumption (C), investment (I), government spending (G) and net export demand ($X - M$). In recent decades, short-term economic growth has been largely consumption-led, though in 2008 and 2009, via its fiscal stimulus, the Labour government tried to achieve government spending-led growth to 'spend the UK economy out of recession'.

Consumption-led growth leads to two big problems. First, since much consumer spending is on goods and services produced in other countries, consumption-led growth 'sucks' imports into the economy, which may soon lead to a worsening deficit in the current account of the balance of payments. A growing payments deficit may then force the government and the Bank of England to deflate aggregate demand, which at best slows the rate of economic growth, and at worst triggers recession.

Second, and perhaps more significant, recent economic history has shown that consumption-led growth is unsustainable. This is because a rapid growth of consumption, fuelled by increased household debt and consumer borrowing, leads to speculative bubbles, particularly in the housing market. When these bubbles are eventually 'pricked', aggregate demand collapses, bringing to an end the 'boom' phase of the economic cycle. The rate of economic growth declines and perhaps becomes negative.

In this scenario, export-led growth and investment-led growth are seen as 'magic bullets' which, if they can be achieved, will increase productivity, competitiveness and supply-side reform within the economy, and allow sustained economic growth to take place. In such a situation, short-term economic growth, brought about by the increase in aggregate demand, will seamlessly move into sustainable long-term growth. This is because export-led growth and investment-led growth are associated with increased productivity and with the modernisation and enlargement of the economy's productive capacity.

Achieving export-led growth and investment-led growth is, however, much easier said than done. At the time of writing this chapter in December 2015, the UK's continuing recovery from recession appears once again to be consumption-led, with little or no evidence of export-led or investment-led growth. Whether this heralds the eventual onset of another recession remains to be seen, and it must be remembered that adverse economic 'shocks' in the wider world economy can also lead to a collapse in aggregate demand in the UK economy.

Government policies to cure or reduce a balance of payments surplus on current account

The policies available to a government for reducing a balance of payments surplus are the opposite of the '3 Ds' of deflation, direct controls and devaluation which are appropriate for correcting a payments deficit. The policies are the '3 Rs' of reflation, removal of import controls and revaluation:

- Reflating demand, via expansionary monetary policy or fiscal policy, increases a country's demand for imports.
- Trade can be liberalised by removing import controls.
- There have been calls on countries with large payments surpluses, such as Japan and China, to revalue in order to reduce global payments imbalances. But because there is much less pressure on a surplus country to revalue than on a deficit country to devalue, such calls have not usually been successful. It is also worth noting that, for a revaluation to reduce a current account surplus, the Marshall–Lerner condition must be met. In addition, a reverse J-curve, illustrated in Figure 10.10, may operate, causing the payments surplus to get bigger immediately after the revaluation, before it eventually starts to get smaller.

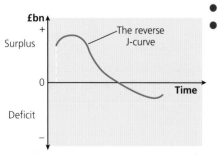

Figure 10.10 The reverse J-curve effect

Three factors that influence a country's current account balance

We have made passing reference throughout section 10.3 to factors which might influence a country's current account balance. Three of these are productivity, inflation and the exchange rate, though primary income flows also need to be considered.

- **Productivity.** Improving labour productivity, or output per worker, is critical to the success of supply-side policies to improve both the price competitiveness and the quality competitiveness of a country's exports in international markets. At this stage, refer back to the earlier sections: 'Supply-side policies and the current account' and 'Export-led growth and the UK economy' (pages 333–34).
- **Inflation.** The key point here is not a country's *absolute* rate of inflation, but its rate of inflation *relative* to those of its trading competitors. If a country's inflation rate is higher than the inflation rates of competitor nations, the country's exports will lose their price competitiveness, which will lead to a deterioration in the country's current account balance. However, our earlier analysis of the price elasticities of demand for exports and imports may complicate things.
- **Exchange rate.** The effect of changes in the exchange rate of a country's currency has a rather similar effect to changes in its relative rate of inflation. In short, a rising exchange rate increases the foreign currency prices of the country's exports and reduces their competitiveness. Meanwhile, imports become more price competitive. As explained earlier, the price elasticities of demand for exports and imports are relevant to the analysis of the effects of a change in a country's exchange rate. Note also that, with respect to a fall in the exchange rate, if a rise in the domestic inflation rate relative to that of other countries exactly matches the fall in its exchange rate, the two effects cancel each other out, and the country's international price competitiveness remains unchanged.

The significance of balance of payments deficits and surpluses

In Book 1, pages 226 and 227, we addressed the issue of whether balance of payments deficits and surpluses on current account pose problems for the country experiencing the deficit or surplus.

It was explained there that, while a short-run deficit or surplus on current account does not pose a problem, a persistent or long-run imbalance indicates fundamental disequilibrium. In the case of a deficit, the nature of any resulting problem depends on the size and cause of the deficit: the larger the deficit, the greater the problem is likely to be. The problem is also likely to be serious if the deficit is caused by the uncompetitiveness of the country's industries. Although in the short run a deficit allows a country's residents to enjoy living standards boosted by imports, and thus higher than would be possible from the consumption of the country's output alone, in the long run, the decline of the country's industries in the face of international competition lowers living standards.

While many people agree that a persistent current account deficit can pose serious problems, we also said few realise that a balance of payments surplus on current account can also lead to problems. Because a surplus is often seen as a sign of national economic virility and success, a popular view is that the bigger the surplus, the better must be the country's performance. This is obviously true insofar as the surplus measures the competitiveness of the country's exporting industries. However, although a small surplus may be a justifiable objective of government policy, a large payments surplus should be regarded as undesirable. This is for two reasons:

● One country's surplus is another country's deficit. Since we don't trade with Mars or any other planet, the balance of payments must balance for the world as a whole. It is therefore impossible for all countries to run surpluses simultaneously. Unless countries with persistently large surpluses agree to take action to reduce their surpluses, deficit countries cannot reduce their deficits. Deficit countries may then be forced to impose import controls from which all countries, including surplus countries, eventually suffer.

● A balance of payments surplus is an injection of aggregate demand into the circular flow of income and this can be inflationary. If there are substantial unemployed resources in the economy, this can have the beneficial effect of reflating real output and jobs. However, if the economy is initially close to full capacity, demand-pull inflation results.

We noted earlier that, in recent years, the UK's current account deficit has increased in size. This has not necessarily been regarded as a problem because it has been financed by inward capital flows. However, the deficit has been increasing as a percentage of national income and some economists believe that, unless the deficit is reduced, it could lead to capital outflows as foreign investors question the ability of the UK to finance its growing overseas debts. It is not a deterioration in the balance of trade in goods and services that has been the main problem in recent years. As Figure 10.11 shows, a significant cause of the growing current account deficit is a deterioration in the primary income balance.

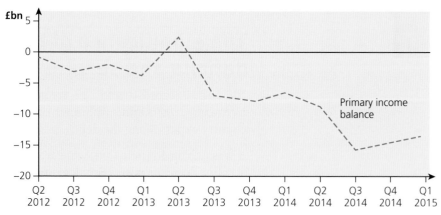

Figure 10.11 The deterioration in the UK's primary income balance within the current account, quarterly data from Q2, 2012 to Q1, 2015

Source: ONS

Primary income is the balance between the income (i.e. profits, dividends and interest payments) received on the UK's foreign investments, and the income paid to overseas investors on their UK investments. Figure 10.11 shows the quarterly deterioration, but on an annual basis, the primary income deficit moved from a £19 billion surplus in 2011 to a £33 billion deficit in 2014. According to **www.parliament.uk**:

the deterioration in the primary account was driven by UK residents receiving lower income on their overseas foreign direct investments (FDI). This in turn was a result of both lower returns on those investments (thanks in part to economic weakness in the eurozone), and a reduction in the total stock of UK overseas FDI. In contrast, foreign residents have continued to expand their holdings of UK assets (something that may be linked to the relative strength of the UK's recovery and its status as a 'safe haven'), and have shifted the composition of their assets from low-yielding debt to riskier, higher-yielding equity, thereby increasing the rate of return on their holdings.

Implications for the global economy of other economies taking action to reduce their current account imbalances

As we have seen, countries are more likely to take action to try to reduce a current account deficit than to reduce a current account surplus. Indeed, surplus countries very often like to keep things exactly as they are, particularly if they benefit from artificial price competitiveness caused by an undervalued exchange rate.

Perhaps not surprisingly, corrective action by an economy to reduce the size of a current account deficit may have very little effect on other economies, first if the deficit is small, and second if the economy forms only a tiny part of the world economy. The same is not true, however, if the economy taking the corrective action is large.

The USA is the country which runs the largest current account deficit, importing far more than it exports. Many of these imports are cheap Chinese manufactured goods and components that American firms such as Apple design before they are assembled into finished consumer goods (often in China). China likes it this way because the USA provides a ready market for its exports. Many American importing firms and consumers also like it this way because they benefit from cheap components and consumer goods. (However, other American manufacturing firms and the workers they employ don't like it this way. Unless these firms move out of the USA and relocate in cheap labour countries, they may be forced to go under, and either way, American workers will lose their jobs.)

To correct the deficit and to save American jobs, the US government may resort to protectionism. Because of US membership of the WTO, overt protectionism is generally not possible, but this has not stopped the USA using its hegemony and power to engage in various forms of covert or hidden protectionism. Such policies undoubtedly harm countries which sell goods to the USA. If a smaller and less powerful country were to take this action, it might suffer 'beggar my neighbour' retaliation, but the size and power of the USA generally make this impractical.

The USA has never really deflated its economy in order to correct its payment deficit, but when the US economy does suffer from a downturn — for example, recession in 2008 and 2009 — other countries have faced a sudden loss of export markets. There is a saying: 'When America sneezes, the rest of the world catches a cold.' Because of the size of the US economy, countries which export to the USA are highly dependent on it continuing to grow.

337

A recession in the USA tends to mean that other countries import recession from it, which is clearly not what the other countries want.

As we have seen, the other action a country can take to reduce a current account deficit is to devalue or encourage a depreciation of its exchange rate. Again, if this policy is viewed by other countries as an attempt to gain at their expense, it might lead to retaliatory devaluations and to an exchange rate war from which nobody benefits. Encouraging the dollar to fall has not always been an effective way of reducing the USA's balance of payments deficit. This is because other currencies, such as China's renminbi (RMB) or yuan, have at times been effectively 'pegged' to the dollar, which means that if the dollar's exchange rate falls, so does the RMB's exchange rate. However, China stunned financial markets in August 2015 by devaluing the RMB on two consecutive days in order to counter a slowdown in its growth rate. This is despite the fact that China had been previously been reluctant to raise the RMB's exchange rate and lose its price competitive advantage.

In the case of the USA and China, the imbalance in the two countries' current accounts is largely resolved by large capital flows from China into the USA. For example, China has purchased large quantities of US government bonds. In 2015, China held US Treasury bonds worth more than $1.25 trillion. These capital flows finance the American trade deficit. Indeed, the world as a whole is generally willing to 'invest' in the USA, irrespective of the state of the US current account, because the US dollar is a reserve currency and is viewed as a 'safe haven'.

Financial markets were stunned by China's devaluation of the yuan or renminbi (RMB) in August 2015

For a smaller country such as the UK, a downward float of the pound's exchange rate might be a viable method of reducing a current account deficit. A fall in the pound's exchange rate would probably have relatively little effect on other economies. However, the effectiveness of a depreciation would depend on how big it was, on whether it provoked retaliation, and on the price elasticities of demand for the UK's exports and imports. A fall in the exchange rate might also provoke a 'hot money' flow out of the pound, leading to a further fall in the value of the currency that might then destabilise the UK economy.

Applying *AD/AS* analysis to the current account of the balance of payments

Section 10.3 concludes with a reminder of the explanation provided in Book 1, Chapter 8, of how *AD/AS* analysis can be used to explain the effect of a change in the current account of the balance of payments on the level of real output and the price level in the economy.

For the sake of simplicity, we assume that exports and imports of goods and services are the only items in the current account. Given this simplifying assumption, there is a current account surplus when net exports are positive, i.e. $X > M$, and a deficit in the current account when net exports are negative, i.e. $X < M$.

As mentioned in Book 1, exports are an injection of spending into the circular flow of income, whereas imports are a leakage or withdrawal of spending from the flow.

Suppose that initially $X = M$, which means there is neither a surplus nor a deficit in the current account. Note also that in this situation, given our assumption that there are no non-trade flows in the current account, foreign trade injections into the circular flow of income exactly equal foreign trade withdrawals from the flow. To put it another way, when $X = M$, the current account has a neutral effect on the state of aggregate demand and on the circular flow of income.

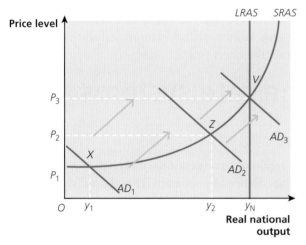

Figure 10.12 How an increase in exports can affect the national economy

However, suppose that at the next stage, overseas demand for UK exports increases, but UK demand for imports remains unchanged. This means there is a net injection of spending into the circular flow of income. The current account moves into surplus, with $X > M$.

In the *AD/AS* diagram drawn in Figure 10.12, the increase in exports shifts the *AD* curve to the right. What happens next in the economy depends on the shape and slope of the *SRAS* curve around the initial point of macroeconomic equilibrium (point X in Figure 10.12).

Point X shows the economy in deep recession, suffering from deficient aggregate demand. In this situation, *any* event that increases aggregate demand increases the level of real output in the economy and causes demand-deficient unemployment to fall. An increase in exports is just such an event. In the diagram, increased exports shift the *AD* curve rightward from AD_1 to AD_2. This causes real output to rise from y_1 to y_2, though at the cost of inflation, since the price level rises from P_1 to P_2.

Following the shift to the right of the aggregate demand curve to AD_2, macroeconomic equilibrium is now shown at point Z. But as the *SRAS* curve becomes steeper, moving up the curve, the diagram tells us that the main effect of a further shift of the *AD* curve from AD_2 to AD_3 falls on the price level rather than on output and jobs. Output increases, from y_2 to y_N (the 'normal capacity' level of real output) but the price level also increases to P_3. As the real output moves toward its 'normal' capacity level, export demand becomes *inflationary* rather than *reflationary*.

Nevertheless, in this situation the growth in export demand eliminates the demand deficiency previously existent in the economy. The economy ends up on its long-run aggregate supply (*LRAS*) curve, with macroeconomic equilibrium at point V.

Once point V has been reached, what may happen next in the economy depends on assumptions made about the nature of short-run and long-run aggregate supply. According to Figure 10.12, when the economy produces on the vertical *LRAS* curve, any further increase in the demand for exports leads only to the price level rising above P_3, without any increase in real output. However, there is another possibility. Foreign demand for a country's exports often creates favourable supply-side conditions and may, for example, lead to a rise in investment, shifting the *LRAS* curve to the right. This means the economy can produce and supply the goods needed to meet the increase in export demand without necessarily generating inflation. This is an example of export-led growth, mentioned earlier in this chapter in the context of successful supply-side policies. The German and Japanese economies certainly enjoyed export-led growth from the 1960s to the 1980s, and China has recently enjoyed similar benefits. However, the growth of demand for Chinese exports has also caused inflation in the Chinese economy.

A fall in export demand and/or an increase in domestic demand for imports triggers an opposite effect to the one just described. There is a net leakage of demand from the circular flow of income, the *AD* curve shifts to the left, and both real output and the price level fall (or, probably more realistically, the rate of inflation slows down). Overall, the effect is *deflationary*.

10.4 Exchange rate systems

Introduction to exchange rates

So far in this chapter, we have made several mentions of exchange rates, particularly in the context of the balance of payments. This should not be surprising: whenever we discuss exchange rates we usually have to make reference to the balance of payments, and vice versa.

Although domestic currencies are used to pay for internal trade within countries, imports are usually paid for in the currency of the country exporting the goods or services. An exchange rate measures how much of another currency a particular currency can buy; it is the external price of the currency quoted in terms of another currency. Exchange rates can also be measured against gold, or against a weighted average of a selection or 'basket' of currencies. Currencies are bought and sold in the foreign exchange market, which is now an international market, dominated by electronic trading. On a global scale, the market never closes, and ICT-based buying and selling takes place throughout the day and night.

The meaning and measurement of an exchange rate

These days the **exchange rate** of a currency is simply the external price of the currency in terms of another currency, such as the US dollar. The convention of quoting exchange rates in terms of the US dollar is fairly recent. Before 1914 most exchange rates were expressed in terms of gold and only after 1945 did the dollar become the near universally accepted standard by which the external values of other currencies were measured.

In recent years, in response to the changing pattern of UK trade, the pound's exchange rate is as often quoted against the euro as it is against the dollar. The sterling exchange rate index (ERI) is also used to measure the pound's exchange rate. The ERI does not measure the pound's external value against a particular currency. Rather it is a trade-weighted average of the pound's exchange rate against a number of leading trading currencies, calculated to reflect the importance of each currency in international trade.

STUDY TIP
Make sure you can use both the *AD/AS* model and the circular flow of income model to analyse how changes in exports and/or imports affect macroeconomic performance, i.e. growth, employment, inflation and international competitiveness.

KEY TERM
exchange rate the external price of a currency, usually measured against another currency.

EXTENSION MATERIAL

The real exchange rate

The different exchange rates mentioned so far are all *nominal* exchange rates. These must not be confused with a *real* exchange rate, which measures the weighted average value of a country's currency relative to a basket of other major currencies, adjusted for the effects of inflation. The real exchange rate of the pound, which is a measure of competitiveness, is calculated by the following formula:

$$\text{pound's real exchange rate} = \text{sterling index} \times \frac{\text{index of the domestic price level}}{\text{index of weighted foreign price levels}}$$

For simplicity, assume that the domestic price level rises by 10%, the foreign price level remains unchanged and the nominal value of the domestic currency depreciates by 10%, then the real exchange rate remains unchanged. The price competitiveness of the country's products has not changed, and the improvement in competitiveness brought about by the fall in the nominal exchange rate has been exactly offset by a higher rate of domestic inflation.

QUANTITATIVE SKILLS 10.4

Worked example: calculating percentage changes in an exchange rate from data presented in index number form

Table 10.14 shows the value of a country's currency against other currencies, in index number form.

Table 10.14 Exchange rate index, 2012–15

Year	Exchange rate index (2013 = 100)
2012	96
2013	100
2014	106
2015	102

Calculate the percentage change in the country's exchange rate between:

a 2012 and 2015

b 2013 and 2014

a Between 2012 and 2015 the index changed by 6 points. The percentage change between these years was therefore (6/96) × 100, which is a 6.25% increase.

b In this example, because the comparison is with the base year index number (100), the change in index points and the percentage change are the same: a 6-point index number change and a 6% change.

The different types of exchange rate system

Figure 10.13 shows the main types of exchange rate system. The two extreme types are **freely floating exchange rates** (also known as cleanly floating exchange rates) and rigidly **fixed exchange rates**. A fixed exchange rate is the most extreme form of managed exchange rate.

KEY TERMS

freely floating exchange rate the exchange rate is determined solely by the interplay of demand for, and supply of, the currency.

fixed exchange rate an exchange rate fixed at a certain level by the country's central bank and maintained by the central bank's intervention in the foreign exchange market.

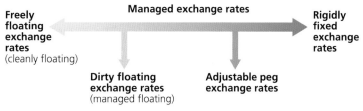

Figure 10.13 The different types of exchange rate system

341

The managed exchange rates that lie between the extremes of freely floating and rigidly fixed exchange rates take two main forms: adjustable peg and managed floating (or dirty floating) exchange rates. Adjustable peg exchange rates resemble fixed exchange rates in many respects, but the rate at which the exchange rate is fixed may be changed from time to time. A formal devaluation reduces the fixed exchange rate, while revaluation increases the fixed rate. With an adjustable peg system, there is usually a band in which the exchange rate is allowed to fluctuate.

Freely floating exchange rates

In a regime of freely floating exchange rates, the external value of a country's currency is determined on foreign exchange markets by the forces of demand and supply alone. Toward the end of this section, we will remind you of how, in recent decades, capital flows and speculation have been extremely significant in influencing the supply of and demand for a currency, and hence its exchange rate. However, we will first simplify by assuming that a currency is demanded on foreign exchanges solely for the payment of trade and that trade flows alone determine exchange rates. We will also assume that any holdings of foreign currencies surplus to the immediate requirement of paying for trade are immediately sold on the foreign exchange market.

EXTENSION MATERIAL

Explaining the slope of the demand and supply curves for pounds

When the exchange rate of the pound falls, UK exports become more competitive in overseas markets. The volume of UK exports increases, leading to greater overseas demand for pounds to finance the purchase of these exports, provided that the demand for UK exports is price elastic. This explains the downward-sloping demand curve for pounds, which is illustrated in Figure 10.14.

But just as UK exports generate a demand for pounds on foreign exchange markets, so imports into the UK generate a supply of pounds. The explanation lies in the fact that UK trading companies generally pay for imports in foreign currencies. Importers must sell sterling on the foreign exchange market in order to purchase the foreign currencies needed to pay for the goods they are buying. As the pound's exchange rate rises, fewer pounds are needed to buy a given quantity of foreign currency. This means that the sterling price of imports falls. UK consumers are likely to respond to the falling price of imports by increasing total spending on imports (which happens as long as the

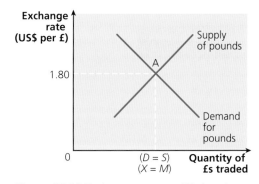

Figure 10.14 Exchange rate equilibrium in a freely floating exchange rate system

demand for imports is price elastic). A greater total quantity of sterling must be supplied on foreign exchange markets to pay for the imports — even though the sterling price of each unit of imports has fallen. The result is the upward-sloping supply curve of sterling depicted in Figure 10.14. This shows that at higher exchange rates, more sterling is likely to be supplied on the foreign exchange market.

Exchange rate equilibrium in a freely floating exchange rate regime

Exchange rate equilibrium occurs at the market-clearing exchange rate at which the demand for pounds on foreign exchange markets equals the supply of pounds. In Figure 10.14 in the extension material, this is determined at point A. The equilibrium exchange rate is $1.80 to the pound.

At this exchange rate, the money value of exports (paid in sterling) equals the money value of imports (paid in foreign currencies). And provided we assume that exports and imports are the only items in the current account, the current account is also in balance.

Because we are assuming away any complications introduced by capital flows, exchange rate equilibrium implies balance of payments equilibrium on current account and vice versa. As we stated at the beginning of section 10.4, the two equilibria are just different sides of the same coin: exchange rate equilibrium is price equilibrium, whereas current account equilibrium in the balance of payments (where $X = M$ in Figure 10.14) means that the quantity of the currency flowing into the country equals the quantity flowing out. Given the simplifying assumptions we have made, once the balance of payments is in equilibrium, there is no pressure for the exchange rate to rise or fall.

The adjustment process to a new equilibrium exchange rate

We shall now assume that some event or 'shock' disturbs the initial equilibrium — for example, an improvement in the quality of foreign-produced goods causes UK residents to increase demand for imports, whatever the exchange rate. In Figure 10.15, the increase in demand for foreign exchange to pay for imports causes the supply curve of the pound sterling to shift to the right from S_1 to S_2. (Remember, when more foreign currencies are demanded, more pounds must be supplied on the foreign exchange market.) In the new situation, the current account of the balance of payments is in deficit by the amount ($X < M$) in the diagram — as long as the exchange rate stays at $1.80. At the $1.80 exchange rate, UK residents supply or sell more pounds than before to pay for imports, but because overseas residents still demand the same quantity of UK goods (assuming that their views on the quality of UK goods relative to foreign goods has not changed), the overseas demand for pounds to pay for UK exports remains at its previous level.

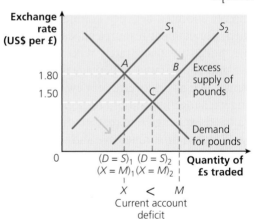

Figure 10.15 How a current account deficit is eliminated in a freely floating exchange rate system

At the exchange rate of $1.80 to the pound, there is now an excess supply of pounds on the foreign exchange market, equal to the distance B minus A. The market mechanism now swings into action to restore equilibrium — both for the exchange rate and for the balance of payments. When the excess holdings of pounds accumulated at the exchange rate of $1.80 are sold on the foreign exchange market, the pound's exchange rate falls. This increases the price competitiveness of UK exports while making imports less price competitive. The exchange rate falls until a new equilibrium exchange rate is reached at point C, where the exchange rate is $1.50 to the pound.

Note that the current account of the balance of payments is once again in equilibrium, but at $(X = M)_2$ rather than at $(X = M)_1$. This means that at the new equilibrium exchange rate, although they are again equal in size, the money values of exports and imports have both increased.

Conversely, if the initial equilibrium is disturbed by an improvement in the quality of UK goods or services, the demand curve for the pound shifts to the right. This moves the current account into surplus, causing the pound's exchange rate to rise or appreciate in order to relieve the excess demand for pounds. Providing UK residents don't change their views on the relative quality of imports, the exchange rate rises until the balance of payments and exchange equilibrium are once again restored.

STUDY TIP
You should practise drawing demand and supply graphs to show a floating exchange rate.

The advantages of floating exchange rates

Economists generally agree that, provided there are no distorting capital flows, freely floating exchange rates have the following advantages.

Balance of payments equilibrium

The exchange rate (which is the external price of the currency) should move up or down automatically to correct a payments imbalance. Provided the adjustment mechanism operates smoothly, a currency should never be overvalued or undervalued for long. In the event of an overvalued exchange rate causing export uncompetitiveness and a payments deficit, market forces should quickly adjust the exchange rate downward towards its equilibrium price, which also achieves equilibrium in the balance of payments. Similarly, undervaluation should be quickly corrected by an upward movement of the exchange rate.

Resource allocation

If the world's resources are to be efficiently allocated between competing uses, exchange rates must be correctly valued. For efficient resource allocation in a constantly changing world, market prices must accurately reflect shifts in demand and changes in competitive and comparative advantage that result from technical progress and events such as discoveries of new mineral resources. In principle, a freely floating exchange rate should respond and adjust to these changes. By contrast, a fixed exchange rate may gradually become overvalued or undervalued, as demand or competitive and comparative advantage move against or in favour of a country's industries. Similarly, different rates of inflation between countries mean that, over time, fixed exchange rates lead to a misallocation of resources between economies.

Domestic macroeconomic policy objectives

It is sometimes argued that when the exchange rate is freely floating, balance of payments surpluses and deficits cease to be a policy problem for the government, as it is then free to pursue the domestic economic objectives of full employment and growth. Market forces 'look after' the current account of the balance of payments, leaving governments free to concentrate on domestic economic policy. If, in the pursuit of domestic objectives, the inflation rate is higher than in other countries, in a freely floating world the exchange rate simply falls to restore competitiveness. However, this adds to the inflationary pressures in the country that already has higher than average inflation.

Inflation

In much the same way, a responsible government achieving a lower than average inflation rate should benefit from a floating exchange rate because the exchange rate insulates the country against 'importing inflation' from the rest of the world. If inflation rates are higher in the rest of the world, a fixed exchange rate causes a country to import inflation through the rising prices of goods imported from high-inflation countries. By contrast, a floating exchange rate appreciates, which lowers the prices of imports, insulating the economy against importing inflation.

Independent monetary policy

As we have noted, with a floating exchange rate, monetary policy can be used solely to achieve domestic policy objectives, such as the control of inflation. This is called an *independent* monetary policy. By contrast, with a fixed exchange rate, interest rates may be determined by events in the outside world (and in particular by capital flows out of and into currencies), rather than by the needs of the domestic economy. To maintain a fixed exchange rate, interest rates may have to be raised to prevent the exchange rate from falling. In this situation, monetary policy is no longer independent, in the sense that it can no longer be assigned to pursuing purely domestic policy objectives.

The disadvantages of floating exchange rates

Freely floating exchange rates nevertheless have some disadvantages, particularly relating to the fact that in the modern globalised world in which financial capital is internationally mobile, capital flows rather than exports and imports are the main determinants of floating exchange rates.

Speculation and capital flows

The argument that a freely floating exchange rate is never overvalued or undervalued for very long depends crucially upon the main assumption of the traditional theory of exchange rates, that currencies are bought and sold on foreign exchange markets only to finance trade. This assumption means that speculation and capital flows have no influence on exchange rates. But this is at odds with how the modern globalised economy works. These days, well over 90% of currency transactions taking place on foreign exchange markets stem from capital flows and from the decisions of individuals, business corporations, financial institutions and even governments to switch wealth portfolios between different currencies.

In the short run, exchange rates are extremely vulnerable to speculative capital or 'hot money' movements into or out of currencies. Just like a fixed exchange rate, a floating exchange rate can be overvalued or undervalued, which means it does not reflect the trading competitiveness of the country's goods and services. In this situation, speculators will buy currencies they perceive to be undervalued in order to make capital gains when selling the currencies at higher exchange rates in the future. Likewise, they will sell currencies they perceive to be overvalued in order to avoid capital losses when selling the currencies at lower exchange rates in the future.

Arguably, however, fixed exchange rates are even more vulnerable than floating exchange rates to speculative capital flows. This is because fixed exchange rates often become overvalued or undervalued. In the case of an overvalued currency, speculators may sell the currency in order to make a profit by buying it back at a lower exchange rate after the currency has been devalued. However, if devaluation does not take place, the speculators can instead enjoy the 'one-way option' of buying back the currency at the exchange rate at which it was sold.

International trading uncertainty

It is sometimes argued that, whereas fixed exchange rates create conditions of certainty and stability in which international trade can prosper and grow, the volatility and instability caused by floating exchange rates slow the growth of, and even destroys, international trade. The prospect of changes in the exchange rate means that companies cannot be sure how much domestic currency they will have to pay for imports or receive from exports, and this uncertainty can deter them from engaging in international trade. By inhibiting trade, resources may be misallocated and world living standards reduced.

In reality, however, *hedging*, which involves the purchase or sale of a currency in the 'forward' market, say 3 months in advance of the actual delivery of the currency and payment for trade, reduces the trading uncertainties associated with floating exchange rates. Indeed, fixed and managed exchange rates may also cause uncertainty, especially when a currency is over or undervalued and a devaluation or revaluation is expected.

Cost-push inflation

Floating exchange rates sometimes contribute to cost-push inflation. Suppose a country has a higher rate of inflation than its trading partners. Trading competitiveness and the current account of the balance of payments both worsen, causing the exchange rate to fall in order to restore competitiveness. This may trigger a vicious cumulative downward spiral of faster inflation and exchange rate depreciation. The falling exchange rate increases import prices, which raise the rate of domestic cost-push inflation. Workers react by demanding pay rises to restore the real value of the eroded real wage. At the next stage, increased inflation itself erodes the export competitiveness initially won by the fall of the exchange rate, which in turn triggers a further fall in the exchange rate to recover the lost advantage, and so the process continues. The resulting downward spiral can eventually destabilise large parts of the domestic economy, causing unemployment and reducing economic growth.

Demand-pull inflation

Floating exchange rates can trigger demand-pull inflation as well as cost-push inflation. With a floating exchange rate, there is no need to deflate the domestic economy to deal with a balance of payments deficit on the current account. But suppose a large number of countries with floating exchange rates simultaneously increase aggregate demand. This can lead to excess demand on a worldwide scale, which fuels global inflation. This happened in the 1970s, when a worldwide expansion of demand created conditions in which oil and primary goods producers could raise prices and still sell in world markets. In countries such as the UK, the resulting inflation appeared to be import cost-push inflation, caused by the rising cost of imported energy and raw materials. However, the true cause lay in excess demand created by the simultaneous effects of demand expansion and floating exchange rates, when world supply could not increase, at least in the short run, to meet the surge in global demand. Similarly, floating exchange rates allow an individual government to over-inflate its economy, provided it is willing to allow the exchange rate to fall.

In contrast, the commitment to a fixed exchange rate prevents a government unilaterally adopting an excessively expansionary monetary policy, since the resulting inflation will cause the balance of payments to deteriorate and put

STUDY TIP
Make sure you understand the links between exchange rates and inflation.

downward pressure on the exchange rate. To prevent this, interest rates will have to be increased, damping down the domestic inflationary pressures.

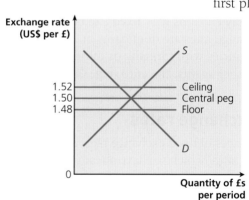

TEST YOURSELF 10.2

All other things being equal, which one of the following is the most likely effect on the UK economy of a change in the exchange rate from $1 = £1.50 to $1 = £2?

A a fall in aggregate demand and a rise in inflationary pressure

B a rise in aggregate demand and a rise in inflationary pressure

C a rise in aggregate demand and a fall in inflationary pressure

D a fall in aggregate demand and a fall in inflationary pressure

Fixed exchange rates

With a freely floating exchange rate system, a currency's external value rises or falls to eliminate a balance of payments surplus or deficit. By contrast, with rigidly fixed exchange rates, a currency's external value remains unchanged, while the *internal* price level, or more usually the level of domestic economic activity and output, adjusts to eliminate a balance of payments disequilibrium on current account.

As the extension material on page 351 explains, there are few examples of fixed exchange rates today. Note also that so-called fixed exchange rates have seldom if ever been rigidly fixed. Modern fixed exchange rates are better thought of as adjustable peg exchange rates. We shall explain this term shortly.

How a central bank manages a fixed exchange rate

Figure 10.16 illustrates the key features of a fixed exchange rate. In the first place, the country's government or its central bank announces that the exchange rate is being fixed at a particular rate and the central bank is then given responsibility for maintaining that rate. In the context of Figure 10.16, the Bank of England would announce that the pound's exchange rate is being fixed at US$1.50. $1.50 would be called the exchange rate's 'central peg', also known as the 'central rate', 'parity' or 'par value'.

Simultaneously, the Bank of England would announce 'ceiling' and 'floor' limits, set respectively just above and below the 'central peg'. Market forces (supply and demand on foreign exchange markets) then determine the currency's 'day-to-day' exchange rate.

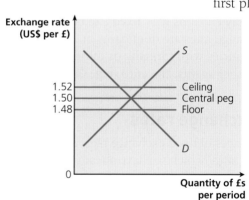

Figure 10.16 The ceiling, central peg and floor of a fixed exchange rate

Provided that the exchange rate remains inside the 'zone or band of flexibility' between the ceiling and the floor, central bank intervention is not needed. However, if either the demand curve for, or the supply curve of, the currency shifts to a new position, in the absence of Bank of England intervention, market forces might take the exchange rate above the $1.52 ceiling or below the $1.48 floor. If this happens, the fixed exchange rate has effectively broken down. To prevent this happening, whenever the ceiling or floor looks as if it is going to be breached, the central bank intervenes.

There are two main ways in which a central bank can intervene in markets to maintain a fixed exchange rate. The first is by buying or selling its own currency on the foreign exchange market. In Figure 10.16, if the exchange rate threatens to rise above the $1.52 ceiling, the Bank of England would sell its own currency on the foreign exchange market to offset excess demand for pounds that would otherwise pull up the exchange rate. Likewise, if the exchange rate is deemed likely to fall below its $1.48 floor, the Bank of England would step into the foreign exchange market and buy its own currency. In this case, by creating an 'artificial' demand for the pound, the Bank would attempt to prevent an excess supply of pounds from pushing the exchange rate below the floor. The policy of buying and selling currencies to support an exchange rate is known as *exchange equalisation*.

The second method of supporting a fixed exchange rate is by the central bank triggering a fall or an increase in domestic interest rates within the economy. In the case of the pound, lower domestic interest rates might cause international holders of the pound to sell pounds and buy other currencies. This would cause the pound's exchange rate to fall, hopefully to a rate below the ceiling of $1.52. Conversely, an increase in UK interest rates attracts 'hot money' into the pound. Through the selling other currencies and the buying of the pound, short-run capital inflows raise the demand for pounds, hopefully taking the pound's exchange rate above its floor rate of $1.48.

In real life, both methods of intervention are likely to be used in tandem to support each other, particularly if an exchange rate crisis has threatened to destroy a fixed exchange rate. Perhaps the most important point to note is that when supporting a fixed exchange rate, a country's central bank may not be able to change its key interest rate (Bank Rate in the UK) to achieve purely domestic macroeconomic policy objectives such as economic growth and low unemployment. Instead, the freedom to use monetary policy to achieve domestic objectives is sacrificed on the altar of supporting a fixed exchange rate. This fact of life probably explains why fixed exchange rates are rare today and why floating exchange rates are dominant. In 2015, however, there were still over 30 countries with formally or informally fixed exchange rates — most were fixed either against the euro (e.g. Denmark), or the US dollar.

The advantages of fixed exchange rates

Because the advantages and disadvantages of fixed exchange rates are closely related to but mirror those of floating rates, which we have already explained in some depth, we shall provide only a brief summary here.

Arguably, the main advantages of fixed exchange rates are:

● certainty and stability
● the anti-inflationary discipline they impose on a country's domestic economic management and on the behaviour of its workers and firms.

The disadvantages of fixed exchange rates

By contrast, the principal disadvantages of fixed exchange rates include:

- a possible increase in uncertainty, which can disrupt the economy if devaluation or revaluation is expected
- continued overvaluation or undervaluation of the currency, leading to a misallocation of resources
- severe deflationary costs of lost output and unemployment for a deficit country and the importing of inflation by a surplus country
- possible recurrent balance of payments or currency crises in a country whose currency is overvalued
- tying up of resources in official reserves (needed to support the fixed exchange rate), which could be used more productively elsewhere

Managed exchange rates

A rigidly fixed exchange rate is, of course, an example (the extreme example) of a managed exchange rate. However, there are two other examples of managed exchange rates: *adjustable peg* (or *fixed* peg) and *managed floating* or *'dirty' floating*. In both cases, a country's monetary authorities hope to achieve the stability and certainty associated with fixed exchange rates combined with a floating exchange rate's ability to avoid overvaluation and undervaluation by responding to market forces.

Adjustable peg exchange rates

An adjustable peg exchange rate is similar to a rigidly fixed exchange rate, except that the central bank may alter the exchange rate's central peg by devaluing or revaluing. If you look back at Figure 10.13, you will see that on the spectrum of exchange rates, an adjustable peg exchange rate is much closer to a rigidly fixed exchange rate than to a freely floating exchange rate. By contrast, a 'dirty floating' (or managed floating) exchange rate is much closer to a freely floating exchange rate.

Nevertheless, adjustable pegs are more flexible than the central pegs of rigidly fixed exchange rates, such as the old nineteenth-century gold standard. This is because the exchange rate can be adjusted upward or downward from time to time by the country's central bank. Adjustments take place because, over a period of time, exchange rates are likely to become over or undervalued as, for example, countries experience different rates of inflation. An upward revaluation corrects an undervalued exchange rate, whereas a downward adjustment or devaluation is used to correct overvaluation.

Figure 10.17, which is a development of Figure 10.16, illustrates devaluation of the pound in an adjustable peg exchange rate system. The exchange rate is initially fixed at a central peg of $1.50. As we explained earlier, the interaction of supply and demand for the currency on the foreign exchange market then determines the day-to-day exchange rate. Provided the exchange stays between a ceiling and a floor set at the time that the central peg was fixed,

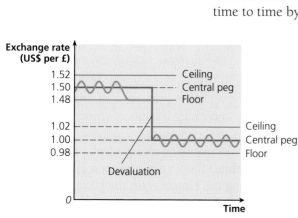

Figure 10.17 A devaluation of an adjustable peg exchange rate

there is no need for central bank intervention. However, the graph shows the sterling exchange rate falling to the floor of $1.48, possibly because of a speculative capital flow against the currency. At this point the Bank of England intervenes, raising domestic interest rates to attract capital flows into the currency and purchasing the pound on the foreign exchange market using its foreign exchange reserves. By selling reserves and buying its own currency, the central bank creates an artificial demand for the pound, bidding up the exchange rate.

Persistent support for a currency almost certainly means that its exchange rate is overvalued, condemning the country to over-priced exports, under-priced imports and a persistent current account deficit. With the rigidly fixed exchange rate shown in Figure 10.16, this is the end of the story. The country's government has to deflate the domestic economy and/or impose import controls, since devaluation and revaluation are not permitted in a rigidly fixed system.

However, Figure 10.17 shows the Bank of England devaluing the exchange rate to a new central peg of $1.00 in an attempt to correct the fundamental imbalance. This illustrates the difference between adjustable peg and rigidly fixed exchange rate systems. But if a country makes frequent changes to the central peg, the benefits of having a fixed exchange rate are lost.

Managed floating or dirty floating exchange rates

Fixed and adjustable peg exchange rate systems have now been abandoned throughout much of the world. Most exchange rates now float, though there is a difference between 'clean' and 'dirty' floating. Clean floating is the same as free floating and pure floating — that is, there is absolutely no central bank intervention to prop up the exchange rate or to manipulate its value. In contrast to clean floating, 'managed' or 'dirty' floating occurs when the exchange rate is officially floating, in the sense that a country's monetary authorities announce that market forces are determining the exchange rate, but in fact they intervene unofficially behind the scenes, buying or selling their own currency in order to influence the exchange rate. (Countries around the world freely admit that they 'manage' their floating exchange rates. Arguably there are currently no countries that have a truly free-floating exchange rate system.)

At the time of writing (in January 2016), it is probably true to say that for most of the period since September 1992, when the pound left an adjustable peg exchange rate system within the EU known as the Exchange Rate Mechanism (ERM) of the European Monetary System (EMS), the pound's exchange rate has been more or less freely floating. Nevertheless, the Bank of England does intervene on a daily basis, as part of a 'smoothing operation' through which it tries to iron out temporary fluctuations in the pound's exchange rate. When in September 1992 there was intense speculative pressure against the pound, 'unofficial' dirty floating took place 'behind the scenes' and for a few days it was difficult to detect when it was going on. However, in the UK currency crises have been rare in recent decades.

A brief history of fixed exchange rates

Although most exchange rates now float, fixed exchange rates have sometimes been important in the last 150 years or so. In a rigidly fixed system, devaluation is ruled out as a means of reducing a current account deficit. This means that deflationary policies that decrease aggregate demand have to be used instead. As a result, deflation harms the domestic economy, increasing unemployment and reducing growth, which explains why modern governments generally reject a return to rigidly fixed exchange rates. Governments prefer a downward float of their exchange rates to deal with balance of payments deficits on current account.

There have been four historical periods in which fixed or adjustable peg exchange rate systems were significant. These were the years of:

- the nineteenth-century gold standard
- the Bretton Woods system
- the Exchange Rate Mechanism
- the fixing of 12 European national exchange rates prior to the introduction of the euro

The gold standard system of fixed exchange rates

The longest period of rigidly fixed exchange rates occurred in the nineteenth century and in the early years of the twentieth century. During this period, most major world currencies were fixed against a particular quantity of gold. A formal gold standard was first established in the UK in 1821, following the introduction a few years earlier of the gold sovereign coin. The full gold standard, in which citizens could exchange paper pounds for gold, came to an end in the UK on the outbreak of the First World War in 1914. The exchange rate then floated, until a temporary return to a more limited gold standard from 1925 until the onset of an economic and political crisis in 1931. Apart from a short period in 1933 when the US dollar left the gold standard, the American currency remained on the gold standard until the break-up, noted below, of the Bretton Woods system of adjustable peg exchange rates in 1971.

The Bretton Woods system of adjustable peg exchange rates

The international gold standard in effect came to an end in 1914 on the outbreak of the First World War, after which exchange rates mostly floated until eventually the Bretton Woods system of adjustable peg exchange rates was created in 1944. The Bretton Woods exchange rates, which were policed by the newly created International Monetary Fund (IMF), were based on a dollar standard. Until 1971, when the Bretton Woods system collapsed, the US dollar remained on the gold standard, with all other Bretton Woods currencies being fixed against the dollar. To find out more about the history of Bretton Woods exchanges rates and the IMF, access the web page: **http://content.time.com/time/business/article/0,8599,1852254,00.html**

The Exchange Rate Mechanism of the European Monetary System

In 1979, the European Union (or European Community as it was then called) created the Exchange Rate Mechanism (ERM) to allow more efficient implementation of common economic policies. Before the ERM, financial assistance granted by the EU to member countries, most notably in the common agricultural policy (CAP), was sometimes distorted by fluctuating exchange rates. A relatively fixed exchange rate system within the EU might reduce or eliminate these distortions. As a result, the ERM was created as an adjustable peg exchange rate system, but not as a single currency system.

The EU national currencies joining the ERM were fixed against each other, although the rules of the European Monetary System (EMS) allowed periodic realignments (devaluations and revaluations) to take place. However, by the time the pound joined the ERM in 1990, the system had fossilised and become much more rigidly fixed. The pound entered at too high an exchange rate, which made the overvalued pound extremely vulnerable to a speculative outward capital flow. It became a question of 'when' rather than 'if' the pound would have to leave the ERM.

A massive run on the pound occurred in September 1992, culminating on 'Black Wednesday' with the pound being forced out of the ERM. Since then, the pound's exchange rate has floated. Following the pound's exit, speculators 'picked off' other ERM currencies, which left the EMS much weaker. Because of this, the European Union eventually decided to go one significant stage beyond an adjustable peg exchange rate system, by replacing national currencies with a single currency, the euro.

The fixing of 12 European national exchange rates prior to the introduction of the euro

From 1999 until the full introduction of the euro in 2002, the national currencies of the 12 countries who were committed at the time to adopting the euro were rigidly fixed against each other in preparation for their eventual disappearance in

2002. (It is a moot point whether the fixing of the 12 currencies had created a new system of fixed exchange rates, or whether they had simply been subsumed into a so-called 'virtual' euro before the release of euro notes and coins in 2002. The national currencies remained as legal tender in all 12 countries until they were withdrawn from circulation.)

These 12 countries, together with other countries such as Malta and Slovenia, which adopted the euro more recently, now form the eurozone. At the time of writing, 19 EU countries have adopted the euro as their currency. The eurozone will grow in size if the national currencies of other new EU member countries are eventually replaced by the euro.

Currency unions, the eurozone and the euro

> **KEY TERM**
>
> **currency union** an agreement between a group of countries to share a common currency, and usually to have a single monetary and foreign exchange rate policy.

The United Kingdom is made up of a number of countries, but all of them use the pound as a common currency. Likewise the 50 states of the United States of America, plus the federal district of Washington DC, all use the US dollar. Both the UK and the USA are examples of a **currency union**, which is a group of countries using or sharing a single currency. A currency union is often known a monetary union.

In the 1990s, the UK, being a member state of the European Union (EU) was given the choice of keeping its own currency (still within the EU), or of adopting the common European currency that at the time was being set up. If the UK had chosen the latter, it would have replaced the pound with the new common currency, the *euro*, and joined what became known as the *eurozone*.

The euro came into existence on 1 January 2002 when euro notes and coins entered circulation. However, economists usually date the euro's introduction as 1 January 1999, as this was the date on which the exchange rates of the 12 countries that became the first members of the eurozone or euro area were irrevocably fixed against each other.

In the early 1990s, the Treaty of the European Union (or Maastricht Treaty) began the process which eventually created monetary union within the eurozone. At the time, monetary union was considered necessary for two reasons. In the first place, although the Single European Act had eventually created almost completely free internal trade in goods and services, the need to exchange national currencies in this trade increased transaction costs. A single currency was thus deemed necessary to complete the single market. In the second place, upward and downward movements of EU national currencies led to undervalued and overvalued exchange rates within the trading bloc. Exchange rate fluctuations artificially increased the competitiveness of those countries benefiting from a falling exchange rate, while reducing the competitiveness of countries whose exchange rates were rising. Monetary union would create a level playing field for all member countries.

The euro was created to facilitate greater economic integration among EU member states. Indeed, the euro is regarded by many as a stepping stone to full monetary union (EMU) between EU states and, possibly in the future, to a much fuller economic union. At this point it is worth noting that EMU can mean two different things. The official EU meaning is *economic and monetary union*. Defined in this way, EMU suggests that common monetary arrangements adopted by EU member countries are part of a grander scheme to integrate the national economies of member states. More narrowly defined, the acronym means *European monetary union*, which involves a common monetary policy applied to all EU member states adopting the euro. In the latter meaning, EMU can be interpreted simply as a step towards making the EU's single market work better and more efficiently.

The impact of the euro upon eurozone economies

When the eurozone first came into existence, it was claimed that member countries would benefit in the following ways: reduced transaction costs, elimination of currency risk, greater transparency and possibly greater competition because prices are easier to compare. According to Paul Krugman:

> The creation of the euro was supposed to be another triumphant step in the European project, in which economic integration has been used to foster political integration and peace; a common currency, so the thinking went, would bind the continent even more closely together.

But Krugman then stated:

> What has happened instead is a nightmare: the euro has become an economic trap, and Europe a nest of squabbling nations. Even the continent's democratic achievements seem under threat, as dire economic conditions create a favourable environment for political extremism. Who could have seen such a thing coming?

But Krugman and many other economists did foresee chaos in some of the countries which use the euro because they realised that the eurozone is *not* an *optimal currency area* (see the extension material on page 354). The USA and the UK, which we mentioned earlier as common currency areas, are much closer to being optimal currency areas. Each uses a single currency, enjoys complete internal free trade, and has a fiscal policy as well as a monetary policy covering the whole of the union. The USA, in particular, also enjoys high mobility of labour which enables workers who lose their jobs in the poorer parts of the country to find jobs in richer states such as California.

Mobility of labour and a common fiscal policy are essential if a common currency area is to become an optimal currency area. Without outward labour mobility from poorer parts of the union to the richer parts or perhaps to other parts of the world, the main way a country can regain jobs that have been lost by lack of competitiveness is through a large fall in real wages to make the region more competitive. Without a single currency, a country could restore its competitiveness by devaluing its currency. But in a currency union this is impossible. A high degree of labour mobility is therefore needed to deal with the unemployment problem. Emigration can shrink the size of the labour force to match the number of jobs available. However, it is often the young and more dynamic workers who move and this can be counterproductive.

A common fiscal policy is also particularly important, since it allows wealth to be transferred by centralised fiscal authority from the richer to the poorer parts of the union. Transfers of wealth, via taxation and public spending, are essential to counter the fact that poorer parts of the union cannot achieve competitive advantage by devaluing their national currencies. Fiscal transfers can help to reduce inequality but can also be used to try to improve the competitiveness of the poorer regions — for example, by spending on improving infrastructure.

An optimal currency area thus requires coordination in fiscal policy as well as in monetary policy. The European Central Bank (ECB) achieves monetary policy coordination, but as Greece has found to its expense, there is no supranational authority in the eurozone similar to the ECB to coordinate fiscal policies and to facilitate significant fiscal transfers.

The lack of fiscal policy coordination has led to some eurozone countries having high levels of government debt. This has built up especially in the so-called 'club-med' countries, such as Greece and Portugal, in the southern eurozone. Governments in the poorer countries of the South believed they would always be bailed out painlessly by the richer governments of countries such as Germany and the Netherlands. Also, prior to 2007/08, 'club-med' countries could borrow cheaply on international capital markets. During that time, any euro-denominated debt was pretty much acceptable to investors, no matter which eurozone country issued the debt.

The single market means that in theory there is complete mobility of both labour and capital within the EU. In practice, however, labour mobility is limited, particularly in comparison with the USA where workers move in large numbers from state to state. With regard to capital, after the creation of the euro, before the financial crisis in 2007, there was massive capital movement from Europe's core — mainly Germany — to its periphery, leading to an economic boom in the periphery and significantly higher inflation rates in the 'club-med' countries than in Germany. But when private capital flows from the core to the periphery came to a sudden stop in 2008, the southern countries were uncompetitive and left with prices and unit labour costs well out of line with those in the core. Suddenly the eurozone faced a major adjustment problem it has yet to deal with fully. (So-called austerity measures appear to have had some success in countries such as Ireland, but not yet in Greece.)

EXTENSION MATERIAL
Optimal currency areas

If several countries/states use the same currency, their inhabitants will benefit from efficiency gains. They no longer have to worry about possible future changes in exchange rates, and the costs involved in currency conversion. These gains will be greater the more economically interconnected the countries are, in terms of their trading relationship, the freedom of labour and capital to move between countries, and a unified fiscal policy covering all member countries. In these circumstances, the advantages of adopting a common currency can lead to benefits for all the member states within the currency union.

The 50 states of the USA satisfy most or all the requirements for benefiting from a common currency, namely a large amount of trade in goods and services, free movement of factors of production across the union, and a unified government budget with fiscal transfers from the richer to the poorer states.

It is not yet clear whether the European countries that have adopted the euro as their common currency satisfy those requirements. Many economists believe that the eurozone countries adopted the single currency for political rather than economic reasons. Although the eurozone countries trade a lot with each other, capital and especially labour are not sufficiently mobile between countries, and the countries lack a unified 'government' budget.

The latter point is really significant. A common fiscal policy provides a mechanism for transferring resources — for example, in the form of subsidies or lower tax rates — from the more prosperous parts of the currency union to the less prosperous countries. This is what happens in the UK, for example, when taxes paid by Londoners are directed into public spending projects in Scotland, Wales and Northern Ireland. The UK and the USA are successful common currency areas, but the eurozone is much less successful, since it lacks a common fiscal policy.

10.5 Economic growth and development

The difference between growth and development

Book 1, Chapter 6 introduced the concept of economic growth, but no mention of economic *development* was made in Book 1. Earlier in this book, in Chapter 7, we briefly explained the difference between the two concepts. There we said that *economic growth* measures changes in the physical quantity of goods and services that an economy actually produces, or has the potential to produce, but that economic development goes further, encompassing not just the increase in *quantity* of output, but also its *quality* and contribution to human happiness.

Economic growth does not necessarily improve the economic welfare of all or most of the people living in a country. Consider, for example, the situation when the ruling elite in a country use the fruits of growth to buy military and police equipment which they then use to suppress and possibly kill those in the population who wish to change how the economy operates. Although economic growth has occurred, economic development has not.

As stated in Chapter 7, economic development can be measured by:

- a general improvement in living standards which reduces poverty and human suffering
- access to resources such as food and housing that are required to satisfy basic human needs
- access to opportunities for human development (for example, through education and training)
- sustainability and regeneration, through reducing resource depletion and degradation
- access to decent healthcare

ACTIVITY

Go back to Chapter 7, page 204, and remind yourself of the difference between resource depletion and resource degradation, and between sustainable and unsustainable economic growth.

STUDY TIP

Don't confuse *sustainable growth* with *sustained growth*. The latter simply means achieving a particular rate of economic growth (on average) over a number of years. For example, from the end of recession in 1992 until the onset of the next recession in 2008, the UK sustained an average annual growth rate of about 2.75% over this period. However, a growth rate which is sustained over quite a long period may nevertheless be unsustainable if it leads to environmental problems, the depletion of vital finite resources and the degradation of others.

The main characteristics of less developed economies

The term 'less developed economies' covers a wide range of economies, from the extremely poor to what the United Nations calls higher middle-income economies. There are various ways of identifying the main characteristics of less developed economies, but we concentrate on only one, which was developed nearly 70 years ago by W. W. Rostow, an economic historian and political theorist.

Rostow used the term 'traditional society' to describe economies that were completely lacking in economic development. He described these as very primitive and usually poor societies in which very little changes from generation to generation, and in which tradition, generally accepted customs and persistent relationships between people govern economic life. Traditional societies face a low limit to their total production which, because of limited available methods of production, is largely agricultural. Today, traditional societies survive very often as tribal societies in remote areas of countries such as Brazil and India, and in parts of Africa.

Higher up the ranking of less developed economies are what Rostow called 'traditional economies preparing for take-off'. These are economies which are becoming more productive and in which various preconditions for successful industrial growth are beginning to appear. Scope for commerce and trade appears, along with banks and other financial institutions for the mobilisation of savings into productive investment.

At the next stage, Rostow identified economies taking off into self-sustaining growth. This involves change from a largely agricultural to an industrialised or manufacturing economy. Output increases, but only a small fraction of society benefits significantly from improved living standards. Growth takes priority over economic development.

At the final stage, higher-income developing economies are the end result of continued self-sustained growth. At this stage of development, countries are in a position to choose to allocate the increased output their economies are producing to social welfare and to other aspects of what we now call economic development.

Rostow's description of economic growth and development has had many critics, who generally argue that it is historically and factually wrong and is too simplistic. Nevertheless, it serves as a starting point for understanding some of the key features of less developed economies and the stages they go through to develop into prosperous societies with high levels of consumption.

Indicators of development

Economists usually use gross domestic product per head or *GDP per capita* as their first indicator of economic development. Unfortunately, for most poor developing countries, GDP is usually greater than another national income **indicator of development**, gross *national* income or GNI. Profit outflows and interest payments out of developing economies to more developed economies, and to banks within these economies, explain why this is the case. (When national income statistics are used as indicators of development, GDP or GNI per capita (per head of population) should be used rather than 'raw' GDP or GNI statistics.)

KEY TERM

indicators of development these include gross domestic product (GDP) per head, information on the distribution of income, mortality rates and health statistics.

ACTIVITY

Research GDP and GNI figures for a number of countries, including the UK, to find out the differences between these two measures of national income or output.

But are measures of national income or output, whether GDP or GNI figures, the best measures of standards of living, economic welfare and economic development? To try to answer this question, it is useful first to identify three components of economic welfare:

Total economic welfare = Economic welfare derived from goods and services purchased in the market economy + Economic welfare derived from public goods and merit goods provided collectively by the state + Economic welfare derived from quality of life factors, including external benefits minus external costs and intangibles

If used carefully, national income figures can provide a reasonable estimate of economic welfare derived from the first two of these three elements, both of which relate to the direct consumption of material goods and services. However, national income fails to provide a satisfactory indication of how externalities and other quality of life factors affect economic welfare and living standards. Intangible factors, which are the third element in people's living standards, are largely ignored. These intangible factors include the value people place on leisure time and living close to work, and the externalities such as pollution and road congestion generated from the production and consumption of national income, which affect people's welfare and quality of life.

National income also fails to reflect the effect of the resource depletion and environmental degradation resulting from producing current income on humankind's ability to produce future income. This means that national income and GDP do not address the issue of sustainability. In addition, whilst national income includes the value of the output of merit goods such as health and education, unless the data are disaggregated it is not possible to determine the extent to which the nation's resources are devoted to producing these services which are vital to economic development. Indicators such as life expectancy, infant mortality rates and literacy rates can be used to supplement national income per head in order to provide a better indicator of the quality of life enjoyed by people.

CASE STUDY 10.3

Why GNP figures provide an inadequate indicator of economic development

The gross national product includes air pollution and advertising for cigarettes, and ambulances to clear our highways of carnage. It counts special locks for our doors, and jails for the people who break them. GNP includes the destruction of the redwoods and the death of Lake Superior. It grows with the production of napalm and missiles and nuclear warheads...And if GNP includes all this, there is much that it does not comprehend. It does not allow for the health of our families, the quality of their education, or the joy of their play. It is indifferent to the decency of our factories and the safety of our streets alike. It does not include the beauty of our poetry or the strength of our marriages, or the intelligence of our public debate or the integrity of our public officials...GNP measures neither our wit nor our courage, neither our wisdom nor our learning, neither our compassion nor our devotion to our country. It measures everything, in short, except that which makes life worthwhile; and it can tell us everything about America — except whether we are proud to be Americans.

US Senator Robert Kennedy, in 1967

When making comparisons between countries that use different currencies, it is necessary to convert values, such as national income (GDP), to a common currency. This can be done by using market exchanges rates, such as £1 equals $1.50, or by using purchasing power parity (PPP) exchange rates.

Market exchange rates can quickly change, which artificially changes the value of GDP in two countries being compared. For example, a 1-month appreciation of the US dollar by 5% against the UK pound would reduce the dollar value of the UK economy by 5%. This would be more to do with changes in the exchange rate than changes in the underlying states of the UK and US economies.

Instead of using market exchange rates we can use purchasing power parity (PPP) exchange rates. The purchasing power of a currency refers to the quantity of the currency needed to purchase a common basket of goods and services. Purchasing power parity means equalising the purchasing power of two currencies by taking into account these cost-of-living and price-level differences in the two countries.

To compare living standards in two countries, we need to know what people can buy with their income. In other words, we want to measure the relative purchasing power of income in different countries. When we translate from local currency into US dollars using market exchange rates, we do not necessarily learn about purchasing power.

Using PPP exchange rates makes a significant difference. For example, compared to the comparison we get using PPP exchange rates, US dollar exchange rates overestimate the purchasing power of local incomes in the advanced countries, but underestimate it for the less-developed countries. For example, for 2012, using PPP exchange rates, China had a GNI per capita of PPP\$9,210, while the estimate for Singapore was PPP\$61,100.

Follow-up question

1 Taking into account what you have learnt earlier in your studies about negative externalities and demerit goods, to what extent does this case study support the view that national income is of little use in measuring economic development?

> **KEY TERM**
> **United Nations Human Development Index** an index based on life expectancy, education and per capita income indicators, which ranks the world's countries into four tiers of human development. These are: (i) very high human development; (ii) high human development; (iii) medium human development; (iv) low human development.

The environmental pressure group Friends of the Earth has argued that measures of national income such as GDP were never intended to be indicators of a country's economic welfare or stage of development. Other indicators of development which are less dependent on 'raw' GNI or GDP are increasingly used to place a value on economic and social progress. One of the earliest of these was the *Measure of Economic Welfare* (MEW) developed by Nordhaus and Tobin in 1972. More recent attempts to adjust conventional national income figures to show developments in economic welfare include the **United Nations Human Development Index** (HDI) and the *Index of Sustainable Economic Welfare* (ISEW).

The HDI is constructed by measuring:

● life expectancy at birth
● mean years of schooling and expected years of schooling
● gross national income (GNI) per head of population, reflecting purchasing power parity (PPP) in US dollars

The maximum value of the HDI is 1 (or unity). The closer a country's HDI is to 1, then the greater its human development, measured in terms of the three indicators specified in the index.

Table 10.15 shows the 15 highest-ranked countries in the HDI for 2014, based on 2013 data, and also the 15 lowest-ranked countries.

In 2013, the Scandinavian country Norway led the way in the HDI 'top 15', with the USA and the UK respectively in fifth and fourteenth positions. At the other end of the spectrum, all the countries in the 'bottom 15' were located in sub-Saharan Africa.

The Index of Sustainable Economic Welfare

Some commentators prefer other methods of measuring welfare and human development to the UN's Human Development Index. One of these is the *Index of Sustainable Economic Welfare* (ISEW). According to Friends of the Earth, the ISEW is significantly better than GDP for looking at how sustainable welfare changes are over time. Although it starts by measuring consumer expenditure in the same way as in the construction of GDP, the ISEW adjusts GDP figures to account for a number of aspects of economic life that GDP ignores. These include pollution, noise, commuting costs, capital growth, health and education spending, urbanisation, and the loss of natural resources.

One of the most recent detailed comparisons of changes in GDP and the ISEW was made in Belgium in 2012. The results are displayed in Figure 10.18. The diagram shows that Belgian GDP per head was about 25% greater in real terms in 2012 than in 1990, with an average year-on-year growth rate of over 2% in real terms. In contrast, the ISEW

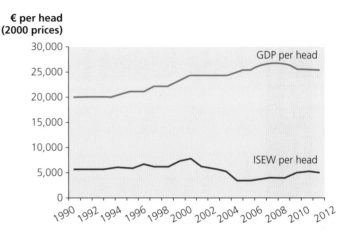

Figure 10.18 Changing economic welfare in Belgium between 1990 and 2012, measured by changes in GDP per head and changes in the ISEW per head

per head was significantly lower than real GDP per head in each of the years in the series, and over the period the gap between the two widened, at least until the onset of the global recession in 2008/09.

The unadjusted HDI is by no means a perfect index of human development, however, since it ignores inequalities in the distribution of income. In 2010 the UN's 2010 *Human Development Report* developed the HDI by introducing a new *Inequality-adjusted Human Development Index* (IHDI). The IHDI estimates the actual level of human development (accounting for inequality) in each of the 187 countries included in the HDI. The HDI itself estimates the maximum IHDI that could be achieved if there were no inequality within countries. The greater the degree of inequality within a country, the greater the difference between the country's HDI and IHDI.

Factors that affect growth and development

A large number of factors affect both growth and development. One of these that we have covered in some depth, especially in Book 1, is investment. Investment in new capital goods and technical progress are two of the main factors leading to long-term economic growth and they are also necessary for economic development. Consider, however, Figure 10.19.

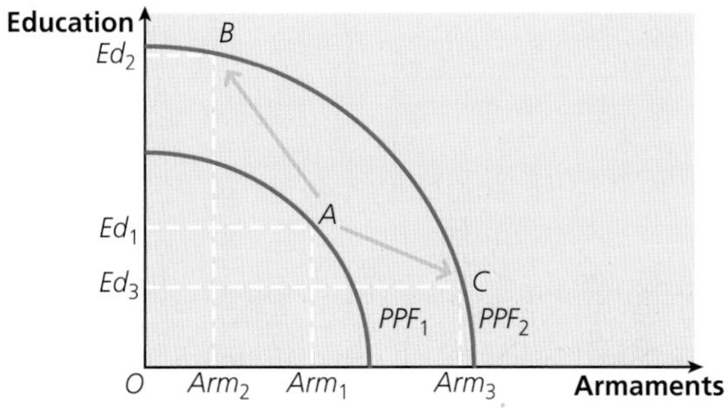

For the simplified economy depicted in Figure 10.19, the outward movement of the economy's production possibility frontier from PPF_1 to PPF_2 illustrates economic growth. However, the movement from point A on PPF_1 to point B on PPF_2 shows that the society is now using more of its available resources to educate its children and is actually devoting fewer resources than before to arms production. The resources devoted

Figure 10.19 Economic growth and development in a country producing just two goods: education and arms

359

Table 10.15 The 'top 15' and the 'bottom 15' countries in the Human Development Index, 2014

HDI rank	Country	Human Development Index (HDI value, 2013	Life expectancy at birth (years), 2013	Mean years of schooling (years), 2012	Expected years of schooling (years), 2012	Gross national income (GNI) per capita (2011 PPP$), 2013	Human Development Index (HDI value) 2012	Changes in rank, 2012–13
Very high human development								
1	Norway	0.944	81.5	12.6	17.6	63,909	0.943	0
2	Australia	0.933	82.5	12.8	19.9	41,524	0.931	0
3	Switzerland	0.917	82.6	12.2	15.7	53,762	0.916	0
4	Netherlands	0.915	81.0	11.9	17.9	42,397	0.915	0
5	United States	0.914	78.9	12.9	16.5	52,308	0.912	0
6	Germany	0.911	80.7	12.9	16.3	43,049	0.911	0
7	New Zealand	0.910	81.1	12.5	19.4	32,569	0.908	0
8	Canada	0.902	81.5	12.3	15.9	41,887	0.901	0
9	Singapore	0.901	82.3	10.2	15.4	72,371	0.899	3
10	Denmark	0.900	79.4	12.1	16.9	42,880	0.900	0
11	Ireland	0.899	80.7	11.6	18.6	33,414	0.901	−3
12	Sweden	0.898	81.8	11.7	15.8	43,201	0.897	1
13	Iceland	0.895	82.1	10.4	18.7	35,116	0.893	0
14	United Kingdom	0.892	80.5	12.3	16.2	35,002	0.890	0
15	Hong Kong, China (SAR)	0.891	83.4	10.0	15.6	52,383	0.889	0
Low human development								
173	Ethiopia	0.435	63.6	2.4	8.5	1,303	0.429	0
174	Malawi	0.414	55.3	4.2	10.8	715	0.411	0
175	Liberia	0.412	60.6	3.9	8.5	752	0.407	0
176	Mali	0.407	55.0	2.0	8.6	1,499	0.406	0
177	Guinea- Bissau	0.396	54.3	2.3	9.0	1,090	0.396	0
178	Mozambique	0.393	50.3	3.2	9.5	1,011	0.389	1
179	Guinea	0.392	56.1	1.6	8.7	1,142	0.391	−1
180	Burundi	0.389	54.1	2.7	10.1	749	0.386	0
181	Burkina Faso	0.388	56.3	1.3	7.5	1,602	0.385	0
182	Eritrea	0.381	62.9	3.4	4.1	1,147	0.380	0
183	Sierra Leone	0.374	45.6	2.9	7.5	1,815	0.368	1
184	Chad	0.372	51.2	1.5	7.4	1,622	0.370	−1
185	Central African Republic	0.341	50.2	3.5	7.2	588	0.365	0
186	Congo (Democratic Republic of the)	0.338	50.0	3.1	9.7	444	0.333	1

to education increase from Ed_1 to Ed_2, whereas those devoted to armaments fall from Arm_1 to Arm_2. Increased investment in the economy has led to economic development as well as economic growth.

By contrast, a movement from point A to point C illustrates economic growth, but almost certainly not economic development, as resources have been shifted from education to armaments. Although new investment has moved the production possibility frontier from PPF_1 to PPF_2, resources have also been shifted from education into arms production. Armament production increases from Arm_1 to Arm_3, but at the expense of education, the output of which falls from Ed_1 to Ed_3. The message is that economic growth can occur without economic development, and indeed at the expense of economic development.

Figure 10.19 also points to the fact that investment in **education and training** is usually an important part of both growth and economic development. Though often considered as meaning the same thing, education and training are in fact slightly different. Education furthers individual knowledge and develops a person's intellect. While a highly educated person is often more employable, however, education is not in itself about getting a job. By contrast, training is about getting a job, or about improving or diversifying skills when in a job. Training is undertaken in order to gain a specific work skill, the possession of which makes a person more employable, either in their existing line of work or through promotion or redeployment into a different type of work

> **KEY TERM**
>
> **education and training**
> education develops individual knowledge and intellect, while training develops work skills. Both are necessary for economic growth and development.

Barriers to growth and development

There are, of course, many barriers which prevent or reduce economic growth, and with it the chance for further economic development. Five of these are corruption, institutional factors, infrastructure, inadequate human capital, and a lack of property rights.

Corruption, which can be defined as dishonest or illegal behaviour, often in the form of bribery, especially payments to powerful people such as government officials, prevents normal economic activity from taking place. Corruption and bribery, which are often endemic features of life in poor countries, but also in richer countries such as Russia, divert scarce resources away from more productive uses to protect less efficient resource use. Production costs and consumer prices also rise — for example, through 'back-handers' paid by customers to corrupt officials and to employees of firms with which they wish to do business.

Institutional factors, which can differ greatly between less developed and more developed economies, include countries' legal and judicial structures, public administration systems, the availability of, and access to, financial institutions such as banks and capital markets, the role, if any, of the civil service, attitudes to work, and the education and training systems. The 'law of contract' is an important part of the legal and judicial systems of more developed economies, but contract law is much less well established in many less developed economies and indeed in eastern Europe. An efficient, policed and enforced 'law of contract' should be viewed as a necessary condition for businesses and consumers to 'do business with each other'. For example, without an enforced law of contract, firms may end up not supplying goods or

> **KEY TERMS**
>
> **corruption** a barrier holding back economic growth and development, especially in less developed economies.
>
> **institutional factors** examples of institutional factors include rules, laws, constitutions, the financial system and defined property rights.

KEY TERM

infrastructure for the most part, the result of past investment in buildings, roads, bridges, power supplies, fast broadband and other fixed capital goods that are needed for the economy to operate efficiently.

SYNOPTIC LINK

Refer back to Chapter 6 and refresh your knowledge of public goods, external costs and benefits, and road pricing.

KEY TERM

human capital the accumulated stock of skills and knowledge, relevant to work, embodied in human beings.

STUDY TIP

Make sure you understand why investment in human capital is important for *both* growth *and* development.

services to consumers and other firms, even though the goods or services have been paid for. In this situation, business transactions may simply not take place.

It goes almost without saying that rich countries, over the course of their development over decades (and sometimes centuries), have built up an **infrastructure** of roads, railways, telephone and communication networks together with other key elements of a modern economy. Poorer developing countries lack such infrastructure, which is an important factor holding back their development. For example, a lack of roads raises firms' costs of production and makes it difficult or impossible for them to access raw materials and to develop their markets.

To a certain extent, as with other consumer and capital goods, developing countries can offset the disadvantage that lack of infrastructure creates, by using the fruits of technical progress to bypass old technology. A good example is provided by mobile phones. Use of these phones has become ubiquitous in many developing economies, which has circumvented the need to invest in an infrastructure of traditional 'land-line' or terrestrial phones. An example in the future could be investment in drone technology to bypass the need to build traditional roads.

Investment in infrastructure is often done by public sector investment in social capital, rather than by the private sector. One reason for this is the fact that, being very expensive to undertake, the investment may only pay for itself after a long period of years. Linked to this, much infrastructure investment creates external economies for the private sector. It may be difficult or impossible for infrastructure providers to charge prices to the private sector firms that yield sufficient profit, and even if prices can be charged, they might deter economic development.

Before beginning our coverage of development economics in this chapter, we had made scant reference to **human capital** in Books 1 and Book 2. Our main reference, in Chapter 7 of Book 1, related the fact that investment in human capital, illustrated in Figure 7.1 of that chapter, can be as important as investment in physical capital goods such as machinery if long-run economic growth and development are to take place. The term 'human capital' is widely used to describe people at work and their collective knowledge, skills, abilities and capacity to develop and innovate. It embodies their accumulated stock of skills and knowledge that are relevant to their employment.

Investment in both physical capital and human capital are of course *flows*, the purpose of which is to build up *stocks* of physical capital such as machines and trained labour that are needed for on-going growth and development to take place. The purpose of investment in labour training, and often investment in education in general, is to build up the stock of human capital.

We have already explained the meaning and importance of *property rights* in our discussion of market failure in Chapter 6. We wrote there that property rights can be defined as the exclusive authority to determine how a resource is used. In the case of a private property right, the owner of private property such as a bar of chocolate in a sweet shop has the right to prevent other people from consuming the bar unless they are prepared to pay a price to the owner.

The traditional, more or less undeveloped, societies that we mentioned earlier in this section often lack private property rights. Most resources are communally owned. While to some this represents an idyllic paradise economy, to others it is a major cause of a lack of economic development.

According to this latter view, the establishment of, and ability to trade in, private property rights is a necessary pre-condition for successful economic development. Tradable private property rights underlie the development of capitalist economies, which are arguably the most successful in achieving economic development.

In contrast, the development of the Russian economy, prior to the collapse of communism, was based to a large extent on state ownership of property rights. Although this successfully created an industrial–military complex, it also created corruption and reduced individual incentives, and it was much less successful in delivering consumer goods to the general Russian population. The absence of sufficient private property rights not only diverted resources away from true economic development, but also led to the eventual disappearance of Russian communism. Unfortunately, it also led to the transfer of previously state-owned property rights to private sector oligarchs such as Roman Abramovich and to other members of a new super-rich elite.

Policies that might be adopted to promote economic growth and development

According to the OECD, sustainable development can be interpreted in economic terms as 'development that lasts' — that is, a path along which the maximisation of human well-being for today's generations does not lead to declines in future well-being.

An obvious point from which to start our analysis of appropriate policies for promoting economic growth and development is the standard macroeconomic and microeconomic government policies explained in earlier chapters. These include demand-side fiscal policy and monetary policy and supply-side policies, all of which can be focused on achieving economic growth and development and overall economic stability.

The danger is that pursuing 'growth for growth's sake' might lead to outcomes in which the costs of growth, such as environment depletion and degradation, exceed the benefits of higher living standards and economic welfare that growth is supposed to bring about. If this is the case, growth may very well be at the expense of development.

Hence the need for appropriate microeconomic policies to reduce or correct the various market failures that growth may bring about. These can include the use of taxes and subsidies respectively, to punish or deter the production of negative externalities and demerit goods, and to encourage the production of positive externalities and merit goods. Redistributive policies may also be deemed necessary to narrow the unjustifiable inequalities in the distributions of income and wealth, though, as we have seen, such policies may harm the incentives provided by markets that many think are essential for sustained growth and development. However, there is a growing consensus that a high level of inequality is a barrier to growth and many would argue that an excessive degree of inequality is incompatible with development. An equitable distribution of income is generally regarded as a characteristic of a developed economy.

Economists and politicians sometimes argue that a higher level of state intervention is required to bring about growth and development in poor countries than in more developed economies. Believers in the virtues of free markets disagree, citing the many cases of government failure that state intervention brings about. In recent decades, pro-free-market approaches have generally gained the upper hand, though not completely so. The strategic trade theory justification of a degree of protectionism in developing countries is a case in point. In practice, there is a strong case for combining market-based instruments with some forms of government intervention.

Some problems which affect growth and development are much more serious in poor countries than in more developed economies. 'Capital flight', which is the sudden withdrawal of money out of a country, affects poor countries much more than it affects economies such as the UK. It occurs, for example, when the ruling elite within an economy move the profits they make from the country's industries into foreign bank accounts, instead of re-investing profits within the country to secure its further development. Capital flight, which is partly the result of free market forces, can be reduced if not completely controlled by government and central bank intervention — for example, through the use of rigorously applied foreign exchange controls.

Capital flight is a major problem in sub-Saharan Africa as it impacts negatively on capital-scarce economies, such as Burundi, which generate very little saving from their own, generally very poor, populations. Trillions of dollars have flown out of Africa over the last four decades. Capital flight has accelerated since 2000, a period that has coincided with a high profits being generated from the exploitation of Africa's mineral resources. Evidence suggests that capital flight has significantly undermined Africa's growth and development, through the siphoning of potential investment funds out of the continent.

The role of aid and trade in promoting growth and development

Economists often debate the issue of whether **aid** is more important than trade (or vice versa) in promoting economic development. The orthodox view in countries such as the UK and the USA is that free trade and trade liberalisation are more important than aid in this respect. Free-market economists believe that international specialisation and complete free trade, undertaken in accordance with the principle of comparative advantage, benefits all the countries involved.

The strategic trade theory argument

However, not all economists agree. The Korean economist Ha-Joon Chang has written that 'History debunks the free trade myth' (**www.theguardian.com/business/2002/jun/24/globalisation**). Ha-Joon Chang's view is that governments in already developed economies are fully in favour of free trade — but only if their countries face little or no competition from developing economies. As soon as such competition emerges, the rich countries 'pull up the drawbridge', arguing that protectionism is necessary to protect themselves from the 'unfair' competition coming from cheap labour countries. Rich countries also argue that they need protecting from countries in the much poorer developing world which steal their technology and clone their products, partly by ignoring

KEY TERM

aid money, goods and services and 'soft' loans given by the government of one country or a multilateral institution such as the World Bank to help another country. Non-government organisations (NGOs) such as Oxfam also provide aid.

international patent laws and other aspects of intellectual copyright. However, transfers of technology can be an important mechanism for stimulating the development of the world's less prosperous economies.

As we explained on page 312, strategic trade theorists such as Paul Krugman have also argued that developing countries can speed up the pace of development by first selecting, and then protecting, key industries deemed vital for successful economic growth.

The counter-argument

Having said this, there is plenty of evidence that the growth of free trade and improved transport links — brought about, for example, by the containerisation of cargo — have been major factors responsible for the huge growth in international trade over recent decades. Moreover, the argument for trade rather than aid is quite broad and is not necessarily just about free trade. Developing countries can benefit from preferential trading arrangements, both with each other, and also with richer developed countries. And countering the strategic trade theory argument, trade may allow a developing economy to build up its own industries and encourages investment in other activities that promote development, such as good governance, property rights, infrastructure and investment in human capital.

The various forms of aid

International aid provided by richer countries and directed at less developed countries takes many forms, some of which are not really aid at all. An example is military aid, which often has to be spent buying the weaponry of the donor country. It is also questionable whether 'hard' loans qualify as aid. A 'hard' loan, usually given in a hard currency, has to be paid back at a market rate of interest. A 'soft' loan, by contrast, has a below-market rate of interest attached and may even be free in the sense that, although the loan must eventually be repaid, little or no interest is charged by the donor country.

Aid also takes the form of disaster relief, much of it dispensed by non-governmental organisations (NGOs) with their headquarters in developed economies. Sometimes this is matched by government-funded relief — for example, in 2015, in response to the devastating earthquake in Nepal, the UK government pledged to match every pound of disaster aid raised by NGOs, such as the Red Cross, with taxpayers' money. However, disaster relief, though very necessary to limit the human cost of events such as droughts and floods, is mostly a form of 'band-aid' relief, applying 'sticking plasters' to the results of natural disasters and civil conflict, but contributing little or nothing in itself to economic development. And in some cases, when drought and war are ongoing and seem never to end, as has been the case in Sudan, disaster relief may build up among sufferers a state of dependency on the generosity of those who feel honour-bound to continue to give.

Another form of aid is 'tied' aid. This can take the form of either a 'soft' loan or a gift of money that has to be spent on the exports of the country granting the aid. Arguably, this can benefit the donor country as much as, if not more than, the recipient country.

Richer donor countries can also give aid by 'lending' their experts to a less developed country to offer advice on matters such as improving the country's governance, its methods of production, how to use advanced technology and the maintenance of transport links and other forms of infrastructure. In recent years, China has gone one stage further by using Chinese workers and managers to build roads and other types of infrastructure in a number of African developing countries — though in return the developing countries have agreed to sell their exports of minerals and other raw materials to China rather than to competitor countries.

Effective and ineffective aid

Of course, economic aid of the right type does promote economic development. For example, in a country where domestic savings are low, aid can be used to finance the domestic accumulation of capital, and it can also provide vital foreign exchange to finance the import of capital goods and resources.

However, it has sometimes been argued that the export of high-technology capital goods in foreign aid programmes, from rich to poor countries, equips less developed countries with the 'wrong sort of technology'. The problem facing the poor country is that when a 'high-tech' piece of equipment breaks down, the country may lack people with sufficient expertise to repair it. Additionally, spare parts produced in developed economies may have to be bought and this uses up foreign exchange which is in short supply. Far better, it has been argued, for developing countries to focus on intermediate, less capital intensive technology, rather than on advanced technology. Intermediate technologies are more suited to the often cheap and plentiful labour in poorer developing countries, while savings needed to finance the purchase of expensive capital goods and foreign exchange are scarce.

The fact that both trade and aid in developing countries are often 'skewed' to the purchase of high-technology goods often results from the desire of the countries' governments and ruling elites to invest in prestige projects such as a national airline which 'flies the flag' for the country.

Trade versus aid: a conclusion

In conclusion, free-market economists argue that trade is more important than aid in relation to economic development. Until quite recently, it was said that aid to Africa actually made the continent poorer rather than better off. This was contrasted with Asia where economic development was the result of increased trade rather than aid. However, in its 2014 report, *Economic Development in Africa*, UNCTAD, the United Nations body responsible for dealing with development issues, particularly international trade, said:

> Africa has experienced high and continuous economic growth in the past decade, prompting analysts to argue that the continent has reached a turning point in its development history and is poised to play a more significant role in the global economy in the twenty-first century. Unlike in the 1980s and 1990s, Africa's average growth rate since the turn of the millennium has also been higher than the average growth rate of the world economy.

UNCTAD believes that international aid has played a significant role in economic development in Africa, although much aid has been disaster relief rather than true economic aid. China is now providing much of the aid given to African countries, albeit with many strings attached, such as the requirement to export minerals and other natural resources back to China.

SYNOPTIC LINK

At this point it would be useful to read once again our coverage of globalisation at the beginning of this chapter.

SUMMARY

- Globalisation is the name given for the increasing integration of the world's economies.
- Trade liberalisation, international capital and labour mobility, and the increased power of multinational corporations (MNCs) are important elements of globalisation.
- International trade widens a country's production possibilities and also its consumption possibilities, and enables countries to benefit from specialisation and economies of scale.
- According to the principle of comparative advantage, specialisation and trade can lead to an increase in world output, which can translate into a net welfare gain. The theory shows that, provided each country has a comparative advantage in the production of a good, each country can benefit from specialisation and trade.
- Import controls and other forms of protectionism have been justified by strategic trade theory, the protection of infant industries and a variety of other economic and non-economic arguments.
- The balance of payments is the part of the national accounts that measures all the currency flows into and out of the country in a particular time period.
- The two main parts of the balance of payments are the current account and the financial account, which records most of the capital flows between countries.
- The expenditure-reducing policy of deflation and/or the expenditure-switching policies of import controls and devaluation can be used to reduce a current account deficit. Sometimes deflation and devaluation should be used in tandem.
- Supply-side policies can also help to reduce a current account deficit.
- An exchange rate is the external price of a currency in terms of another currency.
- There are three main types of exchange rate: freely floating, fixed and managed floating.
- Provided there are no capital flows, a freely floating exchange rate should automatically eliminate a trade deficit or surplus.
- Speculative or hot money capital flows also destabilise floating exchange rates, sometimes leading to severe overvaluation or undervaluation.
- In a rigidly fixed exchange rate system, the exchange rate cannot rise or fall to eliminate or reduce a payments surplus or deficit.
- The advantages of a fixed exchange rate relate closely to the disadvantages of a floating rate, while the disadvantages relate to a floating system's advantages.
- Adjustable peg and 'dirty' floating are types of managed exchange rates.
- The euro has replaced national currencies for the majority of EU member states that are in the eurozone, but this does not include the UK.
- Economic development is not the same as economic growth.
- Free-market economists generally argue that reducing barriers to international trade is more important than aid in promoting economic development.
- Strategic trade theorists, by contrast, advocate the case for strategic protection in developing countries.
- Most economists agree that some forms of aid are good but that other forms are questionable in terms of promoting economic development.

Questions

1 Do you agree that, for a developed economy such as the UK, the advantages of globalisation exceed any disadvantages? Justify your answer.

2 Explain the difference between absolute advantage and comparative advantage.

3 Explain the policies that may be used to reduce a deficit on the current account of the balance of payments.

4 Do you agree that supply-side reforms are needed if the UK's current account is to improve in the long run? Justify your answer.

5 Using a demand and supply diagram, explain how a trade deficit is eliminated in a freely floating exchange rate system.

6 Distinguish between economic growth and economic development.

Macroeconomics key terms

absolute advantage a country has an absolute advantage if it can produce more of a good than other countries from the same amount of resources.

aggregate demand total planned spending on the goods and services produced within the economy in a particular time period.

aggregate supply the aggregate level of real output that all the firms in the economy plan to produce at different average price levels.

aid money, goods and services and 'soft' loans given by the government of one country or a multilateral institution such as the World Bank to help another country. Non-government organisations (NGOs) such as Oxfam also provide aid.

balance of payments the record of all money flows or transactions between the residents of a country and the rest of the world in a particular period, usually monthly, quarterly or annually.

balancing the budget setting government spending equal to government revenue ($G = T$, assuming that taxation is the only source of government revenue).

Bank Rate the interest rate set by the Bank of England which it uses as a benchmark for setting the interest rates that it charges when lending to commercial banks and other financial institutions.

bonds financial securities sold by companies (corporate bonds) or by governments (government bonds) which are a form of long-term borrowing. Bonds usually have a maturity date on which they are redeemed, with the borrower usually making a fixed interest payment each year until the bond matures.

broad money the part of the stock of money (or money supply) made of cash, other liquid assets such as bank and building society deposits, but also some less liquid assets. The measure of broad money used by the Bank of England is called M4.

budget deficit the amount by which government spending exceeds government revenue in a particular time period ($G > T$, assuming that taxation is the only source of government revenue).

budget surplus the amount by which government spending is less than government revenue in a particular time period ($G < T$, assuming that taxation is the only source of government revenue).

capital markets where securities such as shares and bonds are issued to raise medium- to long-term financing, and where shares and bonds are then traded on the 'second-hand' part of the market, e.g. the London Stock Exchange.

capital ratio the amount of capital on a bank's balance sheet as a proportion of its loans.

central bank a national bank that provides financial and banking services for its country's government and banking system, as well as implementing the government's monetary policy and issuing currency. The Bank of England is the UK's central bank.

circular flow of income in the economy, income received by households from selling labour and other factor services to firms circulates back to the firms when spent by households on goods and services produced by the firms. The circular flow becomes more complicated when withdrawals are taken into account — instead of being spent on consumption, some income is saved, spent on imports, or paid in taxes to the government. Similarly, injections of spending, in the form of investment by firms, government spending and overseas spending on UK exports, complicate the circular flow.

commercial bank a financial institution which aims to make profits by selling banking services to its customers. Also known as a retail bank and a 'high-street' bank.

comparative advantage this is measured in terms of opportunity cost. The country with the least opportunity cost when producing a good possesses a comparative advantage in that good.

corporate bonds debt security issued by a company and sold as new issues to people who lend long-term to the company. They can usually be resold second-hand on a stock exchange.

corruption a barrier holding back economic growth and development, especially in less developed economies.

cost-push inflation a rising price level caused by an increase in the costs of production, shown by a shift of the *SRAS* curve to the left. Also known as cost inflation.

coupon the guaranteed fixed annual interest payment, often divided into two 6-month payments, paid by the issuer of a bond to the owner of the bond.

credit when a bank makes a loan it creates credit. The loan results in the creation of an advance, which is an asset on the bank's balance sheet, and a deposit, which is a liability of the bank.

currency union an agreement between a group of countries to share a common currency, and usually to have a single monetary and foreign exchange rate policy.

current account measures all the currency flows into and out of a country in a particular time period in payment for exports and imports of goods and services, together with primary and secondary income flows (previously known as income flows and transfers).

customs union a trading bloc in which member countries enjoy internal free trade in goods and possibly services, with all the member countries protected by a common external tariff barrier.

cyclical budget deficit the part of the budget deficit which rises in the downswing of the economic cycle and falls in the upswing of the cycle.

cyclical unemployment unemployment occurring in the downswing of the economic cycle or business cycle, caused by a lack of aggregate demand in the economy. Also known as Keynesian or demand-deficient unemployment.

debt money people owe.

deflation a persistent tendency for the price level to fall and for the value of money to rise.

demand-pull inflation a rising price level caused by an increase in aggregate demand, shown by a shift of the *AD* curve to the right. Also known as demand inflation.

disinflation a fall in the rate of inflation, but inflation remains positive.

economic growth the rate of increase in the potential output of an economy.

education and training education develops individual knowledge and intellect, while training develops work skills. Both are necessary for economic growth and development.

equity is wealth; shares are known as equities. However, equity can also mean fairness or justness; it depends on the context in which the term is used.

European Union an economic and partially political union established in 1993 after the ratification of the Maastricht Treaty by members of the European Community and since expanded to include numerous central and eastern European nations.

eurozone the name used for the group of EU countries that have replaced their national currencies with the euro. In 2015, 19 of the 28 EU countries were in the eurozone, though this may change in future years. The eurozone is also known as the euro area.

exchange rate the external price of a currency, usually measured against another currency such as the US dollar or the euro.

expenditure-reducing policy a government policy which aims to reduce a current account deficit by reducing the demand for imports by reducing the level of aggregate demand in the economy. Conversely, to reduce a current account surplus, aggregate demand would be increased and spending on imports would rise.

expenditure-switching policy a government policy which aims to eliminate a current account deficit by switching domestic demand away from imports to domestically produced goods. Conversely, to reduce a current account surplus, the policy would aim to switch domestic demand away from domestically produced goods toward imports.

export subsidies money given to domestic firms by the government to encourage firms to sell their products abroad and to help make their goods cheaper in export markets.

financial account the part of the balance of payments which records capital flows into and out of the economy.

Financial Conduct Authority primarily responsible for macroprudential regulation, the FCA aims to make sure that financial markets work well so that consumers get a fair deal, by ensuring that the financial industry is run with integrity and that consumers can trust that firms have their best interests at heart, and by providing consumers with appropriate financial products and services.

financial markets markets in which financial assets or securities are traded.

Financial Policy Committee the part of the Bank of England charged with the primary objective of identifying, monitoring and taking action to remove or reduce systemic risks with a view to protecting and enhancing the resilience of the UK financial system. The committee's secondary objective is to support the economic policy of the government.

fiscal policy the use of government spending, taxation and the government's budgetary position to achieve the government's policy objectives.

Fisher equation of exchange the stock of money in the economy multiplied by the velocity of circulation of money equals the price level multiplied by the quantity of real output in the economy: $MV = PQ$.

fixed exchange rate an exchange rate fixed at a certain level by the country's central bank and maintained by the central bank's intervention in the foreign exchange market.

foreign direct investment investment in capital assets, such as manufacturing and service industry capacity, in a foreign country by a business with headquarters in another country. Very often the overseas company establishes subsidiary companies in the countries in which it is investing.

foreign exchange markets (forex, FX, or currency markets) global, decentralised markets for the trading of currencies. The main participants in this market are large international commercial banks. Collectively, foreign exchange markets are the largest markets in the global economy.

forward guidance attempts to send signals to financial markets, businesses and individuals, about the Bank of England's interest rate policy in the months and years ahead, so that economic agents are not surprised by a sudden and unexpected change in policy.

free trade area member countries abolish tariffs on mutual trade, but each partner determines its own tariffs on trade with non-member countries.

freely floating exchange rate the exchange rate is determined solely by the interplay of demand for, and supply of, the currency.

frictional unemployment short-term transitional unemployment or 'between jobs' unemployment.

full employment occurs when the number of people wishing to work equals the number of workers whom employers wish to hire.

Funding for Lending Scheme incentivises banks and building societies to boost their lending to the UK real economy. FLS is skewed towards small and medium-sized enterprises (SMEs).

globalisation the process of growing economic integration of the world's economies.

government bonds debt security, in the UK known as gilt-edged securities or gilts, issued by a government and sold as new issues to people who lend long-term to the government. They can be resold second-hand on a stock exchange.

gross domestic product the sum of all goods and services, or the value of output, produced in the economy over a period of time, e.g. 1 year.

human capital the accumulated stock of skills and knowledge, relevant to work, embodied in human beings.

indicators of development these include gross domestic product (GDP) per head, information on the distribution of income, mortality rates and health statistics.

inflation a continuous and persistent rise in the price level and a fall in the value of money.

infrastructure for the most part, the result of past investment in buildings, roads, bridges, power supplies, fast broadband and other fixed capital goods that are needed for the economy to operate efficiently.

injections investment spending by firms on capital goods (I), government spending (G) and overseas spending on the economy's exports (X) are injections into the circular flow of income.

institutional factors examples of institutional factors include rules, laws, constitutions, the financial system and defined property rights.

investment bank a bank which does not generally accept deposits from ordinary members of the general public. Traditional 'investment banking' refers to financial advisory work, such as advising private companies on how to become a public company by floating on the stock market, or advising public companies on how to buy up another company. Investment banks also deal directly in financial markets for their own account.

less developed countries countries considered behind in terms of their economy, human capital, infrastructure and industrial base.

liquidity measures the ease with which an asset can be converted into cash without loss of value. Cash is the most liquid of all assets.

liquidity ratio the ratio of a bank's cash and other liquid assets to its deposits.

long-run aggregate supply the real output that can be supplied when the economy is on its production possibility frontier. This is when all the available factors of production are employed and producing at their 'normal capacity' level of output.

long-run economic growth occurs when the productive capacity of the economy is increasing. It is used to refer to the trend rate of growth of real national output in an economy over time.

long-run Phillips curve a vertical Phillips curve, developed by Milton Friedman and Edmund Phelps, along which trade-offs between reducing inflation and reducing unemployment are not possible. Also called the L-shaped Phillips curve.

macroeconomic equilibrium occurs in a circular flow diagram when injections into the circular flow of income equal withdrawals from the circular flow. It can also be shown in an *AD/AS* diagram as the level of real national income at which *AD = AS*. Also known as the equilibrium level of national income.

macroeconomic policy government policy aimed at achieving macroeconomic objectives such as a satisfactory and sustainable rate of economic growth, full employment or low unemployment, control of inflation and a satisfactory balance of payments.

maturity date the date on which the issuer of a dated security, such as a gilt-edged security (long-dated) or a Treasury bill (short-dated), pays the face value of the security to the security's owner.

monetarist an economist who argues that a prior increase in the money supply is always the cause of inflation.

monetary policy implemented by the government and the central bank (in the UK, the Bank of England) to achieve policy objectives (e.g. control of inflation) using monetary instruments (e.g. Bank Rate and quantitative easing).

money primarily a medium of exchange or means of payment, but also a store of value.

money markets provide a means for lenders and borrowers to satisfy their short-term financial needs. Assets that are bought and sold on money markets are short term, with maturities ranging from a day to a year, and are normally easily convertible into cash. The term 'money market' is an umbrella that covers several markets, including the markets for Treasury bills and commercial bills.

money supply the stock of money (coins, notes and bank deposits) in the economy at a particular point of time.

moral hazard the tendency of individuals and firms, once protected against some contingency, to behave so as to make that contingency more likely.

more developed countries countries with a high degree of economic development, high average income per head, high standards of living, usually with service industries dominating manufacturing, and investment having taken place over many years in human capital and infrastructure.

multinational corporations enterprises operating in several countries but with their headquarters in one country.

multiplier the relationship between an initial change in aggregate demand and the resulting usually larger change in national income.

narrow money the part of the stock of money (or money supply) made of cash and liquid bank and building society deposits.

national debt the amount of accumulated debt, resulting from past government borrowing, that is owed by the UK government. It is the stock of debt owed by the UK government both to UK residents and financial institutions, and also to overseas-based individuals and financial institutions. It has built up over many years as many UK governments have run budget deficits.

natural rate of unemployment the rate of unemployment when the aggregate labour market is in equilibrium, i.e. the demand for labour equals the supply of labour. All unemployment is therefore voluntary.

negative output gap occurs when the current level of real GDP is below the potential output of the economy.

Office for Budget Responsibility advisory public body that provides independent economic forecasts and analysis of the public finances as background to the preparation of the UK budget.

output gap the difference between the current level of real GDP and the potential output of the economy.

Phillips curve based on evidence from the economy, a curve showing the apparent relationship between the rate of inflation (originally the rate of increase in money wages) and the rate of unemployment.

portfolio investment the purchase of one country's securities, e.g. bonds and shares, by the residents or financial institutions of another country.

positive output gap occurs when the current level of real GDP is above the potential output of the economy.

primary income flows inward primary income flows comprise income flowing into the economy in the current year, which is generated by UK-owned capital assets located overseas. Outward primary income flows comprise income flowing out of the economy in the current year, which is generated by overseas-owned capital assets located in the UK.

principles of taxation criteria for judging whether a tax is a good tax or a bad tax. Also known as canons of taxation.

profitability the state or condition of yielding a financial profit or gain.

progressive tax when the proportion of income paid in tax rises as income increases.

proportional tax when the proportion of income paid in tax stays the same as income increases.

Prudential Regulation Authority the part of the Bank of England responsible for the microprudential regulation and supervision of banks, building societies, credit unions, insurers and major investment firms.

quantitative easing an unconventional form of monetary policy through which a central bank, such as the Bank of England, creates new money electronically which it then uses to buy financial assets, such as government bonds, on the country's financial markets. Also known as the Asset Purchase Scheme.

quantity theory of money theory that assumes inflation is caused by a prior increase in the money supply.

quotas physical limits on the quantities of imported goods allowed into a country.

real wages wages that have been adjusted for inflation, in contrast to a nominal wage which is simply the money value of the wage. A real wage measures the amount of goods and services that can be bought.

real-wage unemployment a type of disequilibrium unemployment caused by real wage rates being too high to clear the labour market, resulting in excess supply of labour.

recession in the UK and in many other countries a recession is defined as 6 months or more of negative economic growth or declining real national output.

regressive tax when the proportion of income paid in tax falls as income increases.

secondary income flows current transfers, such as gifts of money, international aid and transfers between the UK and the EU, flowing into or out of the UK economy in a particular year.

security secured loans, such as mortgage loans secured against the value of property, are less risky for banks than unsecured loans.

shares undated financial assets, sold initially by a company to raise financial capital. Shares sold by public companies or PLCs are marketable on a stock exchange, but shares sold by private companies are not marketable. Unlike a loan, a share signifies that the holder owns part of the enterprise.

short-run aggregate supply the quantities of real output that businesses plan to produce and sell at different price levels when total productive capacity is fixed but when variable factors of production can be changed.

short-run economic growth occurs when an increase in aggregate demand brings spare capacity into production.

short-run Phillips curve the original downward-sloping Phillips curve, developed by A.W. Phillips.

Single European Market the SEM was intended to establish the 'four freedoms' — free movement of goods, services, workers and capital between the EU member states — from 1993 onward. However, the SEM is only partially complete.

structural budget deficit the part of the budget deficit which is not affected by the economic cycle but results from structural change in the economy affecting the government's finances.

structural unemployment occurs when certain industries decline because of long-term changes in market conditions. It is joblessness caused not by lack of aggregate demand, but by changes in the pattern of demand or technological change.

supply-side improvements reforms undertaken by the private sector to increase productivity so as to reduce costs and to become more efficient and competitive. Supply-side improvement often results from more investment and innovation, often undertaken by firms without prompting from the government.

supply-side policies government economic policies which aim to make markets more competitive and efficient, increase production potential, and shift the *LRAS* curve to the right. Supply-side fiscal policy is arguably the most important type of supply-side policy, but there are also non-fiscal supply-side policies.

systemic risk in a financial context, this refers to the risk of a breakdown of the entire financial system, caused by inter-linkages within the financial system, rather than simply the failure of an individual bank or financial institution within the system.

tariffs taxes imposed on imports from other countries entering a country. Also known as import duties.

taxation compulsory levies charged by central and local government to raise revenue, primarily to finance government spending.

trade in goods exports and imports of visible, or tangible, items such as cars, oil and tea.

trade in services exports and imports of services such as financial services, tourism and shipping.

unemployment occurs when people who are actively searching for employment are unable to find work.

United Nations Human Development Index an index based on life expectancy, education and per capita income indicators, which ranks the world's countries into four tiers of human development. These are: (i) very high human development; (ii) high human development; (iii) medium human development; (iv) low human development.

withdrawals saving (S), tax revenues (T) and spending on imports (M) are withdrawals from the circular flow of income. They are also known as leakages from the circular flow.

World Trade Organization an international body whose purpose is to promote free trade by persuading countries to abolish import tariffs and other barriers to trade. As such, it has become closely associated with globalisation.

Macroeconomics practice questions

In this section you will find a set of multiple-choice questions, followed first by a context question in the style of A-level Paper 2, then by three essay questions for Paper 2, and finally by an investigation question in the style of A-level Paper 3.

Multiple-choice questions

1 The diagram below illustrates the aggregate demand curves (*AD*), long-run aggregate supply curve (*LRAS*) and short-run aggregate supply curve (*SRAS*) for an economy.

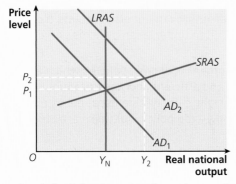

The shift of the *AD* curve from AD_1 to AD_2 will:

A lead to a positive output gap in both the short run and the long run

B increase both real national output and inflation in the short run

C raise output but not the price level in the long run

D leave unemployment at its natural rate in both the short run and the long run

2 A woman earns £20 per hour and the price index = 100. Other things being equal, what would happen to her real hourly wage if the price index rose to 110?

It would be between:

A £15.50 and £16.50

B £17.50 and £18.50

C £19.50 and £20.50

D £21.50 and £22.50

3 Which of the following combinations best illustrates an expansionary fiscal policy?

	Government spending	Taxes
A	Increase	Increase
B	Increase	Decrease
C	Decrease	Decrease
D	Decrease	Increase

4 This question relates to the aggregate demand/aggregate supply (*AD/AS*) diagram below.

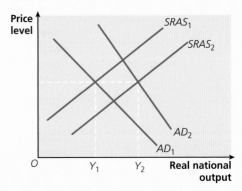

The movement from Y_1 to Y_2 on the diagram could have been caused by:

A an increase in a budget surplus and an increase in business costs

B an increase in interest rates and an increase in the national minimum wage rate

C an increase in consumer spending and an increase in productivity

D an increase in oil prices and a decrease in exports

5 Which **one** of the following newspaper headlines indicates the use of monetary policy?

A 'More money in everyone's pockets as taxes are lowered'

B 'Big reduction in government borrowing announced in the budget'

C 'Government declares its intention to decrease aggregate demand'

D 'Misery for new homebuyers as interest rates are raised'

6 Countries W, X, Y and Z form a customs union. After its formation, the union replaces goods from non-member country V, which is a lower-cost producer, with goods from country X, a higher-cost producer. This is an example of:

A absolute advantage

B diseconomies of scale

C inefficient allocation of resources

D comparative advantage

7 For countries to benefit from international trade in accordance with the principle of comparative advantage, there must be:

A similar opportunity costs in the production of different goods in the same country

B different opportunity costs in the production of the same goods in different countries

C similar opportunity costs in the production of different goods in the same countries

D lower opportunity costs in the production of all goods in one country

8 The diagram below illustrates the case of a good that is supplied to the home market by both domestic and overseas producers. The world price is P_W. After a tariff is imposed, the price is P_{W+t}.

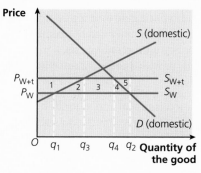

The amount of revenue the country's government collects from the tariff is indicated by the area:

A 1, 2, 3, 4 and 5

B 3 only

C 1, 2 and 3

D 2, 3, 4 and 5

9 The value of the euro is most likely to rise against the US dollar if:

A productivity is greater in the US economy than in the eurozone countries

B interest rates rise only in the eurozone countries

C there is a collapse of confidence in the eurozone

D the eurozone countries have a trade deficit with the USA

10 The diagram below represents the production possibility frontiers for a less developed country (*LDC*) and a more developed country (*MDC*).

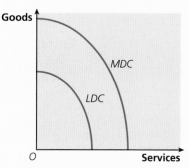

The production possibility frontier of the LDC is to the left of the frontier for the MDC because the LDC is likely to have:

A a higher Human Development Index

B greater productivity of existing resources

C less productive potential

D more resources, particularly capital

Context 1

Total for this context: 40 marks

Monetary policy

Study **Extracts A**, **B** and **C** and then answer **all** parts of Context 1 which follow.

Extract A: UK Bank Rate, actual and forecast, 2007–21

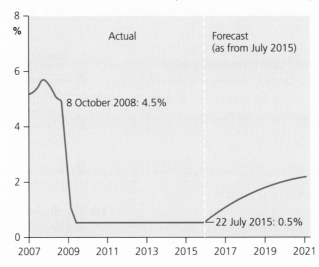

Source: OBR

Extract B: The Bank of England and monetary policy

Monetary policy in the UK usually operates through the price at which money is lent — Bank Rate. The Bank of England raises or lowers Bank Rate, or leaves it unchanged, in order to control inflation. Using Bank Rate to control inflation and to achieve other possible monetary policy objectives is often called 'conventional' monetary policy. 5

However, in March 2009 the Monetary Policy Committee (MPC), which implements monetary policy on behalf of the Bank of England, announced that, in addition to setting Bank Rate, it would start to inject money directly into the economy by purchasing financial assets — often known as quantitative easing (QE). Although quantitative easing has not been extended since 2012, the Bank 10 has maintained the value of bonds purchased at £375 billion. This and other newly introduced monetary policy instruments are often called 'unconventional' monetary policy.

In August 2013 the MPC provided some explicit guidance regarding the future conduct of monetary policy. The MPC said that it intended to maintain the 15 highly stimulative stance of monetary policy until economic slack in the UK economy has been substantially reduced, provided this does not entail material risks to price stability or financial stability.

The Bank of England says that low inflation is not an end in itself. It is, however, an important factor in helping to encourage long-term stability in the 20 economy with sustainable growth and employment.

Source: news reports, 2013–15

Extract C: Conventional and unconventional monetary policy

In his 2013 Budget, while still paying lip service to the 2.0% inflation rate target, George Osborne, the chancellor of the exchequer, instructed the Bank of England to 'deploy new unconventional, but as yet unstated, policy instruments' in an effort to bring about sustained recovery from recession. Mark Carney, the governor of the Bank of England, immediately indicated   5
that this is what he would do.

The first 'unconventional' policy instrument had been introduced in the middle of the recession in 2009. This was quantitative easing. In another new policy known as forward guidance, the Bank of England indicated early in 2014 that, to protect the still 'fragile' economy, Bank Rate would remain at the   10
rock-bottom rate of 0.5% until 2015 at least.

The decision to suspend quantitative easing was partly the result of the Bank of England prioritising its Funding for Lending Scheme over the Asset Purchase Scheme (which is another name for quantitative easing). Launched in 2012, Funding for Lending allows banks and other lenders to borrow   15
money cheaply from the Bank of England. The scheme is designed to make it easier for financial institutions to provide loans at a time when they might otherwise be reducing lending, because of their need — following the 2007/08 financial crisis — to shore up battered balance sheets. Initially, by helping cut mortgage rates for house buyers, Funding for Lending brought   20
about recovery in UK housing markets, though at the potential cost of creating another speculative house price bubble, particularly in London and the southeast. (Because of the fear of this happening, Funding for Lending no longer supports mortgage lending for house purchase.) However, the scheme has been less successful in financing business investment.   25

'Unconventional' monetary policy instruments such as quantitative easing and Funding for Lending were introduced largely because of the ineffectiveness of Bank Rate policy as an instrument for helping to 'spend the economy out of recession'. In trying to promote economic recovery, the 0.5% Bank Rate was ineffective for a number of reasons. These included a 'lower bound', which effectively prevented further cuts in Bank Rate below the historically low   30
rate of 0.5%. And even if Bank Rate could be cut, the existence of a 'liquidity trap' means that the cut would have little or no further effect on the state of aggregate demand.

Source: news reports, 2013–15

01 When UK banks deposit funds with the Bank of England, they usually receive interest on the money deposited at Bank Rate.
If a bank has deposits of £200 million with the Bank of England, with the help of **Extract A**, calculate the difference between the annual amount of interest it would have received if Bank Rate was at the rate ruling on 8 October 2008 and the rate ruling on 22 July 2015. *(2 marks)*

02 Explain why the data in **Extract A** indicate that the Office for Budget Responsibility (OBR) was expecting a rise in inflation after 2015. *(4 marks)*

03 **Extract C** (lines 7–8) states that 'The first "unconventional" policy instrument had been introduced in the middle of the recession in 2009. This was quantitative easing.'
With the help of an *AD/AS* diagram, explain why quantitative easing does not necessarily lead to higher inflation. *(9 marks)*

04 **Extract C** (lines 26–29) states that '"Unconventional" monetary policy instruments such as quantitative easing and Funding for Lending were introduced largely because of the ineffectiveness of Bank Rate policy as an instrument for helping to "spend the economy out of recession".'

Using the data in the extracts and your knowledge of economics, evaluate the effectiveness of monetary policy in the UK in recent years. *(25 marks)*

A-level Paper 2 essay questions

Either

Essay 1

The summer 2015 Budget Statement stated that public sector net borrowing was forecast to fall to 3.7% of GDP in 2015/16 and then to fall each year, returning to a surplus of £10 billion in 2019/20.

09 Explain the likely economic reasons for government borrowing. *(15 marks)*
10 Evaluate the costs and benefits of the UK government aiming to achieve a budget surplus by 2019/20. *(25 marks)*

or

Essay 2

The money market, the capital market and the foreign exchange market are three of the financial markets in the UK economy.

11 Explain the ways in which the money market, the capital market and the foreign exchange market differ from each other. *(15 marks)*
12 Some economists believe that UK macroeconomic performance suffers because the economy is unbalanced in the sense that financial services have grown excessively at the expense of manufacturing. Assess the case for rebalancing the UK economy away from financial services and toward manufacturing. *(25 marks)*

or

Essay 3

Many economists believe that UK macroeconomic performance has benefited from tariff reductions and the liberalisation of international trade, but some economists disagree.

13 Explain the main factors which determine the value of goods and services that a country imports for the rest of the world. *(15 marks)*
14 Evaluate the economic consequences for the UK if the country decides to leave the European Union. *(25 marks)*

A-level Paper 3 investigation question

Source booklet

The UK and global fishing industry

Extract A The tragedy of the commons and the world's fish stocks

Extract B How to conserve fish stocks

Extract C The UK fishing industry, 2003–13: selected key statistics

Extract D UK fishing ports face a bleak future

Extract A: The tragedy of the commons and the world's fish stocks

Over a generation ago, environmentalists sounded the first warnings about the Earth's natural resources running out. Some of the fears then voiced, it was later shown, were partly groundless. For some resources such as oil, the market mechanism has encouraged consumers to economise and producers to search for and to develop new sources of supply. *5*

But with fish it may be different. Unless stocks are managed tightly by all concerned with fishing, they may well collapse, and soon another 'tragedy of the commons' will have been played out. It happens because people think they can take a limitless amount of the Earth's 'free gifts' such as the atmosphere or the sea, or now, we are realising, fish. *10*

For centuries these apparently free goods had no prices attached to them and so nothing to impose restraint on their use. Go ahead, take the atmosphere to dump your smoke in, take the sea to dump your effluent in. Fish to your heart's content, with ever more trawlers. It's all free. And for centuries, nothing harmful happens, such is the seemingly limitless bounty of the Earth. *15* But on a finite globe, the limits logically have to be reached at some stage. A fish stock can make what is known as an 'equilibrium shift'; it can change under pressure to a new level of stable numbers much lower than they were before. Intensive fishing pressure may take out many of the bigger fish so that breeding slows down in a cumulative process, until virtually no new 'recruits' *20* to the breeding stock are coming through.

The decline of many fishing grounds may be irreversible if very stringent measures are not taken. The problems facing global fishing industries result partly from the pursuit of self-interest by fishermen, but also from the failure of governments to manage the world's oceans. *25*

Source: news reports, 2015

Extract B: Reversing the decline of UK fisheries

Four times more fish were being landed in UK ports 100 years ago than today, and catches peaked in 1938. 'Over a century of intensive trawl fishing has severely depleted UK seas of bottom-living fish like halibut, turbot, haddock and plaice,' said Simon Brockington, head of conservation at the Marine Conservation Society. 'It is vital that governments recognise the changes *5* that have taken place and set stock protection and recovery targets that are reflective of the historical productivity of the sea.'

But how could the UK government do this? It could stop subsidising fishermen. There are already too many fishermen, so it does not make sense to spend government money to attract more. Ultimately, fishermen should *10* pay a rent for the fish they catch. The government could also limit access to

fish resources. The oyster is a good example. In the nineteenth century, the
poor living in the UK used to eat around 500 million oysters a year. However,
common ownership of the foreshore, and the discharge of sewage, put paid to
that. Today, the British consume only a few million oysters a year. By contrast,   *15*
nineteenth-century France controlled pollution and passed laws to limit oyster
fishing.

A number of countries have given individual fishermen a fixed share of the
catch caught offshore. These quotas are permanent and can be bought and
sold, with the prices reflecting the value of the fish still in the water. Quotas   *20*
encourage fishermen to think about investing in conserving stock instead of
trying to catch the fish before somebody else grabs them.

Source: academic research, 2002–15

Extract C: The UK fishing industry 2003–13: selected key statistics

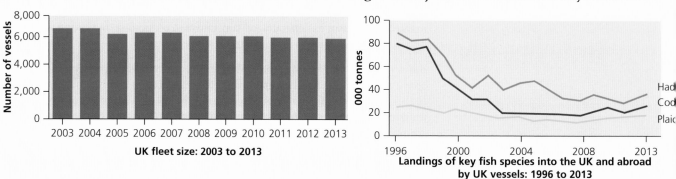

UK fleet size: 2003 to 2013

**Landings of key fish species into the UK and abroad
by UK vessels: 1996 to 2013**

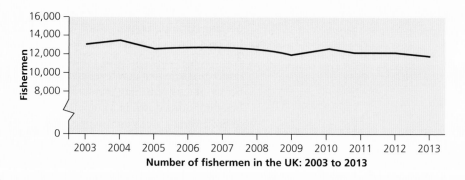

Number of fishermen in the UK: 2003 to 2013

Fish trade flows for the UK: 2003–13

		2003	2004	2005	2006	2007	2008	2009	2010	2011	2012	2013
Imports	(000 tonnes)	632	671	720	753	748	782	721	704	720	755	739
	(£m)	1,439	1,474	1,696	1,921	1,994	2,210	2,177	2,255	2,559	2,570	2,755
Exports	(000 tonnes)	480	478	461	416	467	416	480	517	436	466	453
	(£m)	891	886	939	942	982	1,009	1,166	1,346	1,464	1,344	1,463
Crude trade gap	(000 tonnes)	**152**	**193**	**259**	**337**	**281**	**366**	**241**	**187**	**284**	**289**	**286**

Source: UK Sea Fisheries Statistics, 2013

Extract D: UK fishing ports face an uncertain future

Peterhead is the UK's largest fishing port. In 2013, Peterhead landed 1,134,000 tonnes of fish, out of the total of 2,492,000 tonnes for the UK's 12 largest fishing ports. In terms of value, Peterhead's landings amounted to £112 million out of the total value of £281.2 million for the 12 ports.

However, over the last 15 years Peterhead's fish landings have been extremely *5* volatile, and like all UK fishing ports, the town has had to come to terms with calls for further reductions in the size of its fishing fleet. Without alternative sources of employment, many young men have left the area to seek work elsewhere. Those men and their families who still remain face an uncertain future. Men in Peterhead have earned their living from the sea *10* since the thirteenth century. Today, a third of the town's 23,000 citizens are employed in the industry. It is said that for every fisherman at sea there are five people on shore who depend on him for a living. They include men and women working in fish-processing factories and in wholesale fish markets, buyers, net menders and welders who repair boats. Beyond them are the local *15* shopkeepers, taxi drivers and restaurant owners.

Source: news reports, 2015

Section B

Answer **all** questions in this section.

Refer to source booklet for Extracts A, B, C and D.

Total for this investigation: 50 marks

The UK and global fishing industry

INVESTIGATION

Scenario

You are an economist reporting to the UK Fishing Industry Trade Organisation, a body which represents the owners of many of the commercial fishing boats operating out of UK fishing ports. The organisation has requested that you provide answers to three key questions.

Referring to the source booklet, study **Extracts A**, **B**, and **C** and then use these and your own economic knowledge to help you answer questions 31 and 32. There is also an additional news report, **Extract D**, which is to be used with the other extracts to help answer question 33.

31 To what extent, if at all, do the data support the view that the UK fishing industry is in decline? You must use the data in **Extract C** to support your assessment. *(10 marks)*

32 The UK Fishing Industry Trade Organisation recognises that fish stocks have to be managed, but it is concerned that government policies have damaged the UK fishing industry. Explain how the problems faced by the fishing industry have been affected by government intervention. *(15 marks)*

33 Taking into account the news report concerning Peterhead in **Extract D**, and the other evidence in the extracts, recommend **two** policies that the UK Fishing Industry Trade Organisation should advise the government to adopt in order to protect employment in the UK fishing industry. Justify your recommendations. *(25 marks)*

Index

Note: page numbers in **bold** indicate key terms.

A

abnormal profit **42**, 65, 67, 90
absolute advantage **305–06**, 307, 308
absolute poverty **129**, 130
  and the unwaged/homeless 131
actual (short-run) growth 201, 202, 203, 204
adjustable peg exchange rate 342, 349–50
  Bretton Woods system 351
adverse selection **151**
agency problem 60–61
aggregate demand **190**
  AD/AS model 195–201
  and automatic stabilisers 280–81
  and the credit crunch 211
  deflation reducing 214, 328, 329
  demand-side fiscal policy 275–76, 278
  expenditure-reducing policy 329
  inflation increasing 215, 218, 346–47
  and interest rate policy 249–51
  monetary policy 248
  short-term economic growth 203–04, 333–34
  and unemployment 210
  use of discretionary fiscal policy 288
aggregate supply **190**
aid **364–66**
Akerlof, George 12
allocative efficiency **68**, 69
  in monopoly 71
  negative externalities and 145
  perfect competition 70
  and road use 143, 149
altruism 18
anchoring **17**
Apple Mac
  and creative destruction 52
  innovative 46–47
  method of competing 88
  product differentiation 58
artificial barriers **57**, 106
Asset Purchase Scheme *see* quantitative easing (QE)
assets 217, 226, 229, 230
  see also bonds; shares
  and bank failures 260–61
  decisions about 231
  interest rate effect on prices of 250
  liquidity-profitability trade-off 244–45
  liquidity ratio 262
  portfolio investment 326
  purchase of by central bank 253, 254
  retail banks balance sheet 241–42, 243
  short-dated versus long-dated 233
asymmetric information **11–12**
austerity measures 192–93, 212, 290, 295, 354
automatic enrolment, pensions 137, 138
automatic stabilisers 280–82
automation **48**, 208

availability bias **16–17**
average cost of labour (AC_L) **103**, 104, 105, 107–08, 109
average fixed cost (AFC) **35**, 36
average returns of labour **27**
  and average variable costs 36
  relationship with marginal returns 29
average revenue (AR) **37**
  kinked demand curve 80, 81
  monopolistic competition 73
  in monopoly 40–41
  in perfect competition 38–39
  and price discrimination 84, 85, 86
  profit maximisation 62, 64, 65, 67
average tax rate 280
average total cost (ATC) **35**
  inefficiencies in monopoly 71
  monopolistic competition 73, 74
  profit maximisation in monopoly 67
  profit maximisation in perfect competition 64, 65
  relationship with marginal cost and AVC 36
  $SRATC$ curves 31–32
average variable cost (AVC) **35**
  relationship with marginal cost and ATC 36

B

'bads' (public) 143
balance of payments **322**, 322–40
  see also current account
  capital account 324–25
  export-led growth and UK economy 333–34
  financial account 325–27
  imbalances, policies to cure 328–33, 334
balancing the budget **193**, **276**
Bank of England 238
  balances at 245
  definition of money 229
  exchange rate management 347–48, 350
  and financial regulation 258–59
  forward guidance 256–57
  interest rate policy 250–51
  'lender of last resort' 260
  liabilities 230
  main functions 246–47
  Monetary Policy Committee (MPC) 252–53
  monetary policy implementation 247–52
  quantitative easing 253–56
Bank Rate **192**, **248**
  and LIBOR 251–52
  monetary policies 253, 255, 256, 257
  using to manage demand for credit 249–50
banks
  central bank 246–47
  commercial 238
  credit creation 240–42
  failure of 260–61
  investment 238–40
  liquidity and capital 261–62
  retail banks 243–46
  takeovers 162
barriers to market entry 56–57

removal of 160–61
barter 226, 227
behavioural economics **12**
  and economic policy 18–23
  theory of 12–18
Behavioural Insights Team (BIT) 13
Beveridge, William 206–07
biases, cognitive 15–18
bonds **231**
  calculating current market price 235–36
  capital gains and losses 235
  corporate and government 233
  inverse correlation with interest rates 233–34
bounded rationality **14**
bounded self-control **14**
Bretton Woods system 351
broad money **229**
Brown, Gordon 290
budget deficit **192**, 218, **276–77**, 289
  consequences for macroeconomic performance 288–90
  cyclical and structural 277–78
  demand-side fiscal policy 275, 278–79
  and framing 20
  measures to reduce 193, 211–12, 282
  and the national debt 284–87
  rule-based fiscal policy 282–83
budget surplus **192**, 193, **276–77**
  cyclical and structural 277–78
  and macroeconomic performance 290
  and 'normal times' 284
business objectives 59–63

C

call centres, overseas location 302
Cameron, David 13, 283, 287
canons of taxation 268
capital gains 123, 235, 270
capital account 324–25
capital flight 364
capital flows, financial account 325–27
  from China to the USA 338
  foreign direct investment 326
  'hot money' 326–27
  portfolio 326
  speculative 345, 350
capital markets **232**, 233, 236–37
capital mobility 302–03
capital ratio **262**
Carney, Mark 252–53, 256–57
cartel agreements **78**, 163
central bank **238**
  adjustable peg exchange rate 349–50
  main functions 246–47
  management of fixed exchange rate 347–48
changes in technology *see* technological change
Charter for Budget Responsibility (Fiscal Charter) 282–83, 284
China 304, 314, 315, 337, 338, 340, 366
choice architecture **19**
  mandated choices 20–21
  policy implications 21–22
choices 10, 13, 14
circular flow of income **193–95**, 339, 340

Clegg, Nick 45
climate change 156
Coase, Ronald 25, 156
cognitive biases **15–17**
collective bargaining **107**
collusion 78
  joint-profit maximisation 79–80
  price leadership 82
  tobacco firms and supermarkets 79
  versus market cooperation 78–79
commercial bank **238**
comparative advantage 304–05, **306–08**
  assumptions underlying 308–09
  and competitive advantage 309
  and pattern of world trade 314
competition dynamics 87–88
Competition and Markets Authority
  (CMA) **158**, 159, 161, 163
competition policy **157–58**
  mergers 161–62
  monopoly 158–61
  restrictive trading practice 163
competition spectrum 55
competition, technology-driven 172
competitive advantage 309, 310
competitive oligopoly 78, 80–81
complete market failure **141**
concentration ratio **76**, 77, 89
condition of demand 3
constant returns to scale **30**, 308–09,
  312
consumer behaviour 2–10
consumer surplus **84**, 85, 86, 87
  effect of tariffs on 314
  in monopoly 90
  welfare gains and losses 312–13
consumption externalities **146**, 152–54
consumption-led growth 333–34
contestable markets **89**, 161, 170
contraction of demand 3
contractualisation **168**
corporate bonds **233**
corruption **361**
cost-push inflation **218**, 346
coupon **234**
covert collusion 78–79, 82
creative destruction **51**, 52, 87–88
credit **241**
credit creation 240–42
credit crunch 211, 217, 262, 326
credit ratings, UK 287–88
crowding out 289, 292
currency unions **352**
current account **322**, 323–24
  applying *AD/AS* analysis to 338–40
  deficit, polices to reduce 328–33
  and exchange rate equilibrium
    343–44
  government policies 334
  imbalances, implications of reducing
    337–38
  imbalances, significance of 335–37
  surplus, policies to reduce 328, 334
  three factors influencing 335
customs unions **317**, 319
  versus free trade areas 317–18
cyclical budget deficit **277–78**
cyclical unemployment **194**

D

deadweight debt 286
deadweight loss (*DWL*) **90**, 146, 147
  see also welfare losses
debt **230**
  national debt 193, 282, 284–87
  sovereign debt 287–88
  versus deficit 284, 287
debt rule, fiscal policy 282
decision making
  behavioural economics 12–18
  biases in 15–18
  choice architecture 19, 20–22
  consumer behaviour 2–10
  demand theory 2–4
  framing 20
  and imperfect information 11–12
  utility theory 4–10
decrease in demand 3
decreasing returns to scale **30**, 31, 309
default choice **19**
'deficit bias' 283
deficit financing 275, 285, 289
deficit rule, fiscal policy 282
deficit versus debt 284, 287
deflation **214**, 328
  expenditure-reducing policy 329
  and QE 255
  smoothing economic cycle 288
  supply-side fiscal policy 279
deglobalisation 303–04
demand-led spending 275
demand-pull inflation **215**, 217–18, 219,
  346–47
demand-side fiscal policy 275–76
  AD/AS diagram 278–79
demand theory, individual demand 2–3
demerit goods **150**, 153
  over-consumption of 152
dependency theory of trade 301
depreciation 328, 330, 331, 332, 338
deregulation **169–70**
  contestable markets theory 170
  monopoly power 160–61
  regulatory capture theory 170–71
derived demand **93**, 96
devaluation 328
  adjustable peg exchange rate 349
  China 338
  expenditure-switching policy 330
  J-curve effect 332
  Marshall–Lerner condition 331
  and price elasticity of demand 330–31
development 355–66
  aid and trade promoting 364–66
  barriers to 361–63
  factors affecting 359, 361
  indicators 356–59, 360
  policies promoting 363–64
  versus growth 355
direct controls 328, 329
direct taxes 269, 271–72
dirty floating exchange rates 341, 350
discrimination, labour market 106
  wages 112–15
diseconomy of scale **31**, 32, 33
disequilibrium trading 106

disequilibrium unemployment 208–09
disinflation **200**, 214, 279
disposable income 126, 133, 134
disruptive innovation 49–50
distribution of income **118**
distribution of income and wealth 118–29
  benefits and costs of more equitable 128
  equality and equity 124–25
  factors influencing 119–24
  Lorenz curve and Gini coefficient 125–27
  taxation and public spending 270–71
distribution of wealth **118**
divorce of ownership from control **60–61**
duopoly **51**, 55
dynamic efficiency **46**, **68**, 71

E

earnings trap 135, 137
economic cycle
  and automatic stabilisers 280–81
  cyclical budget deficit 277
  cyclical unemployment 194, 210
  deflating and reflating to 'smooth' 288
  and output gaps 201–02
economic growth **189**, 203–06
  barriers to 361–63
  causes of long-run 205
  and distribution of income and
    wealth 128, 138
  factors affecting 359–61
  long-run 203, 204
  macroeconomic objective 191
  policies to promote 363–64
  short-run 202, 203, 204, 333
  'The Great Moderation' 213
  versus economic development 204, 355
economic integration 317–18
  European Union 320, 352–54
economic sanctions **17**
economic welfare 84, 90
  effect of imposing a tariff 313–14
  indicators of 358, 359
  three components of 357
economies of scale **31**, 32–34, 57, 67–68, 71
education 132, 143, 151, **361**
  consumption of 153–54
  public spending on 274
efficiency 68–71
  minimum efficient scale 32–33
  negative externalities 145
  privatisation promoting 165–66
  and profit 44
  public goods and 143
  taxation principle 268
elasticity of demand for labour **97**
elasticity of supply of labour **101**
emerging markets 314, 315
employment and unemployment 206–13
entry barriers **56–57**
environmental market failures 155–56
equality **124**, 125
equation of exchange **216**
equilibrium exchange rate 343–44
equilibrium level of employment 208,
  295–96
equilibrium unemployment 208, 209
equity **124**, **230**

horizontal and vertical   125
positive and negative   230
shares   236–37
taxation principle   268, 271
euro currency
exchange rate fixing prior to   351–52
impact on eurozone economies   353–54
European Central Bank (ECB)   321, 353–54
European Union (EU)   **302**
brief history of   318–20
as an economic union   320–21
Exchange Rate Mechanism (ERM)   351
merger policy   162
UK's membership of   320
eurozone   **315**, 321, 352–54
examination
assessment objectives and aims ix–x
structure x–xi
exchange rate   **197, 340**, 341–42
effect on import prices   332
fixed   347–49, 351–52
freely floating   342–47
influence on current account balance   335
and interest rate changes   251
managed   349–50
Exchange Rate Mechanism (ERM), EU   351
excise duties   267, 269–70, 272
exit barriers   **57**
expansionary fiscal contractionism (EFC)   295
expectations
and forward guidance   256–57
older people   101
of oligopolists   80, 81
positive cognitive bias   16
expectations, inflation   248
adaptive, Friedman   215, 220–21
rational, free-market economists   215,
221–22
expenditure-reducing policy   **328**, 329
expenditure-switching policy   **328**, 329–30
export-led growth   333–34, 340
export subsidies   **310**
extension of demand   **3**
external economies/diseconomies of
scale   **34**
externalities   **144–49**

F

factors of production   26, 30, 31, 141
and distribution of income   120–21
fairness   **18**
financial account   **325**
and capital flows   325–27
financial assets see assets
Financial Conduct Authority (FCA)   **258**, 259,
260
financial markets   **231–32**
banking sector   238–46
bond prices and interest rates   233–34
capital gains/losses and bond/share
prices   235
capital markets   232, 233, 236–37
central banks and monetary policy
246–57
foreign exchange markets   237
forward guidance   256–57
money markets   232, 233
regulation/deregulation   170, 258–62

Financial Policy Committee (FPC)   **258**, 259
Financial Services Authority (FSA)   258
firms   **25**
objectives of   59–63
optimum size of   32
theory of the firm   13–14, 24
fiscal austerity   192–93, 212, 290, 295, 354
fiscal drag   134–35
fiscal policy   **190, 265**, 265–90
automatic stabilisers   280–82
balancing the budget   276–78, 287–90
demand-side   275–76, 278–79
national debt   284–87
public spending   273–75
rule-based   282–83
supply-side   279, 291–92
taxation   265–73, 279–80
fiscal stimulus   192, 193, 279
versus fiscal restraint   211–12
Fisher equation of exchange   **216**
fixed exchange rate   **341**, 347–49
brief history of   351–52
foreign direct investment (FDI)   **325**, 337
foreign exchange markets   **232**, 237
forward guidance   **253**, 256–57
framing   **20**
freely floating exchange rates   **341**, 342–47
free-market economists   111, 132–33,
190–91, 192, 209–10
deregulation   170
privatisation   165
public choice theory   154–55
free-rider problem   **142**, 144
free trade areas   **317**
versus customs unions   317–18
frictional unemployment   **207**
Friedman, Milton   13, 14, 215, 220, 222
full employment   **189–90**, 208, 209
Beveridge definition   206–07
conflict with inflation control   219–20
Keynesian policy   191, 218, 275
Funding for Lending Scheme (FLS)   256, **257**

G

GDP (gross domestic product)
development indicator   356–59
government spending as share of   273–74
and growth   284
and national debt   285
and output gaps   201–03
gender pay gap   114–15
General Agreement on Tariffs and Trade
(GATT)   311, 322
geographical immobility of labour   **106**
gilts   231, 233–35, 245–46, 289, 294
Gini coefficient   **126**
globalisation   **298–99**
consequences for LDCs   300–01
consequences for MDCs   301–02
features of   299–300
labour and capital mobility   302–03
and power of national governments   303
reversal of   303–04
in the service sector   302
and worker migration   121–22
WTO role in promoting   303
GNI (gross national income)   119, 356–57,
358

GNP (gross national product)   357–58
gold standard   351
Goodhart's Law   229
government bonds   231, **233**
capital gains and losses   235
China's purchase of US   338
and interest rates   233–35
retail banks investment in   245–46
selling of new issues   294
government failure   **154**
government intervention   125
see also regulation
correcting cyclical fluctuation   289
and government failure   154
new growth theory   205
public interest theory   155
to reduce negative externalities   150
versus economic liberalisation   167–68
versus non-interventionist supply-side
policies   293
government policies
balance of payments deficit
reduction   329–33
balance of payments surplus
reduction   334
and choice architecture   19–22
economic growth promotion   363–64
poverty reduction   132–38
government revenue   265–68, 272, 276
government spending   273–75
aggregate demand equation   195, 249,
278–79
and budget balancing issues   192–93, 276
multipliers   276
supply-side fiscal policy   291–92
Great Depression   190, 209
'great recession', and hysteresis   203
gross domestic product (GDP)   **194**
growth of the economy see economic growth
growth maximisation, business objective   61

H

Hardin, Garrett   157
healthcare
government spending on   274
merit good   143, 150–51
private insurance   151
health deprivation–poverty link   132
'high-tech' goods, ineffective aid   366
hit-and-run competition   **89–90**
horizontal equity   125
'hot money' capital flows   326–27, 345
human behaviour see behavioural economics
human capital   205, **362**
Human Development Index (HDI)   **358–59**,
360
hypothesis of diminishing marginal utility   **7**
hysteresis   203

I

ideas, flow of new   205
imperfect competition   24, 55, 56
imperfect information   11–12
in the labour market   106, 207
imperfectly competitive markets   56
goods markets, MRP_L curve   95
labour markets   104–06

monopoly power in 72
non-price competition 76
satisficing 63
wage discrimination 112–15
import controls 329
justification for 310–11
import duties, effect on economic welfare 313–14
import prices
effect of exchange rate changes 251, 331, 332, 346
effect of tariffs 313–14
incentives 4, 22
other than profit maximisation 61
and principal-agent problem 60, 61
profit creating 43–44
redistributive polices reducing 138
and tax system 128, 271, 272, 279
and wage differentials 105
of workers to supply labour 98–99
income **118**
earned versus unearned 121
household, effect of taxes and benefits 133–34
income effect **98**
income inequality 119–20, 122
income tax 269, 271–72
average and marginal rates 279–80
earnings/poverty trap 135–36
fiscal drag 134–35
progressive nature of 268
increase in demand **3**
increasing returns to scale **30**, 31, 34
comparative advantage 309, 312
Index of Sustainable Economic Welfare (ISEW) 359
indicators of development **356–59**
indirect taxes 134, 266–67, 269–70, 272–73
individual demand curve **2–3**
inequality in income distribution 119–20
addressing 128, 138, 270–71
measurement of 125–27
in the UK (2012) 122
infant industries 310
inflation **190**, 213–14
AD/AS analysis 200–01, 339–40
causation theories 215
deflation 329–30
and floating exchange rates 344–45, 346–47
influence on current account balance 335
Keynesian cost-push theory 218–19
Keynesian demand-pull theory 217–18
old quantity theory of money 215–17
Phillips curve 219–21
psychology 223
and rational expectations 221–22
supply-side policies 294
information problems
asymmetric information 11–12
demerit and merit goods 150–51
infrastructure **362**
interventionist policies 293
privatisations 167
inheritance tax 270
inherited wealth 124
injections 193, **194**, 336, 339
innovation **46**
and creative destruction 51, 52
disruptive versus sustaining 49–50

profit as reward for 44
versus invention 46–47
institutional factors **361**
institutional investors 167
insurance
and adverse selection 151
NI contributions 135, 269, 272
inter-bank lending 232, 245, 251–52
interest rates
and bond prices 233–36
effect on demand for credit 249–50
LIBOR 232, 251–52
low level of, winners and losers 255
transmission mechanism 250–51
Zero Lower Bound (ZLB) 290
internal economies and diseconomies of scale **33**
international economic integration 317–18
the EU as an example of 320
international economy 298
balance of payments 322–40
economic growth and development 355–66
exchange rate systems 340–52
globalisation 298–304
trade 304–22
internationalisation 299
interventionist supply-side policies 293
invention **46**
investment
and balance of payments 324–28
in education and training 361
in human capital 362
in infrastructure 362
overseas FDI 325, 337
investment banks **238–40**
investment-led growth 334

J

J-curve effect 332–33
reverse J-curve effect 334
joint-profit maximisation, cartels 79–80

K

Kahneman, Daniel 13, 15
Keynesian economics 190
attack on 191
cost-push theory of inflation 218–19
cyclical unemployment 210–11
demand-pull theory of inflation 217–18
demand-side fiscal policy 275–76, 278–79
long-run aggregate supply curve 200
Phillips curve 219, 220
public interest theory 155
rebirth of 211
rejection of quantity theory of money 217
Keynes, John Maynard 190, 200, 210, 215
King, Mervyn 252
kinked demand curve theory 80–81
Kodak case study 50
Krugman, Paul 312, 353

L

labour immobility 106
labour markets 92–93
demand for labour 93–97

discrimination in 112–15
imperfectly competitive 104–06
national minimum wage 109–12
perfectly competitive 102–04
supply of labour 98–101
trade unions 107–09
labour mobility 302–03, 353, 354
labour productivity **29**, 48
and demand curve for labour 96
improving 205, 335
and wage differentials 121
law of demand **3**
law of diminishing returns **26–27**, 28, 29, 35
Lawson, Nigel, budget speech 276–77
leakages, circular flow 194, 339, 340
'lemons', market for 12
less developed countries (LDCs) **300**
aid targeted at 364–66
barriers to growth 361–62
main features of 355–56
liability 230
and bankruptcy 260
of retail banks 241–42, 243
liberalisation, economic 167–68, 170, 171
LIBOR (London Interbank Offered Rate of Interest) 232, 251–52
limit prices **58**
liquidity **229**, 243
insurance 260
portfolio balance decisions 231
supply of 211
trade-off against profitability 244
liquidity ratio **261**
'living wage' 111–12, 136
loans 211, 230, 233, 241
demand and supply 248
'hard' and 'soft' 365
and interest rates 249, 255
secured 244
London Stock Exchange (LSE) 232, 234, 236, 237, 239
long-run 26–29
long-run aggregate supply **199**
long-run average cost **31**, 37
long-run economic growth **203**, 204, 205
long-run marginal cost **37**
long-run Phillips curve **220**, 296
long-run production theory 30–35
Lorenz curve **125–27**
low-paid workers 110, 121–22, 124, 131, 134–35
developing countries 300–01
and migration 302–03
pension schemes 137–38

M

macroeconomic equilibrium **194**, 196, 199, 218, 219
macroeconomic policy **191**
macroeconomic theory 188–224
AD/AS model 195–201
circular flow theory 193–95
economic growth 203–06
employment and unemployment 206–13
expectations 221–22
inflation 213–15, 217–19, 223
national and international economy 189–93

output gaps 201–03
  Phillips curve 219–21
  quantity theory of money 215–17
managed exchange rates 341, 342, 349–50
mandated choice **20–21**
manufacturing, deglobalisation of 303–04
marginal analysis
  demerit and merit goods 150–54
  externalities 144–49
marginal cost of labour **103**, 104–05, 109
marginal cost (*MC*) **35**
  allocative efficiency, (*P = MC*) 69, 70, 143,
    145
  and average costs 36
  kinked demand curve 81
  long-run 37
  profit maximisation (*MR = MC*) 59–60, 62,
    64, 67, 73
marginal physical product of labour
  93–94
marginal productivity theory 93–97
marginal returns of labour **26**, 35
  and average returns 29
marginal revenue (*MR*) **37**
  in monopoly 40–41
  in perfect competition 38–39
  profit maximisation 59–60, 62, 64, 67, 73
marginal revenue product of labour **94–95**,
  96, 103–04, 105, 108, 109
marginal tax rate **134**, 279–80
marginal utility **4**
  and choice 10
  and an individual's demand curve 8
  law of diminishing 7
  and total utility 5–6
the margin and choice 10
market conduct **77**
market failure **141**
  climate change 156
  and regulation 169
marketisation **168**
market structure **55**, 56–58
  and scale 34
  and technological change 51
Marshall–Lerner condition 331
maturity date **234**, 235
maximising behaviour 9
McArdle, Megan 289
means-tested benefits **135**, 136
mechanisation **48**
merger policy 161–62
merit goods **150–51**
  under-consumption of 153–54
migration 121–22, 205, 303
minimum efficient scale (*MES*) **32–33**, 34, 70
misallocation of resources 67, 141, 145
missing market **141**, 142, 144
mobility of labour 106, 302–03, 353, 354
monetarist **191**
monetary policy **192**, 247–57
  and the Bank Rate 249–52
  conventional and unconventional 253–57
  economic and monetary union
    (EMU) 352–53
  independent 345
  objectives and instruments 247–48
  and supply-side policies 293–94
Monetary Policy Committee (MPC) 252–57

money **226**
  development of 227–28
  functions of 226
  narrow and broad 229
money illusion 221, 222
money markets **232**, 233, 245
money supply **191**, 228–29
  quantitative easing 253–55
  quantity theory 216, 217
monopolistic competition **51**, 72–76
monopoly **66**
  advantages 67–68
  disadvantages 67
  and economic efficiency 70–71
  evaluating using welfare criteria 90
  form of market failure 169
  and privatisation 166
  profit maximisation 67
  unnecessary costs 71
monopoly policy 158–61
monopoly power **72**
  competition policy 157–58, 159, 160
  contestable market theory 88–89
  and inflation 218–19
monopoly profit 67, 68, 86, 160
monopsony **104**
  depression of wages in 110
  effect of trade unions 109
  employment level 105
  wage discrimination 113
  wage rate determination 104–05
monopsony power **104**, 110, 113
moral hazard **151**, 260–61
more developed countries **301**
mortgages 211, 230, 244, 256
multinational corporations (MNCs) **299**,
  300–01, 303, 323, 325
multiplier 193, **194**, 276, 280, 281

N

narrow money **229**
national debt **193**, **282**, 284–87
national economy 189–93
national income
  equilibrium level 196
  measures of 119, 356–58
  multiplier 276
national insurance (NICs) 135, 269, 272
  employers' 296
nationalisation 163–64
nationalised industries 160, 163–64, 166
national living wage (NLW) **111–12**, 136
national minimum wage (NMW) **109–10**
  advantages and disadvantages 110–11
  replaced by national living wage 111–12
natural barriers **57**
natural ('equilibrium') level of
  employment 295–96
natural monopoly 34, 67–68
natural rate of unemployment (NRU) **220–21**
  and rational expectations 222
  and supply-side policy 295–96
negative equity 230
negative externality **144**
  and allocative inefficiency 145
  demerit goods 150, 152
  road use example 148–49

negative output gap **201**
neoclassical growth theory 205
net advantage **99**
new growth theory 205
new-issues (primary) market 233, 236–37
'new wealth' versus 'old wealth' 124
NHS National Programme for IT, failure
  of 48–49
nominal national debt 285, 286
nominal versus real exchange rate 341
non-collusive oligopoly 78
non-excludability **142**
non-pure public goods 142
non-rejectability **142**
non-rivalry **142**
normal profit **42**
'normal times' 284
norms, social, biases based on 17–18
nudges **17–18**, 22
  versus shoves 22–23
Nudge (Thaler and Sunstein) 13

O

objectives of firms 59–63
occupational immobility of labour **106**
Office for Budget Responsibility (OBR)
  282–84
Office for National Statistics (ONS) 123, 194,
  195
old age and poverty 130–31
oligopoly 76–83
  kinked demand curve model 80–81
  and market conduct 77–80
  and prices 82–83
opportunity cost 8, 69, 306–07
optimal currency areas 354
optimum firm size **32**
Osborne, George 20, 212, 282
  compared to Gordon Brown 290
  expansionary fiscal contractionism 295
  national living wage 112
  and 'normal times 284
output gaps **201–02**
  and *AD/AS* 202–03
  and the economic cycle 202
overt collusion 78, 82

P

partial market failure **141**
pensions
  automatic enrolment 20, 137, 138
  private pension wealth 123, 124
  state 130–31, 274, 275
  workplace schemes 137–38
perfect competition 55–56, 63–66
  average and marginal revenue in 38–39
  cost-cutting competition 66
  economic efficiency in 70
  evaluating using welfare criteria 90
  profit maximisation 64–65
perfectly competitive labour markets 102–04
personal tax allowances 134–35, 269
Phillips curve **219–21**
Phillips machine, circular flow 194
plant **30**
portfolio balance decisions 231

portfolio of bills, retail banks 245
portfolio investment **326**
positive externality **144**
    merit goods 150–51, 153–54
positive output gap **201**
pound (sterling)
    demand and supply 342–44, 348
    devaluation of 332, 349
poverty **129**
    absolute versus relative 130
    causes of 130–31
    child poverty 130
    effects of in the UK 131–32
    policies to alleviate 132–38
poverty trap 135, 136
predatory prices **58**
price agreement **82**
price controls 159–60
price discrimination **83–84**
    analysis of 84
    conditions necessary for 85
    limiting case 86–87
    pros and cons of 85–86
    and wage discrimination 113
price elasticity of demand 41
    and devaluation 330–31
    imports and exports 331–32, 335, 342
    required for price discrimination 85
price leadership **82**
price-makers **40**, 55
price-takers **39**, 55, 66
price wars **82**
primary income flows **323**
principal-agent problem 60–61
principles of taxation **268**
private costs and benefits **70**
    externalities 144–49, 169
    merit and demerit goods 150–51
private finance initiative (PFI) **168**
private goods **141**
    private property rights 156
private pension wealth 123, 124
privatisation **164**, 164–68
    of monopolies 160
'pro-cyclicality' 283
producer surplus **84**, 85, 86
    effect of tariffs 314
    in monopoly 90
    welfare gains and losses 312–13
product differentiation **58**
production externalities **146**, 147–48, 149
production methods 47–48
production theory 24
    law of diminishing returns 25–29
    returns to scale 30–35
productive efficiency **49**, **68**
productivity **29**
    see also labour productivity
profit **42**
    in a market economy 43–45
profitability **244**
profit maximisation **42**, 59–60
    alternatives to 61
    in monopolistic competition 73, 75
    in monopoly 67
    in perfect competition 64–65
    versus revenue maximisation 62
profit-sharing, John Lewis PLC 45

progressive tax **128**, **268**, 279–80, 281
property rights **141**, 156–57, 362–63
proportional tax **268**
protectionism 309, 310–12, 329, 337, 364
Prudential Regulation Authority (PRA) **258**, 259, 260
public choice theory 154–55
public expenditure see government spending
public goods **141–42**
    and allocative efficiency 143
    and externalities 144, 148
    and government-provided goods 143
    and property rights 156
    quasi/non-pure 142
    versus public 'bads' 143
public interest theory 155
public ownership **163–64**
    of monopolies 160
public-private partnerships (PPPs) **168**

Q

quantitative easing (QE) **192**, **248**, 253–54
    decision not to extend 255–56
    QE1, QE2 and QE3 254–55
quantity-setter **40**
quantity theory of money **215–16**
    Keynesian rejection of 217
quasi-public goods **142**
    roads 143, 148
quotas **310**
    direct controls on 330

R

rational behaviour **4**, 14
rational expectations theory 221–22
real exchange rate 341
real wages/real wage rate **208–09**, 229–31, 296
real-wage unemployment **209**
recession **192**
redistribution of income and wealth 120, 128, 138
reflation 214, 216, 278, 288, 334
regressive tax **268**
    average and marginal tax rates 279–80
    excise duty and council tax 270
    national insurance 269
    tax on cigarettes 268
regulation **169**
    see also deregulation
    competition policy 158–63
    of financial system 240, 258–60
    and market failure 169
    privatised utility industries 171
regulatory capture **170–71**
relative poverty **129**, 130
    of low-waged poor 131, 135
representative money 226, 227–28
resource allocation 141
    allocative efficiency 69
    and exchange rates 344
    and profits 44
    taxes and subsidies 270
restricted choice **21**
retail banks 238, 243–46
    liquidity and capital ratios 261–62

returns to scale **30**
revaluation 330, 334, 349
revenue 37–38
    maximisation 61–62
reverse causation 217
reverse J-curve effect 334
road pricing 148–49
Rostow, W. W. 356
rule-based fiscal policy 282–83
rule-of-thumb **14**

S

salary differentials 114, 121
sales revenue maximisation 61–62
sanctions, economic **17**
satisficing **62–63**
Say's Law 210
scarcity 7, 9
Schumpeter, Joseph 51, 88
secondary income flows **324**
secondary (second-hand) market 236, 237
second-best theory 311
securities 231, 232, 233, 234, 237
security of assets **244**
self-control, limited 14–15
service sector
    globalisation in 302
    structural unemployment 207–08
shares 231, **233**, 238
    capital gains and losses 235
    new issues of 236–37
    portfolio investment 326–27
shift of a demand curve **3**
short-run 26–29
short-run aggregate supply **196**
short-run average total cost
    (SRATC) curves 31–32
short-run economic growth 201, 202, **203**, 204
short-run Phillips curve **220**, 221
short-run production theory 25–29
'shoves' versus 'nudges' 22–23
Single European Market (SEM) **318**
Smith, Adam 7, 88, 303, 308
Smith, Duncan 130
social costs and benefits **70**
social norms **17**
    biases based on 17–18
sovereign debt problem 286, 287–88
specialisation 227
    and absolute advantage 305–06
    comparative advantage 306–09
    and import controls 310–11
speculation, bonds and shares 235, 237
speculative capital flows 326–27, 345
stamp duty 266–67, 270
state ownership 160, 163–64
state pension 130–31, 274, 275
static efficiency **68**
strategic trade theory 310–11, 312, 364–65
structural budget deficits **277–78**, 289–90
structural unemployment **207–08**, 209
sub-prime mortgages 211
subsidies, export 310, 311
substitution effect **98**
sunk costs **57**, 89
'sunset' industries 207, 310

Sunstein, Cass   13
supermarket industry
   competition in   77
   market shares   76
supernormal profit   42
supply-side fiscal policy   279, 291–92
supply-side improvements   **291**
supply-side policies   **191, 279**, 291–96
   and the current account   333
sustaining innovation   49–50
systemic risk   **239–40**, 262

T

tacit collusion   79
takeovers   161, 162–63
tariffs   **310**
   abolition of, free trade areas   317, 318
   effect on economic welfare   313–14
   welfare gains and losses from   313
taxation   **265**, 268–73
   canons of   268
   on capital and wealth   273
   effect on household income   133–34
   fiscal drag and low pay   134–35
   on income   269, 271–72
   indirect   269–70, 272–73
   of monopoly profits   160
   role and merits of   270–71
   of wealth versus income   124
tax evasion   271, 272, 273
technological change   **45–46**
   and disruptive innovation   49–50
   and efficiency   49
   influence on market structure   51
   innovation versus invention   46–47
   link to creative destruction   51–52
   and production methods   47–48
   and productivity   48–49
   and unemployment   96–97, 207–08
technological progress   205
technology-driven competition   172
Thaler, Richard   13
Thatcher, Margaret   276, 279
theory of the firm   13–14, 24
thinking styles and decision making   15
the 'three Ds' *see* deflation; devaluation;
   direct controls
total net wealth   123
total returns of labour   **27**
total revenue   **37**
total utility   5–6
trade   304–23
   see also European Union
   case for import controls   209–11
   comparative advantage model   304–09
   creation and diversion   319, 320
   and economic development   364–66

international economic integration   317–18
   shift in pattern of world trade   314
   tariffs, effect on economic welfare   313–14
   trading uncertainties   346
   UK pattern of trade   315–16
   welfare losses and gains   312–13
   World Trade Organization   303, 322
trade in goods   **323**
   UK's pattern of   315–16
trade in services   **323**
trade unions   **107–09**, 209–10, 219
traditional versus behavioural
   economics   13–14
tragedy of the commons   157
training   **361**
transfer payments   125
transmission mechanism of interest rate
   policy   250–51
trend (long-run) growth   201, 203, 204, 205
'triple lock', state pensions   131, 274

U

uncertainty
   international trading   346
   in oligopoly   78
   and under-consumption of merit
     goods   151
'unconventional' monetary policy   253–57
under-employment   212
under-full employment equilibrium   200,
   210, 217, 275
unemployment   **190**
   Bank of England inaccurate forecast
     256–57
   cyclical   194, 210
   during Great Depression   190
   equilibrium and disequilibrium   208–09
   forward guidance policy   253, 256–57
   frictional   207
   and full employment   207–08
   natural rate of   221, 222
   and the Phillips curve   219–21, 296
   and poverty   131
   real-wage   209–10
   structural   207–08
unemployment trap   137
United Nations
   Human Development Index (HDI)   **358–59**,
     360
   UNCTAD, trade versus aid   366
universal benefits   **135**
Universal Credit   136
USA   303–04, 322, 337–38, 352, 353, 354
utility   **4**
   marginal   4–8
   maximisation   9
   measurement of   10

utility industries
   privatisation of   171
   rate of return regulation   160

V

VAT (value added tax) 267, 269, 272–73
velocity of circulation of money   216, 217
vertical equity   125
Vickers, Sir John   162

W

wage differentials   100, 105–06, 121
wage discrimination   **112–13**
   types of   113–15
wage elasticity of demand   97
wage elasticity of supply   101
wage rates
   determination in monopsony labour
     market   104–06
   national living wage   111–12, 136
   national minimum wage   110–11
   and supply of individual worker's
     labour   98–99
   trade union influence   107–09
   and unemployment   208, 209
watchdog bodies   171, 172, 283
wealth   **118**
   distribution of   118, 122–24, 128
   net financial wealth, Lorenz curve   127
   taxes on   273
welfare gains   147
   from free trade   312–13
welfare benefits   128, 132–33, 135, 136, 271
welfare, economic *see* economic welfare
welfare losses   90
   over-consumption of demerit good   152
   production externalities   146, 147
   road congestion   149
   from tariffs   314
   under-consumption of merit good   153
withdrawals, circular flow   193, **194**, 339
World Bank, income groupings   119
World Trade Organization (WTO) **299**, 322
   role in promoting globalisation   303
Wren-Lewis, Simon   290

Y

yardstick competition   172
yield, bonds   234

Z

zero-hours contracts   212–13